LUTHER'S WORKS

VOLUME 25

LECTURES ON ROMANS

Glosses and Scholia

HILTON C. OSWALD
Editor

CONCORDIA PUBLISHING HOUSE · SAINT LOUIS

Copyright © 1972 by
CONCORDIA PUBLISHING HOUSE
Saint Louis, Missouri

Library of Congress Catalog Card No. 55-9893

ISBN 0-570-06425-2

Contents

General Introduction

THE first editions of Luther's collected works appeared in the sixteenth century, and so did the first efforts to make him "speak English." In America serious attempts in these directions were made for the first time in the nineteenth century. The Saint Louis edition of Luther was the first endeavor on American soil to publish a collected edition of his works, and the Henkel Press in Newmarket, Virginia, was the first to publish some of Luther's writings in an English translation. During the first decade of the twentieth century, J. N. Lenker produced translations of Luther's sermons and commentaries in thirteen volumes. A few years later the first of the six volumes in the Philadelphia (or Holman) edition of the *Works of Martin Luther* appeared. Miscellaneous other works were published at one time or another. But a growing recognition of the need for more of Luther's works in English has resulted in this American edition of Luther's works.

The edition is intended primarily for the reader whose knowledge of late medieval Latin and sixteenth-century German is too small to permit him to work with Luther in the original languages. Those who can, will continue to read Luther in his original words as these have been assembled in the monumental Weimar edition (*D. Martin Luthers Werke.* Kritische Gesamtausgabe; Weimar, 1883 ff.). Its texts and helps have formed a basis for this edition, though in certain places we have felt constrained to depart from its readings and findings. We have tried throughout to translate Luther as he thought translating should be done. That is, we have striven for faithfulness on the basis of the best lexicographical materials available. But where literal accuracy and clarity have conflicted, it is clarity that we have preferred, so that sometimes paraphrase seemed more faithful than literal fidelity. We have proceeded in a similar way in the matter of Bible versions, translating Luther's translations. Where this could be done by the use of an existing English version — King James, Douay, or Revised Standard — we have done so. Where it could not, we have supplied our own. To indicate this in each specific instance would have been pedantic;

to adopt a uniform procedure would have been artificial — especially in view of Luther's own inconsistency in this regard. In each volume the translator will be responsible primarily for matters of text and language, while the responsibility of the editor will extend principally to the historical and theological matters reflected in the introductions and notes.

Although the edition as planned will include fifty-five volumes, Luther's writings are not being translated in their entirety. Nor should they be. As he was the first to insist, much of what he wrote and said was not that important. Thus the edition is a selection of works that have proved their importance for the faith, life, and history of the Christian Church. The first thirty volumes contain Luther's expositions of various Biblical books, while the remaining volumes include what are usually called his "Reformation writings" and other occasional pieces. The final volume of the set will be an index volume; in addition to an index of quotations, proper names, and topics, and a list of corrections and changes, it will contain a glossary of many of the technical terms that recur in Luther's works and that cannot be defined each time they appear. Obviously Luther cannot be forced into any neat set of rubrics. He can provide his reader with bits of autobiography or with political observations as he expounds a psalm, and he can speak tenderly about the meaning of the faith in the midst of polemics against his opponents. It is the hope of publishers, editors, and translators that through this edition the message of Luther's faith will speak more clearly to the modern church.

JAROSLAV PELIKAN
HELMUT LEHMANN

Introduction to Volume 25

M ARTIN LUTHER had done some teaching either at Wittenberg or at Erfurt ever since he had earned his master's degree in 1505. But his teaching career came into full bloom especially after he turned specifically to theology. By 1508 he was lecturing on Aristotle in Wittenberg, and in the following year at Erfurt on Peter Lombard's *Sentences*. Upon receiving the doctor's degree in theology in 1512, he became lecturer on the Bible at the University of Wittenberg and in that capacity succeeded Johann Staupitz, the vicar general of the German Augustinian Order, his superior but also his close friend. Luther continued in this position the rest of his life.

Luther began his lectures on the Bible with the Psalms, perhaps because this was the book he knew best and the one from which he himself had been led into all the rest of the Scriptures, for he had taken seriously the prescription of his monastic order to read in the Psalter daily. His lectures on the Psalms kept him occupied from 1513 to 1515.

After the Psalms Luther chose to lecture on St. Paul's Epistle to the Romans. He followed the procedure already adopted in the Psalms. He asked Johann Grunenberg, who had a print shop in the Augustinian monastery in Wittenberg, to provide him and his students with identical copies of the Vulgate text of Romans, probably according to the Basel edition of 1509. As in the Psalms, Grunenberg provided the Vulgate text in an edition with generous space between the lines and wide margins on both sides of the text. In these spaces Luther carefully entered the clean copy of his interlinear and marginal glosses in Latin, copied carefully from previously assembled slips of paper. According to the custom of that day, these notes were intended to be dictated almost verbatim in the classroom and entered by the student in his own copy of the Latin text of the Scripture. This procedure also offered a convenient way for Luther to correct the printed version of the text now and then according to the latest version of Faber Stapulensis (1512, 1515) and Erasmus' edition (1516) of the text of Laurentius Valla

(1505). In addition to these glosses, Luther also prepared an extended commentary on various selected passages, written out in detail as a separate preparation for the lectures. This type of added commentary was known as scholia, a plural for which one rarely sees the singular scholion or scholium.

Equipped with this preparation — 28 sheets of glosses and 123 sheets of scholia — Luther entered the lecture hall each Monday and Friday morning at six o'clock for three semesters, from spring 1515 until fall 1516, to dictate and lecture on Paul's Epistle to the Romans in the manner of his time. From a diligent analysis of certain marks in Luther's manuscript Johannes Ficker, the editor of the lectures in the Weimar Edition, concludes that Luther's lectures were distributed as follows: Rom. 1:1—3:4: summer 1515; Rom. 3:5—8:39: winter 1515—1516; Rom. 9:1—16:27: summer 1516.

In addition to Luther's own handwritten copy of both the glosses and scholia, there are extant a number of student notebooks of these lectures. They are not everywhere complete nor all original, that is, as actually taken down in the lecture hall. Some are admittedly copies of originals. But from the composite of these notebooks we get a very fair picture of what Luther actually said in the lectures, and it is interesting to compare the students' record with what the lecturer's own manuscript tells us he had planned to say. What the students heard occasionally helps to explain what we see in Luther's manuscript. It is obvious that Luther dictated his glosses to his students with scrupulous faithfulness to his manuscript, but in the case of the scholia he apparently abbreviated and omitted with complete freedom and occasionally substituted new materials or exposition previously given in his lectures on the Psalms.

From these two sources, Luther's own manuscript of the glosses and scholia (Weimar Edition, Vol. LVI) and the composite student notes of the lectures (Weimar Edition, Vol. LVII), we get a very interesting and reliable account of the lectures. In the manner of the day, Luther read the Latin text of the Scriptures and interspersed it with short explanatory paraphrases of individual words and expressions (interlinear glosses), here and there stopping to dictate somewhat longer interpretations to be written into the margin (marginal glosses). Then again he might announce and launch a still longer discussion of an individual phrase or section of the text (scholia). Here he would adduce standard *auctoritates*, that is, authoritative statements, primarily from the Scriptures but also from the fathers and the more recent teachers of the church. To the latter two he might attach a refutation of the statements adduced, a new interpretation, or praise or criticism of the way Scripture was currently being understood and applied to life.

In using all of these standard devices, Luther was of course in part a traditionalist who quoted again what had been everybody's sources—the *Glossa ordinaria,* assembled from various church fathers by Walafried Strabo (d. 849), and the *Glossa interlinearis,* a kind of spiritual interpretation assembled by Anselm of Laon (d. 1117). But in the lectures on Romans Luther also frees himself of mere repetition of these sources. He may quote them without acknowledgment when they are useful, he may refute them with or without acknowledgment, or he may elucidate them with references to authority of his own choosing, especially the Scriptures but also Augustine, Ambrose, Jerome, Bernard, Lombard, Scotus, Lyra, Occam, Biel, Faber, Reuchlin, Erasmus. In any case, the utterances of men he may at any time take as materials to be criticized and refuted on the way to articulating his own Biblical stance. And on the basis of this stance he may find it worthwhile to make an application to contemporary faith and morals. More often than not, however, such applications, though written out at length and with obvious care in the scholia, were not used in the lecture hall, as the student notes seem to show.

Avoiding both the rigid partition of the fourfold interpretation of Scripture practiced by the scholastics (historical, allegorical, tropological, anagogical) and the literal historical interpretation of Nicholas of Lyra, Luther worked his way toward a historical-Christological interpretation that was to be the core and center not only of his teaching but also of his preaching and living. A prophetic preview as it were of the whole series of lectures on Romans is sounded in the marginal gloss to *de filio suo* in Rom. 1:3: "Here the door is thrown open wide for the understanding of Holy Scripture, that is, that everything must be understood in relation to Christ." In the scholia the same thought is introduced at the very beginning of chapter one with the words: "The chief purpose of this letter is to break down, to pluck up, and to destroy all wisdom and righteousness of the flesh." The one chief topic of Romans for Luther is "the righteousness of God," that is, the righteousness by which God makes sinners righteous through faith in Jesus Christ. We recall Luther's own confession late in life (1545) concerning his struggles with Rom. 1:17 and the consolation afforded him when the context "he who through faith is righteous shall live" permitted him to conclude that he was "altogether born again and had entered Paradise itself through open gates." In that report he also states, "I was more skillful after I had lectured in the university on St. Paul's epistles to the Romans, to the Galatians, and the one to the Hebrews" (*Luther's Works*, 34, pp. 336–337). The whole series of lectures on Romans shows Luther already "skillful" in his understanding of the righteousness of God, even though he still moves about in much of the vocabulary and the teaching forms of his predecessors distant and near.

The story of the transmission of the text of Luther's *Lectures on Romans* is indeed an interesting one. Apparently Luther never intended to publish these notes. They were written for his own use in the lecture hall. Nevertheless, he seems to have preserved them carefully, intending perhaps to use them again for a repetition of the lectures in future years. This purpose never materialized, perhaps because Melanchthon took over the Romans lectures when he arrived at the university in 1518. There is even the surmise that Melanchthon, who is known to have lectured on Romans five times, may have used Luther's notes for his work.

After Luther's death the Romans manuscript was preserved by his son Paul, but his sons in turn sold it among other Martin Luther manuscripts to the margrave of Brandenburg, Joachim Frederick, in 1594. In the meantime the manuscript was generally considered to be lost, expressly so by the Reformation scholar and historian Veit von Seckendorf. For a time it must have been in the possession of that indefatigable scholar and scribe, Johann Aurifaber, who together with other scholars made a copy of the manuscript at the request of Ulrich Fugger (d. 1584), the scion of the famous financier family and a Protestant collector of rare books and manuscripts of the Reformation. Strangely enough, it was through this copy, which in the Thirty Years' War found its way to the Vatican Library, that the search for Luther's original manuscript was resumed at the beginning of our century and through the painstaking efforts of Johannes Ficker carried to a successful conclusion.

The manuscript had for several centuries been in such safe hands that its existence was not even suspected. But in 1846 the Royal Library in Berlin exhibited the manuscript in a special display in connection with the tercentenary of Luther's death under the program title *Lateinischer Kommentar zum Briefe Pauli an die Römer von Luthers eigener Hand; davor der Druck dieses Briefes lateinisch, Wittenberg, 1515.* Then another period of oblivion followed while the manuscript continued its obscure existence in a public display case in the library. But the discovery of the copy in the Vatican Library spurred Johannes Ficker on to search far and wide for the original until he found it. His preliminary edition was published in 1908. The definitive edition prepared by Ficker did not appear until 1938, and then as Vol. LVI of the Weimar Edition of Luther's works.

In Vol. LVII of the Weimar Edition (1939) Ficker also published the extant student notebook manuscripts *(Vorlesungshefte/ Nachschriften)* of the lectures on Romans. The importance of these is outlined by the editor in the statement: "More frequently than is commonly known, student notebooks are extant from the time of the transition from the Middle Ages to the Reformation. Sometimes they are the witness of the lectures held by Luther, at other times, as in the case of the lectures on Romans, they are the indispensable complement to the Reformer's own elaboration and the concrete echo in which the university professor's work for the interpretation of Holy Scriptures and for the instruction of his students can be perceived in its immediate effect."

The present translation reproduces for the first time in English both the complete interlinear and marginal glosses and the scholia (for chapter 16 Luther did not provide scholia). The first section contains the glosses, the second the scholia. The interlinear glosses have been inserted between portions of the Biblical text in order to place them as close as possible to the text they strive to elucidate and in order to approximate the order in which Luther may have read them in the lecture hall. The marginal glosses appear as footnotes with demibold superior numerals. To this we have added, largely from the prodigious apparatus of the Weimar editor, such identifications and references as the reader may wish to have easily at hand. These footnotes appear with superior numbers in regular type below the marginal notes. Scripture references have usually been identified in full, whether Luther identified them or not. The *Nachschriften* of Weimar Vol. LVII were at various times helpful in the editorial process, but their help is not always acknowledged specifically.

The English translation was begun by Walter G. Tillmanns, formerly professor of German at Wartburg College, Waverly, Iowa.

A sudden severe illness leading to an untimely death, however, prevented him from carrying beyond the second chapter a project he dearly loved. The bulk of the translation, chapters 3—16, was supplied by Jacob A. O. Preus, formerly president of Concordia Theological Seminary, Springfield, Ill., and at the time of the conclusion of the project president of The Lutheran Church—Missouri Synod.

Two volumes that have been of inestimable value in the preparation of our edition are the German translation of the scholia and most of the marginal glosses by Eduard Ellwein, published as a supplementary volume to *Martin Luther, Ausgewählte Werke*, ed. H. H. Borcherdt and Georg Merz, 5th ed. (Munich, Chr. Kaiser Verlag, 1965), and the English translation of all the scholia and of the glosses to which Luther himself refers in the scholia by Wilhelm Pauck, published as Vol. 15 in *The Library of Christian Classics* (Philadelphia: The Westminster Press, 1961). Particularly informative concerning Luther's exegetical task and procedure is the 60-page "General Introduction" of the latter volume.

In the present volume the modern reader has before him the full picture of Luther's personal notes for his lectures on Romans, a picture more complete than even those who heard the lectures in Luther's own time could have had. This is a truly remarkable link in the chain of lectures that led to 1517: Psalms, Romans, Galatians, Hebrews.

H. O.

LECTURES ON ROMANS

GLOSSES

Chapters 1–2

Translated by
WALTER G. TILLMANNS

Chapters 3–16

Translated by
JACOB A. O. PREUS

CHAPTER ONE [1]

Summary [1]*: The apostle shows that he loves the Romans and then reproves the faults of those who follow their own lusts.*

1. *Paul, a servant of Jesus Christ.* Because of such a great Lord he is to be received with the same reverence as if he were Christ Himself,[2] Christ who says (Luke 10:16): "He who hears you."

[1] The whole purpose and intention of the apostle in this epistle is to break down all righteousness and wisdom of our own, to point out again those sins and foolish practices which did not exist (that is, those whose existence we did not recognize on account of that kind of righteousness), to blow them up and to magnify [2] them (that is, to cause them to be recognized as still in existence and as numerous and serious), and thus to show that for breaking them down Christ and His righteousness are needed for us. This he does up to chapter 12.[3] From there to the end he teaches in what kind of works we should be involved, once that righteousness of Christ has been received. For in the presence of God this is not the way, that a person becomes righteous by doing works of righteousness (as the foolish Jews, Gentiles, and all other self-righteous people [4] proudly think), but he who has been made righteous does works of righteousness, as it is written: "And the Lord had regard for Abel and for his offering" (Gen. 4:4), not in the first place "for his offering."

[2] The apostle extols his ministry not for the purpose of lording it over them, but that they may receive him in humility as a minister of God and be fearful of belittling him. Although no person should ever think too highly of himself, he should nevertheless, to the best of his ability, think highly of his ministry to the glory of God. At the same time it should not be necessary for him to prove everything he says. They should listen to him as if they were listening to God Himself.

[1] The summaries at the heads of chapters were a part of Luther's printed Scripture text and are derived almost verbatim from the glosses of Nicholas of Lyra (d. 1340).

[2] Consistent with the language of the church in all ages, Luther uses *magnificare* (sometimes *magnum esse agnoscere*) with such diverse objects as "God," "sins," and "grace of God."

[3] For the division of the epistle into two sections (chs. 1—11; 12—16), see *Luther's Works,* 27, p. 381, and also W, IV, 339 f.

[4] Cf. Aristotle, *Nicomachean Ethics,* II, 1: "We become just by doing just acts." This and similar sentences in Aristotle, together with their influence on

Called [5] *to be an apostle,*[3] not an intruder or interloper, driven by ambition, like a false apostle, who "does not enter . . . by the door but climbs in by another way." These false apostles come by their own temerity, therefore they are thieves and not shepherds, as John 10 tells us. Heb. 5:4: "One does not take the honor upon himself, but he is called by God, as Aaron was." *Set apart.* Acts 13:2: "The Holy Spirit said, 'Set apart for Me . . . Paul.'" *For the Gospel of God,* for the Gospel to the uncircumcised, just as Peter was set apart for the Gospel of the circumcision. 2. *Which He had promised before,* in the Old Covenant, because Amos 3:7 reads: "The Lord God does nothing without revealing beforehand, etc.," so that our glorying may cease. *Through His prophets,* not through the prophets of Baal, as we see in Jer. 31:31 and Ps. 109:2 ff. and as it is implied in Hebrews, *passim. In the Holy Scriptures,* from which it follows that while the prophets gave their message in spoken words, yet they wanted to indicate the spirit in the written Word. 3. *Concerning His Son,*[4] not in the general sense, but concerning His incarnate Son, as the following words indicate. *Who was made,* in the Virgin Mary, *(for Him)*[7] *of the seed of David according to the flesh,* as had been promised in Ps. 132:11: "Of the sons of your body." 4. *And predestined,*[5] that is, appointed, or-

[3] Not because "apostle" is to be the name by which he is to be addressed but because he has been called to this great office by God.

[4] Here the door is thrown open wide [6] for the understanding of Holy Scriptures, that is, that everything must be understood in relation to Christ, especially in the case of prophecy. But Scripture is completely prophetical, although not according to the superficial sense of the letter.

[5] *Predestinatus* is a poor translation, because the apostle does not speak here of Christ as predestined for a future kingdom, but as the One who has even now achieved the Kingdom, as if he were saying: "God promised the Gospel of Christ, who has now become incarnate and has been enthroned as King and Lord of the

scholasticism, are frequently attacked by Luther. See W, IV, 3, 32; *Luther's Works,* 31, p. 12, Theses 40—42; 48, p. 25. For a discussion of Luther's polemic against Aristotle, see Gerhard Ebeling, *Luther: An Introduction to His Thought,* trans. R. A. Wilson (London: Collins, 1970), pp. 150—158.

[5] After the word *vocatus* in the printed Scripture text Luther made a mark to call attention to a comment to be made at this point and to be found, in his own hand, in the marginal space nearby. Such marks served in place of our footnote numbering system.

[6] This metaphor was common in the church's literature, but Luther was fond of using it at especially critical points in his own experience. See *Luther's Works,* 54, p. 49, No. 347; 34, p. 337.

[7] Luther bracketed the word *ei* in the Latin text.

dained, prepared,[6] *the Son of God,* so that He Himself, the Man Christ, is the Son of God, not according to the flesh but according to the Spirit, *in power,* that is, through the acceptance of His rule and power above everything, according to Ps. 8:6-8 and Ps. 110:1. *According to the Spirit of sanctification,* that is, according to the Holy Spirit, because He does not have this exalted estate on the basis of His natural birth but because the Spirit elevated Him, *by the resurrection,* because the Spirit did not glorify Him before His resurrection, *from the dead,* from among the dead, *of our Lord Jesus Christ.*[8] 5. *Through whom,* because we indeed have everything from God, but only through Christ, *we have received,* all believers, because all ministry is for the benefit of all, as Eph. 4 teaches. *Grace,* by which he becomes worthy for the ministry,[7] *and apostleship,* the highest ministry existing in the church, *to bring about the obedience of faith,*[8, 9] not for the purpose of dominating and being overbearing, as now. That is, so that all the Gentiles should become obedient and submit themselves to faith. And this makes clear what an apostle to the Gentiles is, as he stated above, "set apart for the Gospel of God." *Among all the nations,* for that reason his ministry is very comprehensive, not merely over one church of the Gentiles but over all, *for the sake of His name,* that is, for, and in place of, the same Christ, as we see in 2 Cor. 5:20. 6. *Among whom are you also,* as part of the Gentiles who are obedient in faith, *the called,* by His grace, *of Jesus Christ,* of such a Person, I say. Paul tells you what follows. 7. *To all who are,* in Greek: "you who are," *in Rome, the beloved of God,* because His

universe," as Heb. 1:2 states: "Whom He appointed the heir of all things," and Acts 2:36: "That God has made this Jesus both Lord and Christ." Ps. 2:8 also applies.

6 Unless "predestined," that is, "destined before others," is understood.

7 Because the Lord looks at the person before He looks at his ministry.

8 He says "of faith," not "of wisdom," which can be proved by reason and testing. He has no intention of proving what he is going to say but wants to be believed simply as one who possesses divine authority. There should be no argument about faith and the things which should be believed.

9 The Greek has "for the obedience of faith." In the church of Christ no prelate is appointed for his own sake, but for the sake of others, that he should bring them to obedience to the Gospel.

---

8 For Luther's explanation of this genitive, see the scholia comment below, p. 148.

love is the beginning of all good things in us.[10] *called* [11] *to be saints,*
sanctified through Christ. *Grace,* which bestows the remission of
sins, *to you and peace,* which removes the torment of the conscience, *from God the Father,* from whom we have everything,
and from our Lord, not from men and the world, because "not as
the world gives peace, do I give to you" (John 14:27), *Jesus Christ.*
8. *First* [12] *I thank my God,* from whom these and all other good
things come, *through Jesus Christ,* who alone is our Mediator,
for all of you,[13] *because your faith,* that is, the faith by which you
believe in Christ and also the faith that justifies, *is proclaimed,*
which is done by the faithful, not by the adversaries, *in all the
world,* throughout all the churches of the world, because this
arouses the others so much more than if you were not Romans.
9. *For God is my witness,* His is the role of a sworn deponent,
whom I serve, that is, whom I attend in the capacity of a servant,
with my spirit,[14] in the spiritual man, "lest after preaching to

[10] Love comes before the call, just as the call comes before sanctification.[9]
Likewise, he wants them to know that they are saints not on the basis of their
merits but on the basis of the love and call of God, so that everything is centered
in God.

[11] No one becomes faithful and holy unless he is called by God. But "many
are called, few are chosen" (Matt. 22:14).

[12] This is the Christian and true way of praising people — not to praise
people for their own sake but to praise God in them first and foremost and to
attribute everything to Him, as Is. 49:3 says: "You are My servant, Israel, in
whom I will be glorified," and Is. 43:21: "This people have I formed for Myself,
they shall show forth My praise." Second, he shows that God is not praised except
through Christ, because as we received everything from God through Him, so
we must return everything to God through Him, since He alone is worthy to
appear before the face of God and to carry on His priestly office for us, as 1 Peter
2:5 tells us: "To offer up spiritual sacrifices acceptable to God by Jesus Christ,"
and Heb. 13:15: "Through Him then let us continually offer up a sacrifice of
praise to God, that is, the fruits of lips that acknowledge His name." Third, he
wants to show those who are being praised that they are still in need of more
help for growth and strengthening, so that they do not become overbearing.

[13] This is the nature of love, that it rejoices in the good gifts of the neighbor,
especially his spiritual gifts, and glorifies God in them; as contrariwise it is characteristic for envy to be sad about a neighbor's good gifts and to curse them.

[14] All are serving God, even the evil ones, consequently also the preachers
of the Gospel, even though they may not have the Spirit. But all this the apostle
says that he may show publicly that he is a doer of the Gospel and that on that
account he is a qualified teacher of the same.

---

[9] *Sanctificatio* is here used by Luther in its most literal sense, "making holy,"
as in Eph. 5:26-27: "Christ . . . gave Himself up for her [the church], that He
might *sanctify* her, . . . that she might be holy." Lyra, *Postillae perpetuae in
universa biblia,* on Rom. 1:7, adds to the word "saints" the explanation "made
holy through Baptism."

others, I myself should be disqualified" (1 Cor. 9:27), *in the Gospel,*
by expounding and teaching, *of His Son,* which is the same "of
His Son" as above [10] and is said of the same Son, because He is the
Lord of all, *that without ceasing I mention you* [15] *always,* not
"always," generally speaking, but in all prayers, *in my prayers.*
10. *Asking* [16] *that somehow by God's will I may now at last succeed,*
thus every faithful pastor is urged to seek out not what the sheep
have, but the sheep themselves, and love accomplishes that completely, *in coming to you.* 11. *For I long,* with a spiritual longing
that arises from the love of friendship,[11] *to see you,* not the city of
Rome or certain persons, as the curious people do, but "you,"
that is, the believers and Christians. And he does this not because
he is vain or has no reason, but he does it, he says, "for you," not
"for myself," *that I may impart to you,* not that I may seek "my"
gain or delight—as the love of concupiscence does—but "yours,"
some spiritual gift, a spiritual gift, namely, the ministry of teaching,
to strengthen you,[17] who are already planted in faith so that you
may be strengthened through additional instruction. 12. *That is,
that we may be mutually encouraged in you,* better: "with you,"
because in God comfort is ours through faith, *by each other's
faith,* through our mutual faith, *both yours and mine.*[18] 13. *I would
not,*[19] that you may know that the trouble was not with me but that
even now I am ready and willing, *have you ignorant, brethren,
that I have often intended to come to you,* I was ready to bring it,
although it would be proper rather to come to get such a great gift,
and thus far have been prevented, that is, I have been burdened

[15] Because prayer is at its best when one prays for the universal salvation
of all, not for one's own only but for everybody's.

[16] Because not even lesser tasks ought to be undertaken without prayer and
the counsel of God; how much more these spiritual tasks.

[17] The perversity of the flesh seeks its own gratification in others, but the
spirit desires only what is good for others, even when it concerns one's own things.
Here he teaches us beautifully by his own example how a prelate should visit the
people who are under him (or one person should visit another).

[18] He places them ahead of himself, saying "yours" before he says "mine,"
as he teaches in Rom. 12:10: "Outdo one another in showing honor."

[19] Here he shows that he is not an "idol" or a slothful prelate but a concerned pastor and faithful minister of God, ready always and for all people to
pay the debt of his strength and of his ministry.

[10] See v. 3 above.

[11] For "love of friendship" and "love of concupiscence," see Gabriel Biel's
discussion of Occam's definitions in *Sent.,* II, d. 1, qu. 5a 2, n. 1, and *Sent.,* III,
d. 27, qu. un. D.

with a large number of places where preaching had to be done, *in order that I may reap some harvest among you,* not only among those whose faith is just beginning but especially among those who are making progress and those who are to be made perfect,[12] *as well as among the rest of the Gentiles,* as I brought forth fruit among the Greeks and the people of Arabia. 14. *To Greeks and to barbarians,*[20] and not only that, but also *to the wise and to the foolish,* both among the Greeks and the barbarians, *I am under obligation,* because of the office of apostleship.[21] 15. *So I am eager,* that is, there is a readiness, *to preach the Gospel also to you who are in Rome.* 16. *For I am not ashamed of the Gospel,*[22] in spite of 1 Cor. 1:23: "A stumbling block to Jews and folly to Gentiles," *for it is the power,*[23] that is, the strength, *of God* [24] *for salvation* [25] *to everyone,* both Gentile and Jew, *who has faith,* and on the other hand, for

[20] He meets two hidden objections: first, if someone should argue that it is temerity for him to extend his apostolate beyond the Greek-speaking world into Latin territory and elsewhere; second, if someone should object that he is presuming to teach also those in the faith who are already filled with wisdom and educated, such as the Romans are, as he has stated above. Or if some one should say that he dares to impose himself as a teacher upon the wise of this world. He answers both objections by stating that he is doing this work not because of his temerity but because of the obligation of his office.

[21] As the Lord says: "Go into the whole world, teach all the nations" (cf. Mark 16:15; Matt. 28:19).

[22] Here the prologue ends and the epistle proper begins. The preceding remarks were made to win the attention and goodwill of his listeners; their attention, in showing the greatness of his office and the glory of the Word, or Gospel; their goodwill, in merely promising to be servant and debtor to their salvation.[13]

[23] "But we preach Christ crucified, a stumbling block to Jews and folly to Gentiles, but to those who are called (to be saints) . . . the power of God and the wisdom of God" (1 Cor. 1:23-24).

[24] That is, that he who believes in Him has power from God and is wise above all things.

[25] That is, it is a power unto salvation for all who believe, or it is the Word that has power to save all who believe in it. And this is given through God and from God. It is as if you should say: "This jewel has this power from God, that he who wears it cannot be wounded." Thus the Gospel has this ingredient from God, that he who believes in it is saved. In this way, therefore, the person who has the Gospel is powerful and wise before, and from, God, even though in the eyes of men he may be considered foolish and weak.

[12] In a sermon of 1516 Luther describes these three traditional stages of "sanctification" in some detail and sums up by saying: "The first stage is that of beginners, the second is that of those making progress, and the third is that of those coming to perfection." See W, I, 90—92.

[13] Cf. 1 Cor. 9:19-23.

damnation to him who does not have faith,[26] *to the Jew first,* because the Jews alone have the Promise,[14] *and also to the Greek,* that is, the Gentiles. 17. *For the righteousness,*[15] by which a person is worthy of such salvation, *of God,* by which alone there are righteous people before God, *is revealed in it,* because formerly it was considered hidden and to consist in a person's own works. But now it is "revealed," because no one is righteous unless he believes, as it is written in the last chapter of Mark (16:16): "He who believes," *from faith to faith, as it is written,* Hab. 2:4: *"The righteous,* namely, in the eyes of God, *shall live by faith,*[16] that is, only through complete belief in God will he be saved. This is the eternal life of the Spirit. 18. *For the wrath of God is revealed,*[27] namely, in the same Gospel it is announced that God is angry, although until now He is postponing punishment, *from heaven against all ungodliness,* on account of their turning away from the true God, *and wickedness,* on account of their turning to idol worship, *of men,* especially of the Gentiles, *who by their wickedness,* that is, by attributing His honor to others, *suppress,* that is, by not glorifying God, giving thanks to Him, and worshiping Him (see below), *the truth of God,* that is, the true known God, or the true knowledge concerning God. But that they have had the truth of God and have held it back he now shows. 19. *For*[28] *what is known of God,* that is, the knowledge of and about God, *is manifest in them,* that is, they have this manifestation about Him in themselves, *because God has shown it to them,* that is, He has shown them amply how they may recognize Him, namely, as follows: 20. *For the invisible things,* such as goodness, wisdom, righteousness, etc., *of Him, ever since the creation of the world,* that is,

[26] John 12:48: "He who rejects Me and does not receive My sayings has a judge; the word that I have spoken will be his judge on the last day."

[27] Here he begins to show that all men are sinners and foolish, so that they may realize that their wisdom and righteousness is of no account and that they need the righteousness of Christ, and he demonstrates this first with the example of the Gentiles.

[28] First he shows that they had the truth of God, second, that they held on to unrighteousness. See below (v. 21): "For although they knew."

---

[14] Luther probably has Rom. 9:4 in mind.

[15] Concerning this passage cf. Luther's "Preface to the . . . Latin Writings," *Luther's Works,* 34, pp. 336—37. See also W, *Tischreden,* V, Nos. 5518, 5553; W, III, 174, 13 ff.

[16] Luther rejects the interpretations of Lyra and the medieval glosses. See the fuller statement in the scholia below, p. 152.

since the act of creation, *by the things that have been made,* that is, from the works, that when they see that there are works, they also recognize that a Creator is necessary, *are clearly seen,* perceived not by the senses but by the understanding, *His eternal power also,* His strength, for this His works declare, *and Deity,* that is, that He really is God. *So they are without excuse,*[29] as much those who have thus sinned knowingly in the first place as those whom they have made their followers through such great ignorance. 21. *For,*[30] therefore they cannot be excused, *although they knew God,* as has been shown before. But this knowledge they suppressed in unrighteousness, *they did not honor Him as God,* but rather claimed the glory of such knowledge for themselves, as if they had learned it by the keenness of their talents, *or give thanks to Him,* for so many good things of creation and for knowledge itself, *but they became vain,* emptied of truth. They became vain and worth nothing, although in the eyes of people they became great and wise and as if they knew everything, *in their thoughts,* that is, in their studies, wisdom, and speculations, *and their senseless minds were darkened,* on account of the blindness of their state of mind, because in their poor conception of nature, or their poor conception of God, they have continued without love and worship.[31] 22. *Claiming,* since they have become so vain that they want to teach everybody, *to be wise,* namely, to know everything, even God Himself, *they became fools,*[32] since they did not know

[29] That is, from the beginning of the world to its end He has always done and does such great things that people, if they would only use their understanding beyond what their senses show them, could easily and clearly recognize God. Thus it was from the beginning of the world, even though gradually the godless more and more obscured it on account of their ingratitude as they went on to idolatry. Thus neither they nor their followers who have been deceived by them have an excuse, as is also the case with the Jews.

[30] Second, he shows that in unrighteousness they suppressed the truth of God which they had.

[31] Just as people would consider a person who seeks gold merely to see it, but not to possess it, a fool; so these people, after they had discovered God, were pleased only with their discovery and became proud of it, and they forgot to worship, and to love the God whom they had learned to know.

[32] This is a golden rule. By inductive reasoning it can be applied to all people. It would be different if someone else would have said it. There are people who say that they are foolish and bad, but they do not say it sincerely, but because they want to hear others say that they are wise and good. This is the most artless cunning of arrogance. But he who confesses honestly that he is foolish is truly wise. Thus those who boast that they are powerful, handsome, noble — even though they may be all these things in the eyes of men — are by that very fact weak, ugly, and ignoble in the eyes of God.

Him and all things with their heart and in love. 23. *And exchanged,*[33] not God Himself, because He cannot be corrupted, *the glory of the incorruptible* [19] *God,*[34] that is, the glorious and incorruptible Deity, *for images resembling,*[35] that is, because they looked upon God as being similar not only to man or animal in the flesh but also to a lifeless picture or likeness, *corruptible,* that is, mortal, *man* [36] *or,* namely, like the image of, *birds* [37] *or animals or reptiles.*[38] 24. *Therefore God gave them up,* that is, some of them,

[33] *And exchanged,* namely, in themselves, through their own faulty evaluation, not in God, who is unchangeable.[17]

[34] For the sin of omission leads by natural inclination to the sin of commission. Therefore, after the apostle has shown how they sinned by omitting to serve the true God, he shows here how they are guilty of the sin of commission by establishing the worship of a false god and idol. The nature of the human mind is so changeable that when it turns away from one thing, it of necessity turns to another. Therefore a person who turns away from the Creator of necessity turns to the creature.

[35] For emphasis the statement here is *for images resembling, etc.* For the idolatrous nations had a number of images of men to whom they believed their gods similar, such as Jupiter, Mercury, Pan, Priapus. These were images of corruptible men, but they believed that the Deity was in their likeness. Therefore the expression *resembling* here should not be understood as implying a formed or molded work of art, such as an image or effigy, but as a perverse and wrong comparison and estimate by which they *exchanged* the Deity *for images resembling,* that is, they made Him resemble them, not in reality but in the way in which they thought of Him, and they looked upon Him as a mere "image." Therefore one might say more clearly: "In likeness to images," or "Like something similar to images," as in Acts 17:29 the same Paul tells the Athenians: "Being then God's offspring, we ought not to think that the Divine (that is, the Deity) is like gold, or silver, or stone, a representation by the art and imagination of man." And Is. 40:18-19: "To whom then will you liken God? or what likeness compare with Him? Will the workman cast a graven statue? etc."

[36] But also man is, according to his soul, "incorruptible." These people have not even shown that much reverence to God, that they have put Him on the same level with their inner hearts. They see Him in a physical likeness and as one that looks like man only according to the body, which is also "corruptible."

[37] It is quite clear that he does not refer to individual Gentiles here but speaks of all of them together, because not only individuals are worshiping images of men and birds, but some worship the image of men, others the image of birds, as is well known.

[38] This is known to all those who have read the books of the Gentiles and others. However, he does not say anything about stars and celestial bodies and other created things, because those who worship things fashioned [18] by men will also worship things created by God, for he is tacitly arguing from the lesser and less noted example.

[17] For Luther's use of *immutabilis* and *incorruptibilis* see also the glosses below on Rom. 2:2 and 4:20 and also his scholia on Rom. 3:5, p. 219 below.

[18] *Ficta,* as compared with facta, "created," by God.

[19] See n. 17 above.

not only to let them have their way but also to teach them a lesson, *in the lusts*, that they should be torn away by them and led away like slaves, *of their hearts*, wise in a carnal way. The explanation is: *to uncleanness*,[39] which is properly [20] called wantonness, *to the dishonoring*, that is, a disgrace that is serious in the eyes of God and in the Spirit, although they themselves may think nothing of it, *of their*, their own, *bodies among themselves*, because there is still another disgrace in the bodies of other people, as he explains below. 25. *Because they*, the Greek says "who," [21] *exchanged*, not in the substance of God but in their own mind, *the truth about God*, the right understanding of the true essence of God, *for a lie*, by putting Him on the same level with the likeness of things, *and worshiped*, venerated, and served, in the service of worship, *the creature rather than the Creator*, to whom alone such worship is due, *who is blessed*, actually: by whom all men are blessed, *forever. Amen.*[40] 26. *For this reason*, namely: idolatry, *God gave*, not only to the above-mentioned disgrace, *them*, some of them, *up to dishonorable passions*, to shameful feelings and desires, before God, although even they, like Sodom, called this sin. *Their women*, some of them, and here he again shows that he is speaking not

[39] The apostle expresses that base manner of life in an embarrassed and indirect way and censures it under the labels "uncleanness" and "disgrace." For as it is a disgrace, physically and in the eyes of men, for one's body to be filthy and deformed but an honor for it to be handsome and well proportioned, so also morally speaking and in the presence of the Spirit in God its honor is chastity and integrity, and its disgrace is wantonness and corruption and riotous living. In the same way we must also speak about cleanness and uncleanness, that is, one is the physical aspect, and here one can be better than the other, as we see when we think of consumption and putrefaction, and the other is the spiritual aspect.

[40] It seems that the apostle holds on to this expression from his religious background as a Jew. For the rabbis of the Jews add the following two words whenever they mention the name of God: "Holy, Blessed One." [22] So he is here saying: "Holy, Blessed." This was the reason why also Caiaphas said: "Tell us, if you are the Christ, the Son of the Blessed God." [23]

---

[20] We have adopted the reading *proprie* suggested in a footnote by the Weimar editor.

[21] Luther's version read *quia*, but the modern Vulgate reads *qui*, as in Luther's gloss.

[22] The Hebrew form is הַקָּדוֹשׁ בָּרוּךְ הוּא , "Holy, Blessed He."

[23] Luther quotes Caiaphas in the form of Matt. 26:63 but adds *benedicti*, "of the Blessed," which is found only in Mark 14:61. Luther makes the same point, quoting the passage from Mark, in a gloss to Ps. 66:6. See W, III, 378, 31—33.

about individuals but about women as a group, *exchanged natural relations,* intercourse with men in matrimony, *for unnatural.* He does not give details of the character of these relations, whether it is mutual abuse or lying with demons or animals. 27. *And the men likewise,* with an overpowering drive of lust, *gave up natural relations* [41] *with women and were consumed with passion,* which overpowered the judgment of their reason, *for one another, men with men,* and thus they deal with each other in mutual disgrace, *committing shameless acts and,* consequently, *receiving the penalty,* punishment, *due for their error,* fitting and just for so great a sin, the sin of idolatry, *in their own persons,* according to the teaching and arrangement of God. 28. *And since they did not see fit,* tried or tested it negligently,[42] *to acknowledge God,* so that their heart would not become blind through the loss of the knowledge of God; to this, I say, they did not pay much attention. Therefore: *God gave them up,* by a fitting punishment and through just condemnation, *to a base mind,* a perverse mind, to have a taste for and be influenced in the direction of things perverse, *to do those things which are not proper,* which are unworthy of human beings. 29. *They were filled with all iniquity,* that is, unrighteousness by which they are unrighteous by themselves before God, *malice,* others [24] have "wickedness," *fornication,*[43] *avarice, wickedness,* others have "spite," *full of envy, murder, contention,* full of discord and quarrels, *deceit, malignity,* others have "depraved habits." 30. *Whisperers,* murmurers against each other, *detractors, hateful to God, contumelious,* insulting with words, *proud,* placing themselves above others, *haughty,* arrogant,

[41] "Natural relations" does not mean those that are without sin, as in marriage, but those according to the analogy of the sex, even outside of marriage.

[42] The statement "They did not see fit" can be understood in a dual sense. First, in the sense of testing, trying, or paying attention to, as in 1 Thess. 5:21: "Test everything," that is, "try and investigate." Second, as "approve," or "esteem worthy." This is the smoother meaning, which would imply: "They did not esteem God worthy of their attention," that is, they did not esteem God worthy or great enough to know Him but rather accepted something else as greater than God, namely, their own vanity.

[43] All this, as I said above, must be understood in this way: Not everybody did all these things, but some did some of these, others did others, some did more of them, others only a few; yet they are one body, and against this the apostle speaks here.

---

[24] By "others" Luther means Faber Stapulensis, whose text reads: *repletos omni iniusticia, fornicatione, naequitia, avaricia, malignitate, plenos invidia, caede, contentione, dolo, depravata consuetudine.*

proud of things which they do not have, *inventors,* so that they hurt others with new types of malice, *of evil lusts,* new ones, *disobedient to parents,* rebels. 31. *Foolish,* not knowing God and the things that are of the Spirit, *dissolute,* in morals and discipline, *without affection,* that is, love for others, *without fidelity,* that is, faithless, or such as do not keep faith, *without mercy,* having no feeling for anyone who is in need. 32. *Though they know the righteousness of God,* by which He Himself is righteous and judges, as stated above,[44] *they did not understand* [45] *that those who do such things, deserve to die,* not only the death of the body but also that of Gehenna, *not only they who do them, but also they who* [46] *approve those who practice them.*

[44] Because we read above (v. 20): "The invisible things of God, etc.," of which one is the righteousness of God itself. For he who knows God knows also that He is righteous, good, and powerful.

[45] The words "they did not understand" are superfluous, they are indeed a bad addition in the Latin text, because they are contrary to, and negate, the preceding passage, "Though they know," unless they are brought into harmony by doing violence to the text.

[46] The pronoun "who" in both places is superfluous.

CHAPTER TWO

Summary: The apostle refutes the faults of the Jews, saying that as far as their guilt is concerned they are the same as the Gentiles and in a certain respect even worse.

1. *Therefore*, since those who act in this way are worthy of death, it follows that *you have no excuse*, just as if you nevertheless believe that you are convicted by your own verdict, *O man, whoever you are*, outside of Christ and not yet spiritual, *who judge*, no matter how well or even better you do things than they and therefore judge them,[1] *For in whatever*, namely, in some special evil thing,

---

[1] All those who are outside of Christ have this fault, for as Prov. 18:17 says, "The just is first accuser of himself,"[1] in heart, word, and deed, and thus the unjust is always the first accuser and judge of his neighbor, at least in his heart. The reason for this is that the just person is always endeavoring to see his own evil works and to overlook those of others, likewise to see the good points in others and to overlook his own good points. The unjust, on the other hand, tries to look only for the good points in himself and for the bad points in others. Therefore the apostle does well that, after he has rebuked those who have really committed such evil deeds, he now declares that those who imagine that they are better than those are just as bad, because they act as if the things that he has said above did not apply to them. From this the apostle concludes that they, too, need Christ and His righteousness, since necessarily all those who are outside of Christ do the same works as those do, no matter how they pretend to do or not do them. This bold assertion has its basis in that the apostle mentions many faults here which some of these people do not have. Therefore they judge these faults in others without noticing that they themselves have different faults which are also enumerated here and which the others perhaps do not have. Thus the usurious miser by forgetting about himself accuses the adulterer and constantly condemns him sharply, and vice versa, the adulterer accuses the miser, etc. The haughty person does the same thing with all others. Therefore, it is impossible that anyone should be free of this false judgment except the man who

---

[1] Luther provides a graphic exegesis for this passage in his Latin letter to Spalatin of February 15, 1518: "O what a long-neglected definition of justice! What is justice? It is self-accusation. What is a just man? One who accuses himself. Why? Because he anticipates the judgment of God and condemns what God condemns, that is, himself, and therefore in all things agrees with God and His judgment." Cf. W, Br., I, 145, 28—32. Already in his first lecture on Ps. 1 (1513) Luther used this exegesis of Prov. 18:17 to elucidate the concept *iudicium*. Cf. W, III, 29, 9—16.

you judge another, reckon him to be an evil person, *you condemn yourself*, although you may not share the same sin, yet,[2] *because*, this gives the reason, *you who[2] judge are doing the very same things*, although not all the things, some of the things mentioned above.[3] For the judge must above all be innocent of the things which he judges in others. 2. *For we know that the judgment of God*, but not your judgment, although it may agree with His, namely, that they are worthy of death, *is according to truth*, for it is itself unchangeable truth, *against those who do such things*, for He is the only one who does not do what He judges, that is, He is the only true judge. 3. *Do you suppose*, such a presumptuous thought, *O man*, you who are wise carnally and in the ways of men, *that when you judge those who do such things*, the above-mentioned vices, *and yet do them yourself*, that is, similar things, *you will escape the judgment of God?* It is as if he were saying: "No, because upon the same evil works the same judgment will be pronounced." [4] 4. *Or do you despise*, as if you were not in need of,

is righteous in Christ. With this sickness the Jews are afflicted more widely than all the Gentiles. Therefore he mentions at the very beginning of this chapter that he is directing his verbal attack against the Jews. All heretics and hypocrites imitate them, and so do those who are at the present time lawyers and priests, and those who have claims against one another. They judge one another, but none of them judge themselves. They even boast of their righteousness and even invoke the punishment of God.

2 Thus it befell David through Nathan, and many people, though they have the same or greater faults, yet because they do not have identical faults, think that they can pass judgment and that they are different.

3 This expression *the very same things* should be applied to all the things mentioned above taken together, and not to individual faults; even if it is expressed in the more common way, it should be understood in the general sense, not individually, and even if it is expressed for classes of such things, it should not be taken for the same members of the classes. Accordingly, although you may not commit one particular evil deed, you still commit another. This holds true of others too. Therefore he says below (v. 22): "You who abhor idols commit sacrilege."

4 Because as he says below (v. 11): "For there is no respect of persons with God." This would be the case if those could escape from the judgment of God who do the same things as they whom they consider worthy of judgment. From this fault very many people suffer in such a way that when they see that others are being punished, they somehow laugh and say: "Aha! Right and good. This is in order. He has well deserved it." They ought rather to say fearfully: "He was punished yesterday, today it will be my turn." — "The puppy is whipped so that the dog may be afraid." [3]

---

2 Following Faber's text, Luther crossed out the Vulgate's *quae* at this point and wrote *qui* above it.

3 A variation of this proverb is quoted in the 12th century by Metellus of

the riches, the abundance, *of His goodness* with which He does good to you assiduously and is always ready to forgive evil, *and patience,* with which He endures your many great vices, *and longsuffering,* which waits patiently for your slow improvement. *Do you not know,* He is so rich toward you not so that you may sin more freely and longer but that you should come to repentance the more quickly, *that God's kindness leads you to repentance?* not to an increase of your sins. But like perverse people, we abuse it the more to the contrary. 5. *But by,* that is, through, *your hard and impenitent heart* **5** *you are storing up,* heaping up, *for yourself,* your very own self, *wrath,* the punishment of the wrath of God, *on the day* **6** *of wrath,* the Last Day, *and of the revelation,* when everything will be revealed and will remain thus revealed forever and,**6** *of the just judgment of God,***7** which will stand forever. 6. *Who will render,* at that time, namely, *to every man,* to the good and to the evil, *according to his works,* 7. *To those,* that is, the good men, *who, by patience in well-doing,* that is, through patience in

5 Bernard says: "That heart is called hardened which is not softened by piety, which does not yield to threats and is hardened even further when whips are used," 4 as in the case of the Jews.

6 The Greek has "against the day," 5 which is better.

7 The apostle talks to them more sternly because "The perverse are hard to correct" (Eccl. 1:15). Such as those who judge others. For it is impossible that they should repent unless they recognize their own evil deeds and forget about those of others, that is, unless they stop judging others. Those who seem wise to themselves are fools, and those who seem just to themselves are sinners. Of them we read in Prov. 26:12: "Do you see a man who is wise in his own eyes? There is more hope for a fool than for him." So it was with Marsyas among the poets.7 From this follows that if they firmly trust that they think

Tegernsee, *Quirinalia,* 36, 46: "The lion is wary that has been mauled as a cub" (*Percusso catulo leo veretur*).

4 This is a rather free paraphrase of Bernard, *De consideratione,* I, 2, *Patrologia, Series Latina,* CLXXXII, 730 f. Luther paraphrases it even more freely in the scholia below p. 176.

5 The student notebooks, too, reflect this note. But the variation *in diem* for *in die* does not rest on a variant Greek reading. Luther may have been thinking of the similar *in die* in verse 16 of this chapter, for which he had adopted Faber's translation *in diem.* In the scholia below (cf. p. 176) Luther quotes *in die* without mentioning the reading *in diem.*

6 Luther placed a large sign for "and" (&) before the text *of the just judgment.*

7 Marsyas was a satyr in Greek mythology who committed the fatal folly of challenging Apollo to a musical contest. Though well-schooled in instrumental performance, Marsyas was woefully deficient in the art of combining music and poetry and so lost the match and his life.

good works, *seek,* by working faithfully and by living a holy life, *glory,*[8] that is, renown and praise, *and honor and incorruption,* in body and soul, *eternal life,* not the vanity of this world. 8. *But to those,* to the evil and impious, *who are contentious,* who do not know patience but assiduously fight against one another, *and do not obey,* believe, or do not want to be persuaded to believe, *the truth,* in an evangelical way, *but obey,* because they seem wise and just to themselves, like the Jews, or only because the Gospel does not seem true to them, as in the case of the Gentiles, *wickedness,* injustice and things contrary to the truth of faith, *wrath and indignation,* that is, the effects of wrath and indignation, which are not in God but in the creature to be punished. 9. *There will be tribulation and distress,* by which a man is held tight so that he cannot escape,[9] *for every soul of man who does evil,* but he does evil who is outside of faith, as is revealed below, no matter how great his work may be, *the Jew first,* because to them everything was told first, *and also the Greek,* that is, the Gentiles. 10. *But glory,* praise, as explained above, *and honor,* reverence, *and peace,* both inwardly and outwardly, *for everyone who does good,* but no good work is done except in faith, *the Jew first, and also the Greek.* The Jew, I say, and also the Greek because: 11. *For there is no respect of persons with God,* namely, for punishing or rewarding both Jews and Gentiles less or more.[10] 12. *All who have sinned,* as Gentiles, *without the Law,* namely, the written law, that is, all people who exist and are living,[11] *will also perish,* will be con-

and act justly and rightly, they will of necessity become hardened and impenitent, because they do not think it fitting to repent of something that is good or to change their ways on account of any admonition.

[8] This is a transposition of words *(hyperbaton).*

[9] Just as joy is a certain freedom and rest for the heart, so tribulation is restlessness and affliction. But anxiety is the affliction in which there is no way out of tribulation.

[10] *For there is no respect.* The apostle opposes the secret excuse of the Jews as well as of the Gentiles, for he had said that each one is rewarded according to his works, whether Jew or Gentile. The Jews perhaps could, or would want to, say: "We have heard the Law, and we know it, and we are the chosen people of God according to the covenant of the Law given on Mount Sinai." But the Gentiles could say: "We did not know the Law. Therefore our lack of knowledge excuses us." To both he says: "I should say not!" As also the Lord says, Matt. 7:22: "On that day many will say to Me: 'Lord, Lord, did we not prophesy in Your name?' etc."

[11] Not as though any person could be without the Law. But *without the Law* here means as much as "without the written law," which is perceived from the outside, or has been made known through man. For otherwise there would be

demned, *without the Law*, namely, such a law, even though they did well according to another law, one in their hearts, *and all who have sinned*, like the Jews, living *under the Law, will be judged*, condemned, *by the Law*, which they have known and accepted. 13. *For not the hearers of the Law*,[12] like those who say: "Lord, in Your name we have prophesied." Such are also those who do the works of the Law, but not willingly, therefore they do not do them. *Are righteous before God*, that is, are considered righteous by God,[13] *but the doers*, who are the only ones who have the grace that conquers the evil will, *of the Law will be justified*, they will be considered righteous before God. 14. *For when the Gentiles*, whom he has described above as being "without the Law," *who have not the Law*, namely, the written law, *do by nature*, only by nature and not by tradition, as the Jews do,[14] *those things*, the works, *which are of the Law*, given or written, *even though they do not have the Law, they*, the Gentiles, *are a law to themselves*, that is, they can instruct themselves without the instruction of such a law. 15. *They show*, prove to others through their performance outwardly and to themselves inwardly, *that the work of the Law*, that is, the law of doing such works, *is written*, namely, with the finger of God, *on their hearts*. By nature and indelibly the law of nature is imprinted on their minds, *while their conscience*[15]

a contradiction in the words of the apostle, namely, that those cannot sin who are without the Law, because, as it is written below, Rom. 4:15: "Where there is no law, there is no transgression," and in another place: "The power of sin is the Law" (1 Cor. 15:56).

[12] As the Lord teaches in the parable of the seed that fell along the path, among thorns, and on the rock. Luke 8:5 ff.

[13] "To be righteous before God" is the same as "to be justified in the presence of God." A man is not considered righteous by God because he is righteous; but because he is considered righteous by God, therefore he is righteous, as we read later in chapter 4. But no one is looked upon as righteous except the one who fulfills the Law in deed, and no one fulfills the Law except the man who believes in Christ. Thus the apostle intends to conclude that outside of Christ no one is righteous, no one fulfills the Law, as he explains in the following chapter.

[14] Here he demonstrates what he has said of the Law that has been handed down: "Whoever without the Law," showing that they will be condemned or saved also without the Law, if only they have done good deeds.

[15] The conscience of any person (so long as it does not err or is not dulled by too much neglect) stings and murmurs when a person has done evil. But it quiets down when he has done good. Therefore also Cicero could say: "The consciousness of a well-spent life is a most pleasant remembrance."[8] Thus it is

[8] Cicero, *De senectute*, 3, 9.

bears witness to them,[16] a good witness about the good works and an evil witness about the evil works. How? Supply "they show it," through their conscience now to themselves and in the Last Judgment before God, *and that among themselves,* mutually against each other, *in turn,* this is exposition of what has been said: what the conscience is which bears witness, *their thoughts* [9] by which they interpret themselves to themselves, what sort of people they are, *accuse,* in the things they have done wrong, *or also defend them,* in the things they have done well. 16. *On the day,* against the day, that is, these things all are done now and take place now so that they may be judged then according to them,[17] *when God will judge the secrets of men,* the sins which are not known to men, that is, even their innermost thoughts, *according to my Gospel,* that is, that which is preached by me, *by Jesus Christ.* For He will be the judge because of His likeness of men, that He may be seen by all. 17. But [18] *if you,* just look, *call yourself a Jew,* although you are not one in truth, but still have the name, *and rely upon the Law,* that is, you are confident and seem secure [10] to yourself because you have the written law, *and boast of your relation to God,* that proved on the other hand from these considerations that they know what one must do and what one must not do, that is, they know the Law.

16 *Bears witness to them,* that is, by the fact that their conscience and their thoughts torture, rebuke, or excuse them "they show" that they know "the work of the Law" and that it "is written on their hearts," even though they do not find it in written books and even though it is not told them to their ears. For if they would know it, they could not be rebuked by their conscience when they do evil nor encouraged when they do good.

17 They will be judged according to their own thoughts, which will either accuse them or excuse them, depending on what they have done. For there our witnesses will be not words or works, which can deceive, but our innermost thoughts. They will witness for us before everybody, as they are now witnesses before ourselves, telling us what kind of people we are and what kind of things we have done. Nor will the case be tried with any other witnesses than those which cannot conceal themselves more closely, because they are the innermost thoughts of men.

18 After he has shown that all the Gentiles are under sin, he shows definitely and expressly here that the Jews are in sin, especially for this reason, that they keep the Law only externally, that is, according to the letter, not in spirit.

---

9 Luther here changes the Latin text from the Greek genitive absolute construction to the Latin ablative absolute.

10 Luther often uses the word *securus* in the sense of "smug" or "fasely secure," but he also uses the concept in the positive sense, especially in the combination "peace and security" and as he must have known it in the ancient collect from Christmas Eve: ". . . may also behold Him without fear *(securi)* when He comes as our Judge."

is, that you have God and are the people of God and have knowledge of Him, 18. *And know*, but don't do, *His will*, which has been made known in the Law, *and approve*, thoroughly approve, *what is excellent*, that is, the things that are good and salutary, *because you are instructed*, to be sure, *in the Law*, which has been given. 19. *And if you are sure*, because of your presumption and arrogance,[19] *that you are a guide*, that is, one who can show the way by means of the example of his life and morals, *to the blind*, when you yourself are blind and in need of a leader, *a light*, pertaining to things that can be known and to the mysteries that can be observed, *to those who are in darkness*, although you yourself are in darkness —and are sure you are: 20. *A corrector*, although you, too, are foolish, *of the foolish*, of people who do not know God and the things of God, *a teacher of children*, not only of the older ones but also of the little ones, that is, you think you are a teacher of them all—and you are confident of: *having in the Law the embodiment*, the measure and pattern by which it is known and truly understood, although you do not have it at all, *of knowledge and truth*, of true understanding, which he proves thus: 21. *You then who teach others*, as you trust, although you are not really teaching, because you are teaching the letter without the spirit, *teach not*, namely, the spirit of the Law, *yourself*, because you, like those whom you teach, are in need. *You who preach*, adopting the commandment from the Law, *that men should not steal*, namely, as far as the external work is concerned, *do steal*,[20] namely, you yourself by an act of your will or in a hidden act. Because if you could, you would do it. But even this will is considered an act in the presence of God. 22. *You who say*, according to the Law, *that one must not*

[19] It is as if he were saying: "All this you take for granted and claim it for yourself, when actually you lack all these things," as follows below (v. 21): "You who teach others, do not teach yourself."

[20] Among these must be numbered the princes and the mighty of the world who take for themselves the goods of their subjects, to be sure, not by violence and robbery but by threatening them with loss of favor and by leaving them in the lurch in their other needs if they do not give in to them. And they say: "We didn't force him. He gave it up of his own accord." You did not force him directly but indirectly. See, this is the nature of the children of men. Thus you will find very few princes who are not thieves and robbers or at least children of thieves and robbers, as blessed Augustine correctly said: "What are the great empires but great dens of thieves?" [11] Yet these people are punishing thieves and judging them, although they are worse thieves in that they are seeking their own and not the public welfare, in that they are enriching themselves by neglecting care and provision for their subjects, etc.

[11] Augustine, *De civitate Dei*, IV, 4, *Patrologia, Series Latina*, XLI, 115.

[W, LVI, 26, 27]

commit adultery, according to the external act only, *you commit adultery,* namely, through inward concupiscence in the presence of God. *You who abhor idols,* you who teach according to the Law that idols should be detested in the sight of men, *you commit sacrilege,* by polluting and violating the true temple of God, which is the heart, with your concupiscence. 23. *You who boast in the Law,* that you have received it and now keep it in your works, *you dishonor God,*[21] because the honor of God is the holiness of His people, and conversely, the contempt of God is the wickedness of His people, *by breaking the Law,* namely, because you willfully neglect to fulfill it, as emphatically required. 24. *For, as it is written,* Is. 52:5, *the name of God,* which is called out over you, because you are called the people of God, *through,* on account of, *you is blasphemed,* just as the glory of a prince is the strength of his people and his shame is the poverty and baseness of his people,[22] *among the Gentiles,* who say: "What kind of God is this who has such a disgraceful people?" 25. *Circumcision indeed,* namely, the external one, lest you think that I disapprove of it, *is of value,* for salvation, *if you obey the Law,* by fulfilling it spiritually.[23]

21 This can be understood also in this way, that even though they did not actually do these things, they performed them with their will, as blessed Augustine says in the eighth chapter of *On the Spirit and the Letter:* "The Jews were so boastful of God, as if they themselves had deserved to receive the Law according to the words of the psalm (Ps. 147:20): 'He has not dealt thus with any other nation; and His judgments He has not made manifest to them.' And yet they imagined that they were fulfilling the Law with their own righteousness, when they were rather breakers of it."[12] And further on he writes: "Because whoever did what the Law commanded, etc." as brought together below.[13] But also the apostle wants it to be seen quite clearly in this way when he says below (Rom. 2:28): "For he is not a real Jew who is one outwardly." In saying so he seems to admit that they have kept the Law outwardly but have not kept it with their innermost will, rather they have done all this as the Lord says, Matt. 5:28: "Everyone who looks at a woman lustfully has already committed adultery with her in his heart." And in this way, I believe, the apostle wants it to be understood that he says at the beginning, "You are doing the same things that you judge," namely, in your will and before God, even though not before men.

22 As it is a disgrace for a prince to have a people without reputation, but a glory to have a famous people.

23 If they object that they are keeping the Law, he answers: "Yes, but only outwardly, like the circumcision of the flesh, but not of the spirit, because it is

12 *Patrologia, Series Latina,* XLIV, 208.

13 With the words *ut infra in collectis* ("as below in the full statements") Luther means to refer to the scholia, where the full quotation is given. But the full quotation is found in the scholia not on the present v. 23 but on v. 12, p. 184.

But if you break the law, also through your will, no matter how much you keep it with works, which is of necessity true for him who is not in Christ, *your circumcision,* in the external work before men, without any in your heart before God, *becomes uncircumcision,* namely, before God, because your heart remains uncircumcised.[24] 26. *So if the uncircumcision,* that is, a Gentile who is uncircumcised in the flesh and yet believes in Christ,[25] *keeps the precepts of the Law,* spiritually, *will not his uncircumcision,* that is, the fact that he is not circumcised is not against him, but will, *be regarded as circumcision?* by God, on account of the circumcision of his heart, just as your circumcision becomes uncircumcision. 27. *Then that which by nature is uncircumcision,* that is, the Gentiles, those who without the restraint of the Law have uncircumcision, *keeping the Law,* fulfilling it from the heart and the spirit, *will judge,* your brief will condemn you, *you,* a Jew, *who by the letter,* external righteousness, *and circumcision,* of the flesh only,[26] *break the Law,* because you have not circumcised your evil will. 28. *For he,* that you are such a person is apparent from this,[27] *is not a real Jew,* that is, of the seed of Abraham, *who is one outwardly,* in the external man and according to the flesh, *nor is that true circumcision*[28] *which is outward,* external in the eyes of the people, *in the flesh,* in imitation of Abraham. 29. *But he is a Jew who is one inwardly,* in the inward man on the basis of faith

without grace, which circumcises the spirit. Therefore he says below (v. 28): 'For he is not a real Jew who is one outwardly.' " With this statement he excludes every kind of righteousness according to the letter as being insufficient. And from this what he charged them with above concerning the inward sins of their will is evident.

24 Therefore we read in Jer. 9:26: "All the nations are uncircumcised, but all the house of Israel is uncircumcised in heart," and also in Jer. 4:4: "Circumcise yourselves to the Lord, and take away the foreskins of your hearts, O men of Judah and Jerusalem."

25 What is meant here becomes clear by a comparison with the passage below (v. 27): "Those who are uncircumcised but keep the Law will do the judging." And the reason given is that he is a Jew in secret and not openly.

26 This can also be understood in this way: "By the letter and by circumcision," that is, through the circumcision of the letter.

27 Here he gives a reason for saying that they were all sinners and for everything else he said above. At the same time he meets the objection of those who say: "We keep the Law, we are circumcised and are Jews." He answers that this is not keeping the Law, because the Law is spiritual. They, however, are keeping the Law only outwardly according to the letter.

28 That is, he is not a Jew who is visibly a Jew, neither is that circumcision which is visibly circumcision.

in Christ, of the faith of Abraham, *and*, this is the real circumcision, *circumcision is a matter of the heart*, away from all forbidden concupiscence,[29] *in the spirit*, that is, in the spiritual man, or in spiritual righteousness, *not in the letter*, that is, in the carnal man or carnal righteousness; *whose praise is not from men*, as is the circumcision and the righteousness of the flesh, but rather there is vituperation and persecution, *but from God*, for God approves it and praises it, that is, He makes it and deems it praiseworthy.[30]

[29] Blessed Augustine says: "Circumcision of the heart he calls the pure will, that is, the will that is free of all forbidden desires. This is not achieved through the letter which teaches and threatens, but through the Spirit who helps and heals. Therefore the praise of such gifts is 'not of men but of God,' who offers them through His grace, therefore they should be praised. About this we have the statement (Ps. 34:3): "In the Lord shall my soul be praised." [14]

[30] What good is it if someone is a Jew before men but not before God? For such a Jew is not a Jew, and such a circumcision is not a circumcision, as it was stated above (v. 25), "Your circumcision becomes uncircumcision." Therefore they are truly such as teach that one should not commit adultery and yet commit adultery, steal, and murder. That the Jews have been of this type is apparent in many passages, first of all in the Gospel, where the Lord says (Matt. 23:27): "Woe to you, scribes and Pharisees, hypocrites! for you are like whitewashed tombs. Outwardly you appear righteous to men, but within you are full of plundering and wickedness." That is the reason also for "They themselves did not enter the praetorium, so that they might not be defiled" (John 18:28), yet they did not think it a defilement to kill Christ by will and word because they did not kill Him by the work of their own hands. Thus when in Acts 4:10 and 7:52 the apostles steadfastly told them, "Whom you have killed," they answered (as in denial): "You intend to bring this man's blood upon us." Thus Josephus criticized the historian Polybius, who had said that King Antiochus had been punished by God because he had wanted to destroy Jerusalem.[15] They all maintain that not the intention but only the actual deed is culpable.

---

[14] Augustine, *De Spiritu et littera*, 8, *Patrologia, Series Latina*, XLIV, 208.

[15] In *Antiquities of the Jews*, XII, ch. 9, 1, Flavius Josephus writes that Antiochus Epiphanes confessed before his death that his calamity was sent upon him "for the miseries he had brought upon the Jewish nation while he plundered the temple and condemned their God." Josephus then criticizes Polybius for saying that "Antiochus died because he had a purpose to plunder the temple of Diana in Persia," adding, "Purposing to do a thing, but not actually doing it, is not worthy of punishment . . . it is much more probable that this king died on account of his sacrilegious plundering of the temple at Jerusalem."

CHAPTER THREE

1. *Then what advantage has the Jew? Or what is the value of circumcision?*

B ECAUSE he had condemned the Jews according to the flesh and the circumcision in the flesh, he seemed to regard it as useless and its practice as vain. But this is not the case. Therefore, in this chapter he shows for what purpose circumcision and Judaism were useful.

1. Its greatest value is that *the oracles of God were believed* (v. 2), that is, circumcision was useful to this end, that in it the promises of God were believed and thus their fulfillment was awaited, and in this the Jews had an advantage over the Gentiles, to whom God promised nothing, but in pure mercy in the fullness of time He deigned to make them equal with the Jews. However, to the Jews He was not only merciful but also truthful, for He demonstrated that mercy which He had promised. Hence these two concepts are frequently joined together in Scripture, mercy and truthfulness. Thus he says below in chapter 15:8-9, "For I tell you that Christ became a servant of the circumcised to show God's truthfulness, in order to confirm the promises given to the patriarchs, and in order that the Gentiles might glorify God for His mercy, etc."

And note that it does not say: "The oracles of God were believed by them," but as the Greek has it: "The oracles of God were believed," not indicating by whom, because immediately the objection was ready which he answers in the following statement that they were not believed by all. Thus the meaning is: The important point is that circumcision does not profit for itself only but for the whole world, because in it the oracles of God are believed, that is, people are found who believe the oracles of God, and thus the promises of the mercy and grace of God are received, which are now given also to the Gentiles. But if the oracles of God had not been believed there, they would nowhere have been believed, and

part, *of them were unfaithful?* that is, did not receive the faith of Christ and the fulfillment of the promise. *Has,* for so it would seem to follow, *their faithlessness,* because of which they were unwilling to receive the fulfillment of the promise, *nullified,* or will it nullify, that is, so that one must say that He did not fulfill it because of their faithlessness, *the faithfulness of God,* that is, His fidelity in holding forth His promises? [5] 4. *By no means,* that is to say, in no way; [6] but *God is truthful,* or, may God be truthful, or let God be truthful, who has promised, no matter how much they refuse to believe or are unworthy, *though every man,* because as man he is outside of faith and not yet a son of God, *be false. As it is written* (Ps. 51:4),[1] for proving that God is truthful, *that Thou mayest be justified,* that Thou mayest be found to have been righteous, truthful, and upright, *in Thy words,* that is, in the statements with which Thou hast promised Thy grace and thus hast demonstrated that we have sin. Through these words Thou also justifiest all those who believe them, *and prevail* by remaining truthful and by proving them to be deceitful, *when Thou art judged,* by unbelievers who are unwilling to justify Thee, but want to justify themselves. 5. *But if,*[7] as it fol-

[5] That the word "faith" *(fides)* is used here for "faithfulness" *(fidelitas)* or "truthfulness" *(veritas)* is clear from the following proof statement, "God is truthful." It is as if he were saying that because He Himself is truthful, therefore no one nullifies His faithfulness, but rather they themselves become destitute of faith and truth, because God is truthful, and man is deceitful.

[6] To me the meaning of this passage "Does their unfaithfulness, etc." seems to be the same as in chapter 9:6 below: "It is not as though the Word of God had failed" (that is, the promise has not been nullified on this account), and in chapter 11:1-2, "I ask, then, has God rejected His people? By no means . . . He has not rejected His people," that is, because of their unfaithfulness. On that account He was not without people for whom to fulfill His promise, so that His faithfulness would be nullified on their account and would not be fulfilled for anyone; no, even if they did not believe, he says (Rom. 11:1), "I myself am an Israelite," to whom He did fulfill His promises and to whom He is truthful, and it is those men rather who are the liars because they do not believe.

[7] From this point on he digresses by the use of this verse adduced from Ps. 51, in the manner of an overflowing stream which leaves its banks and finds whatever place it can fill, and this digression goes as far as "What then" (v. 9). So also the Jordan (which is a symbol of the Gospel) is described as "meandering wherever the terrain permits, presenting itself as it were reluctantly to its neighbors." [2]

---

[1] This is the first of many references to Ps. 51:4 in these lectures. Already in the early lectures on the Psalms Luther had spoken of Ps. 51 as "most commonly known" *(psalmus vulgatissimus)* but also as "most difficult, especially in verse 4, for which there are almost as many interpretations as interpreters." Luther goes on to say, "We choose to follow the apostle in Rom. 3." Cf. W, III, 287, 20 f.

[2] Cf. Pliny, *Natural History,* V, 15, par. 71.

lows from the same psalm (51:4), for it says, "Against Thee, Thee only, have I sinned . . . so that Thou art justified," as if God could be justified and made truthful if we are unrighteous men and liars, and not rather the contrary: if we have been righteous, then He would be justified most of all, *our wickedness, unrighteousness, serves to show the righteousness of God;* but *what shall we say* to his statement "Against Thee have I sinned . . . so that Thou art justified"? It then follows that He ought not to punish but rather reward sinners, but He does just the opposite. *That God is unjust to inflict wrath?* It is as if he were saying: "It is completely ridiculous to think this about God." In other words, because a man would say that this follows from that expression. *I speak in a human way,* that is, according to human judgment, as man is in the habit of speaking about man, because these words should not have been spoken about God, nor should such a question have arisen, since it is certain that He is righteous, and because man would so understand that psalm. 6. *By no means. For then,* if He is unjust, *how could God judge,* since an unjust judgment is really no judgment at all, *this world?* which is partly righteous and partly unrighteous. 7. *But if God's truthfulness,* that is, if from the fact that I am a liar and [3] God is truthful the glory of God abounds, why should I not rather lie, so that He may be more truthful for an even greater glory; indeed, why am I judged a sinner because of my lying? *through my falsehood,* because of my lying, *abounds,* as long as it is commended by it; it is an even more abundant reason for glorification than righteousness, *to His glory,* because through this He Himself is justified, as seemed to follow from the psalm, *why,* as if he were saying that this ought not to be the case, *am I,* that is, any deceitful man, *still being condemned as a sinner?* punished and condemned by God. 8. *And why not,* that is, why is it not so and considered to be true, *as some people slanderously,* because they impute false and unworthy motives to us, *charge us,* treating our words in a perverse and malicious way, *with saying,*[8] *why not do evil,* that is, sins and lies, *that good may come,* namely, the glory and commendation of God's righteousness and truthfulness.[9] *Their condem-*

[8] 2 Peter 3:14 ff.

[9] It is as if he were saying, "If it is true that our lying abounds to the glory of God, why would it not also be true, indeed, it will be completely true what some people charge us with saying, 'Why not do evil, etc.?' But actually in doing this they 'slanderously charge us,' and thus it is not true. Therefore it is also not

[3] We have adopted the reading *et* for *ut.*

nation is just,[10] that is, such perverted and evil men have already been condemned. 9. *What*[11] *then?* that is, what are we to conclude from these words, *are we any better off than they are?*[4] Are we Jews better off than those Gentiles because we are "entrusted with the oracles of God," along with other benefits? *No, not at all. For we have already charged,* that is, we have already stated and given the reasons above, *that all men both Jews,* first, especially the learned ones, *and the Greeks,*[12] the Gentiles, *are under the power of sin,*[13] in the eyes of God, no matter how good and upright they may be before men. 10. *As it is written,* concerning the Jews, which was less generally what people thought; as we read later (v. 19), "whatever the Law says." (1)[6] *None is righteous,* that is, with righteousness that can stand before God, *no, not one.* 11. *No one under-*

true that 'our wickedness serves to show the righteousness of God' " (v. 5). But this does not solve the question posed by the psalm. However, it will be solved in several ways as we proceed.

10 From this text of the apostle it is clear that in this letter he is not speaking primarily against those who are open sinners but against those who appear righteous in their own eyes and trust in their own works for salvation. For he is trying to encourage these people to magnify the grace of God, which cannot be magnified unless sin which is forgiven through this grace is first acknowledged and magnified. This is why the others, when they heard this, were offended and thought that the apostle is preaching that evil should be done, so that the glory of God might be magnified. For in this way do our iniquity and our lying "abound to His glory" (v. 7), when we, humbled through the confession of them, glorify God, who has forgiven such wickedness out of His overflowing grace. He would not be glorified in this way if we did not believe that we are in need of His grace but thought that we were sufficient of ourselves in His sight. Thus he is better off who acknowledges that he has many sins and no righteousness than he who like a Pharisee acknowledges that he has much righteousness and no sin. For the one glorifies the mercy of God, but the other his own righteousness.

11 Having completed the digression, he now returns to the main point.

12 With this expression he counterbalances all the vehement ignorance of the expositors who claim that the things said above in chapter 1 were spoken only of the Romans.[5] Since he himself clearly explains his meaning here and says that he has given the reason why all Gentiles and Jews are under sin, therefore he has not made the charge only against the Romans, as these men like to think.

13 This is the explanation and the correct interpretation of all that has been stated before, namely, that he has said that all are under sin, even though he seems to have said that some fulfill the Law.

---

4 Luther crossed out *eos,* "than they are," and so made his text agree with Faber's.

5 Lyra, for instance, refers the "is plain to them" of chapter 1 to the Romans *(hominibus romanis).*

6 These numerals marking the apostle's quotations were added in the margin by Luther.

stands, that is, with wisdom that avails before God; *no one seeks for God,* as it pertains to man's will and his righteousness.[14] 12. (2) *All have turned aside,* from the true path of righteousness, which is in the Spirit, *together,* that is, all in one group, *they have gone wrong,* that is, vain and empty in performing their own righteousness, *no one does good,* that is, what pleases God, *not even one,* that is, not a single one. 13. (3) *Their throat,* the ministry of their teaching, etc., *is an open grave,*[15] because they devour dead men, and many of them. "Their talk will eat its way like gangrene" (2 Tim. 2:17). *They use their tongues to deceive,* that is, they taught hypocrisy and the outward man, *the venom of asps* with which they have infected the inner man incurably, *is under their lips.* But on their lips they have honey. 14. (4) *Their mouth,* which is an open contradiction against the truth, *is full of curses,* that is, blasphemous words, maledictions, insults, *and bitterness,* that is, with bitter and angry words of slander. 15. *Their feet are swift,* that is, they make haste, and they are full of zeal in intention and in deed, because they think they are thereby "offering service to God" (John 16:2), *to shed blood,* to kill and to persecute those who judge and teach contrary to them.[16] 16. (5) *Ruin,* that is, a loss of what they own, *and misery,* that is, those things which have been lost and which they are attempting to regain do not prosper, *in their paths.* 17. *And the way of peace,* of the heart, which is found alone in God, *they do not know,* because they do not want it. 18. *There is no fear of God,* whose absence always makes them proud and presumptuous, but whose presence makes them humble and reverent, *before their eyes.* 19. *Now we know,*[17] there is no need

[14] For although in their own eyes they "understand and seek God," yet because they are pleased with their own wisdom and righteousness, it really is not so in the eyes of God.

[15] From this passage it becomes clear that the apostle is using the Septuagint translation, because these last three verses are not in the Hebrew text. However, he is not unwise in doing this, for he quotes the Bible which the people had to whom he is writing. Thus also above he uses the expression "that Thou mayest be justified" (v. 4), but the Hebrew text has it this way: "because Thou wilt justify Thyself in Thy sentence and cleanse Thyself in Thy judgment" (Ps. 51:4), which, however, means about the same thing.

[16] For the ungodly not only do not receive the messengers of the truth, but as the Lord says in Matt. 23:37, they "stone" them and "kill" them.

[17] This is a way to counteract their evasiveness, so that if they say, "Who knows whether He is speaking these words about us who are righteous?" the answer is: "He certainly is!" And thus it is manifest that this psalm is to be understood primarily of the Jews. For the Law was not given to the Gentiles, therefore it does not speak of them, at least not in the first place.

of faith, because this is sure, *that whatever the Law says,* either in promising good things or threatening evil, *it speaks,* because it was given to them, *to those who are under the Law,* therefore also that psalm speaks to the Jews and about them, for they had no doubt about the Gentiles that they were sinners, but concerning themselves they were in great doubt, indeed they did not believe it, *so that every mouth,* boasting proudly of its own wisdom and righteousness and telling it to others, *may be stopped, and the whole world,* as a debtor and a guilt-ridden sinner, *may be held accountable,* by recognizing that in actual fact it is already a sinner, *to God,* although in its own eyes it may not be so, for the world previously had proudly made itself equal with God. 20. *For no human being will be justified in His sight by the works of the Law,* but rather, on the contrary, the works of the Law are accomplished as a result of justification and righteousness. For we are not righteous because we act according to the Law, but because we are first righteous, therefore we then fulfill the Law; [18] *since through the Law* [19] *comes,* or is, *the knowledge,* but not the forgiveness, and thus not justification, *of sin,* so that proud men who do not know their sins may be humbled. 21. *But now,* in the day of grace, *apart from Law,* without the necessity of keeping the Law, that is, without the aid of the Law and its works, *the righteousness of God,* by which God justifies us,[20] *has been manifested,* through the Gospel

[18] And thus he concludes the whole discussion with the clear-cut summary statement which he has had in mind, namely, that all men are unrighteous before God.

[19] For what purpose, then, is the Law? That it may humble the proud.

[20] Blessed Augustine in chapter 9 of *On the Spirit and the Letter* says: " 'The righteousness of God'; he did not say 'the righteousness of man' or 'the righteousness of one's own will,' but 'the righteousness of God,' not that righteousness by which God is righteous but that righteousness with which He covers man when He justifies the ungodly. As the term 'the faith of Christ' is used to describe not the faith by which Christ believes but the faith 'by which we believe in Christ,' so likewise this righteousness is not the righteousness by which God is righteous. For both are ours. But it is called God's righteousness and Christ's righteousness because He gives it to us out of His bounty." [7] The same things are said in chapter 11. Augustine continues in the same place,[8] "How can it be witnessed in the Law if it is manifested without the Law? But it is a righteousness without the Law, which God through the Spirit of grace bestows on the believer without the aid of the Law, that is, unaided by the Law. For through the Law He has shown man his weakness, so that through faith he may flee to His mercy for cleansing.

---

[7] Augustine, *De Spiritu et littera,* 9, 15, *Patrologia, Series Latina,* XLIV, 209.

[8] Ibid.

which is preached, *although the Law* [21] *and the Prophets bear witness to it,* for it was foreshadowed and promised by them long ago, but it was not manifested by them, but apart from them. 22. *The righteousness,* that righteousness, I say, *of God,* from God, *through faith in Jesus Christ,*[22] that is, the faith by which we believe in Jesus Christ Himself, *for all,* both Jews and Gentiles, that is, to all, meaning it is manifested and offered to all, so that motion to a place is indicated, such as in "Their voice goes out through all the earth" (Ps. 19:4), *and upon all,* that is, it remains among all of them and is described through the concept of rest, as in Is. 11:2, "The Spirit of the Lord shall rest upon Him," *who believe in Him,*[10] they are made believers, all of them, I say, *for there is no distinction,* as if it were necessary for some but not for others. 23. *Since all have sinned,* have been made and declared to be sinners before God, *and fall short of,* that is, lack, are empty of, *the glory of God,* something they can boast about, by and in God, as he says below in Rom. 4:2, "He has something to boast about, but not before God." [23] 24. *They are justified as a gift,* that is, all, as many as are justified, are not justified except freely, *by His,* God's, *grace,* without merits or works. This grace is not given except *through the redemption* [24] *which is in Christ Jesus.* By this grace He Himself alone has re-

And concerning His wisdom it is said that it carries law and mercy on its tongue,[9] namely, the Law by which He declares the proud guilty and mercy by which He justifies those who have been humbled.

[21] Because if it is "witnessed by the Law," it surely is not without the Law, but because He can, indeed must, be just without being under the Law, it is even better "without the Law," that is, a righteousness which the Law did not give or possess.

[22] He is describing what or of what nature the righteousness of God is, namely, that it is not something by which He Himself is righteous or by which a person could be righteous, but it is that which can be possessed in no other way than through faith. Lest the proud again presume that this righteousness is given to them apart from Christ and on the basis of their own merits, as if Christ were not necessary for it.

[23] They are filled with their own glory. John 5:44 reads: "How can you believe, who receive glory from one another and do not seek the glory that comes from the only God?"

[24] It is as if he were saying that He does not give grace so freely that He has demanded no satisfaction, but rather He has given Christ as the one who makes the satisfaction for us, so that He thus may still freely give His grace to those who make satisfaction through another.

[9] Cf. Prov. 31:26.

[10] Following Faber's text, Luther crossed out *in eum,* "in Him."

[W, LVI, 37, 38]

deemed those who were "sold under sin," Is. 40,[11] making satisfaction for us and freeing us. 25. *Whom God put forward,* established now or foreordained from eternity, *as a propitiation,* or rather, "a place of propitiation" in which alone He willed to be satisfied, *by faith;* our place of propitiation is not won by our merits, but *in His,* Christ's, *blood,* that is, in His suffering, whereby He made satisfaction and merited propitiation for those who believe in Him. *This was to show His righteousness,* to show that His righteousness alone makes men righteous. And He performed this also "in forbearance," even before it was shown in the time of grace, that is, before it was made manifest that He forgives sins, so that He might show, prove, and convince us that He Himself alone justifies, *because He had passed over,* which showing forth of righteousness takes place, I say, when He forgives sins which He has patiently endured until the remission of *former sins,* that is, sins which preceded the remission in His long-suffering, *in His divine forbearance,* that is, toleration or endurance (Augustine calls it "patience"[12]), 26. *It was to prove,* manifest and reveal, or commend and proclaim, *His*[13] *righteousness,* by which He justifies us, *at the present time,*[25] that is, by His grace, *that He Himself is*

25 The passage "whom God put forward, etc.," is an unclear and confusing text. It should be divided and understood as follows: "Whom God put forward" (that is, He has chosen Him from eternity and now has put Him forward thus) "as a propitiation through faith" (that is, that He may be the propitiation for sins, but only for those who believe), because through unbelief the place of propitiation is changed into a tribunal and a place of judgment; "by His blood," because He did not wish us to have this place of propitiation unless He had first made satisfaction for us through His blood. Therefore, by His blood He is made a place of propitiation for those who believe. "To show His righteousness," that is, that He might thereby proclaim that all men are in sin and need His righteousness. For what else does this prove, that Christ suffered and became a place of propitiation through suffering, except that we are unrighteous, for whom He took on that nature, and must seek our righteousness from God alone, having our sins forgiven first through a propitiation of that kind? Hence he says, "For the passing over." For in that He passes over sins through the propitiation and thus justifies, He is showing that His righteousness is necessary, since there is no one to whom He would not remit sin. "Of former sins," that is, those which preceded the manifestation of His righteousness, before it was understood that all who are justified are justified through Him alone. These sins preceded, I say, "in the divine forbearance," that is, unless He had endured them patiently, He would not have come to the point of remission or of showing His righteousness, nor

11 Luther probably had in mind Is. 53:4 ff., which is also the passage cited by Faber. Cf. Rom. 7:14.

12 *De Spiritu et littera,* 13, 21, *Patrologia, Series Latina,* XCIV, 213.

13 Luther crossed out *eius,* "His," which Faber has.

righteous, that is, that He may be known by His nature as the only God, as we have said above, "But let God be truthful" (v. 4) and "that Thou mayest be justified, etc." (v. 4), *and that He justifies,* through His grace, *him,* every man *who has faith,* not the man who is of the Law, *in Jesus Christ.* 27. *Then where,* it is as if he were saying, "nowhere," *is your*[14] *boasting?* whereby they proudly boast of their own righteousness. *It is excluded,* it is thrown out and rejected, and they are made sinners, *On what principle? On the principle of works?* No, this principle actually increases the boasting, because when it is followed, it makes people proud. *No, but on the principle of faith,* because this humbles a man and makes him confess that he is a sinner before God. 28. *For we hold,* recognize and affirm, we conclude from what is said[26] *that a man is justified,* reckoned righteous before God, whether Greek or Jew, *by faith, apart from works of the Law,* without the help and necessity of the works of the Law. 29. *Or is God the God of Jews only?*[27] *Is He not the God of Gentiles also? Yes, of Gentiles also,* of those who believe. 30. *Since God is one,* one and the same God of all, *and He will justify the circumcised,* that is, the Jews after the flesh, *on the ground of their faith,* not works, *and the uncircumcised,* the Gentiles, *through their faith,*[28] mercifully given to them. 31. *Do we then,* through these words, *overthrow,* take away, would He come there now. Therefore He bears them patiently that He may forgive; He forgives that He may show His righteousness or our justification through faith in the propitiation in His blood.

[26] The expression "we hold" in this passage should not really be understood as "having an opinion." For it would be irreverent to doubt or just to be of the opinion that a man is justified by faith. Rather, we should believe and know it with all certainty and firmness. At the very least the term "we hold" means that we are held to hold.

He uses the term "we hold" as a rather weak expression, and he actually means something very strong, as if he were using a kind of antithetical statement: They think *(arbitrantur)* that a man is justified by works, which is merely an opinion and a judgment *(arbitrium);* but "we hold" *(arbitramur),* that is, we know and are sure, etc.

[27] For it would follow that if they were justified by the Law, then only the Jews would be righteous, because they alone have the law of God, and thus He would be "the God of Jews only."

[28] Some people distinguish the expression "on the ground of faith" *(ex fide)* from "through faith" *(per fidem)* in this way, that the Jews moved from a former faith to a new faith, as from a kind of *terminus a quo,* but the Gentiles did not have a *terminus a quo* and thus received only a new faith.

---

[14] Luther crossed out *tua,* "your." Faber's text also omits it.

the Law, as it seems to foolish men,[29] *by this faith? By no means,* because it is good and just. *On the contrary, we uphold the Law,* because through faith and grace it is fulfilled and thus ratified and confirmed. Just as the law of man is most firmly established and strengthened when it is observed.

[29] Hence in Acts 21:28, 27 they said, "This is the man who is teaching men everywhere against the people and the Law and this place," and "they laid hands on him."

CHAPTER FOUR

Summary: Through the example of Abraham the apostle demonstrates that faith is required for salvation, and that the old law does not suffice for salvation.

1. *What* [1] *then shall we say,* it is as if he were saying, "Nothing at all," at least before God, *about Abraham our forefather according to the flesh?* that is, who is our forefather according to the flesh, because you think he found righteousness as a result of works. And inasmuch as a man like Abraham found nothing, neither will we find anything, except to the degree that he is our father in faith. 2. *For if,* he is testing the proposition that Abraham gained nothing before God, *Abraham was justified by works,* as the arrogant Jews and unbelievers think, but this is nevertheless not so, *he has something to boast about,* that is, he has cause to glory and a reason to boast, *but not before God,* no, only in his own presence and before men. 3. *For what does the Scripture say?* It is as if he were saying: Does the Scripture actually say that he was justified by works? Not at all, just the opposite; for it is clear that it says, "He believed, etc." [2] It does not say that he did good works but that "he believed." *Abraham believed God, and it,* this very believing even without works, *was reckoned to him,* by God, *as righteousness,* so that through this he should be righteous before God. And thus it is not a matter of him who works but of God who accepts his faith as righteousness. Therefore he is justified by the grace of God. 4. *Now to one,* [3] whoever he may be, *who works,* that is, who merits

---

[1] To counter the unbelief and pride of the Jews who sought to be justified by their works and who thought of their father Abraham as an example which had been set before them he proves that Abraham was not justified except by faith.

[2] Gen. 15:5-6: "Look toward heaven, and number the stars, if you are able to number them. Then He said to him, 'So shall your descendants be.' Abraham believed God, and He reckoned it to him as righteousness."

[3] The apostle in his argument interprets the Scripture which has been adduced and concludes from it that justification is by faith and not by works. And he does this most effectively by interpreting the force of the word "reckoned"

by his deeds or who by his works is worthy of wages, *his wages are not reckoned,* as is done here, *according to grace,* that is, mercy, *but as his due,* that is, the reward is not reckoned to him on the basis of mercy, as if it were unmerited, but it is owed to him. 5. *But to one who does not work,* that is, even if he does not work or if he is without works or without the aid and necessity of works, but only believes,[4] *but trusts Him,* God, *who justifies,* through grace, *the ungodly,* that is, one who of himself is nothing but wicked before God, *his faith,* such trust, *is reckoned,* freely, by God, *as righteousness,* so that he is righteous before God, *according to the purpose,* that is, according to the predetermination, *of the grace of God,* an expression which is not in the Greek text.[1] 6. *So also David pronounces,* that is, affirms or declares, that there is no other blessedness of man except *the blessedness of a man,* by which he is blessed before God and by God, namely, the blessedness of that man alone *to whom God reckons,* that is, imputes,[5] but He imputes to none but the believer, *righteousness apart from works,* that is, without the aid and cooperation of works, or to men who are undeserving. 7. *Blessed are those,* namely, only the kind of people who do not think that they have no sin, or if they have it, do not believe that they are made righteous by their own works, but *whose iniquities,* as if to say because they all have iniquities, therefore forgiveness is necessary for all, *are forgiven,* that is, by God, who through grace does not impute them, *and whose sins are covered,* which is a repetition of the same thought. 8. *Blessed is the man against whom the Lord has not reckoned sin,* not he who has not imputed sin to himself, for actually the Lord imputes sin to him who has not imputed it to himself. 9. *Is this blessing pronounced—does it remain only* these words are not in

(reputatum est), which expresses the entirely free acceptance by God and not merit for the man who works.

⁴ That is, for him to whom works are necessary or helpful in securing his reward it is no longer by grace, but the reward is given for a debt. But for him who receives no help for his works or has no works which must be performed, it is given by grace, because he believes in God.

⁵ This word "impute" *(reputare)* is used often in this chapter, but our translator ² varies in the way he treats the word; for example, in one place he translates it by "to reckon" *(imputare),* in another "to place to one's credit" *(accepto ferre),* in another "to ascribe" *(reputare),* in the sense of being well disposed.

---

¹ In Luther's manuscript the words *"according . . . grace of God"* are enclosed in parentheses and crossed out, but this was obviously done later.

² The translator of the Vulgate. See also p. 52, n. 10, below.

the Greek [3] — *only upon the circumcised,* that is, only upon the flesh, or upon those who are Jews according to the flesh, *or also upon the uncircumcised,* that is, upon the Gentiles? We *say,*[6] that is, we have already said; and from what has been said, he means to say, it will readily appear that this blessing is on the uncircumcision also, for it is evident *that faith was reckoned to Abraham as righteousness.* 10. *How*[7] *then was it reckoned to him?*[8] *In circumcision,* that is, when he had already been circumcised or before, *or in uncircumcision?* Not in circumcision but, as is sufficiently clear from the text, *in uncircumcision.* 11. *He received,* as is clear in the text of chapter 17,[9] *as a sign or seal,* because it is not the thing itself, but it signified the righteousness of faith by which the heart is purified and circumcised, *circumcision,*[10] that is, for an external testimony *of the righteousness,* which itself is an inner thing, *which he had by faith,* from the faith which had been given to him *while he was*[11] *still uncircumcised,* that is, I say, the faith which had been given to him before his circumcision, or which is in the Gentiles. *The purpose was to make him the father,* that is, the spiritual father, *of all who believe,* and that they through this might be like him in spirit, as a son ought to be like his father,

6 And he proves that it was in uncircumcision.

7 The best argument against the folly of the Jews. For if their father Abraham, in whom they glory so much, was not justified through circumcision or through the works of the Law, but before circumcision and the Law, through faith, why do those who are his sons insist on having righteousness only on the basis of circumcision and the works of the Law, without faith? Therefore they are the sons of circumcision rather than the sons of Abraham.

8 In other words, if there was no need for Abraham to have circumcision in order to have righteousness, it likewise is not necessary for anyone else.

9 Gen. 17:11: "It shall be a sign of the covenant between Me and you."

10 If someone raises the objection that the Lord later commanded circumcision and therefore at that point instituted justification, the reply is an absolute no. For circumcision is not given for the purpose of justification, but for a sign of the justification which has already been accomplished, just as also those who have been justified through faith are now commanded to perform good works, continually to circumcise themselves of evil lusts, and to mortify their flesh with its works and lusts. By these signs they demonstrate in a sense that they have faith and have been justified.

11 The word "is" *(est)* is not in the Greek. Rather we ought to use the term "was" *(fuit),*[4] just as also above (4:9) the word "remain" *(manet).*

---

3 Luther is referring to the words *tantum manet,* which he has crossed out in the text. Faber's second edition of the text also omits them.

4 Luther adopts Faber's text.

without being circumcised, that is, those who are uncircumcised, *who thus have righteousness reckoned to them* because of their believing; just as was the case with Abraham. 12. *And likewise the father,* that is, not only in the flesh but also at the same time in the spirit, *of the circumcised,* of the Jews because of circumcision, *who are not merely circumcised,* that is, who have been circumcised in the flesh only and literally, whose father he is according to the flesh, *but of them also,* Jews by the spirit of circumcision, whose father he is according to both the flesh and the spirit, *who follow the example of the faith,* that is, those who not only are his seed but are also both imitators and seed, *which our father Abraham had before he was circumcised.*[12] 13. *For not through the Law,* that is, because of the Law or through the receiving of the Law, that is, through the righteousness and works of the Law, because it then would be the carnal and temporal possession of the world, *did the promise come to Abraham,* did it become his, but rather what was contrary to the promise, *or to his seed,*[13] his children, *that they should inherit,* become the possessors, as if it had been promised to them, *the world,* but rather the contrary as we see below (v. 15), *but through,* or because of, *the righteousness of faith,* by which he believed God as we see above (v. 1), namely, that through this righteousness the whole world might become his possession and the son of Abraham, because it is proved in this way, namely, that it is not through the Law. 14. *For if they,* those sons of his, *who are of the Law,*[5] that is, only of the flesh, *are heirs,* possessors, of the promise which is to be fulfilled, that is, to possess the whole world, *faith is null,* because under those circumstances faith becomes unnecessary and it suffices that they are sons of the flesh. If they can do this through the seed, what is the need of faith? [14] *and the prom-*

[12] The meaning is that he was justified before he was circumcised, and then he received the sign of circumcision. All of this was done that the future should be understood, that the Gentiles throughout the whole world would imitate his faith and become his sons; and likewise the Jews would become his sons, not only those who were circumcised in the flesh but also those who were also circumcised in the spirit; indeed, for the very reason that they were the sons of his flesh it was necessary that they also should become the sons of the same spirit as their father, so that they thus might be the sons of their father by the flesh and by the spirit.

[13] That is, not because they received the Law and did its works.

[14] And thus it will no longer be necessary to believe God in His every word, because if it is not necessary in one case, it is not necessary in any.

[5] Following the suggestion of the Weimar editor, we have corrected *ex semine* to *ex lege.* Luther's interlinear comments are, however, based on the reading "who are of the seed."

ise is void, that is, it is taken away and need not be fulfilled and is
not fulfilled, and therefore need not be believed.[15] This is obvious,
for 15. *The Law brings wrath,* and therefore it does not merit the
possession. For it is the cause of wrath rather than that it fulfills the
inheritance and promise, therefore the promise in no way is through
the Law,[16] because it is evident that *where*[6] *there is no law, there
is no transgression,* and thus there is no wrath, and thus all wrath
comes about when the Law works it. 16. *That is why it depends on
faith* (that they are heirs), which alone ratifies the promise of God,
in order that the promise[17] *may rest,* that is, be fulfilled, established, ratified, and confirmed,[18] *on grace,* that of God, who does
not impute on the basis of the works of those who are meritorious
by the Law, *and be guaranteed to all his descendants,* namely, to
the spiritual and fleshly seed, to Jew and Gentile, to all the seed,
I say, *not only to those who are,* and because they are, *alone of the
Law,* that is, only from among the Jews, who alone have the Law,
but also to those, to the seed from among the Gentiles, *who share,*
and because they share, *the faith of Abraham,* because through
faith it is the seed of Abraham, *for he is the father,* the spiritual
father in faith, *of us all,* both Jews and Gentiles; 17. *As it is written,*
Gen. 17:5,[19] *I have made you the father,* in spirit and in faith, *of
many nations*[20] *in the presence of the God in whom you be-*

[15] Because faith and the promise are interrelated. When the promise ceases,
faith ceases; and when the promise is done away, faith is made void, and vice
versa.

[16] For the Jews because of the Law were actually deprived of the promise
and the inheritance which they received, since they were not able to preserve
it in spirit.

[17] Which is weakened by the Law, because they were unworthy of fulfilling
it for their own advantage because of their transgression of the Law.

[18] Because the promise is confirmed by fulfillment, just as it is made void
by being cancelled. Jer. 35:16: "They have kept the command which their father
gave them."

[19] Hence the text in Gen. 17:5, "No longer shall your name be Abram, but
your name shall be Abraham; for I have made you a father of a multitude of
nations."

[20] The Jews understood this in a physical sense, as if when all the Gentiles
would be cut down and destroyed, they alone of the seed of Abraham would possess the whole world, just as they possessed the land of Canaan, although it is
an inheritance in the Spirit, that is, through faith, that the whole world now follows the faith of Abraham and confesses him as its father and receives his Seed
(that is, Christ) as its Lord.

---

[6] Although Luther's printed text reads: *Ubi est non est lex,* his comments
here disregarded the first *est,* which seems to have resulted from a mistaken

lieved,[21, 22] these last words are not in the Hebrew but are added as a confutation of the Jews, from whose writings the apostle has doubtless taken them, *who gives life to the dead,* through the raising of the flesh as well as the spirit, *and calls,* He gently draws and does not compel, *the things that do not exist,* both by nature and by grace, *into existence,*[23] in Greek it reads "as though they were." 18. *Against hope,* because there was no natural hope that a son might be born of himself and Sarah, *he believed,* the God who promised, *in hope,* in the thing hoped for, *that*[24, 25] *he should become the father of many nations,*[7] that is, that the prophecy would be fulfilled that he should be made the father, an act which

21 For if God promises and there is no one who believes Him when He promises, then surely there will also be no promise of God and no fulfillment, for it has been promised to no one, since no one has received it. Therefore faith ratifies the promise, and the promise demands faith in him to whom it is made. Wherefore he speaks well when he says: But if the promise of the inheritance is understood to be given without faith, then there will be no promise either. Again, if it is understood to be of the Law, then it will not be by faith, which the followers of the Law reject and, in addition, the Law "brings wrath" (v. 15).

22 It is as if he were saying: How "has he been made a father?" Before men? No, "in the presence of God, whom you believed." Thus in this way he removes carnal paternity and enters into a discussion of spiritual paternity, namely, that before God and in spirit he is a father who according to the flesh and in the eyes of men is not a father at all.

23 These words are encouragements to faith. For Abraham might have said: "This inheritance promised to me cannot be fulfilled in my time nor after me. For if I die and my sons possess it, then it is not I but they alone, even though He promised, saying, 'To you and to your descendants after you.' But if it is fulfilled in my lifetime, then no longer will all of my seed possess it all." And so the promises of God always seem to be contradictory and impossible for the wisdom of the flesh.

24 Not that he believed because of this, but because of the truthfulness of God. Thus the meaning is: He believed, so that God would thus be rendered truthful when he himself would become a father, as God had promised.

25 If he had not believed, he would not have become a father, etc. Thus he is not indicating a sequential cause, however, or taking the *ut* in a sequential sense rather than a causative, which in a negative expression is obvious, thus: If he had not believed, it would not have followed that he would become a father; therefore in order that this should follow and that he might become a father, it was necessary that he believe. And thus "he believed, that he should become the father," because unless it first took place that he believed, it would not take place that he become a father.

realization of the abbreviation *ē* (for *enim*). In the student notebooks the correction to *enim* is given, and in a note to the summary of chapter 7 below Luther quotes: *ubi enim non est lex.*

7 At "of many nations" Luther placed marks in the text to indicate the end of the quotation from Gen. 17:5.

was to be of more benefit to the Gentiles, *as he had been told,*
Gen. 17:5, *So shall your descendants be* [8] *as the stars of the heavens
and the sands of the sea,* these last words are not in the Greek
because they are not in the Hebrew or in the text of the Bible,[9] at
least at this place. For we read in Gen. 15:5, "Look toward heaven
and number the stars, if you are able to number them." Then He
said to him, 'So shall your descendants be.'" Then the words
"Abraham believed God," follow. 19. *He did not weaken,* although
many things exerted pressure on him, as the following shows, *in
his faith,* or trust, *when he considered,* in a way that might make
faith fail, *his own body, which was as good as dead,* as did Zech-
ariah, the father of John the Baptist, *because he was about a hundred years old,* and for this reason incapable of producing a child,
or when he considered the barrenness of Sarah's womb, or uterus,
both by reason of old age and because of the fact that she was by
nature sterile. 20. *Concerning the promise of God,* about a son and
the possession of the world, *he did not waver,* that is, he was not
afraid that God would be diverted, as it were, from His promise or
else might be kept from fulfilling it, *in distrust,* that is, through
lack of confidence, so that when these things did not move forward,
he did not fear with nothing but consternation of heart that God
was changing, a frequent experience when the fulfillment of a
promise is delayed,[26] *but he grew strong in his faith as he gave
glory to God,* because he attributed truthfulness to Him and power
to the man who believes His words. 21. He was *fully convinced,*
through faith, *that God was able to do what He had promised,*
because His truthfulness sees to it that He does not promise what
He cannot perform. But man, because he is a liar, often promises
what he cannot fulfill. But His power sees to it that He cannot be
changed and thus cannot lie.[27] 22. *That is why his faith was*

[26] For these are the two things which make faith hard and difficult. First,
because it is "the conviction of things not seen" (Heb. 11:1), indeed things
which seem contrary to the things which do appear, or things which cannot take
place, where all nature argues against its taking place. And when this handicap
has been overcome, the second is even more difficult, namely, the anxiety of heart
that perhaps God is changing His mind and is doing something else. The first
obstacle considers the power of God, the second His truthfulness. The strength
of both points is God's immutability both inwardly and outwardly.

[27] Num. 24 [23:19], "God is not man, that He should lie, or a son of man,

[8] Luther again indicates the end of the Genesis quotation by means of punc-
tuation.

[9] The Vulgate.

reckoned to him, by God, *as righteousness,* so that he might be righteous before God. 23. *But the words were written not* [28] *for his sake alone,* because he himself did not need to have them written, since both in heart and in action he was not a learner but a teacher of this virtue, and it was written long after him, *it was reckoned to him as righteousness* (the last two words are not in the Greek),[10] 24. *But for ours also,* who need the instruction of his example. *It will be reckoned to us who believe,* if we shall have believed, *in Him,* in God the Father, *that raised from the dead Jesus Christ* (not in the Greek)[11] *our Lord,* 25. *Who,* the risen Christ, *was delivered up,* to death, *for our trespasses,* to destroy them and put them to death, *and raised for our justification,* that it might be established and completed.

that He should repent. Has He said, and will He not do it, Or has He spoken, and will He not fulfill it?" But often man (because he is changeable and not able to accomplish something) breaks his word, even against his own will, because he cannot perform what he has promised, for example, when some hindrance befalls Him which exceeds his ability. This cannot happen with God.

[28] Here he makes his application and brings to a conclusion the point he has wanted to make.

---

[10] Faber's text also omits *ad iusticiam.*

[11] Faber also omits *Christum.*

CHAPTER FIVE[1]

Summary: The apostle demonstrates the power of faith in the justification of the believers, because death reigned from Adam to Christ.

1. *Since we are justified,*[2] through God's imputation, *therefore by faith,* not by works, *we have*[1] *peace,* in conscience and spirit, *with God,* although not yet with men and the flesh and the world and the devil, indeed, we have the more trouble, *through our Lord Jesus Christ,* as through our Mediator and not through ourselves, even though we are already justified by faith. 2. *Through whom,* as our Mediator, *we have obtained access,* to God by loving and knowing and delighting in Him, *by faith,* because there will be no salvation through Christ without faith, *to this grace,* of peace, remission of sins, and justification, *in which we stand,* through the firm confession of faith, *and we rejoice,* not in a present thing before men but *in our hope of sharing the glory,* the exaltation, that is, the glorification in the future life[3] *of the sons of God,*[4] those who are

[1] In this chapter the apostle speaks as one who is extremely happy and full of joy. In the entire Scripture there is scarcely another text like this chapter, scarcely one so expressive. For he describes the grace and mercy of God in the clearest possible manner, telling us what it is like and how great it is for us.

[2] It is more fitting to apply to us the expression "since we are justified" *(iustificati)* rather than "since we are righteous" *(iusti),* and "justification" rather than "righteousness." For Christ alone is righteous and possesses righteousness, but we still are always being justified and in a state of justification.

[3] 1 Peter 1:8: "You believe in Him and rejoice with unutterable and exalted joy."

[4] The Greek has "in the hope of the glory of God" (that is, in the glorification which comes from God alone, John 5:44: "You do not seek the glory that comes from the only God.") Yet this glory does not belong to any except "the sons of God"; therefore our version[2] is not wrong in adding this expression by way of explanation.

---

[1] Luther's printed Latin text read *habeamus* ("let us have"), but he crossed out the second letter *a* in *habeamus* to give the reading "we have."

[2] The Vulgate.

of God. 3. *More than that,* that is, that "we glory in our hope of sharing the glory of God," *but we rejoice also,* but also in the present situation, which is characterized by confusion and persecution, *in our sufferings, knowing,* by our various sufferings, *that suffering produces,* exercises and perfects,[5] *endurance,* for those who stand firmly in their faith, but on the other hand for those who do not stand firmly it works lack of endurance. 4. *And endurance* produces *trial,*[6] that we might be proved by God and found without deceit and guile and hypocrisy, *and trial hope,* that is, of "the glory of God," as has been said (v. 2). 5. *And hope does not disappoint us,* because it neither deserts nor fails us. All these things, I say, happen "because the love, etc.," *because the love,*[7] which creates an insuperable attachment, *of God,* that is, from God, *has been poured,* freely poured out, not received by merit, *into our hearts,* because love performs its works voluntarily; for works done unwillingly and by force do not endure, *by the Holy Spirit, who has been given to us,* through Christ from God the Father. 6. *Why,*[8] "at that time" *(denique),* for our greater exaltation, *did Christ, while we were still weak,* that is, when we were not fulfilling the Law and thus were sinners, as he says later on,[9] *at the right time,* although according to the decree of predestination we have been saints from the beginning, *die for the ungodly?* as if to say, a great reason for hope and glorying, even in our sufferings. 7. *For hardly,* it is extraordinary, I say, to die for the ungodly, *for what is righteous,* that is, for the sake of righteousness and truth,[4] *will one*

---

[5] Because he who has faith also has all of these things, but they are hidden; yet through tribulation they are exercised until they excel.

[6] 1 Peter 1:6-7, "Though now for a little while you may have to suffer various trials, so that the genuineness of your faith, more precious than gold, . . . which is tested by fire, etc."

[7] St. Augustine says regarding this passage: "He progresses step by step to the matter of love, which he says we possess through the gift of the Spirit. He points out all those things which we can attribute to ourselves, with God doing the giving, who deigns through grace to bestow His Holy Spirit upon us."

[8] The "why" *(utquid)* is not in the Greek, but rather it has "still" *(etiam)* or "yet" *(adhuc),* which is equivalent to "precisely at that time" *(denique)* or "besides" *(insuper).*[3]

[9] Thus it follows below (v. 8): "while we were yet sinners."

---

[3] Faber's text reads *adhuc,* but in his commentary *etiam* is given as an alternate. The suggestions *denique* and *insuper* are Luther's own.

[4] Luther takes *pro iusto,* and later *pro bono,* as neuter and therefore interprets

die—though perhaps, it is customary to die, *for what is good,* for its usefulness and desired features, *one will dare even to die.* 8. *But God,* the Father, *shows,* He makes it more commendable and worthy of love than all these things, *His love,* with which He loves us, *for us,* that is, the love which has been given to us, because on His part, *in that while we were yet sinners,* which he earlier (v. 6) expressed with "while we were still weak," *at the right time* (an expression which is not in the Greek at this point but only above) *Christ died for us,* the ungodly, so that we might not die in all eternity. 9. *Much more, therefore,* after we are righteous, *since we are now justified,* and our sins have been forgiven, *by His blood,* that is, by the merit of His blood, *shall we be saved from wrath* of the future judgment, *by Him.* 10. *For if, while we were enemies,* because of our sins, *we were reconciled,* so that we were not deserving of perdition, *to God,* not by our own merits or those of anyone else, except *by the death of His Son; much more, now* that we are reconciled, *shall we,* as His own, *be saved by His life,* in His resurrection to eternal life.[10] 11. And *not only so,* do we rejoice in tribulations, *but we also rejoice in God,* that is, because we have a God and He is our own God, because He has given Himself to us, *through our Lord Jesus Christ,* our Mediator, *through whom we have now received*[11] *our reconciliation,* the remission of sins, so that we may receive God Himself, through One, I say, Christ. 12. *Therefore,* because these things are so, it is therefore also true that *as through one man,* who committed an actual sin, namely, Adam, *sin,* the original sin, *came*[12] *into this world,* that is, among the men who are in the world, without their works, *and through sin,*

[10] The resurrection and life of Christ is not only a covenant *(sacramentum)* but also the cause, that is, the efficacious guarantee *(sacramentum),* of our own spiritual resurrection and life, because it causes those who believe in it to rise again and live, as we read below (Rom. 10:9), "If you confess that Jesus is Lord and believe in your heart that God raised Him from the dead, you will be saved," because in His death we die spiritually, as we read below in 6:3 ff.

[11] Eph. 2:12: "Remember that you were at that time . . . strangers to the covenant of promise, having no hope, and without God in the world, etc."

[12] Which is to say that thus through one man righteousness came into this world. But he deals with that point later on, after the digression which he makes here by taking up one part of the comparison.

with abstract qualities rather than persons. In the student notes we note the lecture hall addition: "as blessed Jerome says." The reference is to the *Letter to Algasia,* in which Jerome expounds this passage. Cf. *Patrologia, Series Latina,* XXII, 869 f.

that of our origin, *death*,[13] both, *and so death spread to all men*,[14] this is an explanation of the meaning of the term "world," namely, all men on earth, from the first to the last, *in which*, in the original sin, *all men sinned*, they have become sinners, even though they have done no evil deed. 13. *Before the Law was given*, the revelation of the Law through Moses, original *sin was in the world*,[15] that is, in the men of the world, *but sin*, original sin itself, even though the actual sins were certainly reckoned, *was not counted*,[5] or reckoned, indeed, it was ignored, *when there was no law*,[16] which actually did exist, but it was not recognized. 14. *Yet death reigned*, because it totally possessed us even to hell. But in the case of the righteous man death was only a servant, indeed it was under dominion, *from Adam*, that is, *to Moses*, who was the first to expose and make this sin known, Gen. 3, *even over those*, especially the children, *who did not sin*, in actual deed, hence, so that he might not contradict himself who said, "in which all have sinned" (v. 12), he adds the words *after the likeness*, that is, with a similar actual sin, *of the transgression of Adam*, which is to say that all have sinned but not in the same way as Adam,[17] *who was a type of the One who was to come*, that is, Christ, an example, a figure insofar as the transmission and propagation of sin is concerned, but not insofar as being that which is transmitted through the propagation or the thing transmitted is concerned. Therefore it follows: [18] 15. *But the free gift is not like the trespass*, that is, the sin is not similar

[13] He adds this in order that he might clearly show that he is speaking of original sin. Because if death comes through sin, then the children who die have sinned. But they certainly did not commit actual sin.

[14] He injects this digression between the points of the comparison in order that it thereby might be better understood that he is speaking about original sin.

[15] It is as if he were saying that the penalty of sin was evident, but sin was not evident.

[16] As below in chapter 7:7, and also as above (4:15): "I should not have known what it is to covet, if the Law had not said, 'You shall not covet'" (Rom. 7:7).

[17] Indeed the sin of Adam, properly speaking, is a transgression *(prevaricatio)* and a violation *(transgressio)*, but original sin is not a transgression *(prevaricatio)* but only "sin" *(peccatum)* and the guilt *(reatus)* of his *(Adam's)* transgression. Just as the righteousness of the saints is not the fulfilling of the Law by them but only the sharing of Christ's fulfillment, which He Himself has accomplished.

[18] Or rather, Adam is indeed the figure of Christ in the transmission, but not in the transmission of the sin, because He Himself has done the transmitting, because "the free gift is not like the trespass."

[5] Though Luther's text has the future *(imputabitur)*, his comment shows that he was working with the correct reading *(imputabatur)*.

to grace, nor is the type similar to grace, because Adam transmitted the offense, but Christ transmitted grace. *For if*, this is the
second point of the comparison, repeating at the same time the
first, *through one man's trespass many*, that is, all, *died*,[19, 20] with
one kind of death or another, *much more the grace of God*, which is
in Christ, *and the free gift*, which He received from God the
Father to give to men, *in the grace*, by which He Himself is pleasing to God in His merit, *of that one Man* [21] *Jesus Christ*, lest anyone
presume upon the grace of God without Christ, *have abounded for
many (plures)*,[22] that is, a great many *(multos)*, for life of every kind,
even by refraining from punishing other sins. 16. *And not like the
effect of that one man's sin (peccatum)*, or that one man who sins
(peccantem); [6] the judgment of death came upon all by only the
one person who sinned, *is the free gift*, that is, the gift is not only
in contradistinction to that one sin [23] of the one person who sinned.

[19] From which it is clear that original sin is the actual sin of Adam himself,
because the apostle says, "Many died through one man's trespass." Therefore
this one sin of the one man is the sin of all, by which all have died with him.

[20] Moreover, original sin is the same as the actual sin itself which Adam
sinned, which all his sons bear, and of which they are all guilty. For together
with his nature he also transmitted his sin to all men, because just as he himself
by a sin of this kind was made a sinner and an evil man, so nothing is born of
him except sinners and evil men, that is, men prone to evil, who find it difficult
to do good.

[21] As the sin of one is, so is the grace of One; just as the former is understood to condemn even without individual commission of sin, so the latter is
understood to give blessing without merits.

[22] The earlier expression "much more" *(multomagis)* ought not be compared
with the expression "for many" *(in plures)*. Thus St. Augustine in chapter 11 [7]
says, "He does not say *in magis multos*, that is, 'unto many more men,' for it is
not that more are justified than are condemned, but rather *multomagis abundavit*,
'has abounded much more.' To be sure, Adam because of his one offense produced guilty sons, but Christ has pardoned even those offenses which men have
added of their own."

[23] That is, the gift leads to righteousness not by "the effect of that one man's
sin," but by the many who sin, that is, by the one who sins all die because of the
one sin, but the gift not only frees us from this sin which we possess because of
the one who sins; not as sin comes "through that one man who sins" does "also
the free gift" take away that one sin alone.

---

[6] Luther underlined *per unum peccatum*, crossed out *peccatum*, and added
peccantem, to indicate that he preferred the reading "of that one who sinned."
Faber suggested the same emendation.

[7] Augustine, *De peccatorum meritis et remissione*, I, 11, 14, *Patrologia, Series
Latina*, XLIV, 117.

For, by laying Himself open He brought upon Himself, as St. Augustine puts it,[8] *the judgment following one trespass,* the sin of Adam, *brought condemnation,* of eternal and temporal death, *but the free gift,* that is, grace, *following many,* insofar as it concerns the multitude of sins and sinners, *trespasses,* that is, of many both collectively and individually *brings justification.* 17. *For if*[24] *because of one man's,* Adam's, *trespass,* through that which the trespass deserved, *death reigned through that one man,* namely, Adam, the one who committed the trespass unto death, *much more will they,* the faithful in Christ, *who receive the abundance of grace,* by which not only that one trespass but all other sins are forgiven, *and the free gift of righteousness,* because our righteousness is free gift and grace, that is, it is given in mercy and grace, and when they have triumphed over death, they will *reign in life through the one Man Jesus Christ,* the Author of the righteousness that brings life. 18. *Then, as one man's trespass led to condemnation for all men,*[25] that is, the judgment of death, *so one Man's,* Christ's, *act of righteousness leads,* by grace, *to acquittal and life for all men,* that is, it came to many, or all who are justified in no other way than through His righteousness, etc.[26] 19. *For as by one man's disobedience many were made sinners, so also by one Man's obedience many will be made righteous.*[27] 20. *The Law came in,* while sin remained, which had "come in"

24 The apostle repeats the same ideas with different words in order to impress upon us the greatness and abundance of the grace of God, etc.

25 This is "the type of Him who was to come" (5:14), wherein Adam is similar to Christ, as he has said previously.

26 Thus blessed Augustine may be cited in chapter 15, as above;[9] "all" and "all" *(omnes et omnes)* are the words used, not because all those who are born of Adam are born again of Christ, but because just as there is no physical generation except through Adam, so there is no spiritual generation except through Christ. Later on he calls the same "all" *(omnes)* "many" *(multos),* etc.

27 Here he uses the term "many" *(multi)* and not "all" *(omnes)* in order to indicate that in the preceding verses he was speaking not of the number of sinners or righteous people but of the power of sin and grace. For if sin was so strong that one sin could destroy many people, indeed, all people, then grace is even stronger still, for the one grace can save many, indeed all people, from many sins, if all are willing.

8 Augustine, *De peccatorum meritis et remissione,* I, 12, 15, *Patrologia, Series Latina,* XLIV, 117 f.

9 Ibid., I, 15, 19, *Patrologia, Series Latina,* XLIV, 119.

(v. 12), it came to those who did not know the Law, *that* [28] *it might increase the trespass,* [29] our own actual sin, beyond original sin, which began without the Law and before it. *But where sin increased* through additional actual sins of our own, *grace,* that of Christ, *abounded all the more,* far beyond every kind of sin, because it had overcome sin. 21. *So that as sin,* of both kinds, through Adam and through ourselves, *reigned in death,* both eternal and temporal, *grace also might reign,* over sin of both kinds, *through righteousness to eternal life,* to life everlasting, *through Jesus Christ our Lord.*

[28] We ought not call this a cause but a result, albeit a negative one, that is, unless the Law had come in, there would have been no sin, and it would not have abounded. He uses the term "came in" *(subintravit),* which means that the Law did not destroy sin, but when sin came in, the Law also "came in" and went deeper *(subintravit)* and cast sin down.

[29] And this in a twofold sense. First, that we might understand what it means to increase; because without the Law it was not understood how abounding and overwhelming sin is. Second, according to St. Augustine, chapter 6, *De Spiritu et littera,*[10] the Law came that it might increase concupiscence by prohibiting it and increase our loathing for the Law by commanding it. And this is the answer if anyone asks on the basis of what has been said: If sin and death reigned till the Law and till Moses, then what? Did the Law take away death and sin? Augustine answers that it has not taken them away, indeed, it has increased sin and made us much more worthy of death. But at that time Augustine intended to speak only about the first sin, which was not imputed till Moses, and death was not understood as being involved.

[10] Augustine, *De Spiritu et littera,* 6, 9, *Patrologia, Series Latina,* XLIV, 205.

CHAPTER SIX

Summary: The apostle declares that we must not continue in our sins but must do what is good.

1. *What shall we say then?* if grace abounds because sin has abounded. *Are we to continue in sin that grace may abound?* [1] as falsifiers understand the passage, when they say, "Let us do evil," that is, let us commit sin, "That good may come" (Rom. 3:8), that is, that grace may abound. 2. *By no means,* because this idea is absolutely contrary to the work of grace, *for we who died to sin,* [2] by a spiritual and saving death, for he dies to sin who determines that he will never again for all eternity desire to sin. Moreover, since it is repugnant to him as long as he lives, *how can we still live in it?* This is the interpretation of the statement "Are we to continue in sin?" for that man does continue in sin who lives for sin. It is as if he were saying: "It is impossible, because a dead man does not rise." Furthermore, that we are dead to sin he proves from the following: 3. *Do you not know, brethren,* as if to say, you ought not be ignorant, *that all of us who have been baptized,* because the threefold dipping of Baptism signifies the three-day death period and the burial of Christ, *into Christ Jesus,* that is, by faith

---

[1] This is an expression concerning which certain people have been scandalized and said, as they did above in chapter 3:8: "Why not do evil that good may come?" erroneously interpreting the apostle's words "where sin increased, grace abounded all the more" (Rom. 5:20), for he spoke these words not to give license to sin but in praise of God's grace. Hence blessed Augustine, in ch. 7 of *On the Spirit and the Letter* says: The apostle Paul "instead of condemnation received mercy, instead of punishment he found grace; rightly then he is loud and eager in his defense of grace; he cares nothing for the hatred of those who do not understand this profound and inscrutible matter, who twist his correct words into a perverted meaning." [1] For in this chapter he is speaking about the mystery of the death and resurrection of Jesus Christ.

[2] Blessed Augustine says: "For grace is necessary that we may die to sin." [2]

---

[1] Augustine, *De Spiritu et littera,* 7, 12, *Patrologia, Series Latina,* XLIV, 207.

[2] Augustine, *Expositio quarundam propositionum ex epistula ad Romanos,* 31, *Patrologia, Series Latina,* XXXV, 2068.

in Christ Jesus, *were baptized into His death,* that is, through the merit and power of His death? Hence "Baptism" *(baptismus),* "dipping" *(mersio),* "to baptize" *(baptiso),* and "to dip" *(mergo)* all mean that 4. *We were buried therefore together (consepulti),* that is, spiritually. The Greek has "we are buried" *(sepulti igitur sumus).* For it is a logical consequence, *with Him by Baptism into death,*[3] namely, a spiritual death, that is, to the world and to sin, *so that as Christ,* after His death, *was raised,* bodily, *from the dead by the glory of the Father,* by the power of His brilliance, *we too,* after this spiritual death, *might walk,*[3] progress, *in newness,* which comes through the grace of Baptism, *of life,* spiritual life. 5. *For if,* he explains what he has just said, *we have been planted with Him,* we spiritually with Him who was planted bodily, *in a death like His,*[4] that is, in resemblance of His death, because we have been buried into a mystical death, *we shall certainly be raised,* to a spiritual resemblance with Him, *in a resurrection like His,* that is, we shall become like it.[5] For it necessarily follows, as he says below (v. 7) "for he who has died is freed from sin." 6. *We know that our,* ours spiritually, *old self,* from Adam and our descent of the flesh, *was crucified with Him,* with Christ who was crucified physically, *so that the body,* the mortal one, which is prone to sin, *of sin,* that is, of concupiscence, *might be destroyed,* through zealous pursuit of the new life, *and that we might no longer be enslaved to sin,*[6] or concupiscence, that is by obeying its lusts. 7. *For he,* he proves the truth of the statement "we have been planted together," *who has died,* that is, in a spiritual death in the good sense of the term, *is freed from sin,* that is, he has risen in a spiritual

[3] This is what he said in the preceding chapter (5:10): "we shall be saved by His life."

[4] With this statement he is alluding to the passage in John 12:24: "Unless a grain of wheat falls into the earth and dies, it remains alone, etc." Thus he uses the term "likeness" so that he may not be understood as speaking of the physical resurrection and death. And in order to show the meaning of this concept of being planted together with Him, He continues in the same passage: "He who hates his life in this world will keep it for eternal life" (John 12:25).

[5] So that "we have been" *(facti sumus)*
　　　　　　　and　　　　　　　　　　　　} correspond to each other.
　　　"we shall be" *(erimus)*

[6] Which sin? It is original sin which is being served when we perform works which are in accord with its desires.

---

[3] Faber's text has "in His death," but Luther preferred "into His death," no doubt to reflect the Greek text.

resurrection. 8. *But if we have died,* in spiritual death through Baptism for the purpose of putting an end to sin, *with Christ, we believe,* because this life has no experiential knowledge of Him, but we have faith. For no one knows that he has life or feels that he has been justified, but he believes and hopes *that we shall also live with Him* in spirit and in a new beginning which will continue into eternity. 9. *For we know,* because we know, *that Christ,* after He had died, *being raised from the dead,* for Himself bodily and for us sacramentally (mystically), *will never die again,*[7] that is, He will die no more; *death no longer,* for all eternity, *has dominion over Him,* as if to say, that it ought not have dominon over your spirit. 10. *The death He died He,* Christ, *died,* bodily, *to sin,* that is, that sin might die, *once for all,*[8] that is, He will not die a second time or again, *but the life He lives,* after His resurrection, *He lives to God,*[9, 10] in righteousness and glory. 11. *So you also must consider yourselves,* understand, be aware that you are, *dead to sin,* 1 Peter 2:24, "that we might die to sin and live to righteousness," *but alive,* with spiritual life, *to God in Christ Jesus,* through faith in Christ. 12. *Let not sin therefore reign,* although it is neither absent nor quiet, *in your mortal bodies,* a statement which he makes

[7] He does not say: "Christ will live," but "Christ will never die again," because a negative statement in Scripture has a stronger meaning and lets an assertion be understood as forever true. Thus the expression "that we might no longer be enslaved to sin" (v. 6) means that we shall be forever righteous.

[8] Heb. 9:12: "He entered once for all into the Holy Place, taking . . . His own blood, thus securing an eternal redemption." And again, (Heb. 9:28): "Christ has been offered once to bear the sins of many."

[9] In the Greek it reads, "That which died to sin died once for all" (ὃ γὰρ ἀπέθανεν, τῇ ἁμαρτίᾳ ἀπέθανεν ἐφάπαξ), and that is much better. "That which lives lives to God," (ὃ δὲ ζῇ, ζῇ τῷ θεῷ). *Quod,* that is the *quodcunque* ("whatever"), is used as a pronoun, not as a conjunction. For it is an expression of the sacrament of Christ's death, which is to say, that just as Christ, who died once, never dies again, so whoever *(quicunque)* dies spiritually to sin once never dies again but will live forever.

[10] From this text it is evident that our translator [4] has not done the work of a translator only, but at the same time that of an expositor. And no greater fault can be found in a translator than this, for he puts his own meaning on the work of others, a meaning which is not in the document he is translating. Hence we cannot agree with blessed Jerome, who says regarding Daniel that he could not translate what he did not first understand.[5] But this is the same as understanding all things and being ignorant of nothing, although if he would apply this statement with moderation, he would be speaking the truth.

[4] I. e., of the Vulgate.

[5] Cf. Jerome, *Contra Rufinum,* II, 32, *Patrologia, Series Latina,* XXIII, 475.

to indicate the difference from our mystical body, which is the
church of Christ, which is an immortal body, as is the Head also,
as he explains his meaning: *to make you obey,* through the consent
of the heart, *their passions,*[11, 12] that is, the passions of the body,
as if to say that they will harass you, to be sure, but they will not
reign over you, if you do not obey them. 13. *But* (and),[6] here he
expounds the same idea even more clearly, *do not yield,*[7] surrender
or offer voluntarily, even though they may be so inclined, *your
members as instruments, tools, of wickedness,* the Greek "unrighteousness" (ἀδικία), which is a better translation, *unto sin,*
which is unbelief, so that they serve sin unto unrighteousness,
but yield, present, even though your sin struggles against it, *yourselves,* your whole selves first, *to God as men who have been
brought from death to life,* spiritually and humbly, living in the
spirit and not in obedience to sin, but consenting to righteousness,
and your members to God as instruments, tools and servants, *of
righteousness,* which comes from faith, that they may serve God
unto righteousness. And you can do this easily: 14. *For sin* [13] *will
have no dominion over you,* unless you want it to. It cannot have
dominion. The reason is: *since you are not under the Law but under
grace,*[14] because you have fulfilled the Law through faith in Christ,
whose righteousness and work of fulfillment is yours by the grace
of a merciful God which is given to you. 15. *What then?* What fol-

[11] The Greek has "that you should be obedient to it" (εἰς τὸ ὑπακούειν),
that is, to sin "in the lusts thereof," that is, of the body.

[12] That "sin reigns" and "to obey" sin is to consent to and do what sin
desires. In Greek it says "that you should be obedient to it in the lusts thereof,"
just as below in Rom. 13:14 it says that "you should make no provision for the
flesh, to gratify its desires."

[13] What sin? Actual? No, original sin. For this kind of sin has dominion
over us first, as Titus 3:3 shows: "For we ourselves were once, etc."

[14] John 8:34: "Truly, I say to you, everyone who commits sin is a slave to
sin." Therefore sin is his master. But those who are under the Law, of necessity
are in sin, since without grace no one can fulfill the Law, at least in his heart.
It is a subtle removal of the reproach of the Law if they were to say: "Who can
sustain the force of sin and its evil desire?" The answer is: "It will not have
dominion or triumph over those who do not want it to, although it will do battle
against them and oppose them." But Christ in John 16:33 gives us this comfort,
"In the world you have tribulation; but be of good cheer, I have overcome the
world." It is as if He were saying: "My victory will be your victory, if you believe."

[6] Luther crossed out *sed* in the text and wrote *et* above it.

[7] Luther preferred to read *exhibete* rather than *exhibeatis.*

lows from this Word? *Are we to sin,* since all things are permitted to those who live without the Law, *because we are not under the Law but under grace?* [15] as if to say: "Is this the way we are to understand the expression 'to be under the Law'?" *By no means.* It certainly is not understood in this way, and it does not follow that this is the meaning. 16. *Do you not know,* it is as if he were saying: "You surely do know," *that if you yield yourselves,* surrender or offer yourselves, *to anyone,* anyone at all, your entire personality, *as obedient slaves,* we are made slaves by this very act of surrender, *you are slaves of the one whom you obey, either of sin,* that is, you are the servants of sin, *which leads to death,* for sin does lead to death and because of this it is no longer under grace; thus there is a struggle between being under grace and sinning. The apostle is trying to point this out. The dialectic is expressed in these words: "either of sin, which leads to death" or of righteousness unto life. But the apostle uses the phrase *or of obedience (obeditio),* compliance *(obedientia),* or faith, *which leads to righteousness,* which in turn is life. 17. *But thanks be,* that is, we give thanks, *to God,* the Greek reads, "But thanks (χάϱις) to God," namely, let there be thanks to God, *that you who were once slaves of sin,* that is, because you now are what you were not, but "you were the slaves of sin," but now you *have become obedient,* through faith, *from the heart* in simplicity and without deceit *to the standard of teaching,* that is, according to the rule of the Gospel *to which you were committed.* [16] 18. *And having been set free from sin,* so that we do not do what sin demands; you are still not entirely free in all respects, but *you have become slaves,* so that we do the things which are according to faith, *of righteousness,* [17] of the kind that is in us through faith in Christ. 19. *I am speaking in human terms,* that is, the kind of thing that is given

---

[15] For thus they are either fools or dolts who think that it is one and the same expression to say that we "are not under the Law" and that we are permitted all things, and on the other hand that we "are under grace" and thus no sin is prohibited.

[16] That is, you have been delivered from the form of error into the form of the Gospel because "Forever, O Lord, Thy Word is firmly fixed in the heavens" (Ps. 119:89). For the Word is not changed, but we are, and we yield to Him; Is. 40:8: "The grass withers . . . but the Word of our God will stand forever"; Matt. 5:25: "Make friends with your accuser," which is to say, give up your usual form and put on the form of the Word. For "the Word became flesh," so that we might be made the Word.

[17] 1 Peter 2:16: "Live as free men, yet without using your freedom as a pretext for evil, but live as servants of God."

attention among men, *because of your natural limitations,* the inability of your flesh [18] to do greater things, by which I mean to say: *For just as,* of your own will, or at least without any violent opposition, *you once yielded,* in the way you act, *your members to impurity,* that is, to the pollutions of the flesh, such as riotous living beyond the limits of wedlock, *and iniquity,* to unrighteousness, which is unfaithfulness, *unto iniquity,* unrighteousness, that is, to an increase of unrighteousness; *so now,* in faith, *yield your members,* in your way of living, *to righteousness,* which comes from faith, *for sanctification,* that is, that they might be purified and made holy from these pollutions.[19] 20. *For when you were,*[8] or better, "since you have been" *slaves of sin, you were free,* that is you were deprived of and had no claim, *in regard to righteousness,* which is in Christ. 21. *But then what return did you get,* it is as if he were saying, "Indeed, a loss and no return at all, as you had believed," *from the things,* the works of sin, the pollutions, and the uncleannesses, *of which you are now ashamed?*[20] *For the end of those things,* the reward of these pleasures and sinful works, *is death,* eternal death. 22. *But now that you have been set free from sin and have become slaves,* through the righteousness of faith, *of God, the return you get,* that is, the merits and joy of a good conscience, *is sanctification,* that is, through purity and chastity of body and soul, *and its end,* reward, *eternal life.* 23. *For the*

[18] It is as if he were saying: "I have taught previously that you should be firm, that is, that even under the fiercest attacks sin must not have dominion over you. But because you are still weak over against this warfare, at least be concerned that you do not sin at peace and quiet, which is not beyond human nature — for the former position is that of a hero, but the latter is the kind of virtue which most people have — so that — if you must yield to your lusts, for example, in marriage, in business, in the exercise of authority, etc., at least remain within the limits of reason."

[19] He has taught previously that he who is dead to sin certainly should not obey his lust, because they live a perfect life who are entirely continent, who despise riches, flee honors, and walk in the counsels of the Gospel. But lest he seem to be imposing this command on all as something absolutely necessary, he teaches less rigorously at this point and dwells only on the command; for he modestly teaches that also in the married state we should avoid the uncleanness of fleshly lust by moderation.

[20] For as long as sin is aglow he seems to have a good and fruitful thing, that is, joy and pleasures, but later, when they have finished, they become detestable and a source of shame to the person who is repentant and has come to his senses.

---

[8] "You were" *(essetis)* is the reading also of Faber's text and other contemporary versions, but Luther's printed text had read "we were" *(essemus).*

wages, the rewards which are the final end, *of sin is death;* he has explained this by saying, "The end of those things is death" (v. 21), *but the free gift,* the present, *of God is eternal life in Christ Jesus our Lord,* that is, the grace which is in us in Christ personally and through faith in Him as we participate in it and receive it through imputation.

CHAPTER SEVEN

Summary: The apostle establishes the cessation of the old law, which is the law of death; and [1] he is dealing here with the law of the tinder.[1]

1. *Do you not know, brethren.* It is as if he were saying: "You surely are not unaware, even though you do not understand the mystery," *for I am speaking to those who know the Law,* therefore you cannot be ignorant of the fact that it follows, *that the Law,* whatever kind it may be, even the human and civil law, *is binding on a person,* and he himself is subject to it right up to the time of his death, *as long as he lives?* The reference here is not to the Law, as some people mistakenly think, but to man, because the apostle wants to say that the Law exercises its dominion and makes its demands over the living and not over the dead. 2. *Thus a married woman is bound by law to her husband,* under his power and rule, *as long as he lives.* And to say the opposite, the law of the man has dominion over her and subjects her,[2] *but if her husband dies,* and also if the woman dies, *she is discharged from the law concerning the husband.*[3] And in this sense she is dead to the law, for

[1] He corroborates and proves more fully what he has said in the preceding chapter concerning the death of the old man and the justification of the new by using the simile of the human temporal law, and (it seems to me) his intent is to explain that remarkable proposition which he has stated in chapter 4:15: "The Law brings wrath, but where there is no law, there is no transgression." 2

[2] He wants to say: Neither party is freed from the law before death. In the same way no one is freed from the law of the letter unless he dies with Christ through Baptism, as he has said in the preceding chapter (v. 4).

[3] Thus also a citizen, if he dies, even though the laws of the state remain in force, yet they no longer have any control over him. Indeed even if he "dies" only as a citizen, the situation is the same, so that a man who moves to another city is "dead" and free from the law of the first city. But the example used by the

---

[1] The summary up to this point is crossed out in Luther's manuscript.

[2] This marginal note is a substitute for the section crossed out in the original summary above the text.

the law has lost its hold on her just as she is lost who dies, and as she herself has become dead to the law, so also she is not held by it. 3. *Accordingly, she will be called an adulteress if she lives with another man while her husband is alive. But if her husband dies, she is free from the law of her husband.* In this example there is no recommendation that a woman enter into marriage a second time, but the freedom to marry is recommended, and to be sure also the freedom to decline the burdens of married life, *so that if she marries another man, she is not an adulteress.* He adds this statement in order to show what kind of "law of her husband" he is speaking about, namely, not a law which her husband has laid down, for a transgression of such a law does not make her an adulteress, but he is speaking about the marriage law which states that she shall not be the wife of a second man while her husband is alive. 4. *Likewise,*[4] *my brethren, you who are a spiritual wife long ago subjected to the old man through the Law, you have died,* as he said above: "Our old man was crucified with Christ" (Rom. 6:6) and "you are not under the Law" (Rom. 6:14), *to the Law,* that is to the dominion of the Law,[5] *through the body of Christ,* that is through His true and mystical body which was also put to death, *so that you may belong to another,* and not to the Law, which lords it over its bond servants by fear, but *to Him who has been raised from the dead,* who rules His children in love, *in order that you may bear fruit for God,*[6] that is, that you may produce good

apostle is the best of all for the purpose because the application of it correctly follows it, both because of the person, since the church is a woman, and because of the putting to death, since the woman dies to the law, but yet she lives, so that she can be made subject to another.

4 Here he applies the simile, for the old law made us subject to the old man and to sin, namely, while the Law aroused our old man, as he says below (v. 9), since without the Law there would be no sin or old man, but through the Law he is aroused.

5 Is. 9:4: "The staff of his shoulder, the yoke of his burden and the rod of his oppressor Thou hast broken."

6 A wonderful and profound summary of this chapter of the apostle, which Nicholas of Lyra and the others have explained not only foolishly but even falsely. The only exception which I have encountered is Augustine.[3] For the apostle wishes to conclude with this point, that there are two men, the old and the new, the one Adam, the other Christ. But the old man was not known before the Law was known and established, but when it was established, then he arose, as it were; and thus through the Law we have been made subject to the old man and to sin (that is, we recognize that we have been made subject). And thus sin ruled

---

3 Augustine's interpretation is from *Expositio quarundam propositionum ex epistula ad Romanos,* 36, *Patrologia, Series Latina,* XXXV, 2069.

works.[7] But if someone arrogantly objects: "Have we not already been bearing fruit for God?" Like the Jews, who presumptuously asserted that they were particularly righteous, the answer is: "No, actually you have been bearing fruit u**n**to death." This he now proves. 5. *While we were living in the flesh*, without grace, *our sinful passions*, our desires, inclinations, and drives toward evil, which make up our old man and man in his unconverted state, *aroused by the Law*,[8] that is, by the dominion of the Law, that is, they were recognized as existing and increased by the Law,[9] *were at work*, that is, they dominated and prevailed, bustled about, and carried on their disturbances, *in our members to bear fruit*, their wicked works, *for death*, that is, unto death because "death came through sin" (Rom. 5:12). 6. *But now*, since we are in the spirit, *we are discharged*, through the grace of faith, *from the law* [10] *of*

over us, just as the husband over the wife through the Law, without which he would not have dominion, that is, he would not be known to have dominion. Therefore, when the old man has died, we also have died to the Law, for he can no longer hold us in subjection to sin, but he has lost this power over us.

7 John 15:16: "I appointed you that you should go and bear fruit, and that your fruit should abide."

8 The Law of Moses; for this is the law of the earlier man, that is, the old man; it was not established by him, but he himself is roused to life by it; therefore Paul uses the term "aroused by the Law" (v.5), because without the Law there was no old man. Therefore the term "the law concerning the husband" is used in a creative sense, because it makes him a man and subjects the soul to him, just as the law of marriage is not made by the husband, but it makes him a husband and subjects some one to the husband. But in the case of marriage the law subjects us in a material way, while in the case of this law it subjects us spiritually (that is, insofar as it concerns the knowledge and increase of concupiscence, even insofar as it pertains to obedience), because through the Law we sin even more as long as grace is lacking. For the Law holds us in subjection as it pertains to work, for the flesh works what it wishes, and so does the old man, whom the Law exposes and arouses, as he says below: "that sin might become sinful beyond measure" (v. 13). But when grace is given, the old man dies, and the Law can no longer produce him or bring him to light. Thus we die to the power and dominion of the Law, but not to the Law in the proper and simple sense, that is, we are not under the Law, even though we have the Law.

9 As he says above (Rom. 4:15): "Where there is no law, there is no transgression, for the Law brings wrath."

10 But how are we "discharged from the Law?" Doubtless because through faith in Christ we satisfy the demands of the Law and through grace are freed and voluntarily perform the works of the Law, but he who does not have this is active unwillingly and almost in fear or ín a desire for his own convenience. Therefore love is necessary, which seeks the things of God, love which is given to him who asks in faith and in the name of Jesus. Therefore, even though we sin often and are not perfectly voluntary, yet we have made a beginning and are progressing, and we are righteous and free. Indeed, we must constantly beware

death, that is, from the dominion of the Law, which causes wrath and death without being weakened itself, *in which we were held captive,* in subjection because of our nonfulfillment, *so that we serve,* so that we are worshipers of God, *in the new life,* which is through the grace of regeneration, *of the Spirit,* that is, of the spiritual man, *and not under the old written code,*[11] that is, of the old man. 7. *What then shall we say?* Because he has said: "our sinful passions were aroused by the Law" (v. 5) and "the law of death" (v. 6). *That the Law is sin?* For this would seem to be the case, because without it there is no sin. *By no means!* Yet we shall say this: *I should not have known,* but should not have escaped, *sin,* as we read above in 3:20: "through the Law comes the knowledge of sin," *if it had not been for the Law. For I should not have known what it is to covet,* therefore coveting existed, but I did not know of its existence, *if the Law had not said: You shall not covet.* 8. *But sin, finding opportunity,* that is, sin taking occasion, although it was not given it by the Law, because where there is no sin, the Law gives no opportunity, as is evident in the case of the saints and righteous men, *in the commandment,* without weakening the commandment or the Law, *wrought,* that is, brought to my understanding, or by arousing itself, *in me all kinds,* that is brought to full consummation, *of covetousness,* of which I was ignorant; which, as far as I was concerned, was not in me before the Law came.[12, 13] *For apart from the Law,* without a knowledge of the

that we may not be under the Law; therefore we must always remain in faith and pray for love. For who knows whether or not he is acting out of fear or a love for his own convenience even in a very subtle manner in his devotional life and his good works, looking for rest and a reward rather than the will of God?

11 The term "written code" *(littera)* ought not to be understood here only in a figurative sense, as Augustine argues at length, *De Spiritu et littera,* chap. 4.[4] Therefore Lyra is in error when he says that Christ has abrogated the Law as it pertains to civil and ceremonial matters, but not as it pertains to moral matters; indeed, he is clearly saying here, when the reference is to moral matters, that this is a law of death and the written code.

12 But in the case of the righteous, who love the law of God, sin does not work concupiscence nor give opportunity, nor is the opportunity received by sin, because it is not there but has truly died.

13 An analogy is the case of a deep and hidden fire in limestone,[5] indeed, it is not known to be there, but when water is poured over it, the fire has an

4 *Patrologia, Series Latina,* XLIV, 203 f. Luther quotes Augustine from this source in the scholia below, p. 325.

5 This analogy may be based on Augustine's observations in *De civitate Dei,* XXI, 4, 3, *Patrologia, Series Latina,* XLI, 713.

Law, sin lies dead. It was not known by me; therefore in explaining his meaning he goes on: 9. *And I was once,* just as anyone else, *alive,* not because there was no law, *apart from the Law,* apart from a knowledge of the Law and therefore also without sin, *but when the commandment came,* came to be known, *sin,* which previously had been dead because it was not known, *revived.*[14] Blessed Augustine says: "Sin began to become apparent."[6] 10. *And I died,* I knew this in my spirit; and in this is the explanation for everything, that I died and I thought I was alive, *and the very commandment which,* by nature and of itself, *promised life proved,* through the knowledge of the Law, indeed it was revealed to me through the Spirit; because Matt. 19:17 tells us: "If you would enter life, keep the commandments," *to be death to me.*[15] For "the written code kills" opportunity of showing itself. Thus the water does not create the fire in the limestone, but it causes it to be made known, and the water itself without the fire is made the occasion of the fire. So it is also with the will of man and the Law, that he is under sin, to be sure, but the sin is not recognized until the man learns to know and perceives the Law; then even without the defect of the Law sin burns more brightly and openly. Grace puts out this fire, just as oil cools the heat of the limestone.

[14] So it is with the arrogant heretics and the self-righteous. Because they do not recognize the Law of God against them, it is impossible for them to recognize their sin; therefore they are also incapable of correction. But if they were to recognize the Law, they would immediately recognize their sin, and what is now dead to them would come to life.

[15] And at this point we must not think, as Lyra and others say,[7] that the apostle is speaking regarding the person of some degraded man and not of his own person. Likewise he is not speaking of that crass darkness of the mind, as if he does not know the Law except in a very superficial way. But he is speaking of his own person and of all the saints [8] and of that abysmal darkness of our heart, by which even the saints and the wisest men have nothing but an imperfect concept of themselves and thus of the Law. As David says (Ps. 19:12): "Who can discern his errors?" Likewise who can understand the Law? For it is im-

---

[6] Augustine, *Expositio . . . ad Romanos,* 38, *Patrologia, Series Latina,* XXXV, 2070.

[7] Lyra says: "The apostle is speaking in the role of the human race that is thus overcome by darkness." Faber, who is often meant by "others" in phrases of this kind, says: "Paul uses himself as an example of carnal man . . . even though he was such least of all . . . he turns himself into a weak man for the sake of the weak . . . yet on occasion he had been weak" (W, LVI, 68, n. 9).

[8] In his comment on Gal. 5:17 (W, XL-2, 88—89, Röhrer's notes) Luther points out that Paul in his Epistle to the Romans is writing to "a church that is renewed, baptized, made righteous, and has forgiveness of sins," and yet he speaks of their flesh as being "opposed to the Spirit." Luther goes on to say: "Jerome and others understand the word 'saints' *(sancti)* to mean only those who are pure and undefiled, but this is to annul the forgiveness of sins and Christ Himself." See also *Luther's Works,* 27, p. 70.

(2 Cor. 3:6). 11. *For sin,* the tinder and law of the members, *finding opportunity,* as above (v. 8), *in the commandment, deceived me,* seduced me in that it made me more concupiscent,[16] because it pretends that what is contrary to the Law is good and sweet and it makes the Law appear harsh and hard, *and by it* (the commandment) it *killed me.* 12. *So the Law is holy,* that is, it is pure and without sin, *and the commandment is holy and just and good,* in itself and in them who are holy and just and good. Blessed Augustine says[9]: "The Law is good, but without grace the Law only shows sins but does not take them away." 13. *Did that,* which is to say: Does it not follow? *which is good,* in itself, *bring death to me,* because this is contrary to it? *By no means!* Thus he now very clearly explains himself here to the end of the chapter and deals with points which he has previously mentioned. *But sin,* which hid itself without the Law, *that it might be shown to be sin through that which is good,* that is, through the Law, *worked,* that is, it made me understand and became the occasion of *death in me,* death of both body and soul, *that sin,* the tinder of sin itself, *by the commandment,* that is, by the opportunity of the commandment, *might become sinful above measure,* a sinner through actual sins. 14. *For we know that the Law is spiritual,* because it requires

possible to understand the Law without understanding every sin. For the Law impinges upon every sin, as we read in Ps. 12:6: "The words of the Lord are purified seven times." Therefore he who thinks that he understands the Law "You shall not covet" even concerning himself is foolish and arrogant, as the heretics are. But with the exception of Christ, any righteous person, as he progresses from evil lust to purity, also progresses from an ignorance of the Law to an understanding of it. Hence what we read in Ps. 25:7: "Remember not the sins of my youth, or my transgressions," must be the prayer of every righteous man. "Sins of my youth" are hidden sins, which also the spiritual and renewed man still possesses. Thus it is only by faith that we can say: "For I know my transgression" (Ps. 51:3), since these words follow: "The uncertain and hidden things of Thy wisdom Thou hast made manifest to me" (Ps. 51:6). These things are the most secret things of the Law: knowledge, which is never understood perfectly, but it is made manifest that it might be believed. Therefore, he who does not wish to confess more sin than he knows and recognizes in himself will confess few sins, and he does not say: "I acknowledge my sin to Thee, etc." (Ps. 32:5).

16 St. Augustine, ch. 4, *De Spiritu et littera,* says: "I do not understand how this very thing for which I lust becomes more delightful when it is forbidden."[10] And again: "The fruit of a forbidden desire is sweeter. This sweetness is the opportunity for sin which is found through the commandment, and when we seek it, it surely deceives us, because it turns us to greater bitterness."[11]

---

9 *Expositio . . . ad Romanos,* 37, *Patrologia, Series Latina,* XXXV, 2070.

10 *Patrologia, Series Latina,* XLIV, 204.

11 *Expositio . . . ad Romanos,* 39, *Patrologia, Series Latina,* XXXV, 2070.

the Spirit and makes demands concerning the possession of the Spirit, *but I,* and any other man you wish to name, *am carnal, sold,* by the transgression of Adam even without my own sin, *under sin.* 15. *For that,* namely, the evil, *which I work,* according to my flesh by my lusting, *I do not understand,* because according to the flesh it appears good and thus the flesh is deceived and falls. *For not the good which I want,* through the spirit of love, that is, not to lust as the Law says, *do I do,* that is, I certainly lust, contrary to the Law, *but the evil,* that is, to lust, *which I hate,* according to the inner man through the Spirit, *that,* because he who is not spiritual does not hate his lustfulness, *I do,* not in act, but by concupiscence it occurs and rises, even though the spirit is unwilling. 16. *Now if I do,* with my flesh, *what I do not want,* in the spirit, namely, to lust, *I agree that the Law is good.* For I want the good in the same way as that which says, "You shall not covet" (Ex. 20:17). Therefore I am at the same time a sinner and a righteous man, for I do evil and I hate the evil which I do. 17. *So then it is no longer I,* as a spiritual man in the Spirit, *that do it,* that is, lust, *but sin,* both the tinder of sin and concupiscence, *which dwells within me,* through my whole life. Blessed Ambrose, in his *De sacramento regenerationis,* says, "Sin works many things in us. Very often pleasures revive and rise again as from the grave, even when we are unwilling." [17] 18. *For I know,* through the spirit and the experience of contending against sin, *that nothing good,* that is, purity or lack of concupiscence, *dwells within me,* as a carnal man, from which it follows, *that is, in my flesh,* in my outer man.[18] *For I can will what is right,* that is, the fact that I will not to lust is because of the Holy Spirit through love, *but to accomplish,* so that it no longer is in me, *that which is good,* that is, not lusting, *I find not,* in this life, but it will be present in the future life.[19] 19. *For I do not do*

[17] St. Augustine, Bk. 2.12

[18] God in Christ restores man as created and cleanses corrupted man of his guilt immediately and of his weakness gradually.

[19] Blessed Augustine, Bk. 2, *Contra Julianum:* "This warfare is characteristic of faithful Christians. In Baptism there is remission of all sins. And there remains with those who have been baptized a kind of civil war against their weaknesses." [13] And again he says: "The law of sin contends against the law of the mind, and

[12] Luther quotes the lost work of Ambrose from the quotation preserved in Augustine, *Contra Julianum,* II, 5, 14, *Patrologia, Series Latina,* XLIV, 683.

[13] *Contra Julianum,* 3, 7, *Patrologia, Series Latina,* XLIV, 678.

the good I want,[20] *but the evil I do not want is what I do.*[21] He repeats it for a more forceful expression of his lament and his complaint. 20. *Now if I do what I do not want, it is no longer I that do it, but sin which dwells within me.*[22] 21. *So I find it,* through experience, *to be a law,* a pleasure and a blessing because grace gives it to me and not my nature, *that when I want to do right,* that is, this law of sin which was present in the members of even the great apostle is forgiven in Baptism, but it does not come to an end." [14]

20 This "doing" means not to fulfill our duty, but to try to do so and to desire to do so. Therefore he also distinguishes "to do" *(facere)* and "to accomplish" *(perficere)* (v. 18). This is blessed Augustine's position, *Contra Julianum,* III, 26, 62.[15] And it is proved through various other passages of Scripture, as for example, Jer. 48:30: "Moab has not tried to do according as he was able," and later on (v. 36): "He has done more than he could." And our Lord said to Judas (John 13:27): "What you are going to do, do quickly," that is, what you are trying and intending to do. Matt. 23:3: "They preach but do not practice." And the whole mistake of those who expound this passage as applying to carnal man is that they do not notice that "to do" *(agere)* and "to do" *(facere)* are clearly distinguished by the apostle from "to accomplish" *(perficere),* so that "to do" *(facere),* "to do" *(agere),* and "to work" *(operari)* do not indicate actual works but the motive or desire to produce works or to try to do them, but "to accomplish" *(perficere)* means to bring those motives to fruition with works and to achieve the desires, as Gal. 5:16 tells us: "Walk by the Spirit, and do not gratify the desires of the flesh," and above ch. 6:12: "Let not sin reign to make you obey its lusts."

21 Blessed Augustine, *Contra Julianum* II, 3, 5, says: "Was not the apostle Paul baptized? Then why did he say such things? Unless because this law of sin which is in the members of the body of this death is both forgiven by spiritual regeneration and yet remains in our mortal body — forgiven in the sense that the guilt is removed through the sacrament by which unbelievers are born again; but sin remains in the sense that it does the things which it desires, things against which believers struggle." And he continues: "Lust is forgiven in respect to its guilt and remains in fact (that is, in activity), as it says here: 'I do what I do not want, etc.'" [16] And Cyprian, commenting on the Lord's Prayer, says: "For there is a struggle and a daily contest between the flesh and the spirit, so that we do not do the things we want to, since the spirit seeks heavenly and divine things, but the flesh lusts after earthly and worldly things. Therefore we pray that harmony might be established between these two by God's help." [17]

22 He uses the term "sin" because according to blessed Augustine although in Baptism there is forgiveness as far as the guilt is concerned, yet it remains in fact and again turns us toward sin.

---

14 Ibid., 4, 8.

15 *Patrologia, Series Latina,* XLIV, 733 f. Luther's manuscript leaves spaces for insertion of book and chapter numbers. See also the scholia below, p. 342.

16 Ibid., 675.

17 Cyprian, *De oratione dominica,* 16, *Patrologia, Series Latina,* IV, 546 f., quoted by Augustine, *Contra Julianum,* II, 3, 6, *Patrologia, Series Latina,* XLIV, 676.

am not lustful, *evil,* that is, concupiscence, *lies close at hand,* in my flesh, even though I am spiritual. 22. *For I delight,* which nothing brings about except love,[23] *in the Law of God,* that is, I am pleased with the Law and willing to obey it, *in my inmost self,* because the outer man hates the Law of God bitterly and is made sad by having it. 23. *But I see,* by experience, *another law,* contrary to the Law of God, that is, the law of the tinder of sin and concupiscence, *in my members at war with,* persuading them to things contrary to, *the Law of my mind,* that is, to love, which is the spiritual law, yes, the spirit itself,[24] *and making me captive,* because I act according to it when I lust, as shown above, inasfar as I am carnal, *to the law of sin which dwells in my members.* He says this in order that it may not be understood of the written law, from which he is made free through the spirit. 24. *Wretched man that I am! Who will deliver me,* that is, "My desire is to depart and be with Christ," *from the* corruptible *body,* which is the body of sin, and therefore also "of death," *of this death?* [25] because this body continually works death to the spirit through sin, although it does not accomplish it fully. 25. *Thanks be to God* [26] *through Jesus Christ,* by faith in

[23] Because "to love righteousness and hate wickedness" is attributed to Christ alone in Ps. 45:7, and in Ps. 1:2: "But his delight is in the law of the Lord," and through the Spirit of Christ to all who are His.

[24] Properly speaking this is the opposite of concupiscence and the law of the members, Gal. 5:17: "The desires of the flesh are against the spirit," that is, the evil desire is opposed to the good desire. And they are both living laws trying to put each other to death. In Gen. 3:15 He does not say "triumph," but "I will put enmities between your seed and her Seed." However, the triumph follows: "He shall crush, etc."

[25] He uses the word "this" because he is not speaking at all of bodily death, which he actually desires. Blessed Augustine, *Contra Julianum,* II, 3, 6, says: "This is what being liberated from the body of this death means, that what is now the body of death becomes the body of life, with death itself dying in the death that is the end of discord but not of nature. That this is not accomplished in this life the same martyr [18] testifies in the epistle concerning immortality,[19] where he says that for this reason the apostle Paul desires to be loosed from his earthly bonds and to be with Christ, so that he may no longer be in danger of the sins and vices of the flesh." [20]

[26] The Greek has "Thanks be to God," [21] as also in 1 Cor. 15:57: "But thanks be to God, who gives us the victory through our Lord Jesus Christ."

---

[18] Cyprian.

[19] The reading should be "mortality," for the reference is to Augustine's *De mortalitate,* 7, where Cyprian is quoted. *Patrologia, Series Latina,* IV, 608.

[20] *Patrologia, Series Latina,* XLIV, 677.

[21] The Vulgate text has *gratia Dei* instead of *gratia Deo.*

Him, *our Lord! So then, I of myself,* that is, as one and the same person am at the same time spiritual and carnal, because *with my mind,* that is, with the inner man and spiritually, *serve the Law of God,* that is, I do not lust, but rather I love God and the things of God, *but with my flesh,* in the outward man, *I serve the law of sin,* the tinder of sin and concupiscence, because I lust and I hate the things of God.[27]

[27] He who sins against this law does well and makes a sin of sin, according to the statement in Ecclus. 42:14: "For better is the iniquity of a man than a woman doing a good turn," that is, the spirit sinning against the law [of sin] is better.[22]

[22] Cf. the use of this passage also on pp. 311 and 513.

CHAPTER EIGHT

Summary: He shows that we must cling firmly to the law of Christ, since His law is the law of life and the law of the Spirit.

1. *There is therefore now no condemnation,* although sin still remains, as we have said, because "with the flesh they serve the law of sin" (Rom. 7:24), *for those who,* through faith, *are in Christ Jesus,* and Christ is in them,[1] *who do not walk according to the flesh,* by fulfilling the lusts of the flesh in their works, although they do feel these lusts and conquer them by the Spirit, in which they walk. The Greek adds the words "but according to the Spirit." 2. *For the law of the Spirit,* "written with the finger of God" (Deut. 9:10), that is, "the love which has been poured into our hearts through the Holy Spirit" (Rom. 5:5), *of life,* because it "gives life," whereas the law of "the written code kills" (2 Cor. 3:6), *in Christ Jesus,* through faith in Him, *has set me free from the law of sin,* as occasions arise, that is, from the desire of my members and my flesh, namely, from the law of the letter, because he had written earlier that it is the "law of the man" (Rom. 7:2), understanding the term "man" to mean sin and the tinder, or "the passions of sin," *and of death.* 3. *For what the Law could not do,* namely, free us from the law of our members, so that it might condemn sin and take it from us, but it only grew weaker, and sin increased, to an impossible degree, *in that it,* the Law itself, *was weakened by the flesh,* because it was not fulfilled; this Law is established only through the spirit of faith; for what is impossible for the Law is possible for faith, and the Law is established, ratified, and grounded on that which is possible, as he says above in ch. 3:31: "But we establish the Law through faith," [2] *God sending His own Son,* through the

---

[1] John 6:56: "He who eats My flesh and drinks My blood," that is, who believes in Me, "abides in Me, and I in him."

[2] "To uphold the Law" is to establish and fulfill it, but "to weaken" it is to make it null and void and not to fulfill it.

incarnation, *in the likeness of sinful flesh*, because He was not "sinful flesh," but yet He was like us in all respects except for sin, as was prefigured in Num. 21 in the account of the brazen serpent, *and for sin*, that is, through the punishment for sin which He bore for us, that is, by virtue of His own sin, which was not in His flesh but which He assumed, as far as the penalty is concerned, in His flesh, *He condemned*, that is, He killed and destroyed, *sin*,[3] that is, the tinder and concupiscence, *in the flesh*, namely, the sin which is in our flesh, 4. *In order that the righteousness of the Law*, that is, the satisfaction which the Law demands, *might be fulfilled*, through the Spirit, who has been poured out for the sake of Christ, *in us*, who believe in Christ, *who walk not according to the flesh*, that is, in the lusts of the flesh by fulfilling them in our works, although we do feel these lusts, *but according to the Spirit*. But they are the works of the Spirit, even when our flesh rebels. 5. *For those who live according to the flesh*, in the native state, not yet born again in the Spirit through Baptism or repentance, *set their minds on the things of the flesh*, that is, the good things of creation; that is, such things are pleasing to them and seem good to them, and therefore they do not "agree that the Law of God is good" (Rom. 7:16), but set their minds and feelings on other things, *but those who live according to the Spirit*, men who are born of the Spirit and of God to become new creatures, *set their minds on the things of the Spirit*, that is, on the good things that are uncreated, that are God Himself.[4] 6. *For the wisdom of the flesh*, that is, setting one's mind on, consenting to, esteeming, and approving the things of the flesh, *is death*, namely, the eternal death of the soul, *but the wisdom*, that

---

[3] 2 Cor. 5:21: "For our sake He made Him to be sin who knew no sin, so that in Him we might become the righteousness of God." And Gal. 3:13, "Christ redeemed us from the curse of the Law, having become a curse for us, for it is written, 'Cursed be everyone who hangs on a tree,'" etc. This is what he is saying here: "and for sin He condemned sin."

[4] Gal. 5:19 ff.: "Now the works of the flesh are plain: fornication, impurity, licentiousness, riotous living, idolatry, sorcery, enmity, . . . but the fruit of the spirit is love, joy, peace, patience, etc." And we must note that here the term "spirit" is used in the sense of the inner man, which is clear from the antithesis of "flesh" and "spirit." And later on (Rom. 8:10) he says: "Your spirit is alive because of righteousness." But the "spirit," that is, the inner man, does not exist unless the man has the Holy Spirit; hence we can correctly permit the expression "fruits of the spirit" to be understood as the fruits of the Holy Spirit. However, it is better to interpret "spirit" of the inner man, like a good tree which brings forth good fruit, and "the flesh" is the evil tree which produces evil fruit. ·But it is better to say that the Holy Spirit makes the tree good rather than to say that the tree is itself good.

is, setting one's mind on, consenting to, and approving the things *of the spirit,* of the new man, *is life,* that is, of the soul and before God, *and peace,* of heart. 7. *For the mind (sapientia),* the same word which above is rendered as "wisdom" *(prudentia),*[1] the German *Gutdünckel,* that is, the thinking, or the judgment, *of the flesh,* of the old man, *is hostile to God,* because it is not from God but from the devil, of which Gen. 3:7 says: "Their eyes were opened."[5] There is a reason for this hostility: *it does not submit to God's Law,* namely, by not lusting, for it lusts and follows its lusts, *indeed it cannot.*[6] But through grace man is well cleansed of it. 8. *And those who are in the flesh,* because of their lusting and their work in keeping with the flesh, *cannot please God,* because very many of them are nevertheless presumptuous, that is, because they are enjoying spiritually good things because of such a "mind of the flesh which is hostile to God." 9. *But you are not in the flesh,* in the old man, and thus neither in his mind nor in his hostility toward God, *but in the Spirit,* in the new man, in the mind of the Spirit and in friendship toward God, *if in fact,* the reason is; in Greek it reads "if indeed," *the Spirit of God,* the Holy Spirit, who makes new men by His indwelling, *dwells in you,* by grace. *If anyone does not have the Spirit of Christ,* even if he bears the name of Christ and has all spiritual gifts and great works, *Christ does not belong to Him,* because he is under the letter of the Law and a dead member. 10. *But if Christ is in you,* through faith, as we have said above at length, *although the body,* your body, *is dead,* that is, made subject to death, that is, under the necessity of dying,[7, 8] *because of sin,* not because of human weakness, but as the penalty of sin, *but* your *spirit,* that is, your inner man, *is alive because of justification.*

[5] Hence the prophet says (Lam. 3:51): "My eye has wasted my soul" (that is, the wisdom of the flesh) and also Job, chapter 3, curses the day of his wisdom, because it is contrary to God and makes the good appear as something different from that highest good, which is God, and it brings about enjoyment of that which is creation.

[6] Because it is impossible for concupiscence to obey God, therefore we must not strive to be cleansed of it, but we must labor to tear it out by the roots, as Matt. 12:33 tells us: "Either make the tree good and its fruit good, etc."

[7] As in Gen. 2:17: "In the day that you eat of it you shall die," that is, you will incur the necessity of dying. For that which of necessity will happen is seen as something which has already happened.

[8] But it is not so dead that it may not live again, indeed, it will be raised.

[1] Cf. p. 350 below for a comparison of *sapientia* and *prudentia.* See also p. 369 and especially p. 428.

The Greek has "righteousness" *(iustitia), that is, by virtue of faith in Christ, which justifies. 11. But if the Spirit, the Holy Spirit, of Him, of God the Father, who raised Jesus from the dead dwells in you, He, God the Father, who raised Christ (Jesus)*² *from the dead, for He did not raise Him alone, will give life, eternal life by raising you, to your mortal bodies, so that they may no longer be either dead or mortal,*⁹ *through His Holy Spirit who dwells in you,* the Spirit who has raised your spirit to eternal life. 12. *So then, brethren, because the Spirit of God dwells in us, we are debtors not to the flesh, that is, to the wisdom and lust of the flesh,*¹⁰ *to live according to the flesh,* by our consent and our action. 13. *For if you live according to the flesh,* by obeying the lusts of the flesh, as he has described above in ch. 6, *you will die,* spiritually and eternally, because now you are alive, *but if by the spirit,* through the spirit, through the grace, of the inner man, *you put to death the deeds,* that is, the actions and desires, *of the flesh,*¹¹ so that they do not prevail, *you will live,* you will continue in the spiritual life

⁹ Earlier he used the expression "the body is dead" (v. 10), but here he speaks of "mortal bodies." Blessed Augustine in his book *On the Merits and Forgiveness of Sins,* I, ch. 5, says: "He very carefully avoids saying 'mortal,' but he rather says 'dead.' For before the body is changed into that state of incorruption which is promised in the resurrection of the saints, it could be "mortal," although not destined to die. Just as this body of ours can be (so to speak) capable-of-illness,³ although never destined to be sick. For whose flesh is incapable of being ill, even though for some reason it may die before it becomes ill? Thus also this body was now already mortal, but this mortal body did not become a dead body except on account of sin. But because in the coming resurrection the change will include not only that there will be no death but also no mortality, he does not say: 'He will make alive your dead bodies,' but, 'your mortal bodies,' so that they will not only not be dead but also not even mortal." ⁴

¹⁰ As above in ch. 6:18: "Having been set free from sin, you have become slaves of righteousness."

¹¹ Here he is explaining what it means "to mortify your members" (Col. 3:5) and "to destroy the body of sin" (Rom. 6:6). And here the "deeds" are not the works themselves, because spiritual men do not have such deeds, but they are the evil desires of which he has said in chapter 7:19: "The evil I do not want is what I do," but he does not use the word "accomplish" *(perficio),* as we have sufficiently pointed out in that discussion concerning the difference between *facere* ("to do") and *perficere* ("to accomplish") and likewise between *facta* ("deeds") and *perfecta* ("accomplishments").

---

² Luther enclosed this name in parentheses, thus following the suggestion of Faber, who omitted it altogether, contending that it was not originally in the text.

³ Augustine apologizes for coining the formation *egrotabilis.*

⁴ *De peccatorum meritis et remissione,* I, 4 f., *Patrologia, Series Latina,* XLIV, 111 f.

for all eternity. 14. *For all who are led,* moved or directed, *by the Spirit of God,* the Holy Spirit, *are sons of God,* as are those who out of a happy and ready will, that is, out of grace, contend against the deeds of the flesh.[12] 15. *For you did not receive,* as do those who are not the sons of God, because they are not led by the Spirit, *the spirit of slavery,* which makes us slaves and not sons, *to fall back into fear,* which drives an unwilling will to do the works of the Law, *but you have received the spirit,* the Holy Spirit, through whom God adopts us as His sons, *of adoption,*[13] that is, of sonship, *of the sons of God,*[5] which is not in the Greek, *whereby we cry,* with the voice of the heart, that is, with the mind of faith and all fear excluded, *Abba,* which means *Father.*[14] 16. *For it is the Spirit Himself,* the Holy Spirit, who is given to us, *who bears witness,* by strengthening our faith in God, *with our spirit that we are the children of God.*[15, 16] For we are and have only as much as we believe. Thus he who believes with full faith and trusts that he is a son of God is truly a son of God, because in Mark 11:24 we read: "Whatever you ask in prayer, believe that you receive it, and you will"; and in Matt. 9:29: "According to your faith be it done to you." 17. *And if children, then heirs,* of all the good things of God, *heirs of God,* of God the Father, *and fellow heirs with Christ,* because by grace we are the brothers of Him who is the Son of God by

[12] For "the mind of the flesh is hostile to God" (Rom. 8:7); therefore the sons of God are hostile to the mind of the flesh, because He Himself is also its enemy.

[13] The apostle creates an antithesis when he says: "You have received the spirit of adoption and not the spirit of slavery." But he did not want to say "of sonship" but "of adoption," in order that he might show the mode of the sonship and give credit to the grace of God. For they are the sons of God not by nature and descent (as Christ alone is), nor by merits (as the Jews presumptuously thought) but by the grace of adoption. And he adds "to fall back into fear" to show the difference between this and the service of righteousness in the spirit of liberty, as above in chapter 6.

[14] The Greek has ἀββὰ ὁ πατήρ, that is, *Abba,* which is Father.

[15] For he who believes with strong faith and hope that he is a son of God, really is a son of God, because without the Spirit no one can. Therefore blessed Bernard writes as he does in his sermon for the Feast of the Annunciation.[6]

[16] Against Eccl. 9:1, "Man knows not whether he be worthy of hatred or love."

---

[5] *Filiorum dei* is omitted in Faber's text, and Luther also crossed out these words.

[6] Cf. p. 359 below and *Patrologia, Series Latina,* CLXXXIII, 383.

nature, *provided,*[7] the Greek has "if only" (εἴπεϱ), *we suffer with Him,*[17] that is, together with Christ and the like, *in order that we may also be glorified with Him,* that we may with Christ receive the glory and the inheritance. 18. *For I consider that the sufferings,* that is, the tribulations, *of this present time,* as if he were saying: "of this brief and limited period," *are not worth,* as indeed they really are not worth,[18] *comparing with the glory* which already has been prepared by God but is not yet revealed, *that is to be revealed in us,* who are the elect. 19. *For*[19] *the expectation,* because it is in captivity and slavery to the unworthy, *of the creation,* that is, the structure, the fabric, which makes up the whole world, *waits for,* longs for, *the revealing,* in the resurrection and glorification, *of the sons of God,* and so it is. Why do you say it is awaiting it? 20. *For the creation was subjected to futility,* that is, to the vain use of the ungodly, that is, it is enslaved, *not of its own will,* not of its own desire, but of necessity, *but by the will of Him,* God, *who subjected it in hope,* that is, made it subject to the unworthy.[20] 21. *Because the creation itself,* Matt. 24:35: "Heaven and earth will pass away," *will be set free from its bondage to decay,*[21] under which it serves corruptibly, into an incorruptible service, indeed,

17 "To suffer with" *(compati)* is usually taken in the sense of "to feel pity" *(misereri),* but here it is taken in the sense of "suffering together" with Christ, that is, suffering the same things that Christ suffered.

18 For it is not through our estimation that they are worthy or unworthy, but our estimation is correct and true if they are estimated as they really are; the proud do not do this.

19 He is speaking of creation, as if it were feeling, living, and suffering it that it has long been compelled to serve the ungodly in their abuse and their ingratitude to God, although it is created so that through it and in it God may be glorified by His saints. Therefore it quite naturally is awaiting this its end.

20 Matt. 5:45: "He makes His sun rise on the evil and the good and sends rain on the just and on the unjust."

21 This is what is referred to in the words, "Heaven and earth will pass away" (Matt. 24:35), not as far as the substance is concerned, but with regard to corruptibility. How the philosophers understand this, they can look into themselves. For my part I do not interpret this of the substance (not that they should no longer exist) but that they should no longer be subject to corruption but be glorious. For the word "will pass away" suggests this, that is, they will be changed. Just as Christ made a change in His "passover," 8 that is, was changed

---

7 Luther crossed out *si tamen* in his text.

8 Reuchlin's *Vocabularius breviloquus* defines *phase* as *transitus domini,* referring first of all to the "Passover of the Lord" as the angel of vengeance in Egypt at the time of the Exodus but also to the staying of God's vengeance against all sin through the atoning blood of Jesus Christ.

into liberty, *into the glorious liberty,*[22] that is, into the glory, *of the children of God,* because this service will be actually His liberty, just as also the righteous can be said to have been delivered from the bondage of sin into the service of righteousness, or rather, into the liberty of righteousness. Because to serve God is to rule. 22. *For we know that the whole creation,* for "all things work together for them who are the elect," as we read below (Rom. 8:28), *has been groaning,* for the redemption and the glory of the children of God and of itself,[23] *in travail,*[24] but has not yet brought forth, *until now.* 23. *And not only the creation,* which is not in the Greek,[10] *but we ourselves,* the believers, the elect, *who have the firstfruits of the Spirit,*[25] we do not yet possess the fullness and the entire harvest or vintage, because we are "the firstfruits of His creation" (James 1:18). But in the future we shall be perfect, according to 1 John 3:2: "We are God's children now; it does not yet appear what we shall be, but we know that when He appears we shall be like Him, for we shall see Him as He is," *groan inwardly,* that is, within ourselves, where no one sees us except God, we pray in our groaning and hope *as we wait,* with a longing for the life to come and a weariness for the present life, *for the adoption as sons*

into the glory of immortality, so also all the saints are called Galileans,[9] that is, those who are crossing over, that is, those who are going to be changed into glory. Thus we read in the last chapter of 2 Peter: "We wait for new heavens and a new earth, etc." (2 Peter 3:13), and in Is. 65:17: "For behold, I create new heavens and a new earth," and in Ps. 102:26: "They will perish . . . and Thou changest them, and they will be changed."

[22] Again he sets up this antithesis: "the bondage to decay" and "the glorious liberty" (in keeping with his custom), because now the creation is in bondage in its own corruption to the abuse of ungodly men, but then when it has been liberated from this corruption, it will serve "to the glory of the sons of God."

[23] And note here how eagerly prayer is spoken on behalf of the righteous and against the ungodly, since the whole creation groans for liberation of the righteous and of itself and in so doing cries out against the ungodly, then we do it, and finally the Spirit Himself also does it.

[24] "In travail," that is, it has been anxiously laboring for the end of this corruption, so that it may bring forth glory, just as a pregnant woman has pain when she is in childbirth, but when she has brought forth, she no longer remembers her suffering (cf. John 16:21).

[25] He is speaking in a metaphor taken from the firstfruits of the earth, which are the beginning of the harvest and the foretaste of the future vintage.

[9] Cf. *Luther's Works,* 27, p. 289. See also W, III, 504, 20 ff.; IV, 363, 1.

[10] Luther underlined the word *illa* to indicate that it is a contested reading. Apparently he agreed with Faber, who omitted the word from his text and explained: "*illa* is superfluous."

of God,[11] which is not from the text, *the redemption of our body,*[26] from mortality to immortality, from corruption to glory. 24. *For in this hope,* "in which we are waiting," *we were saved,* with an eternal salvation. *Now hope,* the thing which through hope is waited for, *that is seen is not hope,* and he explains himself thus: *for what a man sees, why does he hope for it?* because he already has and holds it. 25. *But if we hope for what we do not see,* and do not have and hold, *we wait for it with patience,* for hope which is deferred afflicts the soul. 26. *Likewise the Spirit,* the Holy Spirit, *helps,* with deep groaning and intercession, *our weakness,*[27] our infirmity, our lack of strength (the Greek has "our weaknesses"), *for we do not know what,* so far as what we ask is concerned, *we should pray for as we ought,* so far as the state of mind or the manner of our prayer is concerned, as we read in Matt. 20:22, "You do not know what you are asking," and John 13:7, "What I am doing you do not know now," *but the Spirit Himself,* the Holy Spirit, *intercedes,* makes intercession, *for us with sighs too deep for words,* which cannot be expressed in words by any man, nor can anyone perceive them but only God.[28] They are unlike all other sighs. But God alone, 27. *He who searches the hearts,* the inward part of man, even more exactly than we ourselves do, *knows,* recognizes, understands, and approves[29] *what the Spirit,* the Holy Spirit, *desires,* for to God these sighs are not too deep for words. Therefore I say, He knows, *because the Spirit intercedes,* makes intercession, *for the saints according to the will of God,* that is, for things which are pleasing to God and in accordance with His will. Because he has said that the whole creation and we ourselves and the Spirit sigh for the saints, he proves it by saying: 28. *We know,* I say,

[26] But they who have the spirit of fear do not understand all these things but shrink back in fear, and they would not wish these things to come to pass.

[27] Because man, be he ever so righteous, will never out of his own powers so fervently hope for future glory. Therefore, with unutterable groans the Spirit intercedes for them to the degree that they themselves cannot. Because even when we pray for eternal glory either to be hastened or to be given to us in such and such a way, we still do not know what we should ask for, since glory thus given or hastened could perhaps be harmful to us, how much more could it be so in the case of temporal gifts!

[28] It is as if he were saying that it is such groaning that no one except God can ponder it and rightly perceive it, as we read in Ps. 38:9, "All my longing is known to Thee, my sighing is not hidden from Thee."

[29] As we read in Ps. 1:6, "The Lord knows the way of the righteous."

[11] Luther bracketed the words *filiorum Dei,* probably following Faber's text.

I assert, that the Spirit Himself intercedes, lest this seem strange, *that all things,* both good as well as evil, *work* **30** *for good,* that is, for the increase of salvation, *for those who love Him, who are called according to His purpose,***31** according to His predestination, for not all are called according to the predestination, because "many are called, but few are chosen" (Matt. 22:14), *to be saints,*12 which is not in the Greek; "called," I say, according to His purpose. *29. For those whom He foreknew,* whom He foresaw before they were born, *He also predestined,***32** predetermined, preestablished, chose ahead of time, proposed,13 *to be conformed,***33** in glory and brilliance, just as also in suffering and shame, *to the image,* the example and model, *of His Son,* Jesus Christ, *in order that He might be the firstborn,* the beginning of the firstfruits, the model, the image of all, according to the manhood, because according to the deity He is the only-begotten One, who has no brothers, *among many brethren,* that is, among all the elect, who are many in number.**34** *30. And those whom He predestined,* proposed or chose, *He also called,* to faith through the Word, *and those whom He*

30 The Greek has "works" in the singular, and this is better, because it refers to the Spirit in the sense that it is a matter of amazement that He intercedes, but that He also works together with the saints in doing whatever they do. And this is an explanation of that term "intercedes," which is to say, He intercedes together with us, just as also He does all other things together with us.

31 He uses the term "according to purpose" in an absolute sense, not adding "God's" or "His." For there really is only one purpose, namely, God's, as they who understand God know. For the purpose of no one else is accomplished except that of God, to whom every creature is conformed, as we read in Judith 16:14, "Let all Thy creatures serve Thee."

32 For God does not create or save with His eyes closed, as Joseph surmised in the case of his father Jacob in a type of this kind of predestination (cf. Gen. 48:17 ff.).

33 The construction should be this: Those whom He foreknew to be conformed, these He also predestined to be conformed. Not that He foreknew them to become such people by their merits, for then He would have said: Those whom He foreknew as people who would conform themselves.

34 This expression "many" is used in an emphatic, commendative sense and is not to be understood as teaching that Christ is the firstborn among many but not all brethren, for the Scripture says in Ps. 89:7: "Who among the sons of God will be like God?" But the sense is: He is the firstborn among all His brethren, who are very numerous, as we read above in Rom. 5:19 "many will be made righteous."

---

12 Luther underlined *sancti* in his text to indicate that it is a contested reading. Faber omitted the word in his text.

13 *Prediffinivit, prestituit, preelegit, proposuit.*

*called He also justified,*³⁵ through the Spirit of faith, *and those whom He justified He also magnified,* in place of "glorified," that is, He glorified them in eternal life. 31. *What then shall we say,* it is as if he were saying: "Nothing," *to this?* in opposition to these points which are so immutable. *If God,* He Himself, the very Judge of all men, *is for us,* not our innocent life or the virtue of our righteousness but He who can do all things and performs all things, *who is against us?* ³⁶ for the whole creation is obedient to the Creator. 32. *For He who,* in order that He might show that He is for us and not against us, *did not spare His own,*¹⁴ coeternal, *Son,* as far as His assumed nature is concerned, *but gave Him up for us,* such unworthy people, *all,* because there is no one who does not need Him, *will He not also give* ¹⁵ *us all things with Him?* It is as if he were saying that it is impossible for Him not to, since in His Son He has made and holds all things, Heb. 1:3, "upholding all things by the Word of His power," and Ps. 33:6, "By the Word of the Lord the heavens were made." 33. *Who shall bring any charge,* that is, who will be the accuser and make an accusation, for this is His unbreakable Word,³⁷ *against God's elect?* against us who have been predestined; there is absolutely no one, for these words follow: *It is God who justifies,* that is, who imputes righteousness to them and defends them.³⁸ 34. *Who will* ¹⁷ *condemn?* ³⁹ For no

---

³⁵ Because He does not
        glorify all whom He justifies,
        justify all whom He calls,
        call all whom He foreknew, therefore the apostle sets up this sequence only concerning those predestined, namely, concerning those whom "He foreknew to be conformed, etc."

³⁶ Just as on the other hand: If God were against us, who would be for us?

³⁷ Because this expression "Who shall bring a charge" must be understood in an absolute sense for the expression "who will be the one to bring a charge," or "who will be the accuser," for in addition to appropriateness of the expression, that which follows in the Greek proves the point, "who is the one to condemn?" where in Latin we read, "who is to condemn?" Thus we have: "Who will bring a charge?" that is, "Who will be the one to bring a charge?"

³⁸ See the summary on ch. 2:15, "or perhaps excuse them." ¹⁶

³⁹ Thus who will defend when God brings charges?

---

¹⁴ Luther crossed out *suo* in his text. Faber's text also omits the word.

¹⁵ Luther corrected his text *donavit* to the future tense *donabit.*

¹⁶ Cf. p. 188 below.

¹⁷ Luther adopted Faber's reading *condemnabit,* crossing out the *est qui condemnet* of his printed text.

one can. The reason is: *It is Christ Jesus,* our Mediator and Protector, that is, He is the One *who died, yes, who was raised from the dead,* in order that He might not be devoured by death but rather devour death, *who is at the right hand of God,* in glory, *who indeed intercedes* (he uses *interpello* here instead of the *postulo* above [18]), *for us,* as our High Priest, for if the love of God is so immeasurable for us, how shall we not love Him? 35. *Who therefore shall separate us,* that is, so that we do not love Him, *from the love* [40] *of Christ?* that is, "the will which burns with divine love," as St. Augustine says in his book *On Grace and Free Will,* ch. 17. *Shall tribulation?* Blessed Augustine writes: "This statement grows out of his earlier expression, 'Provided we suffer with Him in order that we may also be glorified with Him' (Rom. 8:17). The entire intent of this passage is directed toward exhortation, lest the hearers be crushed by persecution if they live according to the wisdom of the flesh, which fears temporal evil and seeks temporal goods." *Or distress, or famine, or nakedness, or peril, or persecution, or sword?* which is to say, shall we ever be separated because we suffer these things? Moreover, it is written that we shall suffer these things, etc. 36. *As it is written,* Ps. 44:22, *For Thy sake,* that is because of Thy love and Thy will,[41] *we are being killed,* put to death, *all the day long,* that is, continuously until the end of the world; *we are regarded,* in Thine eyes, *as sheep to be slaughtered,* for there seem to be more "sheep of the pasture" and sheep for breeding who remain in the world. 37. *But in all these,* evil,

[40] Stapulensis wants this passage to be understood of the active love of Christ and in no way of His passive love.[19] But blessed Augustine, on the other hand, in his book *On Grace and Free Will,* ch. 17, says: "The apostle commends this love, that is, a will burning with divine love, and says, 'Who shall separate us from the love of Christ?'"[20] And either interpretation is good, for the fact that our love is unconquerable is not due to its own powers but to the love of God, who loves us and gives us love toward Him, as Augustine says in the next passage: "However, the apostle is speaking of our love, otherwise he would say: 'Who shall separate God from His love of us'? But now he is saying: 'Who shall separate us?' etc."

[41] For the ungodly, too, are killed, but not "for the sake of God."

---

[18] Cf. v. 27 above, p. 74.

[19] In his commentary on this passage, Faber Stapulensis wrote: "There are those who think that this is said of Paul's love for God, as in a state of ecstasy . . . but the apostle seems here to be commending not his own love but that of God toward us" (W, LVI, 85, n. 18).

[20] Augustine, *De gratia et libero arbitrio,* 17, 34, *Patrologia, Series Latina,* XLIV, 902.

things we are more than conquerors, firmly "rooted in love" (Eph. 3:17), *because of,* for the Greek "through," *Him who loved us,* because His love causes us to triumph through our love for Him.[42] 38. *For I am sure,*[43] he does not say "I think," because he holds on with sure faith, *that neither death,* because "he who believes in Christ, though he die, yet shall he live" (John 11:25), and "Do not fear those who kill the body" (Matt. 10:28), *nor life,* because our earthly life is to be despised because of the eternal life which Christ gives, *nor angels,* who have fallen away, that is, devils, *nor principalities,* the devils who have fallen away from such a choir, *nor powers,* also men who have fallen away from such a choir with all their open madness or the secret deception, as in the case of heretics. For Christ has despoiled them, triumphing over them in Himself by faith (Col. 2:15), *nor things present,* that is, the good and evil things of this present world, *nor things to come, nor might* (which is not in the Greek), that is, the power and force which are in this world, 39. *Nor height,* that is, whatever is high and lofty in this world, such as dignities, offices, nobility of family, riches, honors, degrees, *nor depth,* that is, whatever is down, as in the case of subject people, *nor anything else in all creation,* that is, whatever else may be added to what has already been mentioned, *will be able to separate us from the love of God which is in Christ Jesus our Lord.*[44]

---

[42] Because we ourselves do not love Him, but He has first loved us and still loves us. He does not love because we love, but because He loves, we love (cf. 1 John 4:10).

[43] "I am sure," in opposition to Eccl. 9:1: "man does not know whether he is worthy of love or hate." The answer is that the apostle is speaking in his own person and in that of all the elect, because he was certain by revelation that he was a "chosen instrument" (Acts 9:15), and we are all certain of the elect and of all of us. For even though it is certain that the elect of God are saved, yet no one is sure that he has been chosen because of the general rule. And this is what that passage wants to say.

[44] The reason for all this is that "the Lion of the tribe of Judah has conquered" all of these things (cf. Rev. 5:5), as John 16:33 tells us: "Be of good cheer, I have overcome the world," and 1 John 4:4: "He who is in you is greater than he who is in the world," and again, John 10:27 f.: "My sheep hear My voice, . . . and no one shall snatch them out of My hand." And the reason for this is as follows: "My Father, who has given them to Me, is greater than all, and no one is able to snatch them out of My Father's hand" (John 10:29). So Micah 5:8 tells us: "The remnant of Jacob shall be among the nations . . . like a lion among the beasts of the forest, . . . when it goes through, . . . there is none to deliver, etc."

CHAPTER NINE

Summary: The apostle grieves over the obstinacy of the Jews; he shows that the Jews have not been deprived of the promise of the fathers, and he reminds us that the Gentiles have been called.

1. *I am speaking the truth*, namely, concerning my own sorrow, *in Christ Jesus,*[1] that is, in faith and obedience to Christ, *I am not lying*, as the unbelievers say of me, as if I pretended a kind of false sorrow in order to deceive them; [2] *my conscience bears me witness*, that is, I speak from my inmost heart, without lying, *in the Holy Spirit*, because without the Holy Spirit my conscience can deceive and be deceived, 2. *That I have great sorrow*, over their destruction — such is the force of brotherly love, *and unceasing anguish in my heart*, because just as love does not cease to love, so it does not cease to mourn. 3. *For I could wish*, I have prayed just as Moses prayed in Ex. 32:32, *that I myself were accursed*, excommunicated and cut off, *from Christ*, from the fellowship of Him and His saints, *for the sake of my brethren*, so that they might be in Christ, *who are my kinsmen,*[3] not Gentiles, *by race*, although they are my enemies and absolute foreigners according to the spirit, 4. *who are* (1) *Israel-*

[1] The apostle begins in this chapter with a strong attestation and a great oath, that is to say, he is under the compulsion of great necessity. For with these words he who among the Jews was reputed not only to have no zeal for their salvation but most of all to wish to persecute them and their salvation is by means of his words preparing the way for faith. And thus he comes to make mention of his sorrow, for in his line of argumentation he has come to this matter of predestination because of the blindness of the Jews. In their obstinacy he has seen in effect what he already knew with his intellect, namely, that it is not the righteousness of him who runs but the imputation of God, who is merciful, which saves men.

[2] For he who ridicules and is pleased with the damnation of his neighbor and says that he loves his neighbor, he is adding a lie to his hatred.

[3] He lists nine benefits of God which have been given to the Jews in preference to the Gentiles. And this follows from the fact that in chapter three above he began by saying: "Then what advantage has the Jew? Much in every way, etc." (Rom. 3:1-2).

ites, but not Gentiles according to the flesh, *and to them belong,* but not to the Gentiles, (2) *the sonship,* according to the flesh, and (3) *the glory,* of God, because they are the people of God, but in a fleshly sense, and (4) *the covenants,* that is, the testaments of God, namely, the old and the new law, and (5) *the giving of the Law,* that is, of knowledge and grace, the proposing of the laws, and (6) *the worship,* the service, the practices of worship through the priests of Aaron, and (7) *the promises,* concerning Christ and the life to come; 5. *To them belong* (8) *the patriarchs,* the fathers according to the flesh, *and of whom,* my brothers according to the flesh, *is* (9) *the Christ* [4] *according to the flesh,* as man, *who is over all things God blessed forever,* for all eternity. *Amen,* that is, it shall be done, namely, that He be blessed forever. 6. *But it is not,* as I grieve, in hope or in speech, *as though the Word of God had failed,* that is, as though the Word of the God who promises salvation to Israel [5] had been annulled. *For,* the reason is given, *not all,* but a few, *who of the circumcision,*[1] that is, of the flesh, *are,* of, *Israel, these are Israel,* truly Israel. The Greek reads: "for they are not all Israel who are of Israel." 7. *Neither are they who,* "because" or "for the reason that" they, *are the seed of Abraham,* as they nevertheless glory in John 8:33: "We are descendants of Abraham and have never been in bondage to any man," *all sons,*[6] namely of Abraham,[7] *but,* as it is written in Gen. 21:12, *"Through Isaac,* the son of the promise, *shall your seed be named,"* that is,

[4] All these points argue that predestination and the certainty of our election, and not the righteousness of man's will, are the cause of our salvation. For if the people were not saved who had such advantages as these, and those who did not have them were saved, it is clear that election, and not their righteousness, saved them.

[5] The meaning is the same as that above in chapter 3:3: "Does their faithlessness nullify the faithfulness of God?" It is as if he were saying that although they had the promise, and it was not imparted to them, because they did not receive it; yet it was nevertheless imparted to others of the same blood, but not because they were of the blood but because they were of the Spirit.

[6] By means of this nonsense the professors of religion contend fiercely regarding their fathers.

[7] For in this way Ishmael would also have been a son of Abraham, because he was his seed.[2] And yet Isaac alone remained his son.

[1] Luther underlined *qui ex circumcisione sunt Israel hi sunt Israelitae* to indicate that the reading had been challenged. He crossed out altogether *ex circumcisione* and the suffix *-itae.*

[2] Lyra comments: "All the sons who were Abraham's children from Hagar and Keturah were not called his seed."

your posterity. 8. *This means that it is not the children of the flesh who are the children of God,* it is as if he were saying that they are not in Ishmael, who is without the promise, but in Isaac, who was born only by promise; thus those who are like him will be the children and no others; *but the children of the promise,* as Isaac was not the son of the flesh only but of the promise, because he was given not by the flesh but by the promise of God, since at that time his parents were according to the flesh incapable of producing a child, *are reckoned,* estimated, *as seed,* "for seed," [8] or as posterity. 9. *For this is what the promise said,* it proves that the sons of the promise are sons for this reason, that Isaac was the son of the promise, but he wants the sons of the promise also to be understood as the sons of election and predestination, *About this time,* Gen. 18:10, that is, after a year has elapsed, *I will return, and Sarah shall have a son,* as if he were saying: "Sarah shall have no son except the one given to her through the promise and election, and not solely through the flesh." [9] 10. *And not only so,* that is, has she the son of promise, *but also when Rebecca,* the wife of Isaac, that is, received the promise, *had conceived children,* from *cubile* ("bed"), or *torus* ("couch"), *by one man,* namely, the son, *our forefather Isaac,* according to the flesh. 11. *Though* [10] *they were not yet born,* as is clear from the text of Gen. 25:23 ff., *and had done nothing either good,* of their own merit, since I believe they were still in the womb of their mother, *or bad in order that God's purpose of election,* that is, His foreknowledge and predestination, according to grace and not according to merit, *might continue,* might be acknowledged as inviolable, 12. *Not because of works,* that is, his merits, *but because of his call,* by God through grace because of His election of Jacob, *she,* Rebecca, *was told,* 13. *The elder,* that is, Esau the firstborn, *will serve,* that is, will be a servant to, *the younger,* Jacob, who was established as the

[8] Better "unto seed," εἰς σπέρμα,[3] than "in the seed."

[9] Here he is giving a still clearer example, so that if anyone should want to quibble about the first point and say that Isaac is on this account not the example of predestination but rather must be looked upon as a miracle, it is still certain concerning Jacob, who was born of the same parents as his brother Esau and at the same time, and yet was chosen, while Esau was rejected, although between them there was no difference except in God's foreknowledge.

[10] He proves that only from the one did he have the promise.

─────────

[3] In February 1516 Erasmus published his edition of the Greek New Testament. Beginning with the lectures on chapter 9 (probably in the summer semester 1516), Luther regularly takes into consideration the text of the original Greek.

lord, Gen. 27:29, *as it is written*, Mal. 1:2 f., that because by God's call Jacob was going to be the greater, *Jacob I loved*, from eternity, *but Esau I hated*,[11] likewise from eternity. 14. *What shall we say then?* to these examples and to the things which follow from them. *Is there injustice*, inequity, *on God's part?* For so it seems, because He reprobates one without any evil done by him and loves the other without good on his part. *By no means!* 15. *For He*, that is, God, *said to Moses: I will have mercy*, that is, I will give grace both for a time and in keeping with my purpose, *on whom I have had mercy*,[12, 13] I have from eternity determined to give grace, *and I will have compassion*, and I will pardon or remit sins in time and in keeping with my purpose, *on whom I will have compassion*,[14, 15] from eternity I have remitted and pardoned. 16. *So it*, the salvation and righteousness of men, *depends not upon man's will*, his desire through the disposition of love, *or exertion*, that is, his activity through good merits, *but upon the mercy of God*, who gives grace. 17. *For*, here is the reason, *the Scripture says*, that is, he is reported as being told (Ex. 9:16), *to Pharaoh; I have raised you up*, by hardening you against the children of Israel, *for the very purpose*, to this very end, *of showing*, that it is the work of a merciful God, *My power in you*, My strength and your impotence and that of all men,[16] *so that My name may be proclaimed*, preached

11 All these statements have been written and adduced in order that the grace of God might be commended and the presumptuousness of human powers be utterly destroyed.

12 And thus the reason that God is not unjust is in the fact that He has so willed and it has so pleased Him from eternity and He is indebted to no one for His will and His Law.

13 The free will which is subject to no one cannot be unrighteous, since it would be impossible that it be unrighteous unless it should do something against the Law.

14 In Greek it reads: "I will have mercy on whom I have mercy and I will have compassion on whom I have compassion, I will be gracious to whom I will be gracious."

15 A statement such as this appears harsh and cruel, but it is very sweet, because thereby He has summoned to His side every help, every salvation, so that He Himself alone may save us, as we read below (Rom. 11:32): "God has consigned all men to disobedience" (not in a cruel way, but) "that He may have mercy on all," that is, that He can prepare mercy for all, which no one else could or would do as long as the presumptuousness and pride of our self-righteousness are in resistance.

16 That is, "I have wished to show and make known by the fact that I have hardened you and freed Israel that in Me alone there is the power to be ·saved, and not in the power, merit, righteousness, and whatever kind of goodness of anyone else. I had previously shown this same power in the case of the two

and lauded and the name of all other gods be destroyed, according
to Ps. 9:5: "Thou hast blotted out their name forever, etc.," [17] that
is, so that it may become clear that it is the work of the God of
mercy, *in all the earth.* 18. *So then,* it follows, *He has mercy upon
whomever He wills,* in whomever He is well pleased from eternity,
and He hardens the heart of whomever He wills, which was also
pleasing to Him.[18] 19. *You,* carnally wise man, *will say to me then:
Why does He still find,* further, *fault?* that is, why does God complain, which He does by laying down the Law, by threats, by promises, as if He felt despised. *For who can resist His will?* which is
to say, it is impossible,[19] because "He does whatever He pleases"
(Ps. 115:3), and "All My will shall be done, and My counsel shall
stand" (Is. 46:10). 20. And indeed and furthermore, *Who are you,
O man, who answers back to God?* that is, reply against God. *Will
what is molded say to its molder,* the one who molded it, *Why have
you made me thus?* [20] It is as if he were saying: "He should not
reply this way, and he cannot justly do so, and therefore man is not

brothers." It is as if He were saying: "All these things happen, I cause them,
and I have caused them, in order to show that the election of My grace saves;
and those who have been elected are saved, but those who have not been elected
are rejected." But this knowledge of grace would not come to us if God did not
cause it; whoever would persist in the high opinion and presumption of his own
righteousness would have to be saved, as it were, by his own running and not
by God's mercy.

[17] Their names are blotted out, so that those who

	they are wise have been made fools,	
say	they are righteous have been made sinners,	and thus
	they are honest have been made liars and vain people	

only God is called wise, righteous, truthful, good, according to Ps. 8:9: "How
majestic is Thy name in all the earth."

[18] This statement must not read as an interrogative but as an indicative and
affirmative statement. And although many people have labored on this point
concerning the hardening of Pharaoh, as if they wish to free God of the charge
of unrighteousness, saying: "God does not harden but rather 'He hardens' in the
sense of He permits the hardening to take place" — this double talk accomplishes
nothing. For Paul goes straight to the heart of the problem when he says: "He
hardens the heart of whomever He wills." For even if one says that He permits
the hardening to take place, nevertheless by the expression "to permit" they have
to concede that it happens according to the will of God, for the text clearly says:
"He hardens the heart of whomever He wills," that is, He permits the hardening
to take place. For it continues by saying: "Has He not the power?" (v. 21).

[19] It is as if he were saying: "Will not that take place as He has willed it
from eternity? Therefore why does He command and do all things, if He did
not so will and had not so willed?"

[20] Thus Is. 45:9 tells us: "Woe to him who strives with his Maker! Does
the clay say to him who fashions it, 'What are you making?' "

like his Maker. 21. *Has not the potter the power,* the liberty, the ability, *over the clay, to make,* according to his pleasure, *out of the same lump,* which of itself has no form and . . . ,[4] *one vessel for beauty,* an honorable use, *and another for menial use?* [21] that is, for some ignominious purpose. 22. *What if God,* who is the true molder of all, *desiring,* as is evident above in the words to Pharaoh, *to show,* in the vessels for menial use, *His wrath,* which He now conceals, *and to make known His power,*[22] in vessels of His glory and mercy, *has endured,* by sparing and treating well and by overlooking, *with much patience,* for He is offended in many and great ways, *the vessels of wrath,* that is, the reprobate, *made,* that is, prepared, *for destruction,* eternal perdition, 23. *In order to make known,* to make public to all, *the riches,* the abundance which He now hides, *of His glory,* which He now leaves in confusion, *for the vessels of mercy,*[23] the elect, *which He has prepared beforehand,* from eternity, *for glory.* 24. Even us, *whom He has called, not from the Jews only but also from the Gentiles.* 25. *As indeed He says in Hosea* (2:23): *Those who were not My people (plebs),* rather My nation *(populus),* that is the Gentiles, which at that time were not the people of God, *I will call My people,* "My nation," because it reads this way in the Greek and in the original passage: "And He Himself will say: Thou art My God," *And her who was not beloved I will call My beloved, and her who has not obtained mercy, one that has obtained mercy,*[24] 26. *And it shall be,* it will

[21] 2 Tim. 2:20: "In a great house there are not only vessels of gold and silver but also of wood and earthenware, and some for noble use and some for ignoble."

[22] The meaning is: But if it is the case that God wills to show His anger and power, as He said above that He willed to do in the case of Pharaoh, why are you contending against this His will, since you are His vessel, which is to say that if it is permissible for this potter, how much more so if it is God who wills to do this! Therefore this word "God" must be used here with emphasis and accent, corresponding to the clause: "Has not the potter the power over the clay?" Here he argues from the lesser to the greater.

[23] For He sustains the reprobate in order that He may prepare His elect for glory; He sustains them, I say, by permitting them to glory, to rule, and to work their good pleasure against His elect.

[24] These last two clauses are not found in Hosea, and the second one does not occur in the Greek. Thus the apostle has used them more with reference to the sense than the words, just as Peter does in 1 Peter 2:10: "Once you were no people, but now you are God's people: once you had not received mercy, but now you have received mercy." But the background for these words in Hosea is found in what he says in Hos. 2:1: "Say to your brothers and to your sister:

---

[4] A noun such as "character" is missing.

take place, Hos. 1:10, *in the very place,* that is, among the Gentiles, *where it was said to them,* by God: *You are not My people,* My nation, you Gentiles, *there,* among the Gentiles, *they will be called sons of the living God,* which is to say, this prophet says that God will call vessels of mercy from among the Gentiles, 27. *And Isaiah cries out,* just as Hosea did above regarding the Gentiles, *concerning Israel,* that is, about, over, ὑπέρ, Israel,[25] that is, that also from Israel God would call out a vessel of mercy, *Though the number of the sons of Israel be as the sand of the sea,* which is to say, there is no reason for them to glory in this fact, because He does not care about the number of people and their blood line, *only a remnant will be saved,*[26] just a few, while many others will be blinded. 28. *For He,* namely, God Himself, *will finish,* therefore I say "remnant," *His Word,* that is, the doctrine of faith and the Gospel, completing it, reducing it to a summary, *and cut it short,* that is, extend it to a few, *in justice,* in righteousness, which is through faith. He explains what he has said: *because a short,* that is a word which takes in the few after the majority have been left, *Word,* that is the Word of faith, *will the Lord make upon the earth,*[27, 28] that is,

'She has obtained mercy'"; and 1:6: "Call her name Not pitied"; and 3:1: "Go again, love a woman who is beloved of a paramour and an adulteress, even as the Lord loves the people of Israel."

[25] It is as if he were saying: Let no one think therefore that all the Jews are cast off, for Hosea has said: "I will say to Not My people, 'You are my people'" (Hos. 2:23). This seems to mean that He called only the Gentiles to become His people, because the Jews were "His people." Therefore if He calls "Not My people" His people, then He will not call the Jews, who are "His people," "My people." In opposition to this interpretation "He cries out," that is, He speaks with great constancy, because He will also call some out of Israel.

[26] And He speaks of God as being about to reject the entire people, unless He will leave a very few who still remain in the truth and the promise.

[27] Our translation by blessed Jerome [5] of Is. 10:20 ff. reads: "In truth the remnant shall be converted, the remnant, I say, of Jacob, to the mighty God. For if your people, O Israel, shall be as the sand of the sea, a remnant of them shall be converted, the consumption abridged shall overflow with justice. For the Lord God of hosts shall make a consumption and an abridgment in the midst of all the land."

[28] And we must note that we are told from the Word of God that He Himself has made this abbreviation, although more correctly the Jews have been abbreviated by Him, because they did not receive it. But because it is also true that the Word of faith takes *(capit)* more than it is taken *(capiatur),* because it takes captive *(captivat)* the human mind, hence Christ says in John 8:37, "My Word finds *(capit)* no place in you." Therefore those who are unbelievers are not taken, and the Word is abbreviated in them. But it is finished or brought

---

[5] The Vulgate. Our English translation is that of the Douay Version.

Israel. Hence 29. *And, it came to pass, as Isaiah predicted* (1:9): *If the Lord of hosts,* of the armies, *had not left us children,* when the others fell and were cut off, that is, the predicted "remnant," which is to say, not by their own will, but they were left and preserved by the grace of God, who left the remnant, *we would have fared like Sodom,* that is, we would all have suddenly been blinded and destroyed, *and been made like Gomorrah.* This is a repetition of the same idea. Thus Lam. 3:22 reads: "The mercies of God that we are not consumed." 30. *What shall we say then,* it is as if he were saying for what reason these things take place and have taken place, namely, we shall say: *That Gentiles,* as Hosea had prophesied, *who did not pursue,* or seek, *righteousness,* because they practiced idolatry and followed after errors, *have attained,* because they believed in the "finished Word," *righteousness?* not any kind of righteousness you please, mind you, but the righteousness *through faith,* that is, the righteousness by which they are righteous before God; for they have also attained another righteousness, civil righteousness. 31. *But that* carnal *Israel who pursued,* by seeking zealously, *the righteousness which is based on the Law,*[29] which they received from God, *did not succeed in fulfilling that law of righteousness,* that is, the law of faith,[30] but was blinded. 32. *Why?* did they not succeed. *Because they did not pursue it through faith,* that is, they are not of faith, or because they followed the law of righteousness, *but as if it were based on works.* The Greek adds the word "of the Law." In the pride and presumptuousness of their own righteousness *they have stumbled over,*[31] that is, they have

to completion in the believers, because it has accomplished its purpose when it takes those who believe in it.

[29] Here he uses the term "the law of righteousness" rather than the term "the law of wrath" and "law of death" used previously. But for another reason, because it is good and righteous law.

[30] Thus the self-righteous are never justified, because they resist grace, but sinners are justified because they accept grace.

[31] This authority is based on two passages from Isaiah, namely, 8:13 ff. and 28:16, where he speaks in both cases of the same Rock, namely, Christ. Thus he says in 8:13 f. "The Lord of hosts, Him you shall regard as holy, let Him be your fear and let Him be your dread. And He will become a Sanctuary and a Stone of offense and a Rock of stumbling to both houses of Israel, a Trap and a Snare to the inhabitants of Jerusalem. And many shall stumble thereon, and they shall fall, etc." And in 28:16 he speaks thus: "Behold, I am laying in Zion for a foundation a Stone, a tested Stone, a precious Cornerstone, of a sure Foundation. He who believes will not be in haste." And in 1 Peter 2:7 f. we read: "To you therefore who believe, He is precious, but for those who do not believe 'a Stone that will make men stumble, a Rock that will make them fall.'"

been offended and through their unbelief have kicked against *the Stumbling Stone,* that is, Christ, who "is set for the fall and rising of many in Israel" (Luke 2:34). 33. *As it is written* (Is. 28:16): *Behold I am laying in Zion,* for the foundation of the whole church, *a Stone,* Christ, *that will make men stumble, a Rock that will make them fall,* that is, a Stone of offense, *and everyone,* whether Jew or Greek, *who believes in Him,* Christ, *will not be put to shame,* because of his sins, not for all eternity.[32]

[32] For the righteousness of Christ belongs to him who believes in Him, and the sin of the believer belongs to Christ in whom he believes. Therefore sin cannot stand with the believer, just as sin cannot prevail in Christ.

CHAPTER TEN

Summary: The apostle prays for the Jews, showing that the righteousness which renders a man worthy of eternal life comes alone from the law of Christ and faith in Him.

1. *Brethren,*[1] *the will,* in Greek "the good will," *of my heart, from my whole heart, and my prayer to God is for them unto salvation,*[2] that they may be saved. 2. *For I bear them witness,* since I am experienced both in regard to myself as well as to others, *that they have a zeal for God,* a good desire and intention as far as its goal is concerned; therefore they act the more smugly and err incorrigibly, *but it is not enlightened,* insofar as it is a means and a way whereby a zeal for God may be truly pleasing to Him.[3, 4]

[1] "Here he begins to speak of his hope for the Jews," according to blessed Augustine, "lest the Gentiles should dare to vaunt themselves against the Jews; for just as the pride of the Jews had to be repelled because they were glorying in their works, so the glorying of the Gentiles had to be slain, so that they would not become boastful for having been placed ahead of the Jews."[1]

[2] The Greek reads: "My prayer to God for Israel is that they might be saved."

[3] This is what is popularly called a good intention and a sincere purpose but an evil means. The goal which they want is good, but the way by which they seek this goal is wrong, for they want to go to the East, and they are on the road to the West. The pride of zeal and good intentions does this to many people to this day. The apostle uses a mild word when he says, "but it is not enlightened," that is, as it says in Greek, "not according to knowledge." For he wants us to understand that they are acting with a blind zeal, an unwise eagerness, and a foolish intention, which brings the most grave peril. An example for us, that we should be temperate in cataloging the sins of our neighbors.

[4] Good zeal and right judgment produce
   a righteous and pious Christian.
Evil zeal and right judgment produce
   a hypocrite and a sham.
Good zeal and perverse judgment produce
   an idolater, faithless, heretic,
   schismatic, impious, evil man.
Evil zeal and perverse judgment produce
   an evildoer, a worthless person.

---

[1] Augustine, *Expositio quarundam propositionum ex epistola ad Romanos,* 66, *Patrologia, Series Latina,* XXXV, 2082.

3. *For being ignorant,* wilfully and in resistance to those who
would teach them, *of the righteousness that comes from God* which
comes through faith in Christ and humble obedience to the Word
of God, *and seeking,* zealously, *to establish,* to defend, *their own*
(in Greek it reads "their own righteousness") which is of works,
they did not submit to God's righteousness through faith in Christ,
by humbly departing from their own thinking, for this a zealot does
not permit. 4. *For Christ is the end of the Law,* that is, the fulfillment and the consummation, the fullness, and not our works, which
is to say, that the Law without Christ is nothing, for it seeks and
reaches out not for itself but for Him as its end, *unto righteousness
to everyone that believes,* whether he be Jew or Greek. 5. *For
Moses wrote,* or writes, Lev. 18:5, *that the man who practices the
righteousness,* that is, the righteousness of works, *which is based
on the Law,* only that, without grace and without Christ, which is
to say that in doing these things he takes his position here, that
man, as man of flesh, *shall live by it,*[5, 6] according to the flesh, that
is, he will not die, unless he has not practiced it, indeed, no one
practices it, and thus no one will live, for otherwise what is the use
of faith? 6. *But the righteousness based on faith,* without the Law
and good works, *says,*[7] without the prescription of any works, Deut.
30:12 f., *Do not say in your heart,* as those who believe in Christ
do not speak, *Who will ascend,* or is ascending, *into heaven?* Is it
not Christ as He is preached? It is as if he were saying: "Are you
an unbeliever? God forbid!" That is, do not refuse to believe that
Christ has risen, (*that is,* the idea is that to say this "in the heart"
is the same as *to bring Christ down*), that is, to deny that He has
ascended. 7. *Or Who will descend into the abyss?* Is it not Christ,

[5] The Greek says: "For Moses describes the righteousness which is of the
Law, that the man who does these things shall live by them." And for this
reason the apostle cites the words of Moses in Lev. 18:5: "You shall therefore
keep my statutes and my ordinances, by doing which a man shall live." Here
the word "man" is emphatic. It is as if he were saying that a man can do these
things and thus live in them so that he will not die according to the Law. But
this is not sufficient, because beyond man there is the righteousness of faith.

[6] See Gal. 3:12.

[7] That is, he is teaching nothing else but that we must believe that Christ
died and rose again. This faith causes a man to live, even one who has not
performed the works of the Law according to the righteousness of the Law.
For those works are not necessary in order that you may live and be saved, as
is the case with the righteousness of the Law, for faith suffices without these
works. In this way the apostle is comparing these two, the righteousness of the
Law and the righteousness of faith, in the case of the first attributing to it good
works and to the second only faith without good works.

as He is preached? It is as if he were saying: "God forbid!" That is, do not refuse to believe that Christ has died, *(that is,* to say this is the same thing as, *to bring Christ up from the dead),* that is, to bring Him back, to deny that He has died. 8. *But what does it,* the Scripture, *say?* It says, insofar as it pertains to those who believe in Christ: *The Word is near you,* that is, you will believe and confess, *on your lips and in your heart,* that is, you will believe it. But the Word is far away from the unbelievers, farther than beyond the sea, *(that is,* without any need of the Law, *the Word of faith,* which Moses there signified, *which we preach,* we apostles). 9. *Because if you confess with your lips,* for then it surely is "near you, on your lips," namely, through your confession, but if there is no confession, the Word is very far from your lips, *that Jesus is Lord,* that He is Lord Himself over all things, established according to the form of a man, that is, that He has "ascended into heaven," *and believe in your heart,* for so through faith He is "near you, in your heart," *that God raised Him,* that is, that He "descended into the abyss" *from the dead,*[8] *you will be saved.* 10. *For with his heart,* not with his hand, *man believes,* and it is accomplished, *unto righteousness,* that is, so that any person is justified; in other words, it is impossible for anyone to be made righteous unless he believes with his heart, *and with his lips he confesses unto salvation,* that is, it is impossible to be saved if one does not confess with his lips what one believes with his heart. 11. *For the Scripture says,* Is. 28:16, as it also says in the preceding chapter, Rom. 9:33: *No one,* whether Jew or Greek, *who believes in Him,* Christ, the Rock, *will be put to shame.* He will neither blush with shame or flee in terror and confusion. No one, I say. 12. *For there is no distinction,* as the Jews still presume, *between Jew and Greek,* or Gentile. *For the same Lord,* the one God, *is Lord of all and bestows His riches,* in His hearkening, that is, He gives more than is asked, *upon all,* whoever they may be, *who,* whosoever, *call upon Him.* For he uses the expression "whosoever shall call upon Him" in a distributive rather than a collective way, as is immediately obvious

---

[8] For Christ, as has been shown in chapter 4:25, "was delivered for our trespasses and raised for our justification." Therefore the apostle adduces these two mysteries here as he expounds the words of Moses,[2] for the truth is that our righteousness is not by the Law and good works but by the death and resurrection of Christ. For whoever does not deny these two points, as the text continues, "will be saved."

---

[2] Deut. 30:14.

from the following statement, "everyone who." 13. *For, Everyone* [9]
according to Joel 2:32, whether Jew or Greek, *who calls,* or will
call in the time of grace, *upon the name of the Lord,* as it is preached
through the Gospel, not one who merely tosses His name around,
will be saved.[10] 14. *But how are men to call upon Him in whom
they have not believed?* It is as if he were saying that they are
stupidly presumptuous regarding their prayer if they do not believe.
For they will not be saved because they call upon Him, but only
if they call upon Him "in truth," as we read in Ps. 145:18. Note
also Prov. 1:28: "Then they will call upon Me, but I will not answer," and Ps. 18:41, "They cried to the Lord, but He did not answer them." [11] *And how are they to believe in Him of whom they
have never heard?* It is as if he were saying: "It is vain for them to
say that they believe when they call upon Him, while all the time
they do not hear what and how they ought to believe." *And how are
they to hear without a preacher?* It is as if he were saying: "Even
if they say they hear, they are foolish and presumptuous if they do
not hear men who preach the truth, because to hear false teachers
is not to hear at all." Thus they hear, but they do not hear. They
have ears, but not for hearing or listening.[12] 15. *And how shall
men preach unless they are sent?* as if to say: "It is altogether impossible," for if God is not preaching, only a lie is being preached,
even if they preach things that seem true, but they have not been
sent,[13] *as it is written,* Is. 52:7,[14] namely, that men cannot preach
if they have not been sent, *How beautiful,* that is, how pure and
lovely, with no desire for reward or glory, *are the feet of those who
preach,* or announce, *the Gospel,* not in the act of the offering, *of
peace,* but a peace which is hidden under the persecution and
warfare of the cross, *of them that bring glad tidings* [15] *of good*

[9] He proves this statement by citing the prophecy which was given in former
times.

[10] For the prophet Joel is prophesying concerning the time of grace when
he says, "All who call upon the name of the Lord shall be saved."

[11] He is attacking the presumptuousness of the arrogant Jews, indeed, of
heretics and all who are proud in spirit. Oh, that these heretics would only
give ear!

[12] This is directed against arrogant hearers and presumptuous disciples.

[13] This is directed against proud teachers and brash magistrates.

[14] And Ps. 110:2: "The Lord sends forth from Zion a mighty scepter," as if
to say: "He shall not come unless the Lord sends Him."

[15] From this one word "to preach the Gospel" the apostle proves that they
cannot preach unless they are sent. For "to preach the Gospel" is the same as

things, but the good things are deeply hidden under evil things. 16. *But they have not all,* first the Jews and then the Gentiles, *obeyed the Gospel* which has been sent to them. His proof: *For Isaiah says,* in prophesying of their disobedience in chapter 53:1, in the voice of the apostles: *"Lord, who has believed,"* as if to say that because of the small number it seemed as if there were no one, *our report?* that is, the preaching of the Gospel, the words which we only have heard and believed but do not see. 17. *So faith* [16] *comes,* or comes into being, *from what is heard,* [17, 18] that is, the message of faith, *and what is heard,* because such hearing would not take place if the Word did not sound forth, *comes by the Word of Christ.* In Greek it reads "the Word of God." 18. *But I say,* because it says above "How are they to believe in Him of whom they have never heard?" *Have they not heard?* both Jews and Gentiles, as if to say, "They surely have," for the Scripture must be fulfilled, which says (and this is the proof), Ps. 19:4, *Indeed they have, for Their voice*

"to announce." But it is not possible for a man to announce the Word of God and to be a messenger of God unless God has sent him and given him the Word. For no one can snatch the Word of God, but it is taken up only when God commends it and sends it. But if this does not occur, doubtless only a lie is spoken, albeit the message has the appearance of the truth. Finally in the same message he in a wonderful manner describes the nature of peace and of good things, namely, that they are such that they can be heard alone in the Word and comprehended alone by faith, but not visibly demonstrated, as the Jews expected.

[16] Certain people imagine that this statement refers to faith which has already been acquired.

[17] As it says in Hab. 3:2: "O Lord, I have heard the report of Thee, and . . . I fear." Hence we interpret this in the passive sense of a word which has been heard and not in the sense of the act of hearing, since it would be absurd to speak of believing the "hearing" of another person.

[18] Ezek. 7:26: "Rumor follows rumor, disaster comes upon disaster," as if to say that we, too, have nothing except the Word and we are able to show nothing. Therefore they do not believe what we hold only with the ear but cannot show with the hand or the eyes. And this is frequently the method used in the Scriptures, as for example in Obad. 1:1: "We have heard tidings from the Lord," and in Ps. 18:44: "At the hearing of the ear they have obeyed me." Sometimes it is translated with "hearing," as in Ps. 112:7: "He is not afraid of evil tidings ('hearing')," and in Hab. 3:2: "I have heard the report ('hearing') of Thee." And although to Latins the term "hearing" (*audito*) would be clearer than the term "the things heard" (*auditis*), just as "the things done" (*acta*) was better than "the acts" (*actus*) of the apostles, yet he is trying to express the idea of the actual preaching of the Word or the act of transmitting the Word of God to the ears. For the Scripture or the translator speaks in the same way regarding seeing, as in Acts 9:10: "The Lord said to him in a vision (*visu*)," that is, in something seen (*viso*), or a vision (*visione*). And Is. 1:1 speaks of "the vision of Isaiah," that is, the thing or things seen, "which he saw concerning Judea [Luther] and Jerusalem."

has gone out to all the earth, a marvelous statement which points out that they themselves were not the authors of the Word but its instruments, *and their words,* have gone out, *to the ends of the world,* into the whole earth. Just as the sound of a pipe, or a trumpet, belongs to the pipe, but only in an instrumental way, but properly belongs to the art and the player. 19. *But I say,* specifically regarding Israel, *did Israel,* as they heard it as it was spoken, *not understand?* [19] *First Moses,* that is, the Lord through Moses, *said,* Deut. 32:21: *I will make you jealous,* that is, "I will provoke you, I will irritate you, because you have irritated Me," *of those who are not a nation,*[20] that is, of those whom I have raised from a non-people to a people; *with a foolish nation,* that is, in the raising up of the Gentile people who were formerly without the wisdom of the Law. *I will make you angry.*[21] 20. *Then Isaiah,* following Moses, *is so bold as to say,* to speak clearly and to dare confidently in the same spirit,[22] *I have been found,* I Christ, *by those who did not seek Me,* that is, by the Gentiles, "who did not pursue righteousness" (Rom. 9:30); *I have shown Myself,* that is, I have freely manifested Myself, *to those,* to those very Gentiles, *who did not ask for Me,* that is, they did not demand or seek to be taught. 21. *But of Israel,* the jealous one,[23] *He says: All day long I have*

[19] It is as if he were saying that they understood so much that they were even inflamed to zeal by the things that they understood, although they were ignorant of the fact that just as there is no love so also there is no hate.

[20] As if to say: "Just as you have taken up another god in whom you have provoked Me, so also I shall take up another people, in whom when this has taken place I will provoke you by repaying what you have done to Me."

[21] Our translation reads: "They have provoked Me with that which was no god, and have angered Me with their vanities. And I will provoke them with that which is no people, and I will vex them with a foolish nation" (Deut. 32:21). Hence it is obvious that the expression "those who are not a nation" must not be in the accusative but the ablative case.

[22] For the Jews were most unwilling to hear that they had been cast away. Hence they even wished to cast Christ down headlong because He had said (Luke 4:25 ff.) that there were many widows in the days of Elijah, but to no Israelite widow was he sent but to the Gentile widow of Zarephath, and there were many lepers in the time of Elisha, and yet none of them was cleansed except the Gentile Naaman. For because of this they felt that they had been cast off even more than the Gentiles and were regarded as unworthy, which was an intolerable thing for them who were so proud and boastful concerning the blood of the fathers and the righteousness of the Law.

[23] For this is the entire extent of the wrath of the Jews and the main reason for their unbelief, that the Gentiles, whom they did not think worthy and still to this day do not think worthy of life, nor the wisdom, righteousness, and grace of God, seem to be vaunting themselves because of the promises which

held out (and surely Israel "understood") *My hands,* prepared to bless them and to offer grace and mercy and to receive them to Myself, *to a people,* of the Jews, *that believes not,* in the words of the apostles rebellious, stubborn, unbelieving, *and contradicts,* the things heard from the apostles, *Me,* which is not in the Greek.

have been revealed to them, while the Jews are rejected, although they want to be the only people of God. For this reason they consider it almost impossible that the grace of God could be among the Gentiles apart from them. Thus like the devil, so also the Jews and every proud man cannot bear to hear of his own rejection.

CHAPTER ELEVEN

Summary: The apostle turns back the insulting of the Jews by the Gentiles and describes the present blindness of the Jews; he concludes concerning the depth of the wisdom of God.

1. *I ask,*[1] *then, has God rejected,* because He has provoked and repelled them, *His people? By no means!* [2] *I myself am an Israelite,* and yet I have not been rejected; and still I would have been rejected if He had rejected His people, *of the seed of Abraham,* that is, I am a natural born son, *a member of the tribe of Benjamin.* 2. *God has not rejected His people whom He foreknew,* that is, they are not His people who are of the flesh only, but those who have been foreknown. *Do you not know what the Scripture says of Elijah,* the prophet in 1 Kings 19:10, for you have the same idea that he did, therefore just as he was mistaken, so are you; *how he pleads,* that is, intercedes, as above in Rom. 8:26, "the Spirit intercedes": for it is the same word in the Greek,[1] *with God against Israel?* the unfaithful from among Israel. 3. *"Lord, they have killed Thy prophets,* for the sake of the prophets of Baal, whom they strengthened; *they have demolished Thy altars,* for the sake of the altars of Baal; and King Ahab and his princes did all of these

---

[1] He adds this at the end of the discussion so that he might conclude what he began in chapter 3:3, when he said, "Does their faithlessness nullify the faithfulness of God?" and in 9:6: "But it is not as though the Word of God had failed." And he discusses this matter with such seriousness in order that through the absolute constancy of God's truth he may take away the presumptuousness of merits among the Jews. For the Jews had been able to say: "God has promised, therefore He will not reject us. But if this is as you say, He has already rejected us." And thus through the truth of God they try to establish their own presumption, and they are doing it to this day.

[2] It is as if he were saying: "For then the Word of God would fail which He said in Ps. 94:14: 'For the Lord will not forsake His people,' and in Ps. 37:28: 'The Lord will not forsake His saints,' and in Ps. 94:14: 'For the Lord will not forsake His people; He will not abandon His heritage.'"

---

[1] ἐντυγχάνω.

things out of a zeal for God, but not out of an "enlightened zeal" (Rom. 10:2). Hence Ahab called Elijah a "troubler of Israel" and persecuted him as it were justly (1 Kings 18:17). *And I alone am left, and they seek my life,*[3] that they might take it. 4. *But,* as if to say that they were not all rejected except him alone, *what is the divine*[2] *reply to him? I have kept for Myself,* while the others went their way to wickedness,[3] *seven thousand men,* who not only in name but in fact were strong and steadfast in their faith in God, *who have not bowed the knee to,* in Greek γόνυ, that is, they have not worshiped, *Baal,* or an idol of this kind. 5. *So too at the present time,* indeed, it is so in all times, *there is a remnant,* a remnant only is saved, while the majority is damned, *saved according to the election of the grace of God,* that is, they have been chosen. 6. *But if it is by grace,* that is, out of grace or through grace, *it is no longer on the basis of works,* that is, one's own righteousness. He adds that of necessity this is impossible, for, *otherwise,* if this does not stand; but it does stand; therefore that cannot stand, *grace,* if it is bestowed because of the merits of our own righteousness and because of works, *would no longer be grace,*[4] which ought according to its name be given freely — which is a false and ridiculous idea. 7. *What then? Israel,* according to the flesh, *failed to obtain what it sought,* namely, righteousness, because their efforts "were based on works," as we read in Rom. 9:32, and "not through faith." *But*

---

[3] He is arguing against them with the strongest possible example. It is as if he were saying: "If you in any way think that God is a liar or that none of you is rejected, what will you say to this when the same thing has been done?" Thus if it was foolish in those days to feel that the Lord would not reject His people, when it was seen by experience, it is so also now when the experience is the same. And at the same time we see the destruction of the pride of the heretics and the multitudes who say: "Ah, we surely cannot believe that so many Christians will perish, for they are God's people, especially since so many Gentiles are perishing," as if it were necessary that these should not perish, since so many of the others are perishing. Thus also the Jews presumed that they were the people of God for the reason that the Gentiles were not the people of God.

[4] One complete thought is lacking here, namely, the words: "But if it is by works, it is no longer on the basis of grace, otherwise" (unless the former statement were true; it does not stand, and therefore this does stand) "works would no longer be works." This is true and sound, for certainly work is not work, that is, merit is not merit. And here he brings in from the impossible that which is necessary.

---

[2] Luther marked the word "divine" to indicate that it was contested.

[3] A word to complete an ablative absolute with *ceteris* is lacking. The student notes report *ceteris abeuntibus in impietatem* (W, LVII, 95, 4).

the election, that is, the elect (of Israel), *obtained it,*[5] namely,
righteousness through faith, *but the rest were hardened,* because
of the righteousness of other men and their own righteousness,
by hating the former and loving the latter. 8. *As it is written,* in
Is. 6:10: [4] *God gave,* through the Word of the Gospel which was received by others, *to them,* because of their unbelief and their
arrogant presumptuousness over their own righteousness, *a spirit
of stupor,*[6] of zeal and jealousy, which goads, stings and irritates,
and bites,[7] *eyes that should not see,* for envy has a strange way of
making them blind, *and ears that should not hear,*[8] all of which
their zeal and "the spirit of stupor" produce, *down to this very
day.* This is not in Isaiah, but the apostle added it as he also did the
first part. 9. *And David says,* Ps. 69:22 f.,[6] concerning the same
people: *Let their table,* the Holy Scripture,[7] *become,* shall become,

5 As above in chapter 3:3: "What if some did not believe?"

6 But God gives this spirit when He causes them to be roused to indignation
because of the fact that He does what they do not want and destroys what
they do want. And thus He gives them a spirit of envy, in an objective sense,
but not in a causal or formal way. If we understand that God is said to be
giving this spirit to them in an incidental way,[5] or permissively, then the matter
is well understood. Not that God does not will a spirit of this kind to come
upon them, which He surely wills for their punishment, but He does it in accord
with Ps. 112:10: "That the wicked man may see it and be angry; that he may
gnash his teeth and melt away," and finally, "that the desire of the wicked man
may come to naught." Therefore by the very fact that He gives good to some,
He gives evil to those men, because they hate and pursue.

7 As we say popularly: *Sticht mit Worten* ("pricks them with the Word"),
that is, He irritates them; this is what He says above in chapter 10:19: "I will
make you jealous of those who are not a nation, etc."

8 Is. 6:9: "Go and say to this people: 'Hear and hear, but do not understand; see and see, but do not perceive.'" And the apostle brings in the meaning of these words. For the expression "hear and hear" means that those who
have ears, hear, but "not to understand" means not to hear. And the words "see
and see" means to have eyes, but "not to perceive" means not to see. In this
he is expressing the manner in which they have been blinded, namely, by seeing
and hearing those things which they hated and not seeing the things which
they loved.

---

4 With Lyra, Luther specifies "Is. 6," but Is. 29:10 would be at least as
appropriate.

5 For the use of the phrase *per accidens,* cf. p. 200, n. 2, above.

6 Luther has "Ps. 80." The student notebooks give the correct number.

7 Luther's note on "their table" in his lecture on Ps. 68 is: "Their spiritual
table, from which souls are fed, that is, Holy Scripture" (W, III, 414, 29—30).

before them,[9] as if to say: "They themselves are the cause because of their pride," that is, before themselves, seeing and hearing, *a snare,* that is, an ambush prepared for them, *and a trap,* to capture them, as wild animals and fish are captured, *a pitfall,* a stumbling block, *and a retribution for them,* a vengeance on their pride, while bringing grace to others. 10. *Let their eyes be darkened,* while the eyes of other people are enlightened, *so that they cannot see,* through the fact that the eyes of others are enlightened, so that they may see,[10] *and bend their backs,* their minds, that they do not look to grace, which is from above, *forever,*[11] while You excite others to see the grace which is before them. 11. *So I ask, have they,* as if to say that they have not, *stumbled,* sunk down offended, *so as to fall?* namely, to such a degree that no fruit is produced? *By no means! But through their trespass,* by their sin, *salvation has come*

---

[9] This has been added from the Psalm. The apostle does not have it in the Greek.

[10] Under these expressions: "The heart of this people is blinded," "close his eyes," "let their feast become a snare," we must rather understand the opposite, such as: "Enlighten the heart of the faithful and the humble," for to do this is the same as: "You will blind the eyes of the proud." For God has arranged to bless the humble, that is, His elect. But this cannot take place without the proud who see it becoming thereby even more darkened and offended. Therefore it is one and the same thing to say: "Go, blind the heart of this people" and "Go, enlighten the heart of that people." For both are understood to take place under the same Word, as the apostle clearly says when he adds the words (v. 11): "Have they stumbled so as to fall? By no means!" For "through their trespass salvation has come to the Gentiles," where he is explaining that these passages in a hidden way at the same time indicate opposite things. Thus also:

| "Let their table become | for them | a trap | captivity |
| | for the humble | a deliverance | redemption |

| stumbling | retribution | Thus when someone does something good |
| upbuilding | grace. | |

for someone else which he knows will displease another person, he says in popular language: "O how much I have irritated and aroused him!" For God has no need to create a new evil spirit — for the spirit of men is already evil and proud — but only to rouse it up by doing good to someone else. In the Gospel of Luke 15:25 ff. He depicts and exemplifies this in the story of the older and proud son. So the proud man is irritated when the good man gives, or says he is going to give, to someone else what he has promised him, as also is shown in Matt. 20:11 ff., in the Gospel of the workers in the vineyard who murmured against the householder.

[11] This is a metaphorical statement to show that just as those who bend their back cannot look upward, so those men do regard righteousness, which comes from heaven, but rather trust in their own earthly righteousness and rely on it.

to the Gentiles,[12] that is, because they were unwilling, it came to the Gentiles, but it did not come to the Gentiles, except in order that it might go back to the Jews, *so as to make Israel jealous,* of the Gentiles, that the Jews might emulate the faith of the Gentiles. 12. *Now if their trespass,* unbelief, *means riches for the world,* the occasion that the world is made rich by faith, *and if their failure,* that is, that they were deprived and cut off from faith, *means riches for the Gentiles, how much more will their full inclusion mean!* [13] 13. *Now I am speaking to you Gentiles,* that is, about those riches which have been given, *as long,* for "inasmuch," *then as I am an apostle to the Gentiles, I magnify,*[14] adorn and commend *my ministry,* the apostleship. 14. *If by any means I may provoke to jealousy,* that is, so that they may emulate the Gentiles in receiving the Word through my ministry, *them who are of my flesh,*[15] my fellow Jews of the same seed of the fathers, *and thus save some of them,* although not all can be saved, because not all are elect. 15. *For if their rejection,* or loss, through unbelief, *means the reconciliation of the world,*[16] of the Gentiles, *what,* that is, how much, *will their acceptance mean but life from the dead?* It is as if he were saying that the receiving of life can take place much more

[12] Which is to say that, according to blessed Augustine, their "fall was not in vain because it brought profit for the salvation of the Gentiles." [8]

[13] That is, if faith has come to the Gentiles because they have fallen, much more would it come if they had stood firm. Therefore they did not fall "in order that they might fall," but rather that they might rise again, provoked by the example of the Gentiles, as if to say, that He could not gain them simply by teaching, but He tempted them by irritating them, as a dutiful father often does with his son.

[14] And he magnifies it through the fact that he preaches the riches of His grace among the Gentiles, so the Jews in hearing might be provoked to accept his ministration because of their desire for the same riches.

[15] Because he had preached to the Jews and was not accepted, Acts 13:46, therefore he dutifully exercises his office forthwith among the Gentiles, so that the Jews might immediately be provoked by the example of the Gentiles. For we despise what is offered to us, but when others have taken it up, we tend to welcome it ourselves, influenced by their opinion.

[16] Not as a cause but through sequence, because it followed upon their unbelief; no less would it have followed, if they had stood fast, as is entirely clear in Acts 10, where the grace of the Holy Spirit is poured out upon the Gentiles, even while the apostles are still in a state of wonderment and not yet informed regarding the reprobation of the Jews.

[8] Augustine, *Expositio . . . ex epistula ad Romanos,* 70, *Patrologia, Series Latina,* XXXV, 2083.

from life, as it also happened through the apostles. 16. *If*[17] *the first-fruits,* that is, the first samples, *is holy, so is the whole lump,* the whole race of the Jews, hence it is a "firstfruit," *and if the root,* the prophets and patriarchs, the apostles, *is holy, so are the branches,* the sons and the descendants. 17. *But if some of the branches,* the sons and descendants, *were broken off, and you,* the Gentile people, *a wild olive shoot,* a wild olive because of your idolatry, *were grafted,* through the Word of faith, *in their place,* since the roots remained alive, *and made a partaker of the root,* that is, of the prophets and apostles, *to share the richness,* grace and the Holy Spirit *of the olive tree,* the church and the synagog,[18] 18. *do not boast over the branches,* the remnant of Israel which have not been rejected. *If you do boast,* as if to say, "boast in a foolish way," *remember it is not you that support the root,* because the apostles and prophets are the foundation of the church, *but the root that supports you,* for "salvation is from the Jews," John 4:22. 19. *You will say,* still proud over against the Jews who have been broken off: *Branches were broken off so that I,* in consequence, *might be grafted in.* 20. *That is true,* what you say. *They were broken off because of their unbelief, but you,* a Gentile, *stand fast only through faith.* It is as if he were saying: "You do stand, to be sure, but not by your own strength, no, only by faith in Christ." *So do not become proud,*[19] that is, do not try to please yourself in an arrogant way, *but stand in awe,* in humility. And therefore he adds this thought: 21. *For if God did not spare the natural branches,* that is, not His own, but the natural branches of the olive tree, because they were of the natural seed of the fathers and the synagog, *neither will He spare you,* who are not the natural branch, but one "grafted in contrary to nature," as we read below (v. 24). 22. *Note then,* in your awe, *the kindness,* that is, the indulgence and goodness, *and the severity of God; severity toward those,* the

---

[17] He is arguing from a double simile in order to confirm the grace of God and to destroy the presumptuousness of our own righteousness. For in nature it is so that if the firstfruits are good, the whole harvest will also be good; and a good root surely produces an entire good tree. Thus also here, except for the fact that grace is commended, the whole people would be of the same value.

[18] Eph. 2:19: "You are no longer strangers and sojourners, but you are fellow citizens with the saints and members of the household of God, etc." Again, Eph. 2:12: "You were Gentiles, you were without Christ, alienated from the commonwealth of Israel and strangers to the covenants of promise, etc."

[19] It is better to read *alte* ("proudly") rather than *altum* ("proud"). Or *altum* should be taken in an adverbial sense, for in the Greek there is but one concept, ὑψηλοφρονεῖν, that is, to think proudly or arrogantly.

Jews, *who have fallen,* through their unbelief, *but God's kindness to you, provided you continue,* or persevere, through faith *in His kindness; otherwise,* if you do not continue, *you too will be cut off,* just as they were. 23. *And even the others, if they do not persist,* obstinately, *in their unbelief, will be grafted in,* into His olive tree, *for God has the power to graft them in again,* although this is impossible for man and also for them even through their good efforts. 24. *For if you have been cut from what is by nature a wild olive tree,* from those who are by nature the Gentile people, *and grafted, contrary to nature,*[20, 21] but through grace, *into a cultivated olive tree,* for the wild olive tree and the cultivated olive tree are different by nature, *how much more*[22] *will these who by nature are the natural branches be grafted back into their own olive tree?* 25. *Lest you be wise in your own conceits,* by being proud and complacent over against them, *I want you to understand,* for this is necessary in order to curb pride, *this mystery,* this holy secret, *brethren: a hardening has come upon part of Israel,* the people of Israel, *until the full number of the Gentiles,* the completed predestination of the Gentiles, *come in,* into the church of God. 26. *And so all Israel,* all of Israel who are to be saved, *will be saved; as it is written,* Is. 59:20-21: *The Deliverer,* as He has done in the case of the rest of the firstfruits, *will come from Zion,* that is, Christ into the flesh, *and He will banish ungodliness from Jacob,* that is, the unbelief of the Jews. He will do this at the end of the world. 27. *And this will be my covenant with them,* namely, a new covenant in faith for both, *when I take away their sins,*[23] through the

20 For the tame olive and the wild olive tree are so contrary to each other that according to blessed Augustine, *Ad Valerium de nuptiis et concupiscentiis,* Book I, ch. 19,[9] from the tame olive nothing is produced by nature except the wild olive. Therefore, since from the seed of the tame olive comes not the tame olive but the wild olive, much more from the seed of the wild olive comes nothing but the wild olive. And yet the branch of the wild olive through grafting becomes the branch of the tame olive, which the tame could not have done by nature.

21 For the fact that the seed of the olive does not produce the tame olive signifies that the sons of the flesh are not the sons of God, and the Jews therefore, because they are the seed of the fathers, do not thereby possess the glory of their fathers, but actually the contrary.

22 Just as the wild olive does not by nature but by the art of ingrafting become the branch of the tame olive tree, so the Gentiles become the people of God through the ingrafting grace, and not through the righteousness or virtue of their own nature.

23 The old covenant did not take away but increased sin, and the power

9 *Patrologia, Series Latina,* XLIV, 426.

suffering of Christ; for in this way "He banishes ungodliness." 28. *As regards the Gospel,* because they do not receive what you have received, *they are enemies* [24] of God and of the apostles, *for your sakes,* you Gentiles who have been taken up by God, that is, through you, because you have been accepted as friends; *but as regards election,* by which many of them have been chosen, *they are most dear,* "beloved," *for the sake of their forefathers,* [25] from whom they have been born. 29. *For the gifts and the call of God are irrevocable,* that is, He does not revoke or change what He has predetermined to give and call. Therefore He will give, and He will call, and He will not be changed. 30. *For just as you,* Gentiles, *were once disobedient to God,* that is, you were blinded, while they were enlightened and obedient, *but now have received mercy,* so that you might have what they had, *because of,* that is, "through," or as a result of, not because of, *their disobedience,* 31. *So they have now been disobedient,* that is, they have become unbelieving (and the Word has been taken away from them) while you have become believers, *in order that by the mercy shown to you,* that is, in, [26] or according to, the mercy you have received, *they also may receive mercy,* so that they might have what you now possess. 32. *For God has consigned,* that is, He has testified through His Word that all men are in disobedience, in sin, in unbelief. He has shown that all have been thus consigned and surrounded by sins, [27] *all,* namely, the Jews now and the Gentiles previously (in the Greek it reads "all men"), *to disobedience,* that is, to sin, *that He may have*

of men could not take it away; therefore only the new covenant, that is, grace through faith in Christ takes away sin. Moreover, God takes away sin, when He bestows faith, for sins are forgiven to believers. Thus he is trying to say: "This will be a covenant of taking away and forgiving sins, just as the first covenant was one of adding and nonforgiveness." It can also be understood as: "When I will take away their sins," that is, when they acknowledge through faith that I am the one who does it, admitting that it is vain for them to think they can do it themselves. Yet the meaning is the same.

[24] That is, because God classifies them as enemies, Ps. 110:1: "till I make Thine enemies Thy footstool."

[25] That is, I regard them as enemies, insofar as they do not accept the Gospel, for you have accepted it, and you have been made My friends. But yet I love them "for the sake of their forefathers."

[26] Better "in their disobedience" and "in your mercy," so that the antithesis the apostle makes here may be more apt.

[27] As we read in Ps. 40:12: "For evils have encompassed me without number," and Ps. 51:4: "Against Thee have I sinned . . . so that Thou art justified."

mercy upon all,[28] that is, so that they might come to faith through His mercy. 33. *O the depths*,[29] the profundity, or the abyss, *of the riches and wisdom*, by which He dispenses all things and rules them, *and knowledge of God*, that is, of His understanding, because He knows, or sees, all things; *How unsearchable are His judgments*, because there is no way to render a judgment over the things which we see done by Him, *and how inscrutable*, that is, how unsearchable,[30] *His ways!*[31] that is, His works. 34. *For who*[32] *has known*, 1 Cor. 2:11: "No one comprehends the thoughts of God except the Spirit of God," *the mind of the Lord*, that is, His thinking and ideas by learning from Him so that a person might know them, *or who has been His counselor*, by giving Him counsel, so that He might give counsel. 35. *Or who*[33] *has given a gift to Him*, for He Himself first gives to all whatever they possess, *that He might be repaid* by Him? No one has first given to Him, and the reason is: 36. *For from Him and through Him and in Him* (in the Greek it reads "to Him") *are all things. To Him*, alone, *be*[10] *glory forever. Amen*.

[28] Thus Gal. 3:22 reads: "But the Scripture consigned all things to sin, that what was promised to faith in Jesus Christ might be given to those who believe."

[29] This word of the apostle warns us that in this succession of statements there lies hidden something that is more profound than we can comprehend, namely, that he has said "until the full number of the Gentiles come in" (v. 25), "in order that they also may receive mercy" (v. 31), and "that He may have mercy upon all" (v. 32). And in all of these statements he is making the point that God willed that evil should come in order that out of it He might cause the good to take place. But why this happens this way to those people and at the same time both good and evil do not befall the same people is "unsearchable." For these statements cause us great wonder: "They have fallen in order that they might be saved," and "they do not believe in order that they might believe."

[30] Job 5:9: "He does great things and unsearchable," and 9:10: "He does great things beyond understanding, etc."

[31] And therefore they are all thereby fools who seek their knowledge of things through causes, as Aristotle does, although these things are "unsearchable."

[32] This is taken from Is. 40:13.

[33] This is from Job 41:11: "Who has given to Me that I should repay him?"

---

[10] Luther crossed out *honor et* in his text.

CHAPTER TWELVE

1. I appeal to you, brethren.

THE apostle is about to teach Christian ethics, and so no other concern is of such prime importance up to the end of the epistle as to eradicate our own wisdom and self-will. Therefore he begins immediately with this most noxious of all pests, because this alone under the subtle appearance of good works can again dissipate the spiritual birth and kill it by the very works themselves. Moreover, he does this not only in this epistle but in all of them in a most thorough way, because he knows that all our good works are nothing apart from unity, peace, love, and humility, for all of which this wisdom is immediate death. Hence he says also in Phil. 2:1 ff.: "So if there is any affection and sympathy, complete my joy by being of the same mind, having the same love, being in full accord and of one mind; do nothing from selfishness or conceit, but in humility count others better than yourselves. Let each of you look not only to his own interests, but also to the interests of others. Have this mind among yourselves, etc." In the same way we read in 2 Cor. 6:1: "Working together with Him, then, we entreat you not to accept the grace of God in vain." Likewise he says here: "I appeal to you by the mercy of God," as if to say: "By the mercy which you have received, see to it that you do not receive it in vain, but rather 'present your bodies as a living sacrifice.'" Further, what this "presenting of a living sacrifice" means he pursues in the same place (2 Cor. 6:4 ff.): "in much patience, fasting, in watchings, in labors, etc."

2. *But be transformed.* This comment is made by reason of progress. For he is speaking of those people who already have begun to be Christians. Their life is not a static thing, but in movement from good to better, just as a sick man proceeds from sickness to health, as the Lord also indicates in the case of the half-dead man who was taken into the care of the Samaritan. In the same way in Gen. 1:2 the Spirit of God did not rest, but "was moving over

faned, *and acceptable to God,* lest it become pleased with itself
in pride, *which is your reasonable worship,* not beast-like slavery,
that is, your proper service. 2. *Do not,* revert from the new life
which has been begun to the old life which has been left behind,
be conformed to this world, that is, to the men of this world, *but
be transformed by the renewal,* that is, be changed "from one
degree of glory to another," 2 Cor. 3:18, always more and more
laying aside the old state, *of your mind,* your thinking, your judgment, *that you may prove,* that you may discover by your own
experience, *what is the will of God,* because it is hidden under
our evils, *what is good and acceptable,* because it lies hidden
under things which are displeasing to us, *and perfect,* because
it lies hidden under the imperfect. 3. *For I bid,* that is, I admonish,
by the grace, of my apostolic office, *given to me,* for my ministry
among you, because it is not the right of man by nature to admonish
other men, but through the gift of God, *every one among you,*
as if to say, whoever they are, the learned, the unlearned, the great,
the small, *not to think of himself more highly than he ought to
think,* so that he may not think more of himself or seem better
to himself or be more pleased with himself than he ought, as if he
had more power and strength than he actually possesses, *but,* that
is, so that nothing be overdone, *to think with sober judgment,*
modesty, moderation, *and,* let each think, *according to the measure
of faith, which God has assigned,*[3] distributed, given to, *him,*
that is, as his own gift.[4, 5] 4. *For as in one body,* the body is a unit,

[3] He is saying all of these things for the sake of unity, because nothing causes
so many dissensions as when no one works within the limits of his calling, so that
while he leaves his own work undone, he seizes on that of someone else, or if he
does not seize on the work of another, he still neglects his own. From this come
contentions.

[4] It is as if he were saying that God does not give everybody everything, as
we see in 1 Cor. 12, where he fully explores the intent of this text. As a result
of this God distributes, but He does not pour out everything on one person.
Therefore let no one be so proud that he acts as if he alone had received everything and others nothing, because in this way the unity of the church is rent,
as he goes on to show.

[5] And there is the Greek proverb: "Let each practice the art which he has
learned."[1] And there is also in the Greek this very appropriate alliteration of
words, ἀλλὰ φρονεῖν εἰς τὸ σωφρονεῖν, as if to say *Wissen in rechter Weise* ("know
in a knowledgeable way").

[1] A similar line is given in Aristophanes, *Wasps,* 1431 (quoted by Cicero,
Tusculan Disputations, I, 18, 41); Horace, *Epistles,* I, 14, 44. Luther assembled
a group of proverbial statements of similar intent in his *Operationes in Psalmos,*
W, V, 136, 29 ff.

as is also the church, *we have many members*, yet the many members do not divide the unity, thus neither do the many believers divide the church, *and all*, that is, the individual, *the members do not have the same function*, the same duty, as in 1 Cor. 12:4 ff.; 5. *So we, though many, are one body*, a mystical one, *in Christ,* our Head, *and individually members one of another*, the whole body is not the possession of any one individual but of the members, 6. *Having gifts*, not the same gifts, just as the members do not perform the same function, *that differ*,[6] vary as indicated in the following statements, *according to the grace given to us*, according to the measure of the grace given to us — not arrogated by us, *if*, we have the gift of, *prophecy*, whereby the future is predicted, then we ought to possess and use it, *in proportion to our faith*,[7, 8] that is, not in proportion to human wisdom, 7. *If service*, he who has the ministry has the grace of ministering, *in serving*, that is, let him carry out his duty in accordance with the proportion of faith and the measure of this grace; *he who teaches*, he who has the grace of teaching, *in his teaching*, that is, let him do his work within the limits or proportion or measure of this grace; 8. *He who exhorts*, he who has the grace of exhorting, such as those who preach after faith has taken root, *in his exhortation*,[9] let him not be presumptuous in other matters and neglect this; *he who contributes*, who has the ability to contribute, *in simplicity*, not in vainglory or with some other secret intent, because this goes beyond the grace of this service; *he who rules*, who directs others, *with carefulness*, with care for his service; *he who does acts of mercy*, who has the ability to be merciful, *with cheerfulness*, not out of necessity or sadness. 9. *Let love* [10] *be without dissimulation*, that is, "not in word or speech but in deed and in truth" (1 John 3:18). *Hate what is evil*, everything that is evil, not evil men, *hold fast to what is good*,

---

[6] 1 Cor. 7:7: "Each has his own special gift from God," and 1 Cor. 12:4 f.: "There are varieties of gifts" and "there are varieties of working."

[7] The Greek ἀναλογία, that is, the proportion, or the proper degree, that is, so that it does not go beyond the faith and its rubrics. For some trust in their visions, as if they had seen God, and I don't even know all of their monstrous vagaries in the worship of angels.

[8] For an item related to prophecy is faith! For if it reveals the matter itself, it is no longer prophecy, but rather sight and visible proof.

[9] Just as there are the expressions in Greek, such as "in teaching," "in simplicity," so also there is "in service" and "in exhortation" used in place of "in serving" or "in exhorting."

[10] Here are some general instructions for all Christians.

whatever is good; [11] 10. *Love one another with brotherly affection,*[12] for the mutual love of Christians who are brothers ought to be more perfect than that toward enemies; *outdo one another in showing honor,* that is, so that each may honor and elevate the other and humble himself. 11. *Never flag in zeal,* in carefulness, in the interest to be accommodating, in application, that is, eager; *be fervent,* aglow, *in spirit,* and thus cool, yea, frigid,[13] in the flesh, *serve the Lord,* not yourselves, not seeking your own things. 12. *Rejoice in your hope,* because you can surely be sad over the things that are seen and are past, while rejoicing over future and unseen things, *be patient in tribulation, be constant,* that is, faithful, *in prayer.* 13. *Contribute to the needs,* the necessities, the wants, *of the saints,* that is, the believers; moved by compassion and with the purpose of helping them, *practice hospitality,* indeed pursue it. 14. *Bless,* that is, speak well both to their face as well as in absence of, *those who persecute you, Bless,* I say, *and do not curse them,* speak no evil of them, lest you somehow get the idea that it is permissible both to bless and to curse at the same time. 15. *Rejoice with those who rejoice,* for love makes all things common property, the good as well as the bad, because love "seeks not its own interests, but also the interests of others" (1 Cor. 13:5; Phil. 2:4); *weep* [14] *with those who weep.* 16. *Live in harmony,* be of the "same" mind, *with one another,* that is, having the same attitude toward all men, not preferring the rich or despising the poor,

[11] This precept is easily seen, but most difficult because of our disposition to hate, love, fear, and hope.

[12] Stapulensis: "With brotherly love and mutual good will." Erasmus: "Disposed to mutual love toward you through brotherly love." For the expression "brotherly love" is only one word in the Greek, φιλαδελφία, by which the apostle is describing the special love which Christians ought to have among themselves, even beyond that general love which they have toward all men and even all things. Therefore this is better than our translation: "Loving one another with the love of brotherhood." Someone may have corrupted this text by confusing it with 2 Peter 1:7 and changed the case into the accusative. For there he says: "In godliness, affection of brotherhood and in affection of brotherhood, love."

[13] Rev. 3:15-16: "Would that you were hot or cold! So, because you are lukewarm, I will spew you out of My mouth."

[14] Even though in the Greek this is expressed in the infinitive, yet it ought to be translated in the optative.[2]

[2] In the text Luther changed the infinitive *flere* to the imperative *flete.* When he now speaks of the obligation to translate these infinitives in the "optative," he has the imperative in mind. Incidentally, Luther apparently forgot to change *gaudere* to *gaudete* ("rejoice").

do not be haughty,[15] *but associate with the lowly,* humble and despised men, accommodate yourselves to them.[16] *Never be wise,*[17] that is, pleased with yourselves, *in your own conceits,* that is, according to the judgment of yourselves by your own opinion. 17. *Repay no one evil for evil,* but rather bless them, *but take thought for,* provide by doing, *what is noble (not only in the sight of God, but),* these words are not in the Greek,[3] *in the sight of all,* so that even the appearance of evil may be avoided.[18] 18. *If possible,* because it cannot always be the case, *so far as it depends upon you,* as far as it is in you, *live peaceably* [19] *with all,* even Gentiles and strangers. 19. *Beloved,* my dear ones, *never avenge yourselves,* in Greek "take vengeance," *but give place,* patiently yield, *to wrath,* that is, to the future judgment of God, *for it is written,* Deut. 32:35: *Vengeance is Mine,*[20] "it is My revenge," not yours, *and I will repay, says the Lord.* 20. *No, if*[21] *your enemy,* that is, your adversary or someone who has offended you, *is hungry,* Prov. 25:21, *feed him; if he is thirsty, give him drink; for by so doing you will heap burning coals,* that is, according to the Hebrew, lighted coals, *upon his head.* 21. *Do not be overcome by evil,* but if evil has made such progress that even you are made evil by rendering evil, *but overcome evil with good.*

15 The same expression.

16 "Lowly" he calls them here, not "modest," but men of lowly lot, such as poor, common, and unlearned men. For humility is the virtue of being able to accommodate yourselves to these lowly men.

17 φρόνιμοι, from φρονεῖν, φρονοῦντες, that is, "to hold an opinion" or "those who hold an opinion."

18 2 Cor. 4:2: "We would commend ourselves to every man's conscience in the sight of God." And 1 Thess. 5:22: "Abstain from every form of evil." And Matt. 5:16: "Let your light so shine before men." Similar thoughts in Timothy and Titus.[4]

19 Hence the proverb: "No one can have peace longer than his neighbor wishes it." For "a neighbor owes to his neighbor the damage of his fire."

20 Hence we say: "God has reserved to Himself three things: judgment, vengeance, and glory." In this verse the word "vengeance" ought to be in the nominative case, as is clear from the original in Deut. 32:35: "Vengeance is Mine."

21 He adduces the authority of Prov. 25:21-22 as confirmation of this point, for it reads: "If your enemy is hungry, give him bread to eat; and if he is thirsty, give him water to drink; for you will heap coals of fire on his head, and the Lord will reward you."

---

3 Luther bracketed the words in parentheses for the reason given.

4 E. g., 1 Tim. 6:1; Titus 2:5.

CHAPTER THIRTEEN

Summary: The apostle is teaching that subjects should obey their superiors by assisting them and loving them.[1]

1. *Let every person,* without any exception, no matter how lofty, *be subject to the governing authorities,*[2] to the higher powers of whatsoever kind, because the powers are of differing ranks. *For there is no authority except from God,* and thus we are subject to God in them, *and those,* the powers, *that exist have been instituted by God,*[3] even though those who possess the authority may not have been instituted by Him. 2. *Therefore he who resists the*

---

[1] Here the apostle is instructing the people of Christ how they should conduct themselves over against the higher powers that are without, and in contrast to the Jewish idea he teaches that they should be obedient even to evil and unbelieving rulers. As it is written in 1 Peter 2:13 ff.: "Be subject to every human institution, whether it be to the emperor as supreme, or to governors as sent by him. For it is God's will." Even though the powers are evil or unbelieving, yet their order and power are good and of God. Just as the Lord said to Pilate, to whom He was willing to be subject as an example to us all: "You would have no power over Me unless it had been given you from above" (John 19:11). Therefore, in order that Christians should not under the pretext of religion refuse to obey men, especially evil ones, as did the Jews in John 8:33: "We are descendants of Abraham and have never been in bondage to anyone," the apostle commands that they should honor the higher power and not make the liberty of grace a cloak for their iniquity, as blessed Peter says: "Live as free men, yet without using your freedom as a pretext for evil" (1 Peter 2:16). In the preceding chapter he has taught that they should not upset the church order; and now in this chapter he is teaching them that the secular order also ought to be preserved. For both orders are of God; the one to give guidance and peace for the inner man and his concerns, the other for the guidance of the outer man and his concerns. For in this life the inner man cannot exist without the outer man.

[2] "Governing authorities," as if to say: "Let each person be subject to his own superior, even though he himself has been established in a position of power."

[3] In the Greek it reads this way: "What powers there are have been established by God." There are various interpretations of this passage. Stapulensis says: "What powers there are from God, have been ordered." And he adds a comment regarding twofold power, namely, the instituted and the noninstituted. But this comment is not satisfactory. For there is no power which is not instituted, but it is sought and used in a very disorderly way, just as all other good things do not lose their goodness because of misuse; otherwise money would become evil because of theft. Thus the following interpretation is better: "What powers

authorities, who with any pretext of liberty is not in subjection, *resists what God has appointed, and those who resist,* that is, the order of God, *will incur judgment for themselves.*[4] In Greek the word is "receive." 3. *For rulers,* who possess this kind of power, *are not a terror,* they do not terrify or bring fear, *to good conduct,* good works or those who do good do not have to fear them, *but to the bad.*[5] *Would you have no fear of him who is in authority?* It is as if he were saying: "Do not ponder how you might evade authority or seek to have it taken away," but *Do what is good, and you will receive his approval,* that is, he will not punish you but praise you, and on top of it all, also before God. 4. *For he is God's servant,* even though he himself who holds the power may be ignorant of the fact, *for your good,* in order that he may remove you from evil even if it brings him into evil.[6] *But if you do wrong, be afraid,* of his power, as if to say: "Do not think that because of your Christianity you are above punishment," *for he does not bear the sword in vain,* but rather for the punishment of evildoers, as it says in the following passage, as a sign of his wrath and power, *for he is the servant of God to execute,* as an avenger, *His wrath,* in punishment, *on the wrongdoer.* 5. *Therefore,* since he is "God's servant" and "to execute wrath," for these two reasons, I say: *one must be subject,* it is necessary and required that you be subject to him, *not only to avoid the wrath,* which his power inflicts on evildoers, *but also,* as your primary reason, *for the sake of conscience,* for he is God's servant, and God has willed it, 1 Peter 2:15: "For it is God's will." 6. *For the same reason you also pay taxes,*[7] as if to say: "since if this were nevertheless evil, you would certainly have been pro-

---

there are have been instituted by God," that is, because they are powers, they are instituted in their own way by God alone. This is the same as saying: "There is no power but from God," and therefore whatever powers exist and flourish exist and flourish by God's institution.

4 Lest perhaps they think that resistance to the order of God or despising the powers is only a venial sin.

5 That is, they are not a terror to prevent good works from happening, but evil ones. And this is the excuse and commendation for power, as if to say: "Why should you despise the powers even if you would not offend God? For the powers do not force you to do evil, but good.

6 For even if evil men do not serve Him, God yet causes it to happen that the good which they have and which they misuse serves Him. Hence the king of Babylon, a godless idolater, is called a "servant" by God in the writings of the prophets.

7 He adds this expression to confirm the right of taxation, which is justly paid and received. This the Jews have been unwilling to hear.

hibited by us or by God." *For the authorities are the ministers of God,* he has reiterated this so often for the sake of emphasis, *attending,* even though inwardly they do not serve Him, that is, God, *to this very thing,* although there is no merit for them in this. 7. *Pay all of them their dues, taxes to whom taxes are due,* or owed, for what is not owed or claimed should not be paid, *revenue to whom revenue is due,*[8] *respect to whom respect is due, honor to whom honor is due.* 8. *Owe no one,* neither a good man nor a bad one, *anything,* that is, do not remain debtors, *except to love one another,*[9] for this is a debt which is never paid, but rather must continue to be paid forever; *for he who loves his neighbor,* in Greek "another," *has fulfilled the Law.* 9. *The commandments You shall not commit adultery, You shall not kill, You shall not steal, You shall not bear false witness, You shall not covet, and any other commandment, are summed up in this sentence,* that is, are summarized and hence called an *anacephaleosis,* or a summary, or a recapitulation. Here the Greek ἀνακεφαλαιοῦται is translated by the Latin *instauratur,* "summed up," *You shall love your neighbor as yourself.*[10] 10. *The love of our neighbor,* in Greek, "for our neighbor," *works no evil,*[11] therefore it is not in need of the prohibition from evil by the Law. *Therefore love is the fulfilling,* that is, the satisfaction, the completion, *of the Law.* For love requires this. 11. *And besides this*[12] *you know,* that is, since we know because we have been sufficiently instructed by the preceding remarks, *what hour it is,* knowing, I say, that the very time that now is is the time of grace and fulfillment, *how it is full time,* the appropriate hour, *now for you,* the believers in Christ, *to wake from sleep,* that of sin, by the resurrection of the spirit always more and more. *For our salvation,* the time of grace which has been revealed, *is nearer to us now than when we first believed,* although we were

[8] Thus Christ in Matt. 22:21.

[9] It is as if he were saying: "Make yourself free of debt and free of all men except from love, for love must continue, and to this you must bind yourself more and more.

[10] For man loves himself perversely and exclusively. This perversity cannot be directed, unless a person puts his neighbor in the place of himself.

[11] But it does more good to the one loved, because this is the nature of love, that it favors in a good way and does good, even if it suffers evil and is hated.

[12] After he has taught, the apostle exhorts. For previously on one point he has spoken doctrine and on another exhortation, doctrine for the ignorant and exhortation for the understanding. Hence he uses both figurative and metaphorical expressions, a practice which is not suitable for people who are to be taught.

awaiting this revelation in the Law, dealing in figure and letter.[13]
12. *The night*, the letter of the Law, which is the night of the mind
and the flesh, even sin, in which the flesh sleeps, *is far gone, the
day*, the Spirit, the Gospel, the light, righteousness, *is at hand*,
through Christ, the Sun of righteousness, in which we must awake
and arise. *Let us then cast off the works of darkness*, of the Law
and sin and the letter, *and put on the armor*, good works, *of light*,[14]
of righteousness, of the Spirit. 13. *Let us conduct ourselves be-
comingly*, properly, with decorum, *as in the day*, let us live in such
a way as is proper in the daytime, for in the day men walk about
conducting themselves in such a way as to be honest and pure,
not [15] *in reveling*, here he commands abstinence and fasting, *and
drunkenness*, here he teaches temperance and sobriety, *not in
debauchery*, the pleasure of slothfulness and sleepiness, but "be
alert," in which state practice watchfulness and chastity, *and
licentiousness*, that is, be chaste; here he condemns laziness and
lustfulness and teaches watchfulness and purity, for these are the
arms of the faithful, *not in quarreling and emulation*, envy, jealousy,
vindictiveness. 14. *But put on*, through imitation and conforming
to His image, *the Lord Jesus Christ*,[16] in sufferings, abstinence, and
good works, *and make no provision*,[17] none at all, neither care nor
concern, *for the flesh, to gratify its desires*,[18] or lusts.

13 The apostle calls even the old law a state of faith, so that he might not
appear to disparage it, as above in Rom. 1:17: "from faith to faith," and in
ch. 3:30: "He will justify the circumcised on the ground of their faith."

14 He creates a remarkable antithesis whereby he places "light" and "darkness," "works" and "armor" in juxtaposition. And this is surely true, because
the life of the new law is a battle and a war, and therefore we need armor.

15 This is the text by which blessed Augustine was converted.[1]

16 1 Cor. 15:49: "Just as we have borne the image of the man of dust, let
us also bear the image of the man of heaven." And above in Rom. 8:29: "to be
conformed to the image of His Son."

17 That is, do not foster the flesh unto sin, but castigate it unto virtues.
Augustine in his *Regula* says: "Tame your flesh by fasting and abstinence as
much as your health will permit." [2]

18 Thus he says above, Rom. 6:6: "So there might be destroyed," not "the
body" but "the body of sin," that is, to the degree to which it is a sinful body
and the extent to which sin rules in it, not the nature of the body.

---

1 *Confessions*, VIII, ch. 12, tells us how Augustine, following the prophetic
voice of children at play: *Tolle, lege!* ("Take up and read!"), opened the Scriptures and read the first passage to meet his eye, Rom. 13:13. The report goes on:
"Instantly . . . all the gloom of doubt vanished."

2 *Regula beati Augustini*, 11.

CHAPTER FOURTEEN

1. As for the man who is weak in faith, welcome him.

THE word "weak" must not be understood in this passage in the sense of "impotent," as in the following chapter, where he speaks of the "failings of the weak" (Rom. 15:1), that is, of people who are impotent, but rather in the sense of "debility," which is contrasted with strength, or good health. For example, a boy to be sure is impotent in comparison with a man, but he is not weak. Therefore the first term must be understood in a relative and transitive sense, but the second in an absolute sense. For thus the apostle in his letters speaks of some people as weak and others as sound in faith, understanding the term "weak" as referring to people who are overly careful or still superstitious in some respect, who think they ought to do what they really do not need to do. But not that he compliments those who are superstitious and of their own will remain such but rather those who of necessity are still weak in faith, who because of this are not yet in a state of salvation yet are on the way and thus should be cherished and cultivated, so that they might reach the goal. Hence he warns Titus (Titus 2:1): "As for you, teach what befits sound doctrine," and again (2:8): "Show sound speech that cannot be censured," and in the same place (2:2): "Bid the older men be sound in faith," and again (1:9): "So that he may be able to give instruction in sound doctrine." He says all of these things in opposition to Jewish superstition, which certain false apostles were teaching relative to the differences of meats and of days, of whom he says in the same epistle (Titus 1:10, 13): "For there are many insubordinate men, empty talkers and deceivers, especially the circumcision party. . . . Therefore rebuke them sharply, that they may be sound in faith." And in 1 Tim. 1:3 ff. he says: "That you may charge certain persons not to teach any different doctrine, nor occupy themselves with Jewish fables. . . . For the aim of our charge is love that issues from a pure heart and a good conscience and sincere faith. Certain

the weak man, that is, weak in faith, as we said above, *eats only vegetables.* He eats this way because he judges that the meats which others eat are unclean. 3. *Let*[3] *not him who eats,* that is, the man who knows that it is permissible for him to eat, *despise him,* as being weak and useless, *who abstains,* the person who because of a fearful conscience and weak faith does not eat, *and let not him who abstains,* that is, the weak brother, *pass judgment on him who eats,* as if he were a sinner because of his eating something forbidden; *for God has welcomed him,* that is, both the strong man who eats and the weak man who abstains. 4. *Who are you*[4] *to pass judgment on the servant of another?* It is as if he were saying: "He is not your servant, that you should judge him, but rather God's." *It is before his own master that he stands or falls,*[5] as if to say: "Let him be, and do not judge him; what is it to you whether he stands or falls?" *And he will be upheld,* if he has fallen, as you think, *for God is able*[6] *to make him stand,* that is, He has the necessary strength to make him stand, as if to say: "It is not a hopeless case, even if he were to fall." 5. *One man,* who is weak in faith, *esteems,* evaluates and chooses, *one day as better than another,* in other words, he distinguishes one day from another, *while another man,* strong and sound in faith, *esteems,* or judges, *all days alike,* as if he were saying: "He does not prefer one above the other." *Let everyone be fully convinced in his own mind,* thinking, judgment, conscience.[7] Let him be firm and sure, lest he produce a bad conscience through his doubt. 6. *He who observes,* values, esteems, *the day,* that is, he who is concerned in choosing or discerning the day, *observes it in honor of the Lord,* that is, it is a certain kind of day in honor of the Lord and not of yourself. *He also who eats, eats in honor of the Lord,* that is, it is a certain act of eating in honor of the Lord, for thereby he does not detract from the Lord, *since he gives thanks to God* thus he is eating in honor of

---

3 Here he explains what the expression "disputes over opinions" means.

4 And he is speaking to each party regarding the other party.

5 He is formulating a general rule on the basis of a particular case and opposes both groups, because each judges the other as falling and not standing firm in the true faith, and thus the presumptuousness of both groups must be subdued.

6 This expression "able" is used not in the sense of God's will or the power of law or authority, but rather in the sense of His power and efficacy, His ability to do something.

7 He is trying to say: "Let each be strong in his own conscience and not be disturbed at the action of another."

the Lord rather than to himself or to you, *while he who abstains abstains in honor of the Lord and gives thanks to God,* because in all things we must seek those things which belong to God. 7. *None of us,* who believe in Christ, *lives to himself,* whether strong or weak in his own eyes, *and none of us dies to himself.*[8] 8. *If we live,* how much more if we eat or abstain, *we live to the Lord,* and not to ourselves, *and if we die, we die to the Lord,* and not to ourselves;[9] *so then, whether we live or whether we die, we are the Lord's.* Therefore we also live and move and suffer, because he has argued his point from the greater statement. 9. *For to this end,* that is, for this purpose, *Christ died and rose again, that He might be Lord both of the dead and of the living,*[10] and how much more both of the strong and of the weak! 10. *Why do you,* who are weak in faith, *pass judgment on your brother?*[11] who is strong, who eats. *Or,* also, *you,* who are strong in faith, *why do you despise your brother?* who is weak in faith. *For we shall all stand,* that is, we shall be made to stand or be presented as guilty and ready to be judged, *before the judgment seat of Christ,* in order that we may be judged by God, and therefore we are not to be judged by man;[12] 11. *for it is written,* Is. 45:22 ff., *As I live,*[13] *says the Lord,* it is just as true as that I live, *every knee shall bow to Me,* which will come to pass in the future judgment, *and every tongue shall give praise to God."*[14] 12. *So each of us shall give account of himself,* and not

[8] But those who are unbelieving live to themselves and die to themselves and belong to themselves, and thus they perish eternally. And all high-minded men imitate them.

[9] And this is true of those who believe.

[10] Not that He Himself hereby sought only those things that were His own, but that in this action He was obedient to the Father, who willed that He should die and rise again for this very purpose. Otherwise He would have died and risen again not for God but for Himself.

[11] This double question must be applied in both directions.

[12] For by bringing up this judgment and tribunal the apostle deters people from judging; first, because it is foolish of them to judge those who must be judged by Christ Himself; and second, lest, if they should judge, they be judged themselves, Matt. 7:1.

[13] He is swearing by Himself. Hence our translation reads thus: "For I am God, and there is no other. I have sworn by Myself, the word of righteousness shall go out of My mouth and shall not return. For every knee shall be bowed to Me, and every tongue shall swear." And it is clear from what precedes and follows that these words are spoken of Christ, the God incarnate.

[14] It is certain that this is not coming to pass at this time; therefore in this expression there is an irrefutable indication of the resurrection of the dead, both the good as well as the bad. For he uses the expressions "every knee" and "every

of anyone else, *to God*. 13. *Then let us no more pass judgment on one another*, that is, one against another. *But* [15] *rather decide*, make it a point and take care, *never to put a stumbling block*, because of our liberty and faith, that is, an offense, never offend or disturb or cause sorrow to, *or put a hindrance in the way of a brother*, that is, an occasion for his fall into sin. 14. *I know and am persuaded*,[16] I am sure, I am not mistaken, *in the Lord Jesus*, that is, through the Lord Jesus, *that nothing*, no created thing, *is unclean*,[17] impure, *in itself*, that is, by its own doing, but only by our opinion, *but it is unclean for anyone who*, because of his conscience or his ideas, *thinks it unclean*, or impure, it is unclean to him because he violates his conscience if he eats it. 15. (1) *If*,[18] by your guilt and your giving occasion for offense, *your brother is being injured by what you eat*, when he sees you eating it, that is, if he is offended and has conscience scruples, *you are no longer*, because you value your food more than your brother's salvation, which you surely would not want to happen to you, therefore, *walking in love*. (2) *Do not let what you eat*, as if to say: "Don't let so unimportant a good thing ruin so great a good gift," *cause the ruin of one*, namely, your brother, on some occasion, *for whom Christ died*.[19] For all these words have epitasis, that is, strong intention and force. 16. (3) *So do not let your good* (in Greek "to you") *be spoken of as an evil*, tongue," both of which are parts of the body. And he says "every knee" and "every tongue" rather than "all men," in order to express more clearly the complete totality of the resurrection, Rev. 1:7: "Every eye will see Him." Cf. also Phil. 2:10 f.

15 Here he begins his second point, namely, that the strong should not cause the weak to stumble. 1 Cor. 8:9: "Only take care lest this liberty of yours somehow become a stumbling block to the weak, etc."

16 In German we would say: *Ich weiss und bin's gewiss*. It is a kind of parenthetical expression. For before he says in what way the brother might be offended, he brings in this point, as if to say: "although from the side of the guilt, there is no offense."

17 In Scripture the word "common" (*commune*) is the same as "profane" (*prophanum*) or "unclean" (*immundum*); hence in Acts 10:15 and 11:9 we read: "What God has cleansed, you must not call common (*commune*)." Otherwise he would have had to say "unclean" (*immundum*). And this is after the Hebrew manner, where the people were to be holy and separate from the common people and also furnished with holy and separate worship rites, foods, and clothing.

18 There are six reasons for which he admonishes them with great emphasis and vehemence.

19 He compares the matter of food with the death of Christ, as if he were saying: "See to it that your food is not so important to you that you put it ahead of the death which Christ bore for that other person." This is a very strong exhortation.

that is, do not through these matters give opportunity to the Gentiles to speak evil against you because of this dissension. 17. (4) *For the kingdom of God,* which is certainly the eternal good, *is not food and drink,*[20] things which pass away, *but righteousness,* through faith, *and peace and joy in the Holy Spirit,* not joy in the flesh but rather in the crucifixion of the flesh; for this is the joy "in the Holy Spirit." 18. (5) *For he who thus,* the Greek has the plural, "in these respects," and that is a better reading, *serves Christ,* is a servant of Christ because of such qualities, and others like them, *is acceptable to God,* not he who serves in food and drink, *and approved,* receives approbation, is pleasing to, and accepted, *by men,* because in other ways without these qualities men are rightly offended, as also God is. 19. *Let us then pursue,* by word and much more by example, *what makes for peace,* so that there be no dissension in our minds over food for the body, *and keep,* which is not in the Greek, and the word "pursue" is sufficient, *the things which make for mutual*[21] *upbuilding,*[22] for our mutual progress and salvation. 20. (6) *Do not, for the sake of food,* which is such an unimportant thing, *destroy,* which is a much stronger word than "hinder," *the work of God,* which is such an important matter. *Everything,* every created thing, *is indeed clean,* in itself, *but it is wrong,* a sin for him, *for the man who,* contrary to love, in seeking his own advantage and neglecting someone else's, *makes others fall*[23] *by what he eats,*[24] in that he offends, hurts, and saddens his neighbor. 21. *It is right,* that is, meritorious, that in love, which "does not insist on its own way" (1 Cor. 13:5) but on "the interests of others" (Phil. 2:4), *not to eat meat*[25] *or drink wine, or do anything, that makes your brother stumble,* that hurts him or

[20] 1 Cor. 8:8: "Food will not commend us to God. We are no worse off if we do not eat, and no better off if we do."

[21] And it is better that the expression "mutual" be related to "upbuilding" and "peace," as if to say that we pursue mutual peace and mutual edification.

[22] The word "upbuilding" *(edificare)* is peculiar to the apostle as a synonym for "benefiting the other person" by example and word for his salvation. Compare 1 Cor. 10:23: "All things are lawful for me, but all things do not edify *(edificant)*."

[23] In Greek there are two words, πρόσκομμα and σκάνδαλον, which mean an "offense" whereby one is injured, or receives an occasion for falling.

[24] Thus 1 Cor. 10:23: "All things are lawful for me, but all things do not edify."

[25] Thus 1 Cor. 8:13: "If food is a cause of my brother's falling, I will never eat meat."

saddens him, who ought to be made happy even when injured, *or be upset,* suffering occasion for his downfall, when he ought to be edified, *or made weak,* that is, in his faith, when he ought to be supported so that he might be made strong. 22. *The faith that you,* who are strong in faith, *have, keep between yourself,*[26] in your own conscience, *and God,*[27] where no one is made to stumble. *Happy is he,* a man strong in faith, *who has no reason to judge himself,* blame or condemn himself, for such a man both acts and yet judges that some action ought not be taken, and thus he sins against his conscience,[28] *for what he approves,* approves and does. 23. *But he who,* a man weak in faith, *has doubts,* that is, who judges that something ought not be eaten, *if he eats,* nevertheless, against his own judgment, as long as this judgment stands, *is condemned,* because he sins if he acts against what he judges ought to be done, *because he does not act from faith,* that is, he eats, but contrary to his faith, that is, he does not act in accord with his belief but contrary to what he believes, out of concupiscence or some other lust, *for whatever,* even though it is a work which is permissible and good, *does not proceed from faith,* that is, when a person does not act in keeping with what he believes and is thus acting contrary to his faith, *is sin.*[29]

26 For he does not use the expression "he has it with himself" *(seipsum),* which would mean that he shows his faith publicly to the offense of his neighbor. Thus the expression "with yourself" *(teipsum)* belongs to the verb "have" *(habe).*

27 The Greek reads: "Do you have faith? Have it with yourself before God," which, however, blessed Ambrose added, as Erasmus tells us.[3]

28 He judges what ought not be done, and thus he has a law. And yet he does it and thus sins against the law.

29 We should not think, however, that in this passage the apostle is speaking of those people who in an absolute sense believe these things must be preserved and that without them faith in Christ is not sufficient or worth anything but rather he is speaking of those who believe that they are saved through Christ, to be sure, and yet are afraid that they might be sinning in these matters even against Christ.

---

3 Erasmus' reading is thus preferred by Luther to that of Faber, who has *Tu fidem habes apud teipsum: habe et coram deo* ("You have faith with yourself; have it also before God"). Erasmus comments: "Have it in yourself, or in your possession alone," and then attributes the addition "and before God" to Ambrose. Cf. *Patrologia, Series Latina,* XVII, 180.

CHAPTER FIFTEEN

Summary: The apostle encourages the strong to uphold the weak and promote their good; and he excuses himself for not visiting the Romans in person.[1]

1. *We who are strong*, powerful, *ought*, by right and by the law of love, *to bear with the failings*, the weaknesses, the defects, *of the weak*, the powerless, not only in faith, as mentioned above, but also in other virtues; because according to 1 Cor. 13:7, "Love bears all things," *and not to please ourselves*,[2] for to please ourselves is to give cause for dissension, which is opposed to love, but this is a love not of oneself, but of another. 2. *Let each of you*, in Greek it reads "of us," *please his*[1] *neighbor*, not himself, *for his good*, because evil men please themselves for evil, *to edify him*, not to vain ostentation or carnal comfort. 3. *For Christ*, the example and image of us all, *did not please Himself*, and thereby He also taught that we ought not please ourselves, *but, as it is written*, Ps. 69:9: *The insults*, the sins, *of those who insult Thee*, who sin against Thee, *have fallen on Me*,[3] that is, "I have borne them for them." If He had pleased Himself, He would rather have cast them off Himself. 4. *For whatever*, also concerning Christ and concerning anyone else, *was written*, in Greek it reads "was written in former days,"[4] that is, as if it were placed before our eyes, *was written*

---

[1] This chapter is appended to what precedes. For he concludes with the example of Christ, which he had taught in the preceding chapter; he repeats the exhortation that they are to support one another and not despise each other.

[2] On the basis of a particular example he sets up a general teaching. It is as if he were saying: "As I have taught concerning food and the weakness of faith, so in all other forms of weakness and defects we ought to uphold the weak and not despise them, just as Christ has done for us, as shown below.

[3] For just as righteous works honor God, so also evil works dishonor God, as we read above in Rom. 2:23 f.: "You disonor God by breaking the Law. As it is written: 'The name of God is blasphemed among the Gentiles because of you.'"

[4] He is contending against the hidden objection of his readers, namely: "What business is this of ours? This is spoken literally of Christ." The answer

---

[1] Following Erasmus, Luther deleted *suo* from his text.

for our instruction, that is, for our moral upbuilding, to be understood as an example, *that by steadfastness,* in actions, *and by encouragement of the Scriptures,* in words, *we might have hope,* in God. For our encouragement is only in words, but in actions there is distress; therefore steadfastness in necessary here. 5. *May the God of steadfastness and encouragement,* consolation, that is, as if to say: "You do not possess these two qualities of yourselves, but God is the one who gives them," *grant you to live in such harmony,* that is, to be of the same mind in feeling and thought, *with one another,* by turns, so that there be no divisions or schisms among you, *in accord with Jesus Christ,* and not according to the flesh or the world, in those things which belong to Christ or are according to the example of Christ, who did this for you to the honor of God. 6. *That together,* with one heart, *with one voice,* in harmony, *you may glorify the God,* that is, that you may in a harmonious spirit do all things to the praise and glory of the God, *and Father of our Lord Jesus Christ.*[5] 7. *Therefore,* insofar as you can, *welcome one another,* as he said above, the strong welcoming the weak, the powerful the impotent, *as Christ,* the strong Giant, *has welcomed you,* who are weak, even dead, *for the honor of God,* that is, for the glory of God, or that He might glorify God thereby, not seeking His own glory but His Father's. 8. *For I tell*[6] *you that Christ Jesus,* Heb. 3:1: "Consider Jesus, the apostle and high priest of our confession," *became a servant,* an apostle, a messenger sent to them by God, *of the circumcised,* that is, of the Jews, who are of the circumcision, *to show God's truthfulness,* that is, that the promise of

is that what is said regarding Christ is also "written for our instruction," that we should imitate Him. And thus we must understand this not only as something said in a contemplative way concerning Christ but also as an example for ourselves. Hence we derive significant instruction from this passage, for every act of Christ is instruction for us, because here Paul says: "whatever was written."

5 The apostle prays for those people whom he has established in the faith, for it is the duty of a good teacher not only to water but also to seek increase, he who first works, then instructs, and finally prays for them. For thus blessed Bernard explains in *Ad Eugenium*[2] that threefold "Feed" spoken by our Lord to Peter (John 21:15 ff.).

6 He gives the reason why he has admonished them to honor God, namely, that Christ welcomes them purely by grace, not like the Jews, to whom He had been promised, who welcomed Christ as the one who had been promised to them. Thus as soon as he has said: "As Christ has welcomed you" (an expression in which grace freely given is indicated) there immediately follows the reason why it is grace that has been freely given.

---

2 Bernard, *De consideratione ad Eugenium,* III, *Patrologia, Series Latina,* CLXXXII, 776.

God which had been made to them might be fulfilled, whereby the truth of God is declared, *in order to confirm the promises given to the patriarchs,* that is, to fulfill them, as was said above,[3] that the Law is established and confirmed when it is fulfilled and that it is weakened, Rom. 8,[4] when it is not fulfilled. And Rom. 4:16: "In order that through faith the promise may rest on grace." 9. *And in order that the Gentiles might honor,* that is, might glorify, *God for His mercy,* with which they have been welcomed aside from the promise. *As it is written,* Ps. 18:49: *For this I will extol Thee,* the words are Christ's, who is speaking to His Father, *O Lord, among the nations,* that is, "the Gentiles will give honor to Thee through Me," as he says here, *and sing to Thy name,*[7] that is, in the same way among the Gentiles. 10. *And again it is said: Rejoice, O Gentiles, with His people,* the Jews. 11. *And again,* Ps. 117:1, *Praise the Lord, all Gentiles,* they certainly do praise Him because of the mercy they have received, therefore it is written that it has also thereby been spread abroad among the Gentiles, *and let all the people praise Him,* not only some of the Jews. 12. *And further Isaiah says,* 11:10: It will come to pass that[5] *the root of Jesse shall come,* that is, Christ, who is from the root of Jesse,[8] *He who rises,*

[7] The apostle says that the Gentiles do this because the psalm says that Christ does it among the Gentiles. Nor is this an inappropriate or unharmonious comparison, for it is also true that Christ honors God in the Gentiles and the Gentiles honor God in Christ, and this in the Spirit. For bodily Christ was not among the Gentiles, nor was He "praised."

[8] The Septuagint reads this way: "And in that day there will be a Root of Jesse and one who will rise up as Prince of the Gentiles; in Him will the Gentiles hope, and His rest will be glorious." Jerome has it thus: "In that day the Root of Jesse, who stands for an ensign of the people, Him the Gentiles will beseech, and His sepulchre will be glorious." And this "Root" is not, as the artists everywhere picture it, a patriarch in the place of the root of a tree, but the "Root" here is the trunk itself as that which remains after the tree has died, which has miraculously grown into a huge tree, that is, Christ, who is spread forth into the great church. In the same way He has asserted that He Himself is the grain of corn which has been multiplied and the grain of mustard which has been increased, etc. And in Num. 24:17: "A Star shall come forth out of Jacob, and a Scepter shall rise out of Israel, and it shall crush the forehead of Moab." For the term "Root" signifies the death and passion of Christ, that is, Christ humiliated to nothingness and again exalted in the way He is described in Is. 53:2: "And He will ascend before Him like a root out of dry ground," that is, this is a metaphor of His suffering and resurrection.

---

[3] Cf. pp. 34 and 67 above.

[4] Luther writes "Rom. 6," but the reference seems to be to his interlinear comment and marginal note on Rom. 8:3.

[5] Luther deleted *et* and introduced the Isaiah passage with an editorial *erit.*

that is, from the dead, *to rule the Gentiles,*[9] that is, for the purpose of reigning over the Gentiles, *in Him shall the Gentiles,* and not only the Jews, as they wish, *hope.*[10] 13. *May the God of hope,* the Author and Finisher of our hope, because the god of material things is an idol, *fill you with all joy,* which is in hope, for "the God of hope" gives this joy, but the god of material things is an idol, *and peace,* mutual concord, *in believing,* that is, through your faith, *so that you may abound,* that you may be bold and strong, *in hope,* just as you are weak in material things and nothing with Christ, *by*[6] *the power of the Holy Spirit,* that is, through the power of the Holy Spirit; a Hebrew expression which is the equivalent of this preposition "in." Not in your own power, or strength, or that of the world. 14. *I myself am satisfied,* the same word as *confido,* used in the preceding chapter (v. 14), *about you,* not only others of whom I have heard, *my brethren, that*[11] *you yourselves are full of love,*[12, 13] or goodness, for I do not arrogate to myself alone fullness and goodness, and attribute to you wickedness, *filled with all knowledge,* or understanding, which comes from faith, *and able,* in Greek, "having the ability," *to instruct one another,*[14] in Greek, "to instruct others." 15. *But on some points,* that is, to a slight degree, *I have written to you very boldly,* because he has written to those who not only are knowledgeable themselves but are able

---

9 Hence also in Jer. 10:7 He is called "King of the nations," in the statement: "Who would not fear Thee, O King of the nations?" And Gen. 49:10: "And He will be the expectation of the nations," which others translate thus: "To Him shall be the obedience" or "the subjection of the people." Ps. 113:4: "The Lord is high above all nations." And in many other passages.

10 And in all these citations the apostle has settled the contention between Jews and Gentiles, so that they are not in opposition to each other but mutually welcome one another, just as Christ has welcomed them. For not only the Jews, lest they be proud, but also not the Gentiles has He welcomed except out of His pure mercy. Therefore they both have reason to praise God but none for their own contention.

11 Just as the hypocritical Pharisees, on the other hand were certain about themselves and always fearful for others, lest they be empty, while they themselves were the only ones filled.

12 The Greek has ἀγαθωσύνης, and other versions ἀγαπωσύνης.

13 We must always assume better things regarding our neighbor.

14 The apostle excuses himself with shame, because although he had presumed so many things about them, yet they knew next to nothing and he had taught them many things. Now where are those shameless and hateful teachers, those contentious doctors?

---

6 Luther deleted *et* from the text and added the preposition *in* editorially.

also to teach other people,[15] *brothers, by way of reminding you,* not presuming to teach, but only to call to mind, *because of the grace,* that is, because of the apostolic office which has been committed to me out of grace, *given to me by God,*[16] not idly or in vain but: 16. *That I might be a minister,*[17] that is, performer of the sacred duties, *of Christ Jesus,* having been sent by Him, *to the Gentiles,*[18] to the Gentiles or among the Gentiles, *in the priestly service of,*[19] or making a sacrifice, which is, *the Gospel of God, so that,* he continues in this allusion, *the offering of the Gentiles may be acceptable,* because he offers them and they offer themselves through the obedience of faith, as in chapter 1:5: "to the obedience of faith," *sanctified by the Holy Spirit,* not in the flesh and outward garb, as in the Law, but inwardly. 17. *Therefore I have reason to be proud,* that is, I have the reason on account of which I can glory,

[15] For his boldness consists in the fact that they who are wise teach also the teachers of others.

[16] The Greek adds the words "to this end."

[17] In the Greek in this passage we do not have the word διάκονος, which indicates a minister, but rather λειτουργός, which means a minister of sacred ordinances. For the Greeks use the word λειτουργία to describe what we on the basis of a Hebrew word call a Mass *(missa),* which means a sacrifice or a gift, according to John Reuchlin. From this we have the words λειτουργέω, "I perform sacred duties"; λειτουργία, "sacred ministry" or "performance of sacred rites"; λειτουργός, "one who performs sacred rites." Hence by correspondences the apostle says "sanctifying," which in Greek means "in the priestly service of," or "performing the celebration of," in the way the priest carries out his divine work. In this way he commends in a wonderful way his own duties and teaches how the Gospel is to be preached, namely, as a most sacred matter with all sanctity and solemnity. ἱερουργοῦντα, that is, "one who performs sacred rites." For he is alluding to the priestly office, as if to say: "My sacrifice is to preach the Gospel and thus through the Gospel to offer the Gentiles as a sacrifice to God." Hence we have ἱερουργία, "sacrifice"; ἱερουργέω, "I sacrifice," or "I celebrate." For just as among us we say *sacrificio* or *celebro,* so among them they say ἱερουργέω or λειτουργέω. And where we have *sacrificium* and *missa,* they have ἱερουργία and λειτουργία. Therefore the apostle uses both terms and calls himself both λειτουργόν and ἱερουργοῦντα.

[18] It is as if he were saying: "I do not presume to teach, but only to admonish, and even this only in order that I may fulfill the duty laid upon me, because I am 'the preacher of the Gentiles,' 1 Tim. 2:7, and 'the apostle of the uncircumcision,' Gal. 2:7." And from this point on he begins to commend his own office, as if he were saying: "Since you are Gentiles, you belong to my office, the office which I have accepted for the Gentiles," as also he says above, Rom. 1:5: "To bring about the obedience of faith among all the nations, among whom are you also."

[19] It is as if he were saying: "I am a little priest in the priestly service of the Gospel, in which service the Gentiles have been offered and are making offerings in their gratitude to God."

in Christ Jesus,²⁰ certainly not from himself, that is, "from the fact that I am thus a minister to the Gentiles," *for God*, in God's presence; the Greek has: "in those things which" pertain "to God." "In Christ, I say, because since I am a minister, not the Lord." 18. *For I do not*,²¹ or will not, *venture to say anything*, as if to say: "as many crafty people do," *of the things which Christ has not wrought through me*, the understanding is: but only what He has wrought in me; as I speak so it is, for Christ has made me an apostle to the Gentiles, *to win obedience from the Gentiles*, that is, that the Gentiles might be obedient through faith, what he has above called "the offering of the Gentiles" (v. 16), *by word and deed*, through word and work. 19. *By the power*, through the virtue, *of signs and wonders*, miracles, by, that is, through, *the power of the Holy Spirit*,²², ²³ the Greek has "the Spirit of God," *so that from Jerusalem* and *as far round*, that is, from those places which are around Jerusalem, for there he began his work, *as Illyricum*, ²⁴ which is Dalmatia, on the Adriatic Sea,²⁵ *I have fully preached*, that is, I have fulfilled, or perfected, or consummated, *the Gospel of Christ*, not that I glorify myself in all these places for having preached the Gospel. 20. *And I have so preached this*⁷ *Gospel*, that is, of God, *not where Christ has already been named*, that is, known and preached through other disciples, not that I should be proud or despise them,²⁶ *lest I build on another man's foundation*, for this would detract from the apostolic office, since the apostles were sent to establish the church and were themselves the foundation of the church, Rev. 21:14, *but as it is written*, Is. 52:15, 21. *They shall see who have never been told of Him*,²⁷ the Gospel shall

²⁰ Because he has not sought glory among men.

²¹ He strips all arrogance away from himself, and in so doing he cuts down the false apostles who preach because of ambition rather than because of the call from Him.

²² The power of signs is that they give warning; the power of the Holy Spirit is that He causes these signs.

²³ Because both magicians and false christs produce signs and wonders, but not "by the power of the Holy Spirit," as in Dan. 8:24: "And his power shall be strengthened, but not by his own force."

²⁴ It is as if he were saying: "Now it is time that I also come to Italy, since I will be coming so close to it."

²⁵ For Illyria, or Illyricum, stretches all the way to Italy and Venice from the boundaries of the region of Greece.

²⁶ And he very modestly does away with boasting and obviates the suspicion: "Well, what have the other apostles done? Or are you the only one?"

²⁷ He uses the term "another man's" not in the sense that he is preaching

⁷ Following Erasmus, Luther deleted *hoc*.

be preached and they shall know Him, *and they shall understand who have never heard of Him,*[28] which is a repetition or interpretation of what has already been said. 22. *This is the reason,* the office of preaching all the way to Illyricum, *why I have been so often,* again and again, as I said above: "I have often intended to come to you," that is, I have tried, but I have always been prevented, as indicated above, ch. 1:13, *hindered,* in my intentions, *from coming to you,* since it has been necessary for you to come running to me, *and I have been kept away until now,*[9] this seems to have been transposed from the first chapter to this place, because he uses similar words there. 23. *But now since I no longer have any room for work,* which I may fill with the Gospel, for I have covered everything, as shown above, *in these,* Greek, *regions, since I have longed,* as if he were saying: "Why do you not take your rest and remain there?" Answer: "Love does not permit it, *for,* that is, "from," *many past* [10] *years,* the Greek does not have the word "years," *to come to you,* and the reason why he desires to come he has expressed previously in ch. 1:11: "For I long to see you, that I may impart to you some spiritual gift." 24. *I hope to see you in passing as I go to Spain,* for also there I am fulfilling the Gospel. On the basis of the Greek, Stapulensis has: "When I journey into Spain, I will come to you." [11] He speaks very modestly. He does not say: "I will instruct you," but *and to be sped on my journey there by you once I have enjoyed,*[29, 30] been satisfied or another Gospel or another Christ than the other apostles, but in the sense that the preaching has taken place through the ministry of another man, as he has said above in Rom. 2:16: "according to my Gospel" (that is, the Gospel as proclaimed through my ministry).

[28] The apostle applies to himself in particular the statement which has been spoken in general concerning all the Gentiles to whom God was unknown. Hence our translation [8] reads: "He shall sprinkle many nations, kings shall shut their mouth at Him, for they to whom it was not told of Him will see, and they that heard not have beheld."

[29] All these words seem idle, but they are filled with love, for he easily offers himself, since such great good must be sought with all his efforts. "For the manger does not need the cow, but the cow needs the manger," a proverb which is applied here in reverse.

[30] He says all these things to give them an example of what he has taught earlier about love: "Love does not insist on its own way, but that of the neighbor" (cf. 1 Cor. 13:5, 10:24).

---

[8] The Vulgate.

[9] This clause is omitted by both Faber and Erasmus. Luther followed their suggestion and crossed these words out in his text.

[10] With Faber and Erasmus, Luther deleted *praecedentibus* from the text.

[11] Faber Stapulensis, *Epistolae Pauli Apostoli* (1512 and 1515).

filled with, *your company,* society and fellowship and conversation, *for a little,* that is, a little while, as if to say: "I cannot ever get enough of your company, so do I long for you." 25. *At present, however, I am going to Jerusalem,* not because of my own desire, but in the service of love to others, *with aid for the saints,* the Greek has "ministering," that is, that in this undertaking I am ministering to the saints, not myself. 26. *For Macedonia,* that is, the faithful Gentiles of Macedonia, *and Achaia,* the saints of Achaia, *have been pleased,* ηὐδόκησαν, that is, it has pleased them, they have shown a good and free will, *to make some contribution,* a charitable collection, κοινωνία, *for the poor among the saints,* that is, the believing saints converted from Judaism, *at Jerusalem.*[31] 27. *They were pleased,* the same word[12] as the one for which he already used *probaverunt,*[32] *to do it,* and not only this but, *and indeed they,* the Macedonians and Achaians, *are in debt to them,* paupers, *for if the Gentiles have come to share in their spiritual blessings,* in their Gospel and grace, which were surely promised to the Jews and not to the Gentiles, *they ought also to be of service*[33] *to them*[34] *in material,* temporal, *blessings,* to perform a holy work for them. 28. *When therefore I have completed,* or per-

31 With remarkable modesty the apostle is suggesting also to the Romans that they should make some contribution. Otherwise why was it necessary that he point out this matter to the Romans? He wants to bring it about that, moved by the example of others rather than by his coercion, they do what should be done of their own free will and not under compulsion, as if to say: "No one forced it, but they did it willingly. In the same way I am not compelling you, but I would nevertheless be grateful to receive a spontaneous offering." Moreover, this undertaking and ministry had been imposed on the apostle by the other apostles, as we know from Gal. 2:9 f.: "They gave us the right hand of fellowship . . . they would have us remember the poor, which very thing I was eager to do."

32 This expression "they were pleased to do it" (*placuit*), or "they approved of it" (*probaverunt*), really means "they liked the idea, they did it gladly, or willingly." For it is derived from the word εὐδοκία, which our translator translates "good will" in some places and "good pleasure" in others, for example in the verse "peace on earth, εὐδοκία to men" (Luke 2:14), that is "good will" and "good pleasure."

33 Here again the Greek has the word λειτουργεῖν, of which it was said above that it means "performing sacred acts."[13] Thus in order to recommend eleemosynary activity vigorously, he calls it "fruit," or "sacred work" or "ministry," that is, λειτουργία.

34 1 Cor. 9:11: "If we have sown spiritual good among you, is it too much if we reap your material benefits?"

12 That is, the same word in Greek, namely, ηὐδόκησαν. The Latin text has *probaverunt* for this in v. 26, but *placuit* in v. 27.

13 Cf. p. 123, marginal note 17, above.

fected, *this*, the holy work for them, *and have delivered*, handed over what has been pledged, *to them this fruit*, of the offering and collection, *I shall go on by way of you*, with you speeding me on my journey, *to Spain*, in order that I may minister also to Spain according to love.[35] 29. *And I know*, I am sure, *that when I come, shall come, to you, I shall come in the fullness of the blessing*, of the Gospel, *of Christ*, that is, because they hear the Gospel with more fullness and greater blessing, as we hear above in chapter 1:11: "That I may impart to you some spiritual gift to strengthen you." [36] 30. *I appeal to you, brethren, by our Lord Jesus Christ*, because no one ought to have his confidence in himself, but rather he ought to desire the intercessions of other people for him, *and by the love of the Spirit to strive together with me*, that is, labor together with me in this contest, or struggle,[37] *in your prayers*, through your prayers, for with prayers of this kind the saints bring help to themselves, *to God on my behalf*, as I struggle and do battle. 31. *That I may be delivered from the unbelievers*, the unbelieving Jews, *in Judea*,[38] *and that my service*, the Greek has "my ministry," [39] which I am offering, *for Jerusalem may be acceptable to the saints*, that is, to the apostles and others. 32. *So that I may come to you with joy by the will of God*, because it is not fitting to come or to rejoice without the good pleasure of God, *and be refreshed*, be revived, *in your company*. 33. *The God of peace*, that is, the God who is worshiped in peace, as "the God of hope" is He who is worshiped in hope; idols, however, are gods of contention, *be with you all. Amen.*[40]

[35] It is as if he were saying: "See with what great zeal I am prepared to serve other people; and now in your case, what should you do?"

[36] This is the "blessing of the Gospel," to advance mightily in it and grow in understanding of it, as we read in the last chapter of 2 Peter: "Grow in the knowledge of our Lord Jesus Christ" (2 Peter 3:18). For he is not protesting that he is bringing them the blessing of temporal goods, but only the Gospel.

[37] The Greek word has the meaning of "bringing help" to be sure, but in the sense of bringing help to one who is in a contest and is struggling, as if to put it as Stapulensis does: "join me in my struggle."

[38] For he knew of the persecution which was to come to him, which is described from Acts 21 to the end of the book. From this it is clear that this epistle was written after the 30th year reckoned from the suffering of our Lord, for it was in the reign of Nero.

[39] In Greek διαϰονία is used here, and the construction is this: "That my ministry in (for) Jerusalem may be acceptable to the saints."

[40] The question arises whether the apostle ever came to Spain. Stapulensis answers that he did, and quotes apocryphal writings; [14] but I believe that he did not.

---

[14] Faber quotes Sophronius.

CHAPTER SIXTEEN

Summary: The apostle sets forth certain examples of good people to be imitated; and he urges us to persevere.

1. *I commend to you our sister Phoebe,*[1] because of her faith and piety, *a deaconess of the church,* of the faithful, *at Cenchreae,* in such a place as Cenchreae. 2. *That you may receive her in the Lord as befits the saints* [2] *and help her in whatever she may require from you. For she has been the helper of many and of myself as well.* 3. *Greet Prisca and Aquila,* the Aquila of whom Acts 18:2 speaks, *my fellow workers in Christ Jesus.* 4. *Who risked their necks for my life, to whom not only I but all the churches of the Gentiles give thanks;* 5. *Greet also the church in their house. Greet my beloved,* ἀγαπητόν, *Epaenetus, "the one who is praised,"* [2] *who was the first convert to the church of Asia,*[3] *of Achaia, for Christ.*[3]

[1] This epistle was sent through Phoebe, written by the hand of Tertius, as indicated below (v. 22), but dictated by the apostle from Corinth. For Cenchreae is the port and naval station of the Corinthians, as Pomponius Mela [1] tells us.

[2] The term "saints" in this passage must not be understood with reference to those who are to be received but rather to those who do the receiving, for the saints ought not receive only other saints but anyone. For this is befitting the saints and worthy of them, as Christ says (Matt. 5:46): "For if you love only those who love you, what reward have you? Do not even the tax collectors and sinners do the same? etc."

[3] Here the question is properly raised: "Since the apostle as he was writing this epistle had not yet been at Rome and had not seen them, as he mentions above (Rom. 1:11, 15:23) that he desires to see them, how is it that he even lists their names?" The answer is that he had heard of them, as he says above in 1:8: "Your faith is proclaimed in all the world." I really am in doubt as to whether he wishes to greet the people in Rome or that the Romans should greet the Corinthians, for if they are all at Rome, it is remarkable what insight he has

---

[1] A Roman geographer who died A. D. 45. From the student notebooks we learn that Luther also added the authority of Cn. Pompeius Strabo, a Greek geographer of about the same time. W, LVII, 124, 21.

[2] Erasmus adds the explanation of the name in his *Annotationes:* "ἐπαίνετος, which in Latin is *laudatus* or *laudabilis.*"

[3] Following the example of Faber and Erasmus, Luther substituted *Achaiae* for *ecclesiae Asiae.*

6. *Greet Mary, who has worked hard among us.* 7. *Greet Androni-cus, "the manly one," and Junias, of the Junian family, my kins-men, that is, kinsmen in the sense of being of the Jewish nation, and my fellow prisoners, who are men of note among the apostles, and they were in Christ before me.* 8. *Greet Ampliatus,* Amplias,[4] *my beloved,*[4] ἀγαπητόν, *in the Lord.* 9. *Greet Urbanus, our fellow worker in Christ, and my beloved,* above he used the term "most beloved"; it is the same word, *Stachys,* στάχυς, Latin *spica.* 10. *Greet Appelles,* Apelles, *who is approved in Christ.* 11. *Greet those who belong to the family of Aristobulus. Greet my kinsman Herodion. Greet those who belong to the family of Narcissus, who are in the Lord.* 12. *Greet those workers in the Lord, Tryphaena and Tryphosa.*[5] *Greet the beloved,* ἀγαπητήν, *Persis, who has worked hard in the Lord.* 13. *Greet Rufus, eminent in the Lord, also his mother and mine.* Perhaps he was his brother according to the law, born of the same father, but of another mother according to nature. 14. *Greet Asyncritus,* "the incomparable,"[5] *Phlegon,* "who

in their good deeds, when rather he should have learned of them from them. And to point up my argument, note first that Aquila and Prisca, his wife, when they had been expelled from Rome by Claudius with all the other Jews were staying in Corinth, and the apostle was working with them at the tentmakers' craft. Second, note how they had "risked their necks" for the apostle (v. 4), even though he had not been in Rome. Third, Epaenetus is called "the first convert of Achaia" (v. 5) and therefore not of Rome. Fourth, "Mary, who has worked hard among us" (v. 6), not among you; thus she was with the apostle, and to be sure, the apostle was with her. Fifth, "fellow prisoners" (v. 7); was the apostle therefore a prisoner? It was not true at the time he wrote this epistle. Hence I have some rather great uneasiness as to what the purpose of this chap-ter is. Sixth, that he desires to greet his relatives. Seventh, that he asks them to greet one another (v. 16). This seems to indicate that all who were at Rome knew that the others were outside of Rome and with him or elsewhere, unless you argue that all these people had left for Rome and were living there. Eighth, "Urbanus, our fellow worker" (v. 9). Now this term "greet" seems to apply individually and generally, so that if they write, they should send greetings to the people whom the apostle has named. Therefore, at least tentatively it is my opinion that the meaning is that they are all Achaeans and Corinthians whom the apostle is commending to them that they might come to recognize them and greet them. This seems to come from the Hebrew practice according to which the names of all the people were signed and kept in the synagogs accord-ing to their tribes; and for this reason in this chapter he refers to his mother and his kinsmen.

[4] Some careless scribe has inserted "Ampliatus."

[5] τρυφή means "pleasures"; τρυφάω, "to live sumptuously."

[4] Luther changed the superlative degree of the adjective, *dilectissimum,* to the positive, *dilectum.*

[5] ἀσύγκριτος.

burns with me," [6] *Hermas,[6] Patrobas, Hermes, and the brethren who are with them. 15. Greet Philologus and Julia, Nereus and his sister, and Olympas and all the saints who are with them. 16. Greet one another with a holy kiss. All the churches of Christ greet you. 17. I appeal to you, brethren, to take note of those,* those of the circumcision, *who create dissensions and difficulties,* that is, they preach the letter and ceremonies of the Law, as he discusses in Titus 1 and all through Galatians, *in opposition to the doctrine which you have been taught,* which is the doctrine of faith and of the Spirit, *and avoid them.* Do not listen to them. 18. *For such persons do not serve our Lord Christ, but their own appetites,* for they seek to be glorified and enriched, as we read in Gal. 6:13: "that they may glory in your flesh," *and by fair and flattering words*[7] *they deceive the hearts of the simple-minded,* of the innocent.[8] 19. *For your obedience,* of faith, *is known to all,* or among all, as above in chapter 1:8: "Because your faith is proclaimed in all the world," *so that I rejoice over you; I would have you wise,* that is, so that you are not deceived by the evil of other people, *as to what is good,* for the good, for the purpose of the good, *and guileless as to what is evil,*[9] toward evil, that is, so that you are not able or willing to inflict harm. 20. *Then the God of peace may soon crush,* will crush,[8] future, *Satan,* that is, the adversary, the devil, and whoever follows him, *under your feet. The grace of our Lord Jesus Christ be with you.* 21. *Timothy,* that is, "Honor of God," the disciple of Paul and bishop of Ephesus, *my fellow worker, greets you; so do Lucius,* "Brilliant One," *and Jason,* in Latin *Sanus,* "Healthy One," *and Sosipater,* "Father of Salvation"; this is the man to whom Dionysius [9] writes his letter, *my kinsmen.*

[6] From this, by imitation of the Greek, we say "Hermannus" for "Hermas."

[7] There is a play on words in the Greek in the use of χρηστολογία and εὐλογία.

[8] Thus in Titus 1 he calls them "seducers" not of the flesh but of the mind.[7]

[9] It seems that the opposite should be done, namely, that they should be wise toward the evil and guileless toward the good. (Thus in Greek the preposition εἰς indicates motion toward a place, and so in this passage the translator should have said "toward the good" and "toward the evil.") Thus the meaning is: prudent in regard to evil, so that they are not deceived; guileless in regard to good, so that they do not deceive.

[6] φλέγων.

[7] Cf. p. 113, marginal note 1.

[8] Luther corrected *conterat* to *conteret* to make it future tense.

[9] Dionysius the Areopagite. Cf. p. 287, n. 1.

22. *I Tertius*, this was his name,[10] *the writer of this letter, greet you in the Lord.* 23. *Caius*, spelled with a C rather than a G, *to whom* Dionysius writes four epistles, *who is host to me and to the whole church*,[10] the entire congregation, that is, of the Corinthians, *greets you. Erastus,* "the one who loves," *the city treasurer,* in Greek οἰχονόμος ,[11] of Corinth, *and our brother Quartus,* a Latin proper name,[11] *greet you.* 24. *The grace of our Lord Jesus Christ be with you all, Amen.* 25. *Now to Him,*[12] God, *who is able,* strong to accomplish, *to strengthen you,* that is, to perfect what He has begun in you, *according to my Gospel,* that preached by me, *and the preaching,*[13] the proclamation, *of Jesus Christ,*[14] *according to the revelation of the mystery,* that is, of the incarnation of Christ, *which was kept secret,* hidden, *from eternity,*[15] because it is believed to have been unknown even to the angels. 26. *But is now disclosed,* in the time of fulfillment, *and,*[12] that is, *through the prophetic writings* [16] *according to the command of the eternal God,* because "no prophecy ever came by the impulse of man" (2 Peter

10 For he who writes in Greek has a Latin name, and if this were not correct he would have said in Greek: "I Tritos" or "Tritatos," which in Latin is "Tertius."

11 Here the *villicus* ("overseer") of the Gospel is called οἰχονόμος, "manager." And Stapulensis thinks that perhaps *arcarius* was written in place of *aerarius* through the error of copyists. And yet the manager of the public treasury is rightly called *arcarius,* from *arca,* "money chest."

12 Some codices have this passage at the end of chapter 14.

13 The word "preaching" is used here in the passive sense, namely, that activity by which Christ is proclaimed.

14 For the Gospel is nothing else but the preaching of Christ, as shown above in chapter 1:1-3: "The Gospel of God which He promised . . . concerning His Son, etc."

15 He uses the expression "from eternity" not because the times were eternal, nor because the times were in God in which the mystery was hidden, but because of the practice of Scripture whereby the term "eternal" is used to designate an indeterminate time either in the past or the future. Yet this can be understood in the sense that the mystery was hidden from eternity because it was not revealed either before the foundation of the world nor after the end of the world but only now.

16 The question arises how it could be hidden and yet known to the prophets, and thus not only made manifest now but also then.

---

10 Luther deleted *universa ecclesia,* the nominative, explaining that the genitive is called for.

11 As in the case of Tertius (v. 22), Luther maintains that this is a proper noun, not a numeral adjective, as Faber had proposed in both passages.

12 Luther added an & above the line.

1:21), *to bring about the obedience of faith,* that is, that they might obey God through faith, *made known among all nations,* to all nations, through faith and preaching. 27. *To the only wise God, through Jesus Christ, be honor,* reverence toward Him, *and glory,* praise for Him, *forevermore! Amen.*

The End of the Epistle of Paul to the Romans
At Wittenberg in the Shop of John Grunenberg
In the year 1515
At the Augustinian Monastery

LECTURES ON ROMANS

SCHOLIA

Chapters 1–2

Translated by
WALTER G. TILLMANNS

Chapters 3–15

Translated by
JACOB A. O. PREUS

CHAPTER ONE

1. Paul, a servant of Jesus Christ.

THE chief purpose of this letter is to break down, to pluck up, and to destroy all wisdom and righteousness of the flesh. This includes all the works which in the eyes of people or even in our own eyes may be great works. No matter whether these works are done with a sincere heart and mind, this letter is to affirm and state and magnify [1] sin, no matter how much someone insists that it does not exist, or that it was believed not to exist. Therefore blessed Augustine, *On the Spirit and the Letter*, ch. 7, says: The apostle Paul "fights hard against the proud [2] and the conceited and against those who are arrogant on the basis of their works, etc. . . . In the Letter to the Romans this question is treated so persistently and almost to the exclusion of all others that it may really weary the attention of the reader. But it is a profitable and salutary wearying." [3] For there are, and have been, among the Gentiles and the Jews many who believed that it was sufficient if they possessed virtue and knowledge not in order to make a good impression on people or to please them but to possess these qualities in their innermost hearts. This has been the case with many philosophers. But even though they did not parade their righteousness before men and did not boast of it but followed it from a real love of virtue and wisdom, as happened among those who were the purest and the best among them (of whom we know

[1] See p. 3, n. 2.

[2] *Superbia*, one of the seven deadly sins in the medieval catalog, is a frequent subject with Luther. See especially his sermon for St. Stephen's Day, 1514 (W, I, 30 f.), with such trenchant statements as "All rebellion arises from the wisdom of the flesh, which cannot subordinate itself to God" and "The proud always fight against the righteousness of God." In his early lectures on the Psalms Luther says, "Pride, the mother of error, is the chief of all heresies" (W, IV, 437, 28).

[3] Augustine, *De spiritu et littera*, ch. 7, 12—13, *Patrologia, Series Latina*, XLIV, 207.

only a few beside Socrates), they could not refrain from being pleased with themselves in their innermost hearts and from glorying only in themselves—at least in their hearts—as righteous and good men. Of these people the apostle here says (Rom. 1:22): "Claiming to be wise, they became fools, etc."

But here the opposite is to be taught. For in the church we should not merely teach that our righteousness and wisdom are nothing and that therefore we should not exalt them in our boasting or celebrate them in a false imagination, even though the Gospel teaches (Matt. 5:15): "Nor do men light a lamp and put it under a bushel, but on a stand, and it gives light to all in the house," and (Matt. 5:14): "A city set on a hill cannot be hid"; I say, we should not teach this but rather that our righteousness and wisdom be broken down and plucked up in our hearts and in our inner self-satisfaction before our very eyes. For when we consider them base in our own eyes, it will be easy for us not to worry about the criticism and praise of others, as God tells us through Jeremiah (Jer. 1:10): "To pluck up and to break down, to destroy and to overthrow," namely, everything that is within us (that is, everything that pleases us because it comes from ourselves and lies within us), "to build and to plant," namely, everything that is outside of us and is in Christ. This is also the vision of Daniel concerning the stone that shattered the statue.[4] God does not want to redeem us through our own, but through external, righteousness and wisdom; not through one that comes from us and grows in us, but through one that comes to us from the outside; not through one that originates here on earth, but through one that comes from heaven. Therefore, we must be taught a righteousness that comes completely from the outside and is foreign. And therefore our own righteousness that is born in us must first be plucked up. Thus we read in Ps. 45:10: "Forget your people and your father's house, etc." Abraham, too, was ordered to leave his father's house in this way (Gen. 12:1). Thus we read also in the Song of Solomon (Song of Sol. 4:8): "Come from Lebanon, my spouse, and you shall be crowned." Also, the whole exodus of the people of Israel formerly symbolized that exodus which they interpret as one from faults to virtues. But it would be better to understand it as an exodus from virtues to the grace of Christ, because virtues of that kind are often

---

[4] The reference is to Dan. 2:34: "But the stone that struck the image became a great mountain and filled the whole earth." Nicholas of Lyra interpreted the passage as speaking of Christ, the Cornerstone.

greater or worse faults the less they are accepted as such and the more powerfully they subordinate to themselves every human emotion at the expense of all other good qualities. Thus the right side of Jordan was more afraid than the left side.[5] But now Christ wants our whole disposition to be so stripped down [6] that we are not only unafraid of being embarrassed for our faults and also do not delight in the glory and vain joys of our virtues but that we do not feel called upon to glory before men even in that external righteousness which comes to us from Christ. Nor should we be cast down by sufferings and evils which are inflicted on us for His sake. A true Christian must have no glory of his own and must to such an extent be stripped of everything he calls his own that in honor and in dishonor he can always remain the same in the knowledge that the honor that has been bestowed on him has been given not to him but to Christ, whose righteousness and gifts are shining in him, and that the dishonor inflicted on him is inflicted both on him and on Christ. But to obtain such perfection we need much practice, to say nothing of the special gift of grace. Even though a person with all his natural and spiritual gifts may be wise before men and righteous and good, God will not on that account look upon him as such, especially if he regards himself so. Therefore we must in all these things keep ourselves so humble [7] as if we still had nothing of our own. We must wait for the naked mercy of God, who will reckon us righteous and wise. This God will do if we have been humble and have not anticipated God by justifying ourselves and by thinking that we are something, as we read in 1 Cor. 4:3-5: "I do not even judge myself. . . . It is the Lord who judges me. Therefore do not pronounce judgment before the time, etc." To be sure, there are many who for God's sake consider the

[5] Cf. Joshua 3:16 and Ps. 114:1-3.

[6] Expressions like "to strip off" (exuere) and "to be stripped of" (nudus) were commonplace in the language of various medieval writers whose works Luther studied. These expressions signified complete separation from everything objectionable. The Weimar editor cites a number of instances in which Luther adopts such phrases.

[7] "Humility" is the dominant note throughout these lectures and the early lectures on the Psalms as well. In fact, Luther is ready to say that "humility" is the theme of all of Scripture. "What else does all of Scripture teach but humility, in which we are subject not only to God but also to every creature!" he writes below on Rom. 2:11. A typical statement is humilitas . . . est nihil aliud nisi obedientia et tota iustitia (W, IV, 406, 5). "Pride" (superbia) is the very opposite, the root of all evil. Cf. n. 2 above. See also Luther's comment on Is. 40:3: "Prepare the way of the Lord," Luther's Works, 17, pp. 8—9.

goods of the left hand,[8] that is, temporal goods, of no value and gladly give them up, as the Jews and the heretics are doing. But there are few who for the sake of obtaining the righteousness of Christ consider the goods of the right hand, the spiritual goods and righteous works, worth nothing. This is something the Jews and heretics cannot do. And yet, nobody will be saved unless this takes place. For people always wish and hope that their own works will be accepted and rewarded by God. But this statement stands firm (Rom. 9:16): "It depends not upon man's will or exertion, but upon God's mercy."

But let us now turn to the letter. I cannot believe [9] that those to whom the apostle writes this letter, whom he calls the beloved of God, the called, and saints, were of such a type that it was necessary for him to step in on account of their discord and to come to the conclusion that they were all sinners. No, if they were Christians, they knew this on the basis of their faith. I prefer to believe that he wanted to take advantage of this opportunity to write to the faithful so that they would have the witness of a great apostle for their faith and doctrine in their fight against the Jews and Gentiles of Rome who still did not believe and boasted of their flesh and opposed the humble wisdom of the faithful. The believers in Rome were forced to live in the midst of them and had to hear and say things that could not be reconciled, as he also wrote in 2 Cor. 5:12: "We are not commending ourselves to you again but giving you cause to be proud of us, so that you may be able to answer those who pride themselves on a man's position and not on his heart." Now let us look at the text up to the passage which reads: "For the Gospel is the power of God, etc." (Rom. 1:16). It contains practical rather than abstract teachings, for the apostle teaches first through his own example how a pastor should act toward those who are entrusted to him.

It is fitting for a wise servant of God to hold his office in high honor and in respect among those who are entrusted to him.

A faithful servant of God, however, is in duty bound not to exceed the authority of his office and not to abuse it for the sake

---

[8] The phrases "of the left hand" and "of the right hand," in the general distinction of "unfavorable" and "favorable" or "mundane" and "spiritual" respectively, were among Luther's favorite devices, and he used them in a variety of ways.

[9] Nicholas of Lyra had stated the purpose of the letter as "to recall them from the error of a sham faith."

of his own pride but to administer it only for the benefit of those who are entrusted to him.

A servant of God should be a "wise and faithful servant" (Matt. 24:45). If he does not pay attention to the former qualification (wisdom), he will become a mere specter [10] and slothful and unworthy of such honor. Thus in those people who in foolish humility try to get along with everybody everywhere and to be popular with their charges the influence of authority is necessarily lost, and familiarity breeds contempt. How gravely do they sin! They allow the things that belong to God and that have been entrusted to them to be trampled underfoot. They should have seen to it that these things were honored. On the other hand, if he does not pay attention to the latter qualification (faithfulness), he will become a tyrant who always frightens people with his power. He wants to be considered grim. Instead of striving to make their authority as fruitful as possible for others, such people try to make it as frightful as possible, even though according to the apostle that power was given not to destroy but to edify. But let us call these two faults by name: softness and harshness. Concerning the former, Zech. 11:17 says: "O shepherd and idol,[11] you who desert the flock." Concerning the latter, Ezek. 34:4 says: "With force and harshness you have ruled them." These are the two main faults from which all the mistakes of pastors [12] come. No wonder! For softness is rooted in evil desires, and harshness in uncontrolled wrath. These two faults are responsible for everything that is evil, as everybody knows. Therefore, it is difficult to accept an office unless these two beasts are first slain. They would do even more harm, should the power to cause harm be available to them. Throughout the prolog, or preface, of this letter the apostle presents his own person as a most beautiful example of opposition to these two monsters. For first of all, to prevent his being despised as unfit and soft by those entrusted to him, he shows his office in all its glory. In the second place, in order not to be considered a tyrant and a violent man, he

---

[10] See Luther's similar definition of the *idola* of Is. 48:5 on p. 145.

[11] Nicholas of Lyra, commenting on this passage, defines *idolum* as "what is worshiped as God but is not God." See Luther's definition of *idola* on p. 145.

[12] Luther repeatedly emphasizes the important position and responsibility of the clergy, for instance (W, III, 647, 32 f.): "For every clergyman *(prelatus)* is a vicar of Christ, a mystic leader *(caput),* and a mystic Christ"; but Luther also takes note of the opposition these men encounter from those in their charge, for instance, in his commentary on Ps. 1 (W, III, 18, 11 ff.), where the insubordination of monks *(religiosi)* to their superiors *(prelati)* is described.

wins the love of his charges with every expression of good will in order to prepare them for the reception of the Gospel and the grace of God by a mixture of fear and love. Accordingly, every pastor in the church, following the example of the apostle, should, like an animal that parts the hoof and is clean,[13] first of all distinguish with a sharp eye between himself and his office, that is, between "the form of God" and "the form of a servant" (Phil. 2:6-7) and, considering himself always the lowliest of all servants, should administer his office with a mixture of fear and love. He should do only those things that are good and profitable for his charges, so that, knowing that the whole office exists for the benefit of his charges, he should rather resign from the office if his experience should show that the welfare and the good of his charges does not follow or that it is being hindered by him personally. Surely, this is the chief sin of a pastor, when through one or the other of these faults, or through both of them, he hinders the success of his ministry, and he will give a most difficult account of his stewardship.

Therefore he says: *A servant of Jesus Christ.* Both majesty and humility are comprehended in this word: Humility insofar as he does not appoint himself lord and founder, as is the way of tyrants and of the proud, who abuse their power in such a way that they think of nothing but that they have power, as if their power had its origin in themselves and as if they had not received it from someone else. Therefore, they cannot enjoy the blessings which such power gives to them, but they merely enjoy the use of this power. Majesty, however, is implied when he rapturously boasts that he is the servant of such a great Lord. If it is fatal not to honor and to receive the servant of an emperor, what will happen to those who do not honor and receive the servants of God? Thus this word, *A servant of Jesus Christ,* is a terrifying and powerful word. And I believe that the word *servant* in this passage is an expression used for the office and the dignity and not for his own service to, and subjection under, God. Thus the apostle is not, I believe, by this word trying to magnify his own personal works by which he alone and in a very special way is serving God. That would be an indica-

---

[13] Luther's comparison apparently alludes to the allegorical interpretation then commonly given to Lev. 11:3 ff. and Deut. 14:6 ff. According to this, only to "chew the cud" and not to "part the hoof" was to accept only the Law and not to believe in the Trinity and therefore to be "unclean." Cf. the *Glossa ordinaria.*

tion of arrogance. For who would have the courage to claim definitely and conclusively, "I am a servant of God," when he does not know whether he really has done everything that the Lord expects of him, as he himself says [14] 1 Cor. 4:3: "I do not even judge myself." For all judgment is with God and all decisions whether a person is a servant or an enemy. But he expressly calls himself a servant, as has been said, because he wants to confess that he has received his office from God above others, as if he wanted to say: "Yes, I preach the Gospel and teach the church, and I baptize and do all the other works which are the works of God alone, but I do these things not as a master who has been placed over you but as a servant to whom such service among you has been entrusted. And I am a servant in this way, for you; and my service has no other purpose but to do what I am indebted to do for you." This the other service, by which we are all called to render service to God, does not do. That service applies to God alone. To put it briefly: The "servant of God" in the moral and tropological sense is every person by himself and for himself. The "servant of God" in the allegorical sense is a person for others and over others and for the sake of others. For this reason the latter sense signifies dignity and honor, the former complete subordination and humility. Therefore the latter sense has certainty and should inspire confidence, but this is in no way true in the case of the former. In the same way the latter helps others and is adjusted to their needs, but the former benefits only the individual himself. Again, the latter is the special gift of some people, the former should be common to all. The latter has definite tasks and specific boundaries, the former includes all the things a person can do. The latter can exist without grace, the former cannot. Therefore the latter is worth more, but the former [15] is more salutary. The latter is manifest to men in glory, the former is not sufficiently known even to the individual, as I have stated above.

Called to be an apostle. This means, to express it more clearly: "Called as an apostle," or "Called to the office of apostleship." With this statement he expresses even more clearly his service, or his ministry. For there are many servants and ministers of Jesus Christ, but they are not all apostles. But all apostles are also ser-

---

[14] The original text has "2 Cor. 4."

[15] We have followed the Weimar editor's suggestion to read *hoc* in the sense of *illud* at this point.

vants, that is, ministers, that is, people who do the work of the Lord over others and for others, in the place and stead of the Lord. With the first word he strikes three types of people who are not called to offices of honor. The first are the false apostles, who at that time were present in great numbers, whom the devil sowed like weeds (Matt. 13:25) and whom he sent from the north like the boiling pot of Jeremiah (Jer. 1:13). The second are those who enter office with ambitious thoughts. They may not be false apostles or false servants, because they are teaching what is right and true and because they are leading others in a good catholic way. At the same time, however, since they are not called to an office, they stand accused by the word "called." Though they may not be "thieves and robbers" (John 10:1) like the former, they are still hirelings who are thinking of their own interests and not the interests of Jesus Christ. They are interested in their sheep only insofar as they see in them the opportunity to gain honor, gold, and pleasure. Of such people we have an unusual number in the church today. It is true that they are not accused and condemned in Holy Scriptures in the same way as the false prophets and false apostles, that is, the heretics, the schismatics, and the godless people, concerning whom it is written that they run without being sent and talk without commission (Jer. 23:21) and that they seek after lies, etc. (Ps. 4:2). Yet they are not considered acceptable by God, because they take and seek an office for themselves not from free inclination but from mercenary greed. To these the third group is similar, those who enter office by force or are installed by force through others, even if their presence is not desired by their subjects. These people are worse than the second group but not as bad as the first. But since the holy offices are so sublime, one must be on guard against entering these offices without a divine call, yes, more than against all the dangers of this world and the next, for they are absolutely the greatest of all dangers. But alas, how unfeelingly hard many are today; they see all these things but do not give them a moment's thought. Not even the people who are called by God are secure,[16] and those other people, where shall they appear? [17] Judas, the apostle, was ruined, Saul fell, and so did David, the chosen one, and yet they had been called and anointed in a special way. Woe, to those other unfortunate ones!

[16] See p. 20, n. 10.

[17] The allusion is obviously to 1 Peter 4:18.

With the second word, *apostle,* he emphasizes the dignity of his office and inspires greater reverence for his office in his charges and hearers. For if one should receive every servant of God with reverence and love as a person who is doing God's work among us, how much more reverently should one receive an apostle! He is the highest messenger and the highest angel of the Lord of Hosts, that is, of Jesus Christ.

Truly, among the other benefits which God has given to us in such great numbers we should with praise and our most humble thanks recognize also this benefit, that in His great faithfulness He has given to man such power, lest we be frightened too much and our salvation and the work of the Lord be hampered in us through our excessive fear if He should do this work among us Himself or through angels. But like a faithful physician who is concerned about our weakness, He has chosen people who are like us and familiar to us, that is, creatures of whom we do not have to be afraid in the least. In this way His work is to prosper among us in a fruitful and profitable way, for the fright, which in times of old the prophets would suffer whenever they received a message from God or from an angel, has been taken away. Even Moses could not endure this fright. Because the Word had not yet become flesh, we were not yet able to grasp it on account of its sublimity and our weakness. But now it has been made benign to us and has taken on the form of flesh and is being proclaimed to us by flesh-and-blood people. But this does not imply that we should fear and love it less. It is still the same Word as formerly, even if it does not frighten us but inspires love in us. But the time will come when it will be all the more frightening to those who now refuse to honor and love it.

Set apart for the Gospel of God. This sentence can be understood in a twofold way.

First, it can be understood according to the words written in Acts 13:2: "The Holy Spirit said to them, 'Set apart for Me Paul and Barnabas for the work to which I have called them.' " [18] In this case the meaning is that he himself has separately been appointed to the apostleship to the Gentiles, just as Peter and the other apostles have been called to the ministry to the circumcision and the Jews. With this phrase he explains his office in greater detail, for he is not only a *servant* and an *apostle of God* but also one who

---

[18] In a sermon of the year 1524 Luther says concerning this passage: "This is the ordination by the Holy Spirit, as in Gal. 1:1." See W, XVII-1, 509, 21.

has been *separated* from the others to be sent particularly to the Gentiles.

But in the second place, it can be interpreted according to the word in Gal. 1:15-16: "But when He who had set me apart before I was born, and had called me through His grace, was pleased to reveal His Son in me, in order that I might preach Him among the Gentiles." In this case the meaning would be: Already in his mother's womb he was ordained by God above other Jews to become an apostle to the Gentiles. Jeremiah prefigured this, for he was told (Jer. 1:5): "Before you were born I consecrated you; I appointed you a prophet to the nations." But Paul fulfilled these words in real truth. The words "sanctify," [19] "separate," and "set apart" describe almost one and the same thing in Scriptures. But it is more unpretentious and more modest to call himself "separated" rather than "sanctified," lest he speak boastfully of himself. For what is holy and dedicated to God is also set apart and separated, and therefore sanctified, obviously from the union with unholy things. In any case, "Sanctify yourselves" means as much as "Separate yourselves from things of this world." This is the holy will of God, that, in the allegorical sense, you separate yourself from evil people and, in the moral sense, from sin. Thus *set apart for the Gospel of God* is the same thing, that is, "Taken away from preoccupation with other things, I have been dedicated to, initiated in, and sanctified for, this one office, that I teach the Gospel, just as a priest is set apart and separated to offer the sacrifice." This meaning appeals to me more than the first meaning.

Finally, in writing thus he rebukes those who in spite of their separation for the divine ministry and in spite of the fact that they belong to the Lord get involved in other, worldly affairs as if they were of the world. Accordingly, the apostle serves notice that he is separated not for any type of work but for the special work of proclaiming the Gospel. It is as if he were saying: "My chief work consists in preaching the Gospel, as I say in 1 Cor. 1:17: 'For Christ did not send me to baptize but to preach the Gospel.' Even though other apostles may have other tasks, I have been set apart for the preaching of the Gospel."

2. *Which He promised beforehand.* He says this so that we should not think that this gift has been received on account of our merits or that it is the result of human wisdom. This is the greatest

---

[19] For another meaning of *sanctificare* as used by Luther, see p. 321.

power and the proof of the Gospel, that it has the witness of the old Law and Prophets that it would be so in the future. For the Gospel proclaims only what prophecy has said it would proclaim, so that we may say that it has been ordained by God's previous decision to be so before it should happen, and thus God alone should receive the glory for this doctrine and not our own merits and endeavors, obviously because this Gospel was ordained before we existed, as it says itself (Prov. 8:23): "Ages ago I was set up, at the first," that is, in the form of the Law, "before the beginning of the earth," that is, the church, which was of course created by it [wisdom]. For the Gospel, which is the wisdom and the power of God (1 Cor. 1:24), has established the church and does everything that wisdom in that passage says about itself for its own glory and praise. Thus we read in Amos 3:7: "Surely the Lord does nothing without revealing His secret to His servants, the prophets." And Is. 48:5 says: "I declared them to you from of old," that is, in the old law, "before they came to pass, I announced them to you, lest you should say, 'My idols,'" that is, the imaginings of my wisdom, "did them, and my molten images commanded them. You have heard," namely, at the time of the Law and the Prophets; "now see all this," namely, in the time of grace, etc.

Through His prophets in the Holy Scriptures. He says this to indicate distinction from the promise given before all times, about which he says in Titus 1:2: "Which God, who never lies, promised ages ago." For this promise is the predestination from eternity of all things to come. But through the prophets the promise is given in time and in human speech. This is a wonderful proof of the grace of God, that above and beyond the eternal promises He gives the promise also in human words, not only in spoken words but also in written ones. All this has been done so that when the promise of God has been fulfilled, it should in these words be apparent that it was His plan to act thus, so that we might recognize that the Christian religion [20] is not the result of a blind accident or of a fate determined by stars, as many empty-headed people have arrogantly assumed,[21] but that it was by God's definite plan and deliberate

---

[20] Luther has "the religion of Christ." In his day the Latin word *religio* was used in a variety of ways, but especially in the sense of "order of monks" and in the more general sense "service," or "worship."

[21] Luther apparently has in mind contemporary remnants of medieval astrology. See also *Luther's Works*, 1, pp. 44—46; 54; 172—173; 216—217; 219—220; 449; 458—459.

predetermination that it should turn out so. And very fittingly he adds, for another reason, *in the Holy Scriptures*. For if he wanted to say only *through His prophets*, this could have been interpreted maliciously as if he were claiming the authority of dead people, who, with their words, no longer exist. But in this way he refers expressly to their writings, which are still extant.

3-4. *Concerning His Son, who was made for Him of the seed of David according to the flesh and predestined the Son of God in power according to the Spirit of sanctification by the resurrection of Jesus Christ from the dead.* This passage has, as far as I know, never been explained correctly or sufficiently by anyone. The exegetes of the ancient church were hindered by an inadequate explanation, and the more recent exegetes were lacking in Spirit. And yet, aided by the efforts of others, we venture to try our minds at it without doing violence to the piety of our faith. I think the meaning of the apostle is the following: The contents, or object, of the Gospel, or — as others [22] say — its subject, is Jesus Christ, the Son of God, born of the seed of David according to the flesh and now appointed King and Lord over all things in power, and this according to the Holy Spirit, who has raised Him from the dead. Here the Greek text is very helpful, which reads as follows: "Concerning His Son, made of the seed of David, who was chosen,[23] or designated, declared, ordained, etc., to be the Son of God in power according to the Spirit of sanctification by the resurrection from the dead, Jesus Christ, our Lord." Now let us look at the individual expressions. *Concerning His Son.* This is the Gospel, which deals not merely with the Son of God in general but with Him who has become incarnate and is of the seed of David. In effect he says: "He has emptied Himself and has become weak. He who was before all and created everything now has a beginning Himself and has been made." But the Gospel speaks not only of the humiliation of the Son of God, by which He emptied Himself, but also of His glory and the power which after His humiliation He received from God in His humanity. In other words, just as the Son of God became the Son of David by humbling and emptying Himself in

[22] E. g., Nicholas of Lyra.

[23] In his *Epistolae Pauli Apostoli* (1512 and 1515) Faber Stapulensis translated the Greek word ὁρισθείς with the Latin *definitus*, but Luther here follows the translation *destinatus* of Laurentius Valla's *Adnotationes in latinam Novi Testamenti interpretationem* (1505) and then adds the *definitus* of Faber's translation, the *declaratus* of Faber's commentary, and another explanatory synonym, *ordinatus*.

the weakness of the flesh, so on the other hand the Son of David, though weak according to the flesh, has now in turn been established and designated the Son of God in all power and glory. And as according to His divine form He emptied Himself (Phil. 2:7) to the point of the nothingness of the flesh by being born into the world, so in the form of a servant He has brought Himself to completion to the point of fullness of divine essence by ascending into heaven. Observe the fitting expression of the apostle. He does not say: "He who was made the Son of God in power," in the same way as he says: "He who was made according to the flesh." For from the very beginning of Christ's conception, on account of the union of the two natures, it has been correct to say: "This God is the Son of David, and this Man is the Son of God." The first is correct because His Godhead was emptied and hidden in the flesh. The second is correct because His humanity has been completed and translated to divine being. But even though it is true that He was not made the Son of God, but only the Son of Man, nevertheless, one and the same Person has always been the Son and is the Son of God even then.

But this fact was not chosen, declared, and ordained so far as men were concerned. He had already received power over all things and was the Son of God, but as yet He was not exercising that power and was not recognized as that Son of God. This was brought about only through the Spirit of sanctification. The Spirit had not yet been given, because Jesus had not yet been glorified. "He will glorify Me," He says (John 16:14). It was through the apostles that the Holy Spirit designated and declared that He was now the Son of God with power over all things, that all things were subject to Him, and that God the Father had made Him Lord and Christ (cf. Acts 2:36). That is the point which the expression *predestined the Son of God* wants to make. This Man, the Son of David according to the flesh, is now publicly declared the Son of God in power, that is, over all things. For as the Son of David He was weak and subject to all things. All this was done *according to the Spirit of sanctification*. To Him is attributed the glorification of Christ, as stated above. But the Holy Spirit did this only after the resurrection of Christ. Therefore he adds *by the resurrection from the dead,* because the Spirit was not given before the resurrection of Christ. From this statement it is clear that the text has been poorly translated with *predestined,* because the Greek original text reads ὁρισθέντος, that is, "designated," from which we derive "designation" and "determination." By derivation the schools use ὁρισμός for the definition, delineation, and determination of something about which it is declared, set forth, and indicated that it is to be held and believed. For a "designation" is an announcement and declaration of something. Thus also this passage must be understood in this way: Christ is declared in the Gospel by the Holy Spirit and manifested as the Son of God in power over all things. Before the resurrection this was not revealed and manifested but hidden in the flesh of Christ. And when it says *the Spirit of sanctification* instead of "the Holy Spirit," that does not change matters much. In view of His effect, the same Spirit is called "Holy Spirit" and "Spirit of sanctification." Also when the text says *in power*, it must be understood of the power over all things, according to the prophecy in Ps. 8:6 and in Heb. 1:2: "Whom He appointed the heir of all things."

Let us summarize: The Gospel deals with His Son, who was born of the seed of David but now has been manifested as the Son of God with power over all things through the Holy Spirit, given from the resurrection of the dead, even Jesus Christ, our Lord. See, there you have it: The Gospel is the message concerning Christ, the Son of God, who was first humbled and then glorified through the Holy Spirit. To be sure, the genitive *of Jesus Christ, our Lord* is ambiguous. It can be taken either as a genitive or an ablative, because the Greek text cannot be determined with certainty. If genitive,[24] it must be combined with the word *resurrection* in this way: *by the resurrection of our Lord Jesus Christ from the dead.* If ablative, it belongs to the words *concerning His Son, who was born.* And if our translation [25] reads "of the dead," it obscures the meaning, although it leaves it much the same. Therefore we think that it is better to translate sense for sense rather than word for word: *from the dead.*

Corollary

The Gospel is not only what Matthew, Mark, Luke, and John have written. This is clear enough from this passage. For it states expressly that the Gospel is the Word concerning the Son of God, who became flesh, suffered, and was glorified. Therefore, no matter who writes and teaches it, whether Matthew or Thomas, and no

---

24 Valla's text (see n. 23) has the genitive. Lyra and Faber defend the ablative.

25 The Vulgate.

matter in what words or tongues, it is the same Gospel of God. It does not make any difference how many books and writers teach it, because it is all the same thing that all are teaching. Therefore the remarks of the apostle concerning a certain disciple, "whose praise is in the Gospel through all the churches" (2 Cor. 8:18), are not necessarily to be interpreted as referring to the Gospel of St. Luke but rather in this way, that his reputation was in the proclamation of the Gospel, that is, the Word of God. Thus also Apollos [26] and others were esteemed in a similar way, that is, because they knew how to proclaim Christ in eloquent and thoughtful words.

In the same way also the expression "according to my Gospel" (Rom. 2:16; 16:25; 2 Tim. 2:8) does not have to be understood as referring to the Gospel of St. Luke, as if Luke had written down what Paul preached or as if what the former had written down the latter preached. But he says "my Gospel" because he himself preached the message that was the Word of God *concerning His Son*, as he says here.

16. *For it is the power of God.* It should be noted that the word *virtus* here is understood as "strength," or "power," as *Möglichkeit* in the colloquial sense, "possibility." And *power of God* is understood not as the power by which according to His essence He is powerful but the power by virtue of which He makes powerful and strong. As one says "the gift of God," "the creature of God," or "the things of God," so one also says *the power of God,* that is, the power that comes from God, as we read in Acts 4:33: "And with great power the apostles gave their testimony of the resurrection of Jesus Christ"; and in Acts 1:8: "But you shall receive power when the Holy Spirit has come upon you." And in the last chapter of Luke (24:49) we read: "Until you are clothed with power from on high"; also in Luke 1:35: "The power of the Most High will overshadow you."

In the second place, we should note that it says *the power of God* in distinction from "the power of men." The latter is the power by which man gains strength and health according to the flesh and by which he is able to do the things which are of the flesh. But this power God completely canceled by the cross of Christ in order to give His own power, by which the spirit becomes strong and is saved and by which one is able to do the things of the spirit, Ps. 60:11-12: "Vain is the help of man. With God we shall do

[26] Cf. Acts 18:24-28.

valiantly." And Ps. 32:16 f.: "A king is not saved by his great army; a warrior is not delivered by his own great strength. The war horse is a vain hope for victory; and by its great might it cannot be saved." It is the same to say: "The Gospel is the power of God," that is, the Gospel is the power of the Spirit, or the riches, weapons, adornments, and every good thing of the Spirit, from whom it has all its power, and this from God. It is as the saying goes: Riches, weapons, gold, silver, kingdoms, and other things of this kind are the power of men, by which they manage to do what they do and without which they cannot do anything. But all this, as I said, must completely come to naught, at least as far as the desire of it is concerned. Otherwise the power of God will not be in us. For the rich and the powerful do not receive the Gospel. Therefore they do not receive the power of God, for it is written: "To the poor the Gospel is preached" (Luke 7:22), and, as Ps. 49:6 has it: "Men who trust in their own strength and boast of the abundance of their riches."

Therefore it must be noted in the third place that he who does not truly believe is even today not merely ashamed of the Gospel, but he also contradicts it, at least in his heart and in his action. The reason for this is the following. He who finds pleasure and enjoyment in the things that are of the flesh and of the world cannot have a taste or pleasure for the things that are of the Spirit of God. Therefore he is not only ashamed to proclaim the Gospel to others, but he fights against it and does not want it to be spoken to him. He hates the light and loves the darkness. For this reason he does not suffer the salutary truth to be spoken to him. Moreover, to be *ashamed of the Gospel* is a fault of cowardice in pastors, but to contradict it and not to listen to it is a fault of stupidity in church members. This is obvious when the preacher is afraid of the power, influence, and number of his hearers and is silent concerning the essential truth and when the unresponsive hearer despises the lowliness and humble appearance of the Word. Thus it becomes foolishness to him and an insane thing, as 1 Cor. 2:14 says: "The natural man does not receive the gifts of the Spirit of God. For they are folly to him, and he is not able to understand them," and Rom. 8:7: "The mind that is set on the flesh is hostile to God; it does not submit to God's law, indeed it cannot." Thus we arrive at the conclusion: He who believes in the Gospel must become weak and foolish before men so that he may be strong and wise in the power and wisdom of God, as 1 Cor. 1:27, 25 tells us: "The weak and foolish things of the world God chose that He might confound the strong and wise. The weakness and foolishness of God is stronger and wiser than men." Therefore, when you hear that the power of God is soon rejected, you must recognize this as a manifestation of the power of men, or of the world and the flesh. Thus all power and wisdom and righteousness must be hidden and buried and not apparent, altogether according to the image and likeness of Christ, who emptied Himself so that He might completely hide His power, wisdom, and goodness and instead put on weakness, foolishness, and hardship. In the same way he who is powerful, wise, and attractive must have these things as if he did not have them. For this reason the life of the princes of this world, of lawyers, and of all those who have to maintain their position by power and wisdom is threatened by the gravest dangers. For when these advantages do not become apparent and are hidden even to the smallest extent, the people themselves count for nothing. But when they are present, then "there is death in the pot" (2 Kings 4:40), especially if they enjoy it in their hearts that these things are on display before men and are esteemed by them. For it is difficult to hide from your own heart and to despise what is apparent to everyone else and is highly esteemed.

17. *The righteousness of God is revealed.* In human teachings the righteousness of man is revealed and taught, that is, who is and becomes righteous before himself and before other people and how this takes place. Only in the Gospel is the righteousness of God [27] revealed (that is, who is and becomes righteous before God and how this takes place) by faith alone, by which the Word of God is believed, as it is written in the last chapter of Mark (16:16): "He who believes and is baptized will be saved; but he who does not believe will be condemned." For the righteousness of God is the cause of salvation. And here again, by the righteousness of God we must not understand the righteousness by which He is righteous in Himself but the righteousness by which we are made righteous by God. This happens through faith in the Gospel. Therefore blessed Augustine writes in chapter 11 of *On the Spirit and the Letter:* "It is called the righteousness of God because by imparting it He makes righteous people, just as 'Deliverance belongs to the Lord' [28] refers to

[27] Luther's personal struggles with the central concept *iustitia Dei* is best summed up in his preface to the 1545 edition of his Latin writings. Cf. *Luther's Works,* 34, pp. 336—337. See also *Luther's Works,* 29, p. 188, and Luther's reference to the Rom. 1:17-18 passage as *conclusio totius Epistolae b. Pauli ad Romanos* in W, III, 174, 13—16.

[28] Ps. 3:8.

that by which He delivers."[29] Augustine says the same thing in chapter 9 of the same book. The righteousness of God is so named to distinguish it from the righteousness of man, which comes from works, as Aristotle describes it very clearly in Book III of his *Ethics*.[30] According to him, righteousness follows upon actions and originates in them. But according to God, righteousness precedes works, and thus works are the result of righteousness, just as no person can do the works of a bishop or priest unless he is first consecrated and has been set apart for this. Righteous works of people who are not yet righteous are like the works of a person who performs the functions of a priest and bishop without being a priest; in other words, such works are foolish and tricky and are to be compared with the antics of hucksters in the marketplace.

Second, we must note that what is said here, *from faith to faith*, is interpreted in different ways. Lyra wants it understood thus: "From unformed faith to formed faith."[31] But this won't work, because no righteous person lives from an "unformed faith," neither does the righteousness of God come from it. Yet he says both of these things in this passage. It could be that he wants to understand the "unformed faith" as the faith of a beginner and the "formed faith" as the faith of a perfect believer. But the "unformed faith" is no faith at all but rather the object of faith. I do not believe that a person can believe with an "unformed faith." But this he can do well: He can see what must be believed and thus remain in suspense.[32]

Others interpret it in this way: "From the faith of the fathers of the old law to the faith of the new law."[33] This exegesis may be acceptable, even though it may obviously be attacked and contradicted by the argument that the righteous person does not live by

---

[29] Augustine, *De spiritu et littera*, 11, 18, *Patrologia, Series Latina*, XLIV, 211.

[30] *Nicomachean Ethics*, III, 7. The scholastics more often cited the passage in *Ethics*, II, 1: "We become just by doing just acts."

[31] *Ex fide informi ad fidem formatam.*

[32] Commenting on Ps. 74:11 in his early lectures on the Psalms, Luther had said: "So it is today, alas; for faith is ineffectual, a nonfaith *(fides informis)*, since only the things that should be believed are known and the power to believe is not in operation." In the same context Luther equates *informis* and *mortua* as applied to *fides*. Cf. W, III, 490, 25—27.

[33] Cf. the *Glossa ordinaria*.

the faith of past generations, even though he says: "The righteous shall live by his faith." The fathers believed the same as we do. There is only one faith, even though it may have been less clear then; just as educated people now believe the same things as the uneducated, but more clearly. Therefore, the meaning of this passage seems to be: The righteousness of God is completely from faith, but in such a way that through its development it does not make its appearance but becomes a clearer faith according to that expression in 2 Cor. 3:18: "We are being changed . . . from one degree of glory to another," and also in Ps. 84:8: "They go from strength to strength." So also "from faith to faith," by growing more and more, so that "he that is righteous, let him be made righteous still" (Rev. 22:11). In other words, no one should be of the opinion that he has already obtained (Phil. 3:12) and thus stops growing, that is, starts declining. Blessed Augustine says in chapter 11 of his *On the Spirit and the Letter:* "From the faith of those who confess with their mouth to the faith of those who are obedient." [34] Paul of Burgos says: "From the faith of the synagog (as a starting point) to the faith of the church (as a goal)." [35] But the apostle says that righteousness comes from faith, yet the heathen had no faith from which they could have been led to another faith in order to be justified.

19. *What is known about God.* This is a Greek way of expressing what might be better translated in our language in an abstract way; "the known things of God," that is, "the knowledge of God," [36] just as we read in 1 Cor. 1:25: "The weak things of God are stronger than men, and the foolish things of God are wiser than men," that is, the weakness and foolishness of God is stronger, more powerful, and wiser than the strength and the power and the wisdom of men. All of this is said of God not because it is in Him but because it comes to us from Him and is in us. Thus the foolishness and weakness of God is the same as the life according to the Gospel, by which God makes us appear foolish and weak before men in our external being. But the wisdom and the power of God is the life according to the Gospel, or the very rule of the life of the Gospel, by which He makes us wise and strong before Himself

---

[34] *De spiritu et littera,* 11:18, *Patrologia, Series Latina,* XLIV, 211.

[35] Luther paraphrases Paul of Burgos, *Additio V,* on Rom. 1.

[36] *Notitia dei* is Faber's translation (n. 23 above) for the Greek τὸ γνωστὸν τοῦ θεοῦ. Faber adds the comment: "The concrete neuter, . . . more conveniently rendered by means of an abstract noun."

and looks upon us as such in our inner man. Thus the whole matter shows an exchange. The weakness and foolishness of God before men is wisdom and power before God, and vice versa, the wisdom and power of the world is weakness and foolishness and even death before God, as chapter 6 below tells us.

18. *For the wrath of God is revealed.* The apostle directs his chief attack against the powerful and the wise of the world because if they have been humbled, their followers and the uneducated will also easily be humbled, but also because they have opposed the Gospel and the word and the life of the cross of Christ and have incited others against it. Therefore he imputes guilt and sin to them as if they were the only ones who are guilty and announces the wrath of God upon them.

To no one does the preaching of the cross appear so foolish as to philosophers and men of power because it is completely contrary to them and their sensitivities.

20. *From the creation.* Some people (and, if I am not mistaken, also the writer of the *Sentences,* Book I, Distinction II) [37] interpret this to mean: "By the creature of the world," that is, by man, "God's invisible things are seen." But this can easily be rejected on the basis of the Greek text, where we read: "Ever since the creation of the world," or as Matt. 25:34 has it: "From the foundation of the world." Or this way: "From the creation of the world" (that is "ever since creation of the world," not only from the present time on) it has always been true that God's invisible nature is seen and recognized in His works, as will be seen below.[38] Therefore the meaning is: Even if the wise of this world did not perceive the creation of the world, they could have recognized the invisible things of God from the works of the created world, namely, by taking as Word and Scripture those works that testify of God. 1 Cor. 1:21 tells us: "For since, in the wisdom of God, the world did not know God through wisdom it pleased God through the folly of what we preach to save those who believe." This seems to be contradicted here by the statement that they have come to know God. But this apparent contradiction is immediately resolved farther on: Even though they knew God, "they did not see fit to

---

[37] Luther had lectured on the *Sentences* of Peter Lombard 1509—10. The passage referred to is in Book I, Distinction III, *Patrologia, Series Latina,* CXCII, 529.

[38] See p. 156 below.

acknowledge God," that is, by their actions they gave the appearance of not knowing Him.

To gain a clearer understanding, we should note that the apostle with these words does not rebuke the Romans only, as many believe. He rebukes not individuals but all people, Gentiles and Romans alike. This can be seen very clearly from the words of the apostle later in Rom. 3:9: "We have already charged that all men, both Jews and Greeks, are under sin." He does not exempt anyone, since he says "all." Therefore we must interpret this passage to mean that the apostle, as he writes, sees before his eyes the whole world as one body. The members of this body have not individually done all the sins that the apostle charges them with here, because they are individually different. But all the members have done all these things, some this, some that, so that he shows that all the faults mentioned here were present in that body and not in the head only. Without a doubt, not all the Romans did all these things, neither did all the Gentiles, but because they were people living outside of Christ, they were members of that body and are thus rebuked together with all the others. This is the way of Scripture according to the second and fourth rule of interpretation of Scripture, that is, it proceeds from a part to the whole, and, vice versa, from the species to the genus.[39] Scripture speaks in one breath about the good and the evil and does it in the same way. It accuses the former harshly and punishes them together with the evil. On the other hand it blesses and nurtures the evil together with the good. This rule everyone must observe who speaks to a community in which certainly not all men are burdened with the same guilt or are equally praiseworthy, as experience obviously shows. But he rebukes the Romans and the educated people more harshly because they are, and have been, the leaders of the world on the basis of their leadership, power, and knowledge. Therefore he begins with them at the head (in analogy to the order of Baptism) and gradually goes down to the others until he finally includes all when he says (Rom. 1:29): "Filled with all manner of wickedness, etc."

Moral Rule.[40] According to this, he teaches that preachers of

[39] The pertinent statements of Lyra's second prologue in his *Postillae perpetuae* are: "The second rule has to do with our Lord's true body and His mystic body *(vero et simulato)*." "The fourth rule has to do with the species and the genus, or with a part of the whole, as it passes from one to the other and vice versa."

[40] This is the *regula moralis,* an application of the text based on the "moral"

the Gospel should rebuke first and foremost the leaders of the people. To be sure, this must not be done in their own words, which they invent in sick and disturbed minds, but in the words of the Gospel, that is, by showing how and where they live and act contrary to the Gospel. But there are nowadays only few such faithful workers. So John the Baptist is believed to have poured water on our Lord from the head down, not water which he himself had procured, but the water of the Jordan. Take note of this mystery, that you may not proclaim the Gospel in a fit of anger.

Thus the letter of Paul (as it ought to be with all preaching of the Word of God) is like a stream that flows from Paradise and is like the Nile, which inundates all of Egypt. But this inundation must have its source somewhere. Thus the flood which the Lord creates through the apostle Paul covers the whole world and all people. But it begins to enter from the head and the higher authorities of this world and gradually flows on to others. This must be carefully noted. Otherwise, if we follow Lyra and his school, this letter will be very difficult, and there will be no connection between what follows below and what has been said above. For Lyra states that in the first chapter only the Romans are being rebuked (the position supported also by his prolog), and yet in what follows it is necessary to think that all nations are meant, yes, the whole mass of lost humanity. But the apostle is interested in revealing Christ as the Savior of all men, not only as the Savior of the Romans and of the Jews living in Rome, though it is true that he wants to reveal Him primarily to them, but with them also to others.

19. *Because God has shown it to them.* With these words Paul makes it clear that also all gifts of nature must be credited to God as the Giver. The fact that he is speaking here of the natural knowledge of God is clear from the following addition, in which he shows how God has manifested Himself to men, namely, thus (v. 20): *For the invisible things of Him ever since the creation of the world are clearly seen in the things that have been made* (these things are recognized in a natural way by their effects), that is, from the beginning of the world it has always been true that the "invisible things of God, etc." He states this so no one should quibble and say that only in our time could God be known. He could be, and can be, known from the beginning of the world.

interpretation of the passage. In the first prologue of his *Postillae perpetuae,* Lyra defines: "But when the words are read with a view to showing what we are to do, this is the moral sense."

But in order that the apostle might be understood more clearly in these arguments, I shall try to present for my fellow spectators a playlet according to my understanding and then await either their approval or their criticism.

That to all people, and especially to idolaters, clear knowledge of God was available, as he says here, so that they are without excuse and it can be proved that they had known the invisible things of God, His divinity, likewise His eternal being and power, becomes apparent from the following: All those who set up idols and worship them and call them "gods," or even "God," believing that God is immortal, that is, eternal, powerful, and able to render help, clearly indicate that they have a knowledge of divinity in their hearts. For with what reason could they call an image or any other created thing God, or how could they believe that it resembled Him if they did not know at all what God is and what pertains to Him? How could they attribute such qualities to a rock or to Him whom they thought to be like a rock, if they did not believe that these qualities were really suitable for Him? When they now hold that divinity is invisible (a quality to be sure, which they have assigned to many gods) and that he who possesses it is invisible, immortal, powerful, wise, just, and gracious to those who call upon him, when they hold fast to this idea so that they confess it also by works, by calling upon him, worshiping and adoring him of whom they think that divinity resides in him, then it follows most surely that they had a knowledge or notion of divinity which undoubtedly came to them from God, as our text tells us. This was their error, that they did not worship this divinity untouched but changed and adjusted it to their desires and needs. Everyone wanted to see the divinity in the one who appealed to him, and so they changed the truth of God into a lie. Thus they knew that the nature of divinity, or of God, is that He is powerful, invisible, just, immortal, and good. They knew the invisible things of God, His eternal power and divinity. This major premise of the "practical syllogism," [41] this theological "insight of the conscience," is in all men and cannot be obscured. But in the minor premise they erred when they said and claimed: "Now, this one," that is, Jupiter or any other who is like this image, "is of this type, etc." This is where

---

[41] In the "practical" syllogism of the scholastics (in distinction to the "speculative" one), the major premise was called *synteresis*. It was variously defined as "a natural inclination," "an inextinguishable spark of reason," "an inborn habit," "a power tending naturally to the good."

the error began and produced idolatry, for everyone wanted to subsume according to his own interests. If they had stayed with this feeling and had said: "Look, we know this: Whoever this God, or this Divinity, may be whose nature is to be immortal and powerful and able to hear those who call upon Him, let us worship and adore Him, let us not call Him Jupiter and say that He is like this or that image, but let us simply worship Him, no matter who He is (for He must have being)," then without a doubt they would have been saved, even though they had not recognized Him as the Creator of heaven and earth or taken note of any other specific work of His hands. You see, this is the meaning of the words "The things that are known of God are manifest in them." But where and how? Answer: *The invisible things of God are clearly seen in the things that have been made.* One can see how one man helps another, one animal another, yes, how one thing helps and assists another, according as it has superior power and ability. At all times the higher and the more privileged one helps or suppresses the lower and less privileged one. Therefore, there must be that in the universe which is above all and helps all. People measure God by the blessings they receive. This is also the reason why people in ancient times made gods of those who showed them benevolence. In this way they wanted to thank them, as Pliny says.[42]

21. *For although they knew God, they did not honor Him as God, etc.* If they did not *honor* Him as God, or as if He were God, did they honor Him in a different way than as God? Apparently the apostle wants to say this, and the following passage agrees with this meaning:

23. *And exchanged the glory, etc.* That means: They worshiped Him not as God but in the likeness of an image, and so they worshiped not God but a figment of their own imagination. I should be glad to agree with this interpretation, because even the Children of Israel were charged with having worshiped Baal and calves, even though it is clear that with these images and symbols they wanted to worship the true God, but this they were forbidden to do.

But how many people are there even today who worship God not as God but as something that they have imagined in their own hearts! Just look at all our strange, superstitious practices, products of utter vanity. Or is it not exchanging the glory of God into the likeness of an image and fanciful figure if you refuse to do the

---

[42] Pliny, *Natural History*, II, 7 (5), 19.

things which it is your duty to do and if you honor Him with a work which you have chosen yourself and in so doing you imagine God is the kind who has regard for you and your ways, as if He were different from the way He has revealed Himself to you by giving you commandments? Thus even today many people are being given up to their own base mind,[43] as we see and hear.

We can also simply say: "They did not honor Him as God," that is, they did not honor Him as it was fitting for them to render to Him honor and thanks. The word "not" denies the act of honoring Him as it would have been fitting. But if "not" negates the adverb "as," then according to the first interpretation the act of glorifying is admitted and the manner that would have been proper is denied. What follows can be applied conveniently to both interpretations.

Now look at the order and the various levels of perdition. The first level is ingratitude, or the omission of gratitude. Thus Lucifer was ungrateful to his Creator before his fall.[44] Self-satisfaction is responsible for this, for it takes pleasure in things received as though they were not received at all, and it leaves the Giver out of consideration. The second level is vanity. One feasts on oneself and on all of creation and enjoys the things that bring profit. Thus one becomes of necessity vain "in his thoughts," that is, in his plans, endeavors, and ambitions. For whatever one seeks in and through these gifts is completely vain. One seeks only himself, that is, one's own glory, delight, and advantage. The third level is blindness. Bereft of truth and given over to vanity, a person becomes necessarily blind in his whole heart and in all his thoughts, because he has turned completely away from God. Since he is then lodged in darkness, what else can he do except the things for which an erring man or a fool strives? For a blind man errs very easily, yes, he errs all the time. And so the fourth level is the error over against God. This is the worst. It leads directly to idolatry. To have arrived at this point means to have arrived at the abyss. For when a person has lost God, nothing remains except that he be given over to every type of turpitude according to the will of the devil. The result is that deluge of evils and blood-letting of which the apostle goes on to speak in the following passages.

By the same steps people also today arrive at spiritual idolatry of a more refined type, which at present is widespread. Here they worship God not as He is but as they imagine and think Him to be.

[43] Cf. Rom. 1:28.

[44] Cf. Is. 14:12.

Lack of gratitude and love of vanity (that is, a notion of their own importance and righteousness, or, as it is also called, "pious intentions") blind people to such an extent that they are incorrigible and therefore are unable to believe anything but that they are doing extremely well and that they are pleasing to God. And for this reason they fashion a gracious God for themselves, although He is not so. Thus they worship the figment of their imagination more truly than the true God, for they believe that the latter is like the product of their imagination. And therefore "they change Him into a likeness of their imagination," the offspring of a heart that is carnally wise and corruptible. See what great evil this lack of gratitude is! It brings along a love of vanity, which produces blindness; this in turn results in idolatry, and idolatry leads to a whirlpool of vices. On the other hand, gratitude retains the love for God, and thus the heart remains directed toward God. It therefore becomes enlightened, and once enlightened, it worships only the true God, and to this worship of God the whole chorus of virtues [45] is then added.

24. *Therefore God gave them up to the lusts of their hearts.* This "giving up" is not only a permission but a commission and order of God. This is made clear in the last chapter of First Kings (1 Kings 22:22), where the Lord says to the lying spirit that he should entice Ahab, the king of Israel: "You are to entice him, and you shall succeed; go forth and do so." Then follows the word of the prophet addressed to the same king: "Now therefore behold, the Lord has put a lying spirit in the mouth of all these your prophets." Similarly, in 2 Sam. 16:10-11 David said of him who cursed him: "The Lord has said to him, 'Curse David,' . . . Let him alone, and let him curse; for the Lord has bidden him." In the same way the Lord also commands the devil and the flesh to tempt and overwhelm the man who has deserved it in the eyes of the Lord because of his wickedness. If someone should object that God prohibits evil and therefore does not surrender anyone to evil, that is, that He does not raise up evil to let it reign and triumph and never commands that this should happen, the answer is: This is indeed true when God acts in goodness, but when He punishes in severity, He makes those who are evil sin even more against His commandments in order to punish them all the more. To bring these two

---

[45] The *chorus virtutum*, or *collegium virtutum* (cf. p. 476), was often represented in the plastic arts as a group of noble creatures subduing misshapen beasts (cf. p. 139) representing vices.

statements into harmony with each other, the "giving up" here on the part of the man who is being "given up" is a matter of permission, for God withdraws His helping hand from him and deserts him. Then the devil, who is constantly waiting for such an occasion, receives, or thinks he has received, God's authority and command. In this sense it is an order from God. It is certainly not correct to accuse God of ordering man to do evil; but He deserts him so that he is no longer able to resist the devil, who for this purpose has the command and will of God on his side. Whatever we may say about this, it is God's will that that man be overwhelmed by sin. But it is also the will of His good pleasure because He ordains that the man should be overwhelmed by the very thing that God hates most. He makes him a slave to that which He means to punish most harshly. For it is the greatest severity to surrender someone into the hands of him whom you hate most. From this it does not follow that God wills sin, even though He wills that it be done, but it follows that He does not will it at all and that He hates it. For He wills that it be done in order to subject man to what He hates most, so that man may recognize how great the wrath of God's severity is that is hanging over his head, that God would rather let that be done which He hates most, just to punish him. For there is nothing worse than sin. Therefore in order to subject to it a man who is already in the worst way, God permits that to be done which He always forbids. Therefore God wills that sin be done not for its own sake but for the sake of penalty and punishment. Just as a sinner does not want to sin for sin's sake — he would prefer that sin did not exist at all — but for the sake of the good that seems to be in it, so God does not will sin for sin's sake — for He, too, does not will it and hates all that is sin — but for the sake of punishment and of the evil that is contained in it. He is more interested in the punishment than in sin.

But to will such things is God's prerogative alone. He is not forced not to will that there be sin, although by nature He can neither will it nor love it, but He can will and love it not as sin but as punishment. So a father detests dirt and stain on his son, yet when his son gives serious offense, he chooses the dirt, not to please himself but openly to disgrace his son with it. Therefore the conclusion of those who claim that God loves and wills evil is an oversimplification. Still more stupid are those who deny that God wills evil only so that no one can force them to admit that He sins.

God is indeed measuring with just measure when He chooses

the evil that is inherent in sin to punish man with it, for thus He chooses what is good in sin. But the punishment is (not, as Lyra thinks, the sin itself *per accidens* ["incidentally"] but) the vileness of the sin. It hurts to be, or to have been, subjected to such vile sins. This the apostle states clearly when he says (Rom. 1:24): "Therefore God gave them up to sin to dishonor their own bodies." For there is no shameful punishment at all if it is not what happens when one is thrust into sin. It is more shameful to lie in vile sin than in any other kind of punishment whatsoever. Therefore it is not correct, as Lyra says, that the sin is *per accidens* the punishment of sin for this reason, that the withdrawal of the grace of God presumably is the punishment and on that account the man commits sin. Not so! Not so! But sin, or rather the shame which is connected with sin, is itself the punishment of God, not the withdrawal of God's grace. This is what God intends. It is true, He hates sin, yet because He cannot bring about the shame He wills unless sin is committed, He wills that man should commit sin so that that shame may come over him. If it were somehow possible that such shame could become a reality without sin, God would make use of this possibility and prohibit the sin. But this possibility does not exist.

Corollary

This sentence is correct: God wills evil, or sins. Also that other sentence is correct: God knows the meaning of evil, or sins.[46] But people say in surprise: "The whole Scripture says that God does not will evil and that He hates evildoers. You have a contradiction here." [47] Answer: That God wills evil is understood in a dual sense (that is, that evil springs from His own will in the same way in which man wills evil—this is impossible with God). He wills evil in a different way. It remains outside of Him, and a creature commits it, either a man or a demon. This is true. If God did not want it to happen, it would not happen.[48] And vice versa, He does not will the good because, while He wills that all of us should be bound to His laws, yet He does not will that all fulfill them. Therefore all

---

[46] Cf. William of Occam, *Commentarii in quattuor Sententiarum libros,* I, dist. 47, qu. un.

[47] Cf. Peter Lombard, *Sentences,* I, dist. 46, 4 ff., *Patrologia, Series Latina,* CXCII, 645 ff.; Gabriel Biel, *Collectorium super IV libris Sententiarum,* II, dist. 37, concl. 1, 2; ibid., II, dist. 22, qu. 1.

[48] Cf. Peter Lombard, *Sentences,* I, dist. 47, 3, *Patrologia, Series Latina,* CXCII, 650.

these statements are true: God wills evil, God wills the good; God does not will evil, and God does not will the good. But here they loudly object [49] that a free will is involved in guilt. This objection means nothing to theology in depth.[50] It is true that these statements contain the most subtle secrets of theology, such as ought not to be treated in the presence of simple and unlearned people but only among experts. For the former can receive only milk and not this very strong wine, or else they could fall into the abyss of blasphemous thoughts. How these two statements agree and according to which judgment they are correct, namely, that God wills that I and all others should be under obligation and yet gives grace only to whom He wills, and gives it not to all but reserves for Himself an election among them—this, I say, we shall see in the life to come. But for the present it is for us to believe that this is just, for faith is the conviction of things not seen (Heb. 11:1). At the same time it is true that God never wills any sin merely for the sake of sin. But it is rather this way: some He does not will nor like to justify, so that through them He may show forth so much greater glory in the elect. Thus also sin He wills for the sake of something else, that is, for the sake of His glory and for the sake of the elect. This becomes clear below, when he states that God raised up Pharaoh and hardened his heart in order to show forth His power in him (cf. Rom. 9:17). Again He says: "I will have mercy on whom I have mercy" (Rom. 9:15; Ex. 33:19). Thus also through the fall of the Jews salvation came to the Gentiles. In order to show His mercy to the Gentiles more clearly, God caused them to fall (cf. Rom. 11:11). For how could they be evil and do evil unless He permitted it? And how could He permit it unless He willed it? He does not do this against His will. He permits it willingly. He wills it so that the opposite good may shine forth so much more brightly. Now they growl [51] that these people are condemned without guilt because they are bound to laws which they cannot fulfill, or because they are required to do the impossible. The apostle answers: "O man, who are you to answer back to God?" (cf. Rom. 9:20). For if your argument holds water, then it follows that there is no need

---

[49] Cf. Gabriel Biel, II, dist. 30, qu. 1.

[50] In his early lectures on the Psalms, 1513—16, Luther used expressions strikingly similar to the present *profundiorem theologiam*, e. g., *profundissimi theologi Pauli Apostoli* (W, III, 31, 15) and *profunda theologia* (W, III, 283, 19—20).

[51] Cf. Gabriel Biel, II, dist. 28, concl. 2.

to preach, pray, exhort, yes, even for Christ to die. But this is not the way in which God has predestined the elect to be saved; He has done so through all these means (cf. Rom. 8:29, 33-34). But more about this later.

From this text we may therefore deduce that if someone surrenders to these passions, it is a sure sign that he has left the worship of God and has worshiped an idol, or he has turned the truth of God into a lie (cf. Rom. 1:25). Those who do not "see fit to acknowledge God" (Rom. 1:28) are branded in this way, that they are permitted to fall into all kinds of vices. And if such terrible portents are in abundant evidence at the present time, it is a sure sign that idolatry is rampant, on a spiritual level, I mean. It is bad enough to change the glory of God into the likeness of an image. This is the sin of blindness, of lack of knowledge, or of an erring heart. But it is still worse if one does not only err in this way but in the perversion of one's heart also worships those images and adores a creature. But it is less serious "not to acknowledge God." Therefore the apostle distinguishes between these three types of people who have been given up: The first have been given up to uncleanness (Rom. 1:24 f.), the second to unnatural lusts (Rom. 1:28 f.), and the third to "improper conduct" (Rom. 1:28), or what is not right. In the case of the persons belonging to the third type their perversion is not surprising. For where there is no interest in having the knowledge of God, there also the fear of God is of necessity lacking. And where that is lacking, there is an inclination toward all kinds of sins. But as far as the first and second groups are concerned, the question arises why just this penalty should be imposed for their type of sin. The answer is: Just as those who worship God and look to Him are credited with the highest purity of the heart—for this is required if they want to know God and worship Him—so it is only fair conversely that those who do not acknowledge God, or do not want to acknowledge Him, should be catapulted into the lowest and the worst uncleanness, that they have not only an unclean heart (which is the result of their idolatry) but also an unclean body, that those who in their hearts do not want to be clean should also be unclean in their bodies. For as the soul is in relation to God so the flesh ought also to be in relation to the soul, uncleanness to uncleanness, cleanness to cleanness. And as they have not glorified God, neither in their hearts nor in their actions, but have instead transferred His glory to something else and have thus become filled with shame in their hearts, so it is only fair that they should also bring shame upon their own bodies and likewise upon others on their bodies [so those who do not give glory to God must bring shame upon themselves, both upon their own person and upon one another].[52] Thus in the place of glory they must receive shame for two reasons: first, because they put God on their own level and changed Him to their likeness, they had to suffer the shame of uncleanness; second, because they transferred their worship of God to something else, they had to suffer shame in their external bodies, one against another. For what is more just than that those who do not want the glory of God should suffer shame, not only in their hearts (for this is idolatry) but also in their bodies?

However, it must be noted that the sense of the apostle's statement is not that all who are guilty of idolatry have done these monstrous acts but, as he stated repeatedly, that many of them have. Some have done this and others that. But all the acts together became objects of God's vengeance against them. Without a doubt there were many (such as certain Roman consuls) who were not given up to such monstrous vices, since many of them have a reputation for admirable chastity and virtue, and yet they were idolaters.

We should also not think that the apostle wants the three ways of being "given up" which he delineates understood as necessarily being done in different persons. On the contrary, it could happen that some people were given up to all three vices, some to only one, others to two, each according to the judgment of God. For the apostle is interested to show that all were sinners and needed the grace of Christ. Even if the individuals did not commit all the vices, yet, because they individually were idolaters, they were (at least in the eyes of God) the accomplices and equals of all the others who had been given up in the worst condemnation. Against them also the beginning of the second chapter seems to be directed, as if they had been sitting in judgment against the others and yet had done exactly the same things, though not all of them.

To uncleanness to the dishonoring of their own bodies among themselves. From the apostle this vice gets the name uncleanness and effeminacy. Thus we read in 1 Cor. 6:9: "Do not be deceived; neither the immoral, . . . nor adulterers, nor the effeminate, nor homosexuals, etc., will inherit the kingdom of God"; and in Eph. 5:3: "All uncleanness, or covetousness, must not even be named

---

[52] In Luther's manuscript the section in brackets appears in the margin and is written with a different pen.

among you, as is fitting among saints"; and in 2 Cor. 12:21: "They have not repented of the uncleanness, immorality, and licentiousness which they have practiced." He also calls this a dishonor, or shame; for as the nobility of the body (at least in this respect) consists in chastity and continence, or at least in the proper use of the body, so its shame is in its unnatural misuse. As it adds to the splendor of a golden vessel when it is used for exquisite wine, but it contributes to its inelegance when it is used as a container for dirt and refuse, so also our body (in this respect) is ordained either for an honorable marriage or for an even more honorable chastity. But it is dishonored in the most shameful way when it not only violates marriage and chastity but also soils itself with that disgrace which is even worse.

The uncleanness, or effeminacy, is every intentional and individual pollution that can be brought about in various ways: through excessive passion from shameful thoughts, through rubbing with hands, through fondling of another's body, especially a woman's, through indecent movements, etc. I have called it "intentional" in order to differentiate it from the pollution that takes place during the night and sometimes during the day and the waking hours, but which happens to many people involuntarily. Such things are not intended. I have called it "individual," for when it becomes heterosexual or homosexual intercourse, it has a different name.

Rule: When a young person has no spark of reverence for God in his heart but goes his way without a thought about God, I can hardly believe that he is chaste. For as he must live either by the flesh or by the spirit, either his flesh or his spirit must be afire. There is no better victory over the burning of the flesh than to have the heart flee and turn away from it in devout prayer. Where the flame of the spirit is burning, the flesh soon cools off and becomes cold, and vice versa.

25. *And worshiped and served the creature rather than the Creator.* The reason for the second "being given up"[53] is the idolatry in works, as the reason for the first was spiritual idolatry in which people equated God with images. The punishment for this is so much greater, because the guilt is greater. For the shame is greater as it is passed on also to others, so that one defiles one's body not merely in himself but also in another person's body. Therefore also the guilt is greater, for now the error of idolatry and of an empty valuation of God is not only in the mind but also in

[53] Cf. p. 164 above.

hand and deed, an example, a temptation, and an offense for others. If these people, so far as they are concerned, disgrace God (regardless of their reverence for His majesty) by thinking thoughts about Him that are less worthy than He is, it is right and proper that this should fall back on their own heads and that they should think, and also act, less worthily concerning themselves than is proper. But alas, even now very many people think in an unworthy way about God and claim in bold and impudent treatises that God is this way or that way. Not one of them is willing to give to God so much honor that he puts His exceedingly great majesty above his own judgment and understanding. Instead they so raise their own opinion to the skies that they judge God with no more trouble or fear than a poor cobbler judges his leather. They presumptuously assure us that in God, in His righteousness, and in His mercy things are exactly as they imagine them, and although they completely lack the Spirit that searches even the depths of God,[54] they act as if they were filled to the point of intoxication. These are the heretics, the Jews, men of conceit, and all those who are outside the grace of God, for no one can think correctly about God unless God's Spirit is within him. Without Him he teaches and judges falsely, whether it concerns the righteousness and mercy of God or whether he makes a statement about himself or about others, for God's Spirit must give testimony to our spirit.[55]

The third way of "being given up" (which in comparison to the other is less shameful) has its basis in the lack of understanding of God, for

28. *They did not see fit to acknowledge God.* On account of this guilt men have been given up to various vices, that is, various and many are the vices to which, or to some of which, God has given all of them or some of them up. For they were not all murderers or involved in all the other vices, for God does not give up all people in the same way in order to punish them, even though they have sinned in the same way. The reason for this is God's hidden judgment and the fact that one man does some good at the same time and the other does nothing or less than nothing. God wants to silence every impudent mouth so that no one immediately presumes to give God a rule according to which He ought to punish a given sin or reward a good deed. Therefore God permits people to sin

[54] Cf. 1 Cor. 2:10.
[55] Cf. Rom. 8:16.

and yet has mercy on one person and pardons him, while He hardens the heart of the other and condemns him. By the same token He lets some people do good deeds and live a good life, and yet He rejects and casts out one person and takes in another person and crowns him.

29. *Filled with all unrighteousness.* This is the way the Greek text reads, and not "filled with all iniquity." [56] In Holy Scriptures, however, there is (if one were to pay attention to the agreement of our translation [57] with the Hebrew) the following difference between "unrighteousness" and "iniquity." Unrighteousness is the sin of unbelief, the lack of the righteousness that comes from faith, for as we read in Rom. 1:17, Mark 16:16, and in many other passages, he who believes is righteous, he who does not believe is unrighteous. Thus a man who does not believe also does not obey, and he who does not obey is unrighteous. For disobedience is the essence of unrighteousness and the essence of sin, according to the statement of Ambrose, "Sin is disobedience to the heavenly commandments." [58] "Iniquity," however, means the sin of self-righteousness, which man chooses for himself in his foolish zeal. Concerning it Matt. 7:23 says: "Depart from me, you that work iniquity," although in the same place the great deeds which they have done in the name of Christ are mentioned. Therefore we can simply say that iniquity consists in neglecting the duty to which you have been bound and instead doing what you think is right. Uprightness, on the contrary, consists in neglecting the things which seem right to you and doing what you ought to do. This is different with lawyers. Iniquity is therefore considered a more relative term or a term of comparison, especially when compared with true righteousness on the one hand and self-righteousness on the other.

Malice. This is the perverse inclination of the mind according to which man tends to do evil and from which he is not recalled even by the good which he has received. More than that, he abuses for evil works all the good gifts which he has received from God or man.

On the other hand, goodness is the inclination of the mind to do good, even though it may be hindered and kept back by wrongs inflicted on it; it uses the evil for the purposes of the good. For not

---

56 The Vulgate text reads *iniquitate,* but Faber's text translates the Greek ἀδικία with *iniustitia.*

57 The Vulgate.

58 Ambrose, *De paradiso,* 8, 39, *Patrologia, Series Latina,* XIV, 309.

that person is good in spiritual goodness who does good as long as he prospers and nobody opposes him, a practice the goodness of the world is incapable of. In German the precise meaning of *bonus* is *fromm*, and that of *malus* is *bose*. Therefore we read in Matt. 7:18, "A good tree cannot bear evil fruit, nor can a bad tree bear good fruit." This passage is directed against those fools who try to pass their guilt on to others and say, "I could well be good if I could live in good company, or if I could be relieved of the evil people who molest me."

Thus also the terms *benignitas* and *malignitas* are opposites. *Benignitas* is a loving disposition and the ability to get along with other people, a kind attitude, that is, a cordial desire of the mind to do good to others and to be indulgent towards them. It is twofold. The first is the perfect Christian type, which remains one and the same in dealing with those who are grateful and with those who are ungrateful. The other is the human, or worldly, type, that is, the imperfect type, which endures only as long as it finds an echo and ceases over against evil and ungrateful people. We read in Matt. 5:48: "You, therefore, must be perfect, as your heavenly Father is perfect," and in Luke 6:35: "And you will be sons of the Most High; for He is kind to the ungrateful and the evil." *Malignitas*, on the other hand, is the perverted and bitter inclination to take vengeance on others and to do evil to them. This, too, is twofold. The first type is the opposite of the heroic, catholic, Christian kindness; from perverseness of heart it inflicts harm even on good and kind people, not only on evil ones. It does not stop doing so even in dealing with benefactors. This is a brutish type of malice. The other is the opposite of our human imperfect *benignitas,* which seeks revenge and harms others but stops doing so over against those who do good to them. From these considerations we can understand what the apostle writes in Gal. 5:22: "The fruit of the Spirit is goodness and kindness."

Wickedness. This in essence is the perversion of the mind which happens when a person has opportunity to do good to his fellowman and to ward off evil from him but intentionally does not do it. For thus it seems to be described by blessed Augustine in his book *On Order,*[59] where he states that the word *nequitia* ("wickedness") is derived from the word *nequire* ("to be unable"), in the sense

---

[59] Augustine's *De ordine* apparently does not contain such a statement. But a similar etymology is presented in his *De beata vita,* 8, *Patrologia, Series Latina,* XXXII, 964.

that such a person is "unable" to do good, namely, because of ill will. Some people behave this way from envy, others from an overdose of insolence.

31. *Dissolute.* These are the people who are coarse in word, behavior, and dress and who live in dissolute license and do whatever comes to their minds.

Whisperer (v. 29) and *detractor* (v. 30) differ in that the detractor undermines the good reputation of another person, but the whisperer sows discord among those who live in harmony by secretly informing one man of one thing and another man of another thing. Every whisperer is double-tongued, but not every detractor is. See Ecclus. 28:15.[60]

60 Lyra cites this passage as equating "whisperer" *(susurro)* and "double-tongued" *(bilinguis).*

CHAPTER TWO

1. Therefore you have no excuse, O man, whoever you are.

THIS text is interpreted in a threefold way. First, it is applied to those who hold the public office of a judge and who on the basis of their office condemn and punish people whom they themselves resemble in evildoing. In this way some want to twist this passage of the apostle to apply to the Romans, insofar as they judged all evildoers the world over, although they themselves suffered from the sin of idolatry and other vices. They say these are the people singled out by the apostle for rebuke, because they were so haughty and relied on their judicial power and were not worried and concerned about the multitude of their own sins.

But I have stated clearly enough above that the apostle means not only the Romans. Therefore this idea is not very convincing, especially since it is forced. I must admit that the apostle's text can be interpreted as an injunction against those who have been placed into office and that it can be used in the manner of an ordinary proclamation in our churches. But it can be more strikingly directed against those who hold offices in our times, who with a strange madness exercise severe judgment against those who are their subjects, and yet they themselves with impunity perpetrate not lesser crimes but much worse ones. These people the apostle calls and tries to awaken from their deep blindness. Just consider [1] whether both our secular and spiritual leaders are not haughty, seekers of pleasure, adulterers, and, worse than that, thieves, disobedient to God and men, and originators of unjust wars, that is, mass murderers. And yet they continue to punish these crimes most severely in their subjects. But because they have no judge among men, they are careless about themselves. But they will not escape the judg-

[1] The Weimar editor cites Berthold Pürstinger, *Onus ecclesiae* (1524), as an example of contemporary witness and warning against the evil conditions both in church and society, with its eschatological overtones. Chapter 25 of this is entitled "Concerning the Injustice of Dukes and Princes of the World and of Other Magistrates."

ment of God, as the apostle clearly states. Therefore I shall speak more clearly and avail myself of this opportunity to preach about this material and to state the apostle's ideas.

On the basis of what authority do secular princes and secular leaders act when they keep for themselves all the animals and the fowl so that no one besides them may hunt them? By what right? If anyone of the common people would do that, he would justly be called thief, robber, or swindler, because he would take away from common use what does not belong to him. But because the ones who do these things are powerful, therefore they cannot be thieves. Or is it really true that, imitating Demodocus,[2] we can say that princes and the powerful lords are of course not thieves and robbers but that they nevertheless do the things that thieves and robbers do? The vice of Nimrod, the first powerful and strong hunter before the Lord,[3] is so deeply ingrained in them that they cannot rule without also oppressing people and hunting vigorously, that is, violently, which means seizing for themselves things that do not belong to them. Thus blessed Augustine in his book, *On the City of God,* says: "What are the great empires but great dens of thieves?"[4] And he adds the following story: "When Alexander the Great asked a pirate who had become his prisoner of war what business he had to make the sea unsafe, the pirate in boldest defiance answered, 'What business do you have to make the whole world unsafe? To be sure, I do this with a small boat, and I am called a robber; but you do it with a huge fleet and are called an emperor for it.'" He who wants to use this word of the apostle against those thieves should apply it to them about as follows: They are hanging the thieves and executing the robbers, and thus the big thieves act as judges of the little thieves. *Do you suppose, O man, that when you judge those who do such things and yet do them yourself, you will escape the judgment of God?* (v. 3).

Along the same lines they exact taxes from the people without urgent reason and exploit them by changing and devaluating the money, but they fine their subjects for greed and avarice. What is this but stealing and robbing those things which do not belong to

---

[2] In Aristotle, *Nicomachean Ethics,* VII, 8, Demodocus is quoted as saying, "The Milesians are not without sense, but they do the things that senseless people do." Aristotle uses this quotation to illustrate his statement that "incontinent people are not criminal, but they will do criminal acts."

[3] Cf. Gen. 10:8-9.

[4] *De civitate Dei,* IV, 4, *Patrologia, Series Latina,* XLI, 115.

us? Indeed, who will finally absolve of theft people who collect regular tribute and rightful compensation and yet do not fulfill their duties owed to the people by giving them protection, health, and justice? For their eyes are only on tyranny, on collecting riches, and on boasting with empty show of the possessions which they have acquired and kept.

With what profound blindness our spiritual princes do the same and worse deeds even the children in the streets know. Luxury, ambition, ostentation, envy, greed, eating and drinking and a general unfaithfulness to God—all these do not seem to deserve judgment. They are in these things up to their necks. Any diminution of their privileges or income or any reduction of their pensions, as may sometimes occur among their subjects, they consider reason for the harshest judgment and penalty. What kind of thoughts, I ask you, could God—no, not God but an Orestes or someone even worse—have when he sees an ambitious, greedy, immoderate bishop belabor his layman with all the thunderbolts of excommunication for a half florin? Must he not judge him to be twice or seven times an Orestes? Will he not tell him, "Do you suppose, O man, who judge those who do such things, and yet do them yourself, you will escape the judgment of God?" And yet these things are now so common that because of their number they are thought pardonable. What a terrible punishment and wrath of God hangs over us today that He has willed that we live under such conditions so that we see this unfortunate desecration of the holy church and this destruction and ruin that is worse than any inflicted by an enemy.

In the second place, this must also be understood as applying to those who secretly in their hearts are judging others. Yes, they also judge them with their mouth when they denounce them, and yet they are in every respect exactly like those whom they judge. We call it shameless when a conceited person criticizes another conceited person, when one glutton rebukes another, or one miser snaps at another. This shamelessness is so obvious that it looks stupid and ridiculous even to fools, yet there is a strange blindness about it, so that very many people suffer from this plague. The less conceited criticizes the more conceited, and the more conceited the less conceited, the less greedy berates the greater miser, and so forth. To such people we must apply the words, "Do you suppose, O man, that when you judge those, etc." For they are necessarily judging themselves when they judge those who are like them.

They are therefore convicted by their own words, "Judge not that you may not be judged" (Matt. 7:1), that is, so you do not bring the same judgment upon yourselves that you bring upon others. But we are blind to our own mistakes, yet regular Arguses [5] over against those of others.

In the third place, this passage speaks about those people who think that they are holy and, as I said, are affected by sin that is different from the one they are judging. They act as if they were righteous because they do not do quite all the things other people are doing, and not rather as if they were unrighteous because they are doing some of the things which others are doing. They make so great a to-do about the good things they are doing that on account of them they cannot see their mistakes. It is of those people that the apostle is particularly speaking here. To teach that type of people and to correct them is an extremely difficult task, for we should not call them shameless if they merely judge those faults of which in part at least they are free. And yet they do not understand or do not notice that they are unrighteous because they are doing what they are judging. This is well expressed by blessed Augustine in the eighth chapter of *On the Spirit and the Letter,* where he says: "They do the works of the Law according to the letter without the Spirit, that is, from fear of punishment and not from love of righteousness. With their will they would want to do something different if they could get by with it without punishment, but they do so with a guilty will. What advantage can external works have when before God the will is sinful, even though the hand may be righteous before men?" [6] In other words, they are doing the same things that they are judging. They are doing in their minds what others are doing through their actions, and they would do them in their actions too if it were permitted. This is the perversion of the synagog and the reason for its repudiation. In this weakness we are all on the same level. Therefore no one has a right to judge another person unless he wants to judge himself. The apostle wants to call them back to understand themselves, and he begins to teach them that no one who is outside of Christ should be excepted from those sinners, no matter how good he may be and no matter how he sits in judgment over them, he always remains

---

[5] In Greek mythology the giant Argus is described as having eyes all over his body, and he is called "All-seeing."

[6] *De Spiritu et littera,* 8, 13, *Patrologia, Series Latina,* XLIV, 208. Luther paraphrases Augustine freely here.

among them, even though he does not see it. He is always doing the same things that he is condemning, even if he does not believe that to be true.

The apostle now calls attention to three good gifts of God to all sinners, namely, goodness, patience, and long-suffering, or all the riches, that is, the fullness and the greatness, of His goodness, patience, and long-suffering.

The riches of His goodness consist in the abundant fullness both in physical and spiritual gifts, such as the gifts of body and soul, the use and service of everything created, the protection of the angels, etc. The riches of His patience (that is, His forbearance and tolerance; this is the meaning of the Greek [7] and below in Rom. 3:25: *in sustentatione Dei*, "in His divine forbearance") are seen in the immense forbearance with which He bears their ingratitude for all His gifts and on top of it all their evil deeds against Him in the multitude and magnitude of their sins, by which (as far as they can) they insult God, who has dealt kindly with them, and by which they repay Him with evil. They soil His glory and desecrate His name (that is, they do not hallow it), and they desecrate and blaspheme everything that is related to God, as is stated below (vv. 23 f.).

The riches of God's long-suffering appear in His extremely kind delay of the punishment and retribution for such a lack of gratitude and His willingness to wait for their improvement, as if He seemed to hope that they would improve. But the more abundantly God shows His long-suffering, the more severely will He execute judgment if His long-suffering has been in vain. Therefore the statement follows: *You are storing up wrath for yourself* (v. 5). The apostle does not say, "you deserve wrath," but he says, "You are storing up," that is, "a vast and heaped-up wrath is what you deserve!" Thus Valerius Maximus, although he was a pagan, said: "Divine wrath compensates for slowness of vengeance by means of severity of punishment." [8]

From this passage we can deduce what a hardened heart is, namely one that despises the goodness, patience, and long-suffering of God. It receives many good gifts and commits many evil acts. It does not resolve to become better. There are two types of these people. The one type does these things because of the desire and lust of their external personality. The other type does

---

[7] The Greek word ἀνοχή denotes "restraint."

[8] Valerius Maximus, *Factorum et dictorum memorabilium libri*, I, 1, 3.

them because of their own understanding and wisdom and because of stubborn insistence on their own holiness. They include Jews, heretics, schismatics, and other lovers of individuality.[9] Therefore blessed Bernard says in chapter 1 of *De consideratione:* "A heart is called hardened because it cannot be softened by well-doing, frightened by threats, corrected by punishment, or moved by promises." [10] But many of these of the second type are more stubborn and unrepentant on account of their own conceit and their "holiness," and they do not realize that this is only a double foolishness and unrighteousness. Prov. 26:12 reads: "Do you see a man who is wise in his own eyes? There is more hope for a fool than for him."

4. *Do you not know that God's kindness leads you to repentance?* So great is the blindness of the sinner that he abuses to his own harm the things that have been given to him for his own benefit. On the other hand, the light is so bright in a righteous and pious person that he uses for his own benefit the things meant to hurt him. Thus the ungodly person does not know that the kindness of God leads him to repentance. The righteous person, however, understands that even the severity of God is good for his salvation, for it breaks him down and heals him. "The Lord kills and brings to life" (1 Sam. 2:6).

5. *On the day* [11] *of wrath and of the revelation of the just judgment of God.* The Last Day is called the day of wrath and of mercy, the day of trouble and of peace, the day of destruction and of glory. On that day the godless will be punished and will be brought to shame; the godly, however, will be rewarded and glorified. In the same way also the spiritual day, which rules in the hearts of the faithful through the light of faith, is called both the day of wrath and the day of grace, the day of perdition and the day of salvation. In Ps. 110:5 we read: "The Lord is at your right hand; He has shattered kings on the day of His wrath," that is, on the day and in the time of mercy, which is now, and in Zeph. 1:14-16: "The sound of the day of the Lord is bitter, the mighty man (that is, the powerful and proud man) will suffer tribulation there. A day of wrath is that day, a day of tribulation and distress, a day of calamity

[9] See p. 337 below.

[10] Bernard of Clairvaux, *De consideratione,* I, 2, *Patrologia, Series Latina,* CLXXXII, 730 f. See p. 17 above.

[11] See p. 17, marginal note 6.

and misery, a day of darkness and obscurity, a day of clouds and whirlwinds, a day of the trumpet and alarm, etc."

7. *By patience in well-doing.* So necessary is patience that no work can be good when patience is lacking, for the world is so perverted and the devil so wicked that he cannot pass a good work by without challenging it, but it is through this challenge that God in His wonderful good judgment tests the good work that pleases Him. Let us therefore keep the following canonical and practical rule: As long as we are doing good and do not experience as a result of it opposition, hatred, trouble, or harm, so long we have reason to worry that our work has not pleased God as yet, for trial and patience have not been applied as yet, and God has not yet approved it, because He has not yet tested it. For He does not approve what He has not tested before. But if our work is immediately attacked, then let us be of good cheer and firmly trust that it is well-pleasing to God, that is, believe that it is of God Himself, for what is of God must be crucified in the world. So long as it does not lead to the cross (that is, to shameful suffering), it is not recognized as a work that comes from God, inasmuch as the only-begotten Son was not protected against this experience but rather was appointed the example of it. "Blessed are those who are persecuted for righteousness' sake" (Matt. 5:10). "Rejoice and be glad, for your reward is great in heaven" (Matt. 5:12).

Corollary

Those who complain and are impatient when they suffer while doing good deeds show that their good deeds are not of God but have been done on the basis of human righteousness, a righteousness in which a man for his own sake does good things because he seeks to be esteemed and to be honored for it and because he flees and hates being attacked, slandered, and hated on account of it. Thus it is as clear as daylight that he does not do his good deed out of love and humility for God's sake but that he does it for his own sake and for the sake of his own reputation, from a hidden conceit and love of self. For he who wants to do good works on the basis of love and humility for God's sake will say to himself, when he is praised for it: "I did not begin it for your sake, dear praise, therefore I shall not complete it for your sake." And when he is rebuked, he will say: "I did not begin it for your sake, O rebuke, and I shall not stop it for your sake." He will happily continue what he has begun for the love of God, protected on the right and the left.

Therefore James 1:4 states: "Let patience have its perfect work." That is, another virtue can bring about a good work, but only patience can bring about a perfect work, that is, one that is not infected by any vice nor begun in a desire for glory and in self-love nor left undone in fear of rebuke but carried out all the way in the love of God. We read in Heb. 10:36: "For you have need of endurance, so that you may do the will of God and receive what is promised."

Corollary

The pagan word from the mouth of Cicero, "Virtue grows when it is praised," [12] is rightly scorned and rejected by the church of Christ, for the apostle says the exact opposite (2 Cor. 12:9): "Virtue is made perfect in weakness," that is, good works become perfect through patience, for "when I am weak (when I suffer), then I am strong" (2 Cor. 12:10). So it is human virtue that grows through praise, because it looks for praise, but the virtue of Christians grows when it is reproached and when it suffers, and it comes to naught when it is praised (when it takes delight in praise). We read in Ps. 53:5: "God will scatter the bones (that is, the virtues) of those who pleased men; they have been confounded because God has despised them." Now if human virtue grows only when it is praised, what does it do when it is reproached? Does it decrease? Yes, certainly, for it turns into wrath and despair. In short, also those whom Paul here calls *contentious* (v. 8) on account of their lack of patience have undoubtedly done good deeds. But because they did not know patience and wanted to be honored for those deeds, therefore they have become unfaithful towards the truth and have gone away to their wisdom, declaring good what really is evil; that is, by declaring that the thing in which they sought pleasure in themselves and glory among the people is righteousness. Therefore, he threatens them with His *wrath and indignation*.

7. *Glory and honor*, that is, glorious honor. "Glory," Augustine states, commenting on John 17, "as defined in the old Latin classics, is the constant mention of a person with praise." [13] And he writes in the fifth book of *On the City of God*, chapter 12: "Glory is the judgment of men who have a good opinion concerning men." [14]

---

[12] It is doubtful that this saying is to be attributed to Cicero. Lyra quotes it in connection with comments on Heb. 6:10 but does not assign it to Cicero.

[13] Augustine, *In Joannis Evangelium,* Tractate CV, on John 17:1-5, *Patrologia, Series Latina,* XXXV, 1905.

[14] Augustine, *De civitate Dei,* V, 12, *Patrologia, Series Latina,* XLI, 156.

Therefore it is usually called glory and glorification [15] in Holy Scripture, and in accordance with that, being glorified and being transfigured. Honor, however, according to Aristotle,[16] is the high esteem one shows to someone to recognize his ability, or it is the high esteem shown to anyone in word, act, or sign on account of his abilities. Thus it is clear that there is a difference between glory and honor. Glory radiates from one person to another; honor, however, comes from other persons to or into a person. Glory radiates and turns to the outside; honor flows towards us and goes into us. Thus the former takes place in the manner of an exit, but the latter in the manner of an entrance.

8. *Wrath and indignation.* I understand by this the wrath of indignation or the wrath of anger with which God is inflamed against body and soul. It is a wrath of severity. But He is also strict with the righteous as these passages say: "Thou hast been angry and hast had mercy on us" (Ps. 60:1), and again, "When Thou art angry, Thou wilt remember mercy" (Hab. 3:2). This is the wrath of His goodness, the rod of the Father. Thus the psalmist prays (Ps. 6:2), "O Lord, rebuke me not in Thy anger," which means, "You accuse me, this is Your wrath; but do not apply this in anger, but in mercy, so that You may destroy the old man but save the new one."

9. Tribulation and distress. This is to be the explanation of the expression *wrath and indignation.* I take these words as belonging together and meaning the same thing. This does not refer to any kind of tribulation but to a tribulation that is connected with anguish, that is, one from which there is no way out nor hope of a way out, where comfort is lacking in tribulation. To be sure, also the faithful are suffering tribulation, but they are consoled in it, as we read in Ps. 4:2: "Thou hast given me room when I was in distress," and in 2 Cor. 1:4: "Who comforts us in all our tribulation." This comfort hope and trust in God have given us. But the ungodly are tortured by anguish in tribulation through despair. They do not have hope and reliance on anything, because they do not place their hope in God, that they might sometime be freed. Just as joy is a certain freedom of the heart, even in tribulation, so distress represents a certain narrowing and constriction in tribulation.

---

[15] *Claritas et clarificatio,* but *clarificatio* does not occur in the Vulgate. The *Vocabularius breviloquus* adds to the definition of *gloria* a note that *gloria* is related to *clarus* ("bright").

[16] Aristotle, *Nicomachean Ethics,* IV, 3, is probably the source referred to.

God permits also His own from time to time to experience both temporarily, as we read in Ps. 116:3, "I suffered tribulation and anguish," that is, "distress," as the Hebrew text reads. But God lets the ungodly linger in this double distress forever. He indicates this with the words *for every soul*. He does not say "only in their body," as is the case with the elect.

12. *They will perish without the Law.* The Law in this passage, that is, in this entire chapter, means the complete law of Moses, where both the Ten Commandments and also the love of God and of neighbor are enjoined. How is it possible that they will perish without this law and that they have sinned without it? Without it there can be neither sin nor merit, and therefore no punishment or reward.

The answer is as follows. The apostle means it this way: *Without the Law*, namely, without the orally transmitted or the written law (they will perish), even though they may know it in a different way, as he states below (v. 15), "They show that the work of the Law is written on their hearts," or *without the Law* could mean "without the cooperation of the Law," or "without the Law's giving an opportunity for sinning." For a law that is not there is also not an opportunity for sinning. But the law of Moses had not been given among the Gentiles. To be sure, the Gentiles have not received the rites and orders of the law of Moses, nor have these been transmitted to them. Therefore they were neither bound to them, nor have they sinned by not following them, like the Jews, who have accepted the Law, made a covenant through it with God, and received the promise of Christ in it. Nevertheless, they have received a spiritual law which the rites and ceremonies indicated in the moral sense (quite apart from the fact that they symbolized Christ). This law is impressed upon all people, Jews and Gentiles, and to this law all people are bound. Therefore the Lord says in Matt. 7:12: "Whatever you wish that men would do to you, do so to them; for this is the Law and the Prophets." You see, the whole transmitted law is nothing but the natural law, which cannot be unknown to anyone and on account of which no one can be excused. The opinion of the apostle therefore is, as it is most clearly stated, *they will perish without the Law*, that is, "they will perish without having received the Law." It means they have not sinned because they have not received the Law and have not observed it as Jews, and they will not perish because they have not kept the Law. But there is another reason. The same law which they have not received they have learned to know in a different way, and yet they have not kept it. The Jews will be judged according to whether they have kept the Law or not, as Stephen tells them expressly in Acts 7:53, "You who received the Law and did not keep it." *They will perish without the Law* means that it is not the Law that is handed down and received that will condemn them, therefore they will perish without a law of that kind, although not without a law which is the same as that, except that it has not been handed down to them in a written code and has not been contained or represented in it.

One could ask the question whether the Gentiles, who live outside of Christ but still fulfill the Law naturally and according to conscience, are saved, especially since original sin is not taken away without Christ and no commandment is fulfilled without grace (even though they may have the substance of such a deed on their side), and salvation is given through Christ alone. To be sure, the apostle seems to make the point here that some of the Gentiles have done and are doing the things of the Law by nature. But it can arouse one's suspicion that the apostle does not say that they fulfill the Law but that they are observing some certain elements taken from the Law. He says (v. 14): *those things which are of the Law,* that is, something of the Law, although not everything that belongs to the Law. Thus they are all still under sin because of other things that they have not done, as he says below in chapter 3. If one wants to understand the apostle in this way, that they are doing everything that the Law demands, then one must, it seems, answer the above question with "yes," but if one brings up against that the matter concerning Christ, original sin, and grace, then the answer is: "Whoever fulfills the Law is in Christ, and he receives grace because as much as he is able he has prepared himself for it." [17] Original sin God could forgive them (even though they may not have recognized it and confessed it) on account of some act of humility towards God as the highest being that they know. Neither were they bound to the Gospel and to Christ as specifically recognized, as the Jews were not either. Or one can say that all people of this type have been given so much light and grace by an act of prevenient mercy of God as is sufficient for their salvation in their situation, as in the case of Job, Naaman, Jethro, and others. But the first interpretation, according to which they have not done all the works of the Law, does not suit me because the apostle says

---

[17] On the ideas in *per sui preparationem* . . . *quantum in se est,* see Luther's further comments below, pp. 186, 218, 496.

below (v. 27): "Then that which by nature is uncircumcision, keeping the Law, will judge you." Look at this. Here he says that the
"uncircumcision," that is, the Gentile, is fulfilling the Law, and
in the same place he says (v. 26): "If the uncircumcision keeps the
precepts of the Law, will not this uncircumcision be regarded as
circumcision?" They have therefore fulfilled the Law. Whatever
was lacking (and for this lack they are excused on account of
their invincible ignorance) God in His forbearance without doubt
supplied so that it might be made perfect through Christ in the
future. This is not different from what He did for the children who
were uncircumcised and killed for His sake (cf. Matt. 2:16). He
does the same thing today for our children.

11. *For there is no respect of persons with God.* He says these
words primarily against the conceit of the Jews, who boasted about
their reception of the Law and bragged that they were its hearers
and disciples. Therefore they were angry that the Gentiles were
placed on the same level with them as far as good deeds were concerned and that they were placed on the same level with the
Gentiles as far as evil deeds were concerned, for Paul had said,
"The Jew first and also the Greek" (v. 9), and also, "Everyone,
the Jew first and also the Greek" (v. 10). The Jews wanted God to
act in such a way that He would bestow the good on the Jews only
and the evil on the Gentiles only, as if because they were the seed
of Abraham, they should automatically be like Abraham in merits.
Thus the Jews always strive to make of God a judge who considers
the persons. Their foolishness is imitated today by the heretics and
by all spiritually conceited people, who presume that because they
have chosen themselves before all other people because of their
holy lives or their wisdom and because they are pleased with
themselves, therefore God will elect them and find pleasure in
them. They do not understand that God elects and has pleasure
only in a soul that is worthy of contempt and confesses that it is
rejected in the presence of God, a soul that rejects itself, gives
preference to others, and finds pleasure in them. Then Paul
similarly pricks the pride of the Gentiles who inflated themselves
with the excuse that since they did not know the Law, they did not
deserve wrath. He answers, "By no means!" because "They will
perish without the Law" just as they are saved without the Law if
they have kept their law, the law that is inborn [18] and present in

---

[18] Cicero, *Pro Milone*, 10, speaks of the law of self-defense as "a law not
written but born with us" *(non scripta sed nata lex).*

creation, not given; found at hand, not handed down to them; alive, not contained in letters.

If we do to others what we want them to do to us, and we do wish for ourselves only what is good, glorious, and great, then let us wish this first for God—a personal will, judgment, glory, and all the other things that are God's, which we have arrogated to ourselves in alliance with Lucifer. In the second place, let us give them also to our neighbor, whom we generally try to surpass. Let them, too, be our superiors. Then we will have fulfilled total humility both against God and against man, that is, complete and perfect righteousness. What else does all of Scripture teach but humility, in which we are subject not only to God but to every creature? [19] For we, too, want everything to be subject to us, though with a perverse will. But be it ever so perverse, let us do to others what we would like for ourselves according to that will. Immediately this is right and of greatest perfection. For what could be more concise and salutary than this little lesson? But how rarely it is understood in such breadth! And yet the Lord stated it rather briefly when He said about men only this (Matt. 7:12): "Whatever you wish that men would do to you, do so to them." But now you exalt yourself above the sinner, the uneducated, the base, and you desire that they should suffer this at your hands. You must also suffer the same things from them, unless you want to deny that sinful, uneducated, and base people exist.

12. *All who have sinned without the Law.* We must be careful not to connect *without the Law* with the verb *have sinned* or with *will perish.* But we should understand it in this way: Those who have sinned without the Law, that is, without the Law contributing to their sins, without the Law giving them opportunity to sin. Thus *they will perish without the Law.* It means that the Law does not bring witness and sentence against them because such a law has not been given to them. They have a different kind of law. For every law gives occasion for sinning except when grace, love, and will attend the Law. The will always remains opposed and would prefer to do something else if it were allowed to, even though it may outwardly do what the Law commands. Indeed, through the rule of the Law it is enticed to sin rather than helped against it. Blessed Augustine in chapter 5 of *On the Spirit and the Letter* says, "I do not know how it happens that the things which are desired become

[19] Cf. p. 137, n. 7, above.

more enticing when they are forbidden." [20] And the poet says, "We are always intent on forbidden things, and we desire what is denied. So the dam is a threat to the waters impounded." "What is permitted is unwelcome, but what is not permitted entices so much more." "That which follows me I flee, and that which flees from me I pursue." [21] Therefore blessed Augustine also aptly says in chapter 8 of *On the Spirit and the Letter:* "Those who did what the Law commanded without the Spirit of grace did it from fear of punishment and not from love of righteousness. Therefore what was visible before men in the act was not present before God in the will"—and conversely, what was not visible in the external work was nevertheless in the will before God—"and all the more were they held guilty for this reason, that God knew that they would prefer to sin (if that were possible without punishment)." [22] That the Jews were such people is obvious from the Gospel, Matt. 5:20,[23] where the Lord says: "Unless your righteousness exceeds that of the scribes and Pharisees, etc." For these people used to say that being angry in heart was not a sin, but that only actual killing was. Therefore Ps. 1:2 says: "But his delight is in the law of the Lord." But this the Lord gives only by grace through the Holy Spirit. Otherwise sin always takes occasion through the Law and kills through it. No matter how much works may be done, the will still lies dead, as we read in 1 Cor. 15:56 f.: "The sting of death is sin, and the power of sin is the Law. But thanks be to God, who gives us the victory through our Lord Jesus Christ."

13. *But the doers of the Law will be justified.* This passage is interpreted in a twofold way by blessed Augustine in chapter 26 of *On the Spirit and the Letter.*[24] First in this way: *The doers of the Law will be justified* means that through justification they will become, or be made, what they were not before, doers. Second, and in a better way, *will be justified* means that they will be looked upon and thought of as righteous, as stated in the gloss.[25] It is

---

[20] Augustine, *De Spiritu et littera,* 4, *Patrologia, Series Latina,* XLIV, 204.

[21] Ovid, *Amores,* III, 4, 17, 18; II, 19, 3; II, 19, 36. In the first quotation Luther has substituted *agger* ("dam") for *aeger* ("sick man"). The older reading would give us: "Thus a sick man is eager for the forbidden waters."

[22] Augustine, *De Spiritu et littera,* 8, 13, *Patrologia, Series Latina,* XLIV, 208.

[23] The original has "Matt. 7."

[24] Cf. Augustine, *De Spiritu et littera,* 26, 45, *Patrologia, Series Latina,* XLIV, 228.

[25] Cf. p. 19 above.

sufficiently clear from the preceding (v. 13), "For not the hearers of the Law are righteous before God," that, if you should ask who else is righteous before God except the hearers, the answer would be: "The doers will be righteous, that is, they will be justified and looked upon as righteous." Thus Ps. 143:2 says, "For no man living is righteous before Thee," that is, he is not looked upon as righteous. And below, in Rom. 3:20, we read: "No human being will be justified in His sight by works of the Law." And in Luke 10:29: "And he, desiring to justify himself" (that is, he wanted to declare or to state that he was righteous, and he wanted to absolve himself of sin, as though he did not know who was his neighbor whom he was commanded to love), and similarly in many other places.

14. *The Gentiles do by nature those things which are of the Law.* This again blessed Augustine interprets in a twofold way, as he did above in chapter 26. First, by *Gentiles* he understands the believers from among the Gentiles who are justified by the grace of Christ, in contrast to the unbelieving Jews who boast of the Law and of righteousness. From this he interprets the word *by nature* (that is, by the Spirit of the grace of Christ restored from a nature that had been corrupted by sin): "Not as if grace were negated by nature, but rather nature restored by grace." [26] He is inclined toward this interpretation himself. But second, he says this word can be applied to those who, even though they lead an ungodly life and do not truly and properly worship God, are doing one or the other good thing for which reason we might say of them that they are doing some of the things which are of the Law and that they have an understanding of them.[27]

Furthermore, their "thoughts excusing them" should be understood as those thoughts with which they excuse themselves in order to obtain a milder punishment, for just as certain sins which are pardonable and without which one cannot live this life do not exclude a righteous man from life eternal, so a few good works, without which the life of even the worst person is hardly ever found, will be of no help to the ungodly to obtain eternal salvation. But this interpretation is opposed to the word that says they do by nature the things which are of the Law, and those who do the Law are righteous. Therefore Paul does not seem to speak of that type of ungodly people. But neither does he speak of the first group, that

[26] Augustine, *De Spiritu et littera*, 27, 47, *Patrologia, Series Latina*, XLIV, 229.

[27] Ibid., 27, 48, *Patrologia, Series Latina*, XLIV, 229 f.

is, the believers in Christ, for this interpretation of "by nature" is forced, and I cannot see why the apostle wanted to use this particular expression, unless he wanted to hide from his reader what he really intended to say, especially since elsewhere he does not speak in this way. Therefore I prefer to think (as I did above) of the people who are in the middle [28] between the ungodly Gentiles and the believing Gentiles, those who through some good action directed toward God as much as they were able earned grace [29] which directed them farther, not as though this grace had been given to them because of such merit, because then it would not have been grace, but because they thus prepared their hearts to receive this grace as a gift. Unless one must concede that it is to be understood in a restricted sense that he says: "They do by nature those things (that is, some of those things) which are of the Law." Then the text is clear, and the statement of blessed Augustine about the second group is most adequate.[30] In that case the apostle speaks of these Gentiles as having observed the Law as little as the Jews did, even though they have done some of the good works of the Law, on account of which they will excuse themselves from the major punishment on the Day of Judgment. They nevertheless still need the grace and mercy of Christ, just as it will be of no advantage to the Jews that they have observed the Law externally. Thus both are under sin, no matter how much good they may have done, the Jews according to the inner man because they have observed merely the letter of the Law, the Gentiles in a twofold way, because they have fulfilled the Law only in part and not with their whole heart. I accept this interpretation because the whole tenor of this chapter (as Paul himself says below in Rom. 3:9: "For we have charged that both Jews and Greeks are all under sin") is nothing else than a proof that all men, and therefore both of these, are sinners and in need of the mercy of God.

How does this agree with and support the understanding of what the apostle says (v. 15): "The work of the Law is written on their hearts," especially in view of what the prophet says (Ezek. 11:19; 2 Cor. 3:3), that this understanding would be given only to the believers of the future, that God would write His law not on

---

[28] Cf. p. 377.

[29] Cf. pp. 233, 276, 277.

[30] Augustine, *De Spiritu et littera*, chs. 27—29, 47—50, *Patrologia, Series Latina*, XLIV, 229—232.

tables of stone but on their hearts? It seems to me (and I don't want to discredit a better interpretation) that there is a difference between the statement "The works of the Law are written on their heart" and "The Law is written on their hearts," for the apostle did not want to say in this place, even if he knew it and could have said it, that they possessed the Law written on their hearts, but he wanted to say only "the works of the Law." Therefore I believe that the sentence "The law is written on their hearts" is the same as "God's love has been poured into our hearts through the Holy Spirit" (Rom. 5:5). This is, in the real sense, the law of Christ and the fulfillment of the law of Moses. Indeed, it is a law without a law, without measure, without end, without limit, a law reaching far beyond everything that a written law commands or can command. But the words "the work of the Law is written" mean that the knowledge of the work is written, that is, the law that is written in letters concerning the works that have to be done but not the grace to fulfill this law. Therefore until the present they have of necessity remained tied to the letter that kills, for they have had nothing else but the works of the Law written on their hearts.

15. *They show that the work of the Law is written on their hearts.* How do they show this? First, they show it to others by doing those things which are of the Law. Second, they show it to themselves now and to every man in the Judgment through this, that their conscience gives witness to themselves about themselves. But what kind of a witness does it give to them? It gives a good witness of good deeds that have been done. This is done by the thoughts that excuse and defend them. But their conscience also gives an evil witness about evil deeds. This is done by the thoughts that accuse them and torture their conscience. It is as if he were saying: "This proves that the Law was not unknown to them, but that they had a knowledge of what was good and evil, for when they are tortured in their consciences, they see that they have done evil. But they would not be tortured if they did not recognize the evil they have done. Just as they themselves are judged before themselves by themselves while their conscience testifies and their thoughts accuse them or excuse them, so they will also be judged by God on the evidence of the same witness. For they do not judge themselves on the basis of other people's judgments of them or on the basis of the words of such as praise or criticize them, but rather on the basis of their innermost thoughts, which are so deep in their hearts that their souls cannot escape

from these thoughts and get away from them, nor can they silence them, as they can silence the judgments and words of men. Therefore God, too, will judge all people according to them and will reveal our innermost thoughts, so that there is no possibility to flee further inside and to a more private hiding place. The thoughts will of necessity be revealed and open before the eyes of everyone, as if God wanted to say: "See, it's not I who am judging you, but I merely agree with your own judgment about yourself and acknowledge this judgment. If you cannot judge differently concerning your very own self, neither can I. Therefore on the basis of the witness of your own thoughts and of your own conscience you are worthy of either heaven or hell." Thus the Lord says (Matt. 12:37): "By your words you will be justified, and by your words you will be condemned." If this is true about words, it is much more so of thoughts, for they are much more secret and much more reliable witnesses.

And among themselves in turn their thoughts accuse or defend them. To be sure, from our conscience we get only thoughts of accusation, because our works are nothing in the presence of God (unless He Himself by His grace works in us), although it is easy for us to excuse ourselves in our own eyes, because we are easily pleased with ourselves. But what does it profit except that we are thereby convinced that we knew the Law? For any such self-pleasing thoughts testify that we have done good and refrained from evil, but we have not thereby pleased God or fulfilled the Law completely. Whence shall we take thoughts to defend us? Only from Christ, and only in Him will we find them. For if the heart of a believer in Christ accuses him and reprimands him and witnesses against him that he has done evil, he will immediately turn away from evil and will take his refuge in Christ and say, "Christ has done enough for me. He is just. He is my defense. He has died for me. He has made His righteousness my righteousness, and my sin His sin. If He has made my sin to be His sin, then I do not have it, and I am free. If He has made His righteousness my righteousness, then I am righteous now with the same righteousness as He. My sin cannot devour Him, but it is engulfed in the unfathomable depths of His righteousness, for He himself is God, who is blessed forever." Thus we can say, "God is greater than our heart" (1 John 3:20). The Defender is greater than the accuser, immeasurably greater. It is God who is my defender. It is my heart that accuses me. Is this the relation? Yes, yes, even so! "Who shall bring any charge against God's elect?" It is as if he were saying: "No one." Why? Because "It is God who justifies." "Who is to condemn?" No one. Why? Because "It is Christ Jesus (who is also God) who died, yes, who was raised from the dead, etc." Therefore, "If God is for us, who is against us?" (Rom. 8:33, 34, 31).

21. *You who teach others teach not yourself.* How is it possible that a person teaches another person and does not first know something himself or is not taught himself? He who teaches must first know and be taught what he teaches others. But the apostle indicates very clearly that he is speaking here of the spiritual doctrine and instruction in the Law, in which those who are teaching others merely according to the letter are not instructing themselves, I say they do not instruct themselves, to say nothing of others, that the works of the Law must be done with a willing and pure heart. And since the more noble, more important, and more God-pleasing parts of man (that is, heart and will) are lacking in the effort, therefore they certainly do not fulfill the Law as far as God is concerned, no matter how much they exercise the baser part, the body, in the Law against its wishes and without its own free will. And therefore Paul continues in this spirit (vv. 21-22): *You who preach that men should not steal, steal. You who say that one must not commit adultery, you commit adultery.* In the same way Paul could also have said: "You who say that one should not kill, you kill, as is apparent in the murder of Christ." The Lord speaks to the same effect in Matt. 23:2: "The scribes and the Pharisees sit on Moses' seat; so practice and observe whatever they tell you, but not what they do; for they preach but do not practice." How will we recognize that this is true, when these people appear righteous to men in their outward behavior? The Lord Himself says so in the same chapter, and this certainly was not done without works of righteousness. How, therefore, should they not do according to their works, which appear to be good, unless they should, like them, keep the Law only for appearance and according to the letter, without the heart (that is, a resisting heart), as if this were enough. This is the way "they say" (that is, they teach the Law and read it exactly as it is written; for this they are not blamed, and so the apostle does not rebuke them here for teaching the Law to others), but this is what they "do not." They cannot do the Law they teach unless they do it with a joyful and pure will, that is, with a heart that is circumcised of all evil desires, so that they do or do not keep the Law merely in the outward work but do or do not keep

it also with their will and their heart, that is, that they are free of evil works, also of the sinful lust of the heart, not only in the perfection of work, and that they are ready for good works not only from bodily necessity but also willingness of mind. So those people are teaching a correct and complete law, but they are not doing it and accomplishing it, I mean, doing it with their heart and carrying it out with their hands. From this it follows that "they bind heavy burdens, hard to bear, and lay them on men's shoulders, but they themselves will not move them with their finger." These burdens are the commandments of the Law, of which he has said above that they should keep them. But by their literal explanation they become burdens hard to bear, and then they kill and do not make alive. For as long as they teach that the Law is to be fulfilled only with work, even without the fulfillment of the heart, and when they do not show where and how this fulfillment of the Law is to be sought, then they leave those whom they teach in an impossible position, for they cannot fulfill these laws if they do not fulfill them in the heart. But these people are not moving the same laws with a finger, that is, they do not approach them with the slightest attempt of their heart, but they do them only with the external work. Hence they become people who are intent upon receiving empty honors, as the text goes on to say: "They do all their deeds to be seen by men" (Matt. 23:5). See, here Christ says that they are doing works, and yet He has said before that they are not lifting a finger. These apparently contradicting statements still agree with each other, for they are doing the works externally, and to these works attaches a desire of vainglory, but inwardly they do not move them with a finger. Such works of theirs, he has said above, should not be imitated, even though he here admits that they are good. But they are not really good. From this exposition it is clear that in this passage "doing," and in this chapter "committing adultery," "stealing," and "killing," are understood of the desires of the inner man, for the person who desires such things is before God spoken of as doing them, as is stated below in chapter 7:16, 18: "I do what I do not want," but "I cannot do what is right."

Therefore they cannot understand these words nor believe that they are such people as is stated in Acts 5:28 (believing as they do that they have not killed Christ because they had not killed Him with their own hands): "You intend to bring this man's blood upon us," and in Acts 7:52, when St. Stephen accused them of the same sin with the words, "You are the murderers of this Righteous One," they "ground their teeth against him" (Acts 7:54). Also in Prov. 30:20 these people are called "an adulteress" (the synagog, which clings to iniquity with its heart and to righteousness with its body only), "who eats" (that is, has devoured Christ by killing Him), "and wiping her mouth" (clearing herself of her sins), "says, 'I have done no wrong.' " [31] Therefore because they do not understand (as I have said) the words of the apostle nor believe that they are people who preach that one should not steal and yet steal, therefore the apostle, showing further that he is speaking spiritually about spiritual doing, continues by saying (v. 25), *Circumcision indeed is of value,* and very clearly later (v. 28), *For he is not a real Jew who is one outwardly, nor is true circumcision something external and physical,* and again (v. 27), *With the letter and circumcision you break the Law.* "With the letter," he says. Therefore you are a thief in spirit, although not according to the letter. Paul mentioned the letter especially because he wanted to indicate that he has been speaking in the spirit, so that they might understand what they should have known.

But somebody may object and say that this circumcision of the heart is brought about only by grace, for our nature, as I said above,[32] inclines toward evil, is impotent to do good, abhors rather than loves the Law, which drives toward the good and prohibits from the evil, and so by itself it has no desire for the Law but only displeasure. And thus our nature, unless helped from above, remains captive to evil lusts opposed to the Law and is full of evil desires, no matter how much it may produce works when it is prompted externally by fear of punishment or drawn by the love of things secular. But this is not the voice of nature or the old man (Ps. 119:113): "I hate double-minded men, but I love Thy law," nor this (Ps. 119:103): "How sweet are Thy words to my taste, sweeter than honey to my mouth," nor this (Ps. 19:10): "More to be desired are they than gold, even much fine gold; sweeter also than honey and drippings of the honeycomb." But these words represent the voice of the new and spiritual man, who goes on to say (Ps. 19: 11): "For Thy servant has loved them and keeps them." If these things come about through grace, does the apostle, or even the Lord Himself, accuse and charge the Jews? I answer that the whole task of the apostle and of his Lord is to humiliate the proud and to bring them to a realization of this condition, to teach them that they need

---

[31] Luther has adopted Lyra's interpretation of this passage.

[32] Cf. p. 183 above.

grace, to destroy their own righteousness so that in humility they will seek Christ and confess that they are sinners and thus receive grace and be saved. So Paul concludes below in chapter 11:32: "For God has consigned all men to disobedience, that He may have mercy upon all." However, they did not want to hear this and take it to heart. When they heard this voice, they hardened their hearts (cf. Ps. 95:8). Therefore Ps. 95:10-11 says that "they have not known" the ways of the Lord and shall not enter into His rest. The expression "they have not known" is understood in this way: "they did not want to know," just as we say "they have not done it," that is, "they did not do what they should have." This is not an excuse but a stronger accusation that they did not know, because they should have known and did not know. Paul also says in Rom. 10:16: [33] "But they have not all heeded the Gospel," which means that they did not want to heed the Gospel as they should have done.

22. *You who abhor idols, you commit sacrilege.* Sacrilege is robbing and stealing from a holy place. The Jews committed such robbery in a twofold way, first, by diverting their own heart and soul from the truth and the Spirit and subjecting it to their own ideas, second, in a way which applies even more closely to our topic. They removed the letters and words of Scripture, which is not only a holy but a holy of holies, by perverting them and giving to them a false meaning and thus casting and forming a spiritual idol from them. Ezek. 16:17 says: "You also took your fair jewels of My gold and My silver . . . and made for yourself images of men, etc." Sacrilege, therefore, it is that the inhabitants of Jerusalem took away gold and silver (that is, that they arbitrarily took over words of Scripture). But worse is the idolatry that they made idols and pictures of them for themselves, that is, stubborn concepts, dead and stiff, which they have set up in the temple of their hearts. According to the letter they abhor idols, but in spirit they not only embrace them but even fashion them for themselves. We read in Hos. 8:4: "With their silver and gold they made idols for their own destruction." And also in Hos. 6:8, "Gilead is a city of people who are making an idol" (that is, producing false and deceitful doctrine). The apostle calls this sacrilege most of all because it is not so great a sin to invent error as to introduce in the Scriptures a false interpretation, that is, to carry off its sacred character. Therefore this, too, can be understood simply, like the preceding, in this way: You are committing sacrilege in will and desire, even if not in act.

[33] Luther has Rom. 9.

26. *So if the uncircumcision keeps the precepts of the Law.* Here the apostle speaks of the uncircumcised who believe in Christ. He contrasts them with the Jews who boast of their own righteousness. In no other way would the uncircumcised keep the precepts of the Law. This is also clear from what he says below. Wishing to give a reason why the uncircumcised will condemn the Jew, he makes this distinction (v. 28): "For he is not a real Jew who is one outwardly." If "the Jew who is one outwardly" is the one who will be judged by the uncircumcised, then the uncircumcised is not a "Jew outwardly," and therefore he is in secret, namely, by faith in Christ. Otherwise he would not judge the Jew.

28. *For he is not a real Jew who is one outwardly.* We must understand this sentence in this way: Not he who according to outward appearances is a Jew is a real Jew. Neither is that true circumcision which is circumcision outwardly. But he who is a Jew in secret is a true Jew, and the circumcision of the heart is the real circumcision in spirit, not in the letter. This explains what he has said above (v. 25): "Your circumcision becomes uncircumcision," that is, a circumcision which takes place externally is no circumcision before God.

29. *Whose praise is not from men but from God.* This is the same thing as the Lord says about the self-righteous in Matt. 23:5: "They do all their deeds to be seen by men." External righteousness wins praise from people, but rebuke from God. Inner righteousness wins praise from God and rebuke and persecution from people. For the latter looks foolish or even unrighteous to people, but the former is foolish in the eyes of God and a double dose of unrighteousness.

Therefore, the lesson is this: He who has not yet escaped the praise of men and has not suffered shame, rebuke, and persecution in his actions has not yet reached complete righteousness. For this see the explanation above on the passage (Rom. 2:7) "By patience in well-doing." [34]

[34] Cf. pp. 177—179.

CHAPTER THREE

Summary: The apostle shows in what way the Jews were better than the Gentiles, demonstrating that the Gentiles as well as the Jews are in need of the grace of Christ.

1. *Then what advantage,* that is, what does he have more than the Gentile? *has the Jew,* who is one outwardly, *or what is the value,* above and beyond uncircumcision, *of circumcision?* outward circumcision in the flesh. Surely, it was not condemned or useless, was it?[1, 2] 2. *Much,* that is, there is great advantage for him and much value, *in every way,* as below in chapter 9. That is, in all ways; and it is the kind of statement one uses in making an affirmation or in taking an oath as it were. *To begin with,* especially, above all, or particularly. It is as if he were saying that this is the unique and chief reason among others which are stated below in chapter 9, *because the Jews are entrusted with,* that is, the Jew and the circumcision. Among the Jews and in the circumcision, but not among the Gentiles,[3] there were found those who accepted through their faith *the oracles of God,* in which are the promises of God. 3. *For what,* that is, does this hinder the Jew from having an advantage over the Gentile? It is as if he were saying: "Certainly not"[4]; *if some,* from the circumcision, indeed, the greater

---

[1] That is, if because of their unbelief we are compelled to say that the Jews, or the circumcision, have no advantage at all, it follows that "the faithfulness of God," who has made promises to the circumcision in His oracles, "is nullified" (Rom. 3:3). And thus because of their unbelief God is regarded as a liar, which of course is ridiculous.

[2] That is, if he is not a Jew who is so outwardly, if that is not circumcision which is outward and in the flesh, then the Jews had no advantage over the Gentiles, nor was circumcision more useful than uncircumcision. And thus it was in vain.

[3] As Ps. 147:19-20 says, "He declares His Word . . . He has not dealt thus with any other nation."

[4] If someone should object: "It is nothing that 'the oracles of God were entrusted to them,' for they made them of no effect and useless to themselves," the reply is, "This is not a detriment. It is sufficient that they remained effective for some of them."

thus the promise of mercy would not have been received. There-fore circumcision was useful in every way for the coming righ-teousness, although it did not itself justify. Then he answers the objection that the oracles of God were not believed at all there, because not all believed, and therefore the Jew had no advantage and the circumcision was of no value. His reply is: *For what if some of them were unfaithful? Has their faithlessness nullified the faithfulness of God?* (v. 3), that is, since the oracles of God were believed there, the promise surely stands. God has obligated Him-self and because He is truthful, the fulfillment of His promise is expected. But if the promise stands because of their belief, then the unbelief of some can in no way nullify the faithfulness and truthful-ness of God. Therefore circumcision profited wonderfully because through it the promise of God was initiated and confirmed, and thus the fulfillment could be expected with the greatest assurance because of God's truthfulness. Thus our Lord in John 4:22 says, "Salvation is from the Jews," although even the Jews themselves may not be saved; for in His promise God has greater concern for His own truthfulness because of the belief of a few than for the multitude of unbelievers, that He would nullify His promise. For God does not lie, but He is truthful.

2. Or we can understand this passage in the sense of the words of the Gospel, namely, that it was necessary that the Word should be spoken first to the Jews (Acts 13:46) because of the promises of God. And thus it went from the Jews also to the Gentiles. In this way circumcision was marvelously useful, because it was worthy to receive the rule of the Gospel in which the Gentiles also were later made participants. This, therefore, is "the advantage of the Jew," that they did not receive the oracles of God from the Gentiles, but rather that the Gentiles received them from the Jews. But the first interpretation is preferable. For if it refers to the words of the Gospel, there is not only an advantage for the Jew in having the words, but also the gifts and the graces were first given to them, yes, even the apostles, the leaders and the chief and more noble part of the church, are from the Jews.

The sense of the verse is that there is therefore no disadvantage for the Jew or for the circumcision in the fact that some did not believe. It is sufficient that some did believe, and through their faith the promise was fulfilled and received. Thus there was an advantage for them in that they had the oracles of God before the Gentiles did. Thus he says below in chapter 9:6, "But it is not as though the Word of God," that is, the promise, "had failed" because of the fact that many did not believe. For from this fact He seems to have cast off His people and not fulfilled His promises. But His oracles were not believed, and for this reason the Jews had no advantage over the Gentiles. But "their faithlessness will not nullify the faithfulness of God," that is, it will not be the reason why anyone should say that God is not truthful, for "He has not rejected His people whom He foreknew" (Rom. 11:2). For not all are His people who are so of the flesh, but those who are so of the promise; for them He has fulfilled the promise, because to them alone He made the promise. Therefore, let us reconstruct the statement this way:

2. *To begin with* (that is, particularly, or chiefly) *because the Jews are entrusted with the oracles of God,* that is, they became eligible to receive the promises in the Law, something which surely was not given to the Gentiles. Hence he says in chapter 15:8-9 that God has made Christ known to the Jews because He is truthful and to the Gentiles because He is merciful. For He did not promise Him to the Gentiles but to the Jews, among whom His oracles were received through faith. But you may raise the objection: If He made His promise to the circumcision or if His oracles were committed to them, then the promise should also have been made manifest to them, so that all who are of the circumcision might obtain it; otherwise He would not seem to have kept His promise and thus would seem to possess neither faithfulness nor truthfulness, indeed, He might seem not even to have made them a promise, for He is truthful and also keeps His promises, and thus the Jew has actually no advantage and God's oracles have not been entrusted to him. But now the very opposite is the case, for the circumcision has not only not obtained the promise, but the promise has even been given to others, namely, to the Gentiles; since the greater part of the circumcision did not obtain the promise. To this objection Paul replies (v. 3), *For what if some of them were unfaithful* (that is, have not received faith and the promise)? For there is no guilt except for those who were unwilling to receive the fulfillment of the promise. This does not hinder God, however, from being truthful. For God did not so promise, and His oracles were not so believed by the circumcision that it was necessary, whether they wanted to or not, for them to receive the promises. Because then the truthfulness or the faithfulness of God could not be fulfilled unless He were to bestow it upon even the reluctant

and the unwilling, which is an absurdity. And the truthfulness and faithfulness of God would then depend upon man's will, as if God would be faithful only if they had believed in Him or had been willing to receive Him. Therefore, "their unfaithfulness will not nullify the faithfulness of God," that is, because they of the circumcision were unwilling to receive the promise, even though He had made the promise to them who were of the circumcision, we must not contend that God is not truthful. It is sufficient that He has fulfilled His promise to the circumcision, that is, to some of them and not to all, but to the elect. For God cannot lie. Hence it follows: *Let God be true* (v. 4).

But if at this point you insist: whatever He may be, it is still certain that He has made His promise to the Jews, or to the circumcision, but not to the Gentiles; therefore, if He is truthful, the promise should have come to all of them; or else why did He make the promise to the circumcision when He foresaw that He was not going to give them the promise because of their unbelief? He replies to this point in chapters 9 and 11. But at this point he briefly passes over the subject, so as not to be diverted from his main concern, namely, that the promise was not made to all who are the children of Abraham, but to the elect and to those of the circumcision who are to be adopted as the sons of God.

Is. The Greek has: "God shall be" or "let God be truthful," as a statement in which we express not so much the truthfulness of God as a confession of His truthfulness, so that the meaning is: It is right that all should confess and admit that God is truthful. Therefore, let Him be so, let Him be held to be truthful and regarded as faithful in His oracles, no matter how much people refuse to believe Him. Moreover, that we must take this as an imperative is proved by the authority which he quotes, "that Thou mayest be justified," that is, "Let it be so, let all confess, let it be known to all, that Thou art just and truthful in Thy words, no matter how much unbelievers attack Thee and judge Thee, that is, condemn Thee 'in Thy words.'"

If indeed, it is one thing to say simply that God "is justified" and quite another to say that God "is justified in His words," or in His works, so also there is a difference between saying that God "is judged" and He "is judged in His words"; or again between saying that God "overcomes" and "overcomes in His words." For God in Himself can be justified by no one, since He is righteousness itself; and likewise He can be judged by no one, since He

Himself is eternal law and judgment and truthfulness; but He also in Himself conquers all things, and there is no need to wish this for Him or to bespeak it on His behalf. This is the way we also pray that His will may be done, even though it cannot be prevented.

But on the other hand God is justified in His words when we regard and accept His Word as righteous and truthful, and this takes place through faith in His words. But He is also judged in His words when His Word is treated as false and deceitful. This takes place through unbelief and "the pride and imagination of our heart," as the blessed Virgin sang (Luke 1:51). For our wisdom not only does not believe or accept the words of God, but it does not even think they are the words of God; rather it believes that it has the words of God and presumes that it is itself truthful. Such is the foolishness of Jews, heretics, and all stiff-necked men. But He also overcomes in His words when His words prevail over all who attempt the contrary, as is also the case with the Gospel, which always triumphs and always has been triumphant. For truth conquers all things. Therefore He is justified among those who in humility give up their own notion and trust in Him. But He prevails over those who refuse to believe Him and judge and contradict Him. To the former He is a sign "set for the rising," to the latter "for the fall," and "a sign that is spoken against," (Luke 2:34), that is, they judge Him—but in vain. In the same way we also pray that the will of God may be done, that is, that His Word and His work of every kind, whether favorable or adverse, may be accepted by us graciously and willingly.

Corollary

Therefore, the fulfillment of His will is actually the fulfillment of our will for which we prayed, namely, that we might will what God wills. For God wills things that are difficult and hard and far exceed our will. Thus also the justification of God in His words is actually our justification; and the judgment or condemnation of Him actually comes upon us, according to the statement, "He who does not believe will be condemned" (Mark 16:16).

And thus the meaning is: Can it be that God is not truthful just because they do not believe, that is, because they judge Him in His oracles and words and try to make Him a liar and themselves truthful? God forbid. Rather He is all the more truthful and they the greater liars, because truth conquers all the more when it is attacked; it becomes more glorious when it is held down. And it is its nature to advance when it is resisted, as is symbolized in the exodus of Israel and the drowning of Pharaoh. Therefore he says: God is indeed truthful, and man a liar, because it is written that this would happen: "that Thou mayest be justified, etc.," that is, "that Thou mayest come to be regarded as true and mayest show all men to be liars, either in justifying or conquering, that is, in justifying the godly and the believers and in conquering those who judge and those who do not believe." And thus the objection is removed which someone could raise, suggesting that circumcision seems to have been useless and believing the oracles seems to have been of no profit to the Jews, because many — and what a liar He seemed to them — did not seek this advantage. From this there follows the implied corollary that God did not fulfill His promises, because the greater part of the circumcision did not lay hold on them. Or else it follows that they are wrong in saying that God has not fulfilled His promises, and either they themselves are liars or God is. To this reasonable conclusion the apostle replies: "But what if some of them have not believed?" that is, circumcision was not useless just because they did not believe, because God has still fulfilled His promises to the circumcision, and the faithfulness of God is not nullified because of them, but rather they have thereby shown themselves to be liars, since God is truthful and man is a liar. Because He prevails when He is judged by them. *Does their faithlessness nullify the faithfulness of God?* (v. 3), that is, does it follow that because they did not receive the promise, therefore there is no reception of it at all, so that in this respect the Jews have no advantage over the Gentiles? For if this were the case, that they did not have an advantage and did not have the oracles of God entrusted to them because of the fact that many did not believe, it would surely follow that God in His promises would be a liar, for He promised these things to that people. But this conclusion is ridiculous and false. For (as chapters 9 and 11 will more clearly teach on this point) not those who are the sons of the flesh "are the descendents of Abraham" (cf. Rom. 9:7; 11:1), but those who have not believed are the liars, rather than God who has made the promise and fulfilled it, albeit not in all men, but in all the children of the promise.

4. *That Thou mayest be justified.* This authoritative statement must not be taken here in the sense and context it has in its original use in Ps. 51:4 but only insofar as it is quoted as proof of this statement, that God is truthful in His words. For originally it was written

with another purpose. The apostle, to be sure, does not disregard this, for in a passing and incidental manner he does argue from it according to the same meaning that it has in the psalm, saying, "But if our wickedness, etc." (v. 5). For there (Ps. 51:4) [1] we read that God is justified through the confession of our sin. For although He is righteous and truthful in Himself, yet this is not true in us until we confess, "Against Thee only have I sinned, etc."; for then is He alone acknowledged to be righteous. And thus He is also righteous among us.

5. *But if our wickedness*. Some people say that the righteousness of God is commended by our unrighteousness when He punishes it, for then He shows Himself to be righteous in not allowing the unrighteous to go unpunished. And this is a true statement. But it does not pertain in any way to what the apostle is discussing at this point, for he is not talking about the righteousness of God by which he himself is righteous. Rather he is actually denying that the righteousness of God is commended by our unrighteousness, or if he affirms this, it is only in the sense of the psalm, which says, "Against Thee only have I sinned etc." But yet the psalm is not trying to say that our sin justifies God, but rather that confession and acknowledgment of sin humble the proud and righteous man who trusts in his own righteousness and for this reason downgrades the righteousness of God, who alone possesses righteousness along with virtue and wisdom and every good thing. Therefore he who humbly repudiates his own righteousness and confesses that he is a sinner before God truly glorifies God, proclaiming that He alone is righteous. Therefore it is not our unrighteousness, which God forever hates as the enemy of His own glory, but it is the recognition and confession of our own unrighteousness which glorifies God and commends us to Him, for this proves the necessity and saving nature of His righteousness. But others say that our unrighteousness commends the righteousness of God incidentally,[2] "just as opposites which are placed beside one another shine more brightly," as shadows and colors in a picture. But the apostle denies entirely that our unrighteousness commends the righteousness of God in any way at all, but it only seems this way to carnal men from the words of the psalm. This is evident from the

---

[1] See Luther's exposition of this passage, W, III, 284 ff.

[2] *Per accidens.* Lyra uses this expression in contrast to *per se* and quotes the illustration from Aegidius Romanus, who gives Aristotle, *De sophisticis elenchis*, 15, as the source. Luther rejects Lyra's solution also on p. 212 below.

apostle's words when he cites the psalm "that Thou mayest be justified," for from this he infers not the righteousness but the truthfulness of God.

Hence he is not speaking here of the righteousness by which he is righteous himself, but of that by which He who is righteous makes us righteous, and He Himself alone is righteous with respect to us; for our unrighteousness, if it truly has become ours (that is, by being acknowledged and confessed), does commend His righteousness, for it humbles us, makes us bow before our God and seek His righteousness; and when we have received it, we glorify, praise, and love God who has imparted it to us. On the other hand, when our righteousness disparages the righteousness of God, and even destroys and denies it and argues that it is lying and false, as when, for example, we resist the words of God and regard His righteousness as unnecessary and believe in the sufficiency of our own, then we have to say, "Against Thee, Thee only, have I sinned . . . so that Thou art justified" (that is, "that Thou alone mayest be extolled with praise and glory as our righteous Justifier") "in Thy sentence" (Ps. 51:4), that is, "as Thou hast promised and testified."

7. *For God's truthfulness.* That is, if we are to understand that the truthfulness of God is glorious while I am a liar, and the righteousness of God is glorious while I commit unrighteousness (for that is what it means *to speak in a human way* [v. 6], and this is what they thought who said: "Why not do evil?" [3]), how then does God punish the world and condemn me as a sinner, when He really ought to be putting a crown on my head, since His righteousness and truthfulness and glory increase more and more because of this, which is surely in accord with His will? And therefore in doing evil we do His will. Actually, by a question of this kind the apostle forbids such an interpretation of the matter. It is not as the words sound or "in a human way," but, as we have said, it is a matter of righteousness and unrighteousness. Therefore the righteousness of God is not commended because I commit unrighteousness but rather because I confess that I have done unrighteousness and cease to do it, and thus embrace the righteousness of God or what comes from God, since even my righteousness is unrighteousness before Him. Thus I have no glory but only shame before God.

---

[3] Luther has apparently telescoped the passage when he writes *faciamus bonum* for *faciamus mala ut veniant bona* (v. 8).

And thus in the righteousness by which He Himself justifies me He alone is glorified, because He alone is justified (that is, He is acknowledged to be righteous). We must speak the same way about truthfulness, for the truthfulness of God is not glorified because I am a liar but because I recognize that I am a liar and cease being one by embracing the truth which comes from God, so that through it and not through my own truthfulness I may be made truthful, my self-glorification may cease, and only God may be glorified in me, for He alone has rendered, or made, me truthful, because even my truthfulness is a lie before Him.

Now, what we have said here about truthfulness and lying, righteousness and unrighteousness, must be applied to all other perfections and their opposites, for example, strength and weakness, wisdom and foolishness, innocence and sin, etc. For there is an unending controversy about all of these things between God and proud men, especially the Jews, for God in His mercy desires the Jews and all men for the very reason that they are liars, unrighteous, foolish, weak, sinful men to be made truthful, righteous, wise, strong, innocent men through His truthfulness, righteousness, wisdom, strength, and innocence, and thus to be freed from lying, unrighteousness, foolishness, weakness, and sin, in order that His truthfulness, righteousness, wisdom, strength, and innocence may be glorified and commended in them and by them. Then those haughty people, being men who consider themselves truthful, righteous, wise, strong, and innocent by their own powers and of themselves, refuse and speak against God and thus with all their might judge Him and make Him the liar, the unrighteous, foolish, and weak sinner. For they want to establish their own truthfulness, righteousness, wisdom, virtue, and innocence, and they refuse to be looked upon as liars, unrighteous, foolish, weak sinners. Therefore either God or they must be the liars, the unrighteous, and the weak, etc.

This is like the case of the doctor (as Persius [4] tells us) who wishes to heal his patient, but finds that he is a man who denies that he is sick, calling the doctor a fool and an even sicker person than himself for presuming to cure a healthy man. And because of the man's resistance the doctor cannot get around to recommending his skill and his medicine. For he could do so only if the sick man

---

[4] Cf. Persius, *Satires*, III, 90 ff.

would admit his illness and permit him to cure him by saying, "I certainly am sick in order that you may be praised, that is, be a man of health and be spoken of as such, that is, when you have healed me."

Thus these ungodly and arrogant men, although they are sick before God, seem most healthy to themselves. Therefore they not only reject God as their physician, but they even regard Him as a fool and a liar and even sicker than themselves for presuming to heal such wonderfully healthy men and treating them as if they were sick. However, they are not reproving God in His absolute sense, in His essence (since no creature can do this, not even a malicious one), but in His words. Hence he correctly adds the expression, "So that Thou art justified in Thy words." For the words of God which had been sent to them by Him were regarded by them as not from God, but rather as foolish, lying, and stupid. For through His Word He undertook to heal them. They, however, denied that they were sick, considered Him as foolish and sicker than themselves, resisted Him, spoke against Him, judged and condemned Him. But in vain. For His words prevail when they are thus judged, or rather God prevails in words such as those when He is judged by men in them. For because of the fact that they reject Him, it is perfectly clear that they regard Him as foolish and stupid and weak, while they are confessing of themselves that they love nothing but wisdom, virtue, and truth, as if they were saying: "Surely He is not wise, is He, when He thinks that we are foolish? Rather, He is the foolish one, for we possess wisdom for ourselves and follow it. And so it is with all other things. Surely He (that is, God or His Word) is not truthful, righteous, and strong when He contends that we are liars, unrighteous men, and weaklings, whereas we really cling to truthfulness, righteousness, and strength! Actually He Himself is such a person, because He does not know, as we do, where alone these good things are." Thus in the Gospel, in the same manner, they said of Christ (John 9:24), "We know that this man is a sinner," and again (John 9:16), "This man is not from God." Whence also it is said in Ps. 4:6: "Many there are who say, 'O that we might see some good!' " as if to say, "Since we know what is good, anyone who presumes to teach us otherwise must himself be in error, and he will not show us good things." Thus we read in John 9:40-41, "Are we also blind?" And Jesus says, "If you were blind, you would have no guilt. But now that you say, 'We see,' your guilt remains."

Therefore we conclude that

| God in His words cannot be | wise righteous truthful strong good | unless we believe Him and submit to Him by confessing that we are | foolish unrighteous liars weak evil |

Therefore we need humility and faith. What these words seek to establish and maintain is solely this, that inwardly we become nothing, that we empty ourselves of everything, humble ourselves and say with the prophet, "Against Thee, Thee only, have I sinned, so that Thou art justified in Thy words." "In Thy sight I am foolish and weak, so that Thou mayest be wise and powerful in Thy words." For all creation teaches that "there is no need of a physician except for those who are sick" (cf. Matt. 9:12), that no sheep is sought except the one who is lost (Luke 15:4), that no one is freed except the captive, that no one is enriched except the pauper, that no one is made strong except the weak, that no one is exalted except the man who has been humbled, nothing is filled except that which is empty, that nothing is built except that which has been torn down. As the philosophers say: a thing is not brought into form unless there is first a lack of form or a change of previous form; again, a "potential idea" does not receive a form unless at its inception it has been stripped of all form and is like a *tabula rasa.*[5]

Therefore, since every creature proclaims this, it cannot happen that he who is filled with his own righteousness can be filled with the righteousness of God, who fills none but the hungry and the thirsty. Therefore he who is sated with his own truth and wisdom is incapable of receiving the truth and wisdom of God, which can be received only in an empty and destitute heart. Hence, let us say to God: "O how willingly we are empty that Thou mayest dwell in us! How gladly weak that Thy power may dwell in me; gladly a sinner that Thou mayest be justified in me; gladly foolish that Thou mayest be my wisdom; gladly unrighteous that Thou mayest be my righteousness!" Behold, this is the meaning of the statement, "Against Thee have I sinned . . . so that Thou art justified in Thy words" (Ps. 51:4).

And thus to sum up the matter: God is justified in three ways.

---

[5] Cf. Aristotle, *Physics,* I, 5—7. See also Ficker's note, W, LVI, 218, n. 22. The picture of the "slate on which nothing has as yet been written" *(tabula rasa)* to signify a neutral position of the human mind before "knowledge" enters is used in Aristotle, *De anima,* III, 4, and subsequently by many philosophical writers.

First, when He punishes the unrighteous. For then He shows that He is righteous and His righteousness is manifested and commended through the punishment of our unrighteousness. But this is a moderate commendation, because even the ungodly punish the ungodly.

The second way is incidental, or relative, as when opposites which are placed along side each other shine more brightly than when placed by themselves. In the same way the righteousness of God is the more beautiful, the fouler our unrighteousness is. But at this point the apostle is not referring to these ideas, because this is the internal and formal righteousness of God.

Third, when He justifies the ungodly and pours out His grace upon them, or when it is believed that He is righteous in His words. For through such believing He justifies, that is, He accounts people righteous. Hence this is called the righteousness of faith and the righteousness of God. In the same way a good craftsman is commended in three ways. First, when he criticizes the inexperienced and reproves them when they make mistakes. Second, when in comparison with them he appears better trained than they. Third, when he transmits the perfection of his skill to others who did not yet possess it. And this is the true commendation. For to reprove others or to appear as a craftsman, this is not being a praiseworthy artist, but to cause others to become artists, this is being a truly good artist. In the same way, God is truly praiseworthy for being righteous in us. But just as inexperienced men refuse to be taught, so also proud men do not wish to be justified.

God is justified and shown to be truthful in three ways.

First, when He punishes and condemns the unrighteous, the liar, the fool, etc. For then He shows that He is righteous and truthful, etc. And so also His righteousness and truthfulness are commended and glorified through our unrighteousness and lying, because it is made manifest. But this is a moderate commendation, for even a liar often punishes and criticizes another liar, and an unrighteous man another unrighteous man, and yet he is not therefore immediately honored as completely truthful and righteous.

Second, in a relative way. Just as opposites show themselves to greater advantage when they are placed next to each other than when placed by themselves, so also His righteousness is the more beautiful, the fouler our unrighteousness is. The apostle is not speaking of these two modes, because this is the internal and formal righteousness of God, about which he is not speaking.

Third, in an effective way, that is, when we cannot be justified of ourselves and come to Him, so that He Himself makes us righteous when we confess that we cannot overcome our sin. He does this, when we believe His words; for through such believing He justifies us, that is, He accounts us as righteous. Hence it is called the righteousness of faith and the righteousness of God which works effectively in us.

Corollary

The apostle is by no means saying here that "our wickedness serves to show the righteousness of God" (v. 5), but rather he is denying it, for it is not true. However, he is asking the question in the name of those people who thought that this followed from the words of the psalm. But it does not follow. For neither the psalm nor the apostle are trying to say that our sin justifies or commends God, but rather it is our acknowledgment and confession of sin. Hence he says, "For I know my transgressions, etc." (Ps. 51:3), and then follow the words, "Against Thee, Thee only, have I sinned" (that is, "I recognize that before Thee alone I am a sinner." For this admission makes the righteousness of God something to be sought after and this confession makes it commendable. For when I acknowledge that I cannot be righteous before God because it is written, "No man living is righteous before Thee" [Ps. 143:2], and in other places there are many similar statements by which God tells us that we are in our sins), then I begin to seek my righteousness from Him. And thus the acknowledgment of my sin convinced me that God is justified in me (that is, that I should believe in Him and thus He would justify me). And the confession of this then commends and glorifies Him, because He alone is just and our justifier. But He is not commended in this way where sin is not confessed or acknowledged, or where His righteousness is not sought by those who are satisfied and pleased with their own.

For this is similar to a good craftsman who can be commended in three ways. First, when he criticizes and rebukes those who do not understand his art. But this is a small and insolent commendation. Second, when in comparison with others (even though he does not criticize them) he shows himself to be more experienced than they. Third, when he bestows the perfection of his art on those who seek it, because they could not possess it of themselves. This is the true commendation. For to blame others and to appear as an artist, this does not make the greatest artist. But to produce artists similar to oneself, this makes a praiseworthy craftsman. For the first way often involves arrogance and pride, the second envy and presumption. But the third way is true kindliness and generosity. So God is righteous by working in us and praiseworthy because He makes us like Himself.

But just as that craftsman cannot pass on his skill to those who do not have confidence in him and those who are well satisfied with their own skill, and just as he cannot draw praise and commendation from them for his art and mastery unless they first recognize their own lack of skill and believe him when he asserts that they are unskillful — but their pride will not let them believe him — so the ungodly do not believe that they are ungodly and thus do not acknowledge the fact. Hence they do not allow God to be justified in them, or to be declared truthful, and thus glorified or commended.

A Brief Summary

Then what advantage have the Jews? (v. 1), that is, the one who is a Jew outwardly and according to the letter. For if he is not regarded as a Jew, he is then equal in every respect to the Gentiles and has no advantage. *Or what is the value of circumcision?* (v. 1), that is, in the flesh and according to the letter. For if it is not regarded as circumcision, as has been said in the preceding chapter, then has it been useless? *Much* (v. 2), it is of advantage and very useful. *In every way* (v. 2). This is either an assertion and a kind of oath, or it expresses the ways in which circumcision is useful, which he enumerates below in chapter 9:4, when he says, "To them belong the sonship, the giving of the Law, the glory, the covenant, the worship, and the promises; to them belong the patriarchs, etc." *To begin with*, that is, one of the ways, which I now take up first. *The Jews are entrusted with the oracles of God* (v. 2). For the Gentiles did not have this, just as they did not have other things, as Ps. 147:20 says, "He has not dealt thus with any other nation." For this together with other things the Jew alone had as an advantage over the Gentiles, even those who were Jews outwardly and according to the letter. "Entrusted," that is, received through faith. For all Jews received the promises, although not all received the fulfillment. "Oracles," that is, the promises, as he calls them below in chapter 9. The apostle does not have the words "to them" in his text, but it can stand and can refer to "Jew" and to "circumcision" in verse 1. In this sense he says below in chapter

15:8, "Christ became a servant to the circumcised," but not to the Gentiles, "to show God's truthfulness," that is, because God had promised this to them and not to the Gentiles.

What if some were unfaithful? (v. 3). This expression "were unfaithful" *(non crediderunt)* must be taken in an absolute sense and differently from the term "entrusted" used above, for it must not be understood with reference to "oracles." For all of them received the oracles and promises of God, and to this day they are still awaiting the promises of this kind concerning the sending of Christ. Therefore they did believe, but not in the sense that they became believers in Christ and were faithful to Him. The meaning is this: what does it matter?[6] What can we do about it? Who will be harmed by this except them? For surely it will not harm God or us. For it is manifest that neither God's truth nor our faith will be nullified because of their unbelief.

Does their faithlessness nullify the faithfulness of God? (v. 3), that is, the truthfulness and fidelity of God. He says all these things because when he has said that the promises have been committed to the circumcision which is in the flesh and to the Jew who is one outwardly, someone could raise the objection: How then did anyone who is a Jew outwardly and according to the letter receive the promise? For if the promises were to the carnal and literal Jew (in which they do excel the Gentiles) and if none of this kind of Jew has received the promise, but they are lacking it to this very day, then it would seem that they did not have the promise or that God did not fulfill it; for the Jew of the flesh should have received the promise, because it was made to the flesh. The apostle meets this objection and in a sense pounds on one nail with another when he says: "Is the truth of God nullified, is His promise done away, and are His words made vain?" This is impossible, and so also is that which follows from it. To be sure, the apostle does not settle this argument here but defers it to chapter 9. And there he shows how the Israel of the flesh, which at the same time is both the Israel of the promise and election and the Israel of the flesh, obtained the fulfillment, but Israel which is only of the flesh and only according to the seed did not obtain it at all. Therefore even their unbelief cannot annul the faithfulness of God. And thus he sets aside this objection and puts it out of sight, but only for the present; and he gives his attention to the truthfulness of God,

---

[6] Luther uses the German expression *Was leit daran?*

which he had raised up against the objection, and asserts that He has fulfilled His promises everywhere.

By no means (v. 4). He gives the title "Faithfulness of God" to the promise then fulfilled through Christ, according to the statement in Ps. 85:11, "Faithfulness has sprung up from the ground" (that is, the promised Christ has appeared, being born of the Virgin).[7] Therefore the meaning is: God has now fulfilled His promises and is shown to be truthful, and they do not believe Him or receive the promises. Therefore will it be untrue that God has fulfilled His promises, and will this truth which has now been made manifest be taken away, and will it be said that the promise has not been fulfilled, only because they have not believed? By no means. For then the apostles, rather God in the apostles, would be lying when He testifies that He has fulfilled His promises in Christ. But according to my understanding I believe that "faith" (*fides*) here does not refer to the faithfulness of God but means trust in God, which is the actual fulfillment of the promise, as it is clearly seen in many passages. For it is the righteousness which comes from faith which has been promised, for example, in Rom. 1:17, "The righteous shall live by faith." But this difference does not involve a contradiction. For whatever is said concerning the objective truth of faith in a literal sense, the same is understood in a moral sense concerning our faith in this truth. And thus the meaning is entirely clear, namely, what does it matter that they do not believe? Shall we therefore give up faith in God and follow them by denying the fulfillment of the promise rather than believing God when He asserts that He has fulfilled it? The proper answer follows: By no means. We will not follow them, but will cling to the faithfulness of God. *For God is truthful* (v. 4), and therefore we must believe Him. *Though every man be false* (v. 4), and therefore we must not believe or follow him. Or, as the Greek says, "Let God be true" (that is, let us believe God rather than man, for man is a liar). Thus he has removed that objection according to which someone said that fleshly Israel did not receive the promises, and yet they were given to it; therefore they have not been fulfilled as yet. Therefore, do these men speak the truth, and God falsehood? God forbid. They say no, God says yes. The answer is, we must believe God rather than men, because He is truthful. *As it is written*, that is, we must believe Him, following the Greek text, because to be justi-

---

[7] Luther writes almost the same words in his early Psalm Lectures on this passage. Cf. W, IV, 2, 22 f.

fied is to believe, as we shall point out below. *That Thou mayest be justified in Thy words and prevail when Thou art judged* (v. 4). The apostle adduces this authority according to the sense, not according to the reason for the sense, that is, it should be understood in terms of what it points out and not in terms of why it is said, as if one were to say: "Thou wilt be justified in Thy words and Thou wilt prevail when Thou art judged," although later on he makes a digression and does deal with the causal meaning of this passage. Thus God is justified in His words, that is, when we believe Him in the Gospel concerning the fulfillment of the promise, so that He is regarded as truthful and righteous. For these words of His in which He is justified are the word of the Gospel, when people believe Him, that He speaks the truth in them and that what is prophesied in this Word will come to pass. Not only will He be justified by those who believe, but He will also overcome when He is judged, that is, when He is reproved by those who deny that Christ has been sent and that the promises have been fulfilled. For they judge these words and condemn them and never consider them as righteous, that is, they never believe that these words are righteous and true, indeed, they even judge and condemn God in these words, while others justify Him. But these people shall not prevail. For He prevails and obtains the victory, because no matter how much they resist, this faithfulness of God, this "justification of God in His words" (that is, this trust in His Word) continues. The justification of God and trust in God are the same thing. For He prevails and remains, indeed He always goes forward and increases, while they who do not believe will fail and perish.

That "God is justified in His words" (Ps. 51:4) means that He is made just and true in His words or that His words are made just and true. And this takes place in believing them, accepting them, and holding them as true and just. The only thing that can resist this justification is the pride of the human heart through unbelief. For this pride does not justify but condemns and judges. Therefore it does not believe His words, since it does not regard them as true. And it does not regard them as true because it regards its own understanding, which is contrary to them, as true. Hence for God to be judged in His words is the same as that He Himself or His words are condemned and thus become lying and unjust. This takes place through arrogant unbelief and rebellion. For thus it is obvious that this justification and judgment of God are outside of God and His Word, that is, in men. For intrinsically both God and His words are righteous and true. But they have not as yet become such in us until our wisdom yields to them and in faith gives them a place and accepts them. Thus it says in Ps. 51:4: "Against Thee have I sinned," that is, "I yield my righteousness and my understanding, which resists and condemns Thy words, and I confess that I am a sinner, unrighteous, and lying, in order that Thy words may have a place in me, be justified, be true, and become true," that they may become in us what they are in themselves, because in themselves they are justified oracles.

Corollary

Through the fact that "God is justified" we are justified. And this passive justification of God by which He is justified by us is our active justification by God. For He regards that faith which justifies His words as righteousness, as it says in chapter 4:5 and in chapter 1:17, "The just shall live by faith." And on the contrary, the passive justification of God, by which He is judged by unbelievers is their own condemnation. For He rejects as unrighteousness and damnation that unbelief by which they judge and condemn His words. Thus it agrees with the Hebrew, which puts it this way: "Against Thee have I sinned, because Thou wilt justify," [8] that is, Thou wilt bring justification, "in Thy Word and wilt cleanse when Thou art judged." For He justifies, overcomes, in His Word when He makes us to be like His Word, that is, righteous, true, wise, etc. And He thus changes us into His Word, but not His Word into us. And He makes us such when we believe His Word is such, that is, righteous and true. For then there is a similar form of the Word and the believer, that is, truth and righteousness. Therefore when He is justified, He justifies, and when He justifies, He is justified. And thus the same idea is expressed by an active word in the Hebrew and a passive word in our translation.[9] Moreover, God overcomes, that is, He prevails and shows that they all are finally liars and false who do not believe, that is, those who dishonor Him by their judgment, as is manifest in the case of the Jews and will be even more evident at the judgment. Hence, the Hebrew text says, "And Thou wilt cleanse," that is, Thou wilt make a cleansing, "when Thou art judged," that is, Thou wilt make Thy Word clean and those

[8] For the Vulgate's passive *iustificeris* Luther here supports the active form *iustificabis* as promoted by Reuchlin in his *Septem psalmi poenitentiales hebraici cum grammatica tralacione latina*, 1512.

[9] The Vulgate.

who believe in it, and at the same time Thou wilt make Thyself clean in them and wilt gain approbation from the lie which these unbelievers impose upon Thee, and actually Thou wilt defile them, that is, Thou wilt show that they are filthy liars, that is, that their unbelief does not nullify the faithfulness of God.

Corollary

The passive and active justification of God and the faith or belief in Him are the same thing. For the fact that we declare His words righteous is His gift, and because of the same gift He Himself regards us as righteous, that is, He justifies us. And we do not declare His words righteous unless we believe that they are righteous.

But if our wickedness serves to show the righteousness of God (v. 5). This question arises for two reasons, namely, that the authority of Ps. 51 happens to be cited and that the substance and source of the material itself which is being dealt with are such as they are. For the psalm, because it speaks causally (at least in our translation [10] and in the Septuagint) when it says, "that Thou mayest be justified," can appear to a man to be saying that we have sinned in order that God may be justified, and that for this reason we must sin in order that God may be glorified. But the subject under discussion intends to say that God, or His words, cannot be justified and made truthful unless we are made liars and unrighteous men, since they are contrary to us, and it is in this sense that He is made righteous through our sin.

The solution is that the apostle is speaking in the Spirit, and thus is not understood except by those who are in the Spirit. Hence the solution of Lyra, that sin is capable of an effect on the commendation of God incidentally,[11] is not valid, especially if one is thinking of the inner truthfulness of God or of His words, because sin is not capable of an effect on the glory of the truth of God either in its own right [12] or incidentally. But in a moral, or tropological, sense,[13] sin in its own right and in a proper sense is capable of an effect on the commendation of the truthfulness of God, that is, the

---

[10] The Vulgate.

[11] *Per accidens.* Cf. p. 200, n. 2, above.

[12] *Per se.*

[13] For the modes of medieval interpretation, see *Luther's Works,* 1, p. 87, n. 10. A discussion of these modes by Luther is found in his 1519 commentary on Galatians, *Luther's Works,* 27, pp. 311—312.

trust by which we believe God when He says that we are in sins, even though our reason may not know it or believe it—this very thing which confirms us as sinners and gives glory to God by our acceptance of His words of grace and truth as necessary for us. For who would receive the grace and righteousness except the person who confesses that he has sin?

Corollary

The expression "that Thou mayest be justified in Thy words" means the same as the expression "God is truthful though every man be false"; and the clause "that Thou mayest prevail when Thou art judged" has the same meaning as the expression "Does their faithlessness nullify the faithfulness of God?" as is evident from the words. Thus he is correct in putting between these clauses the term *as it is written* (v. 4), establishing both points by Scripture.

Likewise, just as it is said that God or His words are justified, when in faith we believe them to be just and truthful (which they are in themselves even without our faith), so also we must understand that we have to become sinners and liars and fools and that all our righteousness, truthfulness, wisdom, and strength have to perish. And this takes place when we believe that we are sinners and liars, etc., and that our virtue and righteousness are absolutely nothing before God. Thus we become inwardly, inside ourselves, what we are outwardly [14] (that is, before God), even though inside ourselves we are not this way, that is, even though we do not believe that we are such. For as God alone is truthful and righteous and powerful in Himself, so also He wishes to be such outside Himself, that is, in us, so that He may thus be glorified (for it is the glory of any good thing which is in anyone, that it be poured out of itself upon other people), so He wills that just as every man by himself is a liar, unrighteous, and weak outwardly (that is, before God), so he may become such inwardly, that is, he may confess and acknowledge himself to be such as he actually is. And thus God through His own coming forth causes us to enter into ourselves, and through this understanding of Him He gives to us also an understanding of ourselves. For unless God had first come forth and sought to be truthful in us, we could not have entered into ourselves and be made liars and unrighteous men. For man of himself could not know that he is such a person before God, unless God

---

[14] The inward-outward parallelisms of this paragraph imitate the language of the mystics, especially that of the sermons of Johann Tauler (d. 1361).

Himself had revealed it to him. "For who has known the mind of
the Lord, or who has been His counselor?" (Rom. 11:34). Otherwise
man would always believe that he is truthful, righteous, and wise,
especially because in his own eyes and before his fellowmen he is
such. But now God has revealed what He thinks about us and what
He judges us to be, namely, that all are in sin. Therefore we have
to yield to this His revelation, His words, and believe and thus declare them righteous and true and thereby also confess that we ourselves are sinners according to them (a fact we did not know before).
Thus the apostle says (1 Cor. 3:18): "If anyone among you thinks
that he is wise in this age, let him become a fool, that he may become wise." Moreover, what he says concerning foolishness must
be understood of all other imperfections, so that he who wants to
be righteous, truthful, and powerful must become a sinner, a liar,
and a weakling. This pathway is spiritual, not physical or natural,
that is, our whole self-understanding must be destroyed, for it
causes us to misjudge ourselves so badly. Therefore "He has
scattered the proud in the imagination of their hearts" (Luke 1:51).
This is all "the strength He has shown." Hence it follows that this
statement is entirely spiritual when it teaches us to become sinners.
However, when the apostle taught it, many took it in a literal and
carnal sense as to how he becomes a sinner who previously was
righteous, as he says in what follows in this passage.

The same idea also runs through Ps. 51, when it says, "For
I know my transgressions" (v. 3). Therefore, the following thought
is "against Thee have I sinned" (v. 4), that is, I confess that I am
a sinner before Thee, although before men I am righteous. However, I do not for this reason escape being a sinner against Thee,
"so that Thou art justified" (v. 4), that is, that it may come to pass
that I believe Thy words, whereby I, too, am justified. Later on it
speaks of the "uncertain and hidden things of Thy wisdom" (v. 6),
that is, Thou hast revealed to me these hidden things, namely,
that before Thee we are sinners and had nothing of ourselves.
Corollary: The passage "Against Thee only have I sinned" (Ps.
51:4), is not satisfactorily explained by certain men [15] who understand it as if David had spoken this way, because princes have no
one over them except God to whom they can confess and by whom
they can be punished. No, he is speaking for his own person as a
spiritual man, in the way that all men ought to speak, as in Ps. 32:6,
"Therefore (namely, because of the impiety of his sin) let everyone

15 The reference is to the *Glossa ordinaria* and to Lyra.

who is godly offer prayer to Thee," that is, whoever wishes to be holy will confess that he is a sinner and ungodly, and to those who say, "I will confess to Thee," "Thou didst forgive the guilt of their sin" (Ps. 32:5). Hence 1 John 1:10, "If we say we have not sinned, we make God a liar" (which is a double sin). "But if we confess our sins, He is faithful and just and will forgive our sins" (1 John 1:9). And again, "If we say we have no sin, we deceive ourselves, and the truth is not in us" (1 John 1:8). Therefore let us say with the prophet, "And my mouth shall show forth Thy praise" (Ps. 51:15), not ours. And again, "My tongue will sing aloud of Thy righteousness" (Ps. 51:14), not our own.

Therefore, it has now been sufficiently demonstrated that God alone is truthful and that every man is a liar. Thus "Their faithlessness" should not "nullify the faithfulness of God." What effect does it have on our faith that they do not believe? Surely we must not on that account give up our faith, and the faithfulness of God has not been removed; but rather they themselves are liars.

Corollary

Even if we do not recognize any sin in ourselves, it is still necessary to believe that we are sinners. Hence the apostle says, "I am not aware of anything against myself, but I am not thereby justified" (1 Cor. 4:4). For just as through faith the righteousness of God lives in us, so through the same faith sin also lives in us, that is, by faith alone we must believe that we are sinners, for it is not manifest to us, indeed, we often do not seem to ourselves to be aware of the fact. Therefore we have to stand under the judgment of God and believe His words with which He says that we are unrighteous, because He Himself cannot lie. And thus it must be, even though it is not apparent, "For faith is the conviction of things not seen" (Heb. 11:1), and it is content with the words of God alone. And it has been foretold that the reign of Christ will be in this humility and judgment. For thus "He will execute judgment among the nations" (Ps. 110:6). And "there thrones for judgment were set" (Ps. 122:5), for we must strenuously accuse, judge, and condemn ourselves and confess that we are sinful, so that God may be justified in us. The same faith is described in such words as these, "Clear Thou me from hidden faults. Who can discern his errors?" (Ps. 19:12). Likewise, "Remember not my transgressions" (Ps. 25:7).

But we must also seriously consider the fact that it is not sufficient to confess with the mouth that one is sinner, unrighteous, liar, and fool. For what is easier, especially when you are at peace and live without temptation? But when you have confessed with your mouth that you are such a person, then you must also earnestly feel the same way about yourself in your heart, and you must conduct yourself in this manner in every act and in your entire life. For this reason he is a very rare man who confesses and believes that he is a sinner. For how is he to confess that he is a sinner if he is unwilling to endure even a word of criticism against himself or his actions or his ideas, but immediately rushes into the controversy and does not even confess with his mouth that he is a liar but rather contends that he is truthful and well-intentioned and that he has been wickedly resisted and falsely accused? But if he is compelled to endure something, he becomes furious and wears everyone out by complaining of the injury which he alone of all people has suffered. Look at the hypocrite who confesses that he is a sinner but is willing to do and to suffer nothing which befits a sinner but only that which is proper for a righteous man and a saint.

And thus we are all ready to say: "I am a most wretched sinner." But seldom if ever does a man want to be a sinner. For what is it to be a sinner if not to be worthy of all punishment and trouble? And to confess with your mouth that you are such a person but to be unwilling to act like a sinner, this is hypocrisy, this is lying. For it befits a righteous man to have peace, glory, honor, and all good things. Therefore, if you deny that you are righteous, you must also deny these good things. And if you confess that you are a sinner, you must take punishments, injuries, and ignominy as your own and your rightful possessions. But you must flee those things as belonging to someone else which belong only to a righteous man. Therefore if shame or an insulting word, if a beating or an injury, if condemnation or disease befall you, and you say: "I do not deserve it, why must I endure it? An injury has been done me; I am innocent," are you not thereby denying that you are a sinner, are you not resisting God and with your own mouth convicting yourself as a liar? For with all these things (as with His words when "He spoke and it came to be" [Ps. 33:9]) God is proving and asserting that you are a sinner, because He brings to you the things which befit sinners. And He cannot err or lie. But you rise up and contradict Him, resisting and opposing Him, as if God were the one who was acting wickedly, foolishly, and dishonestly. And thus you are like those of whom we spoke above, "for those who are factious and do not obey the truth but obey wickedness" (Rom. 2:8). For you also do not obey the truth (that is, the works of God which have rightly come against you).

But if you say when these things happen: "Indeed, I surely deserve these things, I have been justly treated, I freely admit that I am truly a sinner, so that all these things are just and true; I have certainly sinned against Thee, so that Thy actions and Thy words are justified, and Thou art the truthful and righteous God; Thou art not mistaken concerning me, there is no lying in Thee. For just as in all these things Thou dost show that I am a sinner, so it is true, I am indeed a sinner." Behold, this is simply saying, "Against Thee have I sinned and done that which is evil in Thy sight, so that Thou art justified in Thy words," (Ps. 51:4). Likewise in Daniel 3 [16] we read "All things that Thou hast brought upon us Thou hast done in true judgment, for we have sinned against Thee, etc." It is similar to a situation in which two men are fighting over something, and one of them humbly gives in and says, "I freely admit that you are right and truthful. I am willing to be the one who was wrong, I am willing to be the one who did the wrong, that you might be the one who did right and thought right." Will not the other man say, "I have wronged you. You are right"? For thus they will be of one mind, and otherwise because of their argument they would have remained at odds. Thus it is surely true, "Do not be haughty with one another" (Rom. 12:16).

For this reason I say, how unusual and difficult it is to become a sinner and to speak this verse truly from the heart. For no one is eager to be contradicted in his thinking, reproved in his actions, or despised in his wisdom. However, he who would do this and would say, "Teach me differently, I beg you, and I will gladly do differently," if he would thus always avoid contention, how blessed he would be! But the arrogance of our mind and will is much too great. No one is entirely free of this plague, particularly when things suddenly go against us.

But we have to say something about the way in which a man must spiritually become a sinner. It is not a natural way. For that way every man does not become a sinner but is one. But all the force necessary to bring about this change lies hidden in our mind

---

[16] These additions to Daniel 3 are found in The Prayer of Azariah, 8 and 6.

or in our self-estimation and our opinion of ourselves. Every statement in Scripture and every action of God has the purpose of changing this mind. For here is the "evil eye" (Matt. 20:15) and the incorrigible pride (humanly speaking). Hence the blessed Virgin says, "He has shown strength with His arm. He has scattered the proud in the imagination of their hearts" (Luke 1:51), that is, in a heart which is pleased to be opposed to God in its thinking and self-estimation. Hence this thinking is called "the counsel of the wicked" in Ps. 1:1 and "the golden calf" (Ex. 32) in the desert, mystically interpreted, or the idol Baal or Moloch, because of which "the wicked will not stand in the judgment" (Ps. 1:5). Therefore, to become a sinner is to destroy this way of thinking by which we believe tenaciously that we are living, speaking, and acting in a good, pious, and righteous way, and to adopt another mode of thought (which comes from God) whereby we believe from the heart that we are sinners, that we are acting, speaking, and living wickedly, that we are astray, and thus we come to blame ourselves, to judge, condemn, and hate ourselves. "He who does these things shall never be moved" (Ps. 15:5).

All of the things we have said here must be correctly understood, however, namely, that righteous, good, and holy works must not be understood as being disapproved in the sense that they are to be omitted, but only with respect to the meaning, esteem, and reputation we give them, that is, that we do not trust in them or esteem them or give them such honor as if we had the strength to be sufficiently righteous before God because of them. For it is only this thinking of vanity and this foolish self-esteem that must be driven out by these words. Otherwise good works of this kind should be done with the greatest earnestness and carried out with all seriousness, to the end that through them as through a kind of preparation we can finally become apt for and capable of the righteousness of God; not that they are righteousness, but that they may seek righteousness. For this reason they are now not our righteousness, as long as we do not account them to ourselves for righteousness. For by means of all of these things we must prepare the way of the Lord [17] who will come to us. But they are not themselves the way of the Lord. The way of the Lord is the righteousness of God, which the Lord when He is present alone accomplishes in us after them.

[17] Cf. Is. 40:3; Matt. 3:3; Mark 1:3; Luke 3:4.

Corollary

God is as changeable [18] as possible. This is evident from the fact that He is justified and judged, for we read in Ps. 18:26: "With the pure Thou dost show Thyself pure, and with the crooked Thou dost show Thyself perverse." For as each person is in himself, so God is to him as an object. If he is righteous, God is righteous; if he is pure, so is God; if he is wicked, God is wicked, etc. Hence to the damned He will forever seem evil, but to the righteous, righteous and as He actually is in Himself. But this changeableness is external, which is surely obvious from the expression "Thou art judged." For just as God is judged only from outside and by man, so also He is justified. Thus the expression "that Thou mayest be justified" must be said of God outwardly.

9. *We have charged.* Even though the Jews do excel in those respects which have been mentioned and which will be enumerated below in chapter 9, yet they are not for this reason better before God but under sin equally with the Gentiles. Hence it is clear that the expression which he used above, "The Gentiles do by nature what the Law requires" (Rom. 2:14), did not intend thereby to assert that they are righteous, except with a particular and legal righteousness, but not with the universal, infinite, eternal, and wholly divine righteousness, which is not given to us except in Christ. For it is not sufficient to do the works of the Law outwardly, nor is it sufficient to do them inwardly, unless the justification through Christ is first added. However, if someone must be described as doing the works of the Law inwardly [it is still not enough], since (as Scripture says) from the heart and the mind we are always inclined toward evil (cf. Gen. 8:21) and thus are unwilling to do good things and to obey the Law. Thus we do not do good, as has been sufficiently discussed above.

That all men are under the power of sin. We must understand this entire passage as being spoken in the Spirit, that is, he is not speaking about men as they are in their own eyes and before men, but as they are before God, where all are under sin, namely, both those who even to men are manifestly evil and those who in their own eyes and in the eyes of other men appear to be good.

---

[18] Cf. Luther's glosses on Rom. 1:23 (p. 11, above), where the opposite of our phrase, *Deus immutabilis*, is stated. The paradox is reminiscent of nominalist explanations such as that of Gabriel Biel, *Sentences*, I, dist. 17, qu. 1, c. 2, art. 3, dub. 1, where God is described as being "Without any actual change, but not without any potential change, at least in another."

The explanation is that those who are manifestly evil sin both according to the inner and the outer man and are without any kind of righteousness, even among themselves. But those who appear outwardly good to themselves and to their fellowmen actually sin in the inner man. For although they do good works outwardly, yet they do them out of fear of punishment or of love for money, glory, or some other material consideration, not willingly and joyfully, and thus the outer man, to be sure, is impelled to good works, but the inner man abounds in concupiscence and contrary lusts. For if he were permitted to act with impunity or if he knew that glory and peace would not come to him, he would rather omit doing good and would do evil, just like the others. Therefore what is the qualitative difference between the man who does evil and the man who wants to do evil, granted that he does not do so because he is compelled by fear or lured by the love of some temporal reward? But that man is the worst of all who lets such outward righteousness be sufficient and contends against those who teach an inner righteousness, and who, when accused defends himself and does not think he is meant when he is accused, not because he does no good but because he does not do it out of the simplicity of his heart and because he does not even reform his will, in which he desires to do things which are actually contrary to his actions. In this case his good works are doubly evil, first, because they are not performed out of a good will and thus are evil, second, because they are established and defended as good works by a new pride. Thus Jer. 2:13 reads: "My people have committed two evils, etc." Therefore, unless through the grace of God (which He promised to believers in Christ and bestows upon them) this willfulness is cleansed, so that we are free and happy toward the works of the Law and seek nothing but to please God and do His will and do our work neither out of fear of punishment or self-love, we are always under sin. Therefore, he says:

10. *None is righteous.* But here everyone must watch himself and keep his eyes open and pay close attention. For the just man whom the apostle is seeking is very rare. This is the case because we so rarely analyze ourselves deeply enough to recognize this weakness in our will, or rather, this disease. And thus we rarely humble ourselves, rarely seek the grace of God in the right way, for we do not understand, as he says here (v. 11). For this disease is so subtle that it cannot be fully managed even by very spiritual men. Thus those who are truly righteous not only sigh and plead

for the grace of God because they see that they have an evil inclination and thus are sinful before God, but also because they see
that they can never understand fully how deep is the evil of their
will and how far it extends, they believe that they are always
sinners, as if the depth of their evil will were infinite. Thus they
humble themselves, thus they plead, thus they cry, until at last
they are perfectly cleansed—which takes place in death. This,
then, is the reason why we are always sinners. "We all make many
mistakes" (James 3:2), and, "If we say we have no sin, we deceive
ourselves" (1 John 1:8). For (if I may use an example) who does the
good and omits the evil with that will whereby, even if there were
no commandment or prohibition, he still would do it or omit it?
I believe that if we rightly examine our heart, no one will find himself to be that kind of person except one who is absolutely perfect,
but rather, if he had the freedom, he would omit many good works
and do many evil works. But this is what it means to be in your sins
before God, whom we are compelled to serve freely in the frame of
mind which I have mentioned. Therefore we read (Eccl. 7:20)
"There is not a righteous man on earth who does good and never
sins." Hence, the righteous always plead guilty. And Ps. 32:6
says: "Therefore let everyone who is godly offer prayer to Thee at
a time of distress." Indeed, who knows or who can know, even if it
seems to him that he is doing good and avoiding evil in that frame
of mind, whether it really is so, since God alone will be the judge of
this and since we cannot judge ourselves in this respect, according
to the apostle in 1 Cor. 4:7, "Who sees anything different in you?"
Likewise (1 Cor. 4:5), "Do not pronounce judgment before the
time, etc." The fact that some people think they have such a state
of mind is a dangerous presumption in which many people are very
slyly deceived; since they are confident that they already have the
grace of God, they neglect to search the secrets of their own heart,
and they daily grow colder and finally literally die. For if they were
to inquire as to whether they are moved to do good or avoid evil
because of fear of punishment, love of glory, shame, favor, or some
other desire, they would discover without doubt that they are
moved by the things of which we have just spoken and not solely
by the will of God, or at the very least they would discover that
they do not know whether they do these things purely because of
their love for God. And when they would discover this (as they
must), they surely would be afraid, since we are committed to
finding in ourselves not that which is better but rather that which

is evil, for we of ourselves are by nature evil; they would humble themselves and constantly seek the grace of God with pitiful groans, and thus they would always make progress. That we are commanded to hope surely does not mean that we are commanded to do this in order that we might hope to have done it as we ought, but rather that the merciful Lord who alone can see into this abyss of ours (over the surface of which there are only shadows for us) does not account it to us for sin, as long as we confess it to Him. But it is as Job says (Job 9:21), "Though I am blameless, I regard not myself," and again (Job 9:28), "I became afraid of all my suffering, etc.," that is, because he could not know whether he was working with a double heart or whether he was seeking his own advantages with a completely secret greed. Hence the statement of Seneca is full of arrogance and every sin: "Even if I knew that men would not notice it and that the gods would overlook it, I still would be unwilling to sin." [19] First, because it is impossible for a man to have this intention by himself, since he is always inclined toward evil to such an extent that except for the grace of God he could not be moved to anything good. Thus he who presumes to speak this way about himself does not yet understand himself. To be sure, I admit that it is true that a person with this attitude can do and will some good things, but not all of them, for we are so entirely inclined to evil that no portion which is inclined toward the good remains in us, as is clear in the *synteresis*.[20] Second, even if he says he would not want to sin, even if he knew that the gods would overlook it and men would not notice it, does he also dare to say that he would want to do good, even if he knew that neither the gods nor men would care about it? If he dares to say this, he is as arrogant as before, because he would not entirely escape the glory and boasting, at least not in himself, where he is self-satisfied. For man cannot but seek his own advantages and love himself above all things. And this is the sum of all his iniquities. Hence even in good things and virtues men seek themselves, that is, they seek to please themselves and applaud themselves.

None is righteous, because no man of himself is willing to obey the law of God but all are opposed (at least in the heart) to the will

---

[19] The quotation has not been found in Seneca's writings, but very similar statements are attributed to Seneca by various writers in Luther's time. Cf. W, LVI, 236, n. 32.

[20] Cf. p. 157, n. 41.

of God, since he alone is righteous "whose delight is in the law of the Lord" (Ps. 1:2). So also

11. *No one understands*, because the wisdom of God is hidden, unknown to the world. For "The Word became flesh" (John 1:14), and Wisdom was made incarnate and is thus hidden and unapproachable except by understanding, just as Christ cannot be known except by revelation. Therefore those who are wise only in regard to visible things and in the realm of visible things (such as all men are outside of faith who do not know God and the life to come), do not understand, are not wise, that is, they are not intelligent or truly wise but stupid and blind; and although they may seem to be wise in their own eyes, yet they have become fools. For they are wise only with a wisdom which can be found by human means but not in hidden things.

No one seeks for God. This statement pertains both to those who manifestly do not seek God as well as to those who seek Him or rather think they are seeking Him, because they do not seek Him in the way in which He wishes to be sought and discovered, namely, through faith, in humility, and not through their own wisdom and presumption.

Corollary

Just as the statement "There is none righteous" is to be understood of these two classes of man, namely, those who have strayed to the left and those who have strayed to the right, so also we should interpret the expressions "No one understands" and "No one seeks." For because they are not righteous, the former do not understand and do not seek for God because of a lack of interest and negligence; the latter are in the same situation, but because of excess and overdoing. For these men are too righteous, too understanding, too much given to seeking, so that they are incorrigible in their minds. As the comic writer says, "Do they not make it out with their knowing that they know nothing?" [21] and again, "The highest righteousness is often the highest foolishness," [22] indeed, the highest unrighteousness, when one stubbornly holds to it and refuses to yield to the opposite opinion. Hence we have the

[21] Terence, *Andria*, 17.

[22] Terence, *Heauton timorumenos*, 796; *ius summum saepe summast malitia.* Cicero quotes a variant in *De officiis*, I, 10, 33: *summum ius summa iniuria* and adds the comment, "Already a well-worn proverb in common speech." Also see *Luther's Works*, 46, p. 100.

popular saying *Weiss Leut narrn groblich,* "the wiser the man, the worse the madness."

He says, "No one understands," before he says, "No one seeks." For knowing comes before willing and doing; seeking prompts volition and action. But this itself comes after understanding. Therefore the unrighteous on the left side do not understand, because they are blinded in their vanity by their desire for visible things. But those on the right do not understand because they are hindered in their own minds by their wisdom and righteousness. Thus they were their own bolt [23] against the divine light.

Therefore, according to these two classes a man is properly called righteous if he is blessed with understanding and seeks God according to that understanding. Otherwise, understanding without seeking is dead, just as faith without works is dead, and neither makes alive nor justifies. On the other hand, a man is unrighteous if he neither understands nor seeks. That is also why he began with the premise "None is righteous." As a way of explaining what it means not to be righteous, he says that man does not have understanding and does not seek God.

Corollary

This understanding of which he speaks is faith itself, or the knowledge of the invisible things and the things which must be believed. Therefore it is an understanding in concealment because it deals with those things which a man cannot know of himself, as we read John 14:6 [24]: "No one comes to the Father but by Me," and again (John 6:44): "No one can come to Me unless the Father . . . draws him," and to Peter (Matt. 16:17), "Blessed are you, Simon Bar-Jona! For flesh and blood has not revealed this to you, but my Father who is in heaven." How, therefore, can those on the left, the ungodly and the sensual, know this, because they regard only visible things? And how can those on the right, who consider only their own opinion and give weight only to that? Both groups put up a barrier [25] for themselves and establish a foreign obstacle

---

[23] *Obicem ponere* meant to put a bar, or bolt, in the way of a blessed reception of the Sacrament through impenitence, the *obex,* "bar," or "bolt."

[24] For the three passages cited here, Luther indicates only "John 6" at this point.

[25] See n. 23 above.

blocking out the light of a clear understanding of this matter.

Now the desire for God or the search for Him is the very love of God which makes us will or love what our understanding causes us to know. For even if one understands and believes, yet without the grace of God he cannot love and willingly do what he believes and understands. Therefore he says most appropriately, "No one seeks." For the condition of this life is not that of having but of seeking God. We must always seek Him and search for Him, that is, again and again we must seek Him, as Ps. 105:4 says: "Seek His presence continually," and (Ps. 122:4): "To which the tribes go up, etc." For thus one goes from strength to strength, from splendor to splendor, to the same likeness. For it is not he who begins and seeks, but "he who endures" and keeps seeking "unto the end will be saved" (Matt. 10:22), he who is always beginning, seeking and renewing his quest. For he who does not progress on the way of God regresses. And he who does not renew his quest loses what he has found, since one cannot stand still on the road of God.[26] As St. Bernard says, "When we cease wishing to become better, we cease to be good."[27]

Corollary

Although this psalm may be understood also of the ungodly people on the left, yet it speaks primarily about those on the right. For the former class rarely err so profoundly as to "say in their heart, 'There is no God' " (Ps. 14:1). For they know God and what He has commanded, but in the work of their lives they say, "There is no God." What is said is not true, therefore there is neither truth nor God. But the latter both by their work and their word, but particularly in their hearts, say this, because they do not truly know God but picture Him to themselves in the way they want Him to be. And thus they neither hear what God says, nor do they understand it, but they think and say that they have the Word of God and that they therefore must be heard. Thus they err in their hearts, and if they do hear the voice of God, they harden their hearts, as

[26] Commenting on Ps. 119:88 (W, IV, 350, 15), Luther said: "To advance is nothing else but always to begin again. And to begin without advancing is to fail altogether." Augustine, *Sermo CLXX, Patrologia, Series Latina*, XXXVIII, 926, writes: "On the way [to God] . . . he who does not advance remains behind."

[27] Bernard of Clairvaux, *Epistula XCI, Patrologia, Series Latina*, CLXXXII, 224.

if it were not the voice of God nor God who is speaking. And because the voice of God speaks contrary to their thinking (which seems to them to be righteous and wise and completely filled with God) and thus even in their zeal for God and their love for His truth and especially in their excessive knowledge of Him, they finally say, "There is no God," and deny the truth and become fools because they say they are wise.

All of this happens on a moral plane to all overbearing and self-satisfied men, especially if it touches on things which pertain to God and the salvation of the soul. For here God speaks, but He speaks in such a way that neither the person nor the place nor the time nor the word appears such to the proud people that God is speaking through that person and in such circumstances. And so the unbelieving draw back or resist just like the foolish and say, at least in their hearts, "There is no God there, etc." for none but the humble can receive the Word of God.

12. *All have turned aside; together they have gone wrong.* "All," that is, all the sons of men who have not yet been made the sons of God through faith "by water and the Holy Spirit" (John 3:5). And some of these incline toward the left side, who are slaves to riches, honors, pleasures, and powers of this world. But others incline toward the right. These men are zealous for their own righteousness, virtue, and wisdom, having deserted the righteousness and obedience of God in their spiritual pride, and they attack the humbleness of the truth. Thus Scripture says, Prov. 4:27: "Do not swerve to the right or to the left," that is, from the way which is on the right hand, because these words follow, "For the Lord knows the ways that are on the right hand; but those are perverse which are on the left hand," [28] that is, that to turn to the right from the right is to be overly wise and to be self-righteous, etc.

The term "together" is understood in a collective sense, as if he were saying, "They all have gone wrong," that is, they are vain and are pursuing unprofitable things. For it is correct that those who seek unprofitable things become unprofitable themselves, vain from vain pursuits; just as the rich are called so from their riches, so these men are called unprofitable from their possession of unprofitable things. For we become like the things we love. "If you love God, you are God; if you love the earth, you are earth," says

---

[28] This sentence is not in the Hebrew text.

St. Augustine.[29] For love is a unifying force, which makes the loved and the lover into one.[30]

They can also be said to have "gone wrong" in another sense, in that they are unprofitable to God and to themselves. But the first interpretation is preferable, for he is trying to demonstrate that they have been made vain by the fact that they have fallen away from the truth and the righteousness of God into their own ways.

These three statements can be understood as a device whereby we are led from a lesser to a greater expression, so that the clause "None is righteous" is the same as the expression "All have turned aside," and the expression "No one understands" is the same as "Together they have gone wrong"; and the expression "No one seeks for God" is the same as saying *No one does good.*

Now, "to turn aside" is the same as becoming unrighteous. And to become vain is to lose the truth in our understanding and to turn our minds to vanity. Hence, in many places vanity is ascribed to the thinking of such people. The following expression "not to do good" is the same as not seeking God. For although they do perform good deeds outwardly, yet they do not do them from the heart and thus do not seek God but rather glory and money, or at least deliverance from punishment. And thus they do not *do* good, but rather (if it is permissible to talk this way) they *are made* good, that is, they are compelled by fear or love to do the good which they would not freely do. But those who seek God, do good freely and gladly, purely for the sake of God alone and not for the possession of any kind of creaturely possession, whether spiritual or physical. But this is the work not of our nature but of grace.

13. *Their throat is an open grave.* These three verses show how these men do wrong also to others. For he has shown in the preceding verses how they are wicked and ungodly in themselves, on the one hand, by turning away from God, on the other hand, by

---

[29] Augustine writes: "Such is each one as is his love. Do you love the earth? You shall be earth. Do you love God? What shall I say? You shall be a god? I dare not say it of myself; let us hear the Scriptures: 'I have said, Ye are gods, and all of you sons of the Most High. If then you want to be gods and sons of the Most High, 'Love not the world'" (Homily 2 on the Epistle of John, *Patrologia, Series Latina,* XXXV, 1997). Luther quotes the same passage in his comments on Ps. 114 (W, IV, 263, 38).

[30] Luther may have had Augustine, *De Trinitate,* VIII, 10, 14, in mind, but the text is closer to Thomas Aquinas on Dionysius Areopagita, *Divina nomina: Est enim amor unitio secundum quod amans et amatum conveniunt in aliquo uno* (W, LVI, 241, n. 5).

converting other people to themselves and turning them away from God, as they themselves are also turned away.

And this applies first to those who listen to them and follow them. In these they do three things.

First, they devour the dead. Hence he says, "their throat is an open grave." Just as the grave is the receptacle of the dead and of those who have died without the hope of rising again such as there is in sleep; therefore the psalm (88:5) speaks of those who "lie in the grave, . . . whom Thou dost remember no more, for they are cut off from Thy hand." So also their teaching and their mouth, or throat (that is, the word which comes from their mouth or throat), only swallows up the dead who have gone from faith to unbelief, and swallows them up in such a way that there is no hope of returning from the death of this unbelief, unless they can be recalled by the most wonderful power of God before they descend to hell, as the Lord showed in the case of Lazarus who had been dead for four days. He says, moreover, that the grave is "open" because they devour and seduce many people. "For their talk will eat its way like gangrene" (2 Tim. 2:17), just as earlier he has said, "Have they no knowledge, all the evildoers who eat up my people as they eat bread?" (Ps. 14:4), that is, just as there is no squeamishness about eating bread, even though it is eaten more frequently than other foods, so also they do not cease to devour their dead and their disciples and are never satisfied, because "the barren womb (that is, the infernal doctrine) . . . never says, 'Enough'" (Prov. 30:16). But just as bread passes into him who eats it, so also these men pass into the unbelief of their teachers. But this similarity is also placed here for a distinction, because these same ungodly men devour also the righteous, but not like a piece of bread, since they do not absorb them into their bodies like bread but swallow them alive and raw and thus do not digest them but either perish or are improved by them.

Hence heresy, or faithless teaching, is nothing else than a kind of disease or plague which infects and kills many people, just as is the case with the physical plague.

He uses the word "throat" rather than "mouth" to describe the efficacy or persuasiveness of their doctrine, because they prevail over them, that is, they devour them, just as something which is already down the throat and not only in the mouth, which can be coughed up and spat out. Their teaching is effective, however, because it is described as tasty and pleasant, so that the apostle says (2 Tim. 4:3), "Having itching ears, they will accumulate teachers." As the throat does not have teeth like the mouth, which bites the food with its teeth, so the throat easily devours without any chewing at all.

There is also another reason. Because such teachers do not bite, therefore they do not chew and grind, that is, do not criticize people, do not humble them, do not bring them to repentance, do not pull them down and break them. But as they are they swallow them whole in their faithlessness, as we read in Lam. 2:14, "Your prophets have not exposed your iniquity to call you to repentance." For to criticize a sinner and to castigate him with words is to chew him with the teeth until he is cut into small pieces and made soft (that is, humble and meek). But to flatter and to excuse his sins or to be quick to overlook them, this is to gulp them down the throat, that is, to leave them whole and in large, hard chunks, that is, proud and obdurate toward repentance and unwilling to endure any correction. Hence in the Song of Sol. 4:2 the bride is described as having teeth which "are like a flock of shorn ewes," that is, reproofs taken from Scripture but without any real desire to condemn. Hence he continues with the two remaining expressions to explain what he means when he says, "Their throat is an open grave," and how it happens that they devour them.

Second, they teach *deceitfully*. The reason that their throat is an open sepulcher, the reason that they devour many, is that they teach deceitfully. The reason they devour, the reason their throat is an open sepulcher is that it subtly injects poison. This latter is the way they kill men and deaden them, but in the former way they deaden many. For flattery and subtle persuasion tempt and attract many, but the poison kills them when they have been attracted. Thus it is most aptly said, "Their throat" (because they kill with flattery and guile) "is an open" (because it catches many) "grave" (because they are dead). Therefore, to go back to the beginning, "to use the tongue" is to teach, to warn, to exhort, and to use the tongue in every way as an instrument with which to approach another person. But "to teach deceitfully" is to teach a pleasing and wanton doctrine, as if it were holy, salutary, and from God, so that people who have been thus deceived hear this doctrine as if from God and believe that they are hearing Him, for the message appears good to them and truthful and godly. And this pleasantness and flattery by which a speech of this kind pleases the hearer is emphatically pointed out by the use of the term "their tongues" as well as by the expression "the throat," which is used above. For the tongue is soft, it has no bones, and it licks softly. Thus their every speech only softens the heart of men to be pleased with themselves in their own wisdom, their own righteousness, their own word or work. As it says in Is. 30:10: "Speak to us smooth things. Prophesy not to us what is right," that is, do not speak things which are contrary to our thought. This, yes, this is why they only shudder at the Word of the cross (by which their own thought should have been put to death and torn to pieces by teeth, as it were), and they want to hear those things which cater to their thought. O horrible word! And thus this deceit gets a multitude of people ready, and when they have been made ready, the poison kills them. This is the reason that it is an open and ample grave. Hence:

Third, they kill those who have been taught such things; for *the venom of asps is under their lips.* This is the same flattering and pleasing doctrine that not only does not make alive those who believe it but actually kills them. And it kills them in such a way that they are beyond recovery. For there is no cure for the poison of asps. An asp is a species of serpent in Africa whose sting, as Aristotle says,[31] is incurable. So also a faithless and heretical people are incurable. But the poor wretches do not even recognize this poison as the death of their souls. Therefore he uses the expression "under their lips" as if to say, death lies subtly hidden while outwardly it appears as life and truth in the very words of their doctrine. Therefore, since the poison of asps is incurable and brings irreparable death to life, he is correct in using the term "grave." For the pleasant outward appearance of truth and righteousness is the reason why this is an open sepulcher, an incurable and hopeless poison. For all people love truth and righteousness. Therefore they stubbornly cling to it when it appears attractive; but it is despised when it appears ugly, as it always really appears. This is evident in the case of Christ, for whom "there is no form or comeliness" (Is. 53:2). And it is thus with every truth which goes contrary to our thought.

14. *Their mouth is full of curses.* Notice here that they have a mouth, when it comes to those who do not follow them. Here it is not a "throat" or a "tongue" but a "mouth" which is full of teeth, as the following shows. Thus:

Second, how are they toward those who do not follow them but rather resist them and try to teach them things which are good and

---

[31] Aristotle, *Historia animalium,* VII, 29.

right in an effort to convert them from the death which has been prepared for them? See how they repay them. They likewise do three things.

First, their mouth is full of cursing. An appropriate expression, because their cursing does not pass on to those who have been cursed by them, but it remains with them. They hurt no one but themselves, according to the statement spoken against Christ [32]: "Cursed be everyone who curses Thee." In another psalm (Ps. 58:6) it is put this way: "God will break their teeth in their mouth," and not in the wound or body of others. For He lets them bite, but in such a way that they injure no one, and thus He breaks their teeth in their own mouth. So it is that they do not lack teeth or curses, but these remain only in their mouth, because it is "full." This "cursing" is a matter of openly attacking a person with insults, denunciations, and blasphemies and of wishing him evil. And all of them do this who feel that they have been contradicted in their set way of thinking (because it seems just and true to them), and thus they are prepared to defend the truth as it were and to offer service to God with marvelous zeal, which, however, is not "enlightened" (Rom. 10:2). They do not do this slothfully, but, as I have said, with great zeal. For he uses the expression "their mouth is full," that is, abounding in curses.

Second, with *bitterness*, that is, with the most jealous slander. For jealousy is the bitterness of the heart, just as love on the other hand is the sweetness of the heart. Therefore the proud and the ungodly not only curse the righteous but also among themselves slander others with bitter words. But even this envy remains in their own mouth and does no harm to those whom they hate. Therefore he says it is full, but it does not make other people outside bitter and evil.

15. Third, *their feet are swift to shed blood.* Another striking expression! For they cannot always accomplish with their hands what they want to, but they keep on trying to fulfill their desires. Thus when they cannot overcome the messengers of the truth with their curses or their slanders, they undertake to do away with them and to kill them for fear that their own ideas might be rejected. The Jews (of whom the text is speaking directly) did this most tenaciously, as we see in the Acts of the Apostles. But even now every enemy of the truth does the same thing in the interest of his own

---

[32] For Luther passages such as Gen. 27:29; Ps. 36:22; and Ps. 57:6 apply ultimately to Christ Himself. See W, III, 207, 9 f. and n. 3.

way of thinking in order to reinforce it, for he has good intentions and is acting out of love for God.

16. *Ruin.* Here he depicts their fate. First is ruin, that is, they are ground to pieces, cut down, and humiliated in both body and soul, as is plain in the case of the Jews, who "are like chaff which the wind drives away," as Ps. 1:4 says; for those who were at one time great and powerful are now being destroyed and systematically ground to pieces, "trodden down like the mire of the streets" (Micah 7:10). This physical ruin, moreover, which befalls them before men is matched by an even more terrible spiritual destruction which comes from demons who tread them underfoot and who do not "leave one stone upon another" (Matt. 24:2). At the same time that they are always being cut down in their ways, they are also always becoming more sinful and hardened as long as they persevere in these ways. Just so, on the contrary, those who are in the ways of Christ always grow and become stronger. Thus for the latter there is a strengthening and increase, while for the former only destruction and diminution. Second, *misery,* that is, misfortune, because just as Christ prospers in everything He does, so, on the contrary, they prosper in nothing which they undertake. This is plainly manifest in the Jews, because although they progress in their unbelief, yet they are oppressed in many other ways.

17. *The way of peace they do not know.* Why have they not known it? Because it has been hidden, since it is peace in the Spirit, which is revealed only through much tribulation. For who would think that this is the way of peace when he sees Christians persecuted in connection with their property, their reputation, their honor, and their bodily welfare, and that their whole life through they do not possess peace but the cross and sufferings? But those poeple seek peace in their flesh by their own works of righteousness and lose both. But lying hidden under these sufferings is a peace which no one knows unless he believes and experiences it, but those people are unwilling to believe and abhor the thought of experiencing it. "For great peace have those who love Thy law; nothing can make them stumble" (Ps. 119:165), that is, "those who love Thy law." What does this mean except that those who hate it will have a stumblingblock? But of all the evils which have been mentioned the cause is pride, which makes men incapable of receiving the good. For the fear of God makes all things humble, but humility makes a man capable of receiving all things. Therefore those men receive nothing because they are

proud, and they are proud because they do not fear God. And they do not fear God because they are presumptuous enough to think that God will approve their thinking and their actions, for He appears righteous and upright to them because they are unmindful that if God should judge, He would find nothing righteous and nothing pure. For the judgment of God is of infinite exactness. And nothing is done so minutely that it will not be found gross in His sight, nothing so righteous that it will not be found unrighteous, nothing so truthful that it will not be found to be a lie, nothing so pure and holy that it will not be found polluted and profane in His sight. But if they are aware of this, they claim that there surely is a "respect of persons with God" (Rom. 2:11), so that He will not judge and condemn their righteous and truthful actions, that is, by a remarkably permissive favor they, the impure, are regarded as the pure. And so if they were afraid, they would know that it is Christ alone and His righteousness and His truth which cannot be condemned by God, since they are all infinite. But praise and glory to God forever, who has given all these things to us in Him and with Him, so that through Him we are righteous and truthful and can escape judgment. But standing on our own efforts (even though we are unsure whether they are our own efforts), we must always be afraid before God.

18. But they nevertheless imagine that they have as much *fear of God* as possible. For what virtue will proud men not arrogate to themselves? Just as they consider themselves righteous in their search for God, so also they believe they have the fear of God and all the things which the apostle here denies to them; and all the things which he ascribes to them, these they presumptuously believe are as far away from them as possible. Therefore, unless one believes with faith in these words of the Holy Spirit in this psalm (Ps. 12:3), that they are true and that no one is righteous before God, he will never think this about himself so long as he seems righteous in his own eyes. Hence, it will always be necessary to realize that these things are true about us and that it can be said of each of us that he is an unjust man, without fear of God, so that being thus humbled and confessing ourselves to be ungodly and foolish before God, we may deserve to be justified by Him.

19. *May be held accountable* in this passage is taken as meaning to be under obligation or to be a debtor or bound to a certain thing, so that the meaning as stated in the gloss is that the Law asserts that all are unrighteous, so that all because of this assertion may

recognize that they are unrighteous and may cease considering themselves righteous and cease boasting, keep silent about their own righteousness, and become guilty in the face of God's righteousness. Note Ps. 37:7: "Be subject to the Lord and pray to Him," which the Hebrew renders, "Be still before the Lord, etc."; Is. 41:1: "Listen to me in silence, O coastlands; let the peoples renew their strength," that is, let them be silent and keep their mouth shut, and let them cease boasting that they are righteous in My sight; Ps. 65:1: "A hymn, O God, becomes Thee in Zion," for which the Hebrew reads: "Silence is praise for Thee, O God, in Zion," that is, we owe Thee silence because of our righteousness, because this very silence is a praise to Thee for Thy righteousness. The conjunction "and" may be understood: "Silence and praise are Thine, O God, etc." But this thought is more significantly expressed without the conjunction, so that praising and glorifying God are the same thing, if only we keep silence about praising ourselves and thinking that we are something.

20. The question is asked, "How can justification take place without the works of the Law, and how *by the works of the Law* can there be no justification, since James 2:26 clearly states: 'Faith apart from works is dead' and 'a man is justified by works,' using the example of Abraham and Rahab (James 2:23-25)?" And Paul himself in Gal. 5:6 speaks of "faith working through love," and above in chapter 2:13 he says that "the doers of the Law will be justified before God." The answer to this question is that the apostle is distinguishing between the Law and faith, or between the letter and grace, and thus also between their respective works. The works of the Law are those, he says, which take place outside of faith and grace and are done at the urging of the Law, which either forces obedience through fear or allures us through the promise of temporal blessings. But the works of faith, he says, are those which are done out of the spirit of liberty and solely for the love of God. And the latter cannot be accomplished except by those who have been justified by faith, to which justification the works of the Law add nothing, indeed, they strongly hinder it, since they do not permit a man to see himself as unrighteous and in need of justification.

Here is an example. If a layman should perform all the outward functions of a priest, celebrating Mass, confirming, absolving, administering the sacraments, dedicating altars, churches, vestments, vessels, etc., it is certain that these actions in all respects would be similar to those of a true priest, in fact, they might be performed more reverently and properly than the real ones. But because he has not been consecrated and ordained and sanctified, he performs nothing at all, but is only playing church and deceiving himself and his followers. It is the same way with the righteous, good, and holy works which are performed either without or before justification. For just as this layman does not become a priest by performing all these functions, although it can happen that he could be made a priest without doing them, namely, by ordination, so also the man who is righteous by the Law is actually not made righteous by the works of the Law at all, but without them, by something else, namely, through faith in Christ, by which he is justified and, as it were, ordained, so that he is made righteous for the performance of the works of righteousness, just as this layman is ordained a priest for the performance of the functions of a priest. And it can happen that the man who is righteous by the Law does works which are more according to the letter and more spectacular than the man who is righteous by grace. But yet he is not for this reason righteous but rather may actually be more impeded by these works from coming to righteousness and to the works of grace.

Another example. A monkey can imitate the actions of people, but he is not a man on that account. But if he should become a man, this doubtless would not take place by virtue of these actions, by which he has imitated a man, but by some other power, namely, God's; but then having become a man, he would truly and rightly perform the actions of a man.

Therefore, when St. James and the apostle say that a man is justified by works, they are contending against the erroneous notion of those who thought that faith suffices without works, although the apostle does not say that faith justifies without its own works (because then there would be no faith, since, according to the philosophers, "action is the evidence that form exists" [33]), but that it justifies without the works of the Law. Therefore justification does not demand the works of the Law but a living faith which produces its own works.

But if faith justifies with its own works, but without the works of the Law, then why are heretics regarded as beyond justification,

---

[33] One of Luther's university teachers, Jodocus Trutvetter, in his *Summa in totam physicen*, I, ch. 1, adds to his explanation of the Aristotelian concept "form" a statement very similar to Luther's: "Action shows the presence of form, as change shows the presence of matter." See W, 56, p. 249, n. 9.

since they also believe and from this same faith produce great and sometimes even greater works than the other believers? And all the people in the church who are spiritually proud, who have many and great works which also surely proceed from faith, are such people also unrighteous? Does something other than faith in Christ with its good works seem to be required for justification?

James answers the question briefly: "Whosoever . . . fails in one point has become guilty of all of it" (2:10). For faith is indivisible. Therefore it is either a whole faith and believes all that is to be believed, or it is no faith, if it does not believe one part. The Lord thus compares it to one pearl, to one grain of mustard, etc. Because "Christ is not divided" (cf. 1 Cor. 1:13), therefore He is either completely denied in one unit, or else He is completely affirmed. He cannot be at the same time denied in one word and confessed in another. But heretics are always picking out one thing or many from those which are to be believed, against which they set their minds in their arrogance, as if they were wiser than all the rest. And thus they believe nothing which is to be believed and perish without faith, without obedience toward God, while still in their great works, which are so similar to the real ones. They are not different from the Jews, who themselves believe many things which the church also truly believes. But one only does the thought of their own proud heart oppose, namely, Christ, and thus they perish in their unbelief. So also every proud man in his own mind always opposes either the precept or the counsel of him who is correctly guiding him to salvation. Since he does not believe this counsel, he likewise believes nothing, and his entire faith perishes because of the tenacity of one thought. We must always humbly, therefore, give way in our thinking, lest we stumble over this rock of offense,[34] that is, the truth which in humility stands against us and opposes our own thinking. For since we are liars, the truth can never come to us except as an apparent adversary to what we are thinking, for we presume that we think the truth, and we wish to hear and see as truth only that which agrees with us and applauds us. But this cannot be.

The works of all of these men, therefore, are the works of the Law, not of faith or of grace, indeed they are opposed to and in conflict with faith. Thus justification not only can but must take place without them, and with the apostle must "be counted as refuse for the sake of Christ" (Phil. 3:8).

34 Cf. Rom. 9:32 f.; Is. 8:14; 1 Peter 2:8.

Corollary

It is always safer to listen to things which are contrary to our own thinking, than to listen to those things which approve and applaud our ideas and are in agreement with us.

Indeed, unless a man learns to listen gladly to things which are against him, and unless he enjoys argument against his own opinions and is happy in being contradicted, and on the other hand, unless he is fearful and sorry, or at least suspicious when his word, his opinion, and his work are approved, praised, and upheld, he certainly cannot be saved. For there is no more faithful testimony to the fact that his thinking, his word, and his work are from God than if they are blamed and condemned. For everything which comes from God (as is obvious in the case of Christ) is condemned by men, as stones by the builders. But if it is not from God, then it is much safer, indeed it is necessary, that it be rejected, lest he who continues in it should perish. Hence even the godless king Ahab testifies that he hated the prophet Micah for no other reason than that he always prophesied evil to him. Likewise, King Jehoiakim for the same reason tore up and burned the words of Jeremiah. And all the Jews persecuted the prophets, because they announced things to them which were bad and contrary to what pleased their thinking, although they should have received these messages with humility and acknowledged themselves guilty before God. But rather they said, "Peace, peace"; we are the people of God, He will not do evil to us, He will not punish us, we shall not see evil, for we are righteous. And thus they never listened to the voice of God but always resisted it. Hence the Lord says in Luke 6:26, "Woe to you when all men speak well of you; for so their fathers did to the false prophets." Therefore, to be cursed, abused, reproved is the pathway to safety; to be blessed, praised, approved is the way of danger and destruction. For we must wait for the blessing and praise of God, "for His blessing is upon His people," as Ps. 3:8 says, but not the blessing of men.

22. *The righteousness of God through faith.* This teaches: Since the faith in Christ by which we are justified is not a matter of believing only in Christ or in the Person of Christ, but in all things which pertain to Christ, the proud and the heretics are deceived and yet pleased in their deception that they believe in Christ but are unwilling to believe the things which pertain to Him.

Thus, they plainly divide Christ when they say that it is one thing to believe in Christ and another to believe in the things which pertain to Christ; but actually "Christ is not divided" (1 Cor. 1:13), as the apostle says; and as we have said above, faith in Christ is similarly indivisible, just as Christ and the things which pertain to Him are one and the same thing.

Thus the heretics confess and brag that they believe in Christ according to what the Gospels say of Him, that He was born, suffered, died, etc. But they do not believe in those things which pertain to Him. And what are these things? The church, of course, and every word which proceeds from the mouth of a leader of the church or from the mouth of a good and holy man is the Word of Christ, for He has said, "He who hears you hears Me" (Luke 10:16). They who withdraw themselves, therefore, from church leaders and are unwilling to listen to their words, but follow their own ideas, how do such people believe in Christ, I ask? Or do they believe that He was born and suffered, but not believe the person who teaches it to them? Therefore, "Is Christ divided" (1 Cor. 1:13) because they believe in Him in one place and deny Him in the other? God forbid. But actually in this way they deny Christ entirely, for He cannot be denied and confessed at the same time. This is what the master of the *Sentences* says, "It is one thing to believe that God exists, another to believe God, and still another to believe in God." So also in the case of Christ. For to believe in Christ is to reach out to Him with one's whole heart and to order all things in accord with Him. Hence the Lord says in Matt. 4:4, "Man shall not live by bread alone, but by every word that proceeds from the mouth of God." And what is the mouth of God? The priest and prelate. Mal. 2:7 reads: "Men should seek instruction from his [the priest's] mouth, for he is the messenger of the Lord of hosts." And to Jeremiah He says (Jer. 15:19): "You shall be as My mouth." But why does Christ say "every word"? Because if you fail to believe even one word, you no longer are living in the Word of God. For the whole Christ is in every word and wholly in each individual word. When He is denied, therefore, in one word, He is totally denied, for He is in every word. For thus He is closed off on two sides. In the same way, if you kill one Christian and spare all others, you kill the whole Christ. The same is true in all other instances. If you deny Christ in one sacramental host, you have denied Him in all.

If these things are so, we must humble ourselves greatly. For since we are unable to know whether we really do live in every word of God and deny none (since many words are spoken by the spiritual leader, many by the brethren, many in the Gospel and in the writings of the apostles, and many to us inwardly by God) we can never know whether we are justified or whether we believe. We should, therefore, consider our works as works of the Law and humbly admit that we are sinners, seeking to be justified solely by His mercy. For although we are sure that we believe in Christ, yet we are not certain that we believe in all the words which pertain to Him. And thus it is uncertain that we "believe in Him."

For even in the prophets there is no complaint except that the voice of the Lord is not heard by His people. But a man who fears and humbly confesses will be given grace, that he may be justified and his sins forgiven, even if occasionally he has done something through hidden or uninformed unbelief. Thus, for example, Job was afraid of all his actions. And the apostle was not conscious of any wrong he had done, but yet he did not think that he was thereby justified. And thus righteousness must be left to Christ alone, and to Him alone the works of grace and of the Spirit. But we ourselves are always under the works of the Law, always unrighteous, always sinners, as it says in Ps. 32:6, "Therefore let everyone who is godly offer prayer to Thee."

But the proud man who does not know this humility and does not understand the subtle distinctions of faith but thinks that he believes and possesses all faith perfectly, this man cannot hear the voice of the Lord, and he resists it as false, because it is contrary to his own thinking which he holds to be true.

But you ask: If denial is so great that having denied in one point, a person has denied in all, why is not the acceptance of equal force, so that when one believes in one point, he believes in all? The answer is that the good is perfect and simple, and thus it is destroyed by one denial. But it is not established by the confession of one thing, unless it be one complete confession without any denial. For two contrary things cannot stand in regard to the same subject. And God wants to have all things pure and undefiled. But denial is a stain, and so it renders a confession unclean.

Corollary

Thus in the prophets the term "voice" applies without exception to the "voice of the Lord," so that we must accept every word which is spoken as if the Lord Himself were speaking, no matter by whom it is spoken, and we must believe it, yield to it, and humbly subject our reason to it. For in this way we will be justified, and in no other. But "Who can discern his errors" or notices them everywhere? Therefore we read (Ps. 19:12-13): "Clear Thou me from hidden faults," O Lord.

20. *Through the Law comes the knowledge of sin.* This knowledge through the Law comes in two ways, first, through contemplation, as we read below in chapter 7:7, "I should not have known what it is to covet if the Law had not said, 'You shall not covet.'"

Second, through experience, that is, through the work of the Law, or through the Law that has been adopted together with the work. For in this way the Law becomes an occasion for sinning, since the will of man which is prone to evil is driven toward the good through the Law and thus becomes disinclined toward the good and tired of trying to do good, because it hates to give up what it loves, and it loves evil, as Scripture says. But yet, if it works and does what it is unwilling to do, compelled by the Law, then man understands how deeply sin and evil are rooted in him, which he would not have understood if he did not have the Law and had not attempted to work in accordance with it. The apostle passes over this idea briefly at this point, because he will go into detail on the matter below in chapters 5 and 7. Here he is satisfied with briefly answering the objection that the Law is not of any use because the works of the Law do not justify. Whenever a precept or a prohibition meets us, therefore, and we feel ourselves hostile toward it, let us recognize the fact that we do not love the good, but rather the evil. By this very fact, therefore, we recognize that we are wicked sinners, since a man is not a sinner unless he is unwilling to fulfill the Law, which prescribes good works and forbids evil. For if we were righteous and good, we would consent to the Law with ready will and delight in it, just as we now delight in our sins and evil desires. Hence: "Oh, how I love Thy Law!" (Ps. 119:97) and again: "But his delight is in the law of the Lord" (Ps. 1:2). Behold, thus it has come to pass that through the Law there is knowledge of the sin which is in us, that is, of our evil will which inclines toward the evil and abhors the good. How useful this knowledge is! For he who recognizes it, cries to God and in humility begs that this will may be lifted up and healed. But he who does not recognize it does not ask, and he who does not ask does not receive, and thus he is not justified because he is ignorant of his own sin. Hence, to say: "Through the Law is the knowledge of sin" is the same as saying:

"Through the Law is the knowledge of sinners." For through this, that we are evil and that evil is in us, we recognize that we are sinners and that sin is in us.

Corollary

We do not apply the term "works of the Law" to those works which are preparatory to acquiring righteousness, but to those which are regarded in themselves as being sufficient for righteousness and salvation.

Because he who so conducts himself that through these works he has prepared himself for the grace of justification is already righteous in a certain sense. For a large part of righteousness is the will to be righteous. Otherwise the words and cries of all the prophets by which they called for Christ would have been in vain, and the laments of all the penitents would be fruitless. In vain would Christ and John have taught: "Repent, for the kingdom of heaven is at hand" (Matt. 3:2). Indeed if all the righteous performed such works for no other purpose than that they might be more and more justified, no one would be righteous. Their works, therefore, are good because they do not trust in them but rather through them prepare themselves for justification, in which they trust alone for their future righteousness. But those who conduct themselves in this way are not under the Law, because they desire grace and hate the fact that they are sinners.

For the "works of the Law" are one thing and the "fulfilling of the Law" another. For grace is the fulfilling of the Law, but not works. Well does he say "works of the Law" and not "will of the Law," for they do not will what the Law wills, although they do perform what the Law commands. But the Law wills and demands our will.

Other people work in such a way that they think they are fulfilling the Law and thus are righteous, even though they neither desire grace nor realize and hate the fact that they are sinners; because they have worked according to the outward form of the Law, they do not dispose themselves to seek righteousness but rather boast as if through these works it were already in their possession, being totally unaware in their thinking that they are observing the Law either with no will or with a will which is unwilling and hostile, or at least out of love and desire for earthly things, but not out of a love for God. And thus they stand still, content and without plans for works worth seeking in behalf of grace, by which they might have also willingness in the Law. The fact is that neither the works which precede nor those which follow justify. How much less the works of the Law! The works which precede do not justify because they prepare for righteousness; those which follow do not justify because they demand a justification which has already been accomplished. For we are not made righteous by doing righteous works, but rather we do righteous works by being righteous. Therefore grace alone justifies.

22. *Through faith in Jesus Christ.* This statement is a useful addition against the rebellion of the proud, if they should say: "We agree that we are unrighteous of ourselves, and we believe that we are prone to evil and hostile to the Law in our hearts. Therefore we believe that we must be justified by God, but we ourselves will obtain this as we pray to Him and lament and confess. But we do not want Christ, for God can give us righteousness without Christ."

The answer to this is that He neither wills nor can do this. For Christ also is God. Righteousness will not be given except through faith in Jesus Christ. So it has been established, so it pleases God, and it will not be changed. For who can resist His will? This is only supreme arrogance to wish to be justified without Christ.

But at this point let those men open their eyes of whom I spoke above, who believe in Christ but not in the Word of Christ, who will not heed their spiritual leader but have their pleasure in themselves and in their own ideas. They trust in themselves and not in the word of their pastor or of some good man, that is, the Christ who speaks in such men, for they presume that they can be justified without this obedience, without this faith in God and by performing their own good works. But this cannot be, for the statement still stands: "the righteousness of God by faith in Jesus Christ." From this follows

Corollary

When it says "without the Law," the Law itself with its works is to be understood. Thus when it says "the faith of Christ" (*fides Christi*), we must understand faith in Christ (*fides in Christum*) and in the word of anyone through whom He speaks.

Just as the expression "without the Law" means without the cooperation of the Law and the works of the Law, so also belief in Christ means faith in Him wherever He is and through whomsoever He speaks. Thus we must be very much on our guard that we do not sometime become set in our minds, that we do not resist Christ and refuse to believe in Him, not realizing when, where, how, and through whom He is speaking to us. And almost always it is the case that He speaks to us in the place, the time, the manner, and through the person that we do not think He should. As He Himself says, "The wind blows where it wills (not where we will or think), and you hear the sound of it, but you do not know whence it comes or whither it goes" (John 3:8). For He is near us and in us, but always in a form which is strange to us, not in the appearance of glory but in humility and gentleness, so that He is not thought to be who He really is. Hence the Holy Spirit gives this precept: "Hear, O daughter, consider, and incline your ear, etc." (Ps. 45:10), as if to say that it is necessary that you always and everywhere be swift to hear and to bend your ear and that your entire duty is humbly to listen and receive instruction. As Ps. 2:10 says: "Now therefore, O kings, be wise, be warned."

21. *The Law bears witness.* As Hab. 2:4 says: "The righteous shall live by his faith"; Hosea 2:20: "I will betroth you to Me in faithfulness"; and Jer. 31:31-33: "I will make a new covenant with the house of Judah. . . . I will write My law upon their hearts, etc." We also have in Genesis the example of Abraham and the others who were justified by faith.

Blessed Augustine in the 13th chapter of his *On the Spirit and the Letter* says: "What the law of works commands by its threats, this the law of faith accomplishes by believing. The one says: 'You shall not covet' (Ex. 20:17); the other says: 'When I knew that I could not otherwise be continent except God gave it . . . I went to the Lord and besought Him, etc.' (Wisd. of Sol. 8:21). And through this law of works God says: 'Do what I command.' But by the law of faith we can say to God in humble prayer: 'Give me what Thou commandest.' For the Law commands in such a way that it tells faith what to do (that is, what it ought to do), in other words, so that if the one who is commanded cannot as yet fulfill the command, he may know what he should ask." [35] And in chapter 19 Augustine says: "The Law is given, therefore, in order that grace may be sought whereby the Law in turn may be fulfilled. That the Law is not fulfilled is not the fault of the Law, but it is the fault of the thinking of the flesh. This fault had to be shown by the Law but had to be cleansed by grace. Rom. 8:3-4: 'For God has done what the Law, weakened by the flesh, could not do: sending His own

[35] *Patrologia, Series Latina,* XLIV, 214.

Son in the likeness of sinful flesh and for sin, He condemned sin
in the flesh, in order that the just requirement of the Law might
be fulfilled in us, who walk not according to the flesh.'" [36] John
1:17: "For the Law was given through Moses; grace and truth came
through Jesus Christ."

But now who will reveal to us all the tricks of the messenger
of Satan by which he is trying to deceive us? We all pray: Give what
Thou commandest, and yet we do not receive this power. We all
believe and speak, we confess and act, and yet we are not all
justified. Others who are still rather inexperienced he deceives in
this way, that they do not see their own weaknesses and the inclination of their wicked will, nor have they analyzed themselves to see
how unwillingly they obey the Law and how little they love it, but
actually they believe and act out of a servile fear; yet they think
that they are doing enough and that they must therefore be regarded as righteous before God, because they believe and act;
yet they are in no way anxious to do this work so as to do it gladly
in joy and love and with full will, or even to see their need of God's
grace to accomplish it. But trusting only in their own powers they
go about doing their works, although always with tedium and difficulty, when actually they ought to be seeking God with earnest
prayers that He might take this tedium from them and fill their
will with happiness and through grace take from them their inclination toward evil. For this, I say, there must be earnest prayer,
earnest study, earnest work and reproof, until this old habit is
eradicated and a newness of will comes into being. For grace is not
given without this self-cultivation. But they are snoring so loudly,
they have become so lukewarm, so stultified, so arid and so obdurate, that finally they have lost their faith and have become full of
impatience and evil desires, "unfit for any good deed" (Titus 1:16).

But other people who are more discerning he deceives by a
subtler delusion. He makes these people do their good works with
joy and happiness, so that under this pretense he may hide their
weakness from them, so that they thus come to believe that they
have grace, and in this subtle manner they come to be more pleased
with themselves than with others and are proud, until they have
become completely taken up with their own uniqueness and superstition, as is often the case with heretics and stubborn people
under the appearance of truth and righteousness in a "zeal which
is not enlightened" (Rom. 10:2). Then they become rebels and

[36] Ibid., p. 221.

under the appearance of obedience and fear of God they become disobedient and disdainful of the men of God, that is, Christ's vicars and ambassadors. If we examine ourselves carefully, therefore, we shall always find in ourselves at least vestiges of the flesh by which we are afflicted with self-interest, obstinate over against the good, and prone to do evil. For if there were not this kind of remnant of sin in us and if we were seeking only God, surely this mortal man would quickly be dissolved, and our soul would fly to God. But the fact that the soul does not take to flight is a sure sign that it still clings to the filth of the flesh until it may be freed by the grace of God, and this is to be awaited in death. Meanwhile, we always have to groan with the apostle: "Who will deliver me from the death of this body?" (Rom. 7:24).[37] We must always be afraid of neglecting to drown this sin further. Therefore we must always pray and work so that grace and the Spirit may increase but the body of sin decrease and be destroyed and our old nature become weak. For God has not yet justified us, that is, He has not made us perfectly righteous or declared our righteousness perfect, but He has made a beginning in order that He might make us perfect. Hence we read in James 1:18: "That we should be a kind of first fruits of His creatures." This is pointed out in the story of the man half dead who was brought to the inn. After his wounds had been bandaged He was not yet cured, but he was on the way to being made whole.

But it is easy, if we use any diligence at all, to see the depravity of our will in our love of sensual evils and our flight from things that are good, if, for instance, we are drawn toward lust, greed, gluttony, arrogance, love of honor, and we abhor chastity, generosity, sobriety, humility, shame; but it is easy, I say, to understand how in these things we seek our fulfillment and love ourselves, how we are turned in upon ourselves and become ingrown at least in our heart, even when we cannot sense it in our actions.

In spiritual matters, however (that is, in our understanding, our righteousness, our chastity, our piety), it is most difficult to see whether we are seeking only ourselves in them. For the love of these things, since it is honorable and good, often becomes an end in itself for us and does not permit us to regulate them in accord with God and refer them to Him, so that as a result we do them not because they are pleasing to God but because they delight us and

---

[37] Luther quotes the passage this way, but the Vulgate reads: "From the body of this death."

quiet the fears of our heart, because we are praised by men, and thus we do them not for the sake of God but for ourselves. And this proves to be a temptation. For if we are condemned because of this or if God takes away our enjoyment of these things and the pleasure which they give to our heart, then we neglect to do them or return the condemnations in kind and defend ourselves.

Corollary

Through such presumptuousness and pride it comes about that even the works of grace are turned into works of the Law and the righteousness of God is turned into the righteousness of men, because, when men in grace have done good works, they become pleased with themselves thereby and stop right there and are unwilling to go forward, as if they had thus laid complete hold on righteousness, when actually they should have been progressing and should have been looking upon these good works as only preparatory. Indeed, all righteous works and works which are done in grace are only preparatory for the growth of righteousness which follows, according to the statements "Let the righteous still do right" (Rev. 22:11) and "They go from strength to strength" (Ps. 84:7) and "from one degree of glory to another" (2 Cor. 3:18), with the apostle "straining forward to what lies ahead, forgetting what lies behind" (Phil. 3:13) or has preceded. Thus not one of the saints thinks or says that he is righteous but rather always prays and waits to be justified, and for this reason he is regarded by God as righteous, because He has regard for the humble. Thus Christ is King of the Jews, that is, of those who confess [38] that they are always sinners and yet seek to be justified and hate their sins. Hence "God is wonderful in His saints" (Ps. 68:35), because He regards as righteous those who acknowledge themselves as sinners and grieve over their sins, but He condemns those who think that they are righteous. Thus in Ps. 32:5-6: "I said, 'I will confess against myself my unrighteousness; and Thou didst forgive the iniquity of my sin. Therefore let everyone who is godly offer prayer to Thee" (that is, the righteous, the justified). It is a marvelous thing that a righteous man prays for his sins. Thus also Ecclus. 39:5, 6 speaks of the righteous man: "He will make supplication for his

---

[38] When Leah gave birth to Judah, she exclaimed: "This time I will praise (confess) the Lord!" (Gen. 29:35). Lyra, commenting on this passage, says that Judah means "confessor." Luther refers to Christ as King of the Jews in the sense of what the name Jews (*Judaei*) originally meant.

sins" and "In his prayer he will confess to the Lord," that is, confess his sin. He uses the expression "against myself" which is what I have been trying to say, namely, that the righteous man acknowledges himself to be a sinner and yet hates his sin, just as the ungodly man sees only his righteousness and is pleased with himself in it. So also Ps. 51:3: "For I know my transgression, and (I not only know, but also) my sin is always before me." Therefore, I confess: "Against Thee only have I sinned and done that which is evil in Thy sight, so that Thou art justified in Thy sentence," as if to say, because I acknowledge and hate my sin, therefore Thou dost forgive my sin and justify me, because Thou alone shalt be justified.

In this alone we are saved, therefore, that having sin and living in sin we grieve because we have it and cry to God for deliverance, in accord with John's saying (1 John 1:8-9): "If we say we have no sin, we deceive ourselves, and the truth is not in us. If we confess our sins, He is faithful and just and will forgive our sins and cleanse us from all unrighteousness." In this way, yes, in this way, "The sacrifice acceptable to God is a broken spirit; a broken and a contrite heart, O God, Thou wilt not despise" (Ps. 51:17). "For there is no man who does not sin," says Solomon in his prayer (1 Kings 8:46). And Moses in Ex. 34:7 says: "Before whom no man of himself is innocent." And again, Eccl. 7:20 says: "There is not a righteous man on the earth who does good and never sins." And again, "Who can say, 'I have made my heart clean?'" (Prov. 20:9). Therefore: "There is none righteous. All have turned aside" (Ps. 14:3; Rom. 3:10, 12). Thus we pray: "Forgive us our debts" (Matt. 6:12). And where do these sins and debts come from? Because no one fulfills the Law except Christ. For no living man is justified before God, because his heart is always weak toward the good and prone toward evil. He does not love righteousness without in some way also loving iniquity. But Christ "loves righteousness and hates wickedness" (Ps. 45:7). As the apostle explains later on in chapter 7:25, "With the flesh we serve the law of sin, but with the spirit the Law of God." And thus we are partly righteous, but not wholly so. Thus we have sin and debt. When we pray, therefore, that our righteousness be made perfect in us and that our sin be taken away, we are praying at the same time to finish this life. For in this life this inclination toward evil will never be perfectly cleansed, just as the Children of Israel, to use a figure of speech, could not drive out the Jebusites.[39] Hence, immediately after the petition "Hal-

---

[39] Cf. Joshua 15:63.

lowed be Thy name" (which takes place through our sanctification from sins and evil works) comes the petition "Thy kingdom come" (Matt. 6:10), as if he were saying that it will not be a complete sanctification except in Thy kingdom. But this also will not come except through tribulations. Therefore the words "Thy will be done" follow, just as Christ prayed in the garden in the time of His tribulation.

Who, therefore, can exalt himself against another person as if he were more righteous than the other? When he not only can do the same as the other man does, but also in his heart actually does the same before God as the other man does before men. Therefore no one should ever despise a man who sins, but one should kindly help him as one who shares a common misery, and we should help each other just as two people who are caught in the same mire help each other. Thus "we bear one another's burdens and so fulfill the law of Christ" (Gal. 6:2). But if we despise the other person, we shall both perish in the mire.

23. *And fall short of the glory of God.* The term "glory" must be understood here in the sense of glorying. And the expression "they fall short" is taken in the sense of being deprived of something, that is, they are empty or have no share. So the meaning is: They do not have a righteousness of which they can glory before God, as we read in 1 Cor. 1:29: "So that no human being might boast in the presence of God." And earlier we read (Rom. 2:17): "You boast of your relationship to God." Later, in chapter 5:11: "We rejoice in God through Jesus Christ." Therefore "They fall short of the glory of God," that is, they do not have anything of which they can glory in God and about God, as Ps. 3:3 says: "But Thou, O Lord, art a shield about me, my glory," that is, my glorying. So also below (Rom. 4:2): "If Abraham was justified by works, he has something to boast about, but not before God." Thus also they have a glory before men because of their works of righteousness. "Glory of God" is used in the same way as righteousness, wisdom, and virtue, that is, something which is given to us by God and because of which we can before Him glory in Him and about Him.

25. The Master of the Sentences [40] and certain other writers construe and interpret the passage *in His divine forbearance He had passed over former sins* as meaning that God shows His righteousness, that is, His truth, for the sake of the remission of the

[40] Peter Lombard, *Collectanea in Epistolam ad Romanos, Patrologia, Series Latina,* CXCI, 1362.

sins of those who went before (that is, the fathers under the old law), whose sins He remitted "in forbearance," that is, for the sake of the coming satisfaction of Christ. In forgiving He forbore them, and He allowed the satisfaction to come after the forgiveness; but in our case the satisfaction through Christ came first. And thus the text of the apostle would more clearly be put this way: "To show His righteousness by forgiving, or in forgiving, in the forbearance of God the sins of those who went before." For the sins of all, both those who have gone before as well as those who will follow, are forgiven through Christ alone.

But it makes better sense if the term "He passed over former sins" be taken as an adjective and a substantive, so that the meaning is: God through the remission of the sins which we have committed in the past shows that He is the justifier of all. And thus the remission of sins proves that He is righteous and that He is able to justify. As has been said above: "That Thou mayest be justified in Thy words" (v. 4), which he repeats here by saying:

26. *That He himself is righteous and that He justifies.* He speaks of "former sins," however, because He does not forgive all sins, lest someone should say: "If sins are taken away through Christ, let us then do whatever we wish, for no one can now sin," as those people do who surrender the Spirit for "an opportunity for the flesh" (Gal. 5:13) and make their liberty a cloak for evil (cf. 1 Peter 2:16). For grace and forbearance are not given in order that we may sin or act as we want to, as he later points out when he says that we are not under the Law: "What then? Are we to sin because we are not under Law?" (Rom. 6:15). And he answers: He does not remit sins in such a way that He no longer regards the work of anyone as sin and simply takes the Law away, but He does not punish the sins of the past which He has patiently endured, in order that He may justify. He therefore is not indulgent toward us in order that we may do as we please.

Similarly, it is obvious from this text that God is called righteous by the apostle because He justifies or makes us righteous, as has been said above. And thus it is also evident from the apostle, who interprets himself, that "righteousness of God" (v. 21) is a term which describes that by which He makes us righteous, just as the wisdom of God is that by which He makes us wise.

Through this term "former sins," therefore, the apostle is opposing the foolish and carnal understanding which would interpret the apostle's words thus: "God has fulfilled the Law, He no longer imputes sin, He no longer wishes to regard as sin that which He formerly held to be sin. Therefore, let us perform in safety the same deeds as we did formerly, but now they are not sin."

The expression "to uphold the Law" (v. 31) is understood in two ways, namely, intrinsically and extrinsically. Intrinsically, the Law was formally established when the tenor and the words of the Law were put into use, so that it points out and indicates what must be done and what omitted. On the other hand, the Law is "overthrown" when it is done away with and abrogated, so that it no longer binds and men are permitted to act contrary to it. And in this way carnal people could get the idea that the apostle is overthrowing the Law because he says that we are not justified by the Law, but that "apart from the Law the righteousness of God has been manifested and given" (v. 21). In another way, extrinsically and by way of example, the Law is established and confirmed when we carry out and perform what the Law has prescribed or else omit what the Law has forbidden. Thus we read in Jer. 35:14: "The command of Jonadab . . . which he gave to his sons has been kept, for they have obeyed their father's command." Note that the term "his command has been kept" is the same as saying that it is being obeyed. And later on we read (v. 16): "The sons of Jonadab have constantly kept the commandment which their father gave them, but this people has not obeyed Me," as if to say, they have not upheld, they have not kept my precept, but rather they have overthrown it. So we read in Ps. 11:3: "For they have destroyed the things which Thou hast made"; Ps. 119:126: "It is time, O Lord, to act; for Thy law has been broken"; Hab. 1:4: "So the Law is slacked, and justice never goes forth"; and Jer. 31:32: "My covenant which they broke," that is, by their disobedience. The Law, therefore, is overthrown extrinsically, when what it commands or forbids is either not done or is done. The apostle is speaking of this matter when he says: *On the contrary, we uphold the Law* (v. 31), that is, we assert that it is fulfilled and confirmed by faith. But you people destroy it when you do not fulfill it. You even teach that it should not be fulfilled when you teach that the works of the Law are sufficient even without faith. Below, in chapter 8:3, we read: "For what the Law, weakened by the flesh, could not do . . . ."

Thus we read in Ps. 18:36: "Thou didst give a wide place for my steps under me; and my feet did not slip," that is, the example of my life is strengthened when there are many who imitate it.

Thus we commonly say: "This or that profession or this or that group is strong and solid when there are many who belong to it. But it is weakened and ineffectual when it has no followers.

Thus the Law is upheld both in itself and in us. In itself, when it is promulgated; in us, when we fulfill it with our will and our works. But apart from faith no man does this. We always make the covenant of God null and void, therefore, if we live without the grace of God through Christ.

27. *On what principle? On the principle of works? No, but on the principle of faith.* The principle of works of necessity puffs us up and makes for glorying, because he who is righteous and fulfills the Law doubtless has something of which to glory and exalt himself. Now those people of whom we have been speaking believe that they are of this class, because they have fulfilled outwardly what the Law demands and forbids. For this reason they do not humble themselves, they do not despise themselves as sinners. They do not seek to be justified, they do not cry out for righteousness, because they are confident that they already possess it.

Hence we must note, as we have said above in quoting blessed Augustine,[41] that "the principle of works says: 'Do what I command,' but the principle of faith says: 'Give what You command.'" And thus the people of the Law say to the Law and to God, who speaks in the Law: "I have done what Thou hast commanded, it is done as Thou hast ordered." But the people of faith say: "I cannot do, I have not done, but give me what Thou commandest; I have not done it, but I desire to do it. And because I cannot, I beg and beseech of Thee the power whereby I may do it." And thus the former is made proud and boastful, and the latter humble and vile in his own eyes. And thus there is a very real difference between these classes of people, because the one says: "I have done it," and the other says, "I beg that I might be empowered to do it"; the one says: "Command what Thou dost wish, and I will do it," the other says: "Give what Thou hast commanded in order that I may do it"; the one is confident in the righteousness which he already possesses, the other prays for the righteousness which he hopes to acquire.

For this reason the whole life of the new people, the faithful people, the spiritual people, is nothing else but prayer, seeking, and begging by the sighing of the heart, the voice of their works, and the labor of their bodies, always seeking and striving to be

[41] See p. 243 above.

made righteous, even to the hour of death, never standing still, never possessing, never in any work putting an end to the achievement of righteousness, but always awaiting it as something which still dwells beyond them, and always as people who still live and exist in their sins. Thus when the apostle says that a man is justified *apart from works of the Law* (v. 28), he is not speaking about the works which are performed in order that we may seek justification. Because these are no longer the works of the Law but of grace and faith, since he who performs them does not trust in them for his justification, but he wants to be justified and he does not think that through these works he has fulfilled the Law, but he seeks its fulfillment. But Paul calls those works the works of the Law which those who do them regard as the reason for their justification, and by the performance of which they consider themselves righteous. They do not do these works, therefore, in order to seek justification, but that they may glory in the righteousness which they already possess. Therefore, after they have performed these works, they come to a stop, as if, now that the Law has been entirely fulfilled, no other justification were necessary. And surely this is a proud and arrogant attitude. Indeed, it is also utterly wrong to think that the works of the Law could fulfill the Law, for the Law is spiritual, demanding a heart and a will which we do not possess by ourselves, as we have often said previously. Thus these people do the outward works of the Law but not the inner desires of the Law. And thus the people of faith spend their whole life seeking justification. This is their prayer: "Draw me after Thee" (Song of Sol. 1:3); "Upon my bed by night I sought Him . . . I sought Him but found Him not" (Song of Sol. 3:1); "I called Him, but He gave no answer" (Song of Sol. 5:6), that is, "I never thought that I had apprehended, but I am always seeking." Hence his voice is finally called the "voice of the turtledove" (Song of Sol. 2:12), because he is always groaning and crying. And "blessed are those who hunger and thirst for righteousness" (Matt. 5:6).

Ps. 34:9: "Those who fear the Lord have no want."

Ps. 14:2: "There is no one who seeks after God," as if to say that they think they have found Him.

Ps. 105:4: "Seek His presence continually," as if to say you should not think that you have already found Him.

Ps. 105:45: "That they should observe His laws."

Is. 21:12: "If you will inquire, inquire."

Is. 65:1: "They have sought Me that before asked not for Me."

The same theme runs through the whole octonary psalm,[42] in almost every verse:

"O that my ways may be steadfast in keeping Thy statutes" (Ps. 119:5).

"I will keep Thy statutes" (Ps. 119:145).

"With my whole heart have I sought Thee: let me not wander" (Ps. 119:10).

The apostle likewise also does not think that he himself has attained, but he stretches forward, seeking the things which are ahead, and when he has found them, he forgets the things which are behind (Phil. 3:12-14). For he who thus seeks in heart and work, by the very fact that he seeks to be justified and does not think that he is righteous, is doubtless already righteous before God. For he does not confess himself to be a sinner in such a way that he wants to keep his sins and depart from God, but rather that he may be freed from them and be justified, always saying: "Forgive us our debts" and "Hallowed be Thy name" (Matt. 6:12, 9).

But what does it mean that Is. 65:1 says, "I was found by them that did not seek Me; I appeared openly to them that asked not after Me"? Cf. Rom. 10:20. Are we not to seek Him but only to wait for Him till He is found by chance? This passage is understood in the first place as being directed against the stupid search by those who seek God by a way which they themselves have devised, not the one by which God wishes to be sought and found.

In the second place, the passage is understood as meaning that the righteousness of God is brought to us without our merits and our works, while we are doing and looking for many other things rather than the righteousness of God. For who has ever sought, or would have sought, the incarnate Word, if He had not revealed Himself? Therefore He was found when He was not looked for. But having been found, He now wills to be sought and found over and over again. He is found when we are converted to Him from our sins, but He is sought when we continue in this conversion.

There is a difference, therefore, between sinners and sinners. Some are sinners and confess that they have sinned, but they do not desire to be made righteous; instead, they despair and keep on sinning, so that in death they despair and in life they are slaves to the world. Others, however, are sinners and confess that they sin and have sinned, but they grieve about it and hate themselves for it and desire to be made righteous and constantly pray and cry to

---

[42] Psalm 119, so called because it is usually divided into 8-verse stanzas.

God for righteousness. These are the people of God, who bear the judgment of the cross like a yoke upon their shoulders.

In the same way there is also a difference between the righteous and the righteous. For some affirm that they are righteous and do not care to be justified, but rather they expect to be rewarded and crowned as kings. Others deny that they are righteous and fear condemnation and desire to be justified.

Therefore the fact that we are sinners does not harm us as long as we strive with all our strength to be made righteous.

The devil, therefore, that master of a thousand tricks,[43] lays traps for us with marvelous cleverness. He leads some astray by getting them involved in open sins. Others, who think themselves righteous, he brings to a stop, makes them lukewarm, and prompts them to give up the desire for righteousness, as Rev. 3:14 ff. speaks of the angel of Laodicea. A third group he seduces into superstitions and ascetic sects, so that, for example, in their greater degree of holiness and in their imagined possession of righteousness, they do not at all grow cold but feverishly engage in works, setting themselves apart from the others, whom they despise in their pride and disdain. A fourth class of people he urges on with ridiculous labor to the point where they try to be completely pure and holy, without any taint of sin. And as long as they realize that they are sinning and that evil may overwhelm them, he so frightens them with the judgment and wears out their consciences that they all but despair. He senses the weakness of each individual and attacks him in this area. And because these four classes of people are so fervent for righteousness, it is not easy to persuade them to the contrary. Thus he begins by helping them to achieve their goal, so that they become overanxious to rid themselves of every evil desire. And when they cannot accomplish this, he causes them to become sad, dejected, wavering, hopeless, and unsettled in their consciences. Then it only remains for us to stay in our sins and to cry in hope of the mercy of God that He would deliver us from them. Just as the patient who is too anxious to recover can surely have a serious relapse, we must also be healed gradually and for a while put up with certain weaknesses. For it is sufficient that our sin displeases us, even though we do not get entirely rid of it. For Christ carries all sins, if only they are displeasing to us, and thus they are no longer ours but His, and His righteousness in turn is ours.

43 *Mille artifex* echoes the German *Tausendkünstler.*

CHAPTER FOUR

3. *Abraham believed God*

THE statement that Abraham believed ought to be understood in an absolute and universal sense, and not only with regard to the passage in Gen. 15:6, so that the meaning is: Abraham was a man who was always prepared to believe God. He always believed. This is obvious from the fact that in Gen. 12 and 13 he also believed God when He called him and ordered him to leave his homeland and to migrate to another. Therefore there, too, "it was reckoned to him as righteousness." Likewise in Gen. 22 he believed God when He commanded him to sacrifice his son Isaac, and the same is the case in other passages. And the apostle clearly shows in Heb. 11 that he did all of these things by faith. Hence also the text here follows the preceding clause without any conjunctive particle, so that we should understand that what follows pertains not only to the preceding statement but is stated in an absolute sense to every reference to Abraham's faith. For the text reads thus: "So shall your descendants be" (Gen. 15:5). And as soon as these words of God have been spoken, there immediately follows without any conjunction the statement "Abraham believed God." Likewise, note that it does not say that Abraham believed God in this respect, but he believed Him in an absolute manner. Thus the expression "Abraham believed God" is equivalent to saying that he considered God truthful, for "to believe God" means to believe Him always and everywhere. But these things have been said so that some dolt does not slander the apostle for using the example of Abraham to prove a general statement about faith, and so that no one can say that even before this text was written Abraham had pleased God, and yet there was no mention of that fact that "Abraham believed God and He reckoned it to him as righteousness."

6. *So also David pronounces.* This passage must be understood in this way: *His faith is reckoned as righteousness. So David also*

pronounces (that is, asserts) *a blessing upon the man* (that is, that that man is blessed, or that blessedness is of that man alone) *to whom God reckons righteousness apart from works.* And the expression "apart from works" must be understood, as we have pointed out above,[1] of those works by the doing of which a person thinks he has received righteousness and now possesses it, as if he thereby is made righteous because he has performed those works, or as if God now regards him as a righteous man because he is doing them, although this is not true, because God does not accept a person because of his works but the works because of the person, therefore the person before the works. As it is written, "And the Lord had regard for Abel (first) and (afterwards) for his offering" (Gen. 4:4).[2] Hence it becomes obvious that it is not so much the works of that kind as the foolish opinion or estimation of these works which is disapproved. For the righteous do the same works as the unrighteous, but not from the same heart. That is, the righteous perform the works that they may seek and obtain righteousness through them, but the wicked do them that they may make a display of righteousness through them and boast of it as already found. The former are not content with the works they have performed and seek to have their heart justified and cleansed from sinful desires, but the latter care nothing for their inner life and are content with works performed externally. Therefore they are merely pretenders and are hypocrites, that is, they are like the righteous outwardly, but they are not really righteous inwardly. Thus Job 39:13 says, "The wing of the ostrich is like the wings of the heron and of the hawk."[3] It is as if he were saying: "But it cannot fly and seek its prey as the heron and the hawk do." These people consider themselves righteous, but the others want God to account them as such. The talk and teaching of the former is that he is righteous who has done this or that, but the teaching of the latter is that he is righteous "against whom the Lord will not reckon his sin" (4:8). The one group knows how much and what one must do in order that he may be righteous. The others, however, do not know when they are righteous, because they are righteous only when God imputes righteousness to them, and no man knows His

---

[1] Cf. p. 252 above.

[2] Luther uses this passage similarly in the first marginal gloss of chapter 1 and adds "not in the first place for his offering." Cf. p. 3 above. See also p. 264 below and W, III, 101, 26 f.

[3] The use of the passage is based on Lyra's moral interpretation.

accounting fully, but one must only seek and hope for it. Therefore the former have a time when they do not think that they are sinners, but the latter always know that they are sinners. Thus in order that we may understand the passage

7. *Blessed are they whose iniquities are forgiven,* we must remember:

1 ⁴

The saints are always sinners in their own sight, and therefore always justified outwardly.

But the hypocrites are always righteous in their own sight, and thus always sinners outwardly.

I use the term "inwardly" *(intrinsice)* to show how we are in ourselves, in our own eyes, in our own estimation; and the term "outwardly" *(extrinsice)* to indicate how we are before God and in His reckoning. Therefore we are righteous outwardly when we are righteous solely by the imputation of God and not of ourselves or of our own works. For His imputation is not ours by reason of anything in us or in our own power. Thus our righteousness is not something in us or in our power. As Hos. 13:9 says, "Destruction is your own, O Israel; your help is only in Me," that is, within yourself there is nothing but destruction, and your deliverance is from outside of you. And Ps. 121:2: "My help comes from the Lord," which is to say, it is not from myself. But inwardly we are sinners according to the law of mutual relationship.[5] For if we are righteous only because God reckons us to be such, then it is not because of our mode of living or our deeds. Thus inwardly and of ourselves we are always unrighteous. Thus we read in Ps. 51:3-4, "My sin is ever before me," that is, I always have it in my mind that I am a sinner. "Against Thee have I sinned" (that is, I am a sinner), "so that Thou art justified in Thy Word, etc." And on the contrary, the hypocrites, because they are righteous in their own sight, by force and necessity of this relationship are outwardly unrighteous (that is, in the reckoning of God), as Ps. 95:10 says, "And I said, 'They are a people who err in heart.'" They pervert every word of Scripture, as, for example, this statement, "My sin is ever before me" (Ps. 51:3), for they say: "My righteousness is always before me" (that is, always in view), and "Blessed are they who work

---

⁴ One of the student notebooks here inserts the label *conclusio prima.*

⁵ Aristotle's definitions regarding the *relativum,* the third in his ten "categories," include the statement that "all relatives, if properly defined, have correlatives" (*Categories,* ch. 7).

righteousness, etc." "Before Thee," they say (not, "I have sinned," but), "I do righteous works." Indeed, before themselves they perform such works.

2

"God is wonderful in His saints" (Ps. 68:35). To Him they are at the same time both righteous and unrighteous.

And God is wonderful in the hypocrites. To Him they are at the same time both unrighteous and righteous.

For inasmuch as the saints are always aware of their sin and seek righteousness from God in accord with His mercy, for this very reason they are always also regarded as righteous by God. Thus in their own sight and in truth they are unrighteous, but before God they are righteous because He reckons them so because of their confession of sin. They are actually sinners, but they are righteous by the imputation of a merciful God. They are unknowingly righteous and knowingly unrighteous; they are sinners in fact but righteous in hope. And this is what he is saying here: "Blessed are they whose iniquities are forgiven, and whose sins are covered" (Ps. 32:1). Hence, these words follow (v. 5), "I said, I will confess my transgressions to the Lord" (that is, I am always conscious of my sin, because I confess it to Thee). Therefore, "Then Thou didst forgive the guilt of my sin," not to me only but to all. Hence these words follow (v. 6): "Therefore let everyone who is godly offer prayer to Thee." Note that every saint is a sinner and prays for his sins. Thus the righteous man is in the first place his own accuser. And again (Ecclus. 39:5), the righteous man "will make supplication for his sins." And again, Ps. 38:18: "I confess my iniquity, I am sorry for my sin." Therefore, wonderful and sweet is the mercy of God, who at the same time considers us both as sinners and nonsinners. Sin remains and at the same time it does not remain. Therefore, this psalm must be understood according to its title.[6] On the other hand, His wrath is also wonderful and severe, for at the same time He regards the ungodly as both righ-

---

[6] The title of Ps. 38 is: "A Psalm of David, for a memorial offering." In his comment on this psalm Luther says (W, III, 211): " 'For a memorial offering' means for confessing our sins. . . . This psalm speaks in the person of Christ. In it He recalls and confesses our sins for us before God the Father and asks for His release from them (that is, our release through Him and in Him). Therefore, whoever wants to pray this psalm profitably should pray it not in his own person but in Christ's and, as it were, should hear Him pray it and thus add his own wishes and say 'Amen.' "

teous and unrighteous. And at the same time He both takes away
their sin and does not take it away. Hence

Corollary

He is speaking not only of sins in deed, word, and thought but
also of the tinder,[7] as later in Rom. 7:20: "It is no longer I that
do it, but sin which dwells within me." And in the same chapter
he speaks of "our sinful passions" (Rom. 7:5), that is, the desires,
feelings, and inclinations toward sin which he says produce fruit
for death. Therefore, act of sin (as it is called by the theologians)
is more correctly sin in the sense of the work and fruit of sin, but
sin itself is the passion, the tinder, and the concupiscence, or the
inclination, toward evil and the difficulty of doing good, as he says
below (Rom. 7:7): "I should not have known concupiscence to be
sin." For if these passions "work," then they are not the works
themselves, but they work to bring forth fruit, and thus they are
not the fruit. Conversely, just as our righteousness from God is the
very turning toward the good and the avoiding of evil which is
given to us inwardly through grace, but our works are the fruits of
righteousness, so also sin is the actual turning away from good and
the inclination toward evil. And the works of sin are the fruits of
this sin, as will be seen very clearly later on in chapters 7 and 8.
And all the passages previously cited must be understood in the
light of this kind of sin. Thus (Rom. 4:7; Ps. 32:1): "Blessed are
those whose iniquities are forgiven," and again (Ps. 32:5-6): "I said,
I will confess my transgressions to the Lord . . . Therefore let everyone who is godly offer prayer to Thee," and again (Ps. 51:3): "For
I know my transgression, and my sin is ever before me," and likewise (Ps. 51:4): "Against Thee only have I sinned, etc." For this is
the evil, since it is truly sin, which God forgives through His
nonimputation out of His mercy toward all who acknowledge and
confess and hate their sin and plead to be cleansed from it. This is
the basis for the statement (1 John 1:8): "If we say we have no sin,
we are liars." And the mistake lies in thinking that this evil can be
cured through works, since experience bears witness that in whatever good work we perform, this concupiscence toward evil remains, and no one is ever cleansed of it, not even the one-day-old
infant. But the mercy of God is that this does remain and yet is not

---

[7] The scholastics used the term *fomes* ("tinder," "spark"), especially in the
combination *fomes concupiscentiae,* to designate man's natural attraction toward
evil.

imputed as sin to those who call upon Him and cry out for His deliverance. For such people easily avoid also the error of works, because they so zealously seek to be justified. Thus in ourselves we are sinners, and yet through faith we are righteous by God's imputation. For we believe Him who promises to free us, and in the meantime we strive that sin may not rule over us but that we may withstand it until He takes it from us.

It is similar to the case of a sick man who believes the doctor who promises him a sure recovery and in the meantime obeys the doctor's order in the hope of the promised recovery and abstains from those things which have been forbidden him, so that he may in no way hinder the promised return to health or increase his sickness until the doctor can fulfill his promise to him. Now is this sick man well? The fact is that he is both sick and well at the same time. He is sick in fact, but he is well because of the sure promise of the doctor, whom he trusts and who has reckoned him as already cured, because he is sure that he will cure him; for he has already begun to cure him and no longer reckons to him a sickness unto death. In the same way Christ, our Samaritan, has brought His half-dead man into the inn to be cared for, and He has begun to heal him, having promised him the most complete cure unto eternal life, and He does not impute his sins, that is, his wicked desires, unto death, but in the meantime in the hope of the promised recovery He prohibits him from doing or omitting things by which his cure might be impeded and his sin, that is, his concupiscence, might be increased. Now, is he perfectly righteous? No, for he is at the same time both a sinner and a righteous man; a sinner in fact, but a righteous man by the sure imputation and promise of God that He will continue to deliver him from sin until He has completely cured him. And thus he is entirely healthy in hope, but in fact he is still a sinner; but he has the beginning of righteousness, so that he continues more and more always to seek it, yet he realizes that he is always unrighteous. But now if this sick man should like his sickness and refuse every cure for his disease, will he not die? Certainly, for thus it is with those who follow their lusts in this world. Or if a certain sick man does not see that he is sick but thinks he is well and thus rejects the doctor, this is the kind of operation that wants to be justified and made well by its own works.

Since this is the case, either I have never understood, or else the scholastic theologians [8] have not spoken sufficiently clearly

[8] Duns Scotus, *Sententiarum,* IV, dist. 1, qu. 6, n. 7, 8; dist. 4, qu. 1, art 2,

about sin and grace, for they have been under the delusion that original sin, like actual sin, is entirely removed, as if these were items that can be entirely removed in the twinkling of an eye, as shadows before a light, although the ancient fathers Augustine and Ambrose spoke entirely differently and in the way Scripture does. But those men speak in the manner of Aristotle in his *Ethics*,[9] when he bases sin and righteousness on works, both their performance or omission. But blessed Augustine says very clearly that "sin, or concupiscence, is forgiven in Baptism, not in the sense that it no longer exists, but in the sense that it is not imputed." [10] And blessed Ambrose says, "I always sin, therefore I always go to Communion." [11] And on the basis of this in my foolishness I could not understand in which way I should regard myself a sinner like other men and thus prefer myself to no one, even though I was contrite and made confession; for I then felt that all my sins had been taken away and entirely removed, even inwardly. For if because of sins that were past, which they say must always be remembered (and here they speak the truth, but not strongly enough), I still had to consider myself a sinner, then I felt that these past sins had not been forgiven. Yet God has promised that they are forgiven to those who confess them. Thus I was at war with myself, not knowing that it was a true forgiveness indeed, but that this is nevertheless not a taking away of sin except in hope, that is, that the taking away is to be done, and that by the gift of grace, which begins to take sin away, so that it is not imputed as sin. For this reason it is plain insanity to say that man of his own powers can love God above all things and can perform the works of the Law according to the substance of the act, even if not according to the intentions of Him who gave the commandment, because he is not in a state of grace.[12] O fools, O pig-theologians *(Sawtheologen)!* By your line of reasoning grace was not necessary except because of

concl. 1-3; dist. 14, qu. 1, art. 1, n. 2; William of Occam, *Sententiarum,* IV, qu. 3, 0; qu. 8, 9, A, J.

[9] Cf. p. 152, n. 30.

[10] Augustine, *De nuptiis et concupiscentia,* I, 25, *Patrologia, Series Latina,* XLIV, 430.

[11] Ambrose, *De sacramentis,* IV, 6, 28, *Patrologia, Series Latina,* XVI, 464.

[12] Cf. Duns Scotus, *Sententiarum,* III, dist. 27, qu. un., n. 13, 15, 21; Pierre d'Ailly, *Sententiarum,* I, qu. 2, art. 2J; esp. Gabriel Biel, *Sententiarum,* II, dist. 28K: *homo per liberum arbitrium ex suis naturalibus potest divina precepta quoad actus substantiam implere, sed non ad intentionem precipientis, que est consecutio salutis nostrae.* Cf. also Thesis 13 in the *Disputation Against Scholastic Theology,*

some new demand above and beyond the Law. For if the Law can be fulfilled by our powers, as they say, then grace is not necessary for the fulfilling of the Law, but only for the fulfilling of some new exaction imposed by God above the Law. Who can endure these sacrilegious notions? When the apostle says that "the Law works wrath" (v. 15) and that the Law "was weakened by the flesh" (Rom. 8:3), it certainly cannot be fulfilled without grace. They could have been made aware of their own foolishness and brought to shame and repentance even by their own experience. For willy-nilly they recognize the evil lusts in themselves. For this reason I say: "Hah! Get busy now, I beg you. Be men! Work with all your might, so that these lusts may no longer be in you. Prove that it is possible by nature to love God, as you say, 'with all your strength' (Luke 10:27) and without any grace. If you are without concupiscence, we will believe you. But if you live with and in these lusts, then you are no longer fulfilling the Law." Does not the Law say, "You shall not covet" (Ex. 20:17), but rather, "You shall love God" (Deut. 6:5)? But when a person desires and loves something else, can he really love God? But this concupiscence is always in us, and therefore the love of God is never in us, unless it is begun by grace, and until the concupiscence which still remains and which keeps us from "loving God with all our heart" (Luke 10:27) is healed and by mercy not imputed to us as sin, and until it is completely removed and the perfect love for God is given to the believers and those who persistently agitate for it to the end.

All of these monstrosities have come from the fact that they did not know what sin is nor forgiveness. For they reduced sin to some very minute activity of the soul, and the same was true of righteousness. For they said that since the will has this synteresis,[13] "it is inclined," albeit weakly, "toward the good." And this minute motion toward God (which man can perform by nature) they imagine to be an act of loving God above all things! But take a good look at man, entirely filled with evil lusts (notwithstanding that minute motion). The Law commands him to be empty, so that he may be taken completely into God. Thus Isaiah in 41:23 laughs at them and says, "Do good or evil if you can!" This life, then, is a life of being healed from sin, it is not a life of sinlessness, with the

with its note, "This is in opposition to Scotus and Gabriel," *Luther's Works,* 31, p. 10.

[13] Cf. p. 157, n. 41.

cure completed and perfect health attained. The church is the inn and the infirmary for those who are sick and in need of being made well. But heaven is the palace of the healthy and the righteous. As blessed Peter says in his Second Epistle 3:13 that the Lord will build "new heavens and a new earth in which righteousness dwells." Righteousness does not yet dwell here, but it is preparing a dwelling place for itself here in the meantime by healing sin. All the saints have had this understanding of sin, as David prophesied in Ps. 32:5 ff. And thus they all have confessed that they were sinners, as is clear in the books of St. Augustine. Our theologians, however, have deflected the discussion of sin to the matter of good works only and have undertaken to teach only those things by which works might be safeguarded but not how through much agony men should humbly seek healing grace and confess themselves to be sinners. Thus of necessity they make men proud and cause them to think that they are already entirely righteous when they have performed certain outward works. And thus they are not at all concerned about declaring war on their evil lusts through unceasing prayer to the Lord. And the result is that there is now in the church a great deal of falling away after confession. For the people do not realize that they need to be justified but are confident that they have been justified and thus they are ruined through their own sense of security without any effort on the part of the devil. This is certainly a case of basing righteousness upon works. And although they implore the grace of God, they do not do so rightly, but only for the sake of forgiveness for an act of sin. But those who truly belong to Christ have the spirit of Christ and act rightly, even though they do not understand what we have just stated; for they act before they understand, indeed, they understand more from life than from what they have been taught.

There is still one more point which is raised in objection to what we have just said, namely, that the righteousness of God even without works is imputed to those who believe. We read in the stories of many of the saints that certain of their works or prayers were well regarded by God and commended to others for an example. And thus they were justified by works of this kind. I reply: A great argument, for it both sets forth a glaring error and makes clearer a useful understanding of what we have been saying up to this point. The error is committed by those who immediately want to imitate with their presumed powers all of those things which have been well regarded by God and thus want to be so regarded themselves, because they are doing the same things as the saints to whom works have been reckoned as righteous. This is merely seeking a righteousness of works and in no way an imitation of the saints but rather a perversion of their example. For those saints to whom these works were reckoned for righteousness and commended as an example surely did not do them in order that they might be so reckoned; indeed, they were entirely ignorant that they were reckoned righteous by God, but did what they could in their humble faith, always praying that their works might be pleasing to God according to His mercy. Thus after they had first been reckoned as righteous because of the humble prayer of faith, then also their works were so reckoned and approved. But you stupid perverter, you first begin with the works which have been reckoned, ignoring the inner groaning by which you were already reckoned as righteous, just as these saints were. You want to be reckoned as righteous only by your works, that is, you want first "regard for the offering" and then "for Abel," [14] which cannot be. And this insanity now rages everywhere in the pulpits of those who should be preaching the Word of God.

Exposition of the Psalm Verses

Here three distinct terms for sin are used in the Hebrew. In the translation of John Reuchlin [15] the passage reads: "Blessed is he who is made free in regard to his offense, who is covered in regard to his sin. Blessed is the man, the Lord will not impute iniquity to him" (Ps. 32:1-2). I do not know the difference between these "sins." The first, that is, *crimen*, which is interpreted in various ways, is called פֶּשַׁע in Hebrew. I would understand this as the work of sin. The second, *peccatum*, which is חֲטָאָה in Hebrew and is almost always translated by "sin," I would understand as the root sin or the lust toward evil which is in us. The third, *iniquitas*, which is עָוֹן in Hebrew and is always translated by *iniquitas*, I would understand as hypocrisy, if it weren't for the clash with the words "Wash me thoroughly from my iniquity, and cleanse me from my sin" (Ps. 51:2). Here it seems to apply to the same thing that a person is iniquitous *(iniquus)* because of a turning away and a sinner *(peccator)* because of a turning toward; in the first case, away from the good, in the second, toward the evil;

14 Cf. p. 256, n. 2.

15 Reuchlin, *Septem psalmi poenitentiales*, 1512.

defiled in the first instance because of an omission and in the second because of a commission, if it is indeed iniquitous *(iniquum)* to place God below the creature, and evil *(malum)*, or sinful *(peccatum)*, to cling to the creature, where the good is not found which there has iniquitously been underrated.

Therefore he says in the first place, "blessed (that is, it goes well with him) is he who is made free," that is, who through grace is made free from the burden of his offense, that is, of the sin which he has actually committed. But this is not enough, unless at the same time he "is covered in regard to his sin," that is, his root evil is not imputed to him as sin. For it is covered when it is still there but not seen, not observed, and not reckoned. That he is freed, rather, that he is made free, means that he is freed not by his own powers, but by God, who acts while he is merely passive himself. For he does not say: "Blessed is he who frees himself by his own merits," but, "he who is freed." He is covered, I should add, through Christ who dwells in us, as Ruth in a figurative sense says to Boaz: "Spread your coat over your maidservant, for you are next of kin" (Ruth 3:9). "And she uncovered his feet and lay down" (Ruth 3:7), that is, the soul lays itself down at Christ's humanity and is covered with His righteousness. Likewise, Ezek. 16:8: "I spread my garment over you and covered your nakedness." And in Ps. 63:7: "In the shadow of Thy wings I sing for joy." Again in Ps. 45:9: "Daughters of kings are in Thy glory," that is, in Thy splendor, when they are honored by Thee and Thou in them. And "in your comeliness and your beauty set out, etc." (Ps. 45:8), that is, the evil work is put away and the residue of sin, that is, the tinder,[16] is not imputed until it is healed. Then in the third place it follows that already an ungodly man is justified; for although he is a sinner, he is not ungodly. For that man is called ungodly who is not a worshiper of God but turns away from Him and is without fear or reverence for God. But a person who is justified and whose "sins are covered" is already turned toward God and is a godly man; for he worships God and seeks Him in hope and fear. And for this reason God regards him as a godly and righteous man. Thus it says in the same psalm (32:5): "Thou didst forgive the guilt of my sin." What is here called guilt *(impietas)* is called sin *(peccatum)* above. For it is one and the same thing to say: "Thou didst forgive the guilt of my sin" and "the Lord has not imputed

---

[16] Cf. p. 259, n. 7.

sin." Thus the meaning is: It is not sufficient that we think ourselves to be godly, for it belongs to the Lord to do the reckoning, and He does so only for those "whose transgressions are forgiven and whose sins are covered." For to them their ungodliness will not be imputed, but rather their godliness. For inwardly there "is no deceit" (Ps. 32:2) in them, which of necessity is in those who do not attribute guilt to themselves, and whose sins have not been covered by God and whose iniquities have not been forgiven.

Corollary

It is foolish and absurd to say: God has obligated us to possess grace and thus to the impossible.[17] I excuse our most faithful God. He is innocent of this imposture. He has not done this. He has not obligated us to possess grace, but He has obligated us to fulfill the Law, in order that He might give this grace to those of us who have been humbled and who implore His grace. But these people make of grace a matter of indignation and something hateful. For what does it mean when we say that God has obligated us to possess grace and that He does not want to accept the Law as being fulfilled according to the substance of the act if it is not fulfilled also according to the intention of the Lawgiver—what else does this mean than to say: Look, we can fulfill the Law without grace? Is it not sufficient that He has burdened us with the Law, without now also demanding that we have grace as a new exaction? What pride! What ignorance of the Law! When God therefore offers grace to us wretched people because He sees that we cannot fulfill His law, so that because of this grace we may fulfill it, these people are still not humbled and do not yet realize that the Law cannot be fulfilled according to "the substance of the act" (as they themselves put it), unless they take "the substance of the act" to be some outward activity, which they can by no means accomplish, but they understand it also as an inner action. For they think that the substance of the act is an activity which is performed for the sake of God from the heart by an action of our will naturally motivated, all of which things contribute to the substance of the act. But the fools do not realize that the will, if it were permitted, would never do what the Law prescribes. For the will is hostile toward the good and prone toward evil. This they certainly experience in their own lives, and yet they speak so impiously and sacrilegiously.

---

17 Cf. pp. 163 f.

For as long as the will is hostile toward the Law, it is turned away from the Law and thus does not fulfill it. Therefore there is need for grace, which makes it willing and even glad to obey the Law.

Therefore, I was correct when I said that all our good is outside of us, and this good is Christ, as the apostle says (1 Cor. 1:30): "God made Him our wisdom, our righteousness, and sanctification, and redemption." And none of these things are in us except through faith and hope in Him. Hence all the praise of the church in the Song of Solomon belongs to Christ, who dwells in His church through faith, just as all the light of the earth does not belong to the earth but to the sun which sheds its light upon it. Thus in the Song of Solomon the church confesses that she is often naked [18] and described as having no other desire than for her Bridegroom, saying (Song of Sol. 1:4): "Draw me after Thee, we will run to the odor of Thine ointments." Always she seeks, always she desires, always she praises her Bridegroom. And thereby she shows that she herself is empty and poor in herself, and that only outside of herself is her fullness and righteousness. For if the confessions of the saints are to be understood as only of past sins and that in the present they show themselves pure, why then do they confess not only their past but also their present sins? Is it not that they know that there is sin in them but that for the sake of Christ it is covered and is not imputed to them, so that they may declare that all their good is outside of them, in Christ, who yet through faith is also in them? Thus in Ps. 45:1 the prophet says that his heart is uttering a good word, that is, a sweet and comforting word. What is this word? "Thou art the fairest of the sons of men" (v. 2), that is, Christ alone is beautiful, and all the sons of men are ugly. Therefore, "In Thy comeliness and Thy beauty set out, proceed triumphantly, and reign" (v. 4). We are His kingdom, but the beauty in us is not ours but His, and with it He covers our ugliness.

Hence many give themselves up to laziness and security because of trust in the well-known word which St. Augustine is supposed to have spoken: "A large part of righteousness is the will to be righteous." [19] And thus they equate this "wanting" with the most minute action which is produced but soon relapses and amounts to nothing, in which, however, they go their way snoring

---

[18] Cf. p. 137, n. 6.

[19] Cf. Augustine, *Letter 127, 5, Patrologia, Series Latina,* XXXIII, 485. Also see p. 241 and p. 328.

most smugly. Yet it is true that "wanting" is righteousness, not just a large part but all the righteousness which can be obtained in this life. But this "wanting" is not that of which we have been speaking but that which the apostle mentions later in the epistle (Rom. 7:18): "I can will what is right, but I cannot do it." For this entire life is a time of willing to be righteous, but never achieving it, for this happens only in the future life. And thus "to will" is to show with all our powers, our zeal, our prayers, our works, and our emotions that we desire righteousness but do not yet have it perfectly. Concerning these things, see how beautifully and richly blessed Augustine has written in many of his books, especially in his second book *Against Julian*, where he cites St. Ambrose, Hilary, Cyprian, Chrysostom, Basil, Nazianzen, Irenaeus, Reticius, and Olympius.[20] Therefore the mother of hypocrites and the cause of hypocrisy is this very smugness. For God leaves us in this sin, in the tinder,[21] in our sinful lusts, in order that He may keep us in His fear [22] and humility so that we may always flee to His grace, always in fear of sinning, that is, always praying that He will not impute our sin to us nor let sin have dominion over us. Indeed we sin even by not being afraid of sin. For this evil in us is itself sin, because on account of it we do not succeed in loving God above all things. But it becomes a venial sin [23] and is not imputed to us only when we lament it and ask God not to condemn us on account of it or not to impute it to us, anxiously imploring His mercy and praying that through His grace He would take it from us. And thus by this very act we confess that we are sinners and with tears, penitence, mourning, and weeping we consider ourselves to be sinners. For when this fear and anxiety cease, then very soon smugness takes hold of us, and as soon as this has happened, God's imputation of sin returns, for God has determined that He will impute sin to no one who mourns and fears his sins and anxiously seeks His mercy. By this most merciful counsel our most blessed God compels us to grow weary of this life and to hope for the future life, to a desire for His grace, to a hatred of sin, to repentance, etc.

[20] Augustine, *Contra Julianum*, II, 2, 4-10, 37, *Patrologia, Series Latina*, XLIV, 674—700.

[21] Cf. p. 259, n. 7.

[22] For the relation between *timor Dei* and *securitas*, see Luther's sermon for St. John the Evangelist's Day, 1514 (W, I, 37 ff.).

[23] Cf. p. 276 below. On the question "whether a mortal sin can become a venial sin" see Gabriel Biel, *Sententiarum*, IV, dist. 16, qu. 5, art. 3, dub. 4.

For this reason nothing in the Holy Scriptures is so often described as the cause of pride and laid at the door of hypocrites and those who think themselves holy as this smugness, by which they cast aside the fear of God. Prov. 1:29-30 says: "Because they have hated instruction and did not choose the fear of the Lord, and would have none of My counsel, etc."; Ps. 36:1: "There is no fear of God before their eyes"; and Hos. 10:3: "We fear not the Lord." This misery follows from the fact that they do not seek to purge out that inner sin but recognize only the sin in deed, word, and thought, and when these have been purged by confession they go their way, smug and in no way anxious to cleanse also this inner sin through crying to God that it might not be imputed to them. Thus we read in Rev. 3:17, "For you say, I am rich, I have prospered . . . not knowing that you are wretched, pitiable, naked, and poor." And the apostle says (1 Cor. 5:7), "Cleanse out the old leaven that you may be a new lump, as you really are unleavened." But who of them understands that these two things exist at the same time, that they are unleavened and yet the old leaven must be purged away? This can take place because the one is there in fact but the other because of the humility of faith in fear, in hope and in the nonimputation of God. They have the old leaven, but they grieve because of it and implore grace, and thereby they are unleavened by God's imputation; for He does not impute the old leaven to them but lets it remain to be purged. Hence he who looks only at his actual sin and is concerned only that it be purged, quickly becomes presumptuous and smug, because through the Sacrament and confession he knows that he is purged, and thus he goes his way without any fear and is no longer aware of any sin in him.

Again, others are extremely fainthearted. They sin in a different way, for they are in a hurry to purge out the old leaven and gain perfect health. They would like to root out entirely their internal sin, but because they cannot do it but fall from time to time, they then become sad and downhearted and finally give up hope. And since grace does not cooperate with their excessive zeal and their impetuous haste, they become anxious to accomplish absolute purity by their good works, and they fall most miserably. These people, to be sure, do not have smugness, but yet they are striving toward that which the other group has already achieved. Thus they are both seeking security and are anxious to escape the fear of God, the former in fact, the latter in desire, and thus neither of them fears God. The latter are too afraid, indeed, they are foolishly afraid, for

they think that they would please God only if they were clean; but
then they think that they inevitably displease Him if they are not
cleansed, unaware of the mercy of God which they should have
been imploring, so that He would not impute to them the fact that
they are not clean. And thus they, too, lean dangerously on their
own powers.

Thus those at the right, having given up their fear of God, sin
through their smugness, and those at the left, having turned from
the grace of God, sin through their hopelessness, not understanding
that this inner sin cannot be taken away in this life—which, however, is what they want. The former do not know that it is imputed
precisely to those who do not fear. For both classes of people are
ignorant of this sin and do not pay it proper attention, but, as I have
said, they believe that only actual sin needs to be purged in order
that they may be entirely pure. But since this is not the case, they
think that they are lost. But the others, since they think themselves
to be pure, believe that they are saved, although it is impossible to
be free of all sin as long as that original root sin remains. Therefore
the royal road [24] and the way of peace in the Spirit is to know sin
and to hate it and thus to walk in the fear of God, so that He does
not impute it to us and permit it to rule over us; and at the same time
to pray for His mercy, that He might free us from it and not impute
it to us. Fear excludes the way on the right, mercy the way on the
left; the former takes away smugness, the latter hopelessness; the
former removes self-satisfaction, the latter despair of God. Thus
in order finally to conclude our discussion of these psalm verses,
let us consider again these three terms of which we have spoken [25]
—פֶּשַׁע, which means offenses, crimes, or sins of commission,
violations, and transgressions; חַטָּאָה, which indicates the tinder of
sin, root sin, concupiscence, the sinful disease of our nature; and
עָוֹן, which describes unrighteousness, that is, the absense of righteousness, or the fact that a person is not righteous before God,

---

[24] The "royal road" (here *regia via*, at other times *via media*) represents the
most direct way, one that avoids the aberrations both right and left. The expression is based on Num. 21:22. In his *Von den Schlüsseln*, 1530, Luther points
out that the office of the Keys is given to us by the "faithful Shepherd of our souls,
Jesus Christ," that we may be kept *auf der Mittelstrasse zwischen Vermessenheit
und Verzagen in rechter Demut und Zuversicht* (W, XXX-2, 504, 18). St. Bernard, *De consideratione*, II, 10, *Patrologia, Series Latina, CLXXXII*, 423, 413,
sums up ancient advice in the words *Tene medium . . . Locus medius tutus est.
Medium sedes modi, et modus virtus.* Cf. Luther's use of *medios* above, p. 186
and n. 28.

[25] Cf. p. 264 above.

even if he does many good and righteous acts. This unrighteousness
is imputed to us because of our transgressions or sin. Therefore unrighteousness has to do with God's imputation, just as also righteousness does, and it is a sin of omission and a failure of worship and piety toward God. Concerning this the apostle says in
Rom. 3:10, "None is righteous," that is, he has unrighteousness, and
to have this is to have nothing, or rather, that he is not regarded by
God as a righteous man, even though he does good works, because
works do not establish this righteousness, just as they do not take
away unrighteousness. There is a fourth word in the Hebrew, רֶשַׁע,
which means ungodliness. This is the vice of pride, the denial of
the truthfulness and righteousness of God, the establishment of
one's own righteousness and the defense of one's own wisdom,
which renders men faithless, heretical, schismatic, full of superstition, individualistic or particularistic.[26] Of which the Ps. 80:13
says, "A singular wild beast has devoured it."[27]

Therefore, the meaning of the psalm is: Blessed is the man
(for in Hebrew the singular is used) whose offense, פֶּשַׁע, is lifted
(that is, whose crimes and evil deeds, actual sins, wicked acts,
are remitted, which have been caused by the tinder of sin) and
whose sins are covered; according to the Hebrew, who, or whose
sin, is covered, that is, the very tinder of sin itself, through the
nonimputation of God because of[28] the humility and the cry of
faith for it. Thus the man to whom these two evils are forgiven,
behold, he is the man whom God regards as righteous. Hence it
follows, "Blessed is the man to whom the Lord imputes no iniquity"
(Ps. 32:2). What our text[29] calls "iniquity" more accurately ought

---

26 "Individualistic" and "particularistic" are translations of *moniacus* and
monicus respectively, both extensions of the thought in the Greek μονιός, "singular." In his lecture on Ps. 31:2 Luther had named among the self-righteous the
superstitiosi in singularitate and had described them as people "who reject obedience and faith and set up their own righteousness, because they are unwilling
to have the name of the Lord worshiped above themselves" (W, III, 172, 33 f.).
In his lectures on 1 Timothy in 1528, Luther said: "The monks called this fault
singularitas, that a monk who was dissatisfied with his rule would adopt the hair
shirt. In my order the leaders used to oppose 'individualism' strenuously, and that
was good" (W, XXVI, 7, 23 f.). Cf. Karl Holl, *Gesammelte Aufsätze,* I, pp.
197—203. See also pp. 337 and 422 below.

27 In his commentary on Ps. 80 Luther identifies the "singular wild beast"
with Antiochus or Herod. Cf. W, III, 605, 16.

28 On *propter humilitatem* and similar expressions *(propter confessionem peccati, propter fidem, propter inceptam curationem),* see Karl Holl, *Gesammelte
Aufsätze,* I, pp. 126—129.

29 The Vulgate.

to be understood as "unrighteousness" to be in agreement with the apostle's intention. For by the use of this word he is trying to prove that righteousness is given through imputation without works, and that this takes place through the nonimputation of unrighteousness. It is the same thing, whether we say, "to whom God imputes righteousness," or, "to whom the Lord does not impute sin," that is, unrighteousness. But He will not refrain from imputing this unrighteousness to anyone, no matter how well he performs works, unless his sin has first been covered (that is, the root sin, original sin, natural sin, which is covered through penitence, Baptism, prayer, and the fear of God) and his iniquities have been forgiven, that is, his crimes, or his evil deeds. Thus in this psalm more than in others there is troublesome confusion of these terms. The verse ought to read as follows: "Blessed are they whose crimes are forgiven and whose sin is covered. Blessed is the man to whom God does not impute unrighteousness." And a little later when we read: because "I acknowledged my sin to Thee" (v. 5), where we have the word "fault" (delictum), it is the same word which our version [30] translated with the term "sin" before. "And I did not hide my unrighteousness" (v. 5). This is correctly and very well translated, for it is the same word which our translator previously translated by "sin" in the phrase "the Lord has not imputed sin" (v. 2), with a poor translation of "sin" in the place of "unrighteousness." Then in the words: "I said, I will confess against myself my crimes (scelera) to the Lord" (v. 5), where we wrongly have the expression "my unrighteousness" (iniustitia), because above in the first verse he translated with the plural "iniquities" (iniquitates), and now with the singular "unrighteousness" (iniustitia). "And Thou hast forgiven the wickedness (impietas) of my sin" (v. 5), that is, the unrighteousness of my sin. Here also he changes the word, which in the second [31] verse he translated as "sin" (peccatum) and in the fifth verse as "unrighteousness" (iniustitia), and only in the latter place correctly, as I have said. For the meaning is: "Thou hast not imputed my unrighteousness to me which is in me because of the deep root sin which I possess." "Therefore let everyone who is godly offer prayer to Thee, etc." (v. 6), that is, for the unrighteousness of his sin. "Because all will confess that they really are unrighteous before Thee

[30] Cf. n. 29.

[31] The text has "first," but the translation challenged is "sin" (peccatum) for "iniquity" (iniquitas, עָוֹן) in v. 2.

because of this sin. Therefore Thou wilt forgive and not impute to them their unrighteousness, covering their sin."

And then, "Many are the pangs of the sinner" (v. 10). Here he should have used the word "ungodly" *(impii)*, that is, the man who justifies himself and despises the righteousness of God by establishing his own unrighteousness as a righteousness before God. This is ungodliness and a double sin. These distinctions are very faithfully observed in the Hebrew, but in the translation [32] they are all plainly confused. Thus in Ps. 51:1 "according to Thy abundant mercy blot out my iniquity," that is, "offense" *(crimen)*. Again, "Wash me thoroughly from my iniquity," in place of "unrighteousness" *(iniustitia)*, "and cleanse me from my sin!" (v. 2). "For I know my iniquity" *(iniquitas)*, in place of "my offenses" *(scelera)* or "crimes" *(crimina)*, "and my sin is ever before me" (v. 3). "Against Thee only have I sinned, etc." (v. 4). "Behold I was brought forth in iniquities *(iniquitas)*," in place of "in unrighteousness *(iniustitia)*," and "in sin did my mother conceive me," that is, in the tinder of sin (v. 5). "Hide Thy face from my sins, and blot out all my iniquities *(iniquitas)*," in place of "my unrighteousnesses *(iniustitia)*" (v. 9).

Likewise, "I will teach the unjust *(iniquos)*," in place of "offenders" *(sceleratos)*, "Thy ways, and the wicked *(impii)*," in place of "sinners" *(peccatores)*, "shall be converted to Thee" (v. 13).

Corollary

This verse speaks most explicitly of original sin, according to the Hebrew text: "Behold, I was conceived in iniquities," that is, in unrighteousness *(iniustitia)*, "and in sin did my mother bear me" (Ps. 51:5). For the meaning is that this unrighteousness and sin do not refer to the mother who conceives and bears but to the child who is conceived and brought forth. It is as if he were saying: "Behold when I was conceived, I was in a state of unrighteousness before Thee; I was not righteous because through Adam I had lost this righteousness and thus was conceived without it. For Thou imputest unrighteousness to all those who are conceived because of the sin which is poured out by their parents, even when they do not sin." And "in sin," that is, with the tinder of sin, with sinful lust, "did my mother bear me." Now a mother does not sin by the act of bearing a child, but the son who is born sins, that is, he is a sinner. Surely the psalmist is confessing not someone else's sins

[32] The Vulgate.

but his own, not only in this verse but also in the preceding verses, where he always uses such terms as "my" and "mine." But the reason why in this verse he does not speak of "my" or "mine" is that the sin in which he says that he has been conceived is the common possession of all. And the sin which belongs to all, he asserts, has now become his, too. Therefore he introduces the statement by saying, "Wash me thoroughly from my iniquity, etc." (v. 2). And another reason is that this sin is his own and not his own. Therefore he did not say "in my iniquities" but "in iniquities," as if to say that this iniquity exists whether I perform it or even know about it. I am conceived in it, but I did not do it. It began to rule in me before I began to live. It is simultaneous with me. For if this were only the sin of my parents who conceived me, then surely I would not have been conceived in it, for they would have sinned even before I was conceived. Therefore this iniquity and sin existed and they were not mine; I was conceived in them without my consent. But now they have become mine. For now I understand that I do evil and disobey the Law. The Law commands, "You shall not covet" (Ex. 20:17). And if I do not observe the Law, I am now sinning, and behold, I covet. Therefore the sin is now my own, that is, by my will it has been approved and accepted by my consent, because without grace I have been unable to overcome it in myself; therefore it has overcome me, and I am, because of that same tinder and evil lust, through my work also an actual sinner and not merely under original sin. Therefore I have said, "For I know my transgression, etc." (Ps. 51:3).

Corollary

Scripture uses the terms "righteousness" and "unrighteousness" very differently from the philosophers and lawyers. This is obvious, because they consider these things as a quality of the soul.[33] But the "righteousness" of Scripture depends upon the imputation of God more than on the essence of a thing itself. For he does not have righteousness who only has a quality, indeed, he is altogether a sinner and an unrighteous man; but he alone has righteousness whom God mercifully regards as righteous because of his confession of his own unrighteousness and because of his prayer for the righteousness of God and whom God wills to be considered righteous before Him. Therefore we are all born in iniquity, that is, in unrighteousness, and we die in it, and we are righteous

---

[33] Aristotle, *Categories*, II.

only by the imputation of a merciful God through faith in His Word.

Therefore, let us collect the pertinent statements of Scripture which assert that we are all in our sins.

First, Moses says in Gen. 8:21: "I will never again curse the ground because of man, for the imagination of man's heart is evil from his youth."

Second, he also says in Ex. 34:7: "Lord God, who takest away iniquity and wickedness and sin, and no man of himself is innocent before Thee," as if to say, from the fact that "Thou art the only one who takes away sins" it follows that "no one is righteous in Thy sight," etc. (Rom. 3:20).

Third, Solomon says in 1 Kings 8:46 and 2 Chron. 6:36: "For there is no man who does not sin."

Fourth, he also says in Eccl. 7:20: "Surely there is not a righteous man on earth who does good and never sins."

Fifth, Job, who speaks more fully than the others, says in Job 7:20-21: "I have sinned. . . . Why dost Thou not take away my iniquity"; and later in 9:2: "Truly I know that it is so; for no man will be justified before God," and in 9:15: "Though I am innocent, I cannot answer Him; I must appeal for mercy to my judge." He speaks the same way throughout almost all of the book, although in 27:6 he brings in his own righteousness by saying: "My heart does not reproach me for any of my days." But even the Lord Himself in chapter 1 commended him before Satan.

Sixth, Ps. 32:6: "Therefore let everyone who is godly offer prayer to Thee." And Ps. 143:2: "No man living is righteous before Thee." Likewise Ps. 130:8: "And He will redeem Israel from all his iniquities." And Ps. 72:14: "From oppressions and violence He redeems their life." And there are many similar passages.

Seventh, Is. 64:6: "We have all become like one who is unclean, and all our righteous deeds are like the rag of a menstruous woman."

Eighth (Jer. 30:11) [34]: "I will chasten you in just measure, that you may not seem to yourself innocent."

From the New Testament:

Ninth, the apostle says (1 Tim. 1:15): "Jesus came to save sinners, of whom I am the foremost." Again, he says in Rom. 7:19: "The evil I do not want is what I do, etc." Again (Phil. 3:13): "I do not consider that I have made it my own."

[34] As he did in many other places, Luther left a space here for the insertion of the identification of the quotation.

Tenth, James 3:2: "We all make many mistakes."

Eleventh, 1 John 1:8: "If we say we have no sin, etc." However, farther on he says (1 John 5:18), "Anyone born of God does not sin, etc."

Twelfth, Rev. 22:11: "Let the righteous still do right."

Hence, blessed Augustine says in his 29th Epistle, to blessed Jerome [35]: "Love is the power by which a person loves what he ought to love. In some people this is stronger and in others weaker, and in still others there is none at all; but it is never in its fullest degree, so that it could not be further increased, in any man as long as he lives. But as long as it can be increased, what is less than it ought to be comes from sin. Because of this defect 'there is not a righteous man on earth who does good and never sins' (cf. 1 Kings 8:46). And because of this defect 'no man living is righteous before God' (Ps. 143:2). Because of this defect, 'if we say we have no sin, we deceive ourselves, and the truth is not in us' (1 John 1:8). Also because of this defect, no matter how much we progress, we are forced to say: 'Forgive us our debts' (Matt. 6:12), even though in Baptism all our sins of word, deed, and thought have been forgiven." So far Augustine. But the same relation as for Baptism, indeed, a much stronger one, is in force for penitence and indulgences.

From all of this it is obvious that there is no sin which is venial according to its substance and its nature, but also no merit. For even the good works which are done while the tinder of sin and sensuality are fighting against them are not of such intensity and purity as the Law requires, since they are not done with all of our strength, but only with the spiritual powers which struggle against the powers of the flesh. Thus we sin even when we do good, unless God through Christ covers this imperfection and does not impute it to us. Thus it becomes a venial sin [36] through the mercy of God, who does not impute it for the sake of faith and the plea in behalf of this imperfection for the sake of Christ. Therefore, he who thinks that he ought to be regarded as righteous because of his works is very foolish, since if they were offered as a sacrifice to the judgment of God, they still would be found to be sins. As Ps. 36:2 says, "For he has acted deceitfully in His sight, so that his iniquity is found to be for wrath," that is, before God and within his own spirit there

---

[35] *Patrologia, Series Latina,* XXXIII, 739.

[36] Cf. p. 268, n. 23.

was deceit and not the truth of righteousness, even though before men he makes a display of righteousness in his works. For he could not be righteous within himself without the mercy of God, since he is corrupt because of the tinder of sin. Therefore iniquity will be found in his righteousness, that is, even his good works will be unrighteous and sinful. This iniquity will not be found in believers and those who cry to Him, because Christ has brought them aid from the fullness of his purity and has hidden this imperfection of theirs. For they seek also this and hope for it from Him, but the others do not seek it but presumptuously think they have it.

Corollary

פֶּשַׁע, "offenses" (scelera), "iniquities" (iniquitates), or "crimes" (crimina), etc., has to do with the acts which are in themselves evil works and sins.

חַטָאָה, "sin" (peccatum), however, indicates the tinder of sin (fomes) which inclines toward these evil deeds and is the cause of them. Thus it is the tree of those fruits.

עָוֹן, "iniquity" (iniquitas) or "unrighteousness" (iniustitia), those good works which are done in the face of the sin that contends against us, especially if they are set up as righteousness. But they are not good works through the efforts of the runner, but because of the indulgence of our merciful God. Thus in themselves they are iniquities and unrighteousnesses, that is, they are not righteous acts and do not suffice as equal to what is demanded.

רֶשַׁע, "ungodliness" (impietas). This is the very constituting principle of this kind of unrighteousness. It is a denial of sin, so that people do not confess sin and declare that good works are righteousness and abominate only offenses and crimes. Thus it comes about that they are righteous in the eyes of men and unrighteous before God.

You say, "Then why is there so much preaching about the merits of the saints?" I reply, "Because these are not the merits of the saints but the merits of Christ in them, for whose sake God accepts their works, which otherwise He would not accept. Hence the saints themselves never know that they perform and possess meritorious works, but they do all those things only that they might find mercy and escape judgment, praying for forgiveness with loud groaning rather than presumptuously looking for the crown. "God is wonderful in His saints" (Ps. 68:35). He hides them so that although they are saints, yet they see themselves only as common men. Thus through the hope of mercy "their life is hid with Christ in God" (Col. 3:3). Because of their fear of judgment, their death and their sin are manifest with them, before them, and in their consciences. They always judge themselves in fear, because they know that of themselves they cannot be righteous before God. And thus they fear the judgment of God upon all their works, as Job says (Job 9:28): "I became afraid of all my works, for I know that Thou wilt not hold me innocent." And so that they may nevertheless not despair, they call upon God's mercy in Christ, and thus they are heard. This is the wisdom which is hidden in a mystery (cf. 1 Cor. 2:7), and it is the truth. For just as God and His counsel are unknown to us, so also is our own righteousness which completely depends upon Him and His counsel. Thus Ps. 51:6 reads: "For behold, Thou hast delighted in truth" (that is, true righteousness in contrast to figurative and legalistic righteousness, which pictures it as a sign but not as the actual thing). But how do I know this? "The uncertain and hidden things of Thy wisdom Thou hast made manifest to me" (Ps. 51:6), that is, I know this because this kind of inner righteousness alone is pleasing to Thee, this Thou lovest, because it is truth and fullness. I know, I say, because Thou hast given me a wisdom which is hidden, in order that I might know. Therefore, because of the fact that we cannot fulfill the law of God and thus are always deservedly unrighteous, nothing remains to us except that we live in perpetual fear of judgment and always pray for the remission of our unrighteousness, or rather, for the nonimputation of it. For it is never remitted entirely, but it remains and needs nonimputation. Thus in Ps. 2:11-12, "Serve the Lord" (which cannot be done except with happiness and joy, but because this cannot be done perfectly, then) "with fear," serve Him gladly in fear and "rejoice in Him" (because of His mercy) "with trembling" because of your sin which deserves judgment.

13. *For not through the Law.* Again he proves that righteousness does not come from the Law but from faith, according to the fruit and merit of both. For the Law and faith deserve opposite things. That is, the Law merits wrath and the loss of the promise, but faith deserves grace and the fulfillment of the promise, as if to say, if you do not believe the Scripture and its example, at least believe your own experience. For through the Law you have deserved wrath and desolation, but through faith grace and the possession of the whole world, as is clear in the case of the apostles, who reign with Christ in all the world. Thus also the promise was not

given to Abraham through the Law but through faith, and the same will be the case with you who are his seed.

15. *For the Law brings wrath.* It applies to the Law externally that it works wrath, that is, while it remains standing and is not fulfilled (as it must of necessity stand when faith is absent), those men deserve wrath to whom the Law has been given. Blessed Augustine in chapter 19 of *On the Spirit and the Letter* says, "For it was not its own fault that the Law was not fulfilled but the fault of the judgment of the flesh. This fault had to be pointed out by the Law and healed by grace." [37] Thus the Law works wrath, that is, when it is not fulfilled, it shows the wrath of God to those who have failed to provide for its fulfillment. Thus the Law is not evil, but they are evil to whom it was given and to whom it works wrath, but to the others (that is, the believers) it works salvation; actually it is not the Law that works this but grace. Therefore, if the promise were through the Law, since it works wrath, it would follow that the promise is not a promise, but rather a threat. And thus the promise would be abolished and through this also faith.

14. *For if they who are of the seed,*[38] *etc.* The apostle also shows that faith is made void in another way than through the abolition of the promise because of the wrath of the Law, namely, through the seed of the flesh. For if this is sufficient to make a man righteous and worthy of receiving the promise, that he is a son of the flesh, then faith is not necessary. Then why was Abraham justified by faith and regarded as worthy of the promise? Why was he not justified because of his fleshly descent? Then faith is in vain, and everything said about it in Scripture is vain. For those who could be justified by their flesh and through the Law do not need faith, as they themselves actually think. But the contrary is the case, because they are damned through their flesh and through the Law.

13. *For not through the Law,* that is, through the righteousness and works of the Law. The apostle does not use the term "the righteousness of the Law" but simply the term "the Law" in an absolute sense, because it actually is not righteousness. Yet that he understands "righteousness" by the use of the term "the Law" is clear from the contrasting expression *but through the righteousness of faith,* since it would have sufficed here if he had said: "but through faith." But since the righteousness of the Law is nothing,

[37] Augustine, *De Spiritu et littera,* 19, 34, *Patrologia, Series Latina,* XLIV, 221.

[38] On the reading "seed" see p. 38, n. 5.

he is correct in using the expression "the Law" all by itself. This text confirms the statement made earlier (4:12), where he said that Abraham possessed the righteousness of faith even in uncircumcision, and that the Gentiles follow him in this faith, as sons follow their father, just as the promise of the future had been made to him. And this promise was surely given to him because of this same faith of his and not through the Law. And because he has here tied together the two elements of Law and seed, he then shows that neither of them suffices to obtain the promise. Hence these two statements:

14. *Faith is null, and the promise is void* can be understood both conjunctively and separately. Conjunctively they refer to each other and imply each other, as stated in the gloss,[39] so that the meaning is: not through the Law, nor through physical descent, etc.; because if it were through seed (note below) and through the Law, etc., then faith and the promise would cease. But the fact that faith would cease through the seed suggests and proves that the promise would cease through the Law, because "the Law works wrath" (v. 15). But in this way the text is corrupted and confused. Thus if put in the proper order, the meaning would be as follows: The promise to Abraham and to his seed that they should be the heirs of the world was not through the Law nor through his seed, but through the righteousness of faith. For if they are heirs through the Law and because of their physical relationship, then faith is done away and the promise annulled. "For the Law works wrath" (4:15). But because it is the same thing to be of the seed and to have the Law, and because it is the same people who are involved, therefore he sometimes uses one expression and sometimes the other.

If we understand these expressions separately, so that the first is related to what precedes and the second to what follows in the text, then the meaning is: If seed and physical generation were enough to justify and to make people worthy of the inheritance, it follows that faith is not necessary for justification and for worthiness of that kind, since he who is righteous and worthy needs neither justification nor worthiness. But now this is so false that the very opposite is the case, for the spiritual generation which comes from faith makes us righteous and worthy of the promise, and this is sufficient without the other. But physical generation does not profit at all, indeed it is null and void, for those who are of

[39] Cf. both the interlinear and the marginal glosses on this passage, p. 38.

faith are the heirs, and those who are of the seed are the disinherited, as we read in Ps. 127:2-3: "When He gives sleep to His beloved, lo, sons are an heritage from the Lord, the fruit of the womb a reward"; and in John 1:13: "Who were born, not of blood, nor of the will of the flesh, nor of the will of man, but of God"; again, John 3:5, 7: "You must be born again of water and the Spirit"; and in Ps. 22:30: "A seed that serves Him shall be declared to the Lord, etc."; and Ps. 45:16, "Instead of your fathers, sons are born to you, etc." When this statement is thus proved (that those who are of the seed are not the heirs, but rather that the physical generation is annulled in order that the generation from faith might be established in opposition to those people who seek to annul faith and establish the seed), it follows that the promise would also be abolished by the Law in exactly the same way that faith is abolished by the physical descent. For "the Law works wrath, etc.," as is evident from the text itself, *for where there is no law* (v. 15), as if to say that transgression works wrath, but it would not work it if there were no law.

This statement should be understood as giving the occasion. For actually it is the transgression of the Law which works wrath and makes the promise of no effect. But this would not be the case if there were no law. For the Law, as long as it is without faith which fulfills it, makes all people sinners and establishes the fact that they are guilty and thus unworthy of the promise, indeed worthy of wrath and desolation, and in consequence it turns the promise into a threat. At any rate, it is the occasion for all of these things to happen to man and to befall him, that is, that one recognizes that they happen and befall him, as the apostle has said above (3:20), "through the Law comes knowledge of sin." For he who has the Law without faith and grace will assuredly see that he is a sinner and worthy of wrath and that therefore he is deprived of the promise.

17. *The father of many nations.* The expression "in the presence of God, etc.," is not in the Hebrew text, to be sure, but it is elicited from the text, however, if one correctly considers the fact that Abraham is described as the father of many nations. Now I ask, was he their father according to the flesh or according to the spirit? He cannot be so according to the flesh, because there were then and there were going to be nations always who were in no way descended from him. And yet he was given the promise that he would be their father. But if you say that all the nations are going to be de-

stroyed so that only the sons who are descended from him will reign throughout the world, then he will be the father of only one and not many nations. On the other hand, if all the nations will be reduced to slavery and live in servitude, then he will no longer be their father nor these nations his sons, for they will be slaves and he the lord of the nations; in this case fatherhood is eliminated, and oppression and violence are indicated. Yet the Jews blandly promise themselves this rule and oppression and await it in foolish hope. Therefore we must conclude that the promise was that he would be made the father of the nations "in the presence of God" and in God's sight and in spirit. But again if someone should say that he was going to be the father only in office and name, as Naaman the Syrian was called father by his servants [40] and as the princes of the people are called the fathers of their country, this is to reduce the glory of the promise too much, for that is only a temporal and vicarious paternity which can apply to many men and thus not only to Abraham, etc. Nor would it be perpetual, just as these official fathers are fathers only for the time that they are in office. But if this impudence still does not cease and the objector says that Abraham was going to be a father in the same way that he is and was the father of nations through Keturah, his second wife, then the answer is the same as to the first objection, namely, that most nations were different from them and indeed were much more numerous than they were. Thus he would still not be the father of "many" nations on account of these nations, but rather "the father of a few nations." But not even the Jews themselves understand this promise and await its fulfillment with respect only to these nations. Thus its possession is fulfilled in Christ, who is King and Lord of the nations, which He has obtained by a better victory than the Jews once achieved over the Canaanites. For He kills His enemies spiritually with the sword of the Word by making the ungodly godly and thus ruling over them even in their own land and possession.

Who gives life to the dead. Although this is true historically, yet it should be understood more as a spiritual confirmation of what has just been said; it is as if he were saying: "The nations will be your children, even though they are not so yet and are a long way from becoming your children, yet the Lord has the power to raise them up and call them to become and be your children." As John the Baptist says in Luke 3:8, "Do not begin to say, 'We have Abra-

[40] Cf. 2 Kings 5:13.

ham as our father.' For God is able from these stones to raise up children to Abraham." And thus there is a strengthening of Abraham's faith and a confirmation of God's promise in the fact that Abraham can become the father of many nations, although not by his own powers but by the power of God, etc.

18. *Against hope.* In the first place, "hope" signifies a thing which is naturally hoped for, but this hope was not of this kind. In the second place, however, it also signifies something which is supernaturally hoped for. In both instances "hope" must be taken in the sense of a thing to be hoped for and not in the sense of the power of hoping. And this beautifully suggests the difference between the hope of people generally and the hope of Christians. For the hope of people in general is not contrary to hope but according to hope, that is, what can reasonably be expected to happen. For men do not hope where only that which is contrary to their hopes appears, but rather when that appears which is very similar to their hopes or that which has a definite potentiality to occur. Hence this faith is more a negative than a positive thing, that is, they presume that when certain things have begun, then that which was hoped for will come to pass. And then, finally, they hope that there will be no impediment to prevent what they have hoped for. Thus in regard to what is positively hoped for, this hope wants to be certain and to know, but in regard to the negative it is compelled to remain uncertain. By contrast, the hope of Christians is certain about the negative aspects. For it knows that the thing hoped for must come to pass and will not be hindered, as long as it is hoped for. For no one can hinder God. But with respect to the positive side, this faith is very unsure, since it has nothing certain in which it can trust, for all things are too hidden, and everything appears contrary. Thus this hope is more positive than negative. The apostle here speaks of both aspects of hope, first, positively, when he says that Abraham believed *and did not consider his own body* (v. 19), and second, in the negative sense, that *no distrust made him waver, . . . fully convinced that God was able to do what He had promised* (20-21). The positive aspects militate outwardly against faith and hope, because they are visible, but the negative aspects militate inwardly, because they are essentially the softness and inconstancy of the heart toward believing, while the affirmative aspects are the things which object to or are contrary to the things which should be believed.

20. *He gave glory to God.* From this it follows that just as one

glorifies God by believing, so through contrary unbelief he dishonors Him, 1 John 5:10, "He who does not believe in His Son, makes God a liar, because he has not believed in the testimony that God has borne to His Son." Therefore he who believes God makes God truthful and himself a liar. For he discredits his own feelings as false in order that he might trust in the Word of God as true, which, however, is absolutely contrary to his own feelings, as the apostle says above in chapter 3:4: "That Thou mayest be justified in Thy words, etc." "Let God be truthful, though every man be false," that is, let him cease to believe in himself and believe in God. And thus let him become a liar, but God truthful. Thus blessed Augustine says that God is worshiped by faith, hope, and love.[41] And it is said in a common dictum that God is directly offended by three sins, namely, unbelief, despair, and hatred.

25. *Who was delivered up.* The death of Christ is the death of sin, and His resurrection is the life of righteousness, because through His death He has made satisfaction for sin, and through His resurrection He has brought us righteousness. And thus His death not only signifies but actually effects the remission of sin as a most sufficient satisfaction. And His resurrection is not only a sign or a sacrament[42] of our righteousness, but it also produces it in us, if we believe it, and it is also the cause of it. Of these matters we shall speak in greater detail later. This whole concept the scholastic theologians call one exchange: the expulsion of sin and the infusion of grace.[43]

41 Augustine, *Enchiridion ad Laurentium,* ch. 1, 3, *Patrologia, Series Latina,* XL, 232.

42 For this use of *sacramentum* cf. p. 309 below and W, IX, 18, 20. and W, IX, 18, 20.

43 Duns Scotus (*Sententiarum,* IV, dist. 16, qu. 2, n. 6) says very definitely *una mutatio realis,* but a formal distinction is usually made between two parts of the process. Cf. Luther's reference to the philosophers on this subject, p. 204.

CHAPTER FIVE

1. *We have peace.*

THIS is the spiritual peace of which all the prophets sing. And because this is the case, he adds the words *with God.* And this peace is prefigured in every peace which the children of Israel enjoyed in days of old.

And this is the real peace of conscience and trust in God. Just as on the contrary a spiritual disturbance is the lack of a quiet conscience and a mistrust of God. Thus Hosea says (Hos. 8:7): "For they sow the wind, and they shall reap the whirlwind." For the penalty of a bad conscience is stated in Ps. 1:4: to be "like the chaff which the wind drives away."

Thus Christ is also called the Prince of Peace and a Solomon (cf. Is. 9:6; 1 Chron. 22:9). Eph. 2:14, 17 reads: "He is our peace, who has made us both one. . . . And He came and preached peace to you who were far off and peace to those who were near." The same idea is expressed in Is. 57:19, and in John 16:33: "That in Me you may have peace; in the world you have tribulation." The other kind of peace is carnal, of which He says in Matt. 10:34: "I have not come to bring peace, but a sword." By contrast there is the carnal disturbance and temporal quietness. Hence also Ps. 72:7, "In His days shall righteousness flourish, and peace abound," must not be understood in the sense of the temporal peace which existed under Augustus, as many think, but of this spiritual peace "with God."

But note how the apostle places this spiritual peace only after righteousness has preceded it. For first he says, "since we are justified *(iustificati)* by faith," and then, "we have peace." Thus also in Ps. 85:10, "Righteousness and peace have kissed," the term "righteousness" precedes the word "peace." And again, "In His days shall righteousness flourish, and peace abound" (Ps. 72:7). And here the perversity of men seeks peace before righteousness, and for this reason they do not find peace. Thus the apostle creates a very fine antithesis in these words, namely,

The righteous man has peace with God but affliction in the world, because he lives in the Spirit.

The unrighteous man has peace with the world but affliction and tribulation with God, because he lives in the flesh.

But as the Spirit is eternal, so also will be the peace of the righteous man and the tribulation of the unrighteous.

And as the flesh is temporal, so will be the tribulation of the righteous and the peace of the unrighteous.

Hence we read in Is. 57:21 and 48:22: "There is no peace for the wicked, says the Lord," that is, spiritually, for there surely is a peace for the wicked; in Ps. 73:3: "For I was envious of the arrogant when I saw the prosperity of the wicked"; and in Ps. 28:3: "Who speak peace with their neighbor while mischief (that is, not peace, but disturbance and restlessness toward God) is in their hearts."

2. *Through whom we have obtained access by faith.* In a most useful manner the apostle joins together these two expressions, "through Christ" and "by faith," as he did also above in the expression "since we are justified by faith . . . through our Lord, etc." In the first place, the statement is directed against those who are so presumptuous as to believe that they can approach God without Christ, as if it were sufficient for them to have believed, as if thus by faith alone, but not through Christ, but beside Christ, as if beyond Christ they no longer needed Him after accepting the grace of justification. And now there are many people who from the works of faith make for themselves works of the Law and of the letter, when having received faith by Baptism and penitence, they now think that they are personally pleasing to God even without Christ, when actually both are necessary, namely, to have faith and also always to possess Christ as our Mediator in this faith. Hence we read in Ps. 91:1: "He who dwells in the shelter of the Most High shall abide in the shadow of God in heaven." Faith makes the dwelling place, but Christ the protection and the aid. And later we read (Ps. 91:4): "He will cover you with His pinions, and under His wings you will trust"; and in Mal. 4:2, "But for you who fear My name the Sun of righteousness shall rise with healing in His wings"; and in Ps. 31:2: "Be Thou unto me a God, a protector and a house of refuge" (that is a dwelling place); and again in Ps. 90:1: "Lord, Thou hast been our dwelling place." Thus the apostle is

interpreting these and all similar authoritative expressions of Scripture, together with many other figurative expressions of the Law. But in our day the hypocrites and legalists swell up with horrifying pride and think that they are now saved and sufficiently righteous because they believe in Christ, but they are unwilling to be considered unrighteous or regarded as fools. And what is this except the rejection of Christ's protection and a desire to approach God only from faith but not through Christ? Indeed, then there is not faith at all, but only the appearance. So at sunset the rays of the sun and the light of the sun go down together. But he who is wise does not set such high value on the light that he no longer needs the sun, rather he wants to have both the sun and the light at the same time. Therefore those who approach God through faith and not at the same time through Christ actually depart from Him. Second, the apostle is speaking against those who rely too heavily on Christ and not enough on faith, as if they were to be saved through Christ in such a way that they themselves had to do nothing and show no evidence of faith. These people have too much faith, or actually none at all. For this reason it is necessary to emphasize both points: "through faith" and "through Christ," so that we do and suffer everything which we possibly can in faith in Christ. And yet in all of these activities we must confess that we are unprofitable servants, believing that only through Christ are we made worthy to approach God. For in all works of faith we must strive to make ourselves worthy of Christ and His righteousness as our protection and refuge. "Therefore, since we are justified by faith" and our sins are forgiven, "we have access and peace," but only "through our Lord Jesus Christ." This also applies to those who follow the mystical theology [1] and struggle in inner darkness, omitting all pictures of Christ's suffering, wishing to hear and contemplate only the uncreated Word Himself, but not having first been justified and purged in the eyes of their heart through the incarnate Word. For the incarnate Word is first necessary for the purity of the heart, and only when one has this purity, can he through this Word be taken up spiritually into the uncreated Word. But who is there who

---

[1] This is a reference to the Dionysius the Areopagite to whom certain works of mystical theology were credited which exercised great influence on mediaeval thought. The "inner darkness" mentioned here is a technical term in the theology of Dionysius. In his comments on Ps. 18:11 Luther remarks: "Blessed Dionysius teaches people to enter into uplifting darkness and to rise through denials" (W, III, 124, 32). Later Luther roundly condemned this theology, e. g., *Luther's Works*, 54, p. 112, No. 644; 36, p. 109.

thinks that he is so pure that he dares aspire to this level unless he is called and led into the rapture by God, as was the case with the apostle Paul, or unless he is "taken up with Peter, James, and John, his brother" (Matt. 17:1)? In brief, this rapture is not called an "access."

3. *In our sufferings.* From this text we clearly see the distinction of a twofold wrath and a twofold mercy of God and also of a twofold suffering. For there is a kind of suffering that comes from His severity and another from His kindness. That suffering which comes from His kindness works, because of its nature, only things which are very good, as we see in the following, although by an accident something different may take place; but this is not His fault but the fault of him to whom it happens because of his weakness, for he does not know the true nature of his suffering and its power and working, but he judges and esteems it according to its outward appearance, that is, in a wrong way, since it ought to be adored as the very cross of Christ.

Corollary

1

Of whatever quality suffering finds characteristics and people to be, such it makes them even more. Thus if a person is carnal, weak, blind, evil, irascible, arrogant, etc., when trial comes, he becomes more carnal, weaker, blinder, more evil, more irascible, more arrogant, etc. And on the other hand, if he is spiritual, brave, wise, good, meek, and humble, he becomes more spiritual, braver, wiser, better, meeker, and humbler. In Ps. 4:1 we read: "Thou hast given me room when I was in distress." But concerning the other kind of people, Matt. 7:27 says, "The floods came and the winds blew and beat against that house, and great was the fall thereof."

2

Those people talk nonsense who attribute their bad temper or their impatience to that which causes them offense or suffering. For suffering does not make a person impatient but merely shows that he has been or is still impatient. Thus a person learns in suffering what kind of man he is, just as the glutton does when he itches, etc.

3

Rude, puerile, and even hypocritical are those people who

venerate the relics of the holy cross with the highest outward honor and then flee from and curse their sufferings and adversities. This is obvious, for in Scripture tribulations are expressly called the cross of Christ, as in 1 Cor. 1:17: "Lest the cross of Christ be emptied of its power"; "And he who does not take his cross and follow Me" (Matt. 10:38); Gal. 5:11: "Why am I still persecuted? In that case the stumbling block of the cross has been removed"; and Phil. 3:18: "I tell you with tears that they live as enemies of the cross of Christ." But our theologians and priests today think of nothing else in the term "enemies of the cross of Christ" but Turks and Jews, as the theologians of Cologne did against John Reuchlin, and as the papal bulls and the glosses of the lawyers do.[2]

But they themselves are actually "the enemies of the cross of Christ." For it is true that only the friends of the cross are its enemies, according to the statement in Ps. 38:11: "My friends and companions have stood against Me." "And they who praised Me swore against Me" (Ps. 102:8). For who hates tribulation and suffering more than the priests and the lawyers? Indeed, who seeks riches, pleasures, leisure, honors, and glories more than they do?

4

Whoever is unwilling to suffer tribulation should never think that he is a Christian, but rather a Turk and an enemy of Christ. For here he is speaking about all of us when he says: "We rejoice in our sufferings, etc." In Acts 14:22 we read: "Through many tribulations we must, etc." "We must," he says, not "it just happens" or "it may be the case" or "we are disposed to." And 1 Peter 1:6 we read: "Though now for a little while you may have to suffer various trials, etc." "Have to," he says, that is, it absolutely cannot take place in any other way.

But we must note this: There are two kinds of enemies of the cross of Christ. The first kind is the violent type, and the second is the cunning. The violent are those who want to make the cross of no effect by force, and they attack it with all their forces; they are the ones who seek vengeance against anyone who offends them, and they are neither willing nor able to be at rest until they have been vindicated. They fall into many evils, such as hatred, detrac-

[2] E. g., Arnold von Tungern's preface to *Articuli . . . de iudaico favore nimis suspecto ex libello theutonico domini Ioannis Reuchlin* (1512): *Perfidi canes inimici nominis Christi;* the title of a tract by Pfefferkorn (1514): *Sturm — wider die drulosen Juden, anfechter des Leichnams Christi und seiner glidmossen;* the bull of Julius II (1511).

tions, abuses, rejoicing at the evils which befall their neighbor and sorrow over his good fortune.

But the cunning enemies are those who desert the cross in flight, that is, those who do not want to speak or perform the truth for anyone but are always trying to please, to weedle, to flatter everyone and to offend no one, or else they withdraw into solitude (at least for this reason). The apostle refers to such people in Gal. 6:12, when he says: "It is those who want to make a good showing in the flesh that would compel you to be circumcised, and only that they may not be persecuted for the cross of Christ."

We must note that this climax or gradation is also contrary to those who do not stand in this grace, namely, that suffering works impatience, and impatience rejection, and rejection despair, and despair eternal confounding. And thus finally the hatred of God will be poured out (that is, it will be recognized that it has been poured out whenever this hatred reaches its completion) in their hearts through the wicked spirit under whose dominion they have been delivered, etc. Therefore I said that the impatient man is not yet a Christian, at least before God, because he is found to have been rejected through suffering.

Hence, since the Lord in many passages is given the name of Savior and Helper in suffering, he who is unwilling to suffer as much as he can deprives Him of His true titles and names. Thus to this man there will be no Jesus, that is, no Savior, because he is unwilling to be damned; for him there will be no God the Creator because he is unwilling to be nothing, so that He may be his Creator. God will be no power, wisdom, or good to him, because he does not want Him to uphold him in his weakness, his foolishness, or his punishment.

4. *And endurance.* The different degrees of impatience are known from the degrees of anger which the Lord shows in Matt. 5:21-22, when He is explaining the commandment "You shall not kill." For because impatience is the cause of anger, the effect of both is the same, unless someone should separate impatience from anger. Then its degrees are more intensive than extensive. For an impatient man is patient in nothing. But the apostle here clearly indicates the degrees of endurance. Baptista Mantuanus in the last chapter of Book I [3] distinguishes very carefully among these degrees. The lowest is to bear sufferings only with difficulty and

---

[3] *De patientia,* I, 32. Luther had quoted Mantuanus' poetry previously (W, III, 221, 29).

with a mind which prefers to be delivered from the trial. The second and medium degree is to bear it with joy to be sure and willingly, but not to seek it. The highest degree is to long for suffering, to seek it like a treasure and to bring it about. This is the meaning of the words "we rejoice in our sufferings" and also of the statement in Gal. 6:14: "We must glory in the cross of our Lord, etc."

And trial. The expression "trial" in this passage must be understood in a good sense, namely, as the goal of suffering, as that which is sought through tribulation. For God accepts no one as righteous whom He has not first tested, and He proves him through no other means than through the fire of tribulation, as we read in Ps. 17:3: "Thou hast tried me by fire, and iniquity has not been found in me." And there is this statement of Ecclus. 44:16-17: "He pleased God, . . . and he was found perfect"; and again (Ecclus. 31:8): ". . . he who is found without blemish"; also Ps. 11:5: "The Lord tests the righteous and the wicked, etc." Thus to this testing one comes in no other way than through endurance. And this testing takes place in order that each person may see his own state of mind, that is, that each may know himself, namely, whether he really loves God for the sake of God, which God of course knows even without any testing. Thus we read in Ps. 139:23-24: "Search me, O God, and know my heart" (that is, make it known also to me). "Try me and know my paths. And see if there be any wicked way in me, and lead me in the way everlasting." This passage very beautifully expresses the reason why God brings tribulations to men, in order that He might test them, that is, make them approved through endurance. For

If God should not test us by tribulation, it would be impossible for any man to be saved.

The reason is that our nature has been so deeply curved in upon itself because of the viciousness of original sin that it not only turns the finest gifts of God in upon itself and enjoys them (as is evident in the case of legalists and hypocrites), indeed, it even uses God Himself to achieve these aims, but it also seems to be ignorant of this very fact, that in acting so iniquitously, so perversely, and in such a depraved way, it is even seeking God for its own sake. Thus the prophet Jeremiah says in Jer. 17:9: "The heart is perverse above all things, and desperately corrupt; who can understand it?" that is, it is so curved in on itself that no man, no matter how holy (if a testing is kept from him) can understand it. Thus Ps. 19:12

reads: "Who can discern his errors? Clear Thou me from hidden faults, etc.," and Ps. 32:6: "Therefore let everyone who is godly offer prayer to Thee at a proper time." And the Scripture calls this viciousness by a name most proper to it, עָוֹן, that is, iniquity, depravity, or crookedness. The Doctor of the Sentences, in Book I, dist. 1, deals with this subject at great length in a discussion of enjoyment and use and of the love of friendship and the love of concupiscence. Therefore if we have said that iniquity is this very impatience, or at least the cause of this impatience, then this crookedness is also iniquity, which of necessity is hostile to the cross, since the cross puts to death everything we have, but our iniquity tries to keep itself and its possessions alive. Therefore our good God, after He has justified us and given us His spiritual gifts, quickly brings tribulation upon us, exercises us, and tests us so that this godless nature of ours does not rush in upon these enjoyable sins, lest in his ignorance man should die the eternal death. For they are very lovely and vigorously excite enjoyment. Thus man learns to love and worship God purely for Himself, and not just because of His grace and His gifts; but he worships God for His own sake alone. Thus "He chastises every son whom He receives" (Heb. 12:6). And unless He did this, the son would quickly be drawn away by the sweetness of his new inheritance, he would luxuriate in his enjoyment of the grace which he had received and would offend his Father more deeply than before. Therefore in very good order the apostle says, "Suffering produces endurance, and endurance trial," that is, a proving or a testing.

5. *And hope does not disappoint us.* Without a testing of this sort, as I have said, hope would founder, indeed, it would no longer be hope, but presumptuousness; in fact, it would be worse, for it would be the enjoyment of the creature instead of the Creator. And if a person remained in this state, he would be confounded for all eternity. Therefore suffering comes, through which a man is made patient and tested; it comes and takes away everything he has and leaves him naked and alone, allowing him no help or safety in either his physical or spiritual merits, for it makes a man despair of all created things, to turn away from them and from himself, to seek help outside of himself and all other things, in God alone, and thus to sing in the words of Ps. 3:3: "But Thou, O Lord, art my Protector and my Glory." This is what it means to hope and that hope is created in times of testing, while of necessity the ungodly, who are accustomed to trust in their own powers, are un-

willing to remain calm and to endure their tribulations in order that they may be tested. In the final test, since they do not know how to trust solely in God, after their substance has been ruined and the mountains of their own achievements have fallen down, then they themselves fall into ruin for eternity. "Then they will begin to say to the mountains, 'Fall upon us,' etc." (Luke 23:30; cf. Hos. 10:8). For their hope was not a real hope, but a perverse presumptuousness, a confidence in their own works and their own righteousness.

But yet we must know that suffering is of two kinds.

The first is physical, in which men who are carnal are overcome; they fail because of their concern for physical goods, for things, for the body, for reputation, and they depart from God, lose hope because of their impatience, and thus deliver themselves up to the flesh and forsake God. Of such people the apostle says, Eph. 4:19: "They have become callous and have given themselves up to licentiousness."

The second is the suffering of conscience and spirit, wherein all of one's self-righteousness and wisdom in which people trust are devoured and done away. Of these the Savior says, in a mystical way, "When a strong man fully armed . . . but when one stronger than he assails him and overcomes him, he takes away his armor and binds him and divides his spoils" (Luke 11:21-22), that is, he will strip a man who is fortified with his own righteousnesses and will teach him that they are to be used for the common good and not for his own pleasure.

Because God's love. This expression ought to be understood as an added reason, rather as instruction in the Holy Spirit, as to why and how we can glory in our sufferings, namely, that we might learn that of ourselves and of our own powers it is impossible, but that it is a gift of the love which is given by the Holy Spirit.

Therefore "God's love," which is the purest feeling toward God and alone makes us right at heart, alone takes away iniquity, alone extinguishes the enjoyment of our own righteousness. For it loves nothing but God alone, not even His gifts, as the hypocritical self-righteous people do. Therefore, when physical and spiritual blessings flow in, it does not get excited. Again, when they disappear, and physical and spiritual evils deluge us, it is not crushed. But "Knowledge puffs up" (1 Cor. 8:1), and so does righteousness. Again, ignorance humbles us, and so does sin. "But love bears all things" (1 Cor. 13:7), even glorying in its tribulations. Therefore we must note that

It is called "God's love" because by it we love God alone, where nothing is visible, nothing experiential, either inwardly or outwardly, in which we can trust or which is to be loved or feared; but it is carried away beyond all things into the invisible God, who cannot be experienced, who cannot be comprehended, that is, into the midst of the shadows, not knowing what it loves, only knowing what it does not love; turning away from everything which it has known and experienced, and desiring only that which it has not yet known, saying: "I am sick with love" (Song of Sol. 2:5), that is, I do not want what I have and I do not have what I want. But this gift is far removed from those who still are looking at their own righteousnesses and love them and are sad and despairing when they cannot be seen and trust in them when they are seen and feel secure in them and thus do not "rejoice in sufferings," are not tested, and thus have no hope.

Thus the apostle asserts that this sublime power which is in us is not from ourselves, but must be sought from God. Thus it follows that it *is poured* [4] into us, not born in us or originated in us. And this takes place *through the Holy Spirit;* it is not acquired by moral effort and practice, as our moral virtues are. *Into our hearts,* that is, into the depths and the midst and center of our hearts, not on the surface of the heart, as foam lies on water. This is the kind of love that the hypocrites have, who imagine and pretend that they have love. But a period of testing only proves the pride and impatience which lies deep within them.

Who has been given to us, that is, whom we do not deserve, rather we deserve the direct opposite. But that this is true, he proves, because now follows: "He is really given" and not deserved. For Christ "died for the weak" (v. 6) and not for the strong and the deserving. Thus it is called *love* to indicate the difference between this and the unworthy and low kind of love by which a creature is loved; for the term "love" means to love something very dearly and preciously and to regard as very precious the thing that is loved. For this is what it means to love God above all things and to esteem Him with a rich love, that is, to love Him with a precious love. But to love Him for the sake of His gifts or for some advantage

---

[4] The italicized phrases of verse 5 quoted in these paragraphs were numbered 1—6 in the margin by Luther.

is the lowest kind of love, that is, to love Him with a selfish desire. This is using God but not enjoying Him.[5]

God's love is used because only God is loved in this way, not even the neighbor, except for the sake of God, that is, because God so wills, and one loves His will above all things.

We must also note that love dwells nowhere but in the heart, indeed, in the innermost center of the heart, and for this reason there is that difference between sons and bond servants, because the sons serve Him happily, willingly, and freely, not in fear of punishment or desire for glory, but only to fulfill the will of God; but the bond servants are forced by the fear of punishment, and they serve Him unwillingly and with great difficulty, or they are desirous of a reward, in which case they serve Him willingly enough but with a mercenary intent, but never absolutely out of a desire to fulfill His will. Particularly in time of tribulation does the servant and the hireling run away, but the son perseveres, as John 10:12 says: "But the hireling flees." Thus He says to them in Mal. 1:10: "Oh, that there were one among you who would shut the doors, that you might not kindle fire on my altar in vain!" And then He continues: "I have no pleasure in you, says the Lord of Hosts," for they are actually very presumptuous and believe that they are carrying out the will of God. This is the reason why in the same place (Mal. 1:7-8), when the Lord has said, "You offer polluted bread upon My altar," they reply as if they could not imagine this to be possible, saying, "How have we polluted it?" which is to say, "In our opinion we have done everything which Thou hast commanded." The Lord replies, "When you offer blind animals for sacrifice, is that no evil? And when you offer those that are lame or sick, is that no evil?" That is, they worship God without true love but with a desire for their own advantage, like hirelings, not having the single eye of the bride,[6] with which she sees only the invisible God and nothing of her own things or those of any other creature.

Note again how the apostle unites the spring with the river. He

---

[5] Luther is no doubt indebted to Augustine's discussion of the difference between "using" *(uti)* and "enjoying" *(frui)* in *De doctrina Christiana,* I, 3—5, 22 (*Patrologia, Series Latina,* XXXIV, 20, 26), where Augustine compares the Christian pilgrim to a traveler far from home who "uses" a conveyance to return home but does not "enjoy" the journey for its own sake. In the same way, says Augustine, "if we wish to return to our Father's home, this world must be used, not enjoyed. . . . The true objects of enjoyment are the Father and the Son and the Holy Spirit, who are at the same time the Trinity, one Being."

[6] Cf. Song of Sol. 4:9.

speaks of the "love . . . through the Holy Spirit, who is given to us." For it is not enough to have the gift unless the giver also be present, as Moses also begged in Ex. 33:15: "If Thy presence will not go with me, do not carry us up from here, etc." Indeed, properly it is to love alone that the apostle attributes the presence and at the same time the giving of the Spirit. For all other gifts, as he says in 1 Cor. 12:7 ff., are given by the same Spirit but are not the Spirit Himself. Just so he says here regarding love that it is not given unless the Spirit Himself has first been given, who then spreads this love abroad in our hearts. But in that passage he says: "But all these gifts are inspired by one and the same Spirit" (v. 11). Hence he goes on to say in the same chapter (v. 31): "I will show you a still more excellent way." Or at least, even if He is given in all the gifts, yet He does not pour forth love in all.

6. *At the right time.* Some refer this expression to the statement which follows, so that the meaning is: "When we were still weak, He died for the ungodly according to time," as if to say that, although He is eternal and immortal, yet He died in time. He died because of His humanity which lived in time, but He is alive forever because of His deity, which lives in eternity. Others interpret it thus: "He died at the time when we were weak," that is, He died at the time when we were not yet righteous and whole, but rather weak and sickly, so that the meaning is: "at the right time," namely, at that time when we were still weak. And this interpretation is the better one, as becomes evident in what follows: *For if, while we were enemies we were reconciled to God by the death of His Son* (v. 10). But others refer the expression to the preceding sentence, so that the meaning is: When we were weak according to time, even though before God we were already righteous through His predestination. For in the predestination of God all things have already taken place, even things which in our reality still lie in the future.

12. *Therefore, as sin through one man.* That the apostle is in this passage talking about original sin and not actual sin is proved in many passages, and we assume this to be so from these points:

First, because he says: "through one man." Thus blessed Augustine says in his work *On the Merits of Sins and Their Remission*, Book I, in opposition to the Pelagians: "If the apostle had wanted to point out that sin came into this world not by propagation but by imitation, he would not have spoken of Adam as the one who originated it, but rather of the devil, . . . of whom it is said in Wisd.

of Sol. 2:24: 'And they follow him who are of his side.' " [7] In this sense Adam also imitated him and thus had the devil as the originating cause of his sin. But here the apostle says "through a man." For all actual sins enter and have entered the world through the devil, but original sin came through this one man. In the same place blessed Augustine also says: "Thus when the apostle mentions that sin and the death which passed from this one man to all men through propagation, he makes him the originating cause from whom the propagation of the human race took its beginning." [8] And he makes other pertinent remarks.

And Chrysostom says regarding this passage: "It is clear that it is not the sin which comes from the transgression of the Law but the sin which derives from the disobedience of Adam, which contaminates all things." [9]

Second, he says, "Through one man," because actual sin is committed by many, since every man brings his own sin into the world.

Third, he says, "Sin came into the world." But no actual sin enters the world, for each man's sin hangs over him, as we read in Ezek. 18:20, that each will carry his own sin. Therefore, it does not come upon others but remains on each person individually. And that the term "world" does not mean heaven and earth in this passage but only the men in the world is clear from Rom. 3:6 above, "How could God judge the world?" and 1 John 5:19, "The whole world is in the power of the evil one." In John 3:16 we read: "God so loved the world"; and later on (John 15:18): "If the world hates you, etc."; again (John 15:19): "I chose you out of the world." And the reason is that the physical world is insensitive and incapable of sinning, so that sin and death could not enter it. For it neither dies nor sins, but man both sins and dies: therefore, for sin to enter the world means that the world becomes guilty and sinful because of one man. As we read below (v. 19), "As by one man's disobedience many were made sinners."

Fourth, death through sin, because it is certain that the death of the world (that is, of all men) does not come from the personal sin of each man, since even those who have not sinned die (as the

---

[7] Augustine, *De peccatorum meritis et remissione*, I, 9, 19, *Patrologia, Series Latina*, XLIV, 114.

[8] Ibid.

[9] As quoted by Augustine, *Contra Julianum*, I, 6, 27, *Patrologia, Series Latina*, XLIV, 659.

following passage shows). Therefore, if death comes by sin and if without sin there would be no death, then sin is in all of us. Thus it is not personal sin that he is talking about here. Otherwise it would be false to say that death had entered by sin, but rather we ought to say that it came by the will of God.

Fifth, because he says *death spread to all men*, even if death came because of our personal sin, yet it comes upon only him who commits it, as the Law says (Deut. 24:16): "The fathers shall not be put to death for the children, etc."

Sixth, he uses the term "sin" in the singular, referring to one. But if he had wanted us to understand this passage of actual sin, he would use the plural, as he does below, when he speaks of "many trespasses" (v. 16), where he is clearly comparing that one particular sin with many others, and from this he concludes that the efficacy of grace is greater than that of sin.

Seventh, *in which all men sinned*. There is nothing else "in which all men sinned," but each sins his own.

Eighth, *sin was in the world before the Law was given, etc.* (v. 13). Actual sin also was in the world before Moses, and it was imputed, because it was also punished by men; but original sin was unknown until Moses revealed it in Gen. 3.

Ninth, he says here that their *sins were not like the transgression of Adam* (v. 14), that is, an exact simulation of his sin, as Pelagius insisted, but nevertheless they all sin with actual sin who commit sin.

Tenth, *Adam is a type of the One who was to come*, but not by actual sin; for otherwise all men would be a figure of Christ, but now only Adam is that figure, because of the extension of his one sin to all men.

But now in order to confound and overturn the perversity of future heretics, whom he foresaw in spirit, the apostle in explaining how Adam is the figure of Christ speaks only in the singular, for fear that some impudent sophist might reduce it to nonsense by saying: "He is taking the word 'sin' in a collective sense, using it in the singular rather than the plural, as the Scripture frequently does." Thus he says expressly, "through one man who sinned" (v. 12), and, "the effect of that one man's sin unto condemnation" (v. 16), and again, "because of one man's trespass (v. 17), again, "by one man's trespass" (v. 18), and "by one man's disobedience" (v. 19). This point of comparison is particularly strong, "For the judgment following one trespass brought condemnation, but the free gift following many trespasses brings justification" (v. 16). For "judgment (as blessed Augustine says in chapter 12 of the above-mentioned work) leads from many offenses unto justification." [10] But since he does not say this, however, but rather "by one," it is easy to see that he is speaking of original sin. Likewise, he denies that many sinned, but only the one, when he says "through one man's trespass" (v. 15) and "one man's sin" (v. 18) and "one man's sin" (v. 16), etc. Note how at the same time it is true that only one man sinned, that only one sin was committed, that only one person was disobedient, and yet because of him many were made sinners and disobedient.

What, therefore, is original sin?

First, according to the subtle distinctions of the scholastic theologians,[11] original sin is the privation or lack of original righteousness. And righteousness, according to these men, is only something subjective in the will, and therefore also the lack of it, its opposite. This comes under the category of a quality, according to the *Logic* and *Metaphysics* of Aristotle.[12]

Second, however, according to the apostle and the simplicity of meaning in Christ Jesus, it is not only a lack of a certain quality in the will, nor even only a lack of light in the mind or of power in the memory, but particularly it is a total lack of uprightness and of the power of all the faculties both of body and soul and of the whole inner and outer man. On top of all this, it is a propensity toward evil. It is a nausea toward the good, a loathing of light and wisdom, and a delight in error and darkness, a flight from and an abomination of all good works, a pursuit of evil, as it is written in Ps. 14:3: "They are all gone astray, they are all alike corrupt"; and Gen. 8:21: "For the imagination and thought of man's heart are evil from his youth." For not only this lack does God hate and impute (even as many forget their own sin and no longer acknowledge it) but also this universal concupiscence by which we become disobedient to the commandment "You shall not covet" (Ex. 20:17; Deut. 5:21).

[10] Augustine, *De peccatorum meritis et remissione*, I, 12, 15, *Patrologia, Series Latina*, XLIV, 117.

[11] Preeminently Peter Lombard. Referring to Lombard's *Sentences*, II, dist. 30 (*Patrologia, Series Latina*, CXCII, 721 ff.), Paul of Burgos says in his comments on Rom. 5 that original sin is not purely a lack *(pura privatio)* but a certain corrupted disposition *(quidam habitus corruptus)*. He also adds that the doctors call it "tinder of sin" *(fomes peccati)* and that this is something positive.

[12] Aristotle, *Categories*, ch. 8.

As the apostle most clearly argues later on in chapter 7, this commandment shows us our sin: "I should not have known what it is to covet if the Law had not said, 'You shall not covet.'"

Therefore, as the ancient holy fathers [13] so correctly said, this original sin is the very tinder of sin, the law of the flesh, the law of the members, the weakness of our nature, the tyrant, the original sickness, etc. For it is like a sick man whose mortal illness is not only the loss of health of one of his members, but it is, in addition to the lack of health in all his members, the weakness of all of his senses and powers, culminating even in his disdain for those things which are healthful and in his desire for those things which make him sick. Thus this is Hydra,[14] a many-headed and most tenacious monster, with which we struggle in the Lernean Swamp of this life till the very day of our death. It is Cerberus,[15] that irrepressible barker, and Antaeus,[16] who cannot be overcome while loose here on the earth. I have not found so clear a discussion of the subject of original sin as in Gerard Groote's treatise *Blessed Is the Man,*[17] in which he speaks not as an arrogant philosopher but as a sound theologian.

Corollary

Therefore, to think that original sin is merely the lack of righteousness in the will is merely to give occasion for lukewarmness and a breakdown of the whole concept of penitence, indeed, to implant pride and presumptuousness, to eradicate the fear of God, to outlaw humility, to make the command of God invalid, and thus condemn it completely. At least, this is the situation if these theologians are taken at their word! And as a result, one can easily become proud over against another man, when he thinks that he

[13] The formulation is mainly that of Peter Lombard, *Sentences,* II, dist. 30 (*Patrologia, Series Latina,* CXCII, 722), but this is heavily dependent on Augustine. For Luther *antiqui patres* often means Augustine.

[14] In Greek mythology a monster that inhabited the swamps of Lerna in the Peloponnesus. When one of its nine heads was cut off, it was immediately replaced by two new ones, unless cauterized. Hercules slew this dragon.

[15] The surly, three-headed dog that guarded the gates to Hades. In his most difficult "twelfth labor" Hercules subdued this formidable beast. Cf. Vergil, *Aeneid,* VI, 698.

[16] The giant whose strength was constantly renewed so long as he remained in contact with his mother, Earth. Hercules crushed him while holding him aloft.

[17] Gerard Groote wrote no such tract. Luther must be thinking of Gerard Zerbolt of Zütphen, whose tract *De spiritualibus ascensionibus* begins with these words of Ps. 84:6.

himself is free from a sin in which he sees his neighbor still struggling.

This is why many people, in order that they may have a reason for humility, busy themselves with exaggerating their past sins and those that they possibly could have committed, and they do the same thing regarding their present secret sins, so that they may appear humble because of their attention to them. Here is good instruction. But look, there obviously are also present sins, and they permit no hint of superiority or complacency to gain the upper hand in us at the condemnation of someone else (which often is the case). For the real reason for humility is obvious, namely, that sin remains in us, but "it has no dominion over us" (Rom. 6:14), but it is subject to the Spirit, so that a person may destroy what formerly ruled over him. Therefore, if anyone looks down on another man as a sinner, sin still rules him doubly. For since he himself is a sinner, he compares himself as a righteous man to the other person and thus makes himself a liar and does not realize as a sinner that he is a sinner. Properly speaking, this is iniquity. For it is prohibited to judge, and yet he judges. But a man cannot judge unless he is superior and better. Therefore in this very act he is proudly preferring himself to the other, and in this way he sins, although he has committed no other sin than that he has forgotten that he himself is a sinner and that he has considered himself to be righteous. Therefore, whoever realizes that sin is in him, which he must govern, this man will surely fear to become a servant of sin, especially will he be afraid of judging. For if he judges, he knows that the Lord will say to him: "Why do you judge like a righteous man, when you are unrighteous? And even if you have been righteous, yet because you trust in your own righteousness, you have already polluted it and have created a twofold unrighteousness, since you set up your sin as righteousness and then boast of it as righteousness.

Sin came into the world. The apostle uses this particular expression to indicate that original sin does not come from men but rather that it comes to them. For it is the nature of actual sin that it comes out of us, as the Lord says in Matt. 15:19: "For out of the heart come evil thoughts." But this sin enters into men, and they do not commit it but suffer it, as Moses says in Ex. 32:24: "And there came out this calf."

In which all have sinned. This is unclear in the Greek as to whether it is masculine or neuter. Thus it seems that the apostle wants it understood in both senses. Hence blessed Augustine also interprets it in both ways in the above-mentioned work, chapter 10, saying, " 'in that *(quo)* all have sinned.' It surely is clear and obvious that personal sins, in which only those who have committed them are involved, are one thing and that this one sin in which all have taken part insofar as all were in this one man is something quite different." [18] From this statement of Augustine it would seem to follow that original sin is the very first sin, namely, the transgression of Adam. For he interprets the expression "all men sinned" with reference to a work which has actually been committed and not only with reference to the transmission of guilt. He continues, "But if that one man and not sin is referred to, in that all have sinned in this one man, what can be clearer then than this clear expression?" But the first interpretation is better in view of what follows. For later on the apostle says, "For as by one man's disobedience many were made sinners" (v. 19), and this is the same as saying that all have sinned in the sin of the one man. But even so the second interpretation can be advanced, that is, while one man sinned, all men sinned. Thus in Is. 43:26 f., "Set forth your case, that you may be proved right. Your first father sinned," which is to say, you cannot be justified, because you are the son of Adam, who sinned first. Therefore you also are a sinner, because you are the son of a sinner; but a sinner can beget nothing but another sinner like himself.

13. *Sin indeed was in the world before the Law was given.* In regard to this verse blessed Augustine has this to say in chapter 10: "This means that the Law, either natural or written, could not take away sin. For by the works of the Law no one can be justified." [19] And elsewhere, in his *Exposition of Certain Propositions, etc.,* he says, "The expression 'before the Law was given, sin was in the world' must be understood in the sense 'until grace should come.' For he is speaking against those who think that sin can be taken away by the Law. And he says that sins are made manifest by the Law but are not taken away, since the Scripture says, 'Sin was not counted where there was no Law.' For it does not say that sin did not exist but that it was not imputed. Nor was sin taken away when the Law was given; rather it began to be imputed, that is, to be made manifest. Therefore we should not think that the

---

[18] Augustine, *De peccatorum meritis et remissione,* I, 10, 11, *Patrologia, Series Latina,* XLIV, 115.

[19] Ibid.

expression 'before the Law' is to be understood as if there were no sin under the Law, for the term 'before the Law' is spoken in the sense that he counts the entire time of the Law until the end of the Law, which is Christ." [20]

And in this way blessed Augustine ties the expression "before the Law" to the expression "sin was in the world." But then it becomes necessary to say, as he himself does say, that sin was not only until the Law, but much more so under the Law, which entered that the offense might abound. But if one takes the expression in connection with the negative phrase "sin was not counted," then it is not necessary to take such a harsh interpretation of the phrase "before the Law," which in any case indicates the end, so that the meaning then is: Before the Law, sin (which, however, was always in the world) was not imputed, which is to say, it was not counted or known until the Law came, which brought it forth, not in actual being, for it already was in existence, but in the sense that it became known. Or thus: "Before the Law, sin was in the world," that is, it was merely there, only insofar as it existed, but beyond the fact that it was there and remained, sin was also acknowledged through the Law. And thus it is not understood to mean that sin existed until the Law came and then ceased to exist, but that sin received an understanding of itself which it did not possess before. And the words of the apostle clearly indicate this interpretation: "But sin was not counted where there was no law," as if to say that through the Law, which it had preceded, sin was not abolished but imputed.

14. *Yet death reigned.* It is as if he were saying that the penalty of sin, which was death, was known and recognized experientially by all men, but the cause of death, which is sin, was not recognized. Here again we ought not to understand this passage to mean that death reigned only until Moses, since Moses also died and all men do until the end of the world; and the rule of death hangs especially over those who are lost. But the expression "death reigned to Moses" means that until the time of Moses it was not understood why and whence death reigned. But blessed Augustine understands this reign in the work cited previously, "When the guilt of sin so rules over men that it does not permit them to come to

---

[20] Augustine, *Expositio quarundam propositionum ex epistula ad Romanos,* 27—28, *Patrologia, Series Latina,* XXXV, 2067.

the eternal life, which is the only true life, but drags them down even to the second death (which is eternal punishment)." [21]

In the likeness of the transgression of Adam. Blessed Augustine, in the same work just cited, interprets this passage as applying to those who had not yet sinned in their own volition, as the other man had.[22] And so also blessed Ambrose [23] understands the phrase "in the likeness" to refer to the preceding words "who have not sinned," for otherwise if the apostle had not defined the expression "who have not sinned" in this way, he would have contradicted his earlier statement "in which all have sinned" (v. 12). For how can it be that all have sinned and yet that some have not sinned, unless it means that all have sinned in Adam and in Adam's sin, but not all have sinned in the likeness of Adam's sin or transgression? For sin is one thing and transgression is another; for sin remains as guilt, while transgression is an act which passes on. Thus all have not sinned in action, but they are all in the same guilt; but only Adam sinned by both action and guilt insofar as he committed the first sin.

Faber Stapulensis, however, understands this passage in a different way and reconciles the contradiction between the phrases "in which all have sinned" (v. 12) and "who have not sinned" (v. 14) in a different way. But I doubt, in fact, I fear, that he has not reconciled them correctly. For he refers the phrase "in the likeness" to the term "reigned," and I will accept this because of John Chrysostom, who in explaining this passage says, "How did death reign? In the likeness of Adam's transgression." [24] And thus the phrase "even over them who have not sinned" he takes as being in a parenthetical position. And then the expression "who have not sinned" must be understood as referring to personal sin in a stricter sense than he used above when he said "in which all have sinned." The same Doctor speaks thus also of little children, "For this reason we baptize infants, even though they do not have sin," that is, actual sins of their own, as blessed Augustine clearly proves in his second book against Julian, when he cites this same author.

---

[21] Augustine, *De peccatorum meritis et remissione,* I, 11, 13, *Patrologia, Series Latina,* XLIV, 116.

[22] Ibid., I, 9, 19, *Patrologia, Series Latina* XLIV, 114.

[23] Ambrosiaster, *Commentarius in epistulam ad Romanos, Patrologia, Series Latina,* XVII, 94 f.

[24] Chrysostom, *Homilia X. in epistulam ad Romanos,* as cited by Augustine, *Contra Julianum,* I, 6, 27, *Patrologia, Series Latina XLIV,* 659.

Who is a type of the One who was to come. Chrysostom, as
quoted by blessed Augustine, says concerning this passage: " 'In
the likeness of the transgression of Adam, who is a type of the One
who was to come,' because Adam is also a figure of Christ. And how
is he a figure? they ask. The answer is that just as Adam has become
a cause of death to those who are born of him, even though they
have not eaten of the tree, the death brought on by the eating,
so also Christ was made a provider of righteousness for those who
belong to Him, even though they are entirely lacking in righteousness, and He has given it to us all through His cross." [25] Thus the
likeness of Adam's transgression is in us, because we die, as if we
had sinned in the same way he did. And the likeness of Christ's
justification is in us, because we live, as if we had produced the
same kind of righteousness that He did. Therefore, because of this
likeness, Adam is "the type of the One who was to come," that is,
Christ, who came after him. Indeed, in order that Christ might
take away this likeness and give us His own, "He was born in the
likeness of men" (Phil. 2:7) and sent by the Father "in the likeness
of sinful flesh" (Rom. 8:3). And thus, "as in Adam all die, so also
in Christ shall all be made alive" (1 Cor. 15:22). Hence I lean
toward Chrysostom's view that the expression "in the likeness"
ought to be connected with the word "reigned."

15. *But the free gift is not like the trespass.* Chrysostom says
the following: "If a Jew should say to you: 'How has the world
been saved by the power of the one man Christ?' you can say to
him: 'How has the world been condemned by the disobedience of
one man Adam?' Yet grace and sin are not equal, nor are death and
life, nor God and the devil." "For if sin, even the sin of one man,
had such power, how can it be that the grace of God and the grace
of one Man will not have greater power? For this is much more
reasonable. For it certainly does not seem reasonable that one
person be damned for another, but it appears much more proper
and reasonable that one person be saved for another." [26]

The grace of God and the free gift in the grace of that one Man.
The apostle joins together grace and the gift, as if they were
different, but he does so in order that he may clearly demonstrate
the type of the One who was to come which he has mentioned,
namely, that although we are justified by God and receive His
grace, yet we do not receive it by our own merit, but it is His gift,

---

[25] Augustine, *Contra Julianum,* I, 6, 22, *Patrologia, Series Latina,* XLIV, 656.

[26] Cf. n. 24.

which the Father gave to Christ to give to men, according to the statement in Eph. 4:8, "When He ascended on high, He led a host of captives, and He gave gifts to men." Therefore these are the gifts of God's grace, which Christ received from the Father through His merit and His personal grace, in order that He might give them to us, as we read in Acts 2:33: "Having received from the Father the promise of the Holy Spirit, He has poured out this gift which you see." Thus the meaning is: "the grace of God" (by which He justifies us, which actually is in Christ as in its origin, just as the sin of man is in Adam) "and the free gift," namely, that which Christ pours out from His Father upon those who believe in Him. This gift is "by the grace of that one Man," that is, by the personal merit and grace of Christ, by which He was pleasing to God, so that He might give this gift to us. This phrase "by the grace of that one Man" should be understood of the personal grace of Christ, corresponding to the personal sin of Adam which belonged to him, but the "gift" is the very righteousness which has been given to us. Thus also original sin is a gift (if I may use the term) in the sin of the one man Adam. But "the grace of God" and "the gift" are the same thing, namely, the very righteousness which is freely given to us through Christ. And He adds this grace because it is customary to give a gift to one's friends. But this gift is given even to His enemies out of His mercy, because they were not worthy of this gift unless they were made worthy and accounted as such by the mercy and grace of God.

20. *The Law came in.* He uses a very appropriate word, "came in" *(subintrauit)*, as if he were saying that sin entered in *(intrauit)* and the Law came in on the side, that is, after sin it also entered in, and thus sin was not abolished by the Law; for that the Law came in on the side indicates that sin, which had come in first, still remained and was even increased. For sin entered, and the Law followed sin, arousing it by prescribing things against it and prohibiting the things which sin wished to do. Therefore he says *that sin might abound.* This expression is not causal but consecutive, because the conjunction "that" *(ut)* refers to what follows and not to the final cause of the Law. For the Law did not come because of sin, although he also says this in Gal. 3:19: "Why then the Law? It was added because of transgressions, till the seed should come to whom He made the promise." So here he uses the expression "that sin might abound," that is, for the sake of sin, etc. Thus the meaning is that through the transgression of the Law the first sin is made

known, therefore for the sake of transgression, not in order that transgression should take place but because it necessarily followed upon the establishment of the Law, so that through this transgression of the Law we might learn the sinfulness of our own weakness, our blindness, and our evil desire. For it was not necessary to establish the Law because of the transgression of it, inasmuch as, even if this was not the intention and if the Law was not established because of transgression, yet the transgression of the Law would follow, since without grace it is impossible to overcome concupiscence and to destroy the body of sin. And this affirmative statement, "the Law came in, that sin might abound," is trying to show nothing else than the negative expression: The Law did not make alive, the Law did not take away sin, or the Law did not come in to take away sin or to make alive. Thus this affirmative statement necessarily follows: Therefore the Law did come in to increase sin. And this is true, so that the meaning is: the Law came and without any fault on the part of the Law or in the intentions of the Lawgiver, it happened that it came for the increasing of sin, and this happened because of the weakness of our sinful desire, which was unable to fulfill the Law. Hence blessed Augustine in the above-mentioned book on the *Propositions* of this letter says: "By this very word he has shown that the Jews did not understand the purpose for which the Law was given. For it was not given that it might give life—for grace alone through faith gives life—but it was given to show by how many tight bonds of sin they are held who presume to fulfill the Law by their own powers." [27] This is a common method of speaking, as when a doctor comes to a sick man to console him and cannot help him because the sick man's hopes are in vain; then the sick man can say: "You have come not to comfort me but to make my despair greater." The same is the case with the Law, which the human race most anxiously desires (as is evident in all the philosophers and seekers after truth), but the Law is not a help and a cure; it only serves to increase the disease, as is typified by the woman in the Gospel who had the issue of blood. She had spent all her substance on doctors and yet had been made worse (Luke 8:43 ff.). Hence he has used a most significant word when he says, "The Law came in that sin might abound," that is, God did not establish the Law for this purpose, but it became so when the Law entered "that sin might abound."

[27] Augustine, *Expositio quarundam propositionum ex epistula ad Romanos*, 30, *Patrologia, Series Latina*, XXXV, 2068.

CHAPTER SIX

2. We who died to sin.

BLESSED Augustine says regarding this passage: "With this passage the apostle is giving a complete description of the man who has been placed under grace, where with his mind he is already serving God's law, although with his flesh he is still serving the law of sin." And he continues in his description of these two kinds of servitude of the Law and of sin, saying: "For this man does not obey the desire of sin, no matter how his lusts still continue to trouble him and call him to consent to them, until the time that his body is raised to life and 'death is swallowed up in victory' (1 Cor. 15:54). Thus because we do not surrender to these low desires, we are under grace, and 'sin does not reign in our body' (v. 12). But he over whom sin reigns, no matter how he resists sin, is still under the Law and not under grace." [1]

From this quotation the meaning of the apostle's words is clear. For all these propositions: (1) to be dead to sin; (2) but to live unto God; (3) to serve with the mind the law of God and with the flesh the law of sin, mean nothing else than this, that we do not yield to our evil lusts and to sin, even though sin still remains in us. This is the same as saying: (4) Sin does not have dominion, does not rule; but (5) righteousness does rule, etc. Hence later on, in chapter 13:14, he says: "And make no provision for the flesh, to gratify its desires," as if he were saying: "The desires of the flesh are themselves sin, that is, original sin and the rest of the paternal inheritance from Adam remain, but you must not obey them." Likewise he says, "That the body of sin might be destroyed" (v. 6), which takes place when our spirit resists sin and refuses to give in to it.

Corollary

We are in sin until the end of our life. For this reason blessed

---

[1] Augustine, *Expositio quarundam propositionum ex epistula ad Romanos*, 35, *Patrologia, Series Latina*, XXXV, 2069.

Augustine says: "Until our body is raised to life and death is swallowed up in victory, our evil desires will afflict us." [2] Likewise, we read in Gal. 5:17: "The desires of the flesh are against the Spirit, and the desires of the Spirit are against the flesh; for these are opposed to each other, to prevent you from doing what you would." And below, in Rom. 7:19 Paul says: "For I do not do the good I want, but the evil I do not want is what I do, etc." Again, in James 4:1: "What causes wars, and what causes fightings among you? Is it not your passions that are at war in your members?" And in 1 Peter 2:11: "Abstain from the passions of the flesh that wage war against your soul." And in this way all the apostles and saints confess that sin and concupiscence remain in us, until the body returns to ashes and a new one is raised up without concupiscence and sin, as 2 Peter 3:13 puts it, "According to His promise we wait for new heavens and a new earth in which righteousness dwells," as if to say that sin dwells in this present world. Just so in Jer. 18:4 ff. in regard to the potter who repairs the broken vase by making another, the Lord says that He will do likewise. For the Lord hates this body of sin and is preparing to remake it into another; therefore He commands us to hate it also, to destroy and put it to death and to seek an escape from it and "the coming of His kingdom" (Matt. 6:10).

But this hatred and resistance toward the body of sin is not easy, in fact it is most difficult. As many works of penitence as can possibly be done are necessary for this, especially warnings against idleness.

3. *We are baptized into His death.* Blessed Augustine in Book 4, chapter 3, of *On the Trinity* says: "For our twofold death the Savior pays with His single death, and in order to achieve a twofold resurrection for us, He has set before us and offered us His own single resurrection in His sacrament and example.[3] For having put on our mortal flesh and dying only in it and rising only in it, now only in it He joins these things together for us, for in this flesh He became a sacrament for the inner man and an example for the outward man. With regard to the sacrament for the inner man we have this word: 'We know that our old self was crucified with Him, so that the body of sin might be destroyed' (v. 6). But to the example for the outward man this statement is pertinent: 'And do not fear those who kill the body' (Matt. 10:28). He most strongly encouraged

[2] Ibid.; cf. 1 Cor. 15:54.

[3] Cf. p. 284 above and W, IX, 18, 20.

His followers to this course through His own death, which was of
this kind." [4] The resurrection of the body of the Lord is shown to
pertain to the sacrament of the inner man through this statement
of the apostle in Col. 3:1: "If then you have been raised with Christ,
seek the things that are above." But to the example for the outward
man this statement applies: "Not a hair of your head will perish"
(Luke 21:18), along with the fact that He showed His body to His
disciples after His resurrection. Thus in this passage the apostle is
speaking of the death and resurrection of Christ insofar as they refer
to the sacrament, but not to the example.

Hence we must note that death is of two kinds: natural, or better,
temporal death and eternal death. Temporal death is the separation
of the body and the soul. But this death is only a figure, a symbol,
and like death painted on a wall [5] when compared with eternal
death, which is also spiritual. Hence in the Scripture it is very
often called a sleep, a rest, a slumber. Eternal death is also twofold.
The one kind is good, very good. It is the death of sin and the death
of death, by which the soul is released and separated from sin and
the body is separated from corruption and through grace and glory
is joined to the living God. This is death in the most proper sense of
the word, for in all other forms of death something remains that is
mixed with life, but not in this kind of death, where there is the
purest life alone, because it is eternal life. For to this kind of death
alone belong in an absolute and perfect way the conditions of death,
and in this death alone whatever dies perishes totally and into
eternal nothingness, and nothing will ever return from this death,
because it truly dies an eternal death. This is the way sin dies; and
likewise the sinner, when he is justified, because sin will not return again for all eternity, as the apostle says here, "Christ will
never die again," etc. (v. 9). This is the principal theme in Scripture.
For God has arranged to remove through Christ whatever the devil
brought in through Adam. And it was the devil who brought in sin
and death. Therefore God brought about the death of death and the
sin of sin, the poison of poison, the captivity of captivity. As He
says through Hosea (Hos. 13:14): "O Death, I will be your death;
O Hell, I will be your bite." This is prefigured in all the wars of

---

4 Augustine, *De Trinitate*, IV, 3, *Patrologia, Series Latina*, XLII, 891.

5 Luther is perhaps thinking of the "dance of death" representations common
in his time. In these death is regularly portrayed as the leader of a round dance
who irresistibly confronts men of every station in life with the summons to join the
dance of death.

the children of Israel in the Old Testament, when they killed the
Gentiles. The other kind of death is eternal and very terrible. It is
the death of the damned, where sin and the sinner are not the ones
to die, while man is saved, but man dies, while sin lives on and continues forever. This is "the very evil death of the wicked." [6] And
when the apostle speaks of the death of Christ in a sacramental
manner, he is speaking of the second spiritual death, and thus the
meaning of his words is very plain.

I used the term "sin of sin." What does this mean? The sin of
sin is to act against the law of sin and to transgress the law of the
members (Rom. 7:23) and to sin against the lusts of the flesh. This
kind of sin is very good. Just as the death of death means to act
against death, which is the same thing as life, so the sin of sin is
righteousness. Hence Ecclesiasticus (Ecclus. 42:14): "Far better
is the iniquity of a man than a woman doing a good turn," that is,
it is better that the spirit transgress the law of the flesh and act contrary to the flesh than that the flesh act according to its own law.
These are the works of the Lord in which He delights and causes us
to delight, as it is written: "The Lord shall rejoice in His works"
(Ps. 104:31). And later on, in Rom. 8:3, he says: "For sin He condemned sin." The Spirit uses these negative expressions which are
sweeter than the affirmative ones to describe the eternal nature of
the things about which He is speaking. Because for death to be
killed means that death will not return, and "to take captivity
captive" [7] means that captivity will never return, a concept which
cannot be expressed through an affirmative assertion. For a person
can think of life without eternity. Thus it also says in the same
psalm: "Our God is the God of salvation; and to God the Lord belongs escape from death" (Ps. 68:20),[8] rather than the entrance of
life. For the entering into life can, and necessarily must, become
a departure from life, but the "escape from death" means to enter
into a life which is without death. These are "the delights of Christ"
of which it says in Ps. 16:3: "As for the saints in the land, they are
the noble, in whom is all my delight," and in Ps. 111:2, "Great are
the works of the Lord, sought out according to all His desires."

4. *We are buried therefore.* In the spiritual man all things ought
to appear to men and to himself in the same way that Christ ap-

[6] Cf. Ps. 34:21.

[7] Cf. Ps. 68:18; Eph. 4:8.

[8] Cf. Luther's comment on this passage for an involved study in contrasts.
W, III, 400—401.

peared to the Jews in death and burial. For He is our Precentor that we may address our responses to Him in all things.

First, when Christ had died He no longer felt any of those things which happen in the outside world, even though He was still in that world. Thus the spiritual man, although he is present in all things with his senses, yet in his heart he is entirely withdrawn from these things and dead to all of them. This comes about when a man comes to hate all the things of this life from the very marrow of his bones, indeed, when he detests all the things which go on in this life and yet endures them with patience and even with joy and glories in the fact that he is like a dead body and "the refuse of the world, the offscouring of all things" (1 Cor. 4:13), as the apostle puts it. But we must note that it is not necessary for all men to be found immediately in this state of perfection, as soon as they have been baptized into a death of this kind. For they are baptized "into death," that is, toward death, which is to say, they have begun to live in such a way that they are pursuing this kind of death and reach out toward this their goal. For although they are baptized unto eternal life and the kingdom of heaven, yet they do not all at once possess this goal fully, but they have begun to act in such a way that they may attain to it — for Baptism was established to direct us toward death and through this death to life — therefore it is necessary that we come to it in the order which has been prescribed.

There are thus three kinds of people in this order. First there are those who are impatient with a cross and a dying of this kind, and they are unwilling to die. These people are like the robber on the left, for they blaspheme Christ, at least in their heart and also in their work. The second class, however, are those who endure it, but with great feeling, difficulty, and groaning; yet they finally overcome, so that at least they die with patience. It is very hard for them that they are despised and detested by all. They are like the robber on the right, indeed, a grieving and sympathetic Christ carried them in His body. But the third class are those who, as I have said, enter upon this death with joy, whom Christ Himself prefigured when He died with a loud shout like the most courageous giant.[9]

---

[9] Cf. Matt. 27:50; Mark 15:37; Luke 23:46. The heroic aspect of Christ's death is more likely to be celebrated in Advent and Easter scenes than in those of the crucifixion. Borrowing from the language of Ps. 19:6, *Exultavit ut gigas ad currendam viam,* the mediaeval Advent hymn *Veni, Redemptor gentium* speaks of the Savior as *Geminae gigas substantiae, alacris ut currat viam,* which Luther translated *Gott von Art und Mensch ein Held, Sein'n Weg er zu laufen eilt.*

6. *Our old man.* The term "old man" describes what kind of person is born of Adam, not according to his nature but according to the defect of his nature. For his nature is good, but the defect is evil. However, the term "old man" is used not only because he performs the works of the flesh but more especially when he acts righteously and practices wisdom and exercises himself in all spiritual good works, even to the point of loving and worshiping God Himself. The reason for this is that in all these things he "enjoys" the gifts of God and "uses" God.[10] Nor can he be freed of his perversity (which in the Scriptures is called curvedness,[11] iniquity, and crookedness) except by the grace of God. Eccl. 1:15: "The perverse are hard to be corrected." [12] This is said not only because of the stubbornness of perverse people but particularly because of the extremely deep infection of this inherited weakness and original poison, by which a man seeks his own advantage even in God Himself because of his love of concupiscence. Ps. 72:14: "From usuries and iniquities He redeems their life." Furthermore, this iniquity is so bottomless that no one can ever understand its depth, and in Scripture, by the grace of God, not the iniquity itself but only the love of it is rebuked. Ps. 11:5: "His soul hates him that loves iniquity." And Ps. 32:6: "Therefore," that is, because of iniquity, "let everyone who is godly offer prayer to Thee," because He hates iniquity. This is symbolized in the curvedness of that woman in the Gospel whom Satan had held captive for 18 years, as the Savior said (Luke 13:11).

That the body of sin might be destroyed. The term "to destroy" is understood in a spiritual sense in this context. For if he were intending to speak of a destruction of the body, it would not be necessary that the "old man" be crucified for this. Because he actually will be destroyed anyway, whether we wish it or not, even in the case of those people whose old man is not crucified. Thus what is necessary cannot be command or counsel. Hence, also according to blessed Augustine, the apostle in explaining this destruction goes on to say, "That we might no longer be enslaved to sin" (v. 6). This is an interpretation (says blessed Augustine) of the expression "that the body of sin might be destroyed." [13] Thus to destroy the body of

---

[10] Cf. p. 295 and n. 5.

[11] Cf. p. 291.

[12] Cf. Luther's comment on this passage, *Luther's Works,* 15, p. 26.

[13] Cf. n. 1 above.

sin is to break the lusts of the flesh and of the old man by works of penitence and the cross and thus to diminish them day by day and to put them to death, as Col. 3:5 tells us: "Put to death therefore what is earthly in you." In fact, in this same passage he most clearly describes both the new and the old man.

The titles of some of the psalms refer to this destruction: "Destroy not" (Ps. 57:1; 58:1; 59:1). In Ps. 60:1 we read: "God, Thou hast cast us off and hast destroyed us." And in Jer. 1:10: "to destroy, to overthrow, to pluck up."

Therefore the term "body of sin" ought not be understood as something mystical, as many people do who imagine that "body of sin" refers to a whole mountain of evil works, but rather it refers to this very body which we are carrying around. It is called the "body of sin" because it inclines against the spirit and toward sin. And the seed of the devil dwells in it; hence the Lord in Gen. 3:15 says: "I will put enmity between your seed and her seed." The seed of the woman [14] is the Word of God in the church, because it inclines toward righteousness and good works. The seed of the devil is sin itself, the tinder and evil lust in our flesh. And this enmity is active all the time, as the apostle says in Gal. 5:17: "The desires of the flesh are against the Spirit, and the desires of the Spirit are against the flesh." The flesh has the seed of the devil in it and is seeking to bring forth sin and bear sinful fruit. But the Spirit possesses the seed of God and seeks to bring forth righteousness and the fruits of righteousness. And thus these two "are opposed to each other, to prevent you from doing what you would" (Gal. 5:17).

10. *The death He died He died to sin.* The meaning is that we must undergo this spiritual death only once. For whoever dies thus lives for all eternity. Therefore we must not return to our sin in order to die to sin again. This interpretation is in opposition to the Novatians,[15] for in regard to the necessity and nature of the spiritual life it is to be laid hold on once, because it is eternal. For death does not put an end to this kind of life against its will, as it does with physical life, but this is the beginning of eternal life. Hence we read in John 11:26: "Whoever believes in Me shall never die," that

---

[14] The *Glossa interlinearis* interprets *mulier* with *ecclesia*.

[15] A sect that was active in the years 250—650. They contended that the church could not restore to membership those who had fallen away after Baptism. Ambrose, *De poenitentia*, II, 2, uses Rom. 6:3 and 10 to refute their claims. In his sermon on Matt. 18:21 (W, XLVII, 305—310) Luther preached not only against the original Novatian heresy but also against evidences of contemporary resurgence of the same.

is, as long as he does not willingly turn away from this spiritual life, he cannot die. This spiritual life will be strengthened in the future in such a way that a person cannot be turned away, for no one would want to be turned away who has been given the complete perfection of an eternal will.

For just as the ray of the sun is eternal because the sun is eternal, so the spiritual life is eternal because Christ is eternal; for He is our life, and through faith He flows into us and remains in us by the rays of His grace. Therefore, just as Christ is eternal, so also the grace which flows out of Him is from His eternal nature. Furthermore, just because a man sins again his spiritual life does not die, but he turns his back on this life and dies, while this life remains eternal in Christ. This is what he means when he says: "If we have died with Christ, we believe that we shall also live with Him" (v. 8). How shall we live with Him, "for we know that Christ being raised from the dead will never die again" (v. 9)? So also: "the death He died He died to sin, once for all" (v. 10). He has Christ, who dies no more; therefore he himself dies no more, but rather he lives with Christ forever. Hence also we are baptized only once, by which we gain the life of Christ, even though we often fall and rise again. For the life of Christ can be recovered again and again, but a person can enter upon it only once, just as a man who has never been rich can begin to get rich only once, although he can again and again lose and regain his wealth.

But the life He lives He lives to God. Nothing lives to God, however, except that which lives eternally and spiritually, because God is eternal and a spirit, before whom nothing counts except what is spiritual and eternal; but the flesh and temporal things are nothing with Him. Therefore since this life is eternal, it is necessary that the man who dies to sin should die only once, since only an eternal life can follow this kind of death, and in this life there can be no death, for otherwise it would not be eternal. Nor can a person who died once to sin die to sin again, because eternal righteousness follows this death and this righteousness never sins again. A corollary follows:

The Novatian heresy [16] interpreted this text in a false way, as if those who fell had no hope of rising again, because a person must die to sin once and for all. But this expression "once for all" *(semel)* does not determine the number of acts of repentance, but rather it is a commendation of the eternal nature of grace, and it denies the

---

[16] Cf. n. 15 above.

possibility of some other kind of righteousness, so that the meaning is that whoever has been baptized or has repented has already so escaped sin and acquired righteousness that never again for eternity is it necessary to escape sin or to acquire another righteousness. But this single and only righteousness is sufficient forever. This is not the case at all with the righteousness of men, where according to moral philosophy, as soon as one virtue has been acquired, there are still others which must be acquired. But the meaning here is not that if a person should lose what he has once possessed, he cannot acquire it again. For the Scripture opposes this error in Prov. 24:16: "A righteous man falls seven times and rises again." And the Lord said to Peter: "I do not say to you seven times, but seventy times seven" (Matt. 18:22). Therefore, as I have said, this term "once for all" does not set forth or deny the number of the exchange, but it emphasizes the number of the diversity, or rather the eternal nature of righteousness, which in this life can often be lost and regained without conflicting with its eternal nature. For even blessed Peter after the sending of the Holy Spirit sinned in his dissimulation, for example, in Gal. 2:11 ff., which surely was a mortal sin, because it was contrary to the Gospel and the salvation of the soul, since the apostle Paul expressly says that Peter did not act according to the truth of the Gospel.

14. *Since you are not under the Law.* Therefore sin has dominion over all those who are under the Law. This is entirely clear from what has been said above in chapter 3:27 ff. For he who is without Christ is still in his sins, even if he does good works. Hence we must note that the apostle's mode of speaking appears unusual and strange to those who do not understand it because of its great peculiarity. For those people understand the expression "to be under the Law" as being the same as having a law according to which one must live. But the apostle understands the words "to be under the Law" as equivalent to not fulfilling the Law, as being guilty of disobeying the Law, as being a debtor and a transgressor, in that the Law has the power of accusing and damning a person and lording it over him, but it does not have the power to enable him to satisfy the Law or overcome it. And thus as long as the Law rules, sin also has dominion and holds man captive. Hence 1 Cor. 15:56 tells us: "The sting of death is sin, and the power of sin is the Law" (that is, sin is so powerful and has such dominion because the Law has dominion. The term "power" *(virtus)* here means the same as strength *(potentia)*, so that the sequence of

thought is as follows: Sin is the sting or power of death, through which death is powerful and holds dominion), as above in chapter 5:12 ff.: "death through sin" etc. But the Law is the power or strength of sin, through which sin remains and holds dominion. And from this dominion of the Law and sin no one can be liberated except through Christ, as the following verse says: "But thanks be to God, who gives us the victory through our Lord Jesus Christ" (1 Cor. 15:57). And in John 8:36 He Himself says: "So if the Son makes you free, you will be free indeed," and in John 16:33: "In the world you have tribulation; but be of good cheer, I have overcome the world," and in 1 John 5:4: "This is the victory that overcomes the world, your faith," and in 1 John 5:5: "Who is it that overcomes the world but he who believes that Jesus is the Son of God?" Therefore he says in this passage that we can restrain the reign of sin because "we are not under the Law but under grace" (v. 14). All this means "that the body of sin might be destroyed" (v. 6) and the righteousness which has been begun may be brought to perfection.

17. *To which you were committed.* Although some men [17] wish this statement to be understood by changing it around [18] so that it would read: "which was committed to you," yet the Spirit speaking through the apostle certainly has His purpose in saying what He does say. For the wisdom of the flesh is opposed to the Word of God, but the Word of God is immutable and insuperable. Therefore it is necessary that the wisdom of the flesh be changed and that it give up its form and take on the form of the Word. This takes place when through faith it takes itself captive and strips off its own crown, conforms itself to the Word, and believes the Word to be true and itself to be false. Thus "the Word was made flesh" (John 1:14) and "He took on the form of a servant" (Phil. 2:7), so that the flesh might become the Word and manhood take on the form of the Word; then, as stated in chapter 3, man becomes righteous, truthful, wise, good, meek, and chaste like the very Word itself, to which he conforms himself through faith. Hence "to which you were committed" is a better interpretation than "which was delivered to you." For even to the ungodly the doctrine of the Gospel has been delivered, but they do not deliver themselves over to it or

[17] Faber recommends the figure in his commentary.

[18] *Per hipallagen,* "by interchange" (of syntactical relationships). The classic example of this figure is Vergil's *dare classibus austros* (*Aeneid,* III, 61), "to give the winds to the fleets" instead of "to give the fleets to the winds."

conform themselves to it; but they have not been delivered into it because they do not really believe it from the heart. Very similar is this statement to the Corinthians (cf. 1 Cor. 13:12; Gal. 4:9): "Then you have come to know, even as you have come to be known." And here, too, he could have said: "Which was delivered to you, or rather, to which you were committed," because this is characteristic of believers and saints. Observe chapter 7:4 below, where we die to sin and the Law rather than the contrary.

14. *For sin will have no dominion over you.* This refers not only to sinful lust for temporal goods and prosperity but also to our practice of fleeing from temporal evils and adversities. For the man who has Christ through true faith does not desire any of this world's goods (however much they may allure him), not even life itself, nor does he fear the evils, even death itself (no matter how terrifying they may be). For he stands firm on the solid rock, neither following after a soft life nor fleeing a hard life; not because he is not tempted to flee in the face of overpowering fear or tempted to evil lust by the strong blandishment of sin (for he is not insensitive toward lust and terror), but in the end he does not consent, although it is with tremendous labor and sorrow that he barely resists and triumphs in accord with the statement in 1 Pet. 4:18, "The righteous man is scarcely saved." And the righteous man is always more like a victim than a victor as long as he is contending with temptations. For the Lord permits him to be tempted and attacked right up to the end, like gold in a furnace. "An athlete is not crowned unless he competes according to the rules" (2 Tim. 2:5).

Corollary

1

He who fears death more than Christ and loves his life more than Christ does not yet possess Christ through true faith. For sin has dominion over him, and he is still under the Law. We must fully understand this, as He Himself explains it when He says, John 12:25: "He who loves his life loses it," and in another place (Matt. 10:37): "He who loves father or mother more than Me is not worthy of Me," and again (Matt. 10:38): "He who does not take his cross and follow Me is not worthy of Me." Thus it is not an easy matter to bring sin into subjection. Indeed, unless the Lord were in us, "who is faithful and will not let us be tempted beyond our strength" (cf. 1 Cor. 10:13), surely the waves would overwhelm us. But He permits the unbelievers to be tempted and to fall, indeed, they already have fallen and can never stand before Him, but He is faithful to those who stand and call upon Him by faith.

2

As long as sin only attacks but does not gain dominion over the saints, it is compelled to serve them, as we read later on (Rom. 8:28): "Everything works for good with those who love God." And the apostle says (1 Cor. 10:13): "But with the temptation God will also provide the way of escape, that you may be able to endure it." Thus luxurious living makes the soul more chaste when it attacks, pride makes the soul humbler, laziness makes it more active, avarice makes it more generous, anger, more mild, gluttony, more abstemious.[19] For in all these instances the hatred of the spiritual man increases more and more against the thing which is attacking him. Thus temptation is a most useful thing. Thus also it has dominion over the mortal body when a man yields to it.

But temptation becomes a servant when we resist it, because it then produces a hatred of iniquity and a love of righteousness. And in our future immortal body it will neither have dominion nor rule, nor will it be a servant. Thus let us recognize the marvelous wisdom of God, because by means of evil He promotes the good, and through sin He achieves righteousness, not only in us but also in other people. For He gives us in the sins of other men a reason to hate sin in our neighbor and to get rid of it, and thus a reason to practice love and piety toward him, while in our own case a reason to thirst after righteousness and loathe unrighteousness, yet only if we call upon Him out of a pure and sincere faith.

13. *Instruments of wickedness to sin.* Our version [20] translates "iniquity" here in place of "unrighteousness." And this "unrighteousness" is the complete, general life of unbelief, just as on the other hand righteousness is the complete and general way of the life of faith, or of faith taken together with its works, in the same way that unrighteousness is unbelief along with its works, even the good and the holy.

And the term "sin" in this passage, according to blessed Augustine, *On the Spirit and the Letter*,[21] is not to be understood as the

---

[19] Here Luther lists almost the whole gamut of the so-called "seven mortal sins," omitting only *invidia*, "envy."

[20] The Vulgate. Faber has *iniustitia*.

[21] The reference is probably to Augustine, *De nuptiis et concupiscentia*, I, 30—31, *Patrologia, Series Latina*, XLIV, 432.

work of sin but as the law of sin or the law of the members, as concupiscence, the tinder of sin, the proneness toward evil, and the
difficulty of doing good. Thus the apostle wants to say that the
members of the body must not be surrendered to "sin," that is, to
evil lust and to the tinder of sin, for in obeying sin they become
weapons of unbelief, and out of believers they make unbelievers in
that they perform the works of unbelievers according to the lusts
of sin. But we must obey God, in order that "our members may be
instruments of righteousness to God" (v. 13), that is, of the life of
faith and belief.

19. *I am speaking in human terms because of your natural
limitations.* He has spoken earlier in such a way concerning the
complete mortification of evil lust that we must not consent to it
even in the married state. But here he relaxes his position and
wants to say: "If you must surrender at all to lust because of the
weakness of the flesh, then let it take place in the state of marriage
and sanctified by faith and without any pollution and uncleanness,
since even the heathen, who are outside the faith, observe a purity
of this kind under human custom. Hence the meaning of this text
is the same, though in a shorter form, as 1 Cor. 7, in which he de-
velops the idea throughout the entire chapter, saying, for example
(v. 2): "Because of the temptation to immorality, each man should
have his own wife, etc.," and later on (v. 5): "lest Satan tempt you
through lack of self-control." This is what he is saying here when he
says "because of your natural limitations." Likewise the expression
that he uses in the previously mentioned passage: "I say this by
way of concession, not of command" (1 Cor. 7:6), is stated here in
these words: "I am speaking in human terms." It is as if he were
saying: "I do not command that every man take a wife, but only
that you should avoid fornication, 'because of your natural limitations,' that is, because of your incontinency." For this is a human
mandate and of much less importance than the counsel which he
gives when he says: "I wish that all were as I myself am" (1 Cor.
7:7), but not every person can do this, and therefore he goes on to
say: "But each has his own special gift from God, one of one kind
and one of another." He shows that here, too, he has been speaking
of this kind of counsel and of the complete mortification of the
flesh, when he relaxes the rigor of his position by saying: "I am
speaking in human terms." It is as if he were saying: "If you cannot
be continent at least conduct yourself in a chaste way, so that sin
does not rule over you through the pollution and uncleanness of

the flesh to the detriment of faith and righteousness and to the increase of unrighteousness."

To impurity. Here the apostle turns around and is no longer observing the antithesis, for he says in the first place, "You once yielded your members to impurity and to greater and greater iniquity," and now he is saying: "So now yield your members to righteousness for sanctification," that is, for cleanness. For this reason the Old Testament often says "be holy," "sanctify yourselves," as equivalents of such terms as "be clean" or "purify yourselves," [22] that is, from carnal pollutions. For through the terms "sanctification" and "cleanness" he is trying to convey the same concept, namely, that the body should be pure, but not with just any kind of purity, but with that which comes from within, from the spirit of sanctifying faith. There is also a chastity of the heathen, but it is not a holy chastity or sanctification, because the heathen soul is polluted. Hence he first speaks about yielding your members "to righteousness" and then adds the words "for sanctification." Because through faith first the soul must be cleansed, so that in this way a holy soul can make the body clean for the sake of God; otherwise it would be a worthless chastity. Thus the Lord says to the hypocrites: "Hypocrite, first cleanse the inside of the cup, that the outside also may be clean" (Matt. 23:26), which means, if you are clean inwardly, the body and all outward things will easily and almost of their own accord be clean. Therefore if you serve righteousness, such service brings with it sanctification, as Is. 11:5 tells us: "Righteousness shall be the girdle of His waist, and faithfulness the girdle of His loins," which is to say, he who believes and is righteous in the Spirit will by the same token easily overcome a dissipated life and shall take it into captivity.

On the contrary he who serves uncleanness, that is, dissipation and carnal uncleanness, is already becoming more and more unrighteous, for sin now rules over him, and he has lost his faith and has become an unbeliever.

[22] Cf. p. 144 above.

CHAPTER SEVEN

1. The Law is binding on a person.

IT is evident that the apostle is not speaking of the Law in a metaphysical or moral sense, but in a spiritual and theological sense, as is sufficiently discussed above in chapter 4. That is, he is dealing with the Law as it applies to the inner man and the will and not with respect to the works of the outer man. Once we have understood his customary propositions and his bases and principles, all the rest is easy. The first of these principles is:

Sin and the wrath of God come through the Law. Therefore no one dies to the Law unless he dies also to sin, and whoever dies to sin dies also to the Law. And as soon as a man is free from sin, he is also free from the Law. And when a person becomes a servant of sin, he also becomes a slave of the Law, and while sin rules over him and dominates him, the Law also rules over and dominates him.

Corollary

The apostle's methods of speaking are contrary to the metaphysical or moral methods. For the apostle says what he does in order to indicate (or sound forth) that man rather than sin is taken away, for sin remains as a kind of relic, and man is purged from sin rather than the opposite. But the human mind says the contrary, that sin is taken away while man remains and that man is cleansed. But the apostle's meaning is entirely characteristic of him and completely in accord with God. For the Scripture speaks this way in Ps. 81:6: "He relieved his shoulder of the burden." He does not say: "He removed the burden from his shoulder." Likewise, in chapter 6:17 above: "to which you were delivered." The Exodus is symbolic of this, because it did not take the Egyptians away from the children of Israel, but it led Israel out of Egypt, which remained behind. And in Ps. 21:12 we read: "In Thy remnants [1] Thou shalt

---

[1] In his glosses on this psalm passage, Luther explains "remnants" (reliquiis) with "Thy sufferings and evils, which Thou didst leave behind at Thy ascension and didst not take with Thee" (W, III, 134, 7).

prepare their face, for Thou shalt make them turn their back."
And the reason for this kind of speaking is that grace and spiritual
righteousness picks a man up and changes him and turns him away
from his sin, although sin still remains, so that while it makes the
spirit righteous, it allows concupiscence to remain in the flesh and
in the midst of the sins of the world. And this way of speaking is a
most effective device against the self-righteous. But human righteousness tries first of all to take away sins and change them and
also to preserve man as he is; thus it is not righteousness but hypocrisy. Therefore, as long as a man lives and is not taken away and
changed by the renewing power of grace, he can in no way do anything to prevent his being under sin and the Law.

Therefore, the first proposition is this: "Sin comes through
the Law," as follows below. And therefore the Law is the law of
sin, that is, the law of the husband, to which a man does not die
unless he dies to sin. But when a man has died to sin and has been
removed from it, then sin already has been wonderfully taken
away and put to death. But when a man has not died to sin and has
not been taken from it, in vain does one try to take away sin and die
to it. Thus it is obvious that the apostle means that sin is taken away
by a spiritual means (that is, the will to commit sin is put to death),
but these people want the works of sin and our evil lusts to be taken
away by metaphysical means, as when white paint is taken from
a wall and heat from water. Hence Samuel says in 1 Sam. 10:6:
"And you shall be turned into another man," that is, another person.
He does not say: "Your sins will be turned," but: "you will be
changed first and when you have been changed, then also your
works will be changed." Therefore the hypocrites with amazing
foolishness punish themselves with numerous labors and are
zealous in changing their works before they with true humility
seek the grace which would change them. In Eph. 2:10: "For we
are His workmanship, created in Christ Jesus for good works," he
does not say that good works are created in us. And James 1:18
reads: "that we should be a kind of firstfruits of His creatures."

And therefore unless this putting to death takes place first, sin
remains, so that it may exercise dominion, and because of this also
the Law through which sin has its dominion. Because the man who
is not quickened in his will through the spirit cannot fail to serve
sin, no matter how much he performs good works, but the same
thing that is said in Prov. 11:15 befalls him: "The foolish man shall
be afflicted with pains."

Therefore with marvelous stupidity and with a monkey-sees-monkey-does attitude do these people act who want to imitate the works of the saints and glory in their fathers and ancestors, as the monks do today. But the fools do not first seek the spirit of these great people in order to be like them, but in order to act like them while neglecting their spirit. The Thomists, the Scotists, and the other schools act with the same temerity when they defend the writings and words of their founders with such zeal that they not only disdain to seek their spirit but actually quench it by their excessive desire to venerate them, thinking that it is enough if they merely retain the words even without the spirit. So also the Jews and all those who are proud think that it is enough that they understand the Holy Scriptures, and they care nothing about the spirit of this understanding and the method by which it wants to be understood. Therefore Is. 11:2 quite correctly does not say: "wisdom rests upon Him, etc.," but rather, "the spirit of wisdom, etc." For only the Spirit understands the Scriptures correctly and in accord with God. But otherwise, even if they think they understand, men do not understand, "seeing they do not see and hearing they do not hear" (Matt. 13:13). So also these hypocrites: being holy they are not holy, being righteous they are not righteous, though they do good works they do nothing good.

And so the first thing we must do is beseech grace so that a man might be changed in spirit and with glad heart and will desire and do all things, not with servile fear or childish cupidity but with a free and manly heart. And this alone the Spirit accomplishes.

4. *And likewise you.* Blessed Augustine says on this point: "Three things are spoken of here: the soul as the woman, the passions of sins as the man, and the Law as the law of the husband." And again, "We must note that the similarity ceases at this point, that he does not say that the soul is set free when the sins are dead as the woman is when the husband dies, but rather that the soul itself dies to sin and is freed from the Law and is married to another." [2] Why it does this we have already mentioned.

6. *Not under the old written code.* By the term "written code" in the writings of the apostle Paul refers not only to the symbolical portions of Scripture or the doctrine of the Law but to every teaching which prescribes those things which belong to a good life, whether Gospel or Mosaic Law. For if these things are known and

---

[2] Augustine, *Expositio quarundam propositionum ex epistula ad Romanos,* 36, *Patrologia, Series Latina,* XXXV, 2069.

remembered and the spirit of grace is not present, it is merely an empty written code and the death of the soul. Hence blessed Augustine, *De Spiritu et littera*, ch. 4: "That teaching by which we receive the command to live continently and uprightly is the written code that kills, unless the life-giving Spirit is present. For the term "written code" is not to be understood in the sense that any figurative statement of Scripture whose meaning is absurd if we take it as it reads literally, but also and primarily in the way which the apostle most clearly indicates when he says, 'I should not have known that coveting is sin if the Law had not said, "you shall not covet."' For here it is not something figurative which is being said."[3] And later on, in chapter 14, he says more fully: "When the apostle speaks about the Law, by which, he says, no one can be justified, he wants us to understand not only those sacred acts *(sacramenta)* which had figurative promises but also those works which will enable whoever performs them to live righteously." "And he speaks still more clearly to the Corinthians when he says (2 Cor. 3:6): 'The written code kills, but the Spirit gives life,' for he wants us to understand that he is speaking of no other code than the Decalog itself written on two tables."[4] A corollary follows:

That the so-called moral interpretation of Scripture, which more correctly is the spiritual interpretation, deals with nothing but love and the attitude of the heart, with nothing but the love of righteousness and the hatred of iniquity, that is, when we ought to do something or give up doing something. And we must understand that this must be done or omitted with the whole heart, not with fear of punishment in a slavish manner or because of some puerile desire for comfort, but freely and out of love for God, because without the love which has been poured out through the Spirit this is impossible. That is what the scholastic doctors[5] mean when they say in their obscure and wholly unintelligible way that there is no valid fulfillment of the commandment unless it is formed by love. But this word "formed" *(formatum)* is under a curse, for it forces us to think of the soul as being the same after as before the outpouring of love and as if the form were merely added to it at the time of the action, although it is necessary that it be wholly put to death and be changed before putting on love and working in love.

---

[3] Augustine, *De Spiritu et littera*, 4, 6, *Patrologia, Series Latina*, XLIV, 203.

[4] Augustine, *De Spiritu et littera*, 14, ibid., p. 215.

[5] Scotus, Occam, and Biel are cited by the Weimar editor, W, LVI, 337, n. 16.

(Likewise there is also a distinction between a work done according to the substance of the deed and one done according to the intention of the lawgiver). The apostle agrees with this when he says in 1 Cor. 13:2: "If I understand all mysteries and have all knowledge, even if I have all faith, etc., but have not love, I gain nothing." Therefore it clearly follows that the term "written code" applies to the mysteries, to the whole Gospel, and to every spiritual interpretation of the Scripture. Hence if these people are dead, they are without the Spirit; "for the Spirit gives life, and the written code kills" (2 Cor. 3:6), but these men have been killed and hence are under the written code.

Hence blessed Augustine later on in chapter 21 of the same work says: "What are the Laws of God which He Himself has written in our hearts if they are not the very presence of the Holy Spirit, who is the finger of God and by whose presence love is shed abroad in our hearts? And this love is the fulfilling of the Law and the end of the commandment." [6]

Corollary

They are not the best Christians who are the most learned and read the most and abound in many books. For all their books and all their learning are the "written code" and the death of the soul. But rather they are the best Christians who with a totally free will do those things which the scholars read in the books and teach others to do. But they do not act out of a totally free will unless they have love through the Holy Spirit. Therefore in our age it is to be feared, that by the making of many books we develop very learned men but very unlearned Christians.

Therefore, when the question is asked why the Gospel is called the Word of the Spirit, a spiritual teaching, the Word of grace and a clarification of the words of the ancient law and a knowledge that is hidden in a mystery, etc., the reply is that properly the Gospel teaches where and whence we may obtain grace and love, namely, in Jesus Christ, whom the Law promised and the Gospel reveals. The Law commands us to have love and Jesus Christ, but the Gospel offers and presents them both to us. Thus we read in Ps. 45:2: "Grace is poured abroad in Thy lips." Therefore, if we do not receive the Gospel for what it really is, then it is like the "written code." And properly speaking it is Gospel when it preaches Christ; but when it rebukes and reproves and gives commands, it does

---

[6] Augustine, *De Spiritu et littera*, 21, ibid., p. 222.

nothing else than to destroy those who are presumptuous concerning their own righteousness to make room for grace, that they may know that the Law is fulfilled not by their own powers but only through Christ, who pours out the Holy Spirit in our hearts.

The real difference between the old and the new law is this, that the old law says to those who are proud in their own righteousness: "You must have Christ and His Spirit"; the new law says to those who humbly admit their spiritual poverty and seek Christ: "Behold, here is Christ and His Spirit." Therefore, they who interpret the term "Gospel" as something else than "the good news" do not understand the Gospel, as those people do who have turned the Gospel into a law rather than grace and have made Christ a Moses for us.

7. *For I should not have known what it is to covet.* From this passage on to the end of the chapter the apostle is speaking in his own person and as a spiritual man and by no means merely in the person of a carnal man. St. Augustine first asserted this extensively and repeatedly in his book against the Pelagians.[7] Hence in his *Retractations*, I, 23, taking back a former explanation of this passage, he says: "When the apostle says: 'We know that the Law is spiritual; but I am carnal' (v. 14), I was absolutely unwilling to understand this passage as referring to the person of the apostle who was already spiritual, but I wanted to refer it to him as a man placed under the Law and not yet under grace. This is the way I first understood these words, but later, after I had read certain interpretations of the divine words by men whose authority impressed me, I considered the matter more carefully and saw that the passage could also be understood of the apostle himself." [8] And in Book 2 of his *Contra Julianum:* "Note that it is not, as you think, some Jew who is speaking, but according to most blessed Ambrose, the apostle Paul is speaking of himself when he says, 'I see in my members another law at war with the law of my mind, etc.' (v. 23)." And a little later he cites these words of blessed Ambrose from his *De sacramento regenerationis:* "We must struggle against our flesh. Paul struggled against his flesh. He finally says: 'I see in my members another law at war with the law of my mind.' Are you stronger than Paul? Do not put your trust in the zeal of your flesh and do not put your confidence in it, for even Paul cries out: 'For I know that

---

[7] Augustine, *Contra duas epistolas Pelagianorum*, I, 10, 17, *Patrologia, Series Latina*, XLIV, 559.

[8] *Patrologia, Series Latina*, XXXII, 620.

nothing good dwells within me, that is, in my flesh. I can will what
is right, but I cannot do it' " (v. 18). Likewise he quotes the same
author from his *De paradiso:* "Again in the same work in another
place the same teacher says: 'Paul is under attack and sees the law
of his flesh fighting against the law of his mind. Paul says: "For I do
not do the good I want, but the evil I do not want is what I do" '
(v. 19). And do you think that man is profited by knowledge which
increases his dislike of his sin, etc.?" [9] And he makes the clearest
explanation of all in book six of the same work, from chapter 11 to
the end.[10]

But let us elicit these same ideas from the words of the apostle
himself. In the first place, this entire passage clearly indicates a
complaint and a hatred of the flesh and a love for the good and for
the Law. But this attitude is in no way characteristic of carnal man,
who prefers to hate the Law and laughs at it and follows the desires
of his flesh. For the spiritual man fights with his flesh and groans
because he cannot do as he wants to. But the carnal man does not
fight against his flesh, but yields to it and consents to it. Hence the
well-known statement of St. Augustine: "The will to be righteous is
a large part of righteousness." [11] And in Wisd. of Sol. 9:15 the
Preacher says: "The corruptible body is a load upon the soul, and
the earthly habitation presses down the mind *(sensus),*" that is,
the mind *(mens)* which "muses much" (that is, which plans and devises to do many things), an authority that briefly expounds this
entire text. For *sensus* is the same as what the apostle here calls
mens, against the law of which the law of the members contends.
And where the Preacher uses the expression "muses much," the
apostle here says: "I serve the law of God with my mind" (v. 25),
and again: "When I want to do right, evil lies close at hand"
(v. 21), and: "For I delight in the law of God in my inmost self"
(v. 22). The same idea occurs in Gal. 5:17: "For the desires of the
flesh are against the Spirit, and the desires of the Spirit are against
the flesh; for these are opposed to each other, to prevent you from
doing what you would," and again: "I pommel my body and subdue
it, lest after preaching to others I myself should be disqualified"
(1 Cor. 9:27).

Thus the first expression which proves that these are the words
of a spiritual man is this: *But I am carnal* (v. 14). For it is charac-

[9] Augustine, *Contra Julianum,* 5, 13—14, *Patrologia, Series Latina,* XLIV, 683.

[10] Ibid., pp. 865 ff.

[11] Cf. p. 267 above.

teristic of a spiritual and wise man to know that he is carnal and displeasing to himself, to hate himself and to approve the law of God because it is spiritual. On the other hand, it is characteristic of a foolish and carnal man to know that he is spiritual, to be well pleased with himself, and to love his life in this world.

The second expression is this: *I do not understand my own actions* (v. 15). Blessed Augustine explains this in this way: "That is, I do not approve," [12] perhaps, because a spiritual man who lives by the mind does not understand anything except what belongs to God; therefore he does not understand, does not comprehend the evil which he does. Likewise, on the other hand, he understands and realizes very well what he does not do, namely, the good. Conversely, the carnal man "does not understand the things which belong to the Spirit of God, and he cannot understand them" (cf. 1 Cor. 2:14), but he fully understands, that is, he gives approval to, the things which he does, for, as we read below in Rom. 8:5: "Those who live according to the flesh set their minds on the things of the flesh, but those who live according to the Spirit set their minds on the things of the Spirit." Therefore, to put it the other way, those who are according to the Spirit do not set their minds on the things of the flesh, even though they do them, and those who are according to the flesh do not set their minds on the things of the Spirit. But the passage can also be taken very simply, as I do in the gloss:[13] "I do not understand" can mean I am deceived insofar as I am carnal and sin has deceived me when I do evil. Because as a spiritual man I understand nothing but the good, and yet I do what I neither understand nor desire, namely, the evil, which is to say, I do not do evil out of my intention or by choice, but I choose the good, and yet it happens that I do the opposite. However, the carnal man fully understands this, because he willfully performs the evil by plan, purpose, and free choice. And if he ever does do anything good, it happens by accident.

The third expression is this: *For I do not do what I want, but I do the very thing I hate* (v. 15). But concerning carnal man the Scripture says (Ps. 36:4): "He spurns not evil." For if they hated it, they would not perpetrate it in their actions but would contend and work against it.

The fourth expression is: *I agree that the Law is good* (v. 16),

---

[12] Augustine, *Expositio . . . ex epistula ad Romanos,* 43, *Patrologia, Series Latina,* XXXV, 2071.

[13] Cf. p. 63 above.

because the Law wills what is good and he himself wants the good, and therefore they agree. But the carnal man does not do this, for he always dissents from the Law and would prefer (if it were possible) that the Law did not exist. Therefore he does not want the good, but the evil. And even though he may do good (as I have said), he does not really understand it, because he does his good work only under the compulsion of slavish fear, always having the desire to do the opposite, if he could do so with impunity.

From this we must not think that the apostle wants to be understood as saying that he does the evil which he hates, and does not do the good which he wants to, in a moral or metaphysical sense, as if he did nothing good but only evil; for in common parlance this might seem to be the meaning of his words. But he is trying to say that he does not do the good as often and as much and with as much ease as he would like. For he wants to act in a completely pure, free, and joyful manner, without being troubled by his rebellious flesh, and this he cannot accomplish. It is as with a man who proposes to be chaste; he would wish not to be attacked by temptations and to possess his chastity with complete ease. But his flesh does not allow him, for with its drives and inclinations it makes chastity a very heavy burden, and it arouses unclean desires, even though his spirit is unwilling. He who proposes to watch, to pray, and to help his neighbor will always find that his flesh is rebellious and that it devises and desires other things. Hence we must take special note of the fact that the apostle distinguishes between "to do" (facere) and "to accomplish" (perficere), as blessed Augustine teaches fully at the end of Book 3 of his Contra Julianum.[14] Here he understands "to do" in the sense of trying, devising, having the desire, being willing, etc., such things as without interruption the flesh works against the Spirit and the Spirit against the flesh. For if the expression "to do" were taken in the sense of "fulfilling" by means of one's work, then the apostle could not say: "The evil I do not want is what I do, but I do not do the good I want" (v. 19), words by which he is very clearly describing the battle between the flesh and the Spirit. For this "wanting to do what he does not" means that he has a gracious purpose and, through the love spread abroad by the Spirit, an inclination directed toward the good and a hatred directed against evil, and yet because the flesh resists and because his concupiscence opposes him, he cannot accomplish and fulfill this desire. For if he would accomplish and fulfill it,

14 III, 26, 62, Patrologia, Series Latina, XLIV, 733 f.

he would do good without resistance and cheerfully; for this is what his will desires. But now he does not act in this way; and therefore he does not do what he wants to do, but he does what he does not want to do. Moreover, he who does not have any struggle and who follows his flesh and obeys his evil lusts surely does not put up a resistance and does not say: "I do what I do not want," for he does not take pleasure in the contrary to that which he does, but in the very thing which he is doing. But "to accomplish" is to fulfill what one wishes or desires. Thus the Spirit accomplishes the good that it wishes when without rebellion it does its work in accord with the law of God, which cannot be done in this life, because "I cannot do it" (v. 18). The flesh, however, accomplishes its task when with pleasure and without repugnance and difficulty it does its work according to its lusts. And this is characteristic of this life, rather of death, and it is the destruction of the world; for it is easy to do evil. Therefore I have said that this passage establishes that Paul here is speaking not as a carnal man but as a spiritual one.

The fifth statement is: *It is no longer I that do it, but sin which dwells within me* (v. 20). Therefore it is not he who sins, because his flesh lusts without his consent, indeed he himself does not lust because he dissents from the lusts of the flesh. And yet he says: "I do not do the good I want" (v. 19). Because the same person is both spirit and flesh, therefore what he does in the flesh the whole man is said to do. And yet because he resists, it is rightly said that the whole man is not doing it, but only a part of him. Therefore both expressions are true, that he himself does it and he himself does not do it.

He is like a horseman. When his horses do not trot the way he wants them to, it is he himself and yet not he himself who makes the horse run in such and such a way. For the horse is not without him, and he is not without the horse. But because a carnal man certainly consents to the law of his members, he certainly himself does what sin does. For now it is the mind and flesh not only of one person but also of one will.

The sixth expression: *For I know that nothing good dwells within me, that is, in my flesh.* (v. 18). See how he attributes to himself flesh which is a part of him as if he himself were flesh. Thus he has said above: "I am carnal" (v. 14); and therefore he now confesses that he is not good but evil, because he does evil things. Because of his flesh he is carnal and wicked, for there is no good in him, and he does evil; because of the spirit he is spiritual and good, because he does good. Therefore we must note that the words "I want" and "I hate" refer to the spiritual man or to the spirit, but "I do" and "I work" refer to the carnal man or to the flesh. But because the same one complete man consists of flesh and spirit, therefore he attributes to the whole man both of these opposing qualities which come from the opposing parts of him. For in this way there comes about a communication of attributes, for one and the same man is spiritual and carnal, righteous and a sinner, good and evil. Just as the one and the same Person of Christ is both dead and alive, at the same time suffering and in a state of bliss, both working and at rest, etc., because of the communication of His attributes, although neither of the natures possesses the properties of the other, but are absolutely different, as we all know. But this applies in no way to the carnal man, where the whole man is entirely flesh, because the Spirit of God has not remained in him. Therefore the carnal man cannot say "within me, that is, in my flesh" (v. 18), as if he by his own will were something different from the flesh, but rather he is one and the same with the flesh, because he yields to the lusts of his flesh, just as a man and woman are one flesh in a figurative sense, but in the way of harlots and fornicators.[15] And as a result of this the apostle can be better understood in the comparison which he used earlier, namely, that a woman is free when her husband has died, but the application of this comparison seems inappropriate because he says rather that the soul itself, like the woman, is to die and is thus to be liberated, but the man, that is, the passions of sin, remain but are taken into captivity, etc. But the apostle who has the identity of the person in view sees the marriage union in each and every one, that the flesh is the woman and the soul or mind is the man. When they agree together in their desires, as Adam and Eve did, they are one flesh. But if the mind, the carnal man, dies a spiritual death, we are already dead to the Law in the whole person, and so also we are liberated in our whole person. Whether the apostle now looks at the flesh or at the spirit, we are still the same unit, the man put to death to the Law and the woman set free from the Law, which

---

15 In his interpretation of Gen. 2:18 ff. Nicholas of Lyra speaks of Augustine as the originator of the comparison between "mind" and "sensuality" on the one hand and man and woman on the other. In *De opere monachorum*, 40 (*Patrologia, Series Latina*, XL, 580), Augustine says: "What therefore in a single human being is the mind and the concupiscence (the former ruling, the latter ruled: the former lord, the latter subject), the same in two human beings, man and woman, is in regard to the sex of the body exhibited in a figure."

itself made him a husband and produced this marriage, that is, by its stimulation it increased the desire and by offering the opportunity produced the agreement between the mind and the flesh. Therefore we are the woman because of the flesh, that is, we are carnal, and we are the man because of the spirit which yields to the flesh, we are at the same time both dead and set free. For this double use accrues to the person, even though the two parts are different because of which it accrues. For it is characteristics that tie their individual parts to the totality. Therefore he says: "Likewise you have died" (v. 4), even though only according to the inner man have we died and been freed and loosed from the Law. But again this belongs to the whole man because of the inner man, and it is communicated to the flesh, or the outer man. For the flesh itself no longer serves the Law or sins, but it is freed because of the fact that the inner man has been set free, with whom it makes up one man, whose wife it is and was.

The seventh statement: *I can will what is right, but I cannot do it* (v. 18). This "willing" is the prompting of the spirit which comes from love and of which he says: "I do not do the good I want" (v. 19), and of which we read in Ps. 1:2: "His delight is in the law of the Lord." So he now says: "I can will what is right," that is, the good pleasure and delight in the good which the Law prescribes, as he says below: "I delight in the Law of God in my inmost self" (v. 22), but "to accomplish" it, that is, the good commanded by the Law, this he cannot do because of the resistance of the flesh. He does not want to lust, and he judges that it is a good thing not to lust, and yet he lusts and does not carry out his own will, and thus he is fighting with himself; but because the spirit and the flesh are so intimately bound together into one, although they completely disagree with each other, therefore he attributes to himself as a whole person the work of both of them, as if he were at the same time completely flesh and completely spirit. Yet by these words he makes his position clear and replies to the objection which someone might raise: "If you do not do what the Law commands but rather do what you do not want, and do not do what you want, how then are you not a sinner?" His answer is that he does do the good but does not accomplish it perfectly, because he does not extinguish the concupiscence of the flesh. How then can a thoroughly carnal man who has no desire [16] to do good have this will, a will which

---

[16] Luther contrasts a comparatively rare word, *noluntas* ("nonwillingness") with *voluntas* ("willingness"). He uses the word again in ch. 12 (p. 439 below).

Ps. 1 attributes to the blessed man and which the Spirit alone gives through love? This text cannot be made to say such a thing without extreme violence to it, indeed only with great injury to such words as "I will," "I do not will," "to will," etc.

The eighth expression: *So I find it to be a law that when I want to do right, evil lies close at hand* (v. 21), that is, I find a contrary law when I am willing and ready to act in accord with the Law of God. But a carnal man cannot be said to be willing. For we read in Ps. 112:1, "Blessed is the man who fears the Lord, who greatly delights in His commandments!" In fact, it comes about because of God's dispensation that when this concupiscence resists a willing man and his good will, by this very act it makes his will stronger and increases his hatred of it more than if it did not resist. For it turns the will against it, and thus the more it resists and covets, the more it increases his hatred for it. As in the case of an angry man, if the one who has offended him pushes him, he makes him even more angry. But the carnal man does not have this fire of indignation nor does he feel any resistance, for he is snatched away and meekly follows.

Nor does he realize that "evil lies close at hand." For no one knows the evil which is in him, unless he has been established in the good above the evil, from where he can judge and discern his evil, just as we do not recognize shadows except by the light and we measure contrast by its opposite and judge the valueless by the precious. Thus if the spirit were not in the light, it would not see or lament the evil which lies so close at hand, as is clearly evident in the case of the lost and the proud in this world.

The ninth expression: *For I delight in the law of God in my inmost self* (v. 22). Note that he expressly says that he has an inner man. This is nothing else but the spiritual man, because without the spirit the entire man is the "old man" and only outward. But the inner man is a mind and conscience that is pure and delights in the law of God. Likewise: "I delight in the law of God," that is, "The words of God are sweet for me" (Ps. 119:103) and "The law of Thy mouth is good to me" (Ps. 119:72). But to the carnal man they are bitter and harsh and full of hate, because his will which is suffering from the fever of sin hates God's words, even though in his own eyes and those of others he may almost seem to love them because of the fear of punishment. This delight comes from the Holy Spirit through love, as we have often said, and without this love it is impossible to love the Law and righteousness; indeed, man detests righteousness more when he is under the Law than when he is without it, for he hates to know that he ought to know what he does not want to know, or rather the very contrary of what he wants.

The tenth expression: *I see in my members another law at war with the law of my mind* (v. 23). From this it is obvious that he is speaking of himself as a pugilist between two contrary laws, but not as a defeated fighter for whom there is no longer a war between the law of the members and the law of the mind, because the mind has given in, as is the case with the carnal man. Rather he shows that he is serving the one law, that he is dedicated to it and that he is standing up to the other law which attacks him and is not serving it, rather, that he is struggling against it. We all know that this kind of resistance or reports of resistance are never heard of in the case of the carnal man.

The eleventh expression: *Wretched man that I am! Who will deliver me from the body of this death?* (v. 24). This even more clearly than the preceding statements shows that a spiritual man is speaking these words, for he laments and mourns and desires to be delivered. But surely no man except a spiritual man would say that he is wretched. For perfect knowledge of oneself is perfect humility, and perfect humility is perfect wisdom, and perfect wisdom is perfect spirituality. Therefore only the perfectly spiritual man says: "Wretched man that I am!" But the carnal man does not desire to be liberated and set free but shudders terribly at the freedom which death brings, and he cannot recognize his own wretchedness. But when Paul says here, "Who will deliver me from the body of this death?" he is saying the same thing that he says elsewhere: "I desire to depart and be with Christ" (Phil. 1:23). Thus it is astonishing that the idea could have come into anyone's mind that the apostle is speaking these words in the person of the old man or a carnal man, words which are of such great perfection, as if the apostle like a hypocrite had to think and say nothing but good things about himself, that is, to commend himself and deny that he is a sinner, so that he does not commend grace but denies it.

Rather it is a comfort to hear that such a great apostle was involved in the same sorrows and afflictions as we are when we try to be obedient to God.

The twelfth expression: *So then, I of myself serve the law of God with my mind, but with my flesh I serve the law of sin* (v. 25).

This is the most expressive statement of all. Note that one and the same man at the same time serves the law of God and the law of sin, at the same time is righteous and sins! For he does not say: "My mind serves the law of God," nor does he say: "My flesh serves the law of sin," but: "I, the whole man, the same person, I serve a twofold servitude." Therefore he also gives thanks that he serves the law of God, and he seeks mercy for having served the law of sin. Who will assert this of the carnal man, that he serves the law of God? Now notice what I said above, that the saints at the same time as they are righteous are also sinners; righteous because they believe in Christ, whose righteousness covers them and is imputed to them, but sinners because they do not fulfill the Law, are not without concupiscence, and are like sick men under the care of a physician; they are sick in fact but healthy in hope and in the fact that they are beginning to be healthy, that is, they are "being healed." [17] They are people for whom the worst possible thing is the presumption that they are healthy, because they suffer a worse relapse.

And it is from this sure understanding that the apostle in chapter 2 above speaks so boldly against those people who were righteous in their own eyes and stood in judgment over those who did wrong, while they themselves did the same things; they preached against stealing while they stole, etc. For although he did not know their outward works, he was absolutely sure that as long as they were outside of grace they were also acting against the Law in their hearts. For if a man who is spiritual does not do what he ought, when he is willing to do what he ought, how much more will the carnal man refrain from doing what he ought to do, when he is unwilling to do what he ought to do but is forced. For thus "the spiritual man judges all things, but is himself judged by no one" (1 Cor. 2:15). As a result of this we can at last understand the statement of David: "Therefore let everyone who is godly offer prayer to Thee at the proper time" (Ps. 32:6), and why Christ has repudiated His wife, the synagog, because of her hideousness. For she is unwilling to admit her iniquity and confess it to God's mercy, but rather she thinks she is righteous and holy. We have covered these matters sufficiently in chapter 4 above.

8. *Apart from the Law sin lies dead.* Blessed Augustine explains this passage together with the statement which follows it as applying to the time of infancy before we have the use of reason. In his

---

[17] Luther coins the word *sanificati*, which he explains with *sani fientes.*

second book against Julian he says: "The small child, who does not
yet possess the ability to reason, is neither under the good nor the
bad by an act of his own will. But as the years go by and reason
awakens, the commandment comes and sin revives. And when this
has begun to attack him as he grows up, then will appear what has
been lying dormant in the infant, and it will either conquer him and
rule over him or it will be conquered and he will be healed." [18]
The Law revives and sin begins to make its appearance when the
Law begins to be recognized; then concupiscence which had lain
quiet during infancy breaks forth and becomes manifest. When this
concupiscence breaks forth in adolescence, it immediately shows
what had been lying hidden in the child. So a young plant does not
yet show what fruit it will bear, but when the leaves come forth and
the fruit is developed, then we know what kind of tree it is. But we
can find a still deeper meaning in this. There are people who are
children in their understanding even if they are a hundred years
old. They are the people who are bewitched by the messenger of
Satan under the appearance of some spiritual good, for which they
long more ardently, indeed more tenaciously, than any adulterer
for a woman or a miser for his money. They forsake the Law and
obedience toward God like the Jews, the heretics, the schismatics,
the individualists and particularists.[19] Because the Law has not
yet been given to them they have no sin. But if they knew the
Law against which they are sinning, even though they burn with
great zeal for the Law, they doubtlessly would immediately admit
their sin. Thus when the Law comes to them, sin revives for them.
But now, because they are burning more for their own desires and
pursuits, they are also angered more severely against the Law and
hate it because it prohibits them from the way which they have
chosen as being in accord with the Law, as they see it. Thus when
the Law says: "You shall not covet," coveting is so strongly forbidden, that whatever is coveted besides God, even if one covets
it for the sake of God, becomes a sin. Hence many people who love
piety, prayers, studies, readings, devotions, meditations, and other
good works as if these things were the best and alone pleasing to
God, are really lost, for they murmur and grow angry if they are
called to some lesser service. The stupid fools. They do not know
that God does not require certain kinds of works, or a certain
quality and number, but a quiet, meek, and obedient spirit, as

[18] Augustine, *Contra Julianum*, II, 4, 8, *Patrologia, Series Latina*, XLIV, 679.

[19] Cf. p. 271, n. 26, above.

Ps. 51:16 says: "If Thou hadst wanted it, I would have given a sacrifice, Thou wouldst not be pleased with a burnt offering" (that is, Thou dost not care for our good works, whatever they may be, that we have chosen to perform). What then? "The sacrifice acceptable to God is a broken" (that is, a contrite) "spirit; a broken (that is, contrite) and humble (that is, broken) heart, O God, Thou wilt not despise" (Ps. 51:17), that is, a heart and a spirit that are not hardened by a stubborn attitude but are capable of being guided and broken to do Thy will. Such people do not choose the work they are to do, but wait to be chosen for whatever work may be given to them. And all this that "He may open our lips and our mouth may show forth His praise" (Ps. 51:15). For those people who choose on their own initiative cannot refrain from praising themselves. They please only themselves, and only so do they want to please God. But the other class of people please God and thereby they also please themselves. The devil in this way disturbs every mind, in order that he may make void the calling of every person and to tempt him by seducing him to that for which he has not been called, as if God were a fool and did not know where He wished to call a person. Thus the devil is always fighting against the wisdom of God and trying to make God appear foolish in our eyes, so that he might lead us away into idolatry by trumping up the idea that God wills that which He does not will. These ideas are surely the idols of the house of Israel, now erected on all the street corners throughout all Jerusalem.[20]

17. *So then it is no longer I that do it.* Therefore is it not true that the false metaphysics of Aristotle and the traditional human philosophy have deceived our theologians? For they have come to believe that sin is abolished in Baptism or repentance and consider as absurd the statement of the apostle *but sin which dwells within me.* Thus it was this word which gave them the greatest offense, so that they plunged into this false and injurious opinion, that the apostle was not speaking in his own person but in the person of carnal man, for they chatter the nonsense that the apostle had absolutely no sin, despite his many clear assertions to the contrary which occur in many epistles.

This foolish opinion has led to the most injurious deceptions, such as, that people who have been baptized or absolved think that they are immediately without any sin; they become smug in that they have obtained righteousness and are at rest and relaxed, be-

20 Cf. Jer. 11:13.

cause they are conscious of no sin which they should struggle
against and purge out with laments, tears, groans, and labor.

Therefore sin remains in the spiritual man for the exercise of
grace, for the humbling of pride, for the repression of presumptuousness. For he who does not earnestly strive to drive out sin
certainly still possesses it, even if he has not committed any further
sin for which he might be condemned. For we are not called to
ease, but to a struggle against our passions, which would not be
without guilt (for they really are sins and truly damnable) if the
mercy of God did not refrain from imputing them to us. But only to
those who manfully struggle and fight against their faults, invoking
the grace of God, does God not impute sin. Therefore he who comes
to confession should not think that he is laying down his burden
so that he may lead a quiet life, but he should know that by putting
down his burden he fights as a soldier of God and thus takes on another burden for God in opposition to the devil and to his own
personal faults.

If he does not know this, he will quickly relapse. Therefore, if
a person does not intend to fight thereafter, why does he seek to be
absolved and enrolled in the army of Christ?

Because of their ignorance of this fact the interpreters have
misunderstood this statement of the apostle in Heb. 12:1: "Let us
lay aside every weight, and sin which clings so closely." They have
taken the "weight" to be the devil and the "sin which clings
closely" as evil works, although the apostle says that the works
themselves are the "weight" and that "the sin which clings so
closely" is the internal blemish of sin and the tinder of sin.

Moreover, we must note that the apostle does not wish to be
understood as saying that the flesh and spirit are two separate
entities, as it were, but one whole, just as a wound and the flesh
are one. For although the wound is something by itself, and the
flesh is another thing, yet because the wound and the flesh are
one, and because the wound is nothing else than wounded or weakened flesh, we can attribute to the flesh the properties of the wound.
In the same way man is at the same time both flesh and spirit. But
the flesh is his infirmity, or his wound, and insofar as he loves the
law of God, he is spirit; but insofar as he lusts, he shows the weakness of the spirit and the wound of sin, which is in the process of
being healed. Thus Christ says: "The spirit indeed is willing, but
the flesh is weak" (Matt. 26:41).

And blessed Augustine in his second book against Julian says:

"We generally understand our faults as being those which because of the law of sin resist the law of our mind. When these faults are removed from us, they will not be somewhere else, but when they have been healed in us, they will be nowhere. Then why are they not destroyed in Baptism? Are you not willing to confess that their guilt is destroyed but their weakness remains? Not a guilt by which these faults were guilty, but one by which they had rendered us guilty in the evil works into which they had dragged us. And the weakness of these faults does not remain, as if they were some living creatures that have become weak, but they are our very own weakness." [21] From this clear authority it is evident how concupiscence is that weakness in us toward the good. In itself the concupiscence is guilty, to be sure, but yet it does not render us guilty unless we yield to it and commit sin. From this comes the remarkable fact that we are guilty and not guilty. For we ourselves are this weakness, therefore it is guilty and we are guilty until this weakness ceases and is cleansed. But we are not guilty as long as we do not act in accord with this weakness, since God in His mercy does not impute the guilt of the weakness but only the guilt of the will which consents to the weakness. This twofold idea cannot be better explained than by the parable in the Gospel of the man who was left half dead (Luke 10:30 ff.). For when the Samaritan had poured wine and oil on his wounds, he did not immediately recover, but he began to do so. Thus our sick man is both weak and getting well. Insofar as he is healthy, he desires to do good, but as a sick person he wants something else and is compelled to yield to his illness, which he himself does not actually want to do.

In the light of these points it is obvious that the idea of the metaphysical theologians [22] is silly and ridiculous, when they argue whether opposing appetites can exist in the same subject, and when they invent the fiction that the spirit, namely, our reason, is something all by itself and absolute and in its own kind and integral and perfectly whole, and similarly that our sensuality, or our flesh, on the opposite end likewise constitutes a complete and absolute whole. Because of these stupid fantasies they are driven to forget that the flesh is itself an infirmity or a wound of the whole

---

[21] Augustine, *Contra Julianum*, II, 5, 12, *Patrologia, Series Latina*, XLIV, 682.

[22] Luther has in mind the theologians troubled with the distinctions of philosophy, in this case the question whether the soul consists of separable and independent parts, or potencies. Aristotle's μόρια ϕυχῆς were basic in these discussions.

man who by grace is beginning to be healed in both mind and spirit. For who imagines that in a sick man there are these two opposing entities? For it is the same body which seeks health and yet is compelled to do things which belong to its weakness. The same body does both of these things. *Contra Julianum*, III, 20, says: "Concupiscence is so great an evil that it can be overcome only in actual combat, until, like a wound in the body, it can be healed by the perfect cure." [23] Let us force a rather crude example on these unrealistic theologians: Suppose that a house which has fallen into disrepair is in the process of reconstruction, is then its construction and present condition one thing and its state of disrepair something else? It is one and the same thing. It can be said of the same house that because of its being under construction it is a house and that it is in the process of becoming a house, but because of its incompleteness it can at the same time be said that it is not yet a house and that it lacks what is proper to a house. Thus "we who have the firstfruits of the Spirit" (Rom. 8:23) "are become the beginning of God's creature," according to the apostle James (cf. 1:18), and "are built into a spiritual house" (1 Peter 2:5), and a structure thus "joined together grows into a holy temple in the Lord" (Eph. 2:21).

But sin which dwells within me. In *Contra Julianum*, Book II, blessed Augustine says: "For how is sin dead, when it works so many things in us even when we struggle against it? What are these many things except foolish and harmful desires 'which plunge those who consent to them into ruin and destruction' (1 Tim. 6:9). How then do we say that this sin is put to death in Baptism, and how do we confess that it dwells in our members and works many desires, unless we also confess that it is dead in that guilt by which it held us bound and in which it still rebels even though dead until it is perfectly healed by burial? It is no longer called sin in the sense that it makes us guilty, but because it comes to us as a result of the guilt of the first man and because by its rebellion it strives to draw us into the same guilt." [24]

This sin is the original blemish of the tinder about which we have stated earlier that it would be better to say that we die to it rather than that it dies to us, and that as long as it continues in us, we are turned away from it in this life only by grace, as we read in Ps. 81:6: "He relieved your shoulder of the burden."

---

[23] *Patrologia, Series Latina*, XLIV, 722.

[24] *Contra Julianum*, II, 9, 32, *Patrologia, Series Latina*, XLIV, 696.

And in the first book, chapter 23 of his writing to Valerius, Augustine says: "Concupiscence is no longer a sin in the regenerate, so long as there is no consenting to it, so that even if there is no fulfillment of what is written: 'You shall not covet,' at least there is fulfillment of what we read elsewhere, Ecclus. 18:30: 'Go not after your lusts.' But in a manner of speaking it is called sin because it has been produced by sin and it makes a person guilty if sin conquers the sinner," [25] that is, it is sin with respect to its cause and effect even if not formally.

18. *But I cannot do it.* There is a difference in this passage between "to do" *(facere)* and "to fulfill" *(perficere).* Blessed Augustine, at the end of Book III of *Contra Julianum,* says: "Keep in mind what the apostle writes to the Galatians, who certainly had been baptized: 'But I say, walk by the Spirit and do not fulfill the desires of the flesh.' (Gal. 5:16). He does not say: 'Do not do them,' because they could not be without them, but rather he says: 'Do not fulfill them,' that is, 'do not bring these works to completion by the consent of your will.' Therefore, if a person does not consent to the lusts of his flesh, even though their drives are active in him, they are not fulfilled in his works. Hence when the flesh lusts against the spirit, and the spirit against the flesh, so that we do not do the things we want to do, neither are the lusts of the flesh fulfilled, even though they take place, nor are our good works fulfilled, even though they also occur. For just as the lust of the flesh is fulfilled when the spirit consents to it to do it, so that the spirit no longer lusts against the flesh but with it, so also our good works are fulfilled when the flesh so consents to the spirit that it no longer lusts against it. This is what we want when we desire the perfection of righteousness. But because we cannot fulfill this in our corruptible flesh, therefore he said to the Romans: 'I can will what is right, but I cannot fulfill it,' or as the Greek codices have it: 'I can will what is right, but I cannot fulfill the good,' that is, 'I do not have the ability to fulfill the good.' He does not say: 'to do the good' but 'to fulfill the good.' For to do good is not to go after lusts (Ecclus. 18:30), but to fulfill the good is not to lust at all. Therefore this statement to the Galatians, 'Do not fulfill the desires of the flesh' (Gal. 5:16), is in contrast with the statement to the Romans: 'I cannot fulfill it' (Rom. 7:18). For neither are our lusts fulfilled in evil, as long as our will does not consent to them, nor is our will fulfilled

25 Augustine, *De nuptiis et concupiscentia ad Valerium,* I, 23, 25, *Patrologia, Series Latina,* XLIV, 428.

in good, as long as the activity of our lusts remains, even though we do not consent to it. Therefore the spirit does a good work when it does not consent to evil lust, but the spirit does not fulfill it, for it does not destroy the evil desires. And the flesh causes evil desire, but it does not fulfill it, because as long as the spirit does not consent to it, it does not itself reach the point where its works are subject to damnation." [26]

From this text we have the comfort that, even though the newer doctors [27] say the same things about the primary motives, about putting out the tinder, about delight, and about consent, yet because they speak without the testimony of Scripture, they speak with little authority. But now because the ancient doctors in agreement with the apostles are saying the same things and much more clearly, we are now warmed by the gift of a more quiet comfort and are relieved more easily of the scruples of conscience, apart from the fact that the scholastics, despite their presumption to speak of these matters in a more careful and clear manner, have spoken more intricately and obscurely in their effort to translate divine speech into human form. For this reason their notions are vain and harmful, when on the basis of Aristotle in dark words and metaphors they have taught that virtues and vices stick to the soul like whitewash on a wall, like writing on a beam, and form to its subject. For in so doing a person ceases to understand the difference between flesh and spirit.

[26] Augustine, *Contra Julianum*, 26, 62, *Patrologia, Series Latina*, XLIV, 733 f.

[27] By *recentiores doctores* Luther probably means the men so designated by his teacher Trutvetter, namely, Scotus and Occam. By "ancient doctors" *(antiqui)* Luther means especially Augustine and Ambrose.

CHAPTER EIGHT

3. *For what the Law could not do.*

WHERE now is free will? Where are those people who are trying to affirm that we of our own natural powers can produce the act of loving God above all things? If I said that impossible demands are made of us, I would be roundly cursed. But now the apostle is saying that it was impossible for the Law to condemn sin, indeed, that it was itself infirmity because of the flesh. This is what I have previously said very often, namely, that it is simply impossible for us of ourselves to fulfill the Law, and that it is of no value to say that we can fulfill the Law according to the substance of the deed but not according to the intention of the Lawgiver, as if it were in our power to will and to be able, but not in the way God wills it, namely, in grace. And because of such reasoning grace is useful but not necessary, and we do not incur the wickedness of our nature through the sin of Adam, but we are complete in our natural powers. For this reason philosophy stinks in our nostrils, as if our reason always spoke for the best things,[1] and we make up many stories about the law of nature.

It is certainly true that the law of nature is known to all men and that our reason does speak for the best things, but what best things? It speaks for the best not according to God but according to us, that is, for things that are good in an evil way. For it seeks itself and its own in all things, but not God. This only faith does in love.

Hence knowledge and virtue and whatever good things are desired, sought, and found by natural capacity are good in an evil way. For they are not brought into relation to God but to the creature, that is, to oneself. For how would one relate things to God, if one does not love Him above all things? How would one love Him whom one has not known? How would a man know, when he is under the wickedness of the first sin and in shadows and chains

---

1 This is an echo of Aristotle, *Nicomachean Ethics*, I, 1102b, 15: "The rational principle urges them on to the best objectives."

as far as his intellect and feeling is concerned? Therefore, unless faith gives the light and love makes us free, no man can either have or do anything good, but only evil, even when he performs the good.

Corollary

The common saying that human nature in a general and universal way knows and wills the good [2] but errs and does not will it in particular cases would be better stated if we were to say that in particular cases human nature knows and wills what is good but in general neither knows nor wills it. The reason is that it knows nothing but its own good, or what is good and honorable and useful for itself, but not what is good for God and other people. Therefore it knows and wills more what is particular, yes, only what is an individual good. And this is in agreement with Scripture,[3] which describes man as so turned in on himself [4] that he uses not only physical but even spiritual goods for his own purposes and in all things seeks only himself.

This curvedness is now natural for us, a natural wickedness and a natural sinfulness. Thus man has no help from his natural powers, but he needs the aid of some power outside of himself. This is love, without which he always sins against the Law "You shall not covet," that is, turn nothing in on yourself and seek nothing for yourself, but live, do, and think all things for God alone. For then a man will know the good in every way along with all particular good things, and he will judge all things. Thus the Law is impossible for us.

For this reason blessed Augustine in *On Grace and Free Will*, ch. 16, says: "He commands something which we cannot do in order that we may know what we must ask of Him. For this is faith which demands in prayer what the Law demands." [5]

Corollary

In vain do some people magnify the light of nature and compare it with the light of grace, since it is actually more a shadow and

---

[2] Cf. p. 157, n. 41, above.

[3] Cf. Is. 2:9-22.

[4] Cf. p. 313 above.

[5] Augustine, *De gratia et libero arbitrio*, 16, 32, *Patrologia, Series Latina*, XLIV, 900.

something contrary to grace. Thus it is cursed by Job and Jeremiah,[6] because it is an evil day and a foul sight, because this light came into being right after sin did, as the Scripture says, "Their eyes were opened" (Gen. 3:7). For grace has set before itself no other object than God toward which it is carried and toward which it is moving; it sees only Him, it seeks only Him, and it always moves toward Him, and all other things which it sees between itself and God it passes by as if it had not seen them and directs itself only toward God. This is the "upright heart" (Ps. 7:10) and the "right spirit" (Ps. 51:10).

But nature set for itself no object but itself toward which it is borne and toward which it is directed; it sees, seeks, and works only toward itself in all matters, and it passes by all other things and even God Himself in the midst, as if it did not see them, and is directed only toward itself. This is the "perverse heart" (Ps. 101:4) and the "wicked heart" (Prov. 27:21). Just as grace has placed God in the place of all things it sees, even its own interests, and prefers Him to itself and seeks only those things which belong to God and not its own things, so nature on the other hand, sets itself in the place of all other things, even in the place of God, and seeks only those things which are its own and not the things of God. Therefore it is its own first and greatest idol. Second, it makes God into an idol and the truth of God into a lie, and finally it makes idols of all created things and of all gifts of God. But grace is never content in the things which it sees except as it sees God in and above them, and it wills, hopes, and rejoices in the fact that all things exist, are seen, and are accomplished for the glory of God. Nature, on the contrary, thinks that all the things it sees are nothing unless they serve to its advantage, exist for it and are done for it. And then it esteems them, if it can appropriate them for its own benefit, use, and good.

This is spiritual fornication, iniquity, and a terrible curving in on itself. Therefore, this wisdom is not a light, but it can much better be called darkness, unless someone would call it light because it sees and understands these things by its own reason and sense, but otherwise insofar as it turns all knowledge in upon itself, it is the most complete darkness. Nor can it by its nature do anything else than turn in upon itself. For it cannot love God and His law, as the apostle here says.

---

[6] Cf. Job 3:1 ff.; Jer. 20:14.

And the sign of all of these things is that nature rejoices and is peaceful when these things are flowing in upon it, but it becomes disturbed and disquieted when they go the other way. Not so grace, which remains at rest, in all things loving only to do the will of God and seeking to perform it, so that whatever things befall it, it is content both with itself and with all other things. Whatever God does and wills, grace also wills and takes pleasure in, no matter how unpleasant it may be. Indeed it always praises and blesses God, even when the most contrary and dreadful things befall it. It knows how to rejoice in sadness and to mourn in happiness. This is impossible for the flesh out of its own powers.

In that it was weak. Blessed Augustine says in regard to this passage: "The Law was weakened in that it did not provide the fulfillment for what it commanded, not by its own fault but 'by the flesh,' that is, through men who in seeking after carnal good did not love the righteousness of the Law but preferred temporal pleasures to it." [7] Now this takes place when the Law is observed out of fear of punishment or love of some advantage, and for this reason the heart and the will are not in it, namely, not because God has so willed and commanded but because it promises good things and prevents evils. For only the completely free love of willingness so acts or does not act because it is pleasing to God, without any concern for any other good or fear for any evil apart from doing the will of God. Nature does not have this ability, but grace, which is given through faith in Christ and through the Holy Spirit does have it.

Corollary

The expression "the Law was weak" must be referred to the heart or the disposition rather than to an outward work. For people do indeed observe the Law outwardly, but inwardly in the heart they hate it, as we read in the psalm: "Who speak peace with their neighbor, while mischief is in their hearts" (Ps. 28:3), which is to say they cannot of themselves be as good inwardly as they appear outwardly. Therefore, as I have said, it is with the assurance of this knowledge that the apostle in chapter 2 asserts so boldly that they who teach that we should not steal are themselves thieves, etc., for he knows with certainty that without grace they did not fulfill voluntarily what they taught with their mouth or showed by their works, since without grace they are all equally a part of the

[7] Augustine, *Expositio quarundem propositionum ex epistula ad Romanos*, 48, *Patrologia, Series Latina*, XXXV, 7072.

mass of perdition,[8] of which it is written in Gen. 8:21: "The imagination and thought of man's heart is evil from his youth (and not at all inclined to the good which the Law prescribes)."

And so above all other things let us learn from the perfect knowledge of the Law that we are weak, and let us then see how absolutely necessary Christ was, the bestower of the Spirit and of grace.

For sin He condemned sin. Blessed Augustine says this about this passage: "For the death of the Lord achieved this, that we no longer fear death and no longer seek material goods or fear temporal evils, in which that carnal wisdom was in which the precepts of the Law could not be fulfilled. But when in the Christian man this knowledge has been removed and taken away, the righteousness of the Law is fulfilled, since he no longer walks according to the flesh but according to the Spirit."[9]

From these words it is obvious that the expressions "sin" and "wisdom of the flesh" are to be understood as the same thing here. For "to condemn sin" (blessed Augustine says [10]) is to isolate and take away "the wisdom of the flesh," for when this has been removed, we no longer fear death nor love this life. Thus the Law is fulfilled because God alone is loved. For he who does not fear death because of God, likewise does not love this life more than God, and therefore he inwardly hates himself but loves God above all things. For he who loves God more than himself, surely loves God above all things, since a person loves nothing as much as himself. But this is impossible for the flesh; for the wisdom of the flesh makes a person love himself above all things, even more than God. If it were possible for the flesh to love God perfectly, "then Christ died to no purpose" (Gal. 2:21), since then the flesh would be sound and loving toward God, and the apostle would have said falsely: "It does not submit to God's law, indeed it cannot" (v. 7). Thus again the argument goes against those who say that the will can produce an act of love above all things toward God out of its own natural powers. And their argument is futile when they say: "Whatever the intellect can dictate to be willed or done, the will can

---

[8] For the use of the phrase *massa perditionis* see p. 156 above and p. 394 below. The present passage is from Augustine, *De gratia Christi et de peccato originali*, II, 29, 34, *Patrologia, Series Latina*, XLIV, 301.

[9] Augustine, *Expositio . . . ad Romanos*, 48, *Patrologia, Series Latina*, XXXV, 2072.

[10] Ibid.

will; but the intellect dictates that we must love God above all things, therefore the will can will it." The answer is that this is a wrong conclusion along with what follows from it. Rather the conclusion must be this: the will then can will that God must be loved above all things, as it has dictated. But from this it does not follow that it can love God above all things, but it wills with only a weak activity that this should be done, that is, it has only a small part of the will which has been declared necessary.

If this were not the case, the statement which all commonly make would be useless, namely, that the Law was given to humble the proud who presumptuously rely on their own power.

And how did Christ "condemn sin because of sin," or how by His death did He cause us no longer to fear death or isolate "the wisdom of the flesh from men?" Only by the merit of His death by which He merited that the Spirit be given to us and that "the wisdom of the flesh" be taken from us. For the Spirit kills the "wisdom of the flesh" and makes the inner man alive and causes men to despise death and to give up life and to love only God above all things, as we read in Song of Sol. 8:6: "For love is strong as death, and jealousy as cruel as the grave;" The Spirit also causes concupiscence to be condemned in us. For that we now hate and condemn concupiscence and choose love is not our doing but the gift of God. Therefore he says that God has damned and destroyed the sin in our flesh, but He causes us to destroy it through His Spirit, who is poured out by faith into our hearts.

And also note this, that he does not say: "He condemned sin in the flesh because of the sin in the flesh," for he wants to express the difference between "sin" and "sin in the flesh." For the sin by reason of which sin in the flesh is condemned is itself the penalty of sin which Christ took into His own flesh which was without sin, yet for the sake of the penalties of sin He took on the likeness of sinful flesh. Therefore sin which is in the flesh of all other people is condemned because of the sin of Him in whose flesh there was no sin.

What the Law could not do. The apostle prefers to say, "what the Law could not do" rather than "what we could not do," even though this disability belongs to no one but to us, who were weak or unable to fulfill the Law. But he does this in keeping with his practice and because the occasion requires it. For he is arguing primarily against those who trust in the powers of their own nature and think that no other help is necessary for righteousness and good works than a mere knowledge of the Law, like the Jews and even to this day all proud people, who all are still speaking as did the people in Ex. 20:19: "You speak to us, and we will hear," and also in Ex. 19:8: "All that the Lord has spoken we will do." Now, all these people think that the Law is sufficient for them, and they err the more grievously, the more they think that the Law is fulfilled only by external acts. The apostle argues against their empty faith in the Law and their knowledge of it when he says that it was impossible for the Law to accomplish that which they presumptuously thought, namely, the abolition of sin and the acquisition of righteousness. In this the Law is not at fault, but their opinion of and confidence in the Law is vain and stupid. To be sure, the Law in itself is very good. It is as with a sick man who wants to drink some wine because he foolishly thinks that his health will return if he does so. Now if the doctor, without any criticism of the wine, should say to him: "It is impossible for the wine to cure you, it will only make you sicker," the doctor is not condemning the wine but only the foolish trust of the sick man in it. For he needs other medicine to get well, so that he then can drink his wine. Thus also our corrupt nature needs another kind of medicine than the Law, by which it can arrive at good health so that it can fulfill the Law.

7. *The wisdom of the flesh is hostile to God.* It would be better to use the word "prudence" *(prudentia)* throughout this chapter than "wisdom" *(sapientia)*, as both blessed Augustine and the Greek text do. For there is general agreement that the term prudence is used by all people to apply to our actions while wisdom is applied to our thinking. But here the apostle is speaking in a moral sense and about things we do. Prudence is involved in choosing the good and avoiding the evil. These things are twofold, and therefore he describes a two-fold prudence here.

The "prudence of the flesh" chooses what is good for oneself and avoids what is disadvantageous for oneself, it rejects the common good and chooses what is harmful to community. This is a prudence which directs the flesh, that is, our concupiscence and self-will, which enjoys itself and uses everyone else,[11] including God Himself; in all matters it looks out for itself and its own interests. This prudence makes man feel that he himself is the final and ultimate object in life, an idol, on whose account he does, suffers, attempts, plans, and says all things. He considers

11 Cf. p. 295, n. 5, above.

good only those things which are for his own personal good, and those things only as evils which are bad for him. This crookedness, this depravity, this iniquity is condemned over and over in Scripture under the name of fornication and idolatry, and it is, as we have said earlier in chapter 6,[12] something most profound in our nature, indeed, it is our very nature itself, wounded and totally in ferment, so that without grace it becomes not only incurable but also totally unrecognizable. But in order that we may get a clearer understanding of this crookedness, let us indicate its degrees according to its objectives, which are (as stated elsewhere) the objects of an inordinate enjoyment.

	riches	parents	relatives
External goods	power	friends	children
	honors	family	wife
Physical goods	health	strength	beauty
Spiritual goods	talent memory	intellect	prudence
Knowledge and skills {bodily {mental	powers	{natural {acquired, etc.

Physical, that is, human, wisdom   {liberal arts {philosophy, etc.

Intellectual wisdom, in the knowledge and mysteries   {of Scripture {of creation

Heartfelt grace in righteousness, devotion, gifts of the Holy Spirit, etc., in meditations

God as He is revealed [13] to us in His divine properties

God has given all of these things to men and clothed them as with a garment. But "prudence of the flesh" clings to all of them. Not all men are clothed in all of them, nor are they all equal in each, but in each man one is stronger and another weaker, and one man is clothed with a considerable number and another with fewer. All these, I say, man turns in upon himself, in them he seeks his highest good, and of them he makes for himself horrible idols in place of the true God insofar as he does not refer them to God

[12] Cf. p. 313 above.

[13] *Deus affirmative* and *Deus negative* (cf. p. 352 below) seem to point to statements of Dionysius the Areopagite, *De coelestia hierarchia*, 2, 3, *Patrologia, Series Graeca*, III, 142. See also p. 287, n. 1, above.

and is not content if they are taken from him. Thus he will be despoiled and deprived of all of them only against his will.

Thus there are some people who do not resign themselves to giving up even the lowest of them, such as riches; others, if they give up riches, will not give up honors; if honors, then not children, parents, friends, etc.; and if they give up these, still they cling to their health, their beauty, or their life, and so on through many clutching traps and infinite questions. Even from the smallest of them our nature cannot extricate itself, much less from all of them and from the greatest. But grace quickly opens the way, as the Scripture says (Ps. 25:15): "He will pluck my feet out of the net." These things are "the snare of the fowler" (Ps. 91:3), not as though they become snares as good creatures, but that they do so because of the sinfulness of the prudence of the flesh.

"Prudence of the spirit" is the choice of the common good and the avoidance of the common evil, the rejection of one's own personal good and the choosing of one's personal evil. For this prudence directs the love which seeks "not its own" (1 Cor. 13:5) but the things of God and of all creatures. And it regards as good only those things which are good in the eyes of God and for the benefit of all and as evil only those things which are evil in God's sight and for all men. It has no other object than God in a negative way, and it has all things together with God in a negative way. Hence it also enjoys all things in and with God. And how these things can be, is easy to say, but it belongs only to the Spirit to achieve this and only to the man who has experienced it to understand it. For it is the Spirit's doing that so many things suddenly disappear and become nothing and are regarded as nothing by the soul, and the soul itself is suddenly turned away from everything and with Mary requires only the one thing needful (Luke 10:38). But Martha, as she walks through these things and struggles with them, is troubled about many things, "forgetting what lies behind and straining forward to what lies ahead" (Phil. 3:13).

Clearly there are men who have renounced riches and professed poverty, and their soul has escaped this trap. But look! It falls into a worse one, namely, into self-will or errors of devotion, righteousness, knowledge, study, or something lighter, such as honor and vainglory, etc. Therefore we need to exert many labors that the "wisdom of the flesh," which is entangled in so many snares, may be overcome by the prudence of the spirit through many prayers and tears.

These are the snares which St. Anthony saw in the world,[14] and in his anguish he said: "Who can escape all of these things?" And the answer came to him: "Only humility." For I have listed eight great traps, and if one would subdivide them into their particular parts, they would add up to many more. It is certainly true, that when a man has escaped the trap of riches in one area, for example, in the love of money, he may fall into another one, such as a love for possessions, such as land or something else, and it is the same with other things.

Therefore those things which because of the evil of the "prudence of the flesh" turn into a snare and a stumbling block for a man become a path and an approach toward God for a man through the blessing of the prudence of the spirit.

Therefore he says: "They set their minds on the things of the flesh," that is, on physical goods, which are the objects that they enjoy, all of which we have enumerated above. For the expression "the prudence of the flesh" refers not only to things which are mere carnal pleasures, but to all things which are this side of God and which can be possessed only in this life; for the future life cannot be possessed in the created world, but only in the Creator, who is the good which belongs to the "prudence of the spirit."

On this point blessed Augustine says: "He is called an enemy of God who does not obey His law, and this because of the prudence of the flesh, that is, when he seeks temporal advantages and fears temporal evils. For the common definition of prudence is that a person seeks good things and avoids evils." Then when he has quoted the words "the mind that is set on the flesh is hostile to God," he goes on to show why the apostle said "hostile," namely, because "it does not submit to God's law, lest any Manichaean [15] get the idea that a nature arising from the opposite principle is hostile to God. "But we obey the law of God when this prudence has been destroyed, so that the prudence of the spirit takes its place, and that our hope on that account does not lie in temporal advantages nor our fear in temporal evils. For the same nature of our soul has the prudence of the flesh when it clings to lower desires, and the prudence of the spirit when it chooses the things that are above," and loves them. "In the same way that it is the

[14] This is reported in *Vitae patrum*. Cf. *Patrologia, Series Latina*, LXXIII, 785 and 953.

[15] Manichaeanism developed its system on the basis of a dualism in which light was the original principle from which all good things developed and darkness was the original principle of evil.

nature of water to congeal with cold and to vaporize with heat, so also it is said: 'the prudence of the flesh does not submit to God's law, indeed it cannot.' But when water is vaporized and becomes steam as heat is applied, no one can call it snow." [16] So also the Lord in Matt. 12:33; "Either make the tree good, and its fruit good; or make the tree bad, and its fruit bad," which is to say that if the "prudence of the flesh," which is the evil tree, is not changed into the "prudence of the spirit," which is the good tree, it cannot produce good fruit, even if the fruit looks like good fruit. For the tree does not come from the fruit, but the fruit from the tree. And virtue does not come from acts and works, as Aristotle teaches,[17] but acts come from virtues, as Christ teaches. For a second act presupposes a first one, and the prerequisite of a work is a substance and a power and a cause for the effect. Moreover, these temporal good things must all be understood as things which are outside of God, whether we comprehend them with our senses or our intellect, whether it is life, knowledge, or righteousness, as we have said above.[18] Similarly all those things are evils which are opposed to these things, such as death, ignorance, sin, etc. He who is prudent in the spirit does not fear any of these things, nor does he choose or esteem them. But he who is prudent in the flesh is terribly afraid of death, stupidity, sin, etc.

Therefore, if you feel that you are afraid of death and do not love it, you have a most sure indication that you are still wrapped up on the "prudence of the flesh." Likewise if you dread sin, if you dread the coming judgment, if you have lost hope because of your sin, all these things are signs that the prudence of the flesh still remains and survives in you. Not that we should not fear sin and judgment, but that we should know the prudence of the flesh for what it is, so that the weak may labor to be freed of this horror and come into the hope of security through the grace of God. For such weak people are still under the Law, if they do not sigh for grace and turn their face toward it so that they may be delivered.

But those who have the "prudence of the spirit" love the will of God and welcome it because they are conformed to it. Hence although they know that this is God's will, that there be a final judgment and that all things will be filled with horror and His

[16] Augustine, *Expositio . . . ad Romanos,* 49, *Patrologia, Series Latina,* XXXV, 2073.

[17] Cf. p. 152, n. 30, above.

[18] Cf. p. 351 above.

wrath will be known, yet they are not afraid, but await it with joy and hope that it will come soon. Thus that which to others is the greatest horror is to them the highest joy, because with perfectly attuned wills they desire the same thing that God desires. For wherever there is this will, there will be neither sorrow nor dread but rather the fulfillment of what one has longed for and wanted and the quiet achievement of one's desire. Ps. 97:8 reads: "The daughters of Judah rejoice because of Thy judgments, O God."

And our Lord, when He had predicted the terrors of the Day of Judgment, added these words: "Now when these things begin to take place, look up and raise your heads, because your redemption is drawing near" (Luke 21:28).

Therefore it is a vain thing that some people in human fashion are in anguish over the misery that lies in the future for themselves and others. For we must not consider how through fear we can escape these miseries, nor must we preach about them in such a way that men grow frightened and pale at the thought of them, except for those people who are wallowing in the filth of the world, for whom such preaching is helpful so that they may be terrified to repent, but for the penitent and those who are already lamenting there must be preaching and encouragement that they may learn with joy to await and pray that that Day may come quickly. For not by fearing but by loving shall we escape the wrath of God and the misery and horror of the Judgment, and our conscience is quieted only by conforming to the will of God. For what profit is there in fearing the Day of Judgment? For he who fears it hates it and does not wish it to come. But now it is impossible that it should not come and it is also impossible that it should come for the good and the deliverance of him who hates its coming. For it is the will of God and His good pleasure that it come, but he who dreads its coming resists the will of God and therefore is justly condemned as "a rebel against God" (cf. Num. 14:9). Therefore the apostle is correct when he says in 2 Tim. 4:8: "And not only to me, but to all who love His appearing," and in 2 Peter 3:11-12: "Since all these things are thus to be dissolved, what sort of people ought you to be in lives of holiness and godliness, waiting for and hastening the coming of the day of the Lord," and in Titus 2:12-13: "Let us live sober, upright, and godly lives in this world, awaiting our blessed hope, the appearing of the glory of our great God, etc." And our Lord says in Luke 12:36: "Be like men who are waiting for their master to come home from the marriage feast."

No one has conquered this fear except Christ alone, who has overcome all temporal evils and even eternal death. Therefore those who believe in Him no longer have any reason at all to be afraid, but with a blessed pride they laugh and rejoice in all these evils, for they are not going to perish or be swallowed up, but they are going to experience, await, and see the victory of Christ made complete in those evils. And thus they say: "O death, where is thy victory? O death, where is thy sting?" Therefore death and evil are not overcome by power or might, nor are they avoided by flight and dread, but in weakness (that is, by lack of power) they must be endured, namely by patience and willingly. This is the way Christ teaches us by His example, for He went with confidence to meet death and sufferings.

14. *For all who are led by the Spirit of God are sons of God.* "To be led by the Spirit of God" is to put to death our flesh, that is, the old Adam, and to do it freely, promptly, and gladly, that is, to despise and renounce all that is not God, even ourselves, and thus "not to fear death or the friends of death, the fierce race of penalties," and likewise "to give up the empty pleasures of the world and its corrupt and sordid prizes," [19] and freely to relinquish all good things and embrace evils in their place. This is not characteristic of our nature, but is a work of the Spirit of God in us.

15. *For you did not receive the spirit of slavery.* The apostle sets up an antithesis, that is, a contradistinction or a comparison or a contrast. He puts "slave" and "son" in opposition to each other, as in John 8:35: "The slave does not continue in the house forever; the son continues forever." In this way the spirit of slavery is contrasted with the spirit of sonship, and servile fear with filial love. Hence this term "slavery" ought to be taken in the abstract, so that, if it is permissible to say it,[20] the term "slavery" is derived from slave as "sonship" is from son.

And here the term "slavery" is used in the sense of "slavery to sin," as we read in John 8:34: "Everyone who commits sin is a slave to sin," a slavery from which the Law cannot free us. For only through the fear of threat it forces us to do the works of the Law but does not thereby put to death the works of the flesh but

[19] These two quotations are taken respectively from the hymns *Virginis proles* and *Jesu corona celsior,* both of which were contained in the Augustinian Breviary.

[20] Luther apologizes for coining the word *servietas* for the more usual abstract noun *servitus.*

rather only increases them; for it increases our hatred of the Law and our love and desire of sin.

In two ways this spirit is called the spirit of "fear." First, as we have said, because it compelled unwilling men to do the works of the Law because of fear and the threats of punishment, and thus (since he who is feared must of necessity be hated) in their heart they drew back from the intent and purpose of the Law the more they were compelled to approach it outwardly and in works, as it is described in Ex. 20, where the people stood at a distance and feared to approach the mountain. And thus when the heart and the better part of man turns away from God and rejects His Law, it is nothing that in his lesser part, that is, with his body in outward works and ceremonies he practices obedience to the Law. Thus our Lord says to the hypocrites: "This people honors Me with their lips, but their heart is far from Me" (Matt. 15:8; Is. 29:13). Second, this spirit is called the spirit of fear because this slavish fear also compels men to give up their outward obedience to the works of the Law in the time of trial. This fear ought to be called a worldly fear rather than a slavish fear, for it is not a matter of fulfilling the Law but the slavish fear of losing temporal goods or of suffering impending evils, and thus even worse than slavish fear. Concerning this fear John says in 1 John 4:18: "There is no fear in love, but perfect love casts out fear."

Hence note how profound the words of Scripture are. Never, or rarely, are we without this fear, for no one is without concupiscence or his flesh or the old man. And where there is concupiscence, there necessarily is the fear of losing that which we are lusting after. Thus no one is endowed with perfect love. Again, the statement "every one who commits sin is a slave to sin" (John 8:34) looks easy and seems at first glance not to apply to many people, but when we look into the matter we find that it applies to all. For all men are slaves of sin, because all commit sin, if not in outward works, yet in their concupiscence and inclination, as we have sufficiently described above.

The term "the spirit of fear" according to blessed Augustine's comment on this passage is "he who has the power of death" (that is, the devil) "which they receive who cannot fulfill the precepts of the Law as it has been given because they continue to serve their carnal desires." [21]

[21] Augustine, *Expositio . . . ad Romanos*, 52, *Patrologia, Series Latina*, XXXV, 2074.

But in another and better way, this spirit is the action of the "prudence of the flesh" that dreads the Law; it arises when the Law is laid down and recognized but is quiet before the Law becomes known. This is symbolized in Ex. 4, where Moses fled in terror at the staff which, thrown down, was turned into a serpent. The same thing happens when the Law is proclaimed to a man who is ignorant of the Law and is accustomed to breaking it; he becomes sorrowful and is irked by the Law, grieving over the lost liberty which is now cut off for him. This is the spirit of fear.

And he says: *to fall back into fear.* It is as if he were saying: "Before this you were in the spirit of fear and under a taskmaster, that drove you on, namely, under the Law. Now that you have been freed, you have not received this spirit of fear a second time, but rather the spirit of sonship in trusting faith." And he describes this faith in most significant words, namely, *when we cry Abba! Father!* For in the spirit of fear it is not possible to cry, for we can scarcely open our mouth or mumble. But faith expands the heart, the emotions, and the voice, but fear tightens up all these things and restricts them, as our own experience amply testifies. Fear does not say *Abba,* but rather it hates and flees from the Father as from an enemy and mutters against Him as a tyrant. For those people who are in the spirit of fear and not in the spirit of adoption do not taste how sweet the Lord is (cf. Ps. 34:8; 1 Peter 2:3), but rather He appears to them as harsh and hard, and in their heart they call Him a virtual tyrant, although with the mouth they call Him Father, just as that slave in the Gospel who when he had hidden his master's money said to him: "Master, I knew you to be a hard man, reaping where you did not sow, etc." (Matt. 25:24). Such are the people who are displeased that God accepts no man's merits but has free mercy. Thus they say: "Thou hast commanded the impossible, Thou hast not given grace but only knowledge; this I still have, and I give it back to you." Rather they ought to rejoice because He has not put our hope in ourselves but only in Himself, in His mercy. All who are of this mind are secretly saying in their hearts: "God acts in a tyrannical manner, He is not a Father, but an enemy," which is also true. But they do not know that one must agree with this enemy and that thus, and only thus, He becomes a friend and a Father. For He will not come around to our way of thinking and be changed for us, so that we may become His friends and sons. Therefore we do not have to fear Him nor any of the things which He wills and loves. But this cannot happen unless we have His spirit, so that in the same spirit we love the same things which He loves and hate the things which He hates in the same way that He does. For we cannot love those things which God loves unless we have the love and will and spirit which He has. For if there must be conformity in the things to be loved, there must also be conformity in the feeling of love. And those people are called godlike men and sons of God because they are led by the Spirit of God.

The difference between these two classes of people is symbolized on the one hand by those who gave Christ vinegar, or wine mixed with gall and myrrh at the time of His passion, and on the other hand by those from whom He received a piece of fish and a honeycomb after His resurrection. For the first class signifies that God is more bitter than gall and myrrh. Therefore they give Him what they have, that is, a bitter, sour, and sad heart, that is, a heart without hope. And when the Lord tastes it, He will not drink. But the people in the second class, because God is like honey and the honeycomb to them, they offer Him this sweet happiness of heart, which He takes and eats in the presence of them all. Of the first group it says in Jer. 15:10: "All of them curse Me, says the Lord," and Is. 8:21: "They will curse their king and their God." Or is this not cursing—to think in our hearts that God is an enemy and an adversary, to oppose Him in feeling and will, and, if possible, to take a stand against Him with all of our powers, indeed, of trying to destroy God and His will and change His will to be like ours, that is, making it nothing? For to wish that someone be turned into nothing is the worst curse, which all the damned and those who have the prudence of the flesh hope for God.

Moreover, that this cry is not just a matter of the voice but also of the heart is evident in the statement in Gal. 4:6 f.: "And because you are sons, God has sent the Spirit of His Son into our hearts, crying, 'Abba! Father!' So through God you are no longer a slave, but a son, and if a son, then an heir." These words sound like this passage, and they say the same thing, as is sufficiently clear.

16. *For it is the Spirit Himself.* In his sermon on the Annunciation, blessed Bernard, who was filled with the same Holy Spirit, very clearly shows that this testimony is the faith of our heart in God, saying: "I believe that this testimony consists of three parts. For it is necessary first of all to believe that you cannot have the remission of sins except through the kindness of God. Second, that you could not possess any good work unless God Himself gave

it to you. And last, that you cannot earn eternal life by any of your works, unless it is given to you by grace." [22] But this is not yet enough, but we must consider it as a kind of beginning and foundation of faith. For if you believe that your sins are not taken away except by Him, you do well. But you must still add: That you do believe this; not that you could do this yourself, but the Spirit must cause you to believe this, "because through Him you are given the forgiveness of sins. This is the testimony which the Holy Spirit produces in our hearts, saying: 'Your sins are forgiven you.' For in this way the apostle believes that a man is justified by faith" (that you believe this both of yourself and also of the elect, that Christ died and made satisfaction for your sins). "It is the same in regard to merits, if you believe that you cannot have them except through Him, it is not enough, until the Spirit of truth has produced the testimony that you have these merits through Him." This happens when you believe that the works which you do are acceptable and pleasing to God, whatever they may finally turn out to be. But you can have the confidence that they are pleasing to Him when you realize that through these works you are nothing in His sight, even though they are good and are done out of obedience even though you do no evil works. It is this humility and restraint regarding good works which makes them pleasing to God. "Thus also concerning eternal life it is not enough to believe that He gives it to you freely, but it is also necessary to have the testimony of the Spirit that you will come to eternal life by God's favor."

These three points are clearly seen in this text of the apostle. For he says: "Who shall bring any charge against God's elect?" (v. 33), which is to say that we are sure that no sins will accuse us. Likewise, concerning merits he says: "We know that in everything God works for good with those who love Him" (v. 28), and again concerning eternal glory: "I am sure that neither things present, nor things to come, etc., will be able to separate us from the love of God which is in Christ" (vv. 38 f.).

19. *For the creation waits.* The apostle philosophizes and thinks about things in a different way than the philosophers and metaphysicians do. For the philosophers so direct their gaze at the present state of things that they speculate only about what things are and what quality they have, but the apostle calls our attention away from a consideration of the present and from the essence and accidents of things and directs us to their future state. For

[22] *Patrologia, Series Latina,* CLXXXIII, 383.

he does not use the term "essence" or "activity" of the creature, or its "action," "inaction," and "motion," but in an entirely new and marvelous theological word he speaks of the "expectation of the creation," so that because his soul can hear the creation waiting, he no longer directs his attention to or inquires about the creation itself, but rather to what it is awaiting. But alas, how deeply and painfully we are ensnared in categories and questions of what a thing is; in how many foolish metaphysical questions we involve ourselves! When will we become wise and see how much precious time we waste on vain questions, while we neglect the greater ones? We are always acting this way, so that what Seneca has said is very true of us: "We do not know what we should do because we have learned unimportant things. Indeed we do not know what is salutary because we have learned only the things that destroy us." [23]

Indeed I for my part believe that I owe to the Lord this duty of speaking out against philosophy and of persuading men to heed Holy Scripture. For perhaps if another man who has not seen these things, did this, he might be afraid or he might not be believed. But I have been worn out by these studies for many years now, and having experienced and heard many things over and over again, I have come to see that it is the study of vanity and perdition.

Therefore I warn you all as earnestly as I can that you finish these studies quickly and let it be your only concern not to establish and defend them but treat them as we do when we learn worthless skills to destroy them and study errors to refute them. Thus we study also these things to get rid of them, or at least, just to learn the method of speaking of those people with whom we must carry on some discourse. For it is high time that we undertake new studies and learn Jesus Christ, "and Him crucified" (1 Cor. 2:2).

Therefore you will be the best philosophers and the best explorers of the nature of things if you will learn from the apostle to consider the creation as it waits, groans, and travails, that is, as it turns away in disgust from what now is and desires that which is still in the future. For then the study of the nature of things, their accidents and their differences, will quickly grow worthless. As a result the foolishness of the philosophers is like a man who, joining himself to a builder and marveling at the cutting and hewing and measuring of the wood and the beams, is foolishly content and quiet among these things, without concern as to what

[23] Seneca, *Epistulae,* 45, 4.

the builder finally intends to make by all of these exertions. This man is empty-headed, and the work of such an assistant is meaningless. So also the creation of God, which is skillfully prepared for the future glory, is gazed upon by stupid people who look only at its mechanics but never see its final goal. Thus are we not completely off the track when we turn our thoughts to the praises and glories of philosophy? Look how we esteem the study of the essences and actions and inactions of things, and the things themselves reject and groan over their own essences and actions and inactions! We praise and glorify the knowledge of that very thing which is sad about itself and is displeased with itself! And, I ask you, is he not a mad man who laughs at someone who is crying and lamenting and then boasts that he sees him as happy and laughing? Certainly such a person is rightly called a madman and a maniac. Indeed, if only the rude common people foolishly thought philosophy was of some importance and did not know how to interpret the sighing of the natural order, it would be tolerable. But now it is wise men and theologians, infected by this same "prudence of the flesh," who derive a happy science out of a sad creation, and from the sighings they laughingly gather their knowledge with marvelous display of power.

Thus the apostle is right in Col. 2:8 when he speaks against philosophy, saying: "See to it that no one makes a prey of you by philosophy and empty deceit, according to human tradition." Clearly if the apostle had wanted any philosophy to be understood as useful and good, he would not have condemned it so absolutely. Therefore we conclude that whoever searches into the essences and actions of creation rather than its groanings and expectations is without doubt a fool and a blind man, for he does not know that creatures are also a creation of God. This is clear from the text.

20. *For the creation was subjected to futility.* By the term "creation" most scholars understand "man" in this passage, namely, because man has a share in every created thing. But it is better to understand man through the term "futility," as Ps. 39:5 correctly and truthfully says: "Surely every living man is altogether vanity." For it is certainly true that if man, the old man, did not exist, there would be no vanity. For all the things that God made were "very good" (Gen. 1:31) and are still good, as the apostle says in 1 Tim. 4:4: "Everything created by God is good," and in Titus 1:15: "To the pure all things are pure." Therefore the creation becomes vain, evil, and harmful from outside itself, and not by its own fault,

namely, because it is perverted and regarded as better than it really
is by the erroneous thinking and estimation or love and enjoyment
of man, while at the same time man, who has the capacity to lay
hold on God and be satisfied with only God alone, as far as the mind
and the spirit are concerned, is presumptuous enough to think that
he has this peace and sufficiency in these created things. It is to
this vanity (that is, to a perverted enjoyment) that the creation is
subjected, just as grass in itself is a good thing and not worthless,
necessary and useful for animals, but worthless and useless for
human consumption; yet if it were used for human food it would
be given a higher dignity than belongs to it by nature. This is what
all men do who do not truly love God and fervently thirst for Him.
Every man who is born of Adam and lives without the Holy Spirit
does this. Thus Ps. 14:3 is speaking of us all when it says: "They
have all gone astray," that is, become vain. And because of man the
whole creation has become vanity, even though unwillingly. Hence
we read in Eccl. 1:2 f.: "Vanity of vanities, all is vanity. What does
man gain" (namely, more than vanity) "by all the toil at which he
toils under the sun?" He very significantly adds that man has
nothing more than vanity. Because created things in themselves
are good, and those who know God know also these things, not in
a vain way but in a correct way, and they use them but do not derive
vain pleasure from them.[24] Hence we read in Titus 1:15: "To the
pure all things are pure," but to the impure nothing is pure. Thus
the same things are both pure and impure because of the difference of those to whom they belong.

21. *The creation itself will be set free.* He is saying two things
here. First, that the creation will be set free, namely, from vanity,
when the ungodly have been condemned and taken away and when
the old man has been destroyed. This liberation is now taking place
every day in the lives of the saints. Second, that it will not only no
longer be vain but also it will not be subject to corruption in the
future. Hence we read in Is. 30:26: "The light of the moon will be
as the light of the sun, and the light of the sun will be sevenfold,
as the light of seven days." On this point many scholars say that the
sun in the first seven days, during which the world was created,
was much brighter than it is now but that it was darkened because
of the blemish of the sin of man, who fell into sin on the sixth or
seventh day. And in the future it will be seven times brighter still
than it was then. Although this opinion can be maintained with

[24] Cf. p. 295, n. 5, above.

some degree of logic, yet it cannot be proved from Scripture. Nor does Isaiah's statement compel us to this opinion. For the expression "the light of the sun will be sevenfold" can be understood exegetically "as the light of seven days," that is, as if the brilliance of seven days were one brilliance, that is the brilliance of all seven days taken together.

24. *Now hope that is seen is not hope.* Although grammatically this statement may be figurative, yet theologically it is most direct and affirmative because of the expression of a very intense emotion. Because hope which comes from a desire for something which we love always increases the love by delay. Thus it happens that the thing hoped for and the person hoping become one through the tenseness of the hoping, as blessed Augustine says: "The soul is more where it loves than where it lives." [25] And there is the popular saying "Here is my flame." And the poet says: "My fire, Amyntas." [26] And Aristotle in his *On the Soul*, Book III,[27] says that the intellect and what can be understood, perception and what can be perceived, and in general potentiality and its object become one. Thus love transforms the lover into the beloved. Thus hope changes the one who hopes into what is hoped for, but what is hoped for does not appear. Therefore hope transfers him into the unknown, the hidden, and the dark shadows,[28] so that he does not even know what he hopes for, and yet he knows what he does not hope for. Thus the soul has become hope and at the same time the thing hoped for, because it resides in that which it does not see, that is, in hope. If this hope were seen, that is, if the one who hopes and the thing hoped for mutually recognized each other, then he would no longer be transferred into the thing hoped for, that is, into hope and the unknown, but he would be carried away to things seen, and he would enjoy the known.

26. *For we do not know how to pray.*

Conclusion

It is not a bad sign, but a very good one, if things seem to turn

---

[25] The Weimar editor (W, LVI, 375, n. 10) suggests that this quotation should be credited to Bernard of Clairvaux, *De praecepto et dispensatione*, 20, 60: *Neque enim praesentior spiritus noster est ubi animat quam ubi amat,* rather than to Augustine.

[26] Vergil, *Eclogues*, III, 66.

[27] Aristotle, *De anima*, III, 1, 2, 5, 7.

[28] Cf. p. 294 above.

out contrary to our requests. Just as it is not a good sign if everything turns out favorably for our requests.

The reason is that the excellence of God's counsel and will
are far above our counsel and will, as Is. 55:8-9 says: "For My
thoughts are not your thoughts, neither are your ways My ways,
says the Lord. For as the heavens are higher than the earth, so are
My ways higher than your ways and My thoughts than your
thoughts." And Ps. 94:11: "The Lord knows the thoughts of men,
that they are vain." And Ps. 33:10: "The Lord brings the counsels
of the nations to nought; He frustrates the plans of the peoples and
casts away the counsels of princes."

Hence it results that when we pray to God for something, whatever these things may be, and He hears our prayers and begins to
give us what we wish, He gives in such a way that He contravenes
all of our conceptions, that is, our ideas, so that He may seem to us
to be more offended after our prayers and to do less after we have
asked than He did before. And He does all this because it is the
nature of God first to destroy and tear down whatever is in us before
He gives us His good things, as the Scripture says: "The Lord
makes poor and makes rich, He brings down to hell and raises up"
(1 Sam. 2:7, 6).

By this His most blessed counsel He renders us capable of receiving His gifts and His works. And we are capable of receiving
His works and His counsels only when our own counsels have
ceased and our works have stopped and we are made purely passive
before God, both with regard to our inner as well as our outward
activities. This is what He means when He says: "My thoughts are
not your thoughts, neither are your ways My ways" (Is. 55:8).
Therefore, when everything is hopeless for us and all things begin
to go against our prayers and desires, then those unutterable groans
begin. And then "the Spirit helps us in our weakness" (Rom. 8:26).
For unless the Spirit were helping, it would be impossible for us
to bear this action of God by which He hears us and accomplishes
what we pray for. Then the soul is told: "Be strong, wait for the
Lord, and let your heart take courage and bear up under God"
(Ps. 27:14). And again: "Be subject to the Lord and pray to Him,"
"and He will act" (Ps. 37:7, 5). What is said in Is. 28:21 takes place
here: "He does a strange work in order to do His own work," and
in Ps. 103:11: "As the heavens are high above the earth (that is, not
according to our thoughts), so great is His steadfast love toward us,
etc." Therefore those who do not have this understanding of God

and His will do as those do of whom it says in Ps. 106:13, 24: "They do not bear up under His counsel" and "they despised the pleasant land." These people trust in their own pious intention and presume that they are seeking, willing, and praying rightly and worthily for all things. Therefore when what they have thought of does not immediately come to them, they go to pieces and fall into despair, thinking that God either does not hear them or does not wish to grant their requests, when they should have hoped all the more confidently, the more they saw everything go counter to their desires, for they know that they "are dust and that man is like grass" (Ps. 103:14-15). But they want to be like God, and they want their thoughts to be not beneath God but beside Him, absolutely conformed to His, that is, perfect, which is as possible, or rather as little possible, as that clay which by nature is suitable for a pitcher or some kind of vase can in its present form be like the form or the model which the potter has in mind, into which he intends to shape the clay.[29] They are foolish and proud over this and know neither God nor themselves. For thus Is. 64:8 says: "Yet, O Lord, Thou art our Father; we are the clay, and Thou art our potter; we are all the work of Thy hand." Therefore these people who do not have the Spirit flee and do not want the works of God to be done but want to form themselves. But those who have the Spirit are helped by Him. Thus they do not lose hope but have confidence, even though they are aware of what goes contrary to what they have so sincerely prayed for. For the work of God must be hidden and never understood, even when it happens. But it is never hidden in any other way than under that which appears contrary to our conceptions and ideas. Hence Gabriel says to the Virgin: "The Holy Spirit will come upon you," that is, He will come upon you in a way which is above what you think, "and the power of the Most High will overshadow you" (Luke 1:35), that is, you will not understand, and therefore do not ask how it will come to pass. For in this way He acted in His own proper work, which is the first example of all of His works, that is, in Christ. And then when He wanted to glorify Him and place Him in His kingdom, as the most holy thoughts of all the disciples ardently hoped and expected, He made Him die, be overturned, and descend into hell, contrary to all expectations. Thus He caused also St. Augustine to descend to the depths, and in opposition to

---

[29] Cf. Luther's marginal comments on Johannes Tauler's sermon on "The Stilling of the Storm," written about the same time as the present lectures and containing a strikingly parallel statement (W, IX, 102, 17—27).

the prayers of his mother He caused him to go astray, that He might reward her far beyond what she asked. And so He deals with all the saints.

This is what Ps. 16:3 is saying: "To the saints who are in His land He has made wonderful all my desires in them," and Ps. 4:3: "Know that the Lord has made His holy One wonderful," namely, "because the Lord will hear me when I cry unto Him," and Ps. 111:2: "Great are the works of the Lord, sought out by all who have pleasure in them." For how can it be more wondrous than when He sends the greater temptation of wantonness upon a man who is praying for chastity or greater weakness to the man who is praying for strength? Yet if the man bears up, He achieves even more than was asked for. This is what Eph. 3:20 is saying: "Now to Him who by the power at work within us is able to do far more abundantly than all that we ask or think, etc.," and 2 Cor. 9:8-9: "God is able to provide you with every blessing in abundance, . . . as it is written, 'He has scattered abroad, He has given to the poor,'" (that is, to those who have kept themselves passive).

Corollary

It is always the case that we understand our own work before it is done, but we do not understand the work of God until it has been done, Jer. 23:20: "In the latter days you will understand His counsel," which is to say that in the beginning or at first we understand our own counsel, but in the end we understand God's. John 14:29: "So that when it does take place, you may believe." Because, as I have said, just as in the case of an artist who comes upon some material which is suitable and apt for making into a work of art, the suitableness of the material is in a certain sense an unfelt prayer for the form which the artist understands and heeds, as he gets ready to make what this material calls for through its suitability, so God comes upon our feeling and thinking, seeing what it is praying for, what it is suitable for, and what it desires; then heeding the request He begins to mold the form which suits His art and His counsel. Then of necessity the form and the model of our thinking is destroyed. Thus we read in Gen. 1:2: "The Spirit of the Lord was moving over the waters, and darkness was upon the face of the deep." Notice that it says, "upon the face of the deep," and not just "upon the deep," for according to appearances it seems to be opposed to us, when the Spirit comes over us and is about to do what we pray.

Concerning this patience and endurance of God see Tauler,[30] who has shed more light than others on this matter in the German language. Yes, indeed, this is the meaning of the expression "We do not know how to pray as we ought." Therefore the Spirit who helps us in our infirmities is very necessary. Who would believe that these words are so profound!

Thus Christ says to His disciples in John 14:16: "I will pray the Father, and He will give you another Paraclete, etc." But "Paraclete" is the name used for Comforter and Advocate. By this one word He clearly affirms what the apostle is saying in this passage: "We do not know how to pray as we ought." He who seeks an advocate is confessing that he does not know how to speak or to pray as he ought, and he who needs a comforter confesses that he is certain that he is hopeless and cast down. This is how it is with us when God hears our prayers. For when we ask for nothing but things that are good and salutary and receive the contrary, we must necessarily be sad and afflicted. For all is lost and condemned. Therefore we need someone else to intervene for us, one who understands these things and prays for us and in the meantime sustains us so that we do not lose heart.

Corollary

To the first grace as well as to the glory we always adopt a passive attitude, as a woman does toward conception. For we are also the bride of Christ. Therefore even though we pray and beg for grace, yet when grace does come and the soul is to be impregnated with the Spirit, it ought neither pray nor act, but only be still. This is surely difficult to do and it afflicts us terribly. For that the soul should be without the power of understanding or willing is to have it in darkness, and it is like going into destruction and annihilation, which it violently dislikes. For this reason it often deprives itself of the noblest graces.

I call "first grace" not that which is poured into us at the beginning of conversion, as in the case of Baptism, contrition, or remorse, but rather all that grace which follows and is new, which we call a degree and increase of grace.

For God first gives operative grace, which He allows to be used and worked with up to the point where He begins to pour into us

---

[30] Johannes Tauler, 1300—1361, was one of the leading teachers of mystical piety. For Luther's estimate of him, cf. *Luther's Works*, 31, pp. 128—129; 48, pp. 35—36.

a second kind of grace; and when this has been poured in, He lets
it cooperate, even though when it was first infused it was operative
and first grace, while with respect to the first grace it is second
grace. For it is called first grace always with respect to itself, because it operates first, and then in the second place it cooperates.
Thus fools, as it says in the proverb,[31] do not know how to greet
God when they meet Him, nor how to receive the gifts He offers
them. But the prudent take them with patience and with joy. For
at this point we have the greatest need for prudence, so that we are
not wise in things that are apparent (for then we shall despair)
but rather in future and unknown things which do not appear.[32]

For this reason the apostle in this passage uses a very significant
word: *He knows what is in the mind of the Spirit* (v. 27). The Greek
text has: "He knows what the prudence of the Spirit is." The
Greek φϱόνημα means prudence, as above: "The prudence of the
Spirit is life and peace" (v. 6). For the same word is used here.

And note that when he uses the expression "we do not know
how to pray," the apostle is not trying to say that holy and good
people are asking for things which are contrary or harmful, but
rather that they are asking for too little, things that are too lowly
or insignificant in comparison with what God wants to give them.
Therefore he speaks of "our weakness" (v. 26) and not of "our
iniquity," for we are too weak and impotent to make large requests.
Therefore in heeding our prayers and coming to grant our requests
God destroys our weak thinking and our still too humble ideas, and
He gives us what the Spirit demands for us. It is as if a person
should write his father asking for silver, but the father is disposed to
give him a thousand pieces of gold. The father throws away the
letter and disregards it, and when the son learns of this and realizes
that the silver is not coming to him as he requested, he is made sad.

Therefore the Lord said to the sons of Zebedee in Matt. 20:22:
"You do not know what you are asking," even when they were asking for something good. But then the question follows: "Are you
able to drink the cup that I am to drink?" It is as if He were saying:
"Your petition will not be fulfilled in the way you have asked; you
are not asking for the cup, and yet you shall drink it, and you are
asking for less than you should. Therefore this weakness will be
crucified in you through the cup of suffering, and you will be made
strong." And in John 16:24 He says: "Hitherto you have asked

[31] A German variant of the proverb is *Wenn Gott grüsst, soll man danken.*
[32] Cf. Heb. 11:1.

nothing in My name; ask, and you will receive, that your joy may be full." How can this be true, when He taught them to pray: "Our Father" (Matt. 6:9)? But they asked in their own name, not in the name of Christ, that is, they asked for something less than Christ is, not in the Holy Spirit, but according to the flesh. And thus He continues: "In that day you will ask in My name" (John 16:26). For he prays in the name of Christ who prays also in sufferings.

Let us conclude. There is no better proof that we do not know what we should pray for than the fact that we do not receive as we should the good which God offers to us, but that because of our weakness we become frightened and want to run away, if the Spirit were not praying for us and helping us in this weakness of ours. For he who does not accept, as he should when what he has asked for is offered to him, surely is convicted of not knowing what he asked for. And he deserves to have someone to say of him: "You fool, why did you pray if you do not wish to receive? Therefore it would be in place to accept the terror God gives and to do so with a joy that is greater than the desire with which we prayed for His gift.

But do we not preach the world over that God's power, wisdom, goodness, righteousness, and mercy are great and marvelous without understanding them? For we understand things metaphysically, that is, according to the way we understand them, namely, as things that are apparent and not hidden, although He has hidden His power under nothing but weakness, His wisdom under foolishness, His goodness under severity, His righteousness under sins, and His mercy under wrath. Hence they do not understand the power of God when they see infirmity, etc. Thus Ps. 81:7: "I answered you in the secret place of thunder." Note the expression "the secret place," which means: when the thunder of wrath hid the sweetness of mercy, that is, when He hears us by doing the opposite of our expectations. We ask for salvation, and He, to save us, increases our damnation and hides His answer under this kind of thunder. This is symbolized in Ex. 5:5 ff., where, when He was about to set the people free, He aroused Pharaoh the more strongly against them, so that He seemed to be less desirous of saving them. And in Ps. 31:19 we read: "O how abundant is Thy sweetness," that is, Thy goodness, "which Thou hast hidden from them that fear Thee," which Thou hast not shown in public, "which Thou hast wrought for those who take refuge in Thee in the sight of the sons of men, etc."

28. *We know that to those who love God, who according to His purpose, etc.* On this text depends the entire passage which follows to the end of the chapter. For He wills that to the elect who are loved by God and who love God the Spirit works all things for good, even things which in themselves are evil. He approaches, yes, from this point on begins to discuss the matter of predestination and election, which is not as deep a subject as is commonly thought, but rather is a wonderfully sweet thing for those who have the Spirit, but a bitter thing and harsh above all things for the prudence of the flesh.

For there is no other reason or cause why numerous adversities and evils do not separate the saints from the love of God except the fact that they have not only been called but "called according to His purpose," and therefore to them alone and to no others "He works all things for good." For if it were not the purpose of God, and if our salvation depended upon our will and works, it would depend upon chance, a chance which — I do not say all of these evils together — but one of them might easily hinder or overturn! But now when he says: "Who will bring a charge? Who will condemn? Who will separate?" (vv. 33-35), he is showing that the elect are not saved by chance but by necessity. Here we are shown that neither chance nor wonderfully strong resistance against so many evils impede our salvation. Indeed He saves us in this way and exposes His elect to as many rapacious forces as are mentioned here, all of which are striving to pull the elect down into damnation so that they might be lost, in order to show that He saves us not by our own merits, but purely by His own election and immutable will, in the very face of so many rapacious and terrifying adversaries who try in vain to harm us. For if He did not lead us through so many frightful things, He would leave much room for high opinions concerning our own merits. But now He shows that we are saved by His immutable love. And thereby He gives approval not to our will but to His own unchanging and firm will of predestination. For how could a man possibly break through all of these things in which he would lose hope a thousand times, unless the eternal and fixed love of God led him through them and the Spirit were present to aid our infirmity and to intercede for us with groanings which cannot be uttered? For in such situations man does not even know what he should do or ask for. Indeed he might pray that he not come into these troubles, and this would be foolish, because it would work against his salvation. Therefore "we do not know how to pray," especially in our weaknesses, that is, in these sufferings.

Therefore where is now our righteousness? Where are our good works? Where is our free will and the contingency of circumstances? For one must preach this way. This is to preach correctly. This is to strangle "the prudence of the flesh." Thus far the apostle has cut off its hands and feet and tongue, but now he is quickly strangling it and killing it. For now he sees that in himself there is nothing but that his entire good is only in God. Our theologians,[33] however, brilliant as they are, think that they have accomplished something great when they bring in their concept of "the contingent," saying that the elect are saved necessarily, namely, by the necessity of consequence, but not by the necessity of the consequent.[34] These are only empty words, especially since they try to understand or at least give the occasion to understand the expression "contingency of the consequent"[35] to mean that salvation takes place or does not take place because of our own will. I myself once understood it in this sense. But the expression "contingency of the consequent" is not relevant to our subject, and it solves nothing to ask whether this consequence is contingent, as if it could be necessary, inasmuch as God alone is necessary for this purpose. Therefore it is a ridiculous addition if a person says: The elect are necessarily saved by the necessity of consequence, but not by the necessity of the consequent, that is, the consequent is not God, or because it is not God, therefore a man is saved by the necessity of consequence. For what else does the expression "to be contingent" mean than to be a creature and not God? Thus they twist the meaning of the necessity of an event into the necessity of the essence of a thing. There is no place here for this kind of equivocation. For no one is asking or in doubt as to whether a created thing is contingent in its essence, that is, subject to change and thus not God or something immutable, but the question is con-

---

[33] The Weimar editor cites Scotus, Biel, Occam, d'Ailli, Usingen, and Trutvetter (W, LVI, 382, n. 21).

[34] The "necessity of consequence" (necessitas consequentiae) is the necessity of a logical conclusion once the premises for it are established. But since the premises are subject to review, this necessity is not absolute but relative. The "necessity of the consequent" (necessitas consequentis) is the necessity under which that which follows lies. Thomas Aquinas equates this with necessitas absoluta (Cf. Ludwig Schütz, Thomas-Lexikon, 2d ed., p. 521). Luther dealt with this problem also in De servo arbitrio. Cf. Luther's Works, 33, pp. 36—41.

[35] "Contingency of the consequent" (Consequentis contingere or contingens consequentis) means "nonnecessity of that which follows."

cerning the necessity of the sequel, as to whether what God has
predestined takes place by necessity, and they agree that it is so.
And yet they make this superfluous addition after they have given
the complete answer. For if you know that everything takes place
entirely by the necessity of the consequence, what point is there in
knowing further whether or not at this point it is contingent?

This is like saying: If a son of necessity should kill his father,
must this take place of necessity? And you would reply: It will
happen by the necessity of consequence, but the son is not the
father, or the father has no son. Therefore they who are asking this
question want to know whether contingency can hinder the necessity of the sequel, and they presuppose that they know the contingency and that you are teaching by begging the question when
you say that there are contingent things and that they do not hinder.
Your reply is correct, but you are teaching superfluous and irrele-
vant things. If they are less educated they put this question at any
rate: Does the contingency of an event impede the sure predestination of God? And the answer is that with God there simply is
no contingency, but it is only in our eyes. For not even the leaf of
a tree falls to the ground without the will of the Father. Therefore
like the essences of things, so also the times are in His hands.
Thus they are making a wrong equivocation when they relate the
necessity itself either to the subject or to the connecting clause,
since the question pertains only to the connecting clause or to time
but never to the subject.

We shall deal with this matter in three ways. First, we shall
collect the proofs of an immutable predestination from the words of
Scripture and from the works of God. Second, we shall analyze the
objections, the exceptions, the arguments, and the motives of those
who shift the guilt to God. Third, we shall give consolation to those
who are frightened by these things and show the pleasant aspects
of this matter in order to inspire hope.

I

The apostle in this and the following chapter deals very carefully and almost in every individual word with our first point, beginning, as I have said, with the words: "We know that for those
who love God, etc."

Therefore he says first: *who are called according to His purpose.* Thus it clearly follows that others are not called according
to His purpose. For the term "purpose" in this passage means

God's predestination, or free election and deliberation, or counsel. Blessed Augustine in Book 1 of his *Confessions* says: "Thou art wonderful, O God; Thou changest Thy opinion, but Thou dost not change Thy counsel." [36]

Second, in the following chapter on the basis of the two stories of Isaac and Ishmael, and likewise of Jacob and Esau, the apostle shows that nothing except election distinguished the men, as he expressly says (Rom. 9:8 ff.).

Third, in the same chapter he uses two passages, the first speaking of the elect: "I will have mercy on whom I will have mercy" (Rom. 9:15; cf. Ex. 33:19), and the second speaking regarding the reprobate: "I have raised you up for the very purpose, etc." (Rom. 9:17, cf. Ex. 9:16). And he continues: "He hardens the heart of whomever He wills, and He has mercy upon whomever He wills" (Rom. 9:18). Similarly in chapters 10 and 11 he does the same things, as is clearly evident.

Fourth, from the statements which are taken from John 10:29: "No one is able to snatch my sheep out of the Father's hand."

Fifth, John 13:18: "I am not speaking of you all; I know whom I have chosen." And John 6:44: "No one can come to Me unless the Father who sent Me draws him." And again in the same chapter: "And they shall all be taught by God" (John 6:45; cf. Is. 54:13; Jer. 31:34).

Sixth, Ps. 115:3: "Our God does all things whatever He pleases." And 2 Tim. 2:19: "God's firm foundation stands, bearing this seal: 'The Lord knows those who are His.'"

In the second place we have proofs of God's immutable predestination in His works: first, as in the following chapter in regard to Ishmael and Esau, Pharaoh and the Egyptians.

Second, God exposes His saints to so many evils, which are all like grasping hands, and yet He does not lose His saints. In this way He shows sufficiently clearly the firmness of His election, that it cannot be hindered by any creature, although He leads every creature up against it, as He exemplifies in the case of hardened Pharaoh.

Third, He demonstrates His election by the fact that He permits many people to live a good life from their birth and to do great good deeds, and yet they are not saved; again He permits many people to do great evil, and yet they are suddenly converted and saved. Examples of this are Saul and Manasseh. Likewise Judas the be-

[36] Augustine, *Confessions*, I, 4, 4, *Patrologia, Series Latina*, XXXII, 663.

trayer and the thief on the cross, and many other cases of harlots and open sinners. On the other hand He rejects the learned and those who are brilliant in good works. Thus He rejected one of the 40 martyrs.[37]

II

There are many arguments against predestination, but they proceed from the "prudence of the flesh." Therefore he who has not denied himself and learned to subject his questions to the will of God and hold them down will always keep asking why God wills this and does that, and he will never find the reason. And very properly. Because this foolish wisdom places itself above God and judges His will as something inferior, when actually it should be judged by Him. Therefore the apostle in a few words destroys all the arguments; first restraining our temerity so that we do not sit in judgment over the will of God by saying: "But who are you, O man, to answer back to God?" (Rom. 9:20). It is as if he were saying: "You are under the will of God; why do you presume, therefore, to argue with Him and try to catch Him?" Then he adds the express reason: "Has the potter no right over the clay?" (Rom. 9:21).

Therefore the first argument, which is also the least important, is this: Man has been given a free will by which he either merits or fails to merit something. The answer: The free will without grace has absolutely no power to achieve righteousness, but of necessity it is in sin. Therefore blessed Augustine is correct in his book *Against Julian* when he calls it "a bound will rather than a free will." [38] For when we possess grace, then the will is actually made free, especially with respect to salvation. To be sure it is always free in a natural way, but only with respect to those things which are under its power and lower than itself, but not with respect to the things above it, since it is captive in sin and now cannot choose that which is good in God's eyes.

The second argument is that "God desires all men to be saved" (1 Tim. 2:4), and He gave His Son for us men and created man for eternal life. Likewise: All things exist for man, and he himself exists for God that he may enjoy Him, etc.[39] These points and

---

[37] The reference is to the 40 Christian soldiers of the Roman "Thunderbolt Legion" whom legend describes as having been martyred under Licinius by exposure to severe cold in Sebaste in Armenia. One of the 40 is supposed to have lost courage and to have fled.

[38] Augustine, *Contra Julianum*, II, 8, 23, *Patrologia, Series Latina*, XLIV, 689.

[39] Cf. Augustine, *De doctrina christiana*, 31, 34 ff., *Patrologia, Series Latina*, XXXIV, 32 ff.

others like them can be refuted as easily as the first one. For these verses must always be understood as pertaining to the elect only, as the apostle says in 2 Tim. 2:10 "everything for the sake of the elect." For in an absolute sense Christ did not die for all, because He says: "This is My blood which is poured out for you" and "for many" — He does not say: for all — "for the forgiveness of sins" (Mark 14:24, Matt. 26:28).

Third, God condemns no one without sin, and he who is necessarily in sin is unjustly condemned. The answer: We are all of necessity in sin and damnation, but no one is in sin by force and against his will. For he who hates sin is already beyond sin and belongs to the elect. But those whom God hardens are those to whom He gives voluntarily to will to be and remain in sin and to love iniquity. Such people are necessarily in sin by the necessity of immutability, but not by force.

Fourth, why does He command to be done what He does not want people to do? And what is worse, He hardens the will, so that men prefer to act contrary to His law. Thus the cause is in God that men sin and are damned. This is the strongest and primary objection. And to it the apostle replies principally when He says that God wills it so and in so willing He is not evil. For all things are of Him, as the clay is the potter's. Therefore He gives commands that the elect might fulfill them and the reprobate be enmeshed in them, so that He might show both His anger and His mercy.

Then "the prudence of the flesh" says: "It is harsh and wretched that God should seek His glory in my misery." Note how the voice of the flesh is always saying "my," "my"; get rid of this "my" and rather say: "Glory to Thee, O Lord!" And then you will be saved. For the prudence of the flesh is such that it seeks only its own, and it fears its own misery more than failure to glorify God, and thus it seeks its own will more than God's will. And thus we must have a different mind toward God than toward man. For He owes nothing to anyone. Thus He says to Job (Job 41:11): "Who has given to Me, that I should repay him? Whatever is under the whole heaven is mine." The apostle cites this passage at the end of chapter 11: "Who has first given to Him, that he should be repaid?" (Rom. 11:35).

III

Although this matter is very hard for the "prudence of the flesh," which is made even more indignant by it and brought even to the point of blasphemy, because here it is strangled to death and reduced to absolutely nothing, it understands that salvation comes in no way from something working in itself but only from outside itself, namely, from God, who elects. But those who have the "prudence of the spirit" delight in this subject with an ineffable pleasure, as the apostle makes clear here and as is seen in the case of Hannah, the mother of Samuel in 1 Sam. 2. Among these are those people in the middle [40] who have begun to turn away from the "prudence of the flesh" or are coming close to the "prudence of the spirit," people who gladly want to do the will of God, but they are pusillanimous and tremble when they hear these teachings. Thus even though these words of the most perfect and nourishing food are still not entirely pleasant to them, yet by the process of antiperistasis,[41] that is, through the fact that opposites attract, they find these words soothing and consoling. Thus, for example, no words are more effective than these for terrifying, humbling, and destroying our arrogant presumptuousness regarding merits. But those who are fearful and become pale before them have here the best and happiest sign, for the Scripture says: "Upon whom does My Spirit rest except on him who is humble and trembles at My Word?" (Is. 11:2; 66:2). To these people Christ also says: "Fear not, little flock, for it is your Father's pleasure to give you the Kingdom" (Luke 12:32). And Is. 35:4: "Say to those who are of a fearful heart, 'Be strong, fear not! Behold, your God will come.'" For if He had not seen that they were thinking the opposite, namely, fear and despair of the Kingdom, He would not have said, "You who are of fearful heart, 'Be strong! Behold, your God will come.'" And again: "Blessed is the man who fears the Lord" (Ps. 112:1). And everywhere in the Scriptures, people of this kind who fear the Word of God are commended and comforted. For they despair of themselves, and the Word of God accomplishes its work in them, that is, creating the fear of God in them. For just as those who are hardened toward the Word of God and trust in themselves have a very bad sign so they who tremble before it and are frightened have the very best sign; as it is written in Ps. 144:6: "Send out Thy arrows and rout them."

Therefore he who is overly fearful that he is not elect or is tested concerning his election, let him give thanks for this kind of fear and rejoice that he is afraid, for he knows with confidence that God, who cannot lie, has said: "The sacrifice acceptable to God is a

---

[40] Cf. p. 186 above.

[41] This term appears already in Aristotle, *Physics*, VIII, 267[a], 16.

broken," that is, a despairing "spirit; a broken and contrite heart, O God, Thou wilt not despise" (Ps. 51:17). Moreover, he himself knows what "broken" means. Therefore he should boldly lay hold on the truthfulness of the God who promises and thus free himself from his former idea of a terrifying God and be saved and elect.

It is surely not a characteristic of reprobate men, at least in this life, that they fear the hidden judgment of God, but rather it is a quality of the elect. For the reprobate despise it and pay it no attention, or in desperation they become presumptuous, saying: "If I am damned, I will be damned."

And there are three degrees of the company of the elect.

The first belongs to those who are content regarding this will of God and do not murmur against God but rely on the fact that they are elect and do not wish to be damned.

The second degree is better than the first. They are resigned and content in this feeling or at least in the desire for it, should God not want to save them but consider them among the reprobate.

The third degree is the best and highest of them, who in effect resign themselves to hell if God so wills, as is probably the case with many at the hour of death. These people are perfectly cleansed of their own will and the "prudence of the flesh." They know the meaning of the passage: "Love is strong as death, jealousy is cruel as the grave" (Song of Sol. 8:6). A marvelous comparison, because love is compared with harsh things, although it seemingly is a soft and sweet thing. But it is true that love is the pleasure in someone else, for it enjoys the beloved. But in this world God gives this love to His elect fleetingly and sparingly, for it is a most dangerous thing to have it frequently and for a long time; "for they have their reward" (Matt. 6:2). But this love for something we long for, I say, is like hell, hard and strong, and in this God trains His elect in this life in wonderful ways. Thus the bride says in the Song of Solomon: "I am sick with love" (Song of Sol. 2:5). Therefore under the term "love" or "charity" we must always understand the cross and sufferings, as is clear in this passage. For without these the soul becomes lazy and tepid, neglects the love of God and no longer thirsts for Him, the living Fountain. This love is sweet indeed, but not in passively receiving but in actively demonstrating itself, that is, to speak in common language, it is sweet toward its object but bitter to its subject. For it wishes all good things for others and demonstrates them, but it receives all evils upon itself and takes them as its own. For "it does not seek its own, but bears all things and endures all things" (1 Cor. 13:5, 7).

CHAPTER NINE

2. *I have great sorrow.*

FROM this text it is very clear that love is found not only in sweetness and delight, but also in the greatest sorrow and bitterness. Indeed it rejoices and delights in bitterness and sorrow, because it regards the misery and sufferings of others as if they were its own. Thus Christ even in the final and worst hour of His suffering was aglow with His deepest love, indeed according to blessed Hilary [1] it filled Him with the greatest joy to suffer the greatest pain. For thus it is that "God is wonderful in His saints" (Ps. 68:35), so that He causes them, at the very time they are suffering the greatest pains, also to experience the greatest joys.

3. *For I could wish that I myself were accursed.* I do not know what they are afraid of, but many want this passage to be understood with reference to the apostle before his conversion, when he was outside of Christ and even opposed to Him. But this interpretation has no value for many reasons. In the first place, he says, "I could wish." Now, that he wishes for something a person says when he is not yet what he hopes for. But at that time he was already accursed. In the second place, because he hopes to be accursed from Christ, therefore he is understood to be with Christ when he says this. In the third place, the term "accursed" means the same thing as, for example, excommunication, execration, rejection; therefore he is at this time in communion, consecrated, and taken up in Christ, when he says: "I could wish that I were accursed." In the fourth place, he uses the expression "for the sake of my brethren." But at this time he was accursed and made detestible not for them but with them; at this time he did not wish to be there for their salvation, but he wanted to be associated with their damnation.

But why stop there? In the fifth place, the whole order of the text indicates that he is speaking with most fervent zeal about their salvation. For he wants to bring Christ to them, which he certainly

[1] Cf. Hilary, *De Trinitate*, X, 45, *Patrologia, Series Latina*, X, 379.

was not doing then. For that reason he swore a most sacred oath, because it seems incredible that a man would desire to be damned, in order that the damned might be saved.

And in the sixth place, he alone wishes to be accursed by Christ, which is something less. But before his conversion he hoped that Christ and all His followers might be anathema from the whole world and not that he be alienated from Christ, but Christ from him and from all men. And he wanted to be against Christ in agreement with the Jews, who made Christ anathema to themselves and cast Him out of the city and out of their communion and killed Him and declared themselves chosen and established themselves. For this reason Christ is called "Hermon" [2] in Ps. 133:3: "It is like the dew of Hermon, which falls on the mountains of Zion!" And the church is called "Hermonim" together with Him in Ps. 42:6: "Therefore I remember Thee from the land of Jordan and Hermonim." In Greek the word "Hermon" means anathema and "Hermonim" anathemas. And the word "anathema" means an excommunication or a separation, as lepers are separated as unclean people. Thus Christ predicted to His disciples: "They will put you out of the synagogs" (John 16:2). It is as if he were saying: "You will be Hermonim and anathemas, that is, the rejected and the excommunicated of the people."

Thus the words "I could wish, etc." are a most excellent and entirely apostolic way of speaking here of love both toward Christ as well as toward the Jews. For from the great love for Christ he hopes for great glory from the Jews for Christ. And in order that He might have this, he himself is glad and willing to be separated from Him, but without hating Him. For this love based on its opposite is the strongest and highest love, where the highest sign of hatred for oneself shows the great love for someone else.

Thus he wishes the greatest salvation also for the Jews, and in order that they might have this, he freely is willing to lose his own salvation. He does this also in another place, in 2 Cor. 12:15, where he says: "I will most gladly spend and be spent for your souls."

But we must note that these words seem strange and foolish to those who think that they are righteous and love God with a covetous love, that is, because of their salvation and eternal rest or because of their escape from hell, and not for the sake of God

---

[2] In his comment on Ps. 42:6 Luther compares Hermon to Christ in much the same way. Cf. W, III, 236, 32 ff.

Himself, but for their own sakes, men who babble [3] that ordered love begins with itself and that each person must first desire salvation for himself and then his neighbor's salvation as his own. They have this kind of wisdom because they do not know what it is to be blessed and saved, unless of course it means to be happy and to do well according to their own imagination. Although this is what it means to be blessed, to will to do the will of God and glorify Him in all things and not at all to want one's own interests, neither here nor in eternity.

But to those who truly love God with a filial love and friendship, which does not arise out of nature but only from the Holy Spirit, these words are most beautiful and testimonies of a perfect example. For such men freely offer themselves to the entire will of God, even to hell and eternal death, if that is what God wills, so that His will may be fully done. Therefore they seek absolutely nothing for themselves. But just as they thus conform themselves purely to the will of God, so also it is impossible that they should remain in hell. For it is impossible that the man should remain outside of God who has so completely thrown himself upon the will of God. For he wills what God wills; therefore he pleases God. And if he pleases God, he is loved by Him; and if loved, then saved.

But you ask whether God has ever willed or may ever will that a man should resign himself to hell and damnation or give himself to the anathema from Christ for the sake of His will. I reply that it happens in many cases and especially in those who are imperfect in charity or pure love for God. For in their case the love of concupiscence which is so deeply rooted in them must necessarily be torn out. But it is not torn out except through a superabundant infusion of grace or through this very harsh resignation. For "nothing unclean shall enter into the kingdom of God" (Rev. 21:27). But now no one knows whether he loves God with a pure heart unless he has experienced in himself that if it should please God he would not desire even to be saved nor would he refuse to be damned. For the damned suffer so severely because they are unwilling to be damned and do not resign themselves to this will of God, which they cannot do without the grace of God.

But if this is the penalty of purgatory (as it seems to me to be), that souls of an imperfect love shrink from this resignation, until they actually make the step and consent to be anathematized from

[3] Cf. Scotus, *Sententiae,* III, dist. 29, qu. un.; Biel, *Sententiae,* III, dist. 29, qu. un., art. 2, concl.

God, we are wretched fools, if we put off loving God perfectly in this life with burning zeal and rather await such cruel sadness in the future. However, this purging does not take place unless there is a resignation to hell.

But those who are truly righteous in that they abound in love achieve this resignation without great sadness. For because of their abounding love for God they make all things possible, even enduring hell. And by reason of this facility they immediately escape the penalty of this kind. Indeed they have no need to fear being damned, for they willingly and happily submit to damnation for the sake of God. Rather it is they who are damned who try to escape damnation.

For even Christ suffered damnation and desertion more than all the saints. And it was not easy for Him to suffer, as some imagine. For He really and truly offered Himself to God the Father for the condemnation for us. And in His human nature He acted in no way different than a man to be eternally damned to hell. And on account of this love of His toward God, God immediately raised Him from death and hell and thus devoured hell. This all His saints should imitate, some to a less and some to a greater degree, for the more perfect they have been in their love, the more readily and easily they can do this. But Christ underwent this with the greatest difficulty of all. Hence in many passages He complains about the agonies of hell.[4]

Those who shrink from this interpretation are still being ruled by the imaginings of their flesh, thinking that to love oneself is to want or hope first of all for something good for oneself; but they do not understand what this kind of good is, and thus they do not know what it is to love. For to love is to hate oneself, to condemn oneself, and to wish the worst, in accord with the statement of Christ: "He who hates his life in this world will keep it for eternal life" (John 12:25). But if someone says: "I do not love my life in this world because I am seeking what is good for it in the life to come," I reply: "You are doing this out of love for yourself, which is a worldly love, and therefore you still love your life in this world. He who loves himself in this way truly loves himself. For he loves himself not in himself but in God, that is, in accord with the will of God, who hates, damns, and wills evil to all sinners, that is, to all of us. For what is good for us is hidden, and that so deeply that it is hidden under its opposite. Thus our life is hidden under death, love

---

[4] Luther is thinking of Christological passages in the psalms.

for ourselves under hate for ourselves, glory under ignominy, salvation under damnation, our kingship under exile, heaven under hell, wisdom under foolishness, righteousness under sin, power under weakness.[5] And universally our every assertion of anything good is hidden under the denial of it, so that faith may have its place in God, who is a negative essence and goodness and wisdom and righteousness, who cannot be possessed or touched except by the negation of all of our affirmatives. Thus "the kingdom of heaven is like a treasure hidden in a field" (Matt. 13:44). The field is dirty in contrast to the treasure; while the one is trodden underfoot, the other is picked up. And yet the field hides the treasure. So also "our life is hid with Christ in God" (Col. 3:3), that is, in the negation of all things which can be felt, held, and comprehended by our reason. So also our wisdom and righteousness are not at all apparent to us but are hidden with Christ in God. But what does appear is that which is contrary to these things, namely, sin and foolishness, as the apostle says: "If anyone among you thinks that he is wise, let him become a fool that he may become wise" (1 Cor. 3:18), that is, let him become wise and rich in God, not in himself; let all his own wisdom disappear and nothing but foolishness remain. And thus it is in all other matters too. Thus these are the good things which we should wish for ourselves (that is, every kind of evil). For in this way we conform ourselves to God, who does not regard or consider anything in us as good. And in this way we are already good as long as we recognize nothing as good except God's good and our own good as evil, for he who is wise in this way with God is truly a wise and good man. For he knows that nothing is good outside of God and that in God everything is good. As Christ says: "The kingdom of God is within you" (Luke 17:21). It is as if He were saying: "Outside of you is exile. Outside of you is everything which is seen and touched, but within you is everything which is believed only by faith."

Therefore these people are arguing in a very dangerous manner about the good which can be deduced from philosophy, since God has turned this good into an evil. For even though all things are very good (Gen. 1:31), yet they are not good for us, and even if there are no things which are in any way evil, yet everything is evil for us; and all of this is the case because we have sin. Therefore it becomes necessary to flee the good things and take on the evil

[5] For other delineations of Luther's "theology of the cross," see *Luther's Works*, 31, p. 214; pp. 225—228; 29, pp. 117—118.

things. And we must do this not only with our voice and with a deceitful heart, but with our whole mind we must confess and wish that we might be damned and destroyed. For we must act toward ourselves in the same way that a man does who hates another man. For he does not hate him in imagination, but he sincerely desires to destroy and kill and damn the person whom he hates. Therefore if we so sincerely want to destroy ourselves that we offer ourselves to hell for the sake of God and His righteousness, we have already made true satisfaction to His righteousness, and He will be merciful and free us. "If we judged ourselves truly, we should not be judged by the Lord" (1 Cor. 11:31). For such people seek only this one thing, that they may wash away their sin and win the grace of an offended God; they do not seek the kingdom; they are prepared to lose their salvation, they are ready and willing to be damned, but under the grace of a God who has already been placated, they do not fear punishment but only their offense against God.

This is counter to the ideas of those who imagine that they have merits and picture these to themselves as good and seek them, who shun evils and in their hidden hearts have nothing. For they walk along in blindness wholly absorbed in the good things which they have imagined and desired for themselves.

6. *For not all who are descended from Israel.* This passage is opposed to the presumptuousness of the Jews and as a commendation of grace, for the destruction of all haughty trust in righteousness and good works. For the Jews want to be considered the children of the Kingdom because they are the children of Abraham. Against them the apostle argues with an invincible argument, first, because they themselves cannot deny its validity. For if their presumption were true, then also Ishmael and the sons of Keturah would all be heirs of Abraham and deserving of the same dignity as Isaac, but the text plainly contains the very opposite of this. Therefore their contention is vain that they are of the same status as Isaac on the grounds that they, too, are the children of Abraham. For this does not follow, as the text makes clear. But if they should object and say that Ishmael and the others do not deserve to be on the same plane with Isaac, not only because they were evil and deserved to be deprived of their status because of their sin, but also in the second place because they were not born of the same mother Sarah, he meets them with another example, not refuting their arguments and in a sense granting their objections, although we do not read that the other children of Keturah had sinned, and

Ishmael had sinned only once. But even if this point is conceded, that they were not of the same mother, what about Rebecca? In the first place, in this case there is the same mother; in the second place, the same father; in the third place, two brothers, neither of whom as yet is either good or bad; and yet without any deserving the one is called to be a son and the other to be a servant. Therefore it inexorably follows that flesh does not make sons of God and the heirs of the promise, but only the gracious election of God. Thus and only thus the Spirit and grace of God can arise only when the pride of the flesh has been humbled.

Therefore, why does man take pride in his merits and works, which in no way are pleasing to God? For they are good, or meritorious, works, but only because they have been chosen by God from eternity that they please Him. Therefore we do good works only in giving thanks, for the works do not make us good, but our goodness, rather, the goodness of God, makes us good and our works good. For they would not be good in themselves except for the fact that God regards them as good. And they only are, or are not, what He reputes them to be or not to be. Therefore our reputing or non-reputing is nothing. That is, the man who knows this is always afraid, always trembling at God's reckoning and always awaiting it. Therefore he does not know how to be proud or to argue, as the arrogant self-righteous people do, who are so sure concerning their own good works.

Therefore the definition of virtue in Aristotle [6] is wrong, for this makes us perfect, and its exercise renders us praiseworthy, unless it understands that it makes us perfect and commends our works only before men and in our own eyes. But before God this is an abomination, and the contrary is more pleasing to Him.

10. *But also when Rebecca had conceived by one man.* Although in Greek this can be read in two ways: [7] "Rebecca having shared the bed with one, with Isaac, our father," and "Rebecca having shared the bed with one, the bed of Isaac, our father," yet the second version is better, lest anyone insult Sarah in suspecting that Rebecca had conceived by one man and Sarah by many. For the meaning is that flesh and physical descent do not profit for the adoption of sons, so that even Rebecca, that saintly woman, having

[6] *Nicomachean Ethics*, I, 12.

[7] The Latin for the two versions respectively: *Rebecca ex uno cubile habens Isaac patre nostro* and *Rebecca . . . Isaac Patris nostri.* In respect to the last two words, Erasmus favored the first version, Faber and the Vulgate the second.

shared the bed of no other man but saintly Isaac, the father of all the sons of Israel, received the promise of God for only one of her sons, because only this one and not the other was going to be the lord and heir of the promise. Therefore all of these terms have particular emphasis, such as, "Having shared the bed of Isaac, our father." It is as if he were saying: "It was of no advantage for Esau that he was conceived, like Jacob, of the same great father and the same great mother and of so chaste a bed, and born according to the flesh, yes, even as the firstborn." How much less will it benefit the unbelieving Jews, born long afterwards, that they are the sons of the patriarchs according to the flesh, if they are without faith, that is, if they have not been elected by God!

And finally we should note that the apostle in the Greek speaks modestly, but the translator less so. For the apostle uses the term "bed," [8] but the latter the term "coition." Hence he has given occasion to many to understand the apostle as trying to say that Rebecca had conceived twins by only one coition.

11. *Though they had done nothing either good or bad.* He very nicely uses the term "they had done" rather than "they were." For there is no doubt that both of them were evil because of the disease of original sin, although regarding Jacob some feel that he had been sanctified in the womb. But by their own merit they were the same and equal and belonged to the same mass of perdition.

14. *Is there injustice on God's part? By no means!* The apostle gives no other reason as to why there is not injustice with God than to say: "I will have mercy on whom I have mercy" (v. 15), which is the same as saying: "I will have mercy on whom I wish," or to him who is predestined to receive mercy.

This is a harsh answer for the proud and those who think they know everything, but for the meek and the humble it is sweet and pleasing, because they despair of themselves; and thus God takes them up.

For the fact is that there neither is nor can be any other reason for His righteousness than His will. So why should man murmur that God does not act according to the Law, since this is impossible? Or will it be possible for God not to be God? Furthermore, since His will is the highest good, why are we not glad and willing and eager to see it be done, since it cannot possibly be evil? But do

---

[8] The Greek word κοίτην is translated with *cubile* in Faber's Latin text and with *concubitus* in the Vulgate version. Luther's "the translator" refers to the Vulgate.

I hear you say: "It is evil for me"? Perish the thought! It is evil for no one. But because we cannot affect His will nor cause it to be done, this becomes an evil thing for men. For if they were willing to do what God wills, even if He should will that they be damned and reprobated, they would have no evil. For they would will what God wills, and they would have in themselves the will of God in patience.

15. *I will have mercy on whom I have had mercy.* The Greek reads: "I will have mercy on whom I have mercy, and I will have compassion on whom I have compassion." It is as if He were saying: "To whom I am merciful in the moment of predestination, to him I will also be merciful in fact at a later time, so that the present tense "I have mercy" denotes the intrinsic mercy of the One who predestines, and the future tense the mercy which has been made manifest to the man who has been predestined. The same is the case with the expression "I will have compassion."

The Hebrew reads this way: "I will show mercy on whom I will show mercy, and I will be gracious to whom I will be gracious" (Ex. 33:19). This is said in an indefinite sense as it were and as if He were offering mercy by chance, without reference to predestination. In the same way He also says in Ex. 3:14: "I am who I am," or "I shall be who I shall be."

He seems by these words to be rebuffing those who are anxious and curious about the predestination of themselves or of others, as if to drive them away from thoughts and questions about predestination. As the common saying goes: to whom it comes it comes, and whom it hits it hits. It is as if He were saying: "No one will know to whom I will be merciful and to whom I will be gracious, nor can anyone be certain about it because of his merits or his works or anything else." Thus this word is one of fear and humiliation.

Therefore we must note that in the Hebrew the first mentioned expression "I will show mercy" means to be merciful in the sense that He who shows mercy gives a benefit or a free gift even to him who has not offended or committed a sin, but is only in need and poor. Thus Hannan (which in Hebrew means "one who has shown mercy") signifies "a person who has given a benefit." Hence "Hanna," that is, "grace," "benefit," "free gift," and Johannan, or Johannes with the Greek ending.

But "I will be gracious," or "I will show mercy," means "to forgive" and "to be gracious," which can take place without benefit for him who is guilty and an offender. As when God remits the penalty of hell and the sin, He shows compassion, but when He gives grace and the kingdom of heaven, He is merciful. In the Hebrew this word is "richem." [9]

16. *So it depends not upon man's will or exertion.* This is not to be understood in the sense that this is a matter only of God's showing mercy, as if it were not necessary for a person to will or to exert himself, but rather that the fact that a man does will or exert himself is not of his own power but of the mercy of God, who has given this power of willing and doing, without which man of himself can neither will nor make exertion. As the apostle says in Phil. 2:13: "God is at work in you, both to will and to work." Here he says the same thing, but in different words: "It depends not upon man's will or exertion," that is, not upon man's doing "but upon God's mercy," that is, upon God who gives the gift of His grace. Thus in Ps. 119:32: "I will run in the way of Thy commandments," that is, I have accomplished something, "when Thou enlargest my understanding," that is, when Thou hast made me to will and to be able. And in Ps. 1:2 we read: "And his will is in the law of the Lord." And if someone should ask, "to exert oneself" means "to live and to have one's being in God." Hence the life of the righteous is called the way in Ps. 1:6: "For the Lord knows the way of the righteous." Thus also Jer. 10:23 tells us: "I know, O Lord, that the way of man is not in himself, that it is not in a man who walks to direct his steps." In all of these things there is a kind of contradiction. For if a man's way is not his own, why then does it say: "his way"? The way of man is not his way. So also here: "it depends not on man's exertion," that is, the race he runs, nor does it "depend upon his will," that is, his volition. This is a remarkable thing! The volition is not his who wills, and the race is not his who runs, but God's, who gives it and creates it. In the same way the apostle says in Gal. 2:20: "I live, yet not I." And Christ says: "My teaching is not Mine" (John 7:16). And in Eccl. 9:11 we read: "I saw that the race is not to the swift, nor the battle to the strong, nor bread to the wise, nor riches to the intelligent, nor favor to the men of skill." And then whose are these things? Is the race to those who sit and snore? Is the battle to the weak? Certainly not. But they are all the instrument of God "who works all things in all" (1 Cor. 12:6). So

---

[9] In these last paragraphs Luther is attempting to show the rich content of the two Hebrew words used in the text quoted by Paul from Ex. 33:19 — חָנַן, "be gracious," and רָחַם, "have mercy." His linguistic studies were probably inspired by the lexical contributions of Reuchlin, Faber, and Erasmus.

the cutting of wood is not of the ax but of the cutter and beating the dog is not of the stick but of the man who uses the stick. Hence Is. 10:13 ff. is spoken against those who brag about their own powers to injure and inflict evil on others: "The king of Assyria says: by the strength of my hand I have done it, etc." And it continues (v. 15): "Shall the ax vaunt itself over him who hews with it, or the saw magnify itself against him who wields it? What if the rod should lift itself up against him who lifts it, or a staff should lift itself, which is surely mere wood?" And later on, in Is. 41:23, He laughs at them saying: "Do good or do harm, if you can," that is, "Let us see if you can do good to anyone in need, without My help." And experience abundantly shows that no one can cure or aid those whom God punishes. On the other hand, the same applies to working evil (that is, bringing injury to others); for many people try great things, but they do not prevail when God resists them and does not help them. This was clear in the case of Pharaoh, who wanted to inflict injury on the children of Israel, but could not. And thus God showed His power in him, so that he could not will anything, because he was hardened; and he could run even less than he could will.

But it does not follow from this text that the willing or the running of a man achieves nothing, but that it is not a matter of his own power. For the work of God is not nothing. But the willing and running of a man is the work of God. For he is speaking here about a willing and running according to God, that is, he is speaking about the life of love and the righteousness of God. But the willing and running of any other kind is nothing, of those who do not will and run in the way of God, although they may will great things and run strongly. For these things are not of God and are not pleasing to Him, things of which Isaiah speaks in 41:24: "You are nothing, and your work is of that which does not exist."

Yet here I am issuing the warning that no man whose mind has not yet been purged should rush into these speculations, lest he fall into the abyss of horror and hopelessness; but first let him purge the eyes of his heart in his meditations on the wounds of Jesus Christ.[10] For I myself would not even read these things if the order of the lection and necessity did not compel me to do so. For this is very strong wine and the most complete meal, solid food for those who are perfect, that is, the most excellent theology, of which the

[10] Cf. p. 287 above and Luther's *Meditation on Christ's Passion* in *Luther's Works*, 42, pp. 7—14.

apostle says: "Among the mature we do impart wisdom" (1 Cor. 2:6). But I am a baby who needs milk, not solid food (cf. 1 Cor. 3:1-2). Let him who is a child like me do the same. The wounds of Jesus Christ, "the clefts of the rock," [11] are sufficiently safe for us. The strong and the perfect may discuss the first book of the *Sentences*,[12] which properly should not be the first but the last book. Many today rush into this book heedlessly and strangely also become blinded.

19. *Why does He still find fault?* Some men, like Laurentius Valla,[13] take this expression [*Quid adhuc queritur?*] in a passive sense; Stapulensis [14] takes it as referring to a person, but Erasmus [15] points out that all the Greek interpreters understand it as deponent, and he agrees with them. But we must understand that the apostle introduces this word with reference to the person of those who impiously and arrogantly contend against God and murmur against Him out of indignation as though against an evildoer and someone who is their equal. Thus it does not read in the Greek as we have it in our translation, "Who are you that you should reply to God?" (v. 20), but "that you do reply against," or "in opposition to, God?" It is as if he were saying: "Do you even dare to argue with your Creator and to oppose Him and answer back to Him, not ready to yield to Him in any point?"

Now it surely is no sin if a man out of fear and humility and piety says to God: "Why did You make me thus?" Even if he would commit blasphemy because of the overwhelming violence of his temptation, he would not therefore perish. For our God is not a God of impatience and cruelty, even toward the ungodly. I am saying this for the comfort of those who are perpetually troubled by thoughts of blasphemies and are in great anxiety; since such blasphemies, because they are violently extorted from men by the devil against their will, they sometimes sound more pleasant in the ear of God than a hallelujah or some kind of hymn of praise. For the more

[11] The Weimar editor suggests that "the clefts of the rock" *(foramina petrae)* should be thought of as referring to Song of Sol. 2:14 rather than Ex. 33:22. Both *Glossa ordinaria* and *interlinearis* interpret the phrase as "the wounds of Christ."

[12] In Peter Lombard, *Sentences*, Book I, beginning at dist. 35, the problems of God's foreknowledge, predestination, and the will of God are treated.

[13] Cf. p. 146, n. 23, above.

[14] Ibid.

[15] Cf. p. 81, n. 3, above.

horrible and foul the blasphemy, the more agreeable it is to God, if the heart knows that it does not will this, because the heart did not produce it or choose it. But it is a sign that a man did not will it from his heart and that he is really innocent of it, if he is truly afraid and terrified that he has done such a thing. For the clearest sign of a good heart is the fear of doing evil. Therefore the remedy for these thoughts is not to be worried about them.

So it was also with Job, that very saintly man, to whom the Holy Spirit is witness that he did not sin with his lips nor speak any foolishness against God in all of his trials, although he spoke up against God more than once, as when, for example, he said: "What is man, that Thou dost make so much of him, and that Thou dost set Thy mind upon him? . . . How long wilt Thou not look away from me, nor let me alone?" (Job 7:17, 19). And again: "Against a leaf that is carried away with the wind Thou showest Thy power, and Thou pursuest a dry straw" (Job 13:25). And in his most candid style: "Why didst Thou bring me forth from the womb?" (Job 10:18). Jeremiah and Habakkuk [16] speak the same complaints against God.

17. *For the Scripture says to Pharaoh.* The question is asked: Is the apostle saying these things with any logical connection to what he has said previously? The answer is that he is speaking in a very orderly way, for he has said previously that all things take place according to God's election. Jacob was loved by God because he had been elected, and he obtained mercy because it thus pleased God from eternity, just as also He said to Moses: "I will show mercy, etc." (Ex. 33:19). Having made these statements, he immediately and correctly brings in the corollary which obviously follows what has been said, namely, that it is solely because of a merciful God that anyone is chosen or is righteous, inasmuch as all men are equally a part of the mass of perdition and no one is righteous before God unless he receives mercy. Then follows the statement "For the Scripture says," the sense of which is this: that everything depends on a merciful God and not on someone's will is evident and proved by the fact that in order that God might show this to be the case and that man might know that it is not due to his own running but to the mercy of God, that he wills and runs, God raised up Pharaoh over the children of Israel and drove them to extreme desperation so that they might understand that they

---

[16] Jer. 20:18. Luther seems to be mistaken about Habakkuk. See p. 346 above, where Job and Jeremiah come together on a similar theme.

could not escape Pharaoh by their own powers but only by the power of a merciful God, that their escape was not their own doing but that it was of God, who led them forth. It is the same today; in order to humble the elect and to teach them to trust in His mercy alone, to lay aside every presumption of their own will and achievement, God permits them to be desperately afflicted and to be pursued by the devil, the world, or the flesh, whom He Himself arouses against them. Indeed, in our time He has particularly often aroused the devil to drive His elect into horrible sins and to have dominion over them for a time, or at least always to impede their good intentions and to make them do things contrary to what they want to do, to such an extent that they can even appear to be people who do not desire or make any effort to do good. And yet through all of these things He leads them out and finally frees them unexpectedly while they in despair groan over the fact that they actually will and do such evil things and do not will and do so many good things which they want. Yes, indeed, in this way it comes to pass that "He shows His power" and that "His name may be proclaimed in all the earth" (v. 17).

And please note that the term "power" in this passage is the same [17] as the word used below in "to make known His power" (v. 22), for our translator surprisingly exchanges this for what people otherwise call [18] "strength" (*fortitudo*), "dominion" (*imperium*), or "power" (*virtus, potentia, potestas*). But there is a great difference, for in Greek δύναμις, in Hebrew גְּבוּרָה, in Latin *vis, vires, robur,* or most properly, *virtus,* is the factor by which a person is able actively to overcome and break down what he is trying to break down. In Scripture the opposite of this is "weakness" (*infirmitas*), that is "lack of power" (*impotentia*), not "sickness" (*aegritudo*) or "disease" (*morbus*), as in the expression "My power is made perfect in weakness" (2 Cor. 12:9), and again: "It was weakened, but Thou hast made it perfect" (Ps. 68:9), and Ps. 6:2, "Have mercy on me, O Lord, for I am weak." In German we say *kraftlos, machtlos* ("powerless") in contradistinction to *kräftig,* or *mächtig* ("powerful"). Thus we say: *Er vermag viel, vermag's nicht, er kann's wohl tun* ("He can do much," "he cannot do it," "he is probably able to do it"). So the expression is also applied to

---

[17] The Greek of v. 17 has ἡ δύναμις, v. 22 has τὸ δύνατον.

[18] Faber and Erasmus translate *potentia,* but Faber offers *fortitudo* in his commentary and also uses *potestas* in his translation. On the meaning of *virtus* cf. also p. 149 above.

God: "God is able to perform" (Rom. 4:21), and: "Mighty in battle" (Ps. 24:8).

But ἐξουσία [19] in Greek properly means "power" *(potestas)*, or a free ability and permission to act. This is the power of peace, so to speak, just as the other term *(potentia)* is the power of war. For among the things which we possess and which belong to us we have the free ability and power *(potestas)*, but toward the things which we oppose we are powerful *(potens)* and strong.

And there is still another word in Hebrew for our term "strength" *(fortitudo)*. It is אֵיתָן , that is, something hard and robust, something which is properly speaking a kind of passive power, one that is able to sustain an active power. In German we call this *fest* ("firm"). Num. 24:21 reads: "Enduring is your dwelling place." As a rock is strong, or a castle or a city, concerning which God says in Is. 50:7: "I have set my face like a flint," so a man is called strong who cannot be twisted or overcome, or a man who is stiff-necked and does not let himself be persuaded, but this is in contradistinction to the first meaning of the term, about which we commonly say: "Two hard stones do not grind." For רָשָׁע *(virtus)* and אֵיתָן *(fortitudo)*, if they are equally strong, do nothing. From the balance of equality no action results.

But now to return to our text: God raises up Pharaoh to show forth His power *(virtus)*. For He cannot show His power among the elect unless He first shows them their weakness and hides their power *(virtus)* and reduces it to nothing, so that they may not glory in their own power. But this would not take place if He did not raise up a more powerful *(potentior)* man over them to reduce their power *(virtus)* to nothing and then the power *(virtus)* of the only God alone would appear in the fact that they are liberated. Thus the meaning is: "I have raised you up in order that you may oppress the proud presumptuousness of My people, so that when they have been thus oppressed, they may cry to Me and then My power *(virtus)* may be magnified both in them and in you." This is the meaning which I have followed in the gloss.

Another and perhaps better meaning for this text is possible, namely, that this power should not be applied to salvation but to the perdition of others, so that the meaning from the beginning is that it is due only to a merciful God and not to him who wills or runs. The first example of this is Jacob, who was made good because God had mercy on him; but if God is not merciful, no one becomes

[19] Rom. 9:21.

good, as in the case of Pharaoh. Thus we have examples of both cases, namely, that it is of a merciful God if one does run; and if one does not will or run, it is not of a merciful God but of the God who hardens. And this interpretation seems good to me, because immediately upon both examples follows the statement: *So then He has mercy upon whomsoever He wills, and He hardens the heart of whomsoever He wills* (v. 18). Also, it seems good because He says: *For the purpose of showing My power in you* (v. 17), for He wills that His power be magnified in his perdition.

21. *Has the potter no right over the clay?* Blessed Augustine in chapter 99 of his *Enchiridion* says: "The entire human race in its apostate root was condemned with a divine justice which was so just that even if not a single person were delivered from it, no man could rightly curse the righteousness of God. And even those who are saved must be saved in such a way that from the majority who are not delivered and left in their most righteous condemnation it would be demonstrated what the whole mass would have deserved and to what punishment the righteous judgment of God would bring them, if His unearned mercy had not intervened, so that 'every mouth' of those who want to glory in their own merits 'may be stopped' (Rom. 3:19) and that he 'who boasts, boast of the Lord'" (1 Cor. 1:31).[20] These are important words which should be carefully considered, because they humble and frighten us very much. To be sure, Augustine shows very clearly why the apostle speaks as he does, namely, in order that he might instruct us in humility. For these words do not lead us to horror and hopelessness but to the commendation of grace and the destruction of our presumptuousness, which is the real loss of hope of salvation. Hence, blessed Augustine in chapter 98 of the same work says: "If one refers all things to a very deep and salutary mystery and (so to speak) looking into the face of the Holy Scriptures, the meaning seems to be this: 'Let him who boasts, boast of the Lord'" (1 Cor. 1:31). Again, in the same work he says: "God shows mercy out of His great goodness and hardens with no injustice, so that he who is freed may not boast of his own merits and he who is damned has been overcome by nothing but his own deserts. For grace alone distinguishes the redeemed from the condemned, all having been mingled in one mass of perdition by the common cause of their

---

[20] Augustine, *Enchiridion ad Laurentium*, 99, *Patrologia, Series Latina*, XL, 278.

common origin." [21] Because of such words a man recognizes his own damnation and despairs of saving himself by his own powers, for otherwise he is left cold by the mere thought that he has fallen in Adam, for he hopes that he can raise himself up from that fall by his own free will, indeed he is presumptuous about this. But here he learns that grace has raised him up before every will, including his own.

27. *Only a remnant of them will be saved.* This term "remnant" is common in the prophets as is also the idea expressed in this statement, as, for example, in Is. 4:3: "And he who is left in Zion and remains in Jerusalem will be called holy, everyone who has been recorded for life in Jerusalem."

And Is. 46:3: "Hearken to Me, O house of Jacob, all the remnant of the house of Israel."

Is. 65:8-9: "As the wine is found in the cluster, and they say, 'Do not destroy it, for there is a blessing in it,' so I will do for my servants' sake, and not destroy them all. I will bring forth a seed out of Jacob, that is, a remnant, etc."

Amos 3:12: "As the shepherd rescues from the mouth of the lion two legs or a piece of an ear, so shall the children of Israel be rescued."

Micah 2:12: "I will gather the remnant of Israel."

Micah 5:7: "Then the remnant of Jacob shall be in the midst of many peoples like dew from the Lord."

Therefore in this way and in many other places the apostles and the faithful among the Jews are called the "remnant" or the "remainder", even the "dregs of the people of Israel," as if the better and larger part of them were going to perish. Hence also Is. 49:6 says: "It is too light a thing that You should be My Servant to raise up the tribes of Jacob and to restore the dregs of Israel; I will give You as a light to the nations, etc."

So also Ps. 78:31: "And He slew the strongest of them and laid low the picked men of Israel." It is as if he were saying: "The dregs and the lowly were saved, but the more noble were blinded, just as when the whole cluster is thrown away and only one grape survives."

These dregs are represented by the few poor people who were left behind in the land at the time of the Babylonian exile, when the king and the queen and the princes and the prophets, that is, the powerful, the wise, and the saintly ones went into exile. So

[21] Ibid.

also now the Jews have gone into the true Babylonian exile of unbelief; all the noble ones, with only a few left behind. And it is this exile which Jeremiah laments in his dirges as he sees in spirit even at that time what this thing signified.

These things are likewise signified by that servant of the Amalekite in 1 Sam. 30:11 ff., who was left behind by his master when he had gone ahead with his band of men and his booty. For the same reason Isaiah says of the few who had been left behind in Israel (Is. 10:18-19): "And Israel shall run away in fear, and the remnant of the trees of his forest will be so few that a child can write them down." The trees of the forest are the people of the synagog, very dense and tall in the arrogant multitude of her children.

And so they are called "remnant" because they have been left over, as is clear from this statement of Isaiah. For when the others have been cast into perdition, He preserves these alone to Himself as a seed for another people.

28. *For He will finish His Word and cut it short in righteousness.* This "finishing and cutting short" refers to the Spirit and to the letter, that is, that the flesh and the wisdom of the flesh are in no way capable of comprehending the righteousness and wisdom of God. Therefore it is necessary that this Word of righteousness and wisdom, which is the Word of faith, be contracted and shortened, so that it cannot be extended to the flesh and the wisdom and righteousness of the flesh, nor lay hold upon it nor be captured by it. Hence carnal people must be offended by it, remain outside of it, and be cut off from it.

For before this Word of faith, the Word of the Spirit, was revealed, everything was in shadow and figure because of the slowness of the Jews; the Word was unfinished and incomplete and therefore easily understood by all, because it spoke in figures about things that could be perceived by the senses. But when the figures and the things perceived by the senses were excluded, then God began to speak the hidden Word of the Spirit, which is the Word of faith, and thus He began to bring forth the finished and complete Word, which at the same time must of necessity be also cut off from all figures and signs and symbols. Thereby all those who adhered to those signs and symbols were cut off, or rather the Word was cut off from all of them.

But the very fact that He speaks of "cutting short the Word" rather than the thing itself, that is the reason why those people fell.

For He rejected the reality that could be seen, and the future, which cannot be seen, He did not show, but between these He gave only His Word. Therefore he who does not believe perishes, because he is not content with the Word and is indignant that the reality is denied to him.

But for those who "cut" themselves "short" and "finish" themselves, this Word is finished and cut short for their righteousness; but for the others this is done for their sin and unrighteousness because of their unbelief. For it is a "Word which is finished and cut short in righteousness," that is, all those are righteous who believe in this Word. But they do not believe unless they take their intellect captive to the invisible and cut themselves off from the consideration of all things visible. For the Word is "cut short" also in the sense that it is cut off and separated from all things visible, none of which it promises or exhibits, indeed all of which it denies, cuts short, and commands us to deny. And it does this because it is the "finished" Word, that is, the perfect Word, which cannot signify anything other than the perfect and the complete. For every word which signifies or proclaims the visible or the created is not a finished or a perfect word, because it proclaims only a part and not the entire matter, that is, something which does not satisfy the whole man but tickles only his flesh and his senses. But if it is to proclaim that which is perfect and satisfies the whole man, then it is necessary that it proclaim none of those things which satisfy the flesh, such as something created or visible, but only God. Therefore in the very act of being finished it is cut short, and on the other hand in being cut short it is finished. For its being finished is for the Spirit, for it proclaims the things that are good for the Spirit. But its being cut short is against the flesh, for it denies the things which are good for the flesh. Thus on the contrary the word of the letter or of the old figure was imperfect and unfinished in that it corresponded to and was understood in terms of temporal things and promises and for this reason was extended and stretched out rather than being abbreviated. For it caused the Spirit to be more and more removed from the things which were good in His eyes and from the understanding of these good things.

To put it briefly, as the word of the Law was a carnally understood word, imperfect and extended, or prolonged, so the Word of the Spirit, that is, of the Law spiritually understood, is a finished and abbreviated Word.

It was an imperfect word because it signified but did not demonstrate that which it signified. And for this reason it was extended and prolonged, because it led more and more to the imperfect and the carnal, since it was impossible for it to exhibit what was spiritual as long as it was considered and understood in a carnal way. Just as in the case of a sign, as long as it is accepted in the place of the thing signified, the thing signified is not possessed. And thus in the end this word does not lead "to righteousness" but rather to wickedness, lying and vanity.

On the other hand, the Word of the Gospel is finished, because it bestows what it signifies, namely, grace. Therefore it is also cut short, because it does not defer what it signifies, indeed it actually cuts itself off from all things which prolong and impede the reception of it. Hence it is even abbreviated in righteousness, because it provides for righteousness for those to whom it is finished and abbreviated, and this takes place through faith.

The corollary is that the Word of the new and of the old Law is the same, but only according to our understanding or lack of understanding it is described as perfect or imperfect, short or lengthened. For those who understand the most holy Gospel in terms of their own pride or their own error (as in the case of heretics and individualists) [22] make for themselves an imperfect word out of a perfect one and a lengthened word out of a shortened one, that is, a vain, lying, and useless word.

For the Word of Christ cannot be accepted unless all other things be denied and cut off, that is, that the intellect must be taken captive and every thought be given in humble submission. For because most people persist in their pride and do not receive the Word, or rather are not taken captive by it, therefore barely the remnant is saved, the Word is cut short in those who perish but finished in those who believe. And this is the allegorical "shortening and finishing," that is, the literal meaning of the spiritual Word. And yet it comes from the moral meaning. For because of the fact that the Word of the Spirit says no to all pride and self-satisfaction, therefore of necessity it must likewise say no to all people who are proud and wise in their own conceits and cut itself off from them. Thus the tropological "abbreviation" implies the allegorical one. For because the Word perfects and finishes humility and the emotion of subjecting oneself, therefore it also finishes and perfects all men who are humble and who have put their minds in subjec-

22 For the meaning of *monii*, see p. 271, n. 26, above.

tion. And thus the moral consummation implies also the allegorical.

And thus faith is the finishing and shortening and the compendium of salvation. Indeed the Word which is abbreviated is nothing else but faith. How do we prove this? The Word is abbreviated for no one except him who understands that it has been abbreviated. But only faith can understand this. Thus faith is life and the living Word that has been cut short. Note how this is a brief "conviction of things not seen" (Heb. 11:1), that is, note how it cuts off and abbreviates from everything else; in the same way the believer also cuts himself off from all things by his faith, so that he lives among the things which do not appear. In the second place, faith is a finishing, because it is "the assurance of things hoped for," that is, the possession and the power over the things of the future which are eternal but not present, from which it has cut us off.

And he adds the words *in justice,* or "righteousness." For even the word of the dead letter is finished and shortened, but in a contrary way, namely, in unrighteousness. For just as the Word of the Spirit finishes humility and the humble, shortens pride and the proud, that is, it completes the wisdom of the Spirit and does away with the "wisdom of the flesh," it builds up Jerusalem and tears down Jericho,[23] so also the word of the dead letter on the other hand finishes and hardens the proud and destroys the humble, completes the "wisdom of the flesh," and does away with the wisdom of the Spirit. And it tears down Jerusalem and builds up Jericho. Thus the former word is finished and shortened "in righteousness," and the latter in "unrighteousness."

Thus it is sufficiently obvious that these two terms refer to different things: the term "finished" refers to the end result *(terminus ad quem),* while the term "cut short" refers to the point of departure *(terminus a quo).* For the expression "finished" shows where a word of this kind leads, namely, to the perfection of righteousness; but the term "cut short" refers to what the word leads us from, namely, from the "wisdom of the flesh" and from unrighteousness. Thus those who do not want these two, for them the Word still remains shortened and leaves them in the flesh and in unrighteousness.

And it is the same with this Word as it is with a coat or a blanket which has been shortened; when it covers one part, it leaves the

[23] In Lyra's moral interpretation of Joshua 6 Jericho represents "the city of the devil" and Jerusalem "the city of God."

other bare, as Is. 28:20 says, "The bed is so narrow that the other one falls out, and the coat so short that it cannot cover them both." In the same way the Word of faith is so narrow that two people cannot rest in it, but the one, namely, the old man, falls out and is cut off, because it cannot cover him. The same coat will not cover them both, but only the new man. Thus the Word is truly perfected and finished, because it finishes man wonderfully and overflowingly, but it also is truly abbreviated, because it in no way finishes the old man, for the old man is cut off from everything. Therefore the text wants to tell us that the Lord will make a consummation, but one which is very short and narrow. For in the case of most men it is cut short, because it will cut short the entire old man in accord with the perfection of consummation; thus the greatness of the abbreviation. Now almost all the people were carnal and gloried in the flesh; thus the abbreviation was made exceedingly strong in proportion to the multitude of carnal men. And that is not strange, for they all would have been cut off, because they all were the sons of the flesh and born of their fathers according to the old man, except that God left His seed.

Therefore, the "abbreviated consummation has overflowed with righteousness" (cf. Is. 10:22). It is a strange thing that there should be an overflowing with righteousness and a consummation, and yet one that is both brief and narrow. For who has seen a narrow flood? And who has seen something which is at the same time both consummated and narrowed, both fulfilled and diminished, both made small and magnified, both made full and made empty? And yet this is what has been done here, a thing has been at the same time both magnificently clothed and made almost naked and bare, the promise of God has been both fulfilled and yet cut short from almost all people. But for those for whom it has been fulfilled it has been fulfilled in righteousness which overflows.

33. *He who believes in Him will not be put to shame.* The Hebrew text reads: "He who believes shall not make haste." This can be reconciled by interpreting it to mean that he who believes in Christ is secure in his conscience and righteous and, as the Scripture says, "bold as a lion" (Prov. 28:1). And again, "Whatever befalls the righteous man will not disturb him" (Prov. 12:21), while, according to Prov. 28:1: "The wicked flee when no one pursues," and again in Is. 57:20: "The wicked are like the tossing sea, for it cannot rest." "There is no peace, says my God, for the wicked" (Is. 57:21). And in Ps. 1:4 we read: "The wicked are not so, but are

like chaff which the wind drives away," in Lev. 26:36: "The sound of a driven leaf shall put them to flight," and in Is. 30:15 ff.: "For thus said the Lord God, the Holy One of Israel, 'In returning and rest you shall be saved; in quietness and in trust shall be your strength.' And you would not, but you said, 'No! We will speed upon horses,' therefore you shall speed away; and, 'We will ride upon swift steeds,' therefore your pursuers shall be swift. A thousand shall flee at the threat of one . . ." And this is the meaning, that he who believes in Christ will not be in a hurry, will not flee, will not be terrified, for he fears nothing, he stands quiet and secure, established on the solid rock, as our Lord taught in Matt. 7:24. But he who does not believe in Him, even though he "makes haste," that is, flees, yet he cannot escape the tribulation and the anguish which beset him, and particularly the judgment. For this is the penalty of the damned, and their iniquity is without end, that they flee from God and yet cannot escape Him. This is what every evil conscience which has forgotten Christ does, as we read in Deut. 28:67: "In the morning you shall say, 'Would it were evening!' and at evening you shall say, 'Would it were morning!' because of the dread which your heart shall fear and the sights which your eyes shall see." "For the Lord will give you a trembling heart and a languishing soul" (Deut. 28:65).

Such is the horror and the flight of the hastening conscience, which is the very confusion of the conscience itself. For as Pliny says: "For no living creature is fear more confusing than for man." [24] How aptly therefore our translation agrees with the Septuagint, for when it reads: "He shall not be confounded," [25] it tries to point out the confusion and disturbance of the conscience which comes from terror and fear, so that there is no orderly thinking or planning left, but only a search for flight, which is, however, never found. It is like the confusion caused by the tumults of war; where fear and terror strike, each man runs here and there and is in a state of confusion. Such is the punishment of all who die, rather who suffer outside of Christ; they are so distraught that they do not know what to do.

---

[24] Pliny, *Natural History,* VII, 5.

[25] The Septuagint equivalent, *non confundetur* ("he shall not be confounded"), and the Hebrew equivalent, *non festinet* ("he shall not hasten"), are compared by Erasmus in his *Annotationes,* but he himself translates with *non pudefiet* ("he will not be ashamed").

Blessed Jerome, whom Lyra follows, says: " 'He does not make haste,' that is, the coming of the Lord does not seem near to him, as by contrast the Thessalonians were disturbed and terrified at the imminence of the day of the Lord, which is to say, the man who believes in Christ is not so weak-spirited that he immediately thinks that the day of judgment is at hand whenever some tribulation befalls him." I do not understand what this gloss is aiming at, although I do not reject it; but because there is no time, I will omit discussing it.

Another interpretation is also possible, which I myself once held, but it is a little too forced, that is, that he who believes in Christ, does not make haste with foolish zeal to pass judgment on others in the manner of the noonday demon and to excuse himself, but he thinks humbly, is teachable and capable of taking direction. For many in the fervor of a novice hasten toward heaven and toward righteousness and wisdom with too hot a zeal, which the devil has aroused in them, so that after the first run they are exhausted and useless, filled with disgust at every good effort and lukewarm and languid toward all good, for at the very beginning they were poured out like water. Thus, "An inheritance gotten hastily in the beginning will in the end not be blessed" (Prov. 20:21). And blessed Augustine in his book *On the Blessed Life* says: "What one begins with too great ardor often ends with great disgust." [26]

Likewise some are swift and eager to judge others, to teach others, to be heard by others, but slow to be judged, to be taught, or to hear. Not so the man who believes in Christ, but he is, as blessed James says (James 1:19): "Let every man be quick to hear, slow to speak." But the Jews on the contrary were unwilling to hear, because they were hastening in their heart, etc.

The Greek equivalent of the word *confundetur* does not have the characteristically Latin and specific meaning "he shall be confounded," as we have mentioned above in regard to confusion, or a disturbance; but rather the term *confundetur* means to blush or to be ashamed, and thus hastening and blushing with shame agree with each other because one who is ashamed hesitates to appear in public, he seeks an escape, and he hides. Thus they say: "Fall on us, you mountains" (Luke 23:30). Thus his confusion causes him to make haste, that is, to flee in terror. This the man who believes in

---

[26] This quotation has not been found in Augustine, *De beata vita,* nor elsewhere in his writings.

Christ does not do, for he is not confounded, nor does he blush with shame, for he is secure in Christ.

Therefore, both translations have the same meaning, but the Septuagint expresses the cause, while the Hebrew expresses the effect, as is frequently the case elsewhere. For hurried flight follows confusion and shame, because the person dreads to appear.

CHAPTER TEN

2. *They have a zeal for God, but it is not enlightened*

THIS is a prodigious statement, because it is the essential and sole opponent of faith, it resists obedience, it makes men stiff-necked and incorrigible, as is obvious in the case of heretics and schismatics. As if it were impossible for them to make a mistake, they stand firm and obstinate in their good intention, staking their entire salvation on the fact that they are carrying out their pious intention out of a zeal for God. Scripture very properly calls these men depraved or crooked in heart and corrupt in mind, even though they are not corrupt in the flesh or in bodily vices, but they are corrupt in spiritual matters, spiritually stubborn in their own ideas and good intention. Against these men the blessed Virgin is speaking when she says: "He has scattered the proud in the imagination of their hearts" (Luke 1:51). Today we have in this classification such people as popes and princes who neglect their own duties in their zeal for God and their pious intent and carry on business which does not concern them. Included also is every person who leaves a lower and good task which he ought to do and follows after a greater good, that is, something which has the appearance of a greater good, with the devil deceiving him all the time. For this zeal is the mind and head of the old serpent [1] and the cause of all discord and the source, the father of pride and stubbornness and unbelief, and, [appearing to act] for the sake of salvation, it is a hindrance to salvation.

Therefore we must take note that "to have an enlightened zeal for God" is to be zealous for God in pious ignorance and mental darkness, that is, to regard nothing as so grand and good, even if it appear to be God Himself and all His glory, so as not to be always fearful, always prepared to be led and turned and directed to a lesser kind of good. And thus without understanding, without feeling, without thinking, a person must be indifferent to all things,

[1] Cf. Rev. 12:9; 20:2.

whatever may be required, whether by God or by man or by some other creature. For such people do not know how to choose, but they expect to be chosen and called. Thus Ps. 18:26 reads: "With the chosen Thou wilt be chosen," but it does not say: "By him who chooses Thou wilt be chosen."

These people are gentle and teachable, as gold can be shaped and fashioned to every form. Hence in the Holy Scriptures there is a difference between "upright" and "good," as in Ps. 125:4 f.: "Do good, O Lord, to those who are good, and to those who are upright in their hearts! But those who turn aside into bonds" (that is, into their own crooked ways and away from uprightness) "the Lord will lead away with those who do evil," that is, the good that is vainly evaluated according to their crookedness. This expression "uprightness" is usually translated as "equity," where it is correctly interpreted, so that the right kind of righteousness is the right kind of good, but the wrong kind of righteousness, or self-righteousness, is a wrong and perverted good. Eccl. 1:15 says: "It is difficult to correct the perverse." Hence we read in Ps. 45:6: "Your royal scepter is a scepter of equity," or "of direction," that is, of uprightness. For "it directs the meek in judgment" (cf. Ps. 25:9), that is, those who know nothing, who do not direct themselves according to their own judgment and understanding. Therefore "to have an enlightened zeal" is to know nothing about that for which one is zealous. For to know that one does not know, this is the kind of knowledge according to which the Jews do not have zeal. For they know that they know. For the man who knows that he does not know is gentle, teachable, unresisting, ready to give his hand to all men.

6. *Who will ascend into heaven?* Moses in Deut. 30:12 does not use these words in this sense, but the apostle out of the abundance of his own feeling and spirit brings out the real kernel, teaching us with a strong argument that the entire Scripture deals only with Christ everywhere, if it is looked at inwardly, even though on the face of it it may sound differently by the use of shadows and figures. Hence he also says that *Christ is the end of the Law* (v. 4), as if to say that all Scripture finds its meaning in Christ. That this is absolutely true he proves by the fact that this word which is most alien to Christ yet signifies Christ. These statements are explained in different ways.

In the first place, as in the glosses, it is explained that the apostle is comparing the two kinds of righteousness with each other, so that he attributes works to the righteousness of the Law but the Word to the righteousness of faith. For work was required for the Law, but faith is required for the Word (the Law was required for the deed, so that we might know what ought to be done, but for faith the Word was required, not so that we might know but so that we might believe). Thus the first kind of righteousness depends on the work which has been done, but the second upon the Word which we believe. And what this Word is he describes when he says: *Do not say in your heart, "Who will ascend into heaven?"* (v. 6), as if to say that the Word which must be believed is nothing else than this: Christ died and is risen again.

This is the reason why these negative and questioning forms of expression include some very strong affirmatives, such as, "Who will ascend into heaven?" that is, you should most firmly say that Christ has ascended into heaven, and you will be saved. Do not doubt at all that He has ascended; for this is the Word which will save you. This is the way the righteousness of faith teaches. This is the way of the compendium, the short way to salvation. For the righteousness of the Law is long, winding, and circuitous, as is signified by the wandering of the Children of Israel in the wilderness.

In the second place, Stapulensis [2] interprets the passage in the sense that Moses in these words has introduced the righteousness of Christ and both His descent into hell and His ascension. Hence he translates it in this way: "However, concerning those things which are of faith he says this: 'Who will ascend into heaven?' This signifies Christ's descent. Or 'Who will descend into the abyss?' This signifies Christ's restoration from the dead." Thus he applies the expression "that is" or "this signifies" to the interrogatives "Who will ascend?" and "Who will descend?" and not to the expression "Do not say." But this interpretation is so labored and perplexing that one can get no sense from it.

In the third place, Erasmus [3] thinks there is no difficulty at all here and that the expositors have been laboring in vain. He thinks that the apostle understands Moses by these words to be curbing those people who do not believe unless they see the direct evidence, so that the words: "Who will ascend into heaven?" mean: "Do not say that Christ is not in heaven, even though you do not see Him, but only believe." For he who does not believe this and

2 In his commentary on this passage.

3 In his *Annotationes* on this passage.

says: "Who will ascend into heaven?" does the same as the man who denies that Christ is there or wants evidence for this faith.

But whichever interpretation it may be, the intent of the apostle is that the total righteousness of man leading to salvation depends on the Word through faith and not on good works through knowledge. Hence also in all the prophets God contends against nothing else than that they are unwilling to hear His voice, and through the prophets He has not commended good works but rather His words and His sermons. For example, in Jer. 7:21 ff. He says: "Thus says the Lord of hosts, the God of Israel: 'Add your burnt offerings to your sacrifices, and eat the flesh. For in the day that I brought them out of the land of Egypt, I did not speak to your fathers or command them concerning burnt offerings and sacrifices. But this command I gave them, "Obey my voice, and I will be your God, and you shall be my people."'" And in Is. 1:10 ff. He says, "Hear the Word of the Lord, you rulers of Sodom! Give ear to the teaching of our God, you people of Gomorrah! What to Me is the multitude of your sacrifices?" And He continues (v. 19): "If you are willing and obedient, you shall eat the good of the land." And at the end of the same book He says: "But to whom shall I look except to him who is poor and contrite in spirit and trembles at My word? He who slaughters an ox is like him who kills a man . . . he who makes a memorial offering of frankincense, like him who blesses an idol, etc. All these have chosen their own way" (Is. 66:2 f.).

Nothing but faith can accomplish this, for it puts out the eyes of all wisdom of the flesh, causing men to know nothing, to be prepared to be taught and led and to hear promptly and to give in. For God does not require a magnitude of good works but the mortification of the old man. And he is not mortified except through faith, which humbles our own feeling of self-importance and makes a person subject to that of another. For the whole life of the old man is concentrated in the feelings, mind, or wisdom and prudence of the flesh, just as the life of a serpent is in its head. And so when this head is crushed, the entire old man is dead. As I have said, what causes this is faith in the Word of God. This is not something which sounds forth from heaven only, but rather something which proceeds every day from the mouth of some good man, especially from a preacher. For this reason unbelievers are contentious and are always stumbling at the Word of faith. For where they ought to believe, they want to have it demonstrated to them. They always presume that they see a thing correctly and that others are in error.

For he who does not yield and always thinks that he is infallible is most assuredly a person in whom the old Adam and the old man still lives, and Christ has not yet risen in him.

Hence God hides this most precious obedience equally under great and lesser works, nor does He consider the difference between works, but only the value of obedience. Thus the prudence of the foolish always regards the work as more important than the Word and weighs and estimates the worth of the Word in terms of the worth and nonworth of the works. And where the work is lowly, it immediately regards and despises the Word as lowly. For the "prudence of the flesh" still lives which discerns between good and evil. It was born from the first sin from the tree of the knowledge of good and evil.

On the other hand, the prudence of spiritual men knows neither good nor evil but always looks to the Word and not to the work, and weighs and estimates the dignity of the work on the basis of the Word, where even if the work is the lowliest of all, yet this prudence values it as most precious, for he always puts the highest value on the Word.

By this trickery the ancient serpent deceived Eve, but not Adam; and to this day he is fooling all proud men. For he immediately called Eve away from the Word to works by saying: "Did God say, etc.?" Then when she had begun to look at the meagerness of her work, she also began to despise the Word. In the same way Saul also neglected the Word of God because of the great number of his sacrifices; thus to this day the work-righteous hope to have so much the greater salvation as they have done greater works, recognized as they are by that most certain sign of being unbelievers, proud, and contemptuous of the Word that they strive for quantity of works. For the man to whom the temptation of the great number of works comes, so that he despises little works and stands in awe of great ones, flees the small ones and pants after the great ones, this is the man who, together with the Jews and the heretics, stumbles at the Stone of Stumbling. For in his case Christ remains hidden under the lowly works which are commanded by the Word and leaves these men in their great works which the devil has suggested to them through the wisdom of the flesh.

Therefore we must give our childlike attention to the Word with all zeal, all our powers, all our wisdom, and with completely closed eyes. And whether the Word commands us to do something foolish or base or great or small, let us do it, measuring the work by the Word, and not the Word by the work.

The work-righteous can also be recognized by still another sign, namely, that they seize upon those works which among men are highly esteemed and which people admire. But as soon as people cease to admire them and to regard them as of little account, they immediately tire of them and grow lukewarm toward them, even the very people who have been doing them, so that it becomes apparent that they have not been seeking these works or even God in the works but rather their own ostentation in them. Thus they do not strive for works which are lowly and not esteemed among men, and yet it is these works alone that we should strive for when we act without the Word.

But this is what unlearned preachers are concerned about as they mislead the common people. They preach or read about the great works in the legends of the saints and inculcate and impress on them only these ideas. And when the unlearned people hear that such works are the real thing, they immediately strive to imitate them to the neglect of everything else—this is where so many promises of indulgences come from and so many permits for building and ornamenting churches and for multiplying ceremonies—and in the meantime they care nothing about what every person owes to God according to his calling.

And the pope and the priests who are so generous in granting indulgences for the temporal support of churches are cruel above all cruelty, if they are not even more generous or at least equally so in their concern for God and the salvation of souls, since they have received all they have as a free gift and ought to give it freely too. But "they are corrupt, they do abominable deeds" (Ps. 14:1), seduced themselves and seducing the people of Christ away from the true worship of God.

In this connection I once heard an amusing but most instructive story. A certain ignorant man heard a preacher of this kind, who shouted about examples men should follow and said that in memory of the example of Simeon Stylites in the *Lives of the Pillar Saints* [4] something great should be done for God. In order to ridicule the silly ideas of these "pulpit pounders" [5] and to let it be seen what fruits would follow if people would really obey these ravings, he

---

[4] *Vitae patrum*, I: *Vita S. Simeonis Stylitae*, 5, *Patrologia, Series Latina*, LXXVIII, 528.

[5] Luther sarcastically coins the word *ambonistae*.

decided, by the will of God and out of love for God, not to pass water. After continuing in this for several days, he began to grow ill unto death. When people tried to talk him out of his resolve, he gave them no hearing. But by another counsel of God, see how he was delivered from his decision. A very clever man, informed by the influence of God, came to him and exhorted him to keep on even more zealously with his intention, telling him: "You are doing the right and proper thing. Continue, my brother, as you have begun. For I, too, am going to do what you are doing to show my disdain and hatred for all my friends, for they are against me, just as yours are against you." Now when the man heard this, that his endeavor was thus despised and regarded as nothing among men, so that they said he did it out of hatred for them rather than love, he immediately came to his senses and said: "If they say I am doing this for this reason, I will not do it." This was the deadly ulcer in his heart, that he did it for the sake of men. And as soon as this was cut out, he became well. O what good advice he received, given only by God as the teacher, advice which touched his disease directly. Therefore the works of the saints are not to be preached in an absolute sense, that is, they are not to be commended to men in the sense that they should do exactly the same things, but the added advice should be given: "See here, he lived in his own station in such and such a way as an example for you, so that you in your station may do likewise, but not in such a way that you must do the same things to the neglect of your own station and by jumping over into his."

10. *With his heart man believes unto righteousness.* It is as if he were saying: "One does not arrive at righteousness by works, by wisdom, by zeal, but also not by riches and honors," even though many people today promise themselves release from their sins by paying two pennies. And many people want to appear righteous in their own eyes, because they know, read, or teach great things, or because they shine with great dignity and minister in sacred matters. But this is a new acquisition of righteousness opposed to, or above, Aristotle, who taught that righteousness is produced by actions, especially external and frequent actions.[6] But this civil righteousness is reprobate before God. But true righteousness comes into being by believing the words of God with the whole heart, as has been said above, Rom. 4:3: "Abraham believed God, and it was reckoned to him as righteousness." But this righteous-

[6] Cf. p. 152, n. 30, above.

ness of the philosopher, which is divided into distributive and commutative and finally general righteousness,[7] comes from blindness of the mind or from human wisdom which is concerned only with temporal matters in keeping with the method of dealing with such things, where it can happen that one person is in debt or under obligation to no one, another to a few, and another to many people. But in the case of the righteousness of God a man is indebted to everyone, for "he is guilty of all of it" (James 2:10). To his Creator, whom he has offended, he owes glory and the blamelessness of his life; to the creation he owes good use and cooperation in the service of God. Therefore he is not able to pay this debt unless he humbles himself in subjection to all of these elements, taking the lowest place, asking nothing for himself among all of these things. As the jurists say: "He who surrenders all his goods has made satisfaction." Thus he who gives up God and His creatures, even himself, and gladly and willingly goes into nothingness and death and of his own free will resigns himself to damnation, not believing that he is worthy of sharing in any other of these things, this man plainly has made satisfaction to God and is righteous. For he has retained nothing for himself, he has yielded all to God and His creatures. This takes place through faith, whereby a man makes his own mind captive to the word of the cross and denies himself and denies all things to himself, for he is dead to himself and to all things. And thus he lives only to God, "to whom all things live" (cf. Luke 20:38), even those that are dead.

And with his lips he confesses unto salvation. That is to say, that the faith which leads to righteousness does not arrive at its goal of righteousness, that is, salvation, if it does not arrive at confession. For confession is the principal work of faith by which a man denies himself and confesses God and thus he both denies and confesses to such an extent that he would deny his own life and all things rather than affirm himself. For in confessing God and denying himself he dies. For how can he deny himself in a more forceful way than by dying in his confession of God? For then he forsakes himself in order that God may stand and his confession of Him.

12. *He bestows His riches upon all who call upon Him.* A new expression! For he could have said "ready," "willing," or as the Law says, "merciful to them who cry unto Him to hear them"

[7] The basic discussion of these classifications is in Aristotle, *Nicomachean Ethics,* V.

(cf. Ex. 22:27, Joel 2:13, etc.). We read in Ps. 86:5: "For Thou, O Lord, art good and forgiving, abounding in steadfast love to all who call upon Thee." But the apostle wants to point out this, which he also does elsewhere, namely, that God gives to those who call upon Him even more than they request, so that, just as the request in comparison with the gift is poor and modest, so the one who makes the request could not even have contemplated such great gifts, to say nothing of requesting them. Thus we read in Eph. 3:20: "He is able to do far more abundantly than all that we ask or think," and above in Rom. 8:26: "We do not know how to pray as we ought," and in 2 Cor. 9:8: "God is able to make all grace abound in you." God, therefore, is rich as He hears us, but we are poor as we pray; He is powerful in His fulfilling, while we are weak and fearful in our asking. For we do not ask as much as He is willing and able to give, that is, we do not ask according to His power but far beneath His power and in accordance with our own infirmity. But He cannot give except in accord with His power. Therefore He always gives more than is requested. Thus He says: "Open your mouth wide, and I will" (not let mere drops fall but) "fill it" (Ps. 81:10), that is, "Ask as much as you can, and I will give more, because My giving is more powerful than the power of your petition." Thus "the Spirit helps us in our weakness" (Rom. 8:26) as we pray. Now this "being powerful" which is here posited of God, is not, as in logic, to be understood as the contingent and free power and ability of acting when and where one wishes. But in Greek it is the word δυναμένῳ,[8] that is, "to Him who is able." This has reference to that power which I spoke about above, "strength," or "powers," or "vigor," so that the meaning is: When God gives, He gives so strongly and boldly that we would not have been able even to imagine such things. For He is so powerful, that is, so strong and bold, that He gives more than our weakness asks. But he adds the words "according to the power" (in Greek δύναμιν) "by which He works in us," (Eph. 3:20), whereby he excludes the power of the flesh. For He does not work in us according to the power of the flesh, nor does He hear us on this basis, but rather according to His spiritual power. For this is the meaning of the words "beyond all that we think," which in Greek is νοοῦμεν, that is, "we comprehend," "we understand," from νοῦς, that is, "mind, understanding, judgment." For His way of hearing our prayers goes beyond all our understanding of it, that is, it is not as we have preconceived of it,

---

[8] Luther is thinking of Eph. 3:20 again.

or thought of it, or, as it seems, prudently chosen. For we choose in weakness and impotence, that is, the things which we ask are weak and impotent, if they were to be given to us, since they are only within the limits of our understanding, and thus also things which, being temporal, will immediately become tiresome. In the same way he says in Phil. 4:7: "The peace of God which passes all understanding" (that is, νοῦν), that is, to know, to understand, to comprehend, as we indicated above, "will keep your hearts and minds," that is, νοήματα, that is, what you feel and think through your mind or senses, when we say "your thoughts."

14. *But how are men to call upon Him in whom they have not believed?* All people who are of a proud mind, such as the Jews, heretics, and schismatics, arrogate to themselves these four qualities in this order. They are all deceived by the appearance of piety. For these four points are so interrelated that the one follows upon the other, and the last is the cause and antecedent of all the others, that is, it is impossible for them to preach unless they are sent; from this it follows that it is impossible for them to hear unless they are preached to; and from this, that it is impossible for them to believe if they do not hear; and then it is impossible for them to call upon God if they do not believe; and finally it is impossible for them to be saved if they do not call upon God. Thus the whole root and origin of our salvation lies in God who sends. And if He does not send, those who preach preach falsely; and this preaching is the same as not preaching, indeed it would be better not to preach. And they who hear, hear falsely, and it would be better not to hear at all. And they who believe them believe falsely, and it would be better not to believe. And they who invoke God, invoke Him falsely, and it would be better not to invoke Him. Since preachers of this kind do not preach, the hearers do not hear, the believers do not believe, those who call upon God do not call upon Him, and those who are to be saved are damned. Prov. 1:28: "Then they will call upon Me, but I will not answer." Ps. 110:2-3: "The Lord sends forth from Zion your mighty scepter." And then he goes on: "Rule," that is, be strong, "and your preaching will be effective in the midst of your foes!" But those men rule in the midst of their friends, because they attract them by flattery. And in Ps. 18:41: "They cried for help, but there was none to save, they cried to the Lord, but He did not answer them." Thus these people are images before God; they have ears, but they hear not; a mouth, and they speak not, etc. Why? Because they are not of God. For when God

sends forth His Word, "then there is power afoot" *(so geht's mit Gewalt)*, so that it converts not only friends and those who applaud it, but enemies and those who resist it.

Therefore above all it is necessary to see to it that he who teaches has been sent by God, as John was (cf. John 1:6). This is recognized if he proves through miracles and testimony from heaven that he has been sent, as in the case of the apostles, or if he proves that he has been sent later by some kind of heavenly authority and preaches in humble subjection to this authority, always prepared to stand under the judgment of it, and that he speaks the things which have been committed to him and not merely things which he has invented and which are pleasing to him. Thus we read in Zech. 13:3: "And if anyone again appears as a prophet, his father and mother who bore him" (that is, his religious superior and the church [9]) "will say to him: 'You shall not live,' (that is, you shall be condemned and excommunicated) 'for you speak lies in the name of the Lord'; and his father and his mother who bore him shall pierce him through when he prophesies." This is the sharp spear with which the heretics are pierced. For raised to a high position by the appearance of piety, they are preaching without the testimony of God and without an authority which has been confirmed by God, but only under their own power.

Thus we read in Jer. 23:21: "I did not send the prophets, yet they ran." And yet they dare to say: "We shall be saved because we call upon the name of the Lord; we call upon Him because we believe; we believe because we hear; we hear because we preach." But this they cannot say: "We preach because we have been sent." There, there they lie! Here is all that matters for salvation, and without this all the rest is false, even though they do not realize that it is false. Thus the apostle in Rom. 1:2 beautifully covers this subject, so that no one should think that the Gospel came into the world through man. First, because it was promised long before it came; it was not something newly discovered. Second, it did not come through only one person but through many, through prophets of God, and not only in oral form but also in the Holy Scriptures. A heretic, too, has to give this kind of testimony for his doctrine and heresy. He must show where it was previously promised and by whom. Then through whom it was handed down and finally in which scriptures it has been written, so that he may point to the

---

[9] Priest and church were commonly spoken of as the spiritual parents of the believers.

writings as witnesses. But they are not concerned about these things and foolishly say: "We have the truth, we believe, we hear, we call upon God" — as if it were sufficient proof that something is from God because it seems to certain people that such is the case, and as if it were not necessary that God confirm His Word and cooperate by signs that follow it and promises and prophets which precede.

Therefore the authority of the church has been established, as to this day the Roman church still holds it. They preach safely who preach the Gospel without any defects from outside.

For the word which heretics preach produces great satisfaction [10] for them, because it sounds the way they want it to. But they want the greatest piety (as it seems to them). And thus their own thinking stands unchanged and their own will unbroken. For the Word does not come to them contrary to or above what they think but in accord with what they think, so that they are already equal to the Word or even its judges. But the fact is that if the Word of God comes, it comes contrary to our thinking and our will. It does not allow our thinking to stand, even in those matters which are most sacred, but it destroys and eradicates and scatters everything, as Jer. 23:29 (cf. also 1:10) says: "Is not My Word like fire, says the Lord, and like a hammer which breaks the rock in pieces?" Hence it is an infallible sign that one really has the Word and carries it in himself, if he finds nothing in himself which pleases him, but only what is displeasing, that he is sad at all he knows, says, does, and feels, and finds pleasure only in others or in God. On the other hand, the clearest sign that the Word of God is not in a certain person is if he finds pleasure in himself, and rejoices in what he says, knows, does, and feels. The reason for all this is that the Word of God "breaks the rock in pieces" and destroys and crucifies whatever in us is pleasing to us and does not allow anything to remain in us except that which is displeasing, in order that it thereby may teach us to have pleasure, joy, and confidence only in God, and outside ourselves happiness and pleasure in our neighbor.

15. *How beautiful are the feet of those who preach the Gospel of peace.* In the first place, they are called "beautiful" because of their purity, since they do not preach the Gospel for personal advantage or empty glory, as is now the case everywhere, but only

[10] Luther's word *suaveplacentia* is perhaps a Latinization of the German *Wohlgefallen*.

out of obedience to God as well as for the salvation of the hearers.

In the second place, the term "beautiful" according to the Hebrew idiom has more the meaning of something desirable or hoped for, something favored or worthy of love and affection, in German *lieblich und genehm*. And thus the meaning is that the preaching of the Gospel is something lovable and desirable for those who are under the Law. For the Law shows nothing but our sin, makes us guilty, and thus produces an anguished conscience; but the Gospel supplies a longed for remedy to people in anguish of this kind. Therefore the Law is evil, and the Gospel good; the Law announces wrath, but the Gospel peace. The Law says (as the apostle cites in Gal. 3:10): "Cursed be everyone who does not abide by all things written in the book of the Law and do them." But no one continues in them to do them, as it is written in the same place: "For all who rely on works of the Law are under a curse." But the Gospel says: "Behold the Lamb of God, who takes away the sin of the world" (John 1:29). The Law oppresses the conscience with sins, but the Gospel frees the conscience and brings peace through faith in Christ. Hence we also read above (v. 5): "Moses writes that the man who practices the righteousness which is based on the Law shall live by it." It is as if the apostle were saying: "But no one does this righteousness, and therefore no one shall live by it." Hence we read again in Gal. 3: 11-12: "Now it is evident that no man is justified before God by the Law; for 'he who through faith is righteous shall live'; but the Law does not rest on faith, for 'he who does them shall live by them.'" And above in Rom. 2:13 he has stated: "For it is not the hearers of the Law who are righteous before God, but the doers of the Law who will be justified," as if to say that in God's eyes all those who are outside faith only are hearers. For "he who does them shall live by them," but no one does it; otherwise what need is there of faith?

In the expression "of those who preach the Gospel" the Spirit expresses something more than we have indicated in the gloss, and that is the fact that "peace" and "good things" are not the kind of things which are visible according to the world, for they are so hidden that they are not proclaimed except through the Word and are not grasped except through faith. For these good things and this peace are not exhibited to the senses but announced by the Word and can be perceived only by faith, that is, without personal experience until the future life comes.

And the term "good things" refers to the granting of the gifts of grace, and "peace" to the removal of evils; therefore he places the term "peace" first and then "good things." Thus these good things are under the cross, for no man is able to possess this kind of peace and good things, unless he has renounced the peace and good things of the world and is willing to suffer for his faith in the midst of the evils and tribulations of the world and his own conscience.

But what is meant by the term "feet"? According to the first interpretation the term refers to the attitude and the devotion of those who preach, which must be free of all love of money and glory.

But according to the Hebrew, which is more accurate, although the term "feet" can be taken in a literal sense, namely, that the coming of preachers of good things is something desirable for those who are tortured by sins and an evil conscience, yet more correctly the term can signify their very words themselves or the sound and the syllables, the pronunciation of the words of those who preach, for their voices are like feet or vehicles or wheels by which the Word is carried or rolled or it walks to the ears of the hearers. Hence he says: "Their voice goes out through all the earth" (Ps. 19:4). If it went forth it must have feet. And again: "His Word runs swiftly" (Ps. 147:15). Whatever runs has feet: the Word runs, therefore the Word has feet, which are its pronunciations and its sounds. This must be the case, for otherwise Is. 32:20 would be absurd: "Happy are you who sow beside all waters, who let the feet of the ox and the ass range free." And Ps. 91:13 reads: "You will tread on the lion and the adder, the young lion and the serpent you will trample underfoot." This is not done except through the Word. For while the hearer sits quietly and receives the Word, the "feet" of the preacher run over him, and he crushes him to see whether he can make him better. Thus Micah 4:13 reads: "Arise and thresh, O daughter of Zion, for I will make your horn iron and your hoofs bronze; and you shall beat in pieces many peoples." The term "threshing" here is understood in the sense of the ox treading out the grain with his feet. Thus the feet of the church as it preaches are voices and words by which it cuts and shakes up the people and "beats them to pieces." And the church does this with nothing else than with words and voices. But they are "beautiful" and desirable to those whose consciences are pressed down by sins.

Therefore we have these two sets of contrary terms: Law — sin.

The Law shows up sin and makes man guilty and sick; indeed proves him worthy of being damned. Gospel—grace. The Gospel offers grace and remits sin and cures the sickness unto salvation.

16. *But they have not all obeyed the Gospel.* This refers to what has been said above, so as to confirm those four points which were mentioned in their order. First, the statement which he has made "Everyone who calls upon the name of the Lord will be saved" (v. 13) is pertinent here. For since "they have not all heeded the Gospel," why do they presume to call upon the name of the Lord according to the word of the prophet? And how will they all call upon Him in whom they have not believed? And that they have not believed is evident, because Isaiah says: *Lord, who has believed our report?* Second, he also proves this statement: "How are they to believe in Him of whom they have never heard?" (v. 14) by saying: *Faith comes from what is heard* (v. 17), as if to say: "If they do not hear, they cannot believe," which the same Isaiah passage declares. Third, he also confirms this statement: "How are they to hear without a preacher?" (v. 14). For hearing comes through the Word of Christ. Fourth, the same applies to the statement "how beautiful," as we have already shown sufficiently.

The expression "what has been heard" *(auditus)* is used here as the equivalent of "hearing" *(auditio)* (that is, the perception of the word which has been heard), which we might call its "sound" or its "voice." And he uses the expression "our report" *(auditui nostro)*, because they had only received it. For he is speaking about the Gospel which sounds and is heard or has been heard throughout the world, so that the meaning is very clear: "Lord, who has believed this which we have now heard spoken and preached throughout the world, or what is now being heard?" And he expresses it this way for a very special reason, for he could have said: "Who has believed the Gospel?" inasmuch as the apostle says in this passage: "They have not all heeded the Gospel." But he uses this expression here to show that the Word is the kind of thing which no one can grasp unless it is received by hearing and by faith. The Jews were offended at this, since they were striving for signs and miracles.

19. *Those who are not a nation, a foolish nation.* These are words of grace, that is, they have been spoken to commend grace, because God saves no one but sinners, He instructs no one but the foolish and stupid, He enriches none but paupers, and He makes alive only the dead; not those who merely imagine themselves to

be such but those who really are this kind of people and admit it. For it really was a fact that the Gentiles were not the people of God and were a foolish nation, so that, being saved without any merits or zeal of their own, they might acknowledge the grace of God.

But the proud who trust in their own merits and wisdom become very angry and grumble because to others is given free when they are undeserving what they themselves sought with such great zeal. As Christ expresses it in the Gospel in the parable of the older son who turned away from his prodigal brother and did not want him to come in, and also in the parable of those men who when they had received the denarius for the whole day's work complained because the master treated the last comers equally with the first. But the really "foolish" ones are those who are presumptuous only about themselves and do not rejoice over the salvation of others. And by the same token they prove that they are seeking God not for the sake of God but for their own sake, that is, because of the love of concupiscence and their own comfort (that is, impurely) and they are even proud of this impurity and loathsomeness of theirs, that is, they are twice as loathsome as the people whom they despise. For if they were really seeking God, they would not look down on the salvation of others but would rejoice in it and find pleasure in it, because they would see that they pleased God, and His pleasure must be desired more than anything else. But in contrast to their vain estimation of their own merits *Isaiah is so bold as to say: "I have been found by those who did not seek Me, etc."* (v. 20). It is as if He were saying: "I became known to them through My grace, and not by the zeal or merits of anyone. Then why do you presume that your merits are so great that by them you must find Me?"

There was once a hermit [11] of this kind who, when he saw a robber being taken up into heaven, indignantly returned to the world. And there was another hermit who said to a robber who repented and said that he wished he could be like him: "Very good, you can wish for that, and would that you were." And he was damned. And then there was that nun who was dying. When she heard the people who were standing around her bed praise her, she began to count on her fingers the day of her death, on which

---

[11] The two stories here told of hermits are found in *Speculum exemplorum.* In the same source a story follows concerning a nun who went to hell, but the details are somewhat different from those of the story Luther tells here.

her saint feast would be celebrated. It is true: "Whoever exalts himself will be humbled" (Matt. 23:12). Therefore all of these things have been spoken, written, and done in order that the arrogant pride of men might be humbled and the grace of God commended, so that "he who glories may glory not in his own progress but in the mercy of God" (cf. 1 Cor. 1:31).

For what will a proud man answer, a person who has done many things in his lifetime, if God prefers a little married woman to him and says: "Look, she has served Me only by bearing children; [12] and I regard this work of hers as more than yours, and it is pleasing to Me"? What will he answer? For all of our works have only so much value as they have before God. Now He can regard them as utterly vile and meager, or on the contrary as numerous and very great. Does this mean we should not do good works? Certainly not. But they must be done in humility, and then God will not disregard them. Therefore we have such remarkable fools today, who in their own eyes at least, are piling up many good and grand works, thinking that they must be good because they have been accompanied by so much labor, are so numerous, and seemed good to them. But it is in vain. Only the works of humility are good. And this they are quick to ignore.

16. *Who has believed our report?* Quite frequently Scripture, or rather the translator, uses the term "hearing" *(auditus)* or "seeing" *(visus)* in place of "that which was heard" or "that which was seen," as we have pointed out in the gloss. And this is done first because the things which are announced are invisible and perceptible only by hearing and by faith. Second, and more appropriately, because the Word of God is very good in itself, but as it is spread abroad to men, it is treated in different ways, even though it is not diverse in itself. For it is life to the good, death to the evil; it is a good thing to good men and an evil thing to evil men.

Now, this differentiation applies to the Word only while it is preached and heard. Therefore to the righteous it is something they wish to hear, and they grieve and are amazed that the godless do not hear it as a good word, and they say: "Who has believed the report which we have heard?" that is, that most wonderful message, which we hear and believe; why do not other men also believe it?

[12] Cf. 1 Tim. 2:15, a passage cited often also by Augustine, e. g., *De Trinitate*, XII, 7, 11, *Patrologia, Series Latina*, XLII, 1004.

CHAPTER ELEVEN

1. *I myself am an Israelite.*

HE has established what is less important in order to prove that which is more important, that is, he has argued from the lesser to the greater. For if God had rejected His own people, He surely would have rejected the apostle Paul, who with all his strength had contended against God. But now, in order that God might demonstrate that He will not reject His people, He has taken up even that man who had lost hope, proving thereby how firm His predestination and election is, so that He cannot be impeded even though there is such great despair. Thus he rightly adds the words: *God has not rejected His people whom He foreknew* (v. 2), as if to say: "He has proved this by my example, for He did not reject me; therefore much more He has not rejected others, who have not gone as far away from Him as I had."

4. *I have kept for myself.* They are called a "remnant" from the fact that they were left over, for God kept them for Himself. In this word we see a marvelous commendation for His grace and election. For God does not say: "They remained," although this is true, to be sure, but this act of remaining was not the act of those who remained but of God who kept them, that it might be a matter not "of man's will and exertion, but of God's mercy" (Rom. 9:16). By the same expression indeed He indicates indirectly that He Himself is the author of the reprobation of the others, just as He Himself drove Israel into the Babylonian exile in their time. For the meaning of the expression "I have kept for Myself" is: "Although I myself drove out all of them, I kept for Myself seven thousand men." He does not say: "When all were driven out, there remained, or when Nebuchadnezzar or the devil carried them all away, he left Me seven thousand," but rather: "I myself kept them back, while I took the others away," in order that it might be established firmly that "The potter has the right over the clay, to make out of the same lump one vessel for beauty and another for menial use"

(Rom. 9:21); again: "I will have mercy on whom I will have mercy" (9:15).

Bowed the knee to Baal. Baal was an idol who was worshiped by rites with which I am unfamiliar, except for the fact that the Book of Kings [1] tells us that he was worshiped by kissing of the hands, dancing around the altar, and cutting the skin with knives and lances. Yet the same passage expressly states that they did these things with a pious intent and under the pretext and with the zeal of the worship of the true God of Israel. Thus for this reason Ahab called Elijah the troubler of Israel,[2] because the latter seemed to be working against the worship of God by impeding them. But also in Hos. 2:16 the Lord says that He had been called Baalim by these people: "In that day she will call Me, 'My husband,' and no longer will she call Me, 'My Baal.'" Thus they worshiped the true God, but under a superstitious rite and name, and this was forbidden them in the command that they should not make for themselves any graven image or picture.[3] But misled by foolish zeal, they thought that a graven image was forbidden only if it was the image of a strange god, but if they attributed it to the true God and worshiped it under His name, then they were acting correctly. And as a result of this zeal they killed the prophets as ungodly for saying that any kind of image was forbidden, and all this with a pious intent and out of zeal for God.

Moreover, through the worship of Baal there was depicted a monstrous form of righteousness and superstitious piety which prevails widely to this day. By means of this the Jews, heretics, and monks, that is, arrogant individualists,[4] worship the true God according to their own ideas with most ridiculous zeal; with their excessive piety they are worse than the most ungodly, that is, for the sake of God they are the enemies of God, and for the sake of fearing God they come to despise Him, for the sake of piety they become impious, for the sake of peace, disturbers of peace, for the sake of love and holiness, jealous and profane, and for the sake of humility they become proud. Now the name "Baal" means "man." Hence the term "Beelzebub" means "Lord of the flies," and the term "Beelphogor" "Lord of the corpse," "man," I say, that is,

---

[1] Cf. 1 Kings 18:26-28.

[2] 1 Kings 18:17.

[3] Cf. Ex. 20:4; Lev. 26:1; Deut. 5:8.

[4] Cf. pp. 271 and 337 above.

a hero, a leader, the head man, a prince, the commander, an important person. Here is a case of the opinionated piety of an obstinate mind and the religious wisdom of a stiff neck, which, set up as head by itself and for itself, follows itself on the way of God; it is its own teacher toward God, righteousness, salvation, and all good things; it refuses to bow the neck to true obedience, never hearing the word of the true teacher, contemptuous of God and of all who speak, act, or rule in His name, whom it ridicules and persecutes as fools and errorists, indeed, as idiots.

Hence this idol of the heart is worshiped as a sign of the true God and as truth and righteousness itself. How? By kissing the hands, for example; that is, by a complacent satisfaction with their own works and a high opinion of their own righteousness; then their zeal and their inventiveness take up dance and exult and rejoice; and finally they cut themselves with knives and lances, that is, each accuses himself with words of humility and penitence and says: "O wretched sinner that I am! I am not worthy to see heaven. Have mercy on me, O God, etc." Each man occupies himself before men with grand works and acts of righteousness, and the more he hopes that these works will be well regarded by God and men, the greater is his fervor in doing them. For if he knew that they were going to be held in contempt, he would not do them; so great is his pride and his vain imagining. He cannot believe that these works might be regarded as "a polluted garment" (Is. 64:6), lest he be forced to feel and act on the same level with sinners, which is what he flees and hates with all his might.

5. *So too at the present time there is a remnant.* In Greek it reads: "So too at the present time there is a remnant according to the election of grace." The meaning is that just as in those days there was and could be found a remnant, while the rest perished, so also today a remnant exists and can be found according to the election of grace: so that the expression "there is" is to be related to the term "at the present time," as if he were saying that just as in those days, so also now there is a remnant, and in both times God has kept for Himself some people according to the election of grace. For he explains the expression "I have kept for Myself" by using the term "according to the election of grace." For as I have said above, "I have kept" includes, rather, explains, the election and commends grace.

7. *The elect obtained it.* The term "election" here is used in the passive and collective sense, as equivalent to "the elect." This

corresponds to Gen. 12:2, where God says to Abraham: "I will bless you and you will be a blessing," and to Is. 19:24-25: "In that day Israel will be . . . a blessing in the midst of the earth, whom the Lord of hosts has blessed," and to Is. 65:8: "As a kernel is found in the cluster, and they say, 'Do not destroy it, for there is a blessing in it.'"

8. *God gave them a spirit of stupor.* The word *compunctio* ("stupor") is used in two senses. One is salutary, in the sense of Ps. 4:5: "The things you say in your hearts, be sorry for them *(compungimini)* upon your beds." This makes a man displeased with himself and pleased with all other things, in keeping with the statement in Titus 1:15: "To the pure all things are pure." The other sense is detestable. It causes a man to be pleased with himself and displeased with everything else, in keeping with the statement: "To the corrupt nothing is pure; their very minds and consciences are corrupted" (Titus 1:15). The cause of both of these conditions is the light of the Spirit. When it is absent the one thing occurs; when it is present, the other. For when a man knows himself, he does so only when God gives him light; and without God he does not know himself and therefore is not displeased with himself.

The word "spirit" in this context must not be taken in the sense of some created or infused spirit, but in the sense of the soul itself and the will of man, as we read in 1 Cor. 2:11: "For what person knows a man's thoughts except the spirit of the man which is in him?" And in another place we read (Matt. 27:50): "He yielded up His spirit," that is, He yielded up His soul, and (Eccl. 12:7): "The spirit returns to God who gave it," and in Ps. 104:29: "When Thou takest away their spirit, they die," and in Gen. 6:17: "In which is the breath of life."

The apostle is quoting from Isaiah but adds from his own storehouse the beginning and the end, and the middle part he treats according to the sense and not the words, as has been pointed out in the gloss, so that he says: "God gave them a spirit of stupor, eyes that they should not see and ears that they should not hear, down to this very day."

9. *Let their feast become a snare.* This word "snare" is the divine Scripture itself when it is understood and taught in a deceitful way, so that under the appearance of pious learning the souls of the deceived and the simple are subtly ensnared. We hear of this in Ps. 91:3: "He has delivered me from the snare of the

fowler," that is, from the insidious teaching of the doctors who hunt the souls of the unstable and the wandering. Thus blessed Augustine in his *Confessions* [5] describes Faustus the Manichaean as a great snare of the devil. The word "trap" in this passage can be taken in the sense of a "deception," or more properly a "hunt," a trap whereby animals are caught. And although in the Greek the apostle does not add the words "unto them," yet in the psalm the term is used with great exactness, so that the meaning is that from the same feast, the same Holy Scripture, one man catches death, another life, one man honey, another poison, just as from the same rose, or flower, the spider collects venom and the bee honey. Thus nothing must be touched with such great fear and so little presumptuousness as the Word of God, because it immediately catches those of proud mind and traps them and makes them stumble, to be sure, in an imperceptible manner, often under the loveliest appearance, not by a fault of its own but because of presumptuous pride.

But it is a "pitfall" because those who have been caught continue to stumble without ceasing. For they are trapped in those things which they understand falsely; for they cling to these ideas and find pleasure in them and thus are willingly captured by them, but they do not know it. But they stumbled in those things which are presented to them as the truth, and they turn away from them, or if they cannot escape from it, they corrupt it and deny that it is so understood. Thus it is a "snare" because they do not know it, a "trap" because they want to accept as true only that which seems true to them, a "pitfall" because they turn away from the truth when it is thrown up to them and when it runs counter to their own thinking. As we read in another Psalm (35:8): "Let the snare which he knows not come upon him, and the trap which he has hidden ensnare him."

Thus every arrogant heretic is first caught by his ignorance of the truth; for when he despises this, he is already in the snare. Then he accepts what seems to him to be true; and he is trapped again, because he smugly walks through life as if he were free beyond the snare and the trap. Finally he stumbles against everything which goes contrary to him and thus turns off his hearing. And now he becomes indignant and filled with zeal for his notions, harassing, destroying, and injuring his opponents. And thus he gets the "recompense" he deserves.

[5] *Confessions*, V, 3, *Patrologia, Series Latina*, XXXII, 707.

Then finally their eyes become blurred, so that even though all others are seeing, they themselves are in no way moved to see anything, and while all others stand straight they remain curved in on their own understanding.

11. *But through their trespass salvation has come to the Gentiles.* That is, salvation to be sure has come to the Gentiles by the fall of the Jews, in order that their fall might not entirely be barren of fruit and an evil thing without any good; since for the saints all things work together for good, how much more in the case of Christ and God do evils work out for good! Indeed evils serve the good in greater measure when God is at work, so that the evil works not only for the good of others but also for the good of him who has the evil. For thus their fall was the salvation of the Gentiles, and this is not the ultimate purpose, but rather that those who had fallen might emulate the good of those who had risen.

For this is the final remedy of a dutiful father, that when he has warned his son by precept and command and even punished him and the son has not benefited, he begins to give the son's inheritance to another while the son looks on, in order that when the son sees this he may be terribly grieved and eagerly rushes upon it in order to get it for himself. Thus God willed that the fall of the Jews should be of benefit to them, while at the same time He caused it to benefit the Gentiles, so that He might provoke the Jews when they would see that they themselves had fallen and that they had been deprived of that grace by which the Gentiles were now adorned.

The same thing happens (and this is the moral interpretation) when God allows a man to fall into mortal sin, so that having fallen he may finally recognize his loathsomeness, while previously he appeared in his own eyes to be more virtuous than others.

13. *I magnify my ministry.* How does he magnify his ministry? By glorying in the fact that even though the Jews have fallen, yet he is announcing to the Gentiles the riches of Christ. For he seems to be reproving the Jews for receiving nothing and diminishing themselves and making themselves sinners, whereas through his ministry the Gentiles had been made rich. Therefore if such great good had come to the Gentiles through his ministry, whereas it was taken away from the Jews, by this action he is surely proving the greatness of his ministry. But he does not glorify it in such a way that he brings pleasure to himself thereby, but he does it for the salvation of others, so that the Jews, when they hear that they have fallen and that the Gentiles have been made rich and have accepted

their riches, might be stimulated to seek the riches of the same ministry. But they would not be so stimulated if he said that he had ministered something worthless to the Gentiles or that the Jews had lost nothing.

And this is obvious from the fact that a person is permitted to glory as long as it is done for the benefit of others, for example, out of brotherly love, in seeking not one's own vain pleasure but the welfare of others.

In the second place, he is saying this particularly for the reason that although he himself was a Jew, yet he says nothing but evil and condemnatory things about them, and even though he was not a Gentile, yet he predicates nothing but glorious and enriching things about them; the latter he exalts and praises their gifts, the former he disparages and deplores the condemnation which has come upon them. His answer is that he does this because of the requirements of his office, because as the apostle to the Gentiles he must not say that he has announced an insignificant and despicable message to them, lest no one accept him and his ministry bear no fruit among them. For who would appreciate a gift which you yourself do not think is worth giving? And not only this, but he also does it in order that the Jews through this might be provoked to jealousy so that he might gain a double fruit for his ministry, whereby the Gentiles multiply because of the excellence of the good things shown by his ministry and the Jews because of the multiplication of the Gentiles are also provoked to the same things by their desire to possess those good gifts.

Therefore he said: *Now I am speaking to you Gentiles*, that is, to your glory, because you have been enriched. But he is not permitted to say this to the Jews, lest they be offended even more.

16. *If the firstfruit.* The Latin word *delibatio* is here used for the Greek ἀπαρχή, that is, "firstfruit," or that which is offered from the first and best of the crop. And this is a more apt and fitting way to describe the meaning of the apostle than the term *delibatio*. It is as if he were saying: If the apostles are holy people who have been taken from among the Jews as the firstfruits and as the most precious part, as it were, then the whole nation, since they are of the same stock and nature, must not be despised because of their unbelief.

20. *Do not become proud.* The word *sapere* ("to be of a mind to"), which is the equivalent of the Greek φρονεῖν, is translated

by our translator[6] with remarkable inconsistency. For earlier in
chapter 8:5 he translated the concept both *sapiunt* and *sentiunt*.
In the same chapter, v. 6-7, the expression *sapientia carnis* ("wisdom of the flesh") is the equivalent of *prudentia carnis* ("wisdom
of the flesh") and *prudentia spiritus* ("wisdom of the spirit").
In this chapter 11:25 he uses the word *sapere* again, and likewise
in the following chapter, 12:3: "I bid everyone among you not to
think *(sapere)* of himself more highly than he ought to think
(sapere), but to think *(sapere)* with sober judgment." But the meaning of this word is something else than what is commonly called
sapientia (or in Greek σοφία), and *prudentia*, which in Greek is
called εὐβουλία or προμήθεια. Its proper meaning is to be wise with
a certain complacency, hence in the Greek the meaning is sometimes "to be wise," sometimes "to glory," and sometimes "to
exult." Therefore it is more often referred to the emotions rather
than the intellect. It is commonly applied to people who "think
themselves to be something which they are not" (Gal. 2:6; 6:3).
Hence φρόνησις means a complacency of this kind; and φρόνημα,
the sentiment itself or the act of this φρόνησις; and φρόνιμος, the
person who feels this way. Hence if we should translate in a uniform manner, we would do better to use *sentire* "to feel" in the
sense of understanding with the mind. In popular speech we say
"what seems good" *(bonum videri)*, in German *gutdünken*, which
is commonly said of the proud and sometimes is taken in a good
sense, as when we say: "I feel" *(sentio)* or "I have in mind" *(sapio)*.
But it does not express the force of the Greek word, as is evident
here: "Lest you be wise in your own conceits" (v. 25), that is, lest
you be complacent in your thinking, feeling proud of yourselves.

22. *Note then the kindness.* On the basis of this passage we teach
that when we see the fall of Jews or heretics or others, we should
consider not those who fell but the work of God in them, so we may
learn to fear God by the example of the misery of others and in no
way be proud. For this is the noble teaching of the apostle, who
urges us to a consideration more of the one who works by his work
than to a comparison of ourselves with others.

In opposition to this many people are proud with marvelous
stupidity when they call the Jews dogs, evildoers, or whatever
they like, while they too, and equally, do not realize who or what
they are in the sight of God. Boldly they heap blasphemous insults
upon them, when they ought to have compassion on them and fear

---

[6] The Vulgate.

the same punishments for themselves. Moreover, as if certain concerning themselves and the others, they rashly pronounce themselves blessed and the others cursed. Such today are the theologians of Cologne,[7] who are so stupid in their zeal, that in their articles, or rather their inarticulate and inept writings, they say that the Jews are accursed. Why? Because they have forgotten what is said in the following chapter: "Bless and do not curse" (Rom. 12:14), and in another place: "When reviled, we bless; when slandered, we try to conciliate" (1 Cor. 4:12-13). They wish to convert the Jews by force and curses, but God will resist them.

25. *I want you to understand.* On the basis of this text it is commonly accepted[8] that the Jews at the end of the world will return to the faith, although the text is so obscure that unless one is willing to follow the authority of the fathers who explain the apostle in this way, no one would seem to be convinced of this purely on the basis of the text. But the Lord also agrees with this idea of the apostle in Luke 21:23-24, when He says: "For great distress shall be upon the earth, and wrath upon this people; and they will fall by the edge of the sword and be led captive among all nations; and Jerusalem will be trodden down by the Gentiles, until the times of the Gentiles are fulfilled," that is, as he says here: *until the full number of the Gentiles come in.* And Moses in Deut. 4:30-31, when he had prophesied that they must be led through all nations, followed by saying: "In the latter days you will return to the Lord your God and obey His voice, for the Lord your God is a merciful God." Likewise we read in Hos. 3:4-5: "For the children of Israel shall dwell many days without king or prince, without sacrifice or pillar, without ephod or teraphim. Afterward the children of Israel shall return and seek the Lord their God and David their king; and they shall come in fear to the Lord and to His goodness in the latter days." Again in Hos. 5:12: "I am like a moth to Ephraim, and like dry rot to the house of Judah." And again (5:15): "I will go and return to My place, until you are consumed and seek My face." Again, the Lord says in Matt. 23:38-39: "Behold, your house is forsaken and desolate. For I tell you, you will not see me again until you say, 'Blessed be he who comes in the name of the Lord.' " According to this interpretation, therefore, the meaning of the apostle is: "I want you to understand this mystery, brethren," that is, "Do not be proud; it is a holy secret why the Jews fell,

---

7 Cf. p. 289, n. 2, above.

8 Cf. W, LVI, 436, n. 25.

a secret which no man knows, namely, that the Jews who are now fallen shall return and be saved, after the Gentiles according to the fullness of their election have entered. They will not remain outside forever, but will return in their own time."

A very clear figure of this is Joseph, the symbol of Christ, who was sold by his brothers into Egypt (Gen. 37:28) and there elevated to the position of a ruler and in the end recognized unexpectedly by his father and brothers, as Genesis so beautifully puts it near the end of the book. So also the Jews who threw Christ out to the Gentiles, where He now has the position of ruler, will finally come back to Him, drawn by hunger for the Word, and they will receive Him among the Gentiles.

The apostle indicates this when he cites Isaiah in connection with the statement: *And so all Israel will be saved* (v. 26). In our version Isaiah reads thus in chapter 59:20: "And there shall come a redeemer to Zion, and to them that return from iniquity in Jacob." But they will not return from iniquity unless they are in it, as the Jews now are. For "impiety" or "iniquity", the Greek ἀσέβεια does not signify just any kind of sin, but a sin against the worship of God, that is, against faith, through one's own self-righteousness. In Hebrew this is called רֶשַׁע as in Eccl. 8:8: "Godlessness will not save the ungodly," that is, one's own righteousness (as he thinks) will not save a person, because it is not righteousness but ungodliness.

Furthermore, he adds the expression *when I take away their sins* (v. 27), which is not in Isaiah but is added by the apostle or brought in from other prophets. And this indicates the difference between the two testaments. For the former testament was one in which we increased sin. But the new testament is the one under which God takes away sin. Therefore he is trying to say: "This is the testament of the remission of sin," in which "He will banish ungodliness from Jacob," just as the other is the testament of the commission of sin, under which men were turned to ungodliness. Therefore Christ has not yet come to the Jews, but He will come, namely, at the Last Day, as the writers cited above show. Thus it is necessary that we interpret the apostle as speaking of the mystical coming of Christ to the Jews. In other places this word of Isaiah is clearly fulfilled in the physical coming of Christ. Therefore I said that the apostle speaks in an unclear way and we could not determine his meaning from the text if we did not believe the interpre-

tation of the fathers. Thus in our time "a partial blindness has be-
fallen Israel," but in that future day not a part but all Israel shall
be saved. Now only in part are they saved, but then all shall be.

Corollary

This term "mystery" is taken at this point in an absolute sense,
indicating that which is unknown, but not in the ordinary sense in
terms of the "figurative" or "literal" meaning, as when, for example,
we speak of the "mystical sense," where there is one meaning on
the surface and another in the depth. But this is a mystery in the
absolute sense, because it is hidden to all, namely, that the fullness
of the Gentiles is going to come in while certain Jews fall. He says
the same thing elsewhere, as in Rom. 16:25: "According to the
revelation of the mystery which was kept secret for long ages." And
also in Col. 1:26.

For this entire text has the purpose of persuading his people
to return. Therefore in order that the apostle may be understood
correctly, we must understand that his remarks extend over the
whole mass of the Jewish people and refers to the good among
them, both past, present, and future. Although some among them
are lost, yet the mass of them must be respected because of the
elect. Just as any community must be honored because of the good
citizens, even though they are less in number than the wicked ones.
Hence this one rule applies regarding the interpretation of Scripture,[9] namely, that it speaks at the same time about the good and
the wicked who exist in the one mystical body—for thus the Jewish people are a "holy mass" because of the elect, but "broken
branches" because of the lost; thus they are a "fulfilling" and a
"lessening"; likewise they are "enemies because of the Gentiles"
and at the same time "the well-beloved because of the fathers"—
the Scripture speaking all the time about the same people because
of the diversity found among them. This sounds as if the apostle
wished the same people to be considered both his personal friends
and personal enemies, while he still distinguishes between
persons, but asserts that they belong to the same mass. Therefore
he uses the term "mass," so that he may show that he is speaking
not of individual people but of the entire race, in which are many
unholy people.

28. *As regards the Gospel.* This term *enemies* in this passage is
taken in the passive sense, that is, they are worthy of being hated,

9 Cf. p. 155, n. 40, above.

and God hates them, and for this reason so do the apostle and all who are of God. This is clearly indicated by the antithesis *but they are beloved*, as if to say, they are hated and yet loved, that is, the mass is loved and hated; hated "as regards the Gospel . . . for your sake," that is, because you have been loved according to the Gospel, and thus they are hated as regards the Gospel; but yet they are beloved *for the sake of their forefathers*, that is, because the election adopts some from among them to this very day; therefore they are beloved because of the forefathers, because they, too, are friends.

29. *For the gifts of God are irrevocable.* This is a remarkable statement. For the counsel of God is not changed by either the merits or demerits of anyone. For He does not repent of the gifts and calling which He has promised, because the Jews are now unworthy of them and you are worthy. He is not changed just because you are changed, and therefore they shall turn back and be led again to the truth of the faith. Hence in the Greek we read ἀμεταμέλητα, that is, "God's gifts are irreversible, etc." Hence it is not a matter of our repentence, but of God, who repents of what He changes and destroys.

33. *O the depth of the riches and wisdom and knowledge of God.* "Wisdom and knowledge!" According to blessed Augustine [10] this is the correct distinction, because to wisdom pertains the contemplation of eternal things, but to knowledge the understanding of temporal things. Thus wisdom has been created to deal with those things which are not seen or perceived except by faith alone or a rapture into heaven.[11] But knowledge deals with those things which are outside of God and created. Therefore the wisdom of God is that wisdom by which He contemplates all things in Himself, before and beyond and within their coming into being, but the knowledge of God is that knowledge by which He knows things as they are; and thus it is called "the knowledge of sight."

[10] Augustine, *De Trinitate*, 15, 25, *Patrologia, Series Latina*, XLII, 1010.

[11] Cf. p. 287 above.

CHAPTER TWELVE

Summary: The apostle instructs the Romans both in the things which pertain to God as well as those things which pertain to our neighbor.[1,2]

1. *I appeal to,* which means "I ask you for the sake of that which is holy," in Greek, "I exhort," *you, therefore, brethren, by the mercies of God,* which you have received, *to present,* offer, sacrifice, *your bodies as a living sacrifice,* in a new life, *holy,* abstaining from sin so that the newly born life may not be pro-

[1] Having in the preceding chapters laid the "true foundation, which is Jesus Christ" (1 Cor. 3:11), as the firm rock on which the wise man builds (Matt. 7:24), and having also destroyed the false foundation, our own righteousness and merits, the sand on which the foolish man builds (Matt. 7:26), he now begins to build "with gold, silver, and precious stones" (1 Cor. 3:12). For before all the good works which make up the building, it is necessary to have the sure and faithful foundation upon which one may cause his heart to stand and to trust for eternity, so that, even if he builds nothing on it, yet he may have a building site (so to speak) ready for it. Against this the self-righteous contend, seeking by their good works to establish faithfulness in the conscience and then to satisfy themselves and to become secure, after they have done many things according to their own judgment. To do this is to make the foundation of sand and to cast Christ aside. The apostle in all his letters contends against this, so that this may not happen. For this passage is commonly explained in a superficial and slight fashion, that the "sands" are the riches of this world. But Christ is speaking in this passage about builders (that is, those who do good works), not about greedy and worldly people who destroy themselves rather than build. Therefore He describes as sand the good works which they seek as the foundation for their righteousness and the resting place of their consciences and the comfort of their heart, since Christ is the only foundation before all good works; for by free grace He gives the foundation, the rest for the conscience, and the confidence of the heart, coming ahead of all our satisfaction and building. Was there ever so foolish a builder as to try to build such a foundation? Do they not rather look for one already set in the earth or take a place which offers a foundation? Thus just as the ground without our effort offers a foundation, so Christ offers Himself as our righteousness, peace, and security of conscience without our efforts, so that then we may always build our good works on Him.

[2] Up to this point he has taught how to become a new man, and he has described the new birth which makes the new man (John 3:3 ff.). But now he is teaching concerning the works of the new birth which anyone who has not been made a new man does in vain and presumptuously. For being comes before doing, and suffering comes before being. Therefore the order is: becoming, being, and then working.

the face of the waters." And in Deut. 32:11: "Like an eagle that
stirs up its nest, that flutters over its young." And in Ps. 18:10:
"He ascended and flew, He flew upon the wings of the wind."
Hence blessed Bernard says: "When you begin to cease wishing
to become better, you cease to be good." [1] It is of no value for
a tree to grow green and produce blossoms, unless it also bears
fruit from the blossom. Therefore many die in the blossom stage.
For just as there are five stages in the case of the things of nature:
nonbeing, becoming, being, action, being acted upon, that is,
privation, matter, form, operation, passion, according to Aristotle,
so also with the Spirit: nonbeing is a thing without a name and
a man in his sins; becoming is justification; being is righteousness; action is doing and living righteously; being acted upon
is to be made perfect and complete. And these five stages in some
way are always in motion in man. And whatever is found in the
nature of man — except for the first stage of nonbeing and the last
form of existence, for between these two, nonbeing and being
acted upon, there are the three stages which are always in movement, namely, becoming, being, and acting — through his new birth
he moves from sin to righteousness, and thus from nonbeing
through becoming to being. And when this has happened, he lives
righteously. But from this new being, which is really a nonbeing,
man proceeds and passes to another new being by being acted
upon, that is, through becoming new, he proceeds to become
better, and from this again into something new. Thus it is most
correct to say that man is always in privation, always in becoming
or in potentiality, in matter, and always in action. Aristotle philosophizes about such matters, and he does it well, but people do not
understand him well. Man is always in nonbeing, in becoming,
in being, always in privation, in potentiality, in action, always
in sin, in justification, in righteousness, that is, he is always a sinner, always a penitent, always righteous. For the fact that he
repents makes a righteous man out of an unrighteous one. Thus
repentance is the medium between unrighteousness and righteousness. And thus a man is in sin as the *terminus a quo* and righteousness as the *terminus ad quem*. Therefore if we always are repentant,
we are always sinners, and yet thereby we are righteous and we
are justified; we are in part sinners and in part righteous, that is,
we are nothing but penitents. Likewise, on the other side, the

[1] Luther cites this statement of Bernard's repeatedly. Cf. p. 225 above and
W, I, 649, 18; III, 46, 41; IX, 107, 23.

ungodly, who depart from righteousness, hold a middle position between sin and righteousness, but with a contrary direction. For this life is the road to heaven or to hell. No one is so good that he does not become better, and no one so evil that he does not become worse, until at last we come to our final state. The apostle touches on this in a very effective way. He does not say: "Be transformed to the renewal," but *by the renewal,* or "through the renewal," or still better as it is in the Greek without a preposition: "Be transformed by the renewal of your mind." He adds the expression "by the renewal" so that he should not appear to be teaching through the expression "transformation" something of the transformation of an unstable mind or some renewal of an outward worship, but rather renovation of the mind from day to day, more and more, in accord with the statement in 2 Cor. 4:16: "Our inner nature is being renewed every day," and Eph. 4:23: "Be renewed in the spirit of your minds," and Col. 3:10: "You have put on the new man, which is being renewed."

1. *A living sacrifice.* The true sacrifice to God is not something outside us or belonging to us, nor something temporal or for the moment, but it is we ourselves, forever, according to the statement in Ps. 110:4: "You are a priest forever," and hence He has an eternal priesthood, Heb. 7:17, as Prov. 23:26 says: "My son, give Me your heart." And the apostle speaks of a "living" sacrifice to show the difference (as Lyra says [2]) from animal sacrifices which were formerly offered up dead. Blessed Gregory explains this in the same way.[3] But the better interpretation refers to the spiritual life, in the sense that it is to bring forth good. "In order that," as he says above, Rom. 6:6, "the body of sin may be destroyed." For the "body of sin" is dead before God. But the good works which are performed by polluted people are nothing, and thus he continues by adding the word *holy,* which Lyra interprets as "firm" and persevering, a pious but inept interpretation. For in Scripture the word "holy" is not used in the sense of something firmly established and inviolate, nor in the sense of something which is "without earth," as if the Greek ἅγιος ("holy") were derived from α ("without") and γη ("earth").[4] Such notions are dreams.

[2] The *Additio I* of Paul of Burgos is meant.

[3] Gregory, *Homily on Ezekiel,* II, 10, 9, *Patrologia, Series Latina,* LXXVI, 1069 f.

[4] This curious etymology seems to have enjoyed wide currency. It is quoted by Lyra and Reuchlin.

But rather the word "holy" means something separated, or set apart, kept away from the profane, something which is removed from other uses and applied only to holy purposes worthy of God, something dedicated, as in Ex. 19:10: "Consecrate the people today and tomorrow, and let them wash their garments, etc." And again Joshua 3:5: "Sanctify yourselves; for tomorrow the Lord will do wonders among you." And 1 Sam. 21:4 ff.: "If the young men are clean, especially of women, they shall eat. And David answered: 'Of a truth women have been kept from us; the vessels of the young men are holy,'" that is, clean and chaste. Then the text continues "'Now this way is defiled, but it shall also be sanctified this day.' And he gave them the holy bread." It is clear, therefore, that the word "holy" means the same as clean or chaste, separated, particularly the cleanness which is owed to God. Blessed Gregory in his *Homily on Ezekiel* says: "A living sacrifice is a body which is afflicted for the Lord, and it is called living sacrifice because it lives in virtues and is dead to vices; it is a sacrifice because it is already dead to this world and its depraved works; living because all the things it continues in are good." [5] Therefore the apostle uses the word "holy" in the sense of chaste, so that the bodies are not to be corrupted by dissipation, as he has said above in Rom. 6:19: "Yield your members to righteousness for sanctification," and in 1 Cor. 7:34: "That she may be holy both in body and spirit." In brief, then, "holy" is the same as "sacred," to be pure and clean before God, whereby it is different from the cleanness which is observed among men. Yet in a strange way there is a confusion about the difference between the holy and the sacred, between holiness and sanctification. Hence we are correct in German in saying *heilig* ("holy") rather than *rein* ("pure"). For it is nothing that we perform good works and live a pure life, if we thereby glorify ourselves; hence the expression follows *acceptable to God*. He says this in opposition to vainglory and pride which so often subvert our good deeds. For just as envy pursues someone else's happiness, so pride or vainglory pursue our own. Thus they become foolish virgins who have their lamps, that is, they are living holy lives, but they have no oil, because they are seeking only to please men. And it is more important to please only God than it is to be holy. For it is most difficult for those who have a reason, such as holiness, to be pleased with

---

[5] *Homily on Ezekiel*, II, 10, 19, *Patrologia, Series Latina*, LXXVI, 1069 f.

themselves not to be concerned about the displeasure of others and to be displeased with themselves.

Your reasonable worship. Lyra interprets this as discreet and moderate worship, so that a man does not destroy his natural body but only keeps it under subjection with regard to fleshly lusts. And although this is a good and wholesome observation, yet in this passage this is not the apostle's point. Indeed in the Greek he separates this expression from that which precedes it by using the article, saying: τὴν λογικὴν λατρείαν ὑμῶν, as if he wanted to give a reason why he has been saying that they should offer their bodies as a sacrifice, as if to say: "I am saying this to you because I am trying to teach you that you owe God a reasonable sacrifice, and not one of beasts, in keeping with the new law." For the word λογικός means "rational," just as ἄλογος means "irrational." And the word "worship" *(obsequium)*, or "service" (λατρεία) refers to the sacrifice itself or the actual ritual of this kind of living sacrifice. Thus he is trying to say: "Present your service which is reasonable, that is, your bodies as a living sacrifice."

2. *That you may prove what is the will of God, what is good and acceptable and perfect.* Some interpreters refer the word *good* to those who are beginning, *acceptable* to the advanced, and *perfect* to those who are perfect. And this is not a bad application. It can also be related to the three earlier expressions "living, holy, acceptable to God" (v. 1). It is the "good" will of God that we do good; the "acceptable" will that we live purely and abstain from sin; and "perfect" will that we should desire to be pleasing to God alone. But when the apostle says that the proving of this threefold understanding of the divine will comes from being transformed to a new mind, he is suggesting something even more profound than can be expressed in written words, something which can only be understood by experience. Therefore those "who are led by the Spirit of God" (Rom. 8:14) are flexible in mind and thinking. "The right hand of God leads them wonderfully" (cf. Ps. 45:4) where they neither think nor want to go, but above all thought. And when they are led in this way, the will of God seems to go against them sharply and displeasingly and almost desperately. However, in this leading they show themselves as humbly resigned and enduring all things in faith, and even when they may have been most harshly tested, they then begin to learn how good this will has been, even though hidden, and even misunderstood when it was being fulfilled. But the unbelievers "have spurned

the counsel" (Ps. 107:11) of God, because they act according to their own preconceived notion and want things done that way, nor are they willing to set aside their own ideas or to be transformed. Hence they do not "prove what is the good will of God," but they "are conformed to this world," since they rely only on their own feelings and experience. For faith itself transforms the thinking and leads us to acknowledge the will of God. Eph. 3:18 ff. expresses this same idea: "that you may have power to comprehend with all the saints what is the breadth and length and height and depth, that you may be filled with all the fullness of God." And it continues: "Now to Him who is able to do far more above that we think, etc."

For whenever God gives us a new degree of grace, He gives in such a way that it conflicts with all our thinking and understanding. Thus he who then will not yield or change his thinking or wait, but repels God's grace and is impatient, never acquires this grace. Therefore the transformation of our mind is the most useful knowledge that believers in Christ can possess. And the preservation of one's own mind is the most harmful resistance to the Holy Spirit. We shall prove this by some examples. When Abraham was ordered to go out of his country and did not know the place where he was to go, this was surely contrary to his thinking. Likewise when he was commanded to sacrifice his son, this required a most noble transformation of the mind, as Rom. 4:3 demonstrates; and the will of God concerning Isaac looked sharp, displeasing, and hopeless; and yet afterwards it was proved to have been the best possible, full of blessing, perfect. The same could also be exemplified by the cases of David and of the Virgin Mary. But it is necessary that each man have his own experience and carefully observe his own visitation. For this self-will is a dreadful impediment, indeed, as a result it disagrees with others and it makes a man resist his superiors and to be wise in his own conceits over against his superiors and those through whose words or work God wants to prove His will. Hence he follows with the words: *For I bid,* etc. (v. 3). For in the church God does nothing else but transform this mind, and His transformation they resist who are satisfied with their own thinking; they disturb everything and produce schisms and heresies. They are "men of corrupt mind," as he calls them in another place (2 Tim. 3:8).

And thus just as the wisdom of God is hidden under the appearance of stupidity, and truth under the form of lying — for so the

Word of God, as often as it comes, comes in a form contrary to our own thinking, which seems in its own opinion to have the truth, so it judges that the Word which is contrary to it is a lie, and so much so that Christ called His Word our adversary in Matt. 5:25: "Make friends with your accuser," and Hos. 5:14: "For I will be like a lion to Ephraim, and like a young lion to the house of Judah," that is, I will be contrary — so also the will of God, although it is truly and naturally "good and acceptable and perfect," yet it is so hidden under the disguise of the evil, the displeasing, and the hopeless, that to our will and good intention, so to speak, it seems to be nothing but a most evil and most hopeless thing and in no way the will of God, but rather the will of the devil, unless man abandons his own will and good intentions and submits himself in complete denial of his own righteousness, goodness, and truth. And if he will do this, then those things which previously were most evil to him, which displeased him very much and seemed lost to him, will now taste most sweet, will please him best, and be considered most perfect. Thus our Lord says to Peter (John 21:18): "When you were young, you girded yourself and walked where you would; but when you are old, another will gird you and carry you where you do not wish to go." A marvelous thing! Peter is led where he does not wish to go, and yet unless he willed it, he would not glorify God, but rather would be guilty of sin. Thus at the same time he is both willing and unwilling. Thus Christ in His agony perfected His nonwillingness (so to speak)[6] by a most fervent willingness. For God acts this way in all His saints, so that He makes them do most willingly what they most strongly do not will to do. Philosophers marvel at this contrary state of affairs, and men do not understand it. Therefore I said[7] that a person will never grasp this unless he learns to know it by experience. For if practical experience is necessary in law, which is a shadowy teaching of righteousness, how much more is it necessary in the case of theology! Therefore every Christian ought to rejoice most heartily when something is done which is diametrically contrary to his own thinking, and he ought to be in the greatest fear when it goes according to his own thinking. I say this not only with regard to the lusts of the flesh but also with our greatest acts of righteousness. For this reason the lawyers in our age give most dangerous advice when they persuade us to follow what they know to be righteous

[6] Cf. p. 333, n. 16, above.

[7] Cf. pp. 437 and 438 above.

according to laws. So Pope Julius was advised, and he was called blessed. So also Duke George. And almost the whole world is carried away in this error, cardinals, pontiffs, princes, just as in former times the Jews were when they opposed the king of Babylon.[8] All these people base their arguments on particular rights, therefore they come to no conclusion and thus perish. For God rules the world with universal righteousness, by which He accomplishes what ought to be done in all, by all, and through all; but those people are foolish and blind and appeal to their own righteousness. In this matter no jurist is of any use. For they all speak such stupid notions with boldness and foolish lack of wisdom that not even rustics would dare to speak such nonsense, for example, that even before God one man is righteous and another man is unrighteous, both by divine as well as by human right; and then they move on in all confidence with their notions of good intention and zeal for righteousness. Meanwhile not one of them realizes that this righteousness may be in only one single respect in a person who perhaps in all other respects, or at least in many respects, is unrighteous before God. In this case God must help him as if he were a righteous man, and meanwhile He must not recognize all his unrighteousness and prefer this one point of his righteousness to the entire mass of his iniquity. For example, when Duke George (in order that I may expound the meaning of Scripture in a practical way, so that you may make similar judgments on the basis of parallel accounts) was persuaded that he had followed the course of righteousness in Frisia, no one could be found who would say: "O great prince, your merits and the splendid merits of your whole people are not such that God with righteous divine justice cannot punish you through this rebellious and unrighteous man. Therefore be quiet and recognize in this evil the gracious will of God. Let His will be pleasing to you."[9]

In the same way someone should have advised Pope Julius: "Most Holy Father, the Roman Church of today is not of such a degree of holiness that it does not deserve even greater punishment than the Venetians are inflicting upon it. Be still, it is the will

[8] Cf. 2 Kings 24:20—25:1.

[9] The reference is to the difficulties Duke George of Saxony encountered in his attempts to subdue Count Edzard and to bring East Frisia under his control. He eventually (1515) sold East Frisia to Charles of Burgundy, later Emperor Charles V.

of God." But he said: "No, no. We must pursue justice." [10] Likewise someone should persuade our own bishop of Brandenburg: "Reverend Father, you too have often sinned in every way. Endure, I beg you, this particular injustice." [11] But you, Prince Frederick,[12] thus far you have been protected by a good angel, if you would only acknowledge it! My, what great wrongs have tempted you! What just causes could have made you go to war! But you have quietly endured, whether out of a simple confession of sin or perhaps from fear of an immediate loss.

This is the reason (if I may speak of myself) why even hearing the word "justice" nauseates me to the point that if someone robbed me, he would not bring me such grief. And yet the word is always sounding in the mouths of the lawyers. There is no race of men upon the earth who are more ignorant about this matter than the lawyers and the good-intentioners [13] and the intellectuals. For I in myself and with many others have had the experience that when we were righteous, God laughed at us in our righteousness. And yet I have heard men who dared to say: "I know that I have righteousness, but God does not notice it." That is true, but it is a righteousness only in one particular; but for this God cares nothing. Therefore the only complete righteousness is humility, which subjects everyone to everyone else and thus gives everything to everyone, as Christ says to John: "Thus it is fitting for us to fulfill all righteousness" (Matt. 3:15).

Thus in Dan. 3 Azariah [14] confesses that he and his friends are at one and the same time suffering justly and yet are afflicted with evil, namely, at the hands of the wicked king. For even though he who acts does so unjustly, yet he does not do so to the person who suffers; for that person suffers justly. For by what legal right does

[10] Luther is referring to the futile efforts of Pope Julius II (1503—1513) to conquer and subdue Venice.

[11] Hieronymus Scultetus (Schulz) was bishop of Brandenburg and chancellor to the elector of Brandenburg. Wittenberg belonged to his bishopric, and Scultetus was at first kindly disposed toward Luther's cause. Later he became a bitter enemy. At the Diet of Worms he tried privately to persuade Luther to yield.

[12] Frederick the Wise, the elector of Saxony (1486—1525) and Luther's chief protector in the crucial years to come.

[13] Luther coins the word *bonaeintentionarii,* based on *bonae intentionis,* men "of good intention," or men who constantly boast of good intentions.

[14] The reference is to the apocryphal insertion between vv. 23 and 24 known as *The Prayer of Azariah.* Luther's text reads *Ananias* for *Azarias.* Cf. Dan. 1:7 for the Hebrew and Babylonian names of the three companions of Daniel.

the devil possess men? Or by what legal right does an evil hangman hang a thief? Certainly not in his own right, but by that of the judge. Thus men who glory in their own righteousness are unwilling to listen to the supreme Judge, but only to their own judgment, and because in respect to their victim they are innocent, they think that they really are innocent in every way.

Therefore since before God no one is righteous, absolutely no injustice can be done to a person by any other creature, even though he may have justice on his side. Thus all cause for contention is taken away from men. Therefore, to whomsoever an injury is done or an evil comes in return for his good actions, let him turn away his eyes from this evil and remember how great his own evil is in other respects, and then he will see how good the will of God is even in this evil which has come upon him; for this is what it means to be renewed in one's mind and to be changed into another state of mind and to be wise in the things of God. Thus it is definite that Peter would not have glorified God if he had girded himself and gone where he wanted to go, even though he would not have walked a wicked path, but the highest road of righteousness. But after this road of his own righteousness was prohibited and he went where he did not want to go but where another wanted, then he glorified God. So also we cannot glorify God unless we do what we do not wish, even in the case of our own works of righteousness, indeed, particularly in the case of our own righteousness, our own counsels, or our own strength. And thus to hate our own life and to will against our own will, to be wise in opposition to our own wisdom, to confess sin in the face of our own righteousness, to heed foolishness spoken against our own wisdom, this is "to take our cross" (Matt. 10:38), "to be His disciples" (Luke 14:27), and "to be transformed by the renewal of your mind."

Hence we must note that these terms "good," "acceptable," and "perfect" are not used in a formal way with respect to the will of God, but in relation to their object.[15] For this does not become the will of God through our proving of it, but rather it is recognized to be such; thus it becomes "good" to us, that is, it is acknowledged as being good, "acceptable" because it becomes most pleasing to us, and "perfect" because it makes all things perfect, that is, it becomes "good, acceptable, and perfect" in our eyes. And thus these are words which are overflowing with comfort. For we ought to

---

[15] For another statement of the contrast between the "formal" and the "objective" way, cf. Luther's marginal note 6 on p. 97 above.

have the greatest courage at the very time when evils befall us, for that is where God shows His good will; we should be most pleased at the time when the most unpleasant things happen, for then it is certain that the acceptable will of God is at work, that is, the will which is most pleasing to us; and finally we should be most confident at the time when hopelessness comes over us and the greatest sense of loss, for that is the time when the perfect will of God which makes all things perfect and completely salutary is hardest at work. For this is the nature of the divine will, 1 Sam. 2:6: "The Lord kills and brings to life; He brings down to hell and raises up." That is to say, while doing us evil it does us good; while most unacceptable to us it is most acceptable; while it destroys us, it perfects us. Thus we must not become foolish and "conformed to this world," which judges according to its own sense and wisdom (for it is wise only in what it has experienced and in matters of the present), but rather we must be renewed more and more. For in this way we prove the will of God, when we do not judge according to our experience and our feelings, but rather walk in darkness.

But those who are not willing to be transformed will prove what is the indignation of God, which is evil, unacceptable, and destroying: evil because it brings evil and damnation; unacceptable because it makes people unwilling to bear the evil with patience and acceptance; and destroying because it makes those who will not accept and will not endure fall into obstinate refusal and damnation, where they live in a world of blasphemies and curses, and of death itself.

But the will of God is "good" because out of evil it brings good; "acceptable" because it causes us to love that good with great joy and to be well and rightly pleased with it and even with the evil from which it came; and "perfect" because it brings those who rejoice in it to completion in eternity and thus perfects what it had begun.

Yet all of these things have been said concerning those people who have the power to do this and who are on their own responsibility. But it is different in the case of those who have been placed over other people, for they do not act for themselves but for God. Hence it is their duty to rule with justice over those who are subject to them and not permit them to do harm to one another. For now they do not have the right to tolerate, and patience has no place here. For humility, patience, and endurance are not proper for God, but rather judgment, glory, and vengeance.[16] And these people function as His representatives. But where any of them can do it without becoming guilty himself, even though he may sustain harm and injury, he ought to make concessions, as we have said.

3. *God has assigned the measure of faith.* The term "measure of faith" can at first sight be understood as the measure or mode according to which faith is given in distinction to all other gifts. But here it cannot be understood in that sense, as is obvious from the fact that he states that different gifts are given according to this measure. Therefore we must understand the expression "measure of faith" in a second sense, that is, the measure of the gifts of faith, that is, in faith there are many gifts, and though believers live in the same faith, yet they have a different measure of the gifts of faith. And this is what he calls the measure of faith, because those who act outside of faith do not have these gifts and this measure. For although there is one faith, one Baptism, one church, one Lord, one Spirit, one God, nevertheless, there are various kinds of gifts in this faith, church, lordship, etc. Just as if you were to say: the prince has divided to each citizen a measure of the city or a measure of the household, that is, the things which are in the household or the city.

Or better still: that faith is all of these things. For faith is nothing else than obedience to the Spirit. But there are different degrees of obedience to the Spirit. For one man is obedient and believes in this respect, and another man in another respect, and yet all of us are in the one faith. Thus there is one obedience to the prince but still different methods of obedience, so that no one can presume to adopt the method of obedience of another to the neglect of his own method and there be confusion in the city and sedition and rebellion.

6. *If prophecy, in proportion to our faith.* He has shown above how we ought to conduct ourselves toward God, namely, through the renewal of our mind and the sanctification of our body, so that we may prove what is the will of God. At this point, and from here to the end of the epistle, he teaches how we should act toward our neighbor and explains at length this command to love our neighbor. But it is remarkable how such a clear and important teaching of such a great apostle, indeed of the Holy Spirit Himself, receives no attention. We are busy with I don't know what kind of trifles in building churches, in increasing the wealth of the church, in

16 Cf. p. 108, n. 20.

piling up money, in multiplying ornamentation and gold and silver vessels, in installing organs, and in other forms of visible display. And the sum total of our piety consists of this; we are not at all concerned about the things the apostle here enjoins, to say nothing of the monstrous display of pride, ostentation, avarice, luxury, and ambition which are found in these activities.

Therefore he first turns his attention to the false prophets. For the gift of prophecy ought to be held and used "in proportion to our faith." And they act counter to this who prophesy on the basis of human judgment or according to the probable conjectures based on the workings and signs of nature, such as those who give counsel by the stars or from some plausible opinion of their own. For the prophecy which comes from God comes in such a way that it is against all reason and asserts the impossible, as it were. Thus it provokes many people to unbelief, since all the things which pertain to the truthfulness of this kind of prophecy appears to be beyond hope and seemingly contrary to its promises. This was the case when Jeremiah in the very time of the siege of Jerusalem, when everything was already beyond hope, prophesied, saying in Jer. 32:15: "Thus says the Lord: Houses and fields and vineyards shall again be possessed in this land," although everything had already been laid waste and the citizenry itself was already moving away. For this reason Jeremiah then and there proclaims: "The Lord is great in counsel and incomprehensible in thought" (Jer. 32:19). On the other hand, when he prophesied the ruin of the city and the migration away from it, they did not believe him, since there were no signs of this, but rather signs to the contrary, namely, armaments, armed men, auxiliary strength, so that it seemed so utterly impossible that in Jer. 28:1 ff. Hananiah on the basis of such indications dared to prophesy the very opposite, since he, too, was a prophet. For not only the false prophets but also the true prophets at this point fell into error, because they forgot to prophesy "in proportion to faith." Thus Nathan erred in 2 Sam. 7:3 ff., when he advised David to build the temple. And in Num. 22:21 ff. Balaam erred and became a false prophet in spite of the fact that he foretold remarkable things.

Likewise in the last chapter of 1 Kings Micaiah prophesied contrary to the opinion of all that Ahab was going to perish, although nothing but the strongest indications of a future and certain victory were at hand. (1 Kings 22:14 ff.) Hence, even Zedekiah in reliance on these signs prophesied against him (1 Kings 22:24 ff.).

Thus a prophecy which is based only on experience or human argument is not true. For this reason he says "in proportion to," or "by comparison with," faith. For the Greek ἀναλογία is taken by some to mean "proportion," "comparison", "rule," or "similarity," or in other words, it is as if the apostle were saying: "If you wish to prophesy, do it in such a way that you do not go beyond faith, so that your prophesying can be in harmony with the peculiar quality of faith." In German we say: *Es ähnelt ihm. Es sieht ihm gleich,* that is, it has the same qualities, similarity, likeness to it.

Thus if you see a monastery which is similar to a castle, you say that it is analogous to a castle, that is, it has proportions, characteristics, and a site like that of a castle. In the same way he is trying to say here that prophecy must be in harmony with faith, so that it is concerned "with things not seen" (Heb. 11:1), lest by chance it become the wisdom of the world, which is concerned with things which are seen, either in causes or in effects. This word is worthy of note. And thus an "analogy" is an assimilation, not one that is active and derived from the intellect, but one that is passive, or rather neutral, in which one thing resembles another in its characteristics and becomes like it. Thus one may prophesy new things, but not things that go beyond the bounds of faith, that is, what a person prophesies may not have the experiential proof of things but may be only the signs of things that are in no way apparent, either by signs or other indications, lest faith perish at the hands of prophecy and become a wisdom open to all, one which any wise man can understand and know, and thus he may develop a similar prophecy. And so prophecy is no longer prophecy but an exhibition of facts and evidence of experience.

7. *If service, in our serving.* In Greek it reads διακονίαν, ἐν τῇ διακονίᾳ, that is, "in ministering." "Ministers" are all those who serve in ecclesiastical offices, such as the priest, the deacon, the subdeacon, and all who have to do with sacred rites except the administration of the Word of God, and also those who assist a teacher, as the apostle often speaks of his helpers. Now, there are those who contend against this, first of all the ambitious, who, even though they are not educated, want to teach because they are tired of their own office. This could be endured, but they also lack the ability to teach. For it is not enough to be learned and intelligent, but the gift of grace to teach is also required, in order that a person be chosen by God for teaching. But in our day we rush forward everywhere, ready to teach the whole world, even if we ourselves

do not understand what we teach, and if we do understand it, still the grace and command of the God who sends us is lacking. Thus He says: "Do not send yourselves, because you are servants, not masters." "Pray the Lord of the harvest to send out laborers into His harvest" (Matt. 9:38). Therefore let a person be content with his ministering if he does not know how to preach or has not yet been called, even though he does know how to preach. Matt. 25:14 reads: "He called his servants and entrusted to them his property." First he called. For it is amazing to what extent the good intention is at work here; it imagines that it can produce incalculable fruits if it can but preach, even though untrained in the first place, and even though trained but not called in the second place, and even though trained but without grace in the third place. For the call either discovers grace or confers it. He who preaches without it "beats the air" (cf. 1 Cor. 9:26) and glories in fruit existing only in his own foolish imagination. I will pass over those whom bishops and heads of orders everywhere nowadays are promoting to the pulpit, men who are utterly stupid and incompetent. Even if we should be willing to say that they are called and sent, we could not do so, because incompetent and unworthy men are being called, and this comes from the wrath of God, who because of our sins is taking His Word from us and is multiplying the number of empty talkers and garrulous chatterers.

He who teaches, in his teaching. Many people do have the ability to teach, even if they do not have great learning. Others have both, and they are the best teachers, such as St. Augustine, St. Ambrose, and St. Jerome. The man therefore who neglects this gift and involves himself in other matters sins against this command of the apostle, indeed, of God, especially those men who have been called and placed into such teaching positions, even though they are not as yet called by that name. "Tender ears do not want to listen to the truth that bites." [17] But the apostle here is dealing primarily with those who have been called. For in his epistles he is always stressing his own call, for without the call of God neither the ministry nor teaching succeeds. Hence at the instigation of the devil ministers arrogate to themselves the teaching office, and on the other hand teachers flee the teaching office, so that on both counts the work of God is hindered. Clearly the apostle both here and in 1 Cor. 12:28 puts the order of teachers in the third place.

---

[17] Luther probably has in mind Persius, *Satira,* I, 108: *Teneras mordaci radere vero auriculas.*

8. *He who exhorts, in his exhortation.* The difference between teaching and exhortation is this, that teaching is directed to those who do not know, while exhortation applies to those who do know. The one builds the foundation, the other builds on it. He who teaches hands on knowledge; he who exhorts stimulates and moves his hearers in the direction of the fruit of the knowledge given to them. Thus the one plants, and the other waters, as we read in 1 Cor. 3:6: "I planted, Apollos watered," and later on (3:10): "Like a skilled master builder I laid a foundation, and another man is building upon it." This is the method of almost all the preachers of our age, who are watering a faith which has already been planted, except in cases where they are preaching to people who have not yet been preached to. Therefore those who have this ability and have been called ought not to take time for other matters, although in our day this has become common practice, as also the heathen Horace knew: "The lazy ox longs for the saddle, and the nag longs to plow," [18] for no one is content with his own lot in life, but he praises those who follow other paths.[19] And Terence says: "Most of us are of a mind that makes us dissatisfied with our own lot." [20] Those who are suited for a job dislike it, and the incompetent pant for it.

He who contributes, in simplicity. As his own devil tempts each man in the use of his own ability, so that he does not serve God purely and faithfully in his use of God's gift, so also he who contributes does not lack for his devil. This man is attacked from two points.

In the first place, he is assailed when he gives in a relative sense and not absolutely, that is, with the idea that his gifts will bring him greater returns. This method is now common among Christians, as the well-known proverb has it: "It is the custom in our country today to offer bread to him who has plenty." [21] In German we say: *Geschenk und Ehr'.*[22] As a result those of lower rank give to people of higher rank, to princes, prelates, bishops, rich men, and

---

[18] Horace, *Epistles*, I, 14, 43.

[19] The second half of this sentence is a free paraphrase of Horace, *Satires*, I, 1, 1-3.

[20] Terence, *Phormio*, 172.

[21] *Mos nunc est genti, quod panis praebetur habenti.*

[22] These words, "Gifts and honor," probably were the key words of a German proverb of similar content as the Latin quoted. Example: *Wer nicht ehrt, wird nicht geehrt.*

powerful men. But to these men no one would give if he were giving in simplicity, that is, without the hope of repayment. And
strange to say this evil is very common today. Hence also we read
in Luke 14:12 ff.: "When you give a dinner or a banquet, do not invite your friends or your brothers or your kinsmen or rich neighbors, lest they also invite you in return, and you be repaid. But
when you give a feast, invite the poor, the maimed, the lame, the
blind, and you will be blessed, because they cannot repay you. You
will be repaid at the resurrection of the just." Indeed, if this teaching were observed, how many monstrous evils the church would
be delivered from today! Would the lawyers continue to abound in
their fees? This kind of adulation is very current in all classes of
society. To be sure, this kind of contributing often gives great
pleasure, but the repayment always brings much more pleasure,
and this on the part of lower class people toward their superiors.

In the second place, such a man is attacked when superiors contribute to those beneath them or when equals give to equals. This
gives much greater pleasure, obviously because of vainglory and
boasting. For here "it is more blessed to give than to receive"
(Acts 20:35)! They are like God Himself, but only in their pride.

This latter interpretation does not satisfy me, for the apostle is
actually speaking of the contribution which is made to the teachers
of the Word and those in positions of responsibility, Gal. 6:6 tells
us: "Let him who is taught the Word share all good things with him
who teaches." For this must be done "in simplicity" and not in
hypocrisy, just as He commanded the Children of Israel that they
should take care not to forsake the Levites (Deut. 12:19). Hence he
continues in Gal. 6:7: "Do not be deceived; God is not mocked."
In my opinion, he has reference to this gift in 1 Cor. 12:28: "helps,"
"aids," which people owe to rulers or teachers, who devote themselves to the Word and prayer. For "the Lord is their portion"
(cf. Num. 18:20; Ps. 73:26), and thus "the laborer deserves his
wages" (cf. Matt. 10:10; 1 Tim. 5:18).

This is commonly called *eyn gnade adder fruntschafft*.[23] I do
not know whether I ought to number among these the foundations
and anniversary endowments, etc., of our own time. For they
seem vigorously in pursuit of glory, indeed not only of glory but
of repayment both temporal and eternal, as is plain to see from the
way they lay burdens on people obligated to them. Secondly, they
are given for the sake of future glory. These folks think that they are

[23] *Eine Gnade oder Freundschaft* ("a gracious deed or an act of friendship").

giving "in simplicity" and that they are more sincere than the first class. For they do not appear to be giving temporal gifts in order to receive eternal rewards. But they arrange for certain choir songs in such a way, as if they would not get their due if the choir were to sing less or in a different way. In times past choirs were not so named,[24] as is still evident in the case of the collegiate churches. But even these people are double-minded. For they do not give in simplicity for the glory of God but for the sake of their own future advantage in heaven, and they would not make the gift if it were not for their hope of this advantage. But it is in vain, for they are double-minded. And they do not realize this but go smugly along as if they were absolutely certain of repayment for these gifts, not alert to the fact that they have already here received their reward (cf. Matt. 6:2, 5, 16). I can scarcely believe that they do this for the glory of God, since then they would help support old foundations and renew those which have already been established but have fallen into disuse. But they have made a marketplace out of the worship and service of God.

He who rules, with carefulness. But in our day he who rules, both spiritually as well as in the secular realm, does so in luxury, idleness, riches, pleasure, in glory and honor, in power and terror. Ezekiel 34:2 ff. says of these conditions: "Ho, shepherds of Israel who have been feeding yourselves! You eat the fat, you clothe yourselves with the wool, you slaughter the fatlings. The weak you have not strengthened, the sick you have not healed, the crippled you have not bound up, the strayed you have not brought back, the lost you have not sought, but with force and harshness you have ruled them." Who does not shake at these words and whose hair does not stand on end! These are the men who attack this command. For they do not ascend in order to descend, as did the angels on Jacob's ladder. For to ascend means to rule, but to descend means to be careful. They do not rule in order to serve, although everyone who is exalted is exalted for the purpose that he seek nothing for himself nor seek to live for himself, but that he recognize that he has been made a servant of his servants.

---

[24] The reference is to certain "memorials" in the form of funds to maintain choirs and choir singing at stated points in the services of the churches honored by such gifts. Apparently Luther is saying that it was formerly the custom to provide such memorials anonymously but that the names of donors eventually came to play a more important role. Examples that probably came to mind were the "eternal choir" of the cathedral of Meissen in Saxony and the choirs of the Church of All Saints in Wittenberg itself. Cf. p. 461 below.

Thus the primary measure of every master is his diligence, as the apostle here describes it. Moreover, a man cannot be diligent in the case of other people unless he is negligent of his own interests. For diligence produces negligence, perverse diligence makes evil negligence, but proper diligence a proper negligence. And thus he who rules must do so in diligence, that is, in negligence of his own interests.

He who does acts of mercy, with cheerfulness. 2 Cor. 9:7 has "not reluctantly or under compulsion; for God loves a cheerful giver." This is different from what he has said above: "he who contributes, in simplicity." For in the former case it is a matter of giving to those from whom there is hope of being repaid, but here it refers to giving to the poor and needy.

It seems to me that a person can properly ignore the question under which Lyra labors, namely, that of the order of the items in this catalog of good works, lest we lose the true understanding while we are carried away to an imagined construction of its parts. This happens to Lyra whenever he delights in dividing the Scripture into parts in his learned treatment of it and his belief that he is shedding great light on it.

But he who is forced to come to the aid of the needy out of shame or some kind of threat does not show mercy with cheerfulness. Thus there are many people today who give substantial alms, but without any merit because they are unwilling and sad. Likewise there are those who give alms so that they may not be thought to be greedy or heartless or without mercy.

9. *Let love be without dissimulation.* A necessary and most important connection. For just as nothing ought to be more free of dissimulation than love, so nothing can be more polluted by dissimulation than love. Nothing so shrinks from dissimulation as love, and nothing suffers so much from dissimulation as love. This is the reason why everyone has on his lips the saying: "Faithless is earth, and faithless are the skies," [25] and: "Who can find a faithful man?" (Prov. 20:6).[26] Everything is painted over and concealed under the disguise of friendship. But the dissimulation of love is twofold. The first kind is that which displays outwardly the appearance of love, but inwardly conceals a veritable hatred. This is the "love" of subordinates toward their superiors and the kind that

---

[25] This is John Dryden's expanded translation of the words quoted by Luther from Vergil, *Aeneid*, IV, 373: *Nusquam tuta fides.*

[26] Luther gives *Ecclesiastis* as the source.

exists among equals. And these again fall into two classes. There are some, such as Joab over against Abner in 2 Sam. 3:27, who practice this knowingly. In this class are the detractor, the deceiver, the gossip-monger, the double-tongued. But this kind of dissimulation is so crass that I do not think the apostle is speaking about it here, although this vice with all its filth is very widespread in our day.

But there are also some who do not know that their love is really false until trial and adversity come upon the person whom they love. Ovid says: "When you are happy, you have many friends, but in times of trouble, you will be alone." [27]

This is the way the apostles were at the time of Christ's passion, and the same is the case with many other saints. So deep is this dissimulation that it is a rare man who recognizes it in himself. Indeed, I dare say that no person is completely free of this dissimulation, even though many people think they are. Who is more perfect than the apostles who were strengthened by the time and presence of Christ?

The second kind is that which does not conceal an evil love nor show a good hatred. This is characteristic of superiors toward those of lower class and of equals toward each other.

And these, too, fall into two classes. There are some who clearly understand and see their neighbor when he makes a mistake, or sins, that is, when he brings the greatest harm upon himself, and even though they have the power, they do not reprove him or warn him, or correct him. Rather, they laugh at him and jest with him, as if they were his best friends who did not want to offend him. But this dissimulation of love is so crass and crude that it is difficult to believe that the apostle was thinking of such a thing, although many people do practice this dissimulation even against their own conscience. Some people do it in ignorance; they admire vices as though they were virtues and praise them with a high degree of humility, they are swift to interpret as good the things that seem to be evils, swift to praise, slow to criticize, even the greatest of vices, as long as they are covered with a thin disguise of good to such a degree that, if you are unable to see it on account of the darkness, you may nevertheless feel it. In this case they do not "try all things, so that they might hold to what is good" (cf. 1 Thess. 5:21), but they are satisfied with the mere appearance, they say only good things, and call a man a friend. Thus the one

[27] Ovid, *Tristia*, I, 9, 5.

class does not do the good and the other does not do the evil which
love nevertheless requires. But the former do evil and the latter
good, in both cases against love.

Between these groups come the neutrals, like Absalom speaking
and doing neither good nor evil [28] (cf. 2 Sam. 13:22). These are our
theologians who smugly stand in their elicited acts [29] and never
move forward to an effective deed, thinking that they have abounded
sufficiently if they only hope, desire, and wish good to their neighbor and reject, hate, and deplore the evil act of their neighbor —
and all this by elicited acts. Otherwise they do nothing in the way
of action, or else they do what the aforementioned pretenders do.
And why should I hesitate to say it? It is a simulated love when one
says that to love is to wish someone well by an elicited act. Therefore, as if to expose fabrications of dissimulation, the apostle
continues:

Hate what is evil, hold fast to what is good. There is no man
who would say that he loves the evil and hates the good, and yet
he does not give this command here in vain, because man is prone
to evil and disinclined to good. Therefore the protection of dissimulation lies in ignorance of good and evil, whereby each man calls
that which pleases him good and that which displeases him evil.
Therefore why does he make this commandment that we should
"test everything, and hold fast what is good" (1 Thess. 5:21),
except that we thus do not immediately take hold of something
that is good in its outward appearance only? Thus in this passage
the apostle means the good as that of the new man and the evil as
that of the new man also. For the good of the new man is twofold,
as is also the evil. The one is invisible, and he has it only by faith,
because it is God; the other is visible, and it is everything which
is evil in the sight of sensuality and contrary to the old man, for
example, the chastising of the old man and the stimulation to good
works. Likewise, on the other hand, the visible evil is everything
that is good for the old man and friendly to him, as for example, the
lust of the flesh and the neglect of the Spirit.

Both of these are twofold: the one in our own person and the
other in our neighbor. The apostle here is speaking of the latter,
for in order that "our love may be without dissimulation," it is
necessary that we hate in our neighbor whatever is evil, without

[28] Cf. p. 456 below.
[29] Cf. p. 267 above.

praise or fear, and cling to what is good in him, without deceit or favor.

And he uses the term "hating" what is evil as if he meant to say: "There will never be a time when evil will not exist, and every evil will never be under your control. Therefore hate the evil which you do not do, so that you do not give consent to the evil of another person, but make common cause with the good of another person. Cherish, favor, promote, and preach this; hate and hinder the evil wherever you can. But quite often there is no opportunity to do anything except hate the evil and love the good, as in the case of heretics and those who oppose Christian people and rage against pious folk.

If there were such men in the courts of the popes and the princes, the church would be in a happy state. But now because the very opposite is the case, therefore the church is in a wretched condition, not so much because they wish to do the evil that is their own, but because they do not hate the evil that is present in the church.

However, the hatred or love of a person overturns this whole judgment, as is the case today with John Reuchlin and the theologians of Cologne.[30] When we give our love to a person with complete confidence and intensity, we are prepared to uphold and defend with all our might whatever he thinks is right, and we do not ask how we should recognize whatever he does as good or evil, lest such a person seem to have either good or evil in him. Thus it is the nature of pretended love that it hates the good and clings to the evil. For all love is by nature blind. Who, then, is not blind? For who is without love—I am speaking of the sensual kind— except one who is not alive?

10. *Love one another with brotherly affection.* One Greek text reads "brotherly love" (φιλαδελφία), hence the word *philadelphus* means "brother lover," or "one who loves his brother." In this passage the apostle is dealing with the idea that the love among Christians ought to be a special and more perfect thing than the relationship among strangers and enemies. Thus in another place, Gal. 6:10, he says: "So then, as we have opportunity, let us do good to all men, and especially to those who are of the household of faith." And where we have the word *diligentes* ("loving"), the Greeks have the word φιλόστοργοι (φίλος, "love"). But the word στοργή means "affection," or "sympathy", as we commonly say.

[30] Cf. pp. 289 and 429 above.

Thus a φιλόστοργος is one who is kindly affectioned toward a person with whom he is to practice brotherly love, φιλαδελφία. And thus the apostle is speaking most emphatically when he makes a compound of words meaning love almost in a superfluous way, so that we have *philadelphia estote philostorgi*, that is, "you are to be kindly affectioned toward one another with brotherly love."

Outdo one another in showing honor. Thus we read in Phil. 2:3: "In humility count others better than yourselves." And in Luke 14:10 the Lord says: "When you are invited, go and sit in the lowest place." He is speaking here of that inward honor which is a high regard and esteem for one's neighbor. For the outward honor is very often a simulated and mercenary one which is demonstrated in order that one may receive a greater return. Thus if no return is made, the person becomes angry and ceases to give honor to others. That is what it means when he says: "Count others better than yourselves." He does not say: "Each placing himself above the other." Moreover, a man cannot show this honor to another unless he humbles himself and judges himself worthy of being put to shame and that others are more deserving of honor than he is, that is, unless a man is humble, he does not prefer another in honor above himself.

Pride also gives honor, but it follows others in bestowing it, whereas humility precedes in giving it. The one waits to be preceded, and the other does not even desire others to follow it but believes that it alone ought to take the lead. What a great service to give honor to another! It is easier to give something and to be of service with one's body than to hold only oneself in contempt and to think highly of all other people.

Some people are swift to return honor, or in the manner of the mercenary to give honor with the hope of being honored in return. This is the practice of the Gentiles. Thus the Roman Domitius said: "Why should I regard you as a prince when you do not regard me as a senator?" [31] This is not the Christian way of speaking, but the Gentile way. For we must give honor to one another even if honor from the other person neither precedes nor follows.

11. *Never flag in zeal.* In the Greek: "in diligence," "in zeal," "in service," "with industry."

Note how love keeps nothing for itself and seeks only those things which are in the interest of others. He has taught above how

---

[31] This story is originally told by Cicero about L. Crassus in *De oratore*, III, 4. Luther's version is probably taken from Jerome, *Epistula ad Nepotianum*, 52, 7, *Patrologia, Series Latina*, XXII, 533 f.

we ought to bestow our goods and talents for the benefit of others, namely, by contributing, by showing mercy, and by loving, etc., and then how we should bestow honor and good report among ourselves. And now he teaches that one should offer himself, saying that to help, to serve, and to succor with our own body, so to speak, is to support and stand by those who are in need. On the other side are the Absalomites,[32] that is, the fathers of peace and those who are not willing to be disturbed and helpful over the needs of others. Or if they do do something, they do it unwillingly and grudgingly, as we see in legal actions, lawsuits, and the like.

Be fervent in spirit. Those who snore and yawn and are lukewarm in all their efforts are the people who break this command, and they achieve nothing by their works but only dissipate them, Prov. 18:9: "He who is slack in his work is a brother to him who destroys." But people of this kind are also hateful to men, to say nothing of God. Thus it is that today very commonly the artisans who have been hired do their work as if they were asleep.[33] And the religious and the priests literally snore during their prayers, even physically, to say nothing about the sleepiness of their minds, and they do everything with the greatest laziness. Here the apostle therefore is speaking against this deadly sin of *acedia,* or being tired of doing good works. The Greek word ἀκηδία means "tedium," or "boredom," or "indifference." This sin is so widespread that hardly anyone deigns to be attentive. And because people are unwilling to serve with a fervent spirit, it is necessary that they become fervent in the flesh. For they must be fervent in one of the two, either the spirit or the flesh. And the fervor for one is the freezing out or extinction of the other, except where by God's permission in time of temptation the spirit still is aglow even in the midst of the fervor of the flesh. Therefore the man who does his work with lukewarmness of necessity will be fervent in the flesh. And on that account he is compelled as it were to "waste the work" which he performs, because of the fervor of the flesh. So a lazy cook, about to prepare a meal, does his work in such a way that the food gets cold during the serving. Who would not despise him, and rightly?

[32] The Absalomites are those who do not want their personal peace and well-being disturbed by consideration for the needy. The name is derived from the description of Absalom's attitude in 2 Sam. 13:22. Cf. p. 453 above. But "father of peace" is also the meaning of the name Absalom.

[33] Luther had opportunity to observe such artisans, for in the years 1515 to 1516 a church, a castle, a hospital, and a lecture hall were erected in Wittenberg.

Serve the Lord. This passage is directed not only against those who out of avarice serve the world or their own belly, but even more strongly against those who are persistent in doing a good work, when obedience calls them elsewhere. This latter class of people is like those who have an ass under a yoke and will not permit him to be loosed, in order that he may be used in the Lord's service, that is, they wear themselves out on their own pursuits and permit themselves to be called away to some other area of service neither by piety nor for the sake of God. Therefore they actually are serving themselves rather than the Lord. For they are not prepared to follow every wish of God but only that chosen by themselves, and they excuse themselves by saying: "It is not good to give up what I have just been doing and work in another place." And I would perhaps not be in error if I were to include among this number the princes who are most regular in church attendance and the priests who are most regularly at court.

This is the case with our Duke Frederick and the other officials; when they are needed, they do not want to be found. They are called away by God, and they say: "Oh, I must pray and serve God." They make fools of themselves, so that for the sake of serving God they refuse to serve God, because they do not realize what it is to serve God, namely, that one be indifferent as to where the Lord calls and not insist on remaining fixed in one spot.

12. *Rejoice in your hope.* That is, do not rejoice over things of the present, or things you have experienced and know. For joy is twofold. The first kind has to do with things that are visible, that is, things that are known in some way or other either inwardly or outwardly. This kind is vain, because it is transitory. The other kind has to do with invisible things, that is, things that are unknown but simply accepted in faith; and this is true joy, eternal, firm, and without this kind of hope there is no joy in the other. For who can rejoice in the former if he despairs or doubts that he will receive future joy? And thus the apostle wants Christians to rejoice to the full, but not because of any earthly thing but because of their hope. For the expression "Blessed are those who mourn" (Matt. 5:4) refers to mourning over something, because such people rejoice in their hope. But a person cannot have hope, and thus he cannot have joy in his hope, unless he has renounced everything, has nothing to desire, to trust in, to take pleasure in, and is beset by so many evils besides that he cannot possibly rejoice in any good thing here. And if he bears this willingly, he will achieve

hope and from hope he will proceed to joy. And thus he continues:

Be patient in tribulation. Rom. 5:3 ff.: "Suffering produces endurance, and endurance trial, and trial hope, but hope does not disappoint," that is, it rejoices and is happy and secure. But our subtle theologians [34] have limited hope to elicited acts.[35] For this reason none of them understands what hope is, though it is constantly on everyone's lips. For example, they say that it is possible to elicit an act of hope, even though all things which are in sight and in which we put our trust are in good order. But we shall never arrive at even a taste of hope through such an elicited act. For hope strips a man, at least as it pertains to his disposition, of all his good things and surrounds him with evil things. And thus "you have need of endurance" (Heb. 10:36), which produces hope.

Be constant in prayer. This is spoken in opposition to those who only read the Psalms without any heart. And we must be on our guard that the prayers in church in our day do not become more of a hindrance than a help. First, because we offend God more by reading them when our heart is not in it, as He says: "This people honors Me with their lips, etc." (Matt. 15:8; Mark 7:6; Is. 29:13). Second, because we are deceived and made secure by the appearance of these things, as if we had truly prayed properly. And thus we never become really attached to the desire for true prayer, but when we pray these things, we think that we have prayed and are in need of nothing more. This is a terrible danger. And in return for these things we then at our leisure and in security consume the income and the pensions and subsidies of the people!

This is the reason why he inserted the word "constant," a great watchword that must be noted and respected by all, and especially by clerics. For this word signifies that we must put real work into our praying. And it is not in vain. For as the ancient fathers have said: "There is no work like praying to God." [36] Therefore when a man wants to enter the priesthood, he must first consider that he is entering a work which is harder than any other, namely, the work of prayer. For this requires a subdued and broken mind and an elevated and victorious spirit. But at this point the lawyers introduce a nice explanation, that to pray the hours is not commanded, but rather to "read" them or to "say" them is. For in this

[34] Occam, d'Ailly, Biel, Scotus, Lombard.

[35] Cf. p. 267 above.

[36] *Vitae patrum,* V, *Verba seniorum,* XII, 2, *Patrologia, Series Latina,* LXXIII, 941.

manner they encumber the canon law with words and snore on in peace. But even if we omit the canonical hours, we need to say something about prayer.

Prayer is of two kinds. There is the vocal prayer,[37] of which it is presently the custom to say that a virtual intention is sufficient —a nice little cover for laziness and negligence! For on the basis of this, in the first place, they must by force tear from themselves the good intention, and then being satisfied with this they immediately give up every other attempt.

And in this type of prayer there is a threefold attentiveness: the material, or sensual, attentiveness, whereby one pays attention only to the words, as monks and others, such as simple lay people do, who do not understand even the Lord's Prayer. And this is real prayer no more than material is the real thing, that is, according to its own nature it is not prayer in the proper sense of the word, but only in an extrinsic sense, by which every other good work can be called prayer. To pray in this way is merely to perform an act of obedience which makes it pleasing to God. Such prayer is not to be despised, because in addition to this, that it is a work of obedience, it is good in many other ways. First, because it drives away the devil, even if the prayer is only recited in the simplicity of the heart, that is, if "it is sung in the spirit" (1 Cor. 14:15) and thus brings the Holy Spirit to us. This is symbolized in David's playing the harp before Saul. For the devil cannot endure even having the Word of God read, as we know from many examples. 1 Cor. 14:2: "For one who speaks in a tongue speaks to God." Second, because the divine Word by nature affects the soul, even if it is not understood. For it is a Word of grace, as we read in Ps. 45:2: "Grace is poured upon your lips." Likewise: "Your lips distil nectar" (Song of Sol. 4:11). Third, it gives to the intellect and the emotions an occasion which they would not have otherwise, as we see it symbolized in the minstrel of Elisha.[38] Fourth, although many people who pray this way do not have the full emotional effect of these words, yet they often have a common and elevated spirit toward God.

There is also the intellectual attentiveness, whereby one gives attention to the sense and meaning of the words. The better edu-

---

[37] *Oratio vocalis,* or *exterior,* is the outward, spoken prayer. The *oratio mentalis,* or *interior,* is the prayer of the heart.

[38] The reference is to 2 Kings 3:14 ff.

cated and intelligent must pay attention to this, for each must pay his talent to God.

Then there is the spiritual or emotional attentiveness, whereby one is attentive to the emotional or spiritual effect of the words, as when one laments with those who lament, rejoices with those who rejoice, shouts for joy with those who are shouting for joy, and accommodates himself to every movement of the words. This is true prayer. Of these two points the apostle says, 1 Cor. 14:15: "I will sing with the spirit, and I will sing with the mind also." By using the expression to "sing with the spirit" he is calling attention to the sensual attentiveness, apart from the intellectual attentiveness, and yet intimately connected with the emotional attentiveness, as in the case of devout nuns and uneducated people. By using the expression "to sing with the mind" he is describing the intellectual attentiveness, which can be aroused both without the spirit as well as with the spirit. The mental prayer is the ascent of the mind, as well as the spirit, to God. This is the prayer of which he is speaking when he says: "Be constant in prayer." In this passage he is emphasizing that Christians ought to engage in frequent as well as diligent prayer. For "to be constant" means not only to take a great deal of time, but also to urge, to incite, to demand. For just as there is no work which for Christians ought to be more frequent, so no other work that requires more labor and effort and therefore is more efficacious and fruitful. For here "the kingdom of heaven has suffered violence, and men of violence take it by force" (Matt. 11:12). For prayer in my opinion is a constant violent action of the spirit as it is lifted up to God, as a ship is driven upward against the power of the storm. This is why it is said of blessed Martin to his credit that he had an inconquerable spirit because he never released it from prayer.[39]

This violence decreases and disappears, to be sure, whenever the Spirit draws and carries our heart upward by grace, or surely, when a present and major anxiety compels us to take refuge in prayer. And without these two factors, prayer becomes a most difficult and tedious thing. But its effect is tremendous. For true prayer is omnipotent, as our Lord says: "For everyone who asks receives, etc." (Matt. 7:8). Thus we must all practice violence and

[39] A responsory for the Feast of St. Martin read: "With eyes and hands always directed toward heaven, he would never release his invincible spirit from prayer."

remember that he who prays is fighting against the devil and the flesh.

Now with respect to the prayers of the canonical hours the question is raised, "How is this prescribed?" And the answer is that the church holds us only to the sensual attentiveness, that is, that the individual words be spoken,[40] but not to the intellectual or emotional attentiveness, at least not a personal involvement. For the church requires and presupposes a common emotional response. And it is not within its power to require that we pay intellectual attention or have a personal involvement, but it merely provides an occasion for this by its order.

For this reason it is a strange stupidity that prompts people in our day to establish endowments for canonical hours, obviously under the superstition that the donors do not care what is being prayed but only that much be chanted, since they do wish to have prayer made for themselves. But they prescribe prayer themselves as if it were in their power to buy prayer. How much better their gift would be, if they gave it with no strings attached, so that prayer would be made for them whenever the person who prays could do so! But they are imitating the ancient foundations, they say. My answer is that they are not, for the people of those days sought the glory of God by their prayers and not merely the advantage which prayer bestows. For the wording of our foundation here states "for the salvation of our souls." [41] As if God could not have known the purpose for which you gave! Or could He not have repaid you sufficiently if you had made your gift purely for His sake, without prescribing to Him the purpose for your giving and without blowing your horn before men? What if you are lying? And what if you are not doing it for the glory of God at all? May God make me a false prophet, but I am afraid that this monastery may yet bring great misfortune upon its unfortunate founder [42] and likewise upon the Church of All Saints.

13. *Contribute to the needs of the saints.* By the term "saints" in our day we understand those who are blessed or have been glorified, but the apostle, and indeed the whole Scripture, under-

---

[40] The constitutions of the Hermit Brothers of St. Augustine required "that the divine office be said distinctly, concisely, and scrupulously."

[41] This phrase was a standard feature of many diplomas of endowment for various churches and chapels in the Wittenberg area. Cf. W, LVI, 469, n. 5.

[42] Elector Frederick the Wise, who had ordered extensive building operations for both monastery and church in 1513—1514.

stands the term "saints" to apply to all who are faithful believers in Christ. This is probably why in our day people do not contribute freely to the saints, they do believe that there no longer are any. But why then does the apostle in Rom. 1:7 say that they are "called to be saints"? and why in 1 Cor. 7:14 that "the unbelieving husband is consecrated through his believing wife," and in 1 Peter 1:16: "You shall be holy, for I am holy," the Lord your God?

He is speaking here about the feeling of compassion, that they should have in common the needs of the saints by compassion toward one another, as in Heb. 10:33 f.: "Sometimes being publicly exposed to abuse and affliction, and sometimes being partners with those so treated. For you had compassion on the prisoners, etc." People act contrary to this when they are ashamed of the needs of the saints. However, this passage can also pertain to the effect of helpfulness and to something different from what he mentioned earlier: "He who does acts of mercy, with cheerfulness" (v. 8), for there he spoke in a general way about the wretched and the poor, whether saints or others, but here he is speaking about those under persecution, who are being deprived of their possessions, to whom one can give nothing except sympathy, as St. Anastasia and St. Natalie [43] did in their day by visiting prisoners and encouraging martyrs. Even if it was possible to give them something, it was done not as if they were in need but because they were suffering need for the sake of righteousness; for they were not in need in any other way except that the persecution was raging.

But today the saints are not so visible, and neither are their needs. But yet these people can be regarded as being in the place of the martyrs, when they are pressed down under private poverty and are ashamed to beg or to publicize their need. And this comes under the heading of temporal problems. Other people are in spiritual trouble, in great temptations either from man or from the devil. We must give them support or comfort because they suffer injury. Thus this passage is different from the previous one, "He who does acts of mercy," because there he speaks of needy people who are spared suffering, while here he speaks of suffering people who are spared poverty.

Practice hospitality. The apostle in his epistles to Titus and Timothy commends this duty especially to bishops (Titus 1:8, 1 Tim. 3:2), and here he does so to all people in general. Heb.

[43] Both saints are described as having suffered persecution under Diocletian for their works of love among the martyrs.

13:2: "Do not neglect to show hospitality, for thereby some have been pleased *(placuerunt)* to entertain angels," while in another version it reads "have been unaware of it" *(latuerunt)*, that is, it escaped their notice that they were entertaining angels, as was the case with Abraham and Lot (Gen. 18–19). So also in our day it can happen that we give or refuse hospitality to saints without being aware of it. Moreover, he understands the term "hospitality" here in terms of something freely given and not the mercenary or commercial kind. Hence in Greek the word φιλοξενία, "love of strangers," or "love for the care of strangers," and the term φιλόξενος, "one who loves strangers," are used. Therefore those who are hospitable out of free love and not out of mercenary desire are the ones who are commended in this passage. For the heathen also do this, although it is not an evil work but a meritorious one, if done rightly.

16. *Do not mind high things.* The apostle is speaking of "high" and "humble" things, using the neuter in place of the masculine, as he does also in 1 Cor. 1:27: "God chose what is weak in the world to shame the strong," and again: "The foolishness of God is wiser than men" (1 Cor. 1:25). Thus he is trying to say: "Do not be haughty, that is, do not take pleasure in the great people of this world and disregard the humble, but rather be interested in the humble and find your pleasure in them," as blessed Augustine says in his rule: "Do not glory in the dignity of rich parents but in the company of poor brethren." [44]

Thus we must note that our translation uses the term "humble" *(humile)* in a loose sense, while in the Greek it is one thing to use the terms ταπείνωσις and ταπεινός, and another to use the word ταπεινοφροσύνη. ταπείνωσις and ταπεινός mean "humility" and "humble," in the sense of "lowliness" and "lowly" in the strict sense of the Latin, whereby "humble" is the direct opposite of "high" or "noble." But ταπεινοφροσύνη, which is derived from ταπεινός and φρονεῖν, is being "mindful of humble things." This is humility, namely, the willingness to accommodate oneself to humble things and not to despise the lowly. It describes a person who has regard for things despised and the contemptible, one who avoids the things that are highly regarded. Such an attitude is the humility that is called a virtue. Hence the well-known passage reads: "For He has regarded the low estate (ταπείνωσιν — *humilitatem*) of His handmaiden" (Luke 1:48). But in Phil. 2:3 we

[44] *Regula Augustini*, ch. 5, *Patrologia, Series Latina*, XXXII, 1379.

read: "In humility (ταπεινοφροσύνῃ) count others better than your-selves." And in Eph. 4:2: "With all lowliness (ταπεινοφροσύνης) and meekness."

We can take the terms "high things" *(alta)* and "humble things" *(humilia)* as being neuter, referring to things, but this does some violence to the meaning. In this case the meaning will be that no one should give the appearance of possessing high things, whereby he could be noticed and regarded as a great man, but rather posses-sing lowly things on account of which he could be ignored and despised. And in this sense both statements are used against ambitious men who wish to appear among the great.

It is unnecessary to add here any references to the dissensions, mutual hatreds among kingdoms, duchies, and cities, seemingly to a greater degree than among the heathen, such as among the Venetians, the Italians, the French, the Germans. The German poets prefer the Germans, the French the French. And these things are the greatest virtues, such as they regard of highest worth, almost unmindful of the fact that we are Christians. Thus the word of Christ is fulfilled: "Nation will rise against nation, and kingdom against kingdom" (Mark 13:8).

Never be conceited. This is directed against opinionated, hard-headed, stiff-necked people, whom in popular language we call blockheads [45] but whom Scripture describes as "stiff-necked" and "unbelieving." We all are strongly inclined to this fault with a strange propensity, and most rare is the man who does not possess it. In German it is described by the word *steifsinnig,* which means to yield to the advice of no one, even though we are convinced by the reasoning. And even if one uses the opposite method, they still remain adamant and wait for the chance to rejoice and laugh if the advice of others proves wrong. These people are the authors of contention and the most effective disturbers of the peace and the destroyers of spiritual unity. Paul speaks of this in Eph. 4:3: "Be eager to maintain the unity of the Spirit in the bond of peace," and Phil. 2:2: "Be in full accord and of one mind, etc."

17. *Repay no evil for evil.* We read in Ps. 37:27: "Depart from evil," which blessed Peter explains as meaning not only that we do no evil but that we do not return evil for evil (1 Peter 3:9). Similarly the expression "do good" (Ps. 37:27) refers not only to returning good for good but to offering good. And Christ in Luke 9:55 rebuked His disciples when they wanted to call down fire from heaven, say-

[45] *Immansivos.*

ing to them: "Do you not know of what spirit you are?" So also we are not born "to destroy souls, but to save them" (Luke 9:56).

Providing good things. Thus we read in 1 Peter 2:12: "Maintain good conduct among the Gentiles, so that in case they speak against you as wrongdoers, they may see your good deeds and glorify God"; 1 Tim. 5:14: "I would have them give the enemy no occasion to revile us"; Titus 3:1-2: "Remind them to be ready for any honest work . . . showing perfect courtesy toward all men"; 1 Cor. 10:32-33: "Give no offense to Jews or Greeks or to the church of God, just as I try to please all men in everything I do," that is, I desire to please people as much as I can.

From this statement flows that remarkable statement of blessed Augustine: "He who is unconcerned about his own reputation lacks good feeling. Your own conscience is sufficient for you, but your reputation is necessary for your neighbor." [46] But many people cite this authority in a strangely improper way in justification of their own impatience, contentiousness, and pride, thinking that they must permit themselves to endure no insult or detractor without revenge, although blessed Augustine really is trying to say the same thing that the apostle is, namely, that a person should not do anything that may cause offense because of something which has the appearance of evil, despite his own clear conscience. At any rate, if a person has sustained an insult, he should excuse himself in quiet and calm words and not contend in anger for his position but acknowledge the insult as if it were deserved. So she who was beaten seven times bore the injury but did not admit guilt, nor did she harm her good name, for publicly she remained silent, although inwardly she had a clear conscience. [47]

In contrast to this today there is abroad the monstrosity of freedom not only of conscience but what is more, of intention or of the pretended conscience. Everywhere the higher clergy grant dispensations for whatever pleases them, and the lower clergy, purely on the evidence of good intention, obtain permission to transfer, to exchange, or combine their ecclesiastical benefices and to engage in shady financial deals under strange titles they have invented.

20. *Burning coals.* Blessed Augustine says: "We must understand this expression in the sense that we induce him who has

[46] Augustine, *Sermo* 355, 1, 1, *Patrologia, Series Latina*, XXXIX, 1569.

[47] Jerome tells this story of the woman of Vercellae with all the gory details in *Epistulae*, 1, *Patrologia, Series Latina*, XXII, 325 ff.

injured us to repent of his action, and thus we benefit him." For these "coals" (that is, benefits) have the power to burn, that is, to distress, his spirit. The psalmist speaks of this in Ps. 120:4: "The sharp arrows of the mighty, with coals that lay waste." Thus God also converts those whom He converts with a view of His goodness. And this is the only way to achieve a true conversion, namely, through love and kindness. For he who is converted through threats and terror is never truly converted as long as he retains that form of conversion. For fear makes him hate his conversion. But he who is converted by love is completely burned up against himself and is far more angry with himself than anyone else can be with him, and he is totally displeased with himself. For such a person there is no need for prohibition, for being under surveillance, and for making satisfaction. For love teaches him all things; and when he has been touched by love, he will exhaust himself in seeking out the person whom he has offended.

And thus the good deeds shown toward our enemies are the "burning coals," not those shown to our friends. For a friend does not feel about a good deed the way an enemy does, for he assumes that he has the right to expect good deeds and never receives enough, nor is he surprised at the kindness of his benefactor. But an enemy, because he realizes that he does not deserve an act of kindness, is completely captivated by his benefactor. In the same way God gave His only-begotten Son for His enemies, so that He might make us burn with the warmest love toward Him and that He might bring about in us the greatest possible hatred for ourselves. Christ is the furnace filled with fire, as we read in Is. 31:9: "Thus says the Lord, whose fire is in Zion, and whose furnace is in Jerusalem." We heap "burning coals" on the head of our adversary, but God heaps the Fire itself upon him.

21. *Do not be overcome by evil.* That is, see to it that he who hurts you does not cause you to become evil like him and that his iniquity does not overcome your goodness. For he is the victor who changes another man to become like himself while he himself remains unchanged. But rather by your well-doing make him to become good like you. Let your goodness overcome his wickedness and change him into you. Now he is considered to be the victor among men who is the last to talk or strike blows, while actually he who is the last to strike is worse off, because the evil remains with him when the other man has finished with it. Hence blessed Gregory says: "It is better to escape from anger by silence than to

gain the victory by answering." [48] And Prov. 26:4-5 reads: "Answer not a fool according to his folly, lest you be like him yourself. Answer a fool according to his folly, lest he be wise in his own eyes." Disregarding the preceding words, some people use this passage as a cloak for their own fury, saying that it is right for a wise man to answer a fool with foolish words and to return evil for evil. And even a great many very learned men argue with great erudition that this seems to be the meaning of the passage. But he who is "overcome by evil" and does not change the fool but rather falls into the same violence himself, he it is who answers the fool according to his folly and becomes like him. But he who "overcomes evil with good," with the result that the fool recognizes his own folly and comes to hate and lament it, he it is who replies in such a way that the fool does not seem in his own eyes to be a wise man. For by replying in kind you accomplish nothing to cause the fool to see himself as a fool, but rather you only increase his foolishness by the foolishness with which you repay him. But what does it mean "to answer and not to answer according to folly?" I believe that the word "according to" *(iuxta)* is used here in place of "to" *(ad)* or "against" *(contra)*. Thus when one thing is placed "against" another thing, we say "they are put next to each other," "so that an opposite placed against an opposite causes each to be more distinct," [49] that is, to put them over against each other or to compare them with one another. Thus in this instance the expression "according to his folly" does not mean that one wishes to answer a fool with the same folly, but something different from it should be placed opposite it, by the comparison of which it may be recognized how hideous it is; and that must not be placed opposite it by the comparison of which the folly is increased the more, is ignored the more, and is understood less. For as long as folly sees something like itself, it is not displeased with itself; but it does become displeased when it sees something different from itself.

[48] This quotation has not been identified in the works of Gregory.

[49] Cf. p. 200 above.

CHAPTER THIRTEEN

1. Let every soul be subject to the governing authorities.

Is there some mysterious reason why he does not say "every man" but rather "every soul"? Perhaps because it must be a sincere submission and from the heart. Second, because the soul is the medium between the body and the spirit; so that he thus may show that the believer is exalted once and for all above all things and yet at the same time is subject to them, and thus, being twin-born,[1] he has two forms within himself, just as Christ does. For according to the spirit he is above all things. For all things "work together for good . . . for the saints" (Rom. 8:28). And 1 Cor. 3:22 reads: "All things are yours . . . whether the world or life or death." Because through faith the believer has subjected all these things to himself in the sense that he is not affected by them nor trusts in them, but he compels them to serve him to his glory and salvation. And this is to serve God and so to rule and establish the spiritual realm of which we read in Rev. 5:10: "Thou hast made us a kingdom for our God, and we shall reign on earth."

And the world is conquered and subjected in no better way than through contempt. But this spiritual rule is now so little known that almost everyone with one accord says that the temporal gifts which have been given to the church are spiritual gifts. And now they regard only these as spiritual and rule by means of them, except that they still carry on their juridical actions, the lightning bolts of their decrees, and their power of the keys, but with much less concern and zeal than they use on their "spiritual," that is, their temporal duties.

Thus the spirit of the believers cannot be or become subject to anyone but is exalted with Christ in God, holding all things under its foot, like the woman in Rev. 12:1, who is depicted as having the moon under her feet, that is, all temporal powers. The

---

[1] Here the earlier stirrings of the thoughts later (1520) expressed in Luther's *The Freedom of a Christian* (*Luther's Works,* 31, pp. 343—377) are unmistakable.

"soul," which is the same as man's spirit, insofar as it lives and works and is occupied with visible and temporal matters, ought to be "subject for the Lord's sake to every human institution" (1 Peter 2:13). For by this submission it is obedient to God and wills the same thing that He wills; and thus through this subjection it is victorious over all these things.

Let me digress a little. A person has to be amazed at the impenetrable darkness of our time. Today nothing hurts the spiritual rulers more, those voracious spendthrifts of our temporal gifts, than when the liberties, laws, edicts, or benefits of the church are violated. Then they immediately let fly the lightning bolts of excommunication and with wondrous audacity declare people heretics, enemies of God and of His church and of the apostles Peter and Paul; in the meantime they are utterly unconcerned as to whether they themselves are friends of God or perhaps greater enemies than those they condemn. To such an extent have they established obedience and faith under the custody, enlargement, and defense of temporal things. You may be guilty of pride, wantonness, avarice, contentions, wrath, and you may possess the whole catalog of vices, which the apostle mentions in 2 Tim. 3:2 ff., and even though you may possess them till they cry to heaven, yet you are a most pious Christian, if only you uphold the laws and liberties of the church. But if you neglect them, you are not a faithful son of the church nor her friend.

Moreover, the secular princes have given great riches to the church and have endowed her leaders with many benefits. But look at this marvel. In the time of the apostles, when priests were eminently worthy of the favor of all men, they still paid taxes and were subject to the governing authorities. But now, when the life they lead resembles nothing so little as the life of priests, they enjoy the rights of special exemptions. Do the successors possess what their predecessors should have had? And the life that the present generation ought to live, did the former generation already demonstrate it sufficiently? By some marvelous exchange the earlier age labored and merited but received no fruit, while the later age enjoys the fruit without working for it or deserving it. I do not say that these privileges are evil, but that in our day they are being given to evil and undeserving men, when once they were bestowed only on those who were good.

But if some layman clergy-hater (since we all complain today because the laity are enemies of the clergy, but we do not say why. For why were the laity not enemies of the apostles and saints also in the old days, for the apostles were the ones who led them into poverty, suffering, and death, and they were the first to bring on all the evils of this life?)—if one of them should say: "To you clerics have been given benefits of the law and riches because of your services, as the rule states: "The benefit befits the service" *(Beneficium propter officium)*, they immediately reply and remind us of their murmured prayers and nothing else. The duties of the priests are to say the canonical hours, but these are mumbled in a cold manner, and even suspended and excused by special dispensation, while on the other hand when the apostle described the priest, he did not even mention prayer. And what he does say no one now thinks of putting into practice.

Thus as the priest is, so is the reward; as the service, so also the benefit. Clerics who are only shadows of what they should be have only the shadow of a reward; insofar as they are priests only in appearance, they also possess only the appearance of good things. How much more upright and faithful it would be for the man who wishes to enjoy the privileges of a priest to show himself to be a good priest! Or if he does not wish to be a good one, he should not demand his due in a contentious manner, since in his conscience before God he is an unworthy priest. But if he demands and argues and gets what he wants, what is left for him but that he receive here the pay that is coming to him?

The lawyers complain that it is very bad not to carry out a last will and testament. But who is there nowadays among the priests, who fulfills the will in accord with the wishes of the testators? Or is it because they did not prepare an instrument stating their will that they are now safe and cannot be interfered with? But if we concede that the church is bound to provide for priests who are paupers, and not even because of their praying, but gratis, yet what about avaricious ones and those who are insatiable for riches?

But when the Jews were not willing to submit to the Romans, they were destroyed; likewise under Nebuchadnezzar, all the time prating as we do now: "We are the servants of the God of heaven," [2] we should be servants to no man. But this is to serve neither God nor men. So it is with us, when we do not serve God, we likewise are unwilling to serve men, although men have made us free from serving them in order that we may serve God. But up to this time

[2] Ezra 5:11.

the laity have been ignorant, and they could be easily persuaded and they did not understand, even though they hated it and were rightly offended by it. But now they are surely beginning to understand the mysteries of our iniquity and to show discernment regarding our duties. Thus unless we once more show ourselves to be true clerics, so that the people will be forced to believe not just for appearance, but to take it seriously, it will be vain for us to deceive ourselves regarding our rights and exemptions.

For my part, I do not know, but it seems plain to me that in our day the secular powers are carrying on their duties more successfully and better than the ecclesiastical rulers are doing. For they are strict in their punishment of thefts and murders, except to the extent that they are corrupted by insidious privileges. But the ecclesiastical rulers, except for those who invade the liberties, privileges, and rights of the church, whom they condemn to excessive punishments, actually nourish pride, ambitions, prodigality, and contentions rather than punish them (so much so that perhaps it would be safer if the temporal affairs also of the clergy were placed under the secular power); and not only do they not prevent the unlearned, the dull, and the unfit from entering holy orders, but they actually promote them to the highest positions. Knowingly, with their eyes wide open, and in full possession of their faculties, they destroy the church through these pestiferous men whom they have elevated, and yet they impose judgment upon those who invade their domain, to whom they have actually given the occasion for the invasion in that they have forced them to hate them rather than that they have drawn them to be their friends. And if those who have invaded them have sinned so greatly, how much, I ask you, do they themselves give occasion by the appearance of evil, indeed, by action itself contrary to the apostle? And if Christians, let us suppose, cannot be excused when they are prompted to an evil deed by some occasion, how shall those people be excused who in full knowledge, willfully, and needlessly produce a scandal and an occasion of this kind? Thus they sit like whited walls and according to their laws judge transgressors, while they themselves are the greatest of all transgressors, unconcerned as to how they themselves might be blameless, only considering how they might condemn others, exacting strict righteousness from others, but digging a grave for their own. But if they also had to fear other people, how much more cautiously they would act in all matters!

Thus there is the bishop who in execution of the canon law

wearies a whole city with this tedious case.[3] Why? Because there is the tradition among men not to violate the church. Moreover, if he really desired to carry out the commandments of God, he would not have to leave his house. Not that what he is doing is evil, but that gnats are being strained out while a camel is being swallowed.

And the good Lord God permits this and similar transgressions to happen in order that He may admonish them regarding their duty and the commandments of the Gospel. But paying no attention to this warning of God in a case of this kind, they rush ahead in their ardor to inflict punishment and penance on others and call them sons of Pharaoh and Satan or even worse, only because they have found a speck in the eye of their brother but do not see the log in their own. Hence they themselves are incomparably more like Pharaoh, Satan, and Behemoth than their opponents.

May the Lord God grant that sometime laws of this kind together with their proponents may be destroyed and done away, for example, the idea that the soul is dead which has violated sacred stones by the touch of the hand. But that soul is not dead which has lived in ambition and without faith, and yet curses and judges and condemns the other one!

I beg that no one imitate me in these remarks, because I am speaking under the compulsion of my sorrow and the demands of my office. For in order to understand it is most important to make an application to our present life of the doctrine that is taught. At the same time I am performing my work of teaching by apostolic authority. It is my duty to speak of whatever I see not being done correctly, even in the case of those in high places.

So the Venetians, too, committed a very great sin against Julius II in taking away the small contributions of the church, and he regained them for the church with great merit, by killing and destroying a large number of Christians. But there is no sin at all in the terrible corruptions of the whole Curia and the portentous collection of the filth of all wantonness, prodigality, greed, ambition, sacrilege. Blessed Bernard is correct in the fourth book of his *De consideratione*, when he says in ridicule: "It is a marvelous thing! The bishops have at hand more than enough people to whom

---

[3] This is a reference to the case of the City of Strasbourg vs. one Hepp von Kirchberg, a canon of St. Thomas Church, who had raped a citizen's daughter. The city appealed to the bishop and the archbishop for justice in vain. The criminal meanwhile managed to procure indictments against three members of the city council of Strasbourg from the Curia in Rome, and so the plaintiff became the defendant.

they can entrust souls, but they cannot find people to whom to entrust their little secular affairs; obviously they are men of the best judgment, for they devote the greatest care to the least important matters and little or none to the most important.

But this is enough. Let us return to the apostle.

As I was saying, there are three elements in a man, the body, the soul, and the spirit. And the soul is the midportion. The body is subject to the power of the state, but with the consent and willingness of the soul, and under the direction of the spirit, which is free and above all. But the question arises:

Why then does the apostle in Gal. 5:13 say: "You were called to freedom; only do not use your freedom as an opportunity for the flesh"? And in chapter two of the same epistle he says: "False brethren were secretly brought in to spy out our freedom . . . that they might bring us back into bondage" (Gal. 2:4). And in another place, 1 Cor. 6:12: "All things are lawful for me, but I will not be enslaved by anything." And in 1 Cor. 7:23: "You were bought with a price; do not become the slaves of men." The apostle is frequent in his assertion of liberty and his rejection of slavery. Indeed in 1 Cor. 9:19 ff. he even says: "For though I am free from all men, I have made myself a slave to all, that I might win the more. To the Jews I became as a Jew, in order to win Jews." And again he later says: "I have become all things to all men, that I might save all" (1 Cor. 9:22). What shall we say to these things? How do they harmonize?

The reply is that the apostle, just as he has been made all things to all men, so also he speaks to all, and to each on his own terms. Hence of necessity he is equivocal in his use of the terms "liberty" and "slavery." For to those who were slaves but free according to the law of the Gentiles, he speaks in the proper terms so that he commands slaves to obey their masters, and if they can, they should become free (1 Cor. 7:21 and in almost all of his letters). But he makes the statement in 1 Cor. 6:12: "All things are lawful for me . . . but I will not be enslaved by anything," and 1 Cor. 7:23: "You were bought with a price; do not become slaves of men," and other such statements he makes with reference to a metaphorical slavery, whereby if one involve himself in temporal matters and in business negotiations with men, he will lose his liberty. For he must cling to those people with whom he does business and if he wants to remain faithful, he must make mutual confidence serve the business operations. Thus in one way or another people of this kind become captives to each other. For they become distracted and occupied with temporal matters and cannot direct their attention toward God.

He calls the other kind of servitude the very best of all, Gal. 5:13: "Through love be servants of one another." About this kind of love he says that though he was free, yet he made himself the servant of all. This kind of servitude is the highest freedom, for it lacks nothing and receives nothing, but rather gives and bestows. Thus it is truly the best freedom and one which is the peculiar property of Christians. He has this in mind in this chapter when he says: "Owe no one anything, except to love one another" (Rom. 13:8). This is the good spiritual servitude: all things serve them who possess it, and "all things work together for good" (Rom. 8:2) for them who have it; but they themselves are in slavery to no one, for they need nothing, as I have said.

And the fourth kind of servitude is equally spiritual, but it is very bad, and against this he contends on behalf of the Christians with all his might. This is a matter of being subjected to the Law and all of its burdens, that is, to believe that it is necessary for salvation to fulfill all the external works of the Law. For they who think and believe this, remain slaves and will never be saved. For they are the servants of the Law, and the Law rules over them because of this foolish faith and conscience of theirs. And such are all those who desire to be saved in some other way than through faith in Christ, for they are greatly concerned how they can satisfy the Law by their many works and their own righteousness. To be sure, the apostle and spiritual men also performed these works and still do so, but not because they have to but because they want to; not because the works are necessary but because they are permitted. But these hypocrites have tied themselves up in their good works as necessary works, and therefore they do them because they have to of necessity and not because they want to. Indeed they wish they were not necessary, as in fact they seem to them. In our day this is a very common form of servitude.

From this we can easily understand how in the Book of Acts the apostle wished to purify himself (Acts 21:26) and why he circumcised Timothy (Acts 16:3), while at the same time preaching the exact opposite everywhere. Thus all these external matters are free for them who are in the Spirit.

But with respect to the secular power the apostle does not raise the question of liberty. For this is not a servitude, since it deals with all the people in the world, which is not the case with the works of the Law.

10. *Love is the fulfilling of the Law*. The commandment "You shall love your neighbor as yourself" is understood in a twofold manner, as it reads in Matt. 19:19 or as in Lev. 19:18, where it reads: "Love your friend as yourself." First, we can understand it in the sense that both the neighbor and one's own self are to be loved. But in another sense it can be understood that we are commanded to love only our neighbor, using our love for ourselves as the example. This is the better interpretation, because man with his natural sinfulness does love himself above all others, seeks his own in all matters, loves everything else for his own sake, even when he loves his neighbor or his friend, for he seeks his own in him.

Hence this is a most profound commandment, and each person must test himself according to it by means of a careful examination. For through this expression, "as yourself," every pretense of love is excluded. Therefore he who loves his neighbor on account of his

money		poor	clearly
honor	and does	lowly	has a
knowledge	not love the	unlearned	hypocritical love,
favor	same person if he	hostile	not a love
power	is	dependent	for him
comfort		unpleasant	himself,

but a love for his neighbor's goods for his own benefit, and thus he does not love him "as himself," for indeed, he does love himself, even if he is a pauper, or a fool, or a plain nothing. For who is so useless that he hates himself? But no one is such a nothing that he does not love himself and does not love others in the same way. Therefore this is the hardest commandment of all, if we really think about it. And thus it is that no one wishes to be robbed, harmed, killed, to be the victim of adultery, to be lied to, victimized by perjury, or have his property coveted. But if he does not feel the same way also about his neighbor, he is already guilty of breaking this command. Therefore this commandment also includes the idea of Matt. 7:12: "So whatever you wish that men would do to you, do so to them; for this is the Law and the Prophets." Thus although this commandment when viewed in a superficial and general way seems quite a small matter, if we apply it to particular cases, it pours forth infinite salutary teachings and gives us faithful direction for all of our dealing. But the fact that this commandment is not observed and that we sin against it countless times and that it is ignored by those who are thoughtless proves that people do not apply it to their own actual undertakings but are content with their good intentions. For example, rich men supply the priests with treasures for the building of a church or a memorial. But if they would put themselves in the position of the poor and ask themselves whether they would want it donated not to themselves but rather to the churches, they would easily learn from themselves what they ought to do.

Likewise our prince and our bishop compete with each other for relics.[4] Each wants the other to concede to him, and yet each proceeds in his show of good works, granting nothing to the other.

Also the Observants contend with one another for the sake of God.[5] But they pay no attention to the commandment to love.

But he who wishes to think seriously about this commandment and apply it ought not to depend on his own actions which are elicited from within, but rather he must compare all the acts, words, and thoughts of his whole life with this commandment as a rule and always say to himself about his neighbor: "What would you wish done to you by him?" And when he has seen this, let him also begin to do the same toward his neighbor, and immediately the contention, the detraction, the dissension will cease, and there will be present the whole host of virtues, every grace, every act of holiness, and as it says here, "the fulfilling of the Law." For this is how Moses taught the children of Israel in Deut. 6:6 ff.: "These

---

[4] Both Elector Frederick the Wise of Saxony and Albert of Brandenburg, archbishop of Magdeburg, bishop of Halberstadt, and archbishop of Mainz, were ardent collectors of relics and were pursuing their hobby with particular vigor during the time of these lectures.

[5] The monks of the Augustinian monastery at Erfurt, where Luther was a brother from 1505 to 1524, were *Observantes,* practicing a strict observance of the monastic rules. But as Luther indicates here and in many other places, there was a constant struggle going on within the order between the "strict" and the "lax" cloisters and persons. The efforts of Staupitz to reconcile and unite these two elements failed. Although Luther supported the efforts of Staupitz, his own observance was of the strictest sort. In 1533 he wrote: "I kept the rules of my order so strictly that I can say: if ever a monk went to heaven on account of his monkery, I should get there too. . . . If it had lasted any longer, I would have killed myself with vigils, prayers, readings, and other work" (W, XXXVIII, 143). Luther never hesitated to criticize his nonobserving brothers by asides in his lectures, such as: "This is what happens to all proud, stubborn, superstitious, rebellious, and disobedient people, and I fear to our Observants too, for under the guise of life according to rule they commit disobedience and rebellion (W, IV, 83). Cf. p. 139, n. 12, above.

words which I command you this day shall be upon your heart; and you shall teach them to your children, and you shall talk of them when you sit in your house, and when you walk by the way, and when you lie down, and when you rise." And then he continues by saying: "And you shall bind them as a sign upon your hand, and they shall be as frontlets between your eyes. And you shall write them on the doorposts of your house and on your gates." It was not the wish of Moses that we wear Pharisaic phylacteries, but saying that they are to be as "a sign upon your hand" means that all our efforts must be applied and directed to this end. And the expression "between your eyes" means that all our thoughts must be directed by these words, and the phrases "to write them on the doorposts of your house and on your gates" means that all our senses and particularly our tongue must be directed and applied according to these words.

He who would do this would come to a complete knowledge of his faults and to humility and fear of God; otherwise he remains secure and saintly in his own opinion. For he would often discover not only that he is sluggish in helping his neighbor—while at the same time he nevertheless finds that he wants everyone to be kindly affectioned, loving, and favorably disposed toward him—but that he himself is actually an enemy and a false brother toward his brothers, indeed, a detractor and full of every kind of sin. For this reason the apostle describes the essence of this commandment when he says in Phil. 2:4: "Let each of you look not only to his own interests but also to the interests of others," and in 1 Cor. 13:5: "Love does not insist on its own way," that is, it causes man to deny himself and to affirm another, to put on affection for the neighbor and put off affection for himself, to place himself in the person of his neighbor and then to decide what he wants him to do for him himself and what he himself and others might do for him. And then he will discover by this infallible teaching what he ought to do. But when this process is omitted then commandments multiply and yet a man will not arrive where he is going.

As often as he wants benefits, either spiritual or physical, to come to him, as for instance, that prayer be made for him, and how it ought to be done (that is, perfectly), he becomes mixed up in vices by this very prayer, because he owes the same things to others, and then he finds that he does not want to do the same things for others. Or he may come to hate himself and desire no good from others, and then he will also owe nothing to others. Why?

Because he who is dead is righteous. Behold how deep and wide is this commandment!

11. *It is full time now for us to wake from sleep.* It says the same thing in 1 Cor. 15:34: "Awake, you righteous, and sin not," and Eph. 5:14: "Awake, O sleeper, and arise from the dead, and Christ shall give you light." There is no doubt that with these words also in this passage he is speaking of spiritual sleep, where the spirit is sleeping when it lives in sins and is content. Christ in many ways in the Gospel wakes us up against this kind of sleep, admonishing us that we must be watchful. And we must take note that he is not speaking of those people who are dead in the sin of unbelief, nor about those believers who are lying in mortal sin, but rather about Christians who are living lukewarm lives and are snoring in their smugness; for he wants them to advance carefully, as we read in Micah 6:8: "I will show you, O man, what is good; and what the Lord requires of you, namely, to do justice and to love kindness and to walk humbly with your God." For those who are unconcerned and are not watchful and fearful, they are the ones who make a beginning but do not progress, they put their hand to the plow and look back (Luke 9:62); they have the appearance of godliness but deny the power thereof (2 Tim. 3:5); with their body they depart from Egypt, but with their heart they return; they are smug, going their way without fear of God, hardened, impious, insensitive. Of these people blessed Bernard says: "He who does not constantly hasten to repent says by this action that he does not need repentance." [6] And if he does not need repentance, he does not need mercy; and if he does not need mercy, then he does not need salvation. This is something which cannot happen, unless one is without sin, as God and His angels are.

Thus it is well that the apostle speaks to Christian people and exhorts them that they should arise out of sleep, even though they would not be Christians if they had not already arisen; but to stand still on the way to God is to retrogress, and to advance is always a matter of beginning anew. Hence the Preacher does not say: "When a man has made progress" but "when a man has finished, then shall he begin" (Ecclus. 18:7). St. Arsenius prayed in this way to God every day: "Help me, Lord, that I may begin to live for You." [7] And surely, just as the apostle said about knowledge: "If

[6] *Sermo II in vigilia nativitatis Domini, Patrologia, Series Latina,* CLXXXIII, 90.

[7] *Vitae patrum, Verba seniorum,* III, 190; V, 15, 5, *Patrologia, Series Latina,* LXXIII, 801; 953.

anyone imagines that he knows something, he does not yet know as he ought to know" (1 Cor. 8:2); so we must infer regarding each of the individual virtues: He who thinks he has already taken hold of them and made a beginning does not yet know how he ought to begin.

And this species of men in our day is most portentous and numerous. They practice the repentance established by Christ in the form of temporal and external matters, and when they have done this, they think they are righteous. The result is that this kind of confession is frequently practiced to the detriment of this wretched trust in oneself, because it does not take away what they presume it does.

The word "sleep" is used in Scripture in various ways. In the first place, it is used in the literal sense with reference to physical death, as in John 11:11: "Our friend Lazarus has fallen asleep." And in the Old Testament, very frequently in the Books of Kings and Chronicles we read: "He slept with his fathers."

In the second place, it is used with reference to spiritual sleep and in a twofold manner. First, in a good sense, as in Ps. 127:2: "For He gives to His beloved sleep," and again in Ps. 68:13: "If you sleep among the midst of lots." [8] And in Song of Sol. 5:2 the bride says: "I slept, but my heart was awake." Accordingly, "to sleep" is not to be turned aside to temporal advantages but to regard them as imaginary things and shadows rather than real things, because of one's concern for eternal matters, which people see through the illumination of faith by means of a watchful heart. Thus they snore and act negligently regarding temporal matters.

In the third place the word "sleep" is used with reference to spiritual sleep but in an evil sense and contrary to the usage already mentioned. The apostle speaks of this in 1 Thess. 5:6 f.: "So then let us not sleep, as others do, but let us keep awake and be sober. For those who sleep sleep at night, and those who get drunk are drunk at night," using the term "night" here with reference to spiritual evil. Likewise we read in Ps. 76:5: "They sank into sleep, and all the men of riches found nothing in their hands." Thus the term "to sleep" in this sense means not to turn to and not to be concerned about eternal values. And so people of this kind snore away,

---

[8] Luther quotes the Vulgate: *Si dormiatis inter medios cleros*. His glosses in the *Dictata super Psalterium* are, for *si dormiatis*: "resting from the tumult of desires," and for *inter medios cleros*: "between the two testaments, or to live in faith between things temporal and heavenly." Cf. W, III, 386, 15. In his glosses on Ps. 127:2 Luther defines "sleep" as "contempt of things temporal, about which I have spoken at Ps. 68:13." Cf. W, IV, 415, 10.

indifferent toward eternal things, but very active regarding temporal matters, which they watch with vigilant cupidity. Thus they are the antithetical counterpart [9] of the sleepers mentioned previously, for the night of the one is the day of the other, and the watchfulness of the one group is the sleep of the other, and vice versa. Thus we note conflicting values, conflicting effects, and thus conflicting men. In brief we may describe these three as the sleep of nature, the sleep of grace, and the sleep of guilt, but this distinction is a little obscure.

And just as there are three ways in Scripture of describing sleep, so also there are different ways of talking about night and day, indeed about almost all the metaphorical uses of language. For "day" in the spiritual sense refers to faith, "night" to unbelief. On the contrary, faith is night, and unbelief is day, as in Ps. 19:2: "Day to day pours forth speech, and night to night declares knowledge," that is, the carnal man [10] speaks to the carnal and the wise man to the wise; the fool of God to the fools of men, the wise in Christ to the wise of the world. And thus it is also obvious that in this passage the apostle is not speaking about physical sleep or of the darkness or of the night that is felt by the senses — of which he speaks later on when he says: "not in reveling and drunkenness" (v. 13), that is, in sleep and lustfulness. These things are certainly done in the night.

Therefore the works of darkness are the works of those who are asleep in the spirit, in the bad sense, that is, those who are snoring away in the desires of the world — not only those works which are popularly thought to be evil but also those which are considered good, and yet are evil because of the inner evil, for men do them without the watchfulness of faith.

Salvation is nearer to us now. The meaning here is the same as that which he expresses in 2 Cor. 6:1-2, where he says: "Working together with Him, then, we entreat you not to accept the grace of God in vain. For He says, 'At the acceptable time I have listened to you and helped you on the day of salvation.' Behold, now is the acceptable time; behold, now is the day of salvation." What the apostle here touches on in a brief and incidental way, he there deals with at great length, describing fully what he means here with the expression *the armor of light and the works of darkness* (v. 12), saying: "We put no obstacle in anyone's way, so that no fault may

---

[9] Luther seems to have a new coinage in the word *antithesiaci.*

[10] Luther wrote "spiritual man," but this ruins the parallelism he is setting up. He must have meant "carnal man."

be found with our ministry, but as servants of God we commend ourselves in every way, through great endurance and . . . hunger." And a little later he continues: "with the weapons of righteousness for the right hand and for the left" (2 Cor. 6:3-7). Here he uses "armor of light," there "weapons of righteousness"; therefore righteousness and light are the same thing.

13. *Not in reveling.* Just as the term *graecari* ("to live in the Greek manner") is derived from *Graecus* (Greek), so the word *comessari* ("reveling") comes, it seems, from *comos* ("a revel"). For the Greek κῶμος means a banquet, or rather a luxurious, wasteful, and immoderate preparation and celebration of a banquet. Indeed, the god of drunkenness is called Comus, and his feast bears the same name. In this the Greeks outdo the Germans and indeed the whole world, because they gave attention to banquets so enthusiastically that they even devised a god who was in charge of this as a useful activity. But the apostle teaches contrary to this in this passage and the positive side in 2 Cor. 6. For he wants us to devote ourselves to fasting and temperance and sobriety. And certainly anyone who reads the histories, at least St. Jerome, will discover that these six vices not only abounded in Rome but actually ruled and tyrannized the people—look at Suetonius' *Lives of the Caesars* —so that even Juvenal, the old heathen, exclaims: "A stronger enemy, namely, luxury, has come to lodge with us and takes vengeance upon a conquered world." [11] And thus the apostle is trying to frighten the faithful, so that they do not give in to the wild examples of Rome. Nor is blessed Peter silent about the wantonness of the same city when in 1 Peter 4:4 he calls attention not only to the wantonness but also to "the riotousness and vileness mingled with it." Indeed because of this he does not hesitate to call this city a Babylon, because everything there was in confusion, as even Catullus testifies: "Everything, right or wrong, is mixed with insane raving," [12] so that the city, now brought to the last insanity of corruption, seems to have cried to highest heaven either for apostles, and the greatest of them, or for a punishment like that of Sodom and Gomorrah. Hence 1 Peter 4:3 ff. says: "Let the time that is past suffice for doing what the Gentiles like to do, living in licentiousness, passions, drunkenness, revels, carousing, and lawless idolatry. They are surprised that you do not now join them in the same wild profligacy, and they abuse you." And in 2 Peter

[11] Juvenal, *Satyrae,* VI, 292.

[12] Catullus, LXIV, 406.

2:13 we read: "They count it pleasure to revel in the daytime. They are blots and blemishes, reveling in their dissipation, carousing with you." But now Rome, having returned to her former morals, draws almost the whole world after her in keeping with her example, if the Rome of today does not even exceed ancient Rome in her outgushing of riotousness so that it would seem to demand apostles again, but with even greater urgency. Would that their coming be kindly before they come as judges.

Incidentally, we must take note that the word *luxuria* (wantonness) must not be understood in this passage in the sense of "lust" *(libido)*, but rather of "reveling" or "an outpouring of prodigality," like the Greek ἀσωτία , ἄσωτος.

Opposing the same vice in 1 Tim. 2 and 3, and Titus 1 and 2, the apostle orders that bishop, deacon, elders, young men, and women are to be sober, and to all he forbids drunkenness and reveling like a plague. Thus a comparison of those passages with this one, and of this with those, gives us a correct understanding of the apostle's thinking, when in this passage he shows what he does not want and in the others what he does want.

Not in debauchery and licentiousness. That is, they should be watchful and chaste. For in the foregoing passages he has prescribed chastity and watchfulness, beginning with the bishops and then applying it to the elders and to others. And this is clearly a proper order. For reveling and drunkenness foment unchastity, or as the Greek says, lasciviousness. Thus the holy fathers [13] stated that he who wishes to serve God must above all fight against the vice of gluttony, because it is both the first and the most difficult vice to overcome. If this is not rooted out, even if it does not lead to chambering and lasciviousness, as sometimes happens with older men, yet it renders the mind unprepared over against divine matters. For this reason fasting is one of the strongest weapons of Christians, but gluttony is one of the most potent machines of the devil. But there is much on this subject in the writings of the saints.

Not in quarreling and emulation. Just as in the foregoing where he has instructed man with regard to himself, namely, that he be temperate, watchful, and chaste, so here in this passage he is giving him instruction regarding his relationship with his neighbor, that they live together in peace, unity, and love. He orders this in all of his epistles at great length and with much solicitude, as he has also done in the preceding chapter. In 1 Tim. 2:8 he says: "I desire

[13] Cf. Johannes Cassianus, *De coenobiorum institutis et de octo principalibus vitiis*, V, 1 ff., *Patrologia, Series Latina*, XLIX, 201 ff.

then that in every place the men should pray, lifting holy hands without anger or quarreling." And in the third chapter of the same epistle (1 Tim. 3:3) as well as in Titus 1:7 he commands the bishop not to be a quarrelsome person. And according to blessed Jerome, this means that he should not have a sharp tongue. Thus he wants them to be meek, kind, and generous toward each other in their attitudes. A "contention" is a verbal sword fight, and "to contend" is to fight with words, in which each contender wants to be considered correct, right, and the winner, all the rest being considered as refuted, a situation in which neither gives in to the other. On the other hand, the term "emulation" is a very broad word. "To emulate" means to follow after or to pursue. And just as the term "to follow" or "to pursue" is used in both a good and a bad sense, so the word "to follow after eagerly" *(consector)*, "to follow after" *(insector)*, "to pursue" *(prosequor)*, "to follow" *(persequor)*, and also "to emulate" *(emulor)* can be used in these different ways. And it does not properly mean "to imitate" *(imitari)*. For the word "emulate" means to pursue in such a way that one obtains or lays hold on or even excels, thus expressing not merely a simple pursuit, but a real attempt to excel. Thus if one emulates in a good sense, he is a person who so imitates his teacher or his example that he even tries to surpass the example, which a person does not do if he is only imitating. And on the other hand, he who is emulating in an evil sense is one who strives to overcome the one with whom he is contending, or as we say in popular parlance, he wants to have the last word or to inflict the final blow, that is, to conquer evil by evil; if the other person says or does something evil, he tries to do or say something even worse. Thus emulation is the sister or handmaiden of contention. And hence we use the term "rival" *(emulus* or *emula)* either as an adjective or as a noun.

But with these remarks the use of this term is still not yet exhausted, although we have said sufficient for this passage. God is called a *zelotes* ("a jealous one," Ex. 20:5, etc.), and an *emulator.* The apostle says (2 Cor. 11:2): "I emulate you with the emulation of God," that is, "I am jealous of you with the jealousy of God." And in Song of Sol. 8:6 jealousy is described as "cruel as the grave," a passage in which the term emulation cannot be taken in the sense of a mutual contention, it would seem. Moreover, because everyone who emulates tries to be the only one in the matter over which he is contending with another, that is why the husband contends with the adulterer, God with the idol, the wife against the adulteress, or mistress, in the way that a man wants sole possession of his wife and thus tries to exclude the other man, so God wants to be the only God, so the apostle is jealous over his Corinthians as wanting to be their only teacher to the exclusion of all others, disliking to share this glory with others, but this with a holy jealousy. For he was afraid that their mind might be corrupted through the wiles of Satan, even though he had betrothed them to Christ. He also was afraid of false prophets. Thus emulation embraces the good which is beloved and thereby excludes the sharing of this good with someone else, and thus it is a kind of hatred of him who wishes to share and not want to leave it to him alone. Thus emulation both loves and hates at the same time. Sometimes the object of this jealousy is what is loved and sometimes what is hated, as when we say, "a man is jealous of his wife," and also "a man is jealous of an adulterer"; in the first instance the term is used more properly, as in 1 Cor. 12:31: "Be jealous for the better gifts."

Emulation is loving jealousy or jealous love. There is a simultaneous mixture of love and hatred, bitter love and loving bitterness. Just so, repentance is sweet sorrow and sorrowful sweetness. For the sweetness of his love makes the emulator do what he does and willing to do it, but the bitterness of his hatred makes him unwilling. But the term is not always used so properly, but often it is used in the sense of the effort which a person uses to surpass and to reach his goal, even without the concept of hatred, as for example in 1 Cor. 10:22: "Do we emulate the Lord?" that is, are we trying to surpass the Lord or do more than He does? Are we stronger than He is?

14. *And make no provision for the flesh, to gratify its desires,* that is, to gratify its lusts, but make provision for its necessities or in its necessities. The apostle is trying to say that the flesh should not be encouraged in its lusts. For so Hugo of St. Victor rightly says: "He who cherishes his flesh nourishes an enemy," and again on the other hand, "he who destroys his flesh kills a friend." [14] But it is not the flesh but the vices of the flesh, that is, the lusts, which must be destroyed. And Prov. 29:21 says: "He who pampers his servant from childhood will in the end find him stubborn."

---

[14] The Weimar editor was unable to find these words in the works of Hugo of St. Victor and suggests that the following words of Gregory, *Homilia in Ezechielem*, II, 7, may be in the background: "Sometimes our flesh is a helper in a good deed, and sometimes it is a seducer to an evil one. Now, if we give it more than its due, we nourish an enemy. But if we do not give it its due, we kill a fellow citizen."

CHAPTER FOURTEEN [1]

Summary: The apostle encourages those who are greater (stronger in faith) that they not despise those who are less (weaker) and that they should not cause them to stumble but should edify them in peace.

1. *As for the man who is weak in faith,* who is of a weak faith, *welcome him, but not for disputes,*[1] that is, adjudications,[2] *over opinions,* that is, ideas, that is, that one person does not judge the opinion or thinking of another. 2. *For one,* who has a strong and mature faith, *believes he may eat anything,* that is, whatever he wishes, that is, because he is permitted to eat everything, for "to the pure all things are pure" (Titus 1:15), *while,* another, namely,

---

[1] The apostle is prohibiting two things in this chapter. First, those who are strong in faith or weak should not despise or judge one another. Second, the strong should not offend the weak, cf. below, v. 13, "but rather decide . . ." The background for this teaching is this, that under the old law many kinds of food were prohibited, and this as a prefigurement of things to come. Therefore those who were so uneducated and weak in faith that they failed to understand that the figure had ceased and that all created things were clean or that they because of the ritual they were accustomed to could not eat those things should be tolerated and not despised; and again, those who did know this should not be condemned as if they were doing wrong because they were eating everything. A very great controversy arose over these matters. The first church council devoted itself to this question, Acts 15, and even Peter himself was taken to task by Paul for this very reason, Gal. 2:14 ff. And in almost all of his epistles the apostle deals with this matter in opposition to false apostles from among the Jews, who were teaching that it was necessary to keep these regulations in order to be saved, as we read in 1 Tim. 1:7: "desiring to be teachers of the Law without understanding either what they are saying or the things about which they make assertions," and in Titus 1:10, "deceivers of minds." In another place he says: "To the Jews I became as a Jew. . . . to those outside the Law as one outside the Law" (1 Cor. 9:20 f.). A similar cause for offense was given in the case of meats offered to idols by those who believed from among the Gentiles, as we see in 1 Cor., throughout chapters 8—10, where he says: "Eat whatever is sold in the meat market" (1 Cor. 10:25).

[2] The translator [2] does not bring out the meaning of the Greek original.

---

[1] Luther improves the spelling of *disceptionibus* to *disceptationibus.*

[2] Jerome.

persons by swerving from these have wandered away into vain discussion, desiring to be teachers of the Law, without understanding either what they are saying or the things about which they make assertions." Likewise in Gal. 4:9 ff. he says: "How can you turn back again to the weak and beggarly elemental spirits, whose slaves you want to be once more? You observe days and months and seasons and years! I am afraid I have labored over you in vain." And he is even more explicit in Col. 2:16 ff.: "Therefore let no one pass judgment on you in questions of food and drink or with regard to a festival or a new moon or a sabbath. These are only a shadow of what is to come, but the substance belongs to Christ. Let no one seduce you, insisting on self-abasement and worship of angels, taking his stand on visions, puffed up without reason by his sensuous mind, and not holding fast to the Head, from whom the whole body, nourished and knit together through its joints and ligaments grows with a growth that is from God. If with Christ you died to the elemental spirits of the universe, why do you live as if you still belonged to the world? Why do you submit to regulations, 'Do not handle, Do not taste, Do not touch' (referring to things which all perish as they are used), according to human precepts and doctrines? These have indeed an appearance of wisdom in promoting rigor of devotion and self-abasement and severity to the body, but they are of no value in checking the indulgence of the flesh." And Heb. 13:9: "Do not be led away by diverse and strange teachings; for it is well that the heart be strengthened by grace, not by foods, which have not benefited their adherents." And in 1 Cor. 8:1 ff. and 10:16 ff. he speaks extensively on the point mentioned in this chapter.

Thus the meaning of the apostle is that in the new law all things are free and nothing is necessary for those who believe in Christ, but love is sufficient for them, as he says (1 Tim. 1:5): "from a pure heart and a good conscience and sincere faith," and in Gal. 6:15: "For in Christ Jesus neither circumcision counts for anything, nor uncircumcision, but a new creation and the observance of God's commands." [1] And our Lord in the Gospel says (Luke 17:21-22): "The kingdom of God is not coming with signs to be observed, nor will they say, 'Lo, here it is!' or 'There!' for behold, the kingdom of God is in the midst of you." Likewise in Matt. 24:11, 26 He says: "And many false prophets will arise and lead many astray. . . . So if they say to you, 'Lo, He is in the wilderness,' do not go out;

[1] This quotation adds an element from 1 Cor. 7:19.

if they say, 'Lo, He is in the inner rooms,' do not believe it." And in Is. 66, at the end of the chapter, we read: "From new moon to new moon, and from sabbath to sabbath." And again in Is. 1:13 f.: "Your new moons and solemnities I cannot endure." And there are many such expressions throughout the whole book.

Thus it does not belong to the new law to set aside certain days for fasting and others not, as the law of Moses did. Nor does it belong that we make an exception of and a distinction between certain kinds of food, such as meat, eggs, etc., as again is done in the law of Moses, for example, in Lev. 11 and Deut. 14. Nor does it belong to designate some days as feast days and others not. Nor does it belong to the new law that we build this or that church or that we ornament them in such and such a way, or that the singing be of a certain kind or the organ or the altar decorations, the chalices, the statues and all of the other paraphernalia which are contained in our temples. Finally it is not necessary that the priest and other religious wear the tonsure or go about in distinctive garb, as they did under the old law. For all of these things are shadows and signs of the real thing and thus are childish. For every day is a feast, all food is permitted, every place is sacred, every time is a time of fasting, every kind of apparel is allowed, all things are free, only that we observe moderation in their use and that love and the other things which the apostle teaches us be practiced. Many false apostles have preached against this liberty which has been asserted by the apostle, so that they might lead the people to consider these matters as being necessary for salvation. These things the apostle resists with magnificent zeal. To what end? Are we now going to confirm the heresy of the Picards? [2] For they brought themselves to this rule. And thus are we going to say that all churches, all their ornamentation, all offices in them, all sacred places, all fast days, all feast days, finally all the distinctions between priests, bishops, and religious in rank, garb, and ceremonies observed for so many centuries right up to this day, and so many monasteries, foundations, benefices, and prebends — are we going

---

[2] The name Picards is a corruption of Beghards, a mystical libertine religious movement traceable from the 13th century in Europe. Because a group of Beghards flourished in Bohemia and won some adherents among the Hussites, the name eventually became a derogatory designation for the Moravian Brethren in general. Luther characterizes the Picards as extremely self-centered and vain when he writes: "The Picard is more ready to lead than to follow the Lord, so that not he might be called 'Christian,' after Christ, but that Christ might be called 'Picardian,' after the Picard" (W, IV, 361, 16 f.).

to say that all of these should be abolished? For that is what the Picards are doing, and this is what the liberty of the new law requires. God forbid!

Because if we understand the apostle in this way, then there will immediately follow the objection that used to be raised to one teaching such things: Then "let us do evil that good may come" (Rom. 3:8), let us cease doing good, we shall get to heaven while at ease. It is obvious that this conclusion follows. For if the apostle did reject all these works which we have just mentioned, surely no other works remain which are not also rejected. For none of them is necessary for salvation, as is obvious in the case of infants and children, and also in the case of those who are sick or prisoners or paupers, for whom these works of piety are not necessary or even possible, at least not all of them, indeed for no one are all of them necessary or even possible. But "love from a pure heart" suffices, as we have said above.

In opposition to this notion is the statement of the apostle himself that certain widows "incur condemnation for having violated their first pledge . . . and desired to marry" (1 Tim. 5:11-12). Thus it was necessary that they remain widows ("because they have grown wanton in Christ," that is, elegant and fat). And in the Gospel the Lord said about the most insignificant things: "These you ought to have done without neglecting the others" (Matt. 23: 23; Luke 11:42). And likewise in Jer. 35:5 ff. He highly commends the house of the Rechabites because they did not drink wine and build houses, indeed, because they had been obedient to their father Jonadab in these matters. And the apostle himself in the Book of Acts (16:3) circumcised Timothy, and offered sacrifices and made purification in the temple (Acts 21:26).

The answer is that it is true on the basis of the new law that none of these things is necessary, but not in such a way that when one thing has been omitted it is permissible to do the opposite or something entirely different. As Hilary says, "We must understand the meaning of statements on the basis of the reasons why they were spoken." [3] For the apostle is speaking in opposition to the Jews and people like them, who were teaching that such things were absolutely necessary, and that unless they were performed, faith in Christ was not sufficient for salvation. Hence they said in Acts 15:1, even to those who were at that very time baptized believers in Christ: "Unless you are circumcised according to

---

[3] Hilary, *De Trinitate*, IV, 14, *Patrologia, Series Latina*, X, 107.

the custom of Moses, you cannot be saved." And a little later: "It is necessary to circumcise them and to charge them to keep the law of Moses" (Acts 15:5). And the same idea is obvious in Gal. 2:14, where the apostle says to Peter: "How can you compel the Gentiles to live like Jews?" It is as if he were saying: "You compel them, that is, you make them think that it is necessary to salvation for them to abstain from the food of the Gentiles. And in the same chapter (Gal. 2:3) he says: "But even Titus was not compelled to be circumcised, even though he was a Gentile." The same meaning is here drawn from the word "to judge," which he uses several times in this passage. For he who judges another certainly believes that he is doing things that are opposed to his salvation and that he must necessarily do otherwise. Now, when this weakness of faith, along with the superstitious opinion, ceases to be influential, everyone is permitted to observe the whole law and every commandment in keeping with the vow he has taken. In this way the primitive church for a long time was permitted to observe the Jewish ceremonies, a matter about which blessed Augustine had a long argument with blessed Jerome in Letters 28, 40, 71, and 82.[4]

Therefore, as it was foolish at that time to give so much weight to these matters that they became matters of salvation, while both faith and love, which alone are sufficient, were neglected (this was completely in opposition to Christ, so that He said in Matt. 23:24: "You strain out a gnat and swallow a camel"), so also in our day and at all times it is both foolish and preposterous to make the Christian religion synonymous outwardly with these displays (as is the custom in our time) with distinctions of feast days, meats, dress, and holy places, while in the meantime the commandments of God are rejected along with faith and love.

Hence although all of these things are now matters of the greatest liberty, yet out of love for God each is permitted to bind himself by oath to this or that goal. But he is thereby no longer bound to these matters by the new law but by his own oath, which he has taken upon himself by reason of his love for God. For who is so foolish as to deny that a person can give up his liberty out of deference to another person and make himself a servant and bind himself to a certain place on such and such a day with such and such

---

[4] Luther gives the numbers of the letters according to the older editions, respectively 8, 9, 10, 19. We have supplied the numeration of the Benedictine edition.

a work? But this must be done out of love and the faith that does not believe that he is doing these things as necessary for salvation but only of his own free will and out of a sense of freedom.

And thus all things are free, but because of our oath and out of love they can be offered up. And when this has been done, then these works are necessary, not because of their own nature but because of the oath freely given. And thus we must take care that our oaths are fulfilled with the same love with which they were promised, for without this they cannot be fulfilled. And if they are fulfilled without it, that is, in an unwilling spirit, it would be better not to have made the vow. For he who makes a vow and does not keep it is like this: he keeps it with his body, but he has reservations in his heart, and thus he is sacrilegious, since he does not perform it willingly. Thus there are many apostates, but they do not appear as such. However, he who omits love and directs his attention to various commandments which he considers necessary for salvation, as now is the case everywhere among the priests and the religious, indeed, even among the seculars who are preoccupied with their own laws and the doctrines of men—then we surely have returned to superstitions of the Jews and have reestablished the Mosaic servitude. For we do these things not only unwillingly but in the belief that without them there is no salvation and that with them there is salvation without everything else. But then what about the general commandments of the church, about fasts and feasts? The answer is: Whatever has been imposed on us by the ancient consensus of the whole church and by the love of God and righteous causes, must surely be kept, not because they are themselves necessary or immutable, but because we owe God obedience out of our love for Him and the church. However, the higher clergy ought to carry on their work in such a way that they make as few commandments as possible and be on their guard as to when, how much, and how these commandments either promote or hinder love, and change them accordingly. For example, when they fill the churches with a loud noise, make the organs resound, and perform the Mass with all pomp, they think they have done such a good work that they can consider help given to the poor as worth nothing. For perjury, lying, slander are committed even on feast days, and nobody cares. But if a person eats meats or eggs on the sixth day of the week, the people are stunned. So stupid is everybody today. The result is that today we should abolish the fast days and many of the feast days. For the common people

observe them with such conscience that they believe there is no
salvation without them. And yet nearly all of them are acting
against their conscience. The people have come to this foolish
idea because of the neglect of the preaching of the true Word,
so that again the people are in need of the apostles so that they
might learn true piety.

For this reason it would be useful to revise and reform nearly
the entire book of decretals and to curtail displays, and especially
the ceremonies of prayer services and vestments. For every day
these increase, and they increase to such an extent that under the
load of them faith and love decrease, but avarice, pride, vainglory
are fostered, and what is still worse, that men hope in these things
for salvation and are not at all concerned about the inner man.

The question therefore is whether it is good to become a religious in our day. The answer is: If you think you cannot have
salvation in any other way except by becoming a religious, do not
even begin. For the proverb is so true: "Despair makes a monk,"
actually not a monk but a devil. For there will never be a good monk
who is one out of despair of this kind, but only when he becomes
a monk out of love, namely, when he sees that his sins are very
serious and he wishes to do something great for God because of
his love, when he willingly gives up his liberty and dons the habit
as a fool and subjects himself to degrading duties.

For this reason I believe that it is better to become a monk
today than it was at any time in the last two hundred years, because
up to this time the monks drew away from the cross and there was
a glory in being a religious. But now again it has become displeasing to men, even to those who are good, because of the foolish
garb. But this is what it means to be a religious, that one be hated
by the world and regarded as a fool. And he who out of love submits
himself to this situation does a very good work. For I am not afraid
when the bishops and the priests persecute us. For this has to
happen. But this alone displeases me, that we give them such
a poor reason for their dislike. Moreover, those who have no reason
and yet dislike the monks, not knowing why they dislike them,
are the best friends that the religious have in the whole world. For
the monks should rejoice as able to fulfill their vows by being
despised and shamed for the sake of a vow taken to God, for they
wear their foolish habit to induce all men to hold them in contempt. But in our day they do something entirely different, having
only the appearance of the religious. But I know that they would

be the happiest of men if they had love, and they would be more blessed than the hermits in the desert because of the fact that they are exposed to the cross and the shame every day. But now there is no more arrogant class of people than they are, sad to say!

And now let us return to the text. The apostle desires above all that those who are weak be tolerated and helped by those who are stronger, and secondly, that the weak should not make hasty judgment. And thus he is encouraging them to peace and unity. For even though a weak faith is not sufficient for salvation, as is evident in the Epistle to the Galatians, yet such people are to be welcomed in the meantime, so that they may be strengthened and not allowed to remain in their weakness, as those do who are disdainful of them and are concerned only about their own salvation. He has showed an example of this attitude both in regard to all men but especially in regard to the Galatians, so that with his own hand he wrote an epistle to them. Hence the word "welcome" *(assumite)* in the Greek corresponds to the concept of "join to yourselves," [5] as if to say: "Not only must you not haughtily reject or leave him, but you must take him to yourself, so that you nourish him, until he is perfected. But if you do not do this, but look down upon him as a useless person, be on your guard that God Himself does not make him stand." Thus he speaks to both groups: Those who are strong should instruct the weak, and those who are weak should permit yourselves to be instructed, and there will be peace and love for both.

But not for disputes over opinions. This is not a satisfactory translation. For where our version [6] says "in disputes," the Greek reads "in distinctions." And where our text has "thoughts," the Greek has διαλογισμῶν, [7] which is more properly "the process of making a decision" or "weighing a reason," as above in Rom. 1:21: "They became vain in their thoughts," that is, what we in popular speech call motives or reasons. Thus the apostle is trying to say that no one should judge the decisions or reasons of another person by which he is moved to do so and so. For the strong man has his own opinion and is moved by his own reasons, and likewise the

---

[5] Erasmus translated the Greek word προσλαμβάνεσθε with *vobis adiungite* ("join to yourselves").

[6] The Vulgate.

[7] Erasmus defines διαλογισμός in his comments on Rom. 1:21 as follows: *non simplex cogitatio, sed cogitatio ratiocinantis et expendentis ac diiudicantis* ("not a simple thought but the thought of one who reasons, calculates, and distinguishes").

weak by his. Hence he says a little later: "Let everyone be fully convinced in his own mind" (v. 5), that is, leave him in peace and let him be satisfied with his own motives (or to say it in more popular language) let him stand secure and immovable in the directions of his own conscience.

But it is no longer necessary in our time to be tolerant toward these superstitious practices of piety or these shows of piety on the grounds of weakness, because people do them out of crass ignorance, not knowing that they themselves and not their works have to be changed. However, the apostle warns the Galatians that they were not to "use this freedom as an opportunity for the flesh" (Gal. 5:13), as they do now in Rome, where they care nothing at all for the things that have been spoken; for they have all been devoured by dispensations. They take possession of this kind of liberty in an absolutely perfect way. But the other things which the apostle has commanded they completely disregard, and they use this liberty "as an opportunity for the flesh and as a pretext for evil" (Gal. 5:13; 1 Peter 2:16), obviously because they are not bound by those commands, which is true. But O how many in our day, if they knew of this liberty, would enter religious life or some other holy state? Indeed, how many would most gladly leave their ceremonies, prayers, rules, if only the pope would annul them, as he surely can! Thus in our day nearly all fulfill their vocations without love and unwillingly, and if they do anything, they do it in such fear that they put their trust in this most wretched cross of conscience. But perhaps God wants us in our time to be bound by these different kinds of ordinances and rules and regulations, so that He may at least compel us to come in (Luke 14:23). But if this liberty is given again, that is, that fasts, prayers, obedience to ordinances, the services of churches, etc., should be committed to each of us on the basis of our own free will and conscience to do as much as he wishes, moved by his love for God, I believe that in one year all of the churches would fairly be closed and the altars deserted. And yet so it ought to be, and we should approach all of these things as people about to serve God freely and happily and not out of fear of conscience or punishment, nor in the hope of reward or honor.

For example, if the mandate should go out that no priest, unless he so wished it, had to be without a wife, wear a tonsure, be dressed in special garb, or be bound to the canonical hours, how many, I ask you, would you find who would choose this form of life in which they are now living? Would it not be as people say: "Let your conscience be your guide"?[8] And yet this is exactly what ought to be done, namely, that it be left to their own decision to do as much as they think they can defend in the sight of God. But people say: "Who would then not want to be a priest?" The answer is that those who speak this way clearly demonstrate that they are seeking liberty as an occasion for their flesh and that they are unwillingly in their state of servitude, deserving nothing before God.

I am afraid that we shall all perish this day. For who follows this rule? And what about the people, what would they give? They are equally foolish, for they make their contributions to hired servants and not to free brothers.

Therefore examine yourself when you pray, when you make a sacrifice, when you enter the choir or do anything else whether you would do the same thing if you had your liberty, and then discover who you are in the eyes of God. For if you would not do it, if you would rather be free and without restraint, then you are doing nothing, because you are a servant and a hireling. However, there are some who know this and set themselves down in some corner and say: "I will arouse in myself a good intention and a will if this is necessary." Meanwhile the devil laughs and replies to him: "Preen your fur, little kitten, we are going to have company,"[9] then he gets up, goes to the choir, and prays and says: "Little owl, how beautiful you are! Where did you get the peacock feathers?"[10] If I did not know (according to the fable) that you were an ass, I would believe that you were a lion, such is your roar; but put on your lion's skin, your ears will cause you to be recognized. Then the tedium begins, he counts the pages and the verses, wondering if the prayer is almost finished, and comforting himself, he says: "Scotus proved that a virtual intention suffices and an actual intent is not required." Then the devil says to him: "Well said, you are right, be secure."

O God, what a laughing stock we are for our enemies! A good intention is not so easy as that, nor (good God!) is it given into your power, O man, to arouse it in yourself, as Scotus and his school

---

[8] *Wenn's bis auf die Conscientz kommt.*

[9] Luther quotes: *Schmück' dich, liebes Kätzchen, wir werden Gäste haben,* a German saying used by children when they see a kitten preen its fur. This means company is coming.

[10] The German proverb quoted is: *Sieh, Eulchen, wie schön du bist! Hast du nun Pfauenfedern?*

teach and learn to our harm. For in our time this presumptuousness is most pernicious, that we can form good intentions of ourselves, as if we were sufficient of ourselves to think up anything, in direct opposition to the express statement of the apostle. Hence we snore on in our smugness, relying on our free will that we have at hand whenever we wish the power to make a pious intention. Why then does the apostle pray: "May the Lord direct your hearts and bodies" (2 Thess. 3:5)? [11] And why does the church pray: "May our words be spoken and our thoughts and works directed always to doing Thy righteousness." [12] But these ideas are the snares of the unrighteous, of which we read in Ps. 5:9: "Their heart is a snare," and in Prov. 11:6: "The unrighteous shall be caught in their own snares."

Not so, you unrighteous men, not so! But it is necessary that you prostrate yourself in your chamber and pray to God with all your strength that He give to you also the intention which you have presumed to arouse in yourself. You cannot walk in a security which has been produced of and by yourself, but rather in one which has been sought and looked for from His mercy.

Thus the whole error in this idea is that we fail to consider that if we are pleasing to God, all of these things must be done not by the compulsion of necessity or by the drive of fear but in happiness and a completely free will. For he who does these things in such a way that if it were possible, he would prefer to omit them, really does nothing, all things being equal. Yet he does these things and thinks that he is making satisfaction, since he has done them and is not conscious of anything more. But when he has failed to do them, he has a bad conscience. This defect abounds everywhere, also among the religious. For they feel secure in these things which they do without a will, indeed, compelled by necessity or fear or habit, and are thus free of compunction. But if they omit something, then they make confession and do penance. The first ones do not differ from these, except that they have a pretext for their iniquity and a covering for their external activity under which they fail to recognize the weakness of their will, while in the second case they recognize quite properly their failure, except that they repent more strongly for the omission of a work than for the lukewarmness of their will. Hence we ought in all of our works to pay close attention, not as to what we do or ought to do, nor what

---

[11] The Breviary adds the words "and bodies."

[12] A prayer for Prime in the Roman Breviary.

we have omitted or should omit, not what good we have done or failed to do, nor what evil we have done or not done, but rather with what kind of willingness and with how great a willingness, with how much and what kind of happiness in our hearts we have done everything or wanted to do it. Thus in the last chapter of 1 Cor. the apostle says that he had strongly urged Apollos, although he could have compelled him. And yet he says: "I strongly urged him to visit you, . . . but it was not at all His will." Likewise he beseeches Philemon on behalf of a slave, though he could have commanded him, "that your goodness might not be by compulsion but of your own free will" (Philemon 14).

But in our day the boys who are princes and the effeminate men who rule in the church [13] carry out their work only in such a way that they compel their subjects by severity and power in fear, when they should have acted with wisdom, so that they might first make them willing, and only if they were unwilling to do their work might compel them by shaming and frightening them.

The whole substance of this error is a Pelagian notion.[14] For although there are now no Pelagians by profession and title, yet there are many people who in truth and in their thinking, although ignorantly, are Pelagians. For example, there are those who think that unless they attribute doing what is in their own power, before grace, to the freedom of their will, they are being forced by God to sin and thus of necessity must sin. And although it is extremely godless to have such an idea, they smugly and boldly think that because they form a good intention, they have infallibly obtained the infused grace of God. Then they go their way completely secure, completely certain that the good works they do please God, and thus they have no more fear or concerns about imploring the grace of God. For they have no fear that in this very action they might be doing evil but are certain that they are doing good (Is. 44:20). Why? Because they do not understand that God allows the ungodly to sin even in their good works. To be sure they

---

[13] Cf. Is. 3:4: "I will make boys their princes, and babes shall rule over them." Perhaps Albert of Brandenburg, archbishop of Magdeburg at 23 and archbishop of Mainz at 24, and as such one of the electors of the empire, is meant especially.

[14] Reuchlin's *Vocabularius breviloquus* describes the Pelagians as follows: "They think more highly of free will than of the grace of God, saying that it is enough to have a willingness to fulfill the commandments of God." This description is distilled from Augustine, *De haeresibus, Patrologia, Series Latina,* XLII, 27.

are not then compelled to sin, but they do what they want to and according to their good intention. But if they understood it, they would walk in that fear in which Job walked, and they would say with him: "I feared all my works" (Job 9:28); and again, another says: "Blessed is the man who fears the Lord always" (Prov. 28:14). Hence they who truly do good works, do nothing without always considering: Who knows that the grace of God is acting with me in this work? Who let's me know that my good intention is from God? How do I know that what I have done as my own or what is in me is acceptable to God? These people know that man of himself can do nothing. Hence it is most absurd and gives strong support to the error of Pelagius to use the commonly accepted statement: "God infallibly pours His grace into him who does what is within his power," [15] if we understand the expression "to do what is within his power" to mean that he does something or can do something. For as a result of this the whole church has almost been overturned, obviously because of confidence in this statement. And in the meantime each smugly sins, since he at all times has in his free will the capability to do what is within his own power and therefore also grace. Therefore they go about in fearlessness, ready to do in their own good time what is within their power and thus to possess grace. Is. 44:20 says of these people: "They will not say: 'Is there not a lie in my right hand?'" And in Prov. 14:16 we read: "A wise man is cautious and turns away from evil, but a fool throws off restraint and is careless," that is, he is not afraid that there might possibly be "a lie in his right hand," nor does he fear that perhaps his good is evil, but he is confident and smug.

And this is the reason why the apostle Peter also commands: "Fear God" (1 Peter 2:17), and Paul says: "Knowing the fear of the Lord, we persuade men" (2 Cor. 5:11), and again: "Work out your own salvation with fear and trembling" (Phil. 2:12). And in Ps. 2:11 we read: "Serve the Lord with fear, and with trembling rejoice unto Him." Now how can one fear God or his own works unless he regards these things as evil or suspect? For fear comes from evil. Thus the saints are concerned about constantly imploring the grace of God. They do not place their trust in their good intention or their general diligence, but they are always still afraid that they are

---

[15] In W, IV, 262, 4, Luther introduces this statement with *dicunt doctores*. Closely parallel statements are found in Aquinas, Biel, and others. Cf. W, LVI, 503, n. 2.

doing something wrong. And humbled by this fear, they seek and sigh, and by this humility they cause God to be favorable toward them. And thus the most pestilent class of preachers today is that group which preaches about the signs of present grace, so that it makes men secure, when in fact the very best sign of grace is that we fear and tremble, and the surest sign of God's wrath is to be smug and self-confident. And yet everyone pants for this with marvelous ardor. For in this way grace is found through fear, and through grace a man is made willing for good works, and without grace he is unwilling. And yet through this unwillingness (if I may say so) [16] he is fearless, strong, and secure, because he accomplishes outwardly the works which are good in his own eyes and in the eyes of men.

14. *I know and am persuaded.* This term "I am persuaded" is not to be understood in this passage in the sense of "I hope," but in an absolute sense of "I am secure and certain and very bold," or "daring," as he has also said above: "Then Isaiah is so bold as to say" (Rom. 10:20), that is, he speaks with confidence and boldness. In Latin people who are rather high-spirited are called "*confidentes*," as for example in Plautus. [17] In German we say *keck*. And then we have the same in 2 Tim. 1:12: "I know whom I have believed, and am sure," as if to say: "I am not mistaken." Thus the meaning of the apostle is: I know and am sure; in German: *Ich weiss und bin keck, darfs kecklich sagen.* Otherwise he should have said: "I have confidence in the Lord Jesus Christ," if he wanted it understood in the sense of "having hope." But now he says *in the Lord Jesus*, that is, because of the fact that I am in Christ, for this reason I feel bold. And he uses this word boldly because of the fears of others who were timid and diffident with respect to this idea, and then also because of the false apostles who were teaching the contrary.

Nothing is unclean in itself. The word "common" means the same as "unclean," but according to the Hebrew way of speaking, for among the Hebrews this word is the direct opposite of that which "holy" indicates, namely, separate, or set apart. Hence we read in Ps. 4:3: "The Lord has set apart the godly for Himself." Some translate this thus (as Reuchlin bears witness to its proper meaning): "God has set him apart who has received His mercy, or

16 Luther apologizes for the boldness involved in the new coinage *invititas.*

17 Plautus, *Amphitruo*, I, 1, 1: *Qui me alter est audactior homo, aut qui confidentior?* Cf. also *Captivi*, III, 5, 8.

His grace, or His sanctification." Hence the apostle also says in Rom. 1:1 that he was "set apart for the Gospel of God," that is, set apart from a common occupation for the work of the Gospel. Hence also in a figurative way it says in the Law: "Consecrate to me all the firstborn" (Ex. 13:2). Likewise: "I have separated you from the peoples" (Lev. 20:24), and the same expression is used there frequently. Thus what is not separated in this way, in the Hebrew is called "common." Hence as time went on, the term "separate" came to be used in the sense of clean, holy, pure, and "common" for unclean, profane, impure. Thus Acts 10:15 and 11:9 read: "What God has cleansed, you must not call common." Here it ought to read: "What God has cleansed, you must not call unclean; except that "common" and "unclean" mean the same thing.

7. *None of us lives to himself.* The apostle is arguing from the greater, that if we do not live to ourselves or belong to ourselves (which is the greater), much less do we eat or drink to ourselves or do or suffer anything to ourselves, but rather all things are the Lord's. Hence in 1 Cor. 6:19: "Do you not know that your body is a temple of the Holy Spirit? . . . You are not your own." And again: "Glorify God in your body and in your spirit, which are God's" (cf. 1 Cor. 6:20). And Gal. 2:20: "It is no longer I who live, but Christ who lives in me."

5. *Let everyone be fully convinced in his own mind.* The holy fathers and doctors again and again make use of this passage as a general statement to the effect that each should be fully convinced in his own mind regarding the understanding of Scripture.[18] But the apostle has something special in mind in this verse, namely, that he wants each person to be content in his own mind, or as it is commonly phrased, in his own thinking, and not judge another man in his thinking, nor should the other spurn him in return, lest perhaps he who is weak in faith, having his own mind, thinking, or conscience, but being disturbed or offended at the "mind" of another person, begin to act contrary to his own "mind" and thus conclude one thing and do something else and so be at odds with himself. For although because of his weakness he cannot come to any other conclusion than that this or that is not permitted, yet so

---

[18] The Weimar editor points out that this interpretation has not been found in scholastic and patristic exegesis and that Luther is in all likelihood thinking of a general application of the phrase "let everyone be fully convinced in his mind" *such as he himself made repeatedly without reference to the subject at hand,* e. g., *Luther's Works,* 27, p. 380, line 13; p. 409, line 17.

that he should not be despised by those who are strong, he does the things which they are doing; and yet he concludes that he ought not to do these things. With such matters the apostle deals in 1 Cor. 8:4, 7: "As to the eating of food offered to idols, we know that an idol has no real existence in the world. . . . However, not all possess this knowledge. But some, through conscience, being hitherto accustomed to idols, eat food as really offered to an idol; and their conscience, being weak" (that is, being unable to conclude in any other way except that it is not permitted) "is defiled," because he has eaten contrary to his own judgment. And the cause of this defilement is the pride of the strong who eat meats sacrificed to idols in the sight of these people and with contempt for them, when rather they ought to be upholding them and strengthening them, or if they cannot strengthen them because of their weakness, they ought for the sake of love to become weak with them and abstain with them so that faith may be preserved within the bounds of conscience. For although all things are lawful for them, yet for the sake of the brother's salvation a person ought not make a show of his liberty. For it is better that one openly deprive himself of his own liberty than that his weak brother perish. For if a person has a weak conscience and is spurned because of it, nothing else happens than that he is by that contempt forced to do what the others are doing, and yet he concludes that what they are doing ought not to be done. Because of the difference of consciences, in the selfsame permissible work one man sins, and the other does a good work. Thus he says: "Let everyone be fully convinced in his own mind," that is, let him be certain and quiet; and the strong should not change his faith because of the scruples of the weak, nor should the weak because of the strong act against his own judgment; he should let them do as they want, and he himself should act in accord with his own conscience.

14. *Nothing is unclean in itself.* It seems that the expression "in itself" *(per ipsum)* can be referred either to "the Lord Jesus" or to the word "unclean." For nothing is unclean through Jesus Christ, or nothing is unclean in itself, or by its own nature and inner substance, but only because of external opinion and conscience. And this is more in agreement with the statement that follows, for he says: *But it is unclean for anyone who thinks it unclean.* For if he wanted the statement to be understood in the sense that through Jesus nothing is unclean, we would also here have to understand: "it is unclean for anyone who thinks it un-

clean" through Jesus. Therefore the translator [19] should have avoided the ambiguity which is in the Greek and simply said "as such" *(per se)* rather than "in itself," as Erasmus does.[20]

Therefore let us give a summary of this chapter, which has two parts: First, let not the strong despise the weak; second, let them not offend them.

For both of these are contrary to love, which receives the weak, not seeking its own interests but those of the weak, as an example of which the apostle presents himself, 2 Cor. 11:28-29: "There is the daily pressure upon me of my anxiety for all the churches. Who is weak, and I am not weak? Who is made to fall, and I am not indignant?" And again in 1 Cor. 9:22: "To the weak I became weak, that I might win the weak. I have become all things to all men, that I might win all." That he was thus indignant (for he could not be offended with those who were offended) the passage before us shows, for here he speaks with very strong words against those who despise the weak and give offense. For he impresses the first point in this way:

First: *God, he says, has welcomed him* (v. 3). By the use of this very strong word he is impressing on them that it is no longer man but God whom a person despises or judges when he despises or judges. Thus with a very powerful argument he compels them to mutual humility and acceptance.

Second: *Who are you to pass judgment on the servant of another?* (v. 4). For it is contrary to the law of nature and offensive to all men to pass judgment on another man's servant, and thus it is not only against God but also against every human judgment that people of this kind act. He also destroys their motives:

First: That the weak judges that the strong is falling, and the strong thinks that the weak has already fallen. The answer is: "What is this to you?" *It is before his own master that he falls,* or if he stands, *he stands to his own master* (v. 4). Therefore you are not freed of the guilt of judging or despising, even if your judgment is right, for you do not have the right to spurn him.

Second: That they judge: "Who knows if he will stand?" The answer to this is: *God is able to make him stand* (v. 4).

Third: That everything we do, are, or live we do, live, and are to the Lord; therefore it is not right to despise another person. For *none of us,* he says, *lives to himself* (v. 7).

[19] The Vulgate.

[20] That is, Erasmus has *per se* for *per ipsum.*

Fourth: That *Christ died and rose again, that He might be Lord of all* (v. 9). Therefore it is also against Christ to take the power of judging and to hold men in contempt.

Fifth: He opposes them with *the judgment seat of Christ* (v. 10). For we are all to be judged there. See with what kind of thunderbolts, I beg you, He frightens us away from contempt for one another, especially for the weak. He brings in God, man, the suffering of Christ, His reign, and the final Judgment. There is nothing that he does not bring to bear. With similar sharpness he makes his second point:

1

First: *If your brother is being injured by what you eat, you are no longer walking in love* (v. 15). Note his climaxes and his emphases by the use of individual words. "By what you eat," he says, as if to say: "For so minor a matter you despise the eternal salvation of your brother! It would be less offensive if you did it for the sake of gold or honor or at least for your own life and the health of your body or some other permanent matter rather than for food, which is of only momentary use and pleasure. This then is a sharp rebuke, and he sharply criticizes him for lacking love when a man despises his brother on account of food.

Second: He uses equal emphasis in the expression "your brother." He does not say "your enemy." Nor does he even say "associate" or some other acquaintance, but brother, to whom a man owes more than to anyone else, since he is his brother, almost the same as his neighbor. Why then does a person favor his belly and his gullet, which are going to perish, over his brother, who will live forever?

Third: He uses the word "injured," disturbed, wounded in his conscience, which is much more than if he were deprived of his money or material things or were even wounded. And this because of food! Also notice that he does not say "if you grieve him," but rather "if he is grieved." Here he very adroitly rejects their excuse if they should say: "It is not my fault, I am not doing anything to him. I am not grieving him, I am only doing what I am permitted to do. Or am I not permitted to make use of my rights and do what I wish in those matters which pertain to me?" This is the righteousness of the jurists of our own day as they interpret, or rather pervert, their own laws. But it is not enough that you live by your own law and do what you wish with your own things, unless you also look out for your brother, according to God. Indeed, you do not have the right or the power to do something, nor are those things only yours when your brother is offended in them. To be sure, they are yours temporarily, but spiritually they belong to your brother, because he clings to them with his conscience scruples. Therefore you act according to an alien law, that is, you commit a wrong, if you act in such a way that through you your brother is grieved. For thus today nearly everyone pays attention only to what is his own and what is permitted him under his own rights, but not to what he owes another and what is expedient for both. "All things are lawful for me," he says, "But not all things are helpful or edifying" (1 Cor. 6:12).

Fourth: "You are no longer walking in love," as if to say: "You are walking in vain, even if you walk in great and marvelous works." 1 Cor. 13:2: "If I have not love, I am nothing." It is strangely terrifying that because of food a man can destroy all his good works, and yet fools wear themselves out with their many good works, while love is everywhere neglected, so that the statement of Eccl. 10:15 is fulfilled: "The toil of a fool wearies him, so that he does not know the way to the city" (Eccl. 10:15).

2

Do not let what you eat cause the ruin of one for whom Christ died (v. 15). It is as if he were saying: "It is less offensive that you hurt, that you offend, that you fail to show love; on top of it all you are a cruel murderer, for you are destroying a brother, indeed, you are guilty of fratricide, which is most cruel. Moreover—and this surpasses all the cruelty and ingratitude—you are despising the death of Christ in your brother, for whom Christ died." See what he does who walks about despising your brother and failing to show love. Thus we read in 1 Cor. 8:12: "Thus, sinning against your brethren and wounding their conscience when it is weak, you sin against Christ." And in 1 Cor. 8:11: "And so by your knowledge this weak man is destroyed, the brother for whom Christ died."

3

So do not let what is good to you be spoken of as evil (v. 16). It is as if he were saying: "You are sinning against the church as well as against yourselves. For what is good to you, that is, that which you are and have from God appear to the Gentiles in such a light that they flee from it rather than desire it, and thus you will be the cause of the damnation of many of them, who might other-wise be saved." It is a grave and serious matter, that not only your evil but also your good is blasphemed because of a little food. He in this passage calls "good" everything we are through Christ, as if to say: "Be careful that the Gentiles do not downgrade your faith and religion and all your Christianity, for they ought to be drawn to it by its good reputation and built up by its goodness through you." Thus he says in 2 Cor. 6:3: "So that no fault may be found with our ministry," as has also been sufficiently discussed above in chapter 12 under the heading "take thought for what is good" (Rom. 12:17).

4

For the kingdom of God is not food and drink (v. 17). It is as if he were saying: "Your presumption that the kingdom of God is yours is in vain if you disturb the peace because of food and are so eager to defend what you eat and drink, as if the kingdom of God consisted in these things, as now is very frequently the case." The outward food arouses more storms than the inward religion pro-duces peace, and they continue their disturbance during both peace and war. *But righteousness*, as over against God, which comes through faith or by believing; *and peace*, as over against our neighbor, which comes about through love for one another and by receiving and upholding one another; *and joy in the Holy Spirit*, as over against oneself, which comes about through hope, by having trust in God and not in those things which one does toward his neighbor or toward God. Be pleasant toward yourself, peaceful toward your neighbor, righteous before God. And nothing so dis-turbs this peace as the temptation and the offense of the brother, especially in those things which injure his conscience. Hence the word "peace" must be understood in several ways.

1. Peace with God, as above in chapter 5:1: "Therefore, since we are justified by faith, we have peace with God." This peace is broken by sin.

2. Peace with oneself, which a person has through this joy in the Holy Spirit, through hope and patience, as above in chapter 12:12: "Rejoice in your hope, be patient in tribulation." This peace is disturbed by impatience or through tribulations which are borne impatiently, that is, through love of carnal and useless peace.

3. Peace with one's neighbor, which a person has through the fulfillment and upbuilding of mutual love. And it is broken by con-tempt for the weakness of the other party and through the violation

of the conscience of those who have peace with God and with themselves through faith and patience, but not with their neighbors. And this in the passive sense, in that they do not leave others in peace. Therefore he would have us not only be at peace but also bring peace, be quiet and modest toward one another. Therefore he continues:

He who thus serves Christ is acceptable to God (v. 18) (because of his righteousness), and he is approved by men (because of his peacefulness), and in this sentence he puts the joy in the Holy Spirit in the last place. For first one ought to be acceptable to God, and then one ought to seek not one's own things but the neighbor's. Hence it is common to say of those who are restless and who disturb others that they do not have peace, because they will not allow others to live their lives in peace, but they disturb them. These people the apostle calls restless, 1 Thess. 5:12-14: "Be at peace with those who are over you . . . rebuke the restless, encourage the fainthearted, help the weak, be patient with them all." And in Acts 15:19 James, in speaking on the same subject, says: "Therefore my judgment is that we should not trouble those of the Gentiles who turn to God," that is, in regard to their observance of the Law. And in Gal. 5:12 he says: "I wish those who unsettle you would mutilate themselves." And in 2 Thess. 3:6 he says: "We command you . . . that you keep away from any brother who is walking disorderly." Therefore people of this sort are not "approved by men" but are displeasing to men.

And of this peace he now says: *Let us then pursue what makes for peace* (v. 19), that is, those things which do not disturb others but which edify and calm them. And what are these things? The answer is: Love teaches us what they are as the time and the place require. For they cannot be given to us in the particular.

5

Do not, for the sake of food, destroy the work of God (v. 20). He calls his brother "the work of God," just as in 1 Cor. 3:9 he says: "You are God's field, God's building." And later in 1 Cor. 9:1: "Are you not my workmanship in the Lord?" And Heb. 3:6: "We are His house, etc." And again, in 1 Cor. 3:17: "God's temple is holy, and that temple you are. If anyone destroys God's temple, God will destroy him." But who destroys it but the all-wise self-righteous? Of whom he goes on to say immediately: "Let no one deceive you. If anyone among you thinks that he is wise in this age, let him become a fool that he may become wise" (1 Cor. 3:18). Understand now what it means "for the sake of food to destroy the work of God." It means not only to offend God, but also to fight against Him and to destroy what He builds, to be in constant warfare against God (like the giants of mythology with their gods).

23. *For whatever does not proceed from faith is sin.* See blessed Augustine, *Contra Julianum*, IV, 3, F.[21] Here the apostle is speaking in a very general way regarding faith, and yet in so doing he is alluding to the singular faith which is directed toward Christ, outside of which there is no righteousness but only sin. Moreover, it is faith in God, faith in one's neighbor, faith in oneself. And by faith in God any person is made righteous, because he acknowledges that God is truthful, in whom he believes and puts his trust. And by faith in his neighbor he is called a faithful, true, and trustworthy man, having become over against his neighbor what God is to him. And this faith in the neighbor is also called an active faith, by which he believes in his neighbor. And the nature of this faith is that if a person acts differently from what he believes or if he has doubts about this neighbor, he offends against his neighbor, because he does not do for him what he has promised. Likewise he also sins against God when his actions differ from what he has been told and what he believes. In the same way he believes in himself and the dictates of his conscience, and if he acts against it, he is already doing differently from what he believes, and thus contrary to his faith. Thus "whatever does not proceed from faith is sin" because it is contrary to faith and conscience, for we must avoid with great effort everything which works against conscience.[22]

Therefore the question is whether the ungodly person sins, when he does not believe, because he is not acting out of faith, and thus not contrary to conscience, in fact, he believes falsely; and thus acting falsely out of this kind of faith, does he not sin? The answer is this: The passage "whatever does not proceed from faith is sin" means that every person who does not wish to sin must believe. For faith alone is without sin. Therefore he who does something he does not believe sins. Thus he who eats what he thinks is unclean sins, not so much because he sins against his thinking as because he is lacking in faith, whereby he would know that it is not unclean. And thus weakness of faith which is present and

---

[21] *Contra Julianum*, IV, 3, 24, *Patrologia, Series Latina*, XLIV, 750.

[22] The words remind us of Luther's closing words at the Diet of Worms: "To act against one's conscience is neither safe nor salutary."

strength of faith which is lacking brings it about that he sins when he eats. Therefore he who does not have faith must not eat, that is, he must not perform a work of faith. For a work of faith must come from faith, otherwise he who eats because he does not believe it is permissable but concludes that it is forbidden (this is lack of faith) sins and thus goes against his own conscience. A corollary of this is that everyone who is lacking in faith sins even when he does a good work. For this is the meaning of this passage.

But you say: "If this means that a weak man sins not so much because he goes counter to his conscience as that he does not operate out of faith, then he also sins whether he eats or does not eat, because the deficiency in his faith always remains in him." The answer: quite so, he is always in sin, that is in the deficiency of faith. But yet this condition ought not be irritated further so that he sins even more. For this weakness of faith is a venial sin, that is, one which God does not impute to him as a mortal sin, although by nature it might be a mortal sin. For God has "taken him up" to perfect him and make him healthy, as the Samaritan did with the man who was left half dead (Luke 10:33 ff.). Therefore he must not be stimulated to act in keeping with this weakness of his faith, but rather he must be nourished and cultivated so that he may increase in his knowledge of our Lord Jesus Christ, as St. Peter says in 2 Peter 3:18: "Grow in the grace and knowledge of our Lord and Savior Jesus Christ."

This is similar to the situation of a person who is baptized or doing penance and remains in the weakness of his concupiscence, which is still contrary to the law "You shall not covet" and surely a mortal sin if God were not merciful and did not refrain from imputing it as such because of the cure which has been begun. This man is certainly in his sins, and yet he must not be stimulated by others and offended, that is, he must not be given the occasion so that he will act according to this weakness of his, but rather he must be nourished and perfected. Otherwise everything which he does, because he does not do it out of purity, would be a total sin and his weakness would because of his work become a mortal sin, even though his weakness in itself would be a venial sin because of God's grace. In the same way that man of weak faith would be obedient to his weakness and perform a work which would not proceed from faith.

Therefore the word "faith" must be taken in a double sense in this passage. One way is to take it in the sense of opinion and conscience. Many interpret this passage in this way. Another way would be in the absolute sense in the fashion of the apostle, as identical with faith in Christ. For my part, with due respect for others, I understand this passage in this sense. For just as one can go against his conscience while in faith, so one can also in any other virtue. For he who is weak in the area of chastity sins against his conscience if he fornicates, for his conscience dictates to him that he must not fornicate in keeping with his chastity. And yet because he is weak, he is made to stumble and act against the dictate of his conscience. So also he who is weak in faith believes and yet does not believe. Because he believes, he does good; because he does not believe, he sins. But if he is moved not to believe, he sins in deed.

CHAPTER FIFTEEN

1. *We who are strong ought to bear, etc.*

THUS love bears all men and "all things" (1 Cor. 13:7), thus Moses and the prophets bore the people of Israel. Moreover this expression "to bear" means that one makes the sins of all his own and suffers with them. For this is what love does, and these are the words of love: "Who is weak, and I am not weak? Who is made to fall, and I am not indignant?" In the same way he encourages in Gal. 6:2: "Bear one another's burdens, and so fulfill the law of Christ." And again in the same place (v. 1): "Brethren, if a man is overtaken in any trespass, you who are spiritual should restore him in a spirit of gentleness, looking to yourself, lest you too be tempted." And in 1 Cor. 10:12: "Let anyone who thinks that he stands take heed lest he fall." And (Gal. 6:3): "If anyone thinks he is something, when he is nothing, he deceives himself." Phil. 2:5-7: "Have this mind among yourselves, which you have in Christ Jesus, who, though He was in the form of God, did not count equality with God a thing to be grasped, but emptied Himself, taking the form of a servant." The relation is like that of the natural body, in which the bones sustain the flesh and the weak members are not rejected by the strong ones but are cared for more than the strong ones, and the honorable members cover the less honorable, as we read in 1 Cor. 12:22 f.: "The parts of the body which seem to be weaker are indispensable, and those parts of the body which we think less honorable we invest with greater honor, and our unpresentable parts are treated with greater modesty." Consider in the first place the individual social orders. God has not deserted any of them to such an extent that He did not place some good and honorable people in them to serve as the covering and honor of the others. Thus bad women are spared because of the good women, good priests protect the bad ones, unworthy monks are honored because of the worthy ones. But here foolish people rise up against a whole order, as if they themselves were pure and had no dirt on themselves, although actually before and behind and within they are nothing but a meeting place and a workshop of sows and hogs. From this source comes neither woman, nor priest, nor monk. From this source comes the word of the apostle: "Why are you so self-satisfied, you foolish man, and think you are something, when you are nothing?" (cf. Gal. 6:3). Again there are those who see that they are honorable and serve as a cover for others and as a result run away from the others to whom they have been given as a cloak of respectability. These are the most foolish of all, because they think that they are this way of themselves, not realizing that they are what they are because of other people. Hence they dislike them and do not want to be in their company. Heretics are like this, and so are many other arrogant people. They would not do these things if they were not self-satisfied. Thus a woman does not want to associate with women unless they are all pure. To her the apostle says: "Listen, sister, listen. Are you standing? To be sure, but see to it that you do not fall." For no woman stands so firmly that she cannot fall. And none falls so low that she cannot rise again. Why? "God can make her stand" (Rom. 14:4). And He is also able to forsake her. Many women have fallen who had stood most firmly and more strongly than the towers of Babylon. On the other hand, many have risen up who had fallen to the depths. The former because they had become pleased with themselves, the latter because they had become displeased. Likewise, if a priest does not wish to be a priest, because he cannot deal with evil people, it will be said to him: "Master John, you stand and you are pleased with yourself; see to it that you do not fall and become more displeased with yourself than these people now are with you." So it is with those religious who go to pieces because they are compelled to serve useless men and associate with them; they complain and beg that they rule over, associate with, and be friendly with none but honorable, perfect, and sensible companions. Hence they run from place to place. But in vain, for thus it has been ordained: "Each must bear the shame of the other" [1] (like the citizens on account of the councilman in the case right here).[2] And although it may be hard to bear the shame of another

---

[1] *Einer muss des Anderen Schanddeckel sein.*

[2] The reference is to a quarrel between the bishop of Brandenburg and the town council of Wittenberg. The council had imprisoned a priest in spite of the immunity he claimed because he had taken refuge in a monastery. The bishop countered with the interdict for the city, but the local clergy sided with the council and refused to carry out the interdict. Eventually, after the archbishop

and to share in it when one is innocent, yet it is a good and meritorious act. And it will be easy, if one recognizes that Christ gladly bore our shame, even though it was hard for Him. Thus "none of us lives to himself" (Rom. 14:7).

But the most beautiful fools of all are those who (as I have said) forget that they themselves are the dirtiest of all when they inveigh against priests, monks, and women and impute to all of them what one person has done. To such a person the answer is: Did you never make a stench in your mother's lap? Or is there no filth on any part of you now? Or doesn't any part of your body stink? For if you are so clean, it is a wonder that the druggists did not buy you long ago in place of the balsam shrub, inasmuch as you smell like nothing but balsam. If your mother had treated you this way you would have been consumed in your own filth.

This is the reason why God gave Daniel and his friends to the people of Israel in the Babylonian captivity (Dan. 1:6), and this is why he gave Esther and Mordecai in Persia before Ahasuerus (Esther 2:7 ff.).

And thus the expression "to please oneself" means to be displeased with oneself in all respects. For it cannot be that at the same time others can please a person and he be pleased with himself. Such people do not want to bear another's burdens (Gal. 6:2) but his benefits; indeed they want only to be carried by everyone else, but they themselves want to carry no one. These people do nothing but revile, judge, accuse, despise others. They have no mercy on others but rather rage against them, and nothing is clean but they themselves. Of them Isaiah says, Is. 65:5: "They say, 'Keep to yourself, do not come near me, for I am set apart from you.' These are a smoke in My nostrils, a fire that burns all the day." And such a person was that Pharisee in the Gospel who only reviled, accused, and condemned the publican and other men in his completely empty joy in his own righteousness. All these people are alike. Hence blessed Augustine in his exposition of Psalm 71 says of this same Pharisee: "Does it give you pleasure that you are good and that he is evil? And then what does he add? 'Unjust, extortioners, adulterers, as also is this publican.' (Luke 18:10). Here he is no longer rejoicing but being scornful." [3] And

and Rome itself became involved, the matter was settled when the council apologized (1515) and the interdict was lifted. For another reference, cf. p. 441 above.

[3] Augustine, *Enarrationes in Psalmos*, Ps. 70, n. 4, *Patrologia, Series Latina*, XXXVI, 877 f.

thus it is a characteristic of these people to be scornful over the unrighteousness of others rather than to rejoice over the fact that they are righteous; and they would not rejoice at all if others were as righteous as they are. For this would be very displeasing to them.

2. *Let each of us please his neighbor.* "In this way," as blessed Gregory says, "love reaches out to another person, so that it can be love. For no one is said to have charity for himself." [4] And in the gloss I pointed out that charity is love not for oneself but for another. Likewise as soon as the apostle rejected self-complacency, he immediately went on to teach that we should please our neighbor. Therefore to please our neighbor means not to please oneself. But this statement of Gregory's and our own statement appear to be contradicted by the famous definition of the different ways of loving and their order. For in accord with blessed Augustine, the Master of the Sentences affirms: "First we must love God, then our own soul, then the soul of our neighbor, and finally our own body." [5] Ordered love therefore begins with itself. The answer to this is that this is one of the things by which we are led away from love as long as we do not fully understand it. For as long as we first use each good for ourselves, we are not concerned about our neighbor. But true love for yourself is hatred of yourself. As our Lord said: "For whoever would love his life, will lose it, and he who hates his life will find it" (cf. Mark 8:35). And the apostle in Phil. 2:4 says: "Let each of you look not only to his own interests, but also to the interests of others." And 1 Cor. 13:5: "Love does not insist on its own way." Therefore he who hates himself and loves his neighbor, this person truly loves himself. For he loves himself outside of himself, thus he loves himself purely as long as he loves himself in his neighbor.

Hence with all respect for the judgment of others and with reverence for the fathers, I want to say what is on my mind, even if I speak like a fool: This does not seem to be a correct understanding of the law of love toward our neighbor when it is interpreted in such a way that we say that in this commandment the person who loves is the model *(forma)* by which one loves his neighbor, obviously because the commandment says "as yourself." Thus people

---

[4] Gregory, *Homiliae in Evangelia,* I, 17, 1, *Patrologia, Series Latina,* LXXVI, 1139.

[5] Augustine, *De doctrina christiana,* I, 23, 22, *Patrologia, Series Latina,* XXXIV, 27; Peter Lombard, *Collectanea in epistulas Pauli,* on 1 Tim. 1:1-5, *Patrologia, Series Latina,* CXCII, 329.

conclude: It is necessary that you first love yourself and thus in keeping with this example (exemplar) of your love you then love your neighbor. And to support this they adduce the statement of the wise man (Ecclus. 30:21): "Have pity on your soul, pleasing God," namely, by putting the emphasis on the pronoun "your," as if to say: "First pity your own soul and then your neighbor's." But I do not reject this interpretation, although I believe that the emphasis is on the word "soul," as if to say: "Do not spare your body, in order that the soul may be saved. Be cruel toward the Old Adam, in order that you may be merciful toward the new man. For "better is the wickedness of a man than a woman who does good" (Ecclus. 42:14), that is, it is more salutary if the soul inflicts evil and injury on the flesh than if the flesh pets and flatters the soul or "does good," according to what seems "good" to it. It is better that man as spirit do what seems bad to his flesh than that he allow it to do what seems good to it. For the "wisdom of the flesh" is wondrously wise for its own advantage "more subtle than any wild creature" (Gen. 3:1). And the will of a superior is better, even if it causes a loss, than the will of a disobedient servant which might be advantageous.

Therefore I believe that with this commandment "as yourself" man is not commanded to love himself but rather is shown the sinful love with which he does in fact love himself, as if to say: "You are completely curved in upon yourself[6] and pointed toward love of yourself, a condition from which you will not be delivered unless you altogether cease loving yourself and, forgetting yourself, love your neighbor. For it is a perversity that we want to be loved by all and want to seek our interests in all people; but it is uprightness that if you do to everyone else what in your perverseness you want done to yourself, you will do good with the same zeal as you used to do evil.[7] In this we surely are not commanded to do evil, but the zeal should be the same. Just as Adam is the "type of the one who was to come" (Rom. 5:14), that is, of Christ, the second Adam. Just as in Adam we are all evil, so also in Christ we ought to be good. This is said for the sake of comparison, but not for imitation. So it also says here: "Love your neighbor as yourself," but not in the sense that you should love yourself; otherwise that would have been commanded. But now it is not commanded in this way, that the com-

[6] Cf. pp. 291 and 313 above.

[7] Luther has *tanto studio facias malum, quanto fecisti bonum*, but he must have meant *malum* and *bonum* interchanged, as we have translated.

mandment is founded on this principle. Thus you do wrong if you love yourself, an evil from which you will not be free unless you love your neighbor in the same way, that is, by ceasing to love yourself. But if you do this, this law will also pass away, for it will not longer be necessary to love another person as you love yourself, inasmuch as you no longer love yourself. Nor will it be necessary for you to love yourself as you do your neighbor, inasmuch as by this very fact you most truly love yourself, and all in turn love you.

Notice the careful language of the apostle. He does not say "we ought not please ourselves" but "we ought to please others." [8] For if they were pleasing to us, it would no longer be necessary to bear with their weaknesses, that is, to endure their unpleasant qualities. But on the contrary, we ought to please others, as we read in 1 Cor. 10:32-33: "Give no offense to Jews or to Greeks or to the church of God, just as I try to please all men in everything I do." Blessed Augustine speaks of this beautifully and completely in a homily on words of our Lord,[9] saying why a person should do this, namely, as the apostle says in the same context, "Not seeking my own advantage but that of many, that they may be saved" (1 Cor. 10:33). For he is not opposed to the proverb "No one can please everyone." [10] Indeed, he is pleasing to all people, that is, in the sense that he does as much as he can that he may be pleasing to all men in a proper way. And as a result he also continues by saying:

For his good, that is, toward the good, that is, that the person may be moved in the direction of the good which is pleasing; not to the good per se, but *to edify him,* that is, toward the good that edifies, since there are also good things which do not edify. And we must note that the apostle has a way of contrasting edification with giving offense, and vice versa, as he also says above (Rom. 14:19): "Let us pursue what makes for peace" (namely, that they are not offended) "and for mutual upbuilding" (that is, that they may not be made to stumble)—peace as the opposite of offense, edification as the opposite of causing to stumble, taking care of the weak as the opposite of weakening them. Thus he has used these three concepts above (Rom. 14:21): "make the brother stumble"

---

[8] Luther's *alii debent nobis placere* does not fit his argument. He must have meant either *alii non debent nobis placere* or *aliis debemus nos placere.* We have preferred the latter.

[9] Cf. Augustine, *Sermo 54, Patrologia, Series Latina,* XXXVIII, 374.

[10] *Nemo placet omnibus.*

(that is, that he becomes disquieted rather than to be at peace), or "be upset" (that is, that he falls instead of being built up, and thus becomes worse), or "be weakened," the opposite of being received.

3. *The reproaches of those who reproached Thee.* This refers not only to the reproaches of the Jews, for then it would not apply to what is being discussed. For the apostle wants to bring Christ in as an example, as one who bore the infirmities of all, as Is. 53:4 says: "Surely He has borne our griefs and carried our sins." Likewise in the same sense he says in Phil. 2:5: "Have this mind among yourselves which is yours also in Christ Jesus." For just as we glorify God when we do good — "that they may see your good works," He says in Matt. 5:16, "and give glory to your Father who is in heaven" — so likewise with our evil works we dishonor God and call down reproach and blame on Him, that is, we give occasion for reproach, as he says above in 2:23-24: "You dishonor God by breaking the Law. As it is written: 'The name of God is blasphemed among the Gentiles because of you.' " Hence we also pray: "Hallowed be Thy name," that is, may it be honored and feared as sacred. Someone perhaps will want the term "reproaches" to be understood as being penalties to be paid because of our sins, which fall upon Him. But he cannot escape the fact that penalties do not reproach God, but our guilt does. Therefore our guilt has fallen upon Him, that is, He has paid the penalty for them and made satisfaction for us. If He had wanted to please Himself and love Himself, He surely would not have done what He did. But now He has loved us and hated and humiliated Himself, He has completely given Himself up for us. Thus love is the reason why our neighbor is not displeasing to us and why we can have patience with him. Love does not allow us to please ourselves, inasmuch as it is patient itself, and without it every haughtily righteous person is impatient and self-pleasing. Thus he is saying that these things have been said about Christ, and yet they have been written "for our instruction," "that by patience" with our neighbors "and the encouragement of the Scriptures we might have hope."

4. *That by steadfastness and by the encouragement of the Scriptures.* What a beautiful combination, that hope is possible through patience and the comfort of the Scriptures! To be sure, if hope is not a material thing. "For who hopes for what he sees?" (Rom. 8:24). Hope therefore removes all material things. Hence we need patience. And in place of material things he gives us the

Word of comfort by which we are sustained so that we do not lack
in patience. Thus to give up a tangible thing for words and the
Scripture is truly a big order. And people do not do this unless they
have died to all material things, at least in their feelings, even
though in practice they still use them out of necessity rather than
willingly. These are the Christians who have heard the statement
of their Teacher: "Whoever does not renounce all that he has cannot be My disciple" (Luke 14:33). They are "those who deal with
the world as though they had no dealings with it" (1 Cor. 7:31), and
they do good works as though they were not doing them. For they
do all of these things to God, whom they serve in all of these
matters, seeking nothing of their own in them.

7. *Welcome one another, therefore, as Christ has welcomed you,*
for the glory of God, that is, to the glory of God, or that God may
hereby be glorified. The glory of God is a wondrous thing! For He
is glorified when sinners and the weak are received. For His glory
lies in the fact that He is our benefactor. Therefore it is for His
glory, that is, an occasion for His kindness, when those are brought
to Him who will receive His blessing. Thus we are not to bring the
strong, the holy, the wise. For in them God cannot be glorified,
since He cannot be a blessing to them, for they do not need Him.

10. *Rejoice, O Gentiles, with His people.* Lyra thinks that the
background of this statement is Is. 35:1: "The wilderness and the
dry land shall be glad." Others think it is Is. 44:23: "Shout with
joy, O ends of the earth." But in my opinion Is. 66:10 is the source:
"Rejoice with Jerusalem, and be glad for her, all you who love her."
For when this word comes forth from Jerusalem, that is, from God's
people to others, it surely goes to none but the Gentiles, who are
not Jerusalem, which is what the apostle is saying when he adds
the word "Gentiles" and explains "Jerusalem" with "His people."
On the other hand, if he is using only the prophetic sense, the
oracle seems to be a conglomerate of several psalms, such as Ps.
67:4: "Let the nations be glad and sing for joy, for Thou dost judge
the peoples with equity," and Ps. 97:1: "The Lord reigns; let the
earth rejoice; let the many coastlands be glad!"

12. *The root of Jesse shall come.* As we have said in the gloss,
the term "root" does not here refer to Jesse himself, but to Christ,
on the basis of Is. 53:2. Otherwise he should have said: "the rod of
Jesse" or "the flower of Jesse," as Is. 11:1 does: "There shall come
a shoot from the stump of Jesse," etc. Likewise in Rev. 22:16:
"I am the root of David." Therefore Christ according to the flesh

has His root in David and the patriarchs, from whom He has arisen, but according to the Spirit He Himself is the root from which has arisen the universal church. In the first sense He is the flower, but in the second sense they are His flower.

On top of this we ought to take a look at how the translations agree with one another. Blessed Jerome reads: "Who stands for an ensign of the people" (Is. 11:10). The Septuagint reads: "Who will rise up that He might be Prince of the Gentiles." Paul says: *He who rises to rule the Gentiles.* But he who stands surely has risen up, and he who is an ensign to the people is surely guiding them. Therefore He is an ensign in order that the Gentiles may be led to Him. And here we have an expression of the nature of Christ's rule, for it is a ruling in faith, in a sign, in things that do not appear, not in a material way. The princes of the world, however, rule the people in a material way, namely, by their bodily presence and with bodily things. And thus the expression "they shall beseech Him" (Is. 11:10) can easily be reconciled with "in Him shall they hope" (Rom. 15:12), for he who beseeches does so in hope.

And the expression "His resting place will be honor" (Is. 11:10), that is, glory, which Jerome thinks he is translating more clearly when he says: "And His sepulcher shall be glorious," in the sense that in the Latin usage the word "rest" *(requies)* does not commonly denote the sleep of death.[11] But to my way of thinking this seems to make the expression even more unclear. For on the basis of this some [12] understand that the sepulcher of Christ was glorious because it was cut out of stone and He Himself had been anointed with precious ointments, although neither blessed Jerome nor the Septuagint nor the Spirit wanted to say this; but blessed Jerome was trying to describe the glory of the contents by means of the container. For the meaning is that the death and grave of Christ will be honored and celebrated throughout the whole world forever. Yet this is something that is naturally contrary to death, since the death and grave of other people usually drag away with them their glory and fame and honor and bury them "whose very memory has perished with a noise" (Ps. 9:6). But here the opposite occurred: He was not only not swallowed up by death and the grave, but He made His own death glorious.

---

[11] Jerome, *Commentarius in Esaiam,* on Is. 11:10, *Patrologia, Series Latina,* XXIV, 152, comments: "To make the meaning clear to the reader, we have used a different but equivalent word for 'sleep' and 'rest,' namely, 'sepulcher.'"

[12] Lyra.

13. *May the God of hope fill you.* What a wonderful title, the "God of hope"! But this is the sign by which the apostle distinguishes between false gods and the true God. For false gods are demons, gods of material things, because they possess those people who in their reliance on material things do not know how to hope. For he who relies on the true God, when all material things have been taken away, lives by pure hope alone. Therefore the "God of hope" is the same as the God of those who hope. For He is not the God of those who are timorous and despairing, but rather their enemy and their judge. And in short He is the "God of hope" because He is the one who bestows hope. He is that even more because hope alone worships Him, for as He is called "the God of Abraham and Isaac and Jacob" and "the God of Israel," so also He is called "the God of hope," because where there is hope, there He is worshiped.

With all joy and peace, that is, with a trusting conscience and with mutual concord. He puts joy first and then peace, because joy makes a man peaceful and composed in himself, and when he has become composed, it is easy for him to make peace with others. But he who is sad and disturbed is easily upset at others and of a stormy mind. But all these things take place *in believing,* because our joy and peace do not consist in something material, but are beyond material things, in hope. Otherwise the God of hope would not give them, for He gives good things which are hidden, joy in sadness and personal affliction, peace in the midst of tumult and outward persecution. Where faith is lacking, a person falls in sadness and persecution, because material things, in which he had placed his trust while they were available, fail him. But persecution causes hope to abound, as he said above in chapter 5:4: "Trial produces hope." And this is *by the power of the Holy Spirit.* It is not because we trust in our own abilities that "trial produces hope," since then we would still be weak and powerless under persecutions, but "the Spirit helps us in our weakness," so that we cannot only hold out but be made perfect and triumphant.

14. *You yourselves are full of goodness.* Note the careful order of his remarks: "full" first "of goodness," then *filled with all knowledge.* For knowledge without love which edifies puffs a man up. Nor can they *instruct one another* if they are not first filled with love or goodness. For knowledge, if it is all by itself, stays confined to itself and puffs up and does not deign to instruct another but only desires to be seen and despises others. But love overflows

with knowledge and edifies. Neither does love without knowledge edify, however. To be sure, a holy simplicity that proceeds from a meritorious and exemplary life does edify, but an educated love does so both in itself and in its word, while knowledge both by example and by its message offends and does not instruct. Thus love in company with knowledge and knowledge by itself are totally contrary to one another. Knowledge by itself seeks its own, is pleased with itself and despises other people; thus it does not fear to cause offense by its example, and yet it refuses to give an account with a single word. But love by contrast teaches by its word and even refrains from any work which it will not be able to teach by a word that is offensive.

17. *In Jesus Christ, then, I have reason to glory.* By this expression the apostle is trying to say that it is not he himself who speaks or performs the things which he speaks or does *for the obedience of the Gentiles* (v. 18) but Christ, as he says in 2 Cor. 13:3: "Do you desire proof that Christ is speaking in me?" Thus he says that he does not dare to say anything except what Christ speaks in him. And he causes the word "to speak" to correspond with the word "He works," so as to express the idea both of word and work. For it is the same as if he were saying: "I do not dare to speak or to do anything except what Christ speaks and does through me," but in order to avoid wordiness, since in the first part he had discussed the matter of "speaking," it was not necessary to add the idea of "working," because he put this into the second part. And here it was not necessary to repeat "speaking," since he who works will thereby all the more speak of Him, because it is even easier to speak than to do something. Moreover, since the "working" includes in itself both the speaking and the doing, he wanted to emphasize especially *what Christ has wrought through me* in order that he might express that not only his speaking but also everything he was doing was Christ's. And while I am not unaware that in the opinion of others [13] the apostle is speaking this way in order to exclude all arrogance, by suggesting that although he is glorying before God in Christ, yet he does not dare to glory over the things in which false apostles glory, namely, in something which God is not working in them, for they boast about the things which they have not done and which God has not done in them. But the first interpretation seems to me to be more rational, namely, that the negative expression stands for an affirmative one, which the

[13] Erasmus.

following statement indicates: "for the obedience of the Gentiles." For Christ did not "work nothing" for the "obedience of the Gentiles," but He accomplished all things in the apostle, and in these the apostle gloried, not in the things which he himself did. So the meaning is: "I glory because I am a minister to the Gentiles sanctifying the Gospel. And I glory because I did not do this but Christ did it through me, and through Him it comes about that this glorying of mine is valid even before God."

20. *And I have so preached the Gospel.* The translator seems to have been afraid that it might sound offensive the way the apostle said it. For he plainly says in the Greek: "I have been ambitious to preach the Gospel." And it is not a case where the word "ambitious" is used in its common meaning, as when Pliny speaks of the Jordan: "As far as local sites permit, it is *ambitiosus*." [14] (Thus the word *ambitiosus* is used in the sense that a person desires to encompass many places and strives to extend and enlarge himself everywhere, as when a river overflows and spreads over many areas.) But φιλοτιμούμενος, that is, "desirous of glory or honor," is used here. Therefore for our word "I have preached" there are two words in the Greek, namely, "I have been ambitious *(ambitiosus)* to preach" or "impelled by a desire for honor, I have preached." And now what is the answer to this question? Was the apostle ambitious? Is he here giving to ambitious men an example by which to defend themselves? God forbid. For previously he had said: "In Christ Jesus, then, I have reason to be proud of my work" (v. 17), and in 1 Cor. 9:15: "For I would rather die than have anyone deprive me of my ground for boasting." If he were seeking this glory for his own sake, his glory would be null and void. But he certainly sought it for the sake of others, namely, as follows:

First, that his apostolic authority might not be diminished, which would be an impediment to the faith of the Gentiles, to whom he had been ordained as an apostle, as shown in the gloss. [15]

Second, he says these things out of an abundance of love, namely, because he desired to save as many as possible, he did not want to preach in a place where Christ had already been made known, lest he might meanwhile be hindered from preaching to those who did not know Him. And he indicates this by citing Isaiah: *They shall understand who have never heard of Him* (v. 21;

---

[14] Pliny, *Natural History*, V, 15, par. 71. Cf. also p. 26, marginal note 7, above.

[15] That is, Luther's own gloss on Rom. 15:16, p. 123, marginal note 18, above.

Is. 52:15), as if to say: "It is necessary to preach Christ where He is not known, lest if He be preached where He is known, time may be lost in which He should be preached to others." It is also not without significance that he does not say: "Where the other apostles preached I did not preach," for this would have been a sign of an ambitious and proud man, as if he despised preaching where the others had preached, but rather he says: "where Christ has not already been named," to indicate that he had abstained from preaching where it was not necessary, in order to preach where it was necessary.

But in all of these points we have sufficient reason for his doing what he did, but not yet for his use of the word φιλοτιμούμενος. For a person can do all of these things even if he does not say that he is desirous of honor. But now he is saying expressly that he has done these things out of zeal for honor and glory. Therefore we must not ask here to what extent he did these things not out of a desire for glory, but rather what this glory was. Therefore:

Third, we must note that to preach the Gospel was a despised and ignominious duty, just as it still is, void of all honor and glory, exposed to every kind of insult, reproach, persecution, etc., to such a degree that Christ says: "Whoever is ashamed of me before men, I will be ashamed of him before the angels of God" (cf. Luke 9:26). And Jeremiah (20:8) confesses that the Word of God "has become a reproach and a derision all the day long." And Ps. 14:6 says: "You would confound the plans of the poor, but the Lord is his refuge." And also Christ confesses everywhere in the Psalms that He was despised and that "shame had covered His face" (Ps. 69:7). Likewise He says: "God, Thou knowest My folly" (Ps. 69:5) and the irreverence which has been heaped upon Me. And what happens to Christ, who is the truth, for Christ is the truth, this also happens to the ministers of Christ, that is, of the truth, as we read in 1 Cor. 4:9-10: "For I think that God has exhibited us apostles as last of all, like men sentenced to death; because we have become a spectacle to the world, to angels, and to men. We are fools for Christ's sake, but you are wise in Christ. We are weak, but you are strong." And he says a little later (v. 13): "We have become, and are now, as the refuse of the world, the offscouring of all things."

Therefore since preaching the Gospel is not a matter of honor, with marvelous and apostolic love he regards that which is its shame as being his glory, only in order that he may be of benefit to others. For to preach where Christ is known is not disgraceful, because there the first shame of the Gospel is endured and overcome. But where He is not yet known, the disgrace poured upon the Gospel is still new and very great. He is also speaking in this context in chapter 1:14, when he says: "I am under obligation both to Greeks and to barbarians, both to the wise and to the foolish." And in 1:16: "For I am not ashamed of the Gospel," as if to say: "I consider preaching the Gospel as an office of honor, and I am ambitious for it, for the very reason that others abhor it because of its dishonor." Thus we read in Acts 5:41: "Then the apostles left the presence of the council, rejoicing that they were counted worthy to suffer dishonor for the name of Jesus." Does the word "rejoicing" here mean anything else than that they accepted this disgrace as an honor? Therefore he also has said earlier (Rom. 15: 17): "In Christ Jesus, then, I have reason to be proud of my work for God," as if to say: "even though before the world I have dishonor and confusion among men." Thus we read in Ps. 119:46: "I also spoke of Thy testimonies before kings and was not put to shame," that is, "I did not blush to speak of Thee, but considered it an honor." But in other cases people who do blush are offended, since they are afraid of being put to shame. In the same psalm he often prays to be freed from this "scorn," saying: "Take away from me their scorn and contempt" (Ps. 119:22). And again he says: "Turn away the reproach which I dread" (Ps. 119:39). And in another place: "We are a reproach to the rich and contempt to the proud" (Ps. 123:4).

Fourth, which however differs only slightly from the third point, he declares this, namely, that he understands this glory to be the glory of the conscience before God, that is, that he does not have the testimony of an evil conscience, but a good conscience, as when he says (2 Cor. 1:12): "For our boast is this, the testimony of our conscience." Therefore in order that he might have a rich conscience before God because he had performed his duty most faithfully, he hastened to preach Christ only where He had not been known before. Just as in 1 Cor. 9:15, as mentioned above, he says that it would be better to die than that his glory should be nullified, that is, than that he should not have an uninjured conscience. For the conscience is that which either puts us to shame or honors us before God. Not that anyone's conscience is such that it does not at some time shame him (otherwise Christ would have died in vain), but that a person must strive to violate or injure his conscience as little as possible and to keep it as clear and honorable as he can, and then what is left over and remains hidden is covered, excused, and forgiven through faith and hope in Christ. In this sense he was ambitious to preach, because he strove to enrich his conscience, which cannot be enriched in a better way than by serving others out of love, even if this leads to ignominy and the cross. Such ignominy is its glory because of the glory of the conscience. And I believe that this was the mind of the apostle, that in this open shame he might seek the hidden glory, outwardly disgraced but honored in conscience, despised among men but glorified before God. For truth gives birth to hatred. But this hatred brings forth grace. Hence we must ambitiously seek hatred, that is, grace, even through hatred.

But lest we appear to reject the opinion of others completely, men such as Erasmus and others like him, we concede that the apostle also strove with a kind of holy ambition to be the apostle of the Gentiles (although this passage does not teach it, because he does not say that he only refrained from preaching where the other apostles had preached, but wherever Christ was named; but even among the Gentiles His name was known, as for example at Rome). But let us concede that because he was "Set apart for the Gospel of the uncircumcised" (Rom. 1:1), he strove with pious ambition to fulfill his office as if he alone wanted to bring the light to the Gentiles, a task in which he most strongly gave proof of his love. For the ambition to do good is truly rare and thoroughly apostolic. Moreover, to preach the Gospel is to bestow the greatest benefit, even if it is done through the greatest persecutions and enmities of the whole world. Therefore to strive as it were for this glory (and this is the strongest of all desires) of bringing the greatest benefit and blessing, and this as a free gift, and what a free gift it is, and to receive nothing but every kind of reproach for it—is this not something that is beyond man and truly apostolic, indeed a divine kind of ambition? How far from this lofty position, I ask you, is the man who is benevolent without receiving any return? Think about this. The Gospel is an indescribable gift, which cannot be compared with any other riches, honors, or pleasures. Furthermore, he who gives good things, even to his enemies and those who render him evil in return, what is his benefit in comparison with the Gospel? Yet the man who gives good things only to his friends is less than this man, who is really very rare; and lesser still is the man who only lends his goods; and below him is the one who shares nothing; and worst of all is he who even takes away these gifts either by thought (which nearly the whole human race is doing) or by deed, which a great many are doing. Therefore when he boasts about his office, the apostle is merely speaking commendations of the Gospel. And what is more necessary for men who despise or attack the Gospel than to hear it praised thus? So he does seek glory, but a glory that is the salvation of those among whom he seeks it.

Index

By JOHN H. JOHN

INDEX TO SCRIPTURE PASSAGES